O9-BHL-132

PSYCHOLOGY of LEARNING and TEACHING

PSYCHOLOGY of LEARNING and TEACHING

third edition

HAROLD W. BERNARD

Division of Continuing Education
Oregon State System of Higher Education

7 5591

YORK COLLEGE
PENNSYLVANIA
Servire est vivere

LIBRARY

McGRAW-HILL BOOK COMPANY
New York   St. Louis   San Francisco
Düsseldorf   Johannesburg   Kuala Lumpur
London   Mexico   Montreal   New Delhi
Panama   Rio de Janeiro   Singapore
Sydney   Toronto

Library of Congress Cataloging in Publication Data

Bernard, Harold Wright, 1908-
  Psychology of learning and teaching.

  Bibliography: p.
  1. Educational psychology. I. Title.
LB1051.B37 1972   370.15   70-39309
ISBN 0-07-004925-4

PSYCHOLOGY of LEARNING and TEACHING

Copyright © 1965, 1972 by McGraw-Hill, Inc. All rights reserved. Copyright 1954 by McGraw-Hill, Inc. All rights reserved. Printed in the United States of America. No part of this publication may be reproduced, stored in a retrieval system, or transmitted, in any form or by any means, electronic, mechanical, photocopying, recording, or otherwise, without the prior written permission of the publisher.

1234567890KPKP798765432

This book was set in Press Roman by Allen-Wayne Technical Corp., and printed and bound by Kingsport Press, Inc. The designer was Ursula Pross; the drawings were done by Vantage Art, Inc. The editors were Robert C. Morgan, Alison Meersschaert, and Claudia A. Hepburn. Matt Martino supervised production.

LB
1051
B37
1972

8/28/72   pub. 1975

To our children—
may they have teachers who help
develop their potential

Contents

Preface

Psychology of Learning and Teaching, third edition, focuses on the imperative of change in approaches to teaching, with special emphasis on the individual needs of the pupil, the cultural setting, and the process of learning, as well as on innovation in curriculum, methods of testing, and classroom techniques. Cultural and technological changes, as well as further insights into the nature of human development and learning, demand a reexamination of the aims and purposes of education. Perhaps the greatest change in this new edition is the shift from the concept of the teacher as an instructor and leader to the idea of the teacher as a facilitator, a catalyst, in the teaching-learning process. Pupils need to be encouraged and guided in learning activities much more than they need to be taught. The human transaction between pupil and teacher, involving mutual respect, dignity, personal responsibility, and ego identity, is highlighted.

The phenomenon of rapid technological and cultural change is readily and widely acknowledged. However, observers of the educational system have noted the resistance of schools to the process of change. Schools today, it is said, are remarkably like those of thirty years ago. In this book the view is taken that beneficial change could take place more rapidly and that classroom teachers can and should take the initiative to improve themselves, their aims, and their methods.

A number of scholars have referred to rapid change in the nature of pupil personality. The generation now in school, having grown up in a period marked by a series of wars and the threat of nuclear catastrophe, places priority on the present rather than on future goals. Economic prosperity (despite periodic slumps) and government programs of assistance to lower-income groups have made survival goals and the need for being economically competent less insistent. There has been a shift to a striving of youth for identity—being an individual of worth—rather than for professional and occupational proficiency. A stance of sophistication in the younger generation and an accompanying insistence on relevance of school curricula is attributed to the many more hours of exposure to television than to formal schooling. Schools today must meet the needs of a greatly increased pupil variation, given the gradual obsolescence of unskilled labor in a society with little future for the dropout student, as well as a deepened concern for the education of minorities. Other factors influencing the generation now in school are urban problems, population explosion, and increased mobility in modern society.

School personnel have long recognized nascent forms of these changes and have attempted to alter teaching practices to fill the needs of the present school population. However, the needs are intensifying and the rationale of educational psychology is becoming increasingly cognizant of the merit of new outlooks on pupil needs. Among the important concepts emphasized in this book are:

The centrality of the ego concept in effective learning

The importance of group processes

The need for self-actualization rather than competitive striving

The fundamental importance of recognizing individuality and fostering creativity

The need to make the processes of learning gratifying so that a base is laid for the lifelong habit of continuous learning

This presentation of the psychology of learning and teaching is based on several assumptions. Among these are that pupils learn by means of different styles and that teaching (to be effective) must capitalize on these varied styles. Pupils learn, in part and sometimes unintentionally, by imitation, and teachers teach what they *are* as well as what they do. Learning is highly complex, and different psychological orientations, or viewpoints, emphasize different aspects of the learning process. The "whole child" comes to school, and his physical needs, his parental and sibling relationships, his emotional responses and potentials, his peer relationships influence his success in learning about what his culture demands of him. In this intricate world of rapid change, the teacher's role shifts from that of tutoring or instructing to that of managing a learning milieu. The pupil's goal in this world must be that of achieving gratification with the process of continuous learning rather than concern about his comparative-competitive standing.

These assumptions are based on a survey of what I hope is the seminal literature on school learning. They are based on the successes and failures observed and experienced in four decades of work in public schools, colleges, and federal government activities. The assumptions are based on personal convictions about the nature of human beings; e.g., we learn, on the basis of inherited *potential*, our intelligence; we learn, with genetic predispositions, our personality; and the healthy human being is born with an urge to learn. He does not have to be cajoled or coerced into learning—though this zest for creative living can be dampened.

Different teaching methods are mentioned—drill, problem solving, discovery, cooperative projects, experience—but none is espoused as the panacea to educational problems. As there are different styles of learning, there are different styles of teaching, and all styles will work with some pupils and all will "turn off" some other pupils. Hence, the practical *Psychology of Learning and Teaching* is viewed as that which suggests some things to individual teachers that can be seen as being appropriate to their style of teaching and living. Educational psychology should provide some basis for the teacher's continuous experimentation and his continuous innovation. It should provide an incentive to his personal involvement in the processes of continuous learning.

Harold W. Bernard

Part one

Bases for a Psychology of Learning and Teaching

The first five chapters of this book deal with human beings in school and the underlying processes of how they get to be what they are.

Psychology (herein accompanied by sociology, biology, and politics) in education begins with the teacher, not because he is most important but because he is most able to control his own behavior. Furthermore, no matter what the teacher teaches or what techniques he uses, his effectiveness is determined by his personality.

Whatever teachers and their pupils become, they do so in numerous, sequential steps. Despite differences in rate and direction of growth, the processes of maximizing one's potential are orderly and, generally speaking, predictable.

Both children and adolescents are studied because their needs and attitudes toward learning are different. Children are not miniature adults and adolescents are not children. Children, for instance, need psychological safety—rules, regulations, directions, structure—but they also need freedom to explore and become. Adolescents need to establish an identity, to be someone. They need freedom *and responsibility* to become a unique person.

It is postulated that we are not born human beings but are endowed with great potential for becoming human. Children, adolescents, and teachers learn to be what they are as a function of their culture, as mediated by the school and family. This concept provides an optimistic orientation, because culture is man-made and can be changed.

1

1

Teacher Personality— A Major Factor in Learning

Children learn certain behaviors and attitudes so thoroughly without going to school that we are tempted to think those reactions are innate characteristics. Food preferences, cruelty toward enemies— or children—friendliness or hostility, cunning or candor, being garrulous or taciturn are examples. These differences are noted even as we admit that the differences within a group are greater than the differences between groups. Sociologists and cultural anthropologists have emphasized that children learn these behaviors as a part of the process of "enculturation." This assimilation of values and adoption of behaviors is not taught—at least in the sense that one thinks of teaching as a classroom activity. Learning how to behave, live, and value is a matter of watching, listening, playing, trying, imitating, and being with someone.

Parents, in this sense, are the most effective teachers. They influence the child in his initial experiences; they are with him at the most impressionable time; and they have their children for comparatively continuous time intervals. But teachers run second, albeit often a poor second, in terms of their influence. Hence, in terms of the realities of how children learn, it seems appropriate to begin the study of teaching-learning transactions with a careful consideration of teachers—their influence and their being.

The Role of Teachers in Pupil Behavior

Influence of Teacher Personality

Three decades ago, Fairbank (1933), reporting on a longitudinal, communitywide study of handicapped children, assessed teacher personality as being the prime item in pupil success. A survey made in 1916 revealed that 166 pupils in a school population of 1,502 were so subnormal and emotionally unstable that dependency, delinquency, immorality, and alcoholism were predicted for them. Seventeen years later, during the depression, 122 of the original students were located. Ninety-two of these had never had contact with any agency, either welfare or legal. The remainder had been temporarily identified with an agency or were on welfare. The admirable adjustment of these pupils, said Dr. Fairbank, was primarily due to highly able and involved teachers—especially selected for their concern and their sympathetic and understanding efforts with children.

The situation is no different today. How pupils achieve in school, how they behave, and particularly how they view themselves is, to a remarkable degree, a function of teacher personality. Rist (1970) reports that much of the difficulty which culturally different pupils encounter in schools may be attributed to how a teacher views the pupil, what he expects of the pupil, and how he deals with the pupil.

May 1, 1970

Dear Dr. Bernard:*

As you were interested in our son, Kermit, while I was enrolled in your class last term, I thought you might be interested in the latest development. During finals week last term, Dr. Edith M. of the Medical School called him in to make a video tape for her files. She was impressed with his progress, and as she was disappointed in the results of his last intelligence test, she arranged for retesting. This time with a different tester and a nonverbal test given in her presence, he showed quite different results. Complete evaluation of the tests had not been made when last I talked to her. However, he tended to verify earlier tests [showing comparatively higher scores] rather than the one just previous. The last test may well put him back in the Special Education range [rather than being excluded from school].

She discussed the results with a psychologist there who has not previously been involved with Kermit. After analyzing the results, he diag-

---

*Omissions are made because they relate to earlier conversations regarding Kermit and explanations of the references would not enhance the main reason for reproducing the letter.

College Newsphoto Alliance

nosed Kit as a youngster who responds to different people in either a definitely negative or positive manner! Which, of course, was no news to us, though few would agree with us.

What will happen schoolwise now, I don't know. We will have to prove that he is capable of returning to the classroom. He cannot return to the Special Ed teacher who would normally have him for three years; as she is a champion "turner offer" for Kit. Maybe the school district will pay tuition to send him elsewhere.

I wanted you to know these results as I felt you might be able to impart in some manner just what teachers can do to their students with their attitudes. Kit, with his mental defect, was just not allowed to react as a normal youngster would to someone who the child instinctively knows regards him as a failure.

Sincerely,

——————— ————————— —————

Numerous experimental and observational studies confirm the fact that pupils learn what a teacher is as well as what he says. Pupils absorb his attitudes, they reflect his moods, they share his convictions, they imitate his behavior, and they quote his statements. Experience attests to the fact that such problems as motivation, discipline, social behavior, pupil achievement, and above all, the continuing desire to learn all center around the personality of the teacher.

Personality is all that a person is and might be—it includes knowledge, skills, ideals, and attitudes, as well as the perceptions he has of other people. It is with these qualities, rather than personal appearance, that this chapter deals. Attention is directed to you as learner and teacher because in the helping professions the person who performs the service is important. No matter how excellent one is today, further growth is demanded in order to remain effective and become more so.

It has been said that the prime requisite for a nation's mental health is a corps of properly trained and personally adequate teachers. It is a simple, and gigantic, matter of *as the teacher so is the school.*

The Lives of Pupils—And of Teachers

Mr. A., a sixth-grade teacher, was just under 6 feet tall, quite thin, had a large nose, and smiled easily but not effusively. He dressed neatly but informally. He exercised his sense of humor by telling jokes and laughing with his pupils. He spoke correctly and distinctly in a voice that was somewhat high-pitched for a man.

Alex, his largest and brightest pupil, was told three times within an hour to stop eating candy wafers—at the end of the period, there was a wafer in his mouth. There was some confusion in the room—some pupils were moving about, jostling and giggling, but others were seriously engaged in work. Mr. A. worked with those who wanted to work and sought ways to stimulate the laggards. At recess, most of the pupils went outside in a somewhat orderly manner, but one girl insisted that she wanted to stay with Mr. A. She was urged to go out, but she had some problems she wanted to talk over, so she stayed.

When the principal was asked why Mr. A. was so "easy" on pupils, he replied, "Easy? He's very effective with pupils over a period of time." The girl who stayed in was under the care of a psychiatrist. Another teacher had asked to be relieved of responsibility for her. The disobedient wafer chewer was accepted, and later tests showed that his achievement was appropriately high. Subsequent visits to this classroom showed a great improvement in orderly behavior, with most pupils seriously engaged in work.

Mr. A. was effective because of what he was and what he did. He liked children. *He genuinely accepted them as they were.* He expressed his appreciation of the attentive workers. He recognized that the emotionally disturbed "clinging vine" girl needed support. At the end of the year, the wafer eater had satisfied his appetite and was a staunch defender of Mr. A. and his excellence as a teacher; the girl's emotional condition had improved; and the hard workers continued to be diligent.

Mr. D., a high school teacher, presented a sharp contrast, but he too was effective in his own way. He was a stocky, red-faced, heavily bearded, sparse-haired athlete. His movements were quick, and his jaw was prominent and tight. He smiled rarely, talked rapidly, and barked orders like the proverbial sergeant. In fairness to him, it must be said that he was employed after the pupils had laughed another teacher out of the school in the first two weeks. No one laughed at or with Mr. D. When he spoke, pupils listened. Pupils were to be seen and not heard, even if they had a question. They studied algebra and general science earnestly. It is possible that some learned to like these subjects because they acquired some competence in them. But most of the pupils learned also to dislike Mr. D., and a junior who had a good bit of prestige as an up-and-coming middleweight at the time showed particular animosity. There was considerable verbal sparring, and pupils were relieved when it was announced that Mr. D. would continue his study of law the following year.

Mrs. Doe had a great zest for life. She was continually on the go. In addition to a busy social life, she was interested in art, music, drama, and politics. She had firm opinions about most subjects and would defend them vigorously with other adults; she tolerated no criticism of her pupils, always finding reasons, and very sound reasons, for interpreting misbehavior in an understanding manner.

Mrs. Doe's classroom conduct accorded with her personality. Her room was virtually a three-ring circus, with something going on in every corner. Whether she was teaching the second grade, the fifth, or the eighth, it was the same story, except for content. Being truly creative, she found ways to incorporate drawing, painting, drama, music, and dance into the various disciplines of arithmetic, writing, history, and geography. She listened to and respected the opinions of her pupils. Not all students responded with the same degree of enthusiasm; some appeared to be confused by the variety of activities, and although they worked diligently at the academic tasks, they did not participate in all activities. Most, however, were productive, and their pictures, poems, and science projects were frequently so outstanding that they well deserved the publicity that Mrs. Doe got for them outside the classroom. A lad who had previously been a persistent problem was, in Mrs. Doe's room, achieving at the level that was indicated by aptitude tests.

Miss R. was hardly ever observed in conversation with other teachers; she rarely found occasion to come to the principal's office. Her whole life appeared to center around school and her pupils. Achievement test data showed that her pupils consistently ranked above those in other sixth grades. Miss R. was with her pupils all the time. She took no coffee break, she accompanied students to the playground and kept them in the room for the lunch hour, though others in the school ate together in the cafeteria. If she had discipline problems, no one heard about them. In terms of pupil achievement there could be no criticism of her work. But one wonders about the development of the whole child. It must be concluded that a mother-hen personality in a teacher is not conducive to the development of the independence that is so much needed to get along in life.

Fortunately for the child and society, pupils meet many teachers in the course of formal education. Psychology teaches that pain is more readily forgotten than pleasure. Perhaps the errors made by some teachers will be erased by others. In addition, there is evidence that what makes one teacher good for certain pupils is the very thing that makes him less valuable for others; therefore, there is no one "best" teacher personality. The task for educational psychology is to diminish the obvious weakness by helping teachers in self-analysis and enabling them to offer effective instruction and wise supervision. Because the needs of pupils differ, *there should be no attempt to cast all teachers in the same mold.*

Studies of Teacher Personality and Pupil Behavior

Lest the timid become apprehensive about the great responsibility of being a teacher, let it be known that pupils, in their turn, have a great capacity for tuning teachers out of their lives. An effective teacher can be a marked and positive influence, a poor one can contribute to pupils' disliking school and formal learning, but many teachers might just as well not have been there. Allport (1968, p. 172) found, in a study of 100 successful pupils and 4,632 teachers, that about 8 percent had a strong influence on pupils, 15 percent had a well-remembered but not strong influence, and about 77 percent were remembered vaguely if at all.

Studies of school achievement may suggest similar discouraging conclusions. Children learn about as much under one set of conditions as another. Clements (1968), summarizing a number of studies, reported that in most schools, instructional methods, type of teacher, and class size made no noticeable difference in test performance. He then suggested that perhaps the teachers and their methods are not so much at fault as are the research objectives and methods. He recommends that instead of examining achievement alone we look at the school as a whole—as a social system, with interrelationships and statuses. Curiosity is more important than cumulative scores. More important than **grade equivalent*** index is the child's belief in himself as a person of worth and capa-

---

*Words that are in boldface, as above, are listed and defined in the Glossary.

bility. Teachers do influence that concept, and it is the bias of this author that self-concept should be a focal concern for the really professional teacher.

There are more optimistic researches than those indicated above. Children who have experienced difficulty at home, in the community, and with earlier teachers have also been positively influenced. Their adjustive behaviors and learning skills and interests have improved markedly when they encountered certain teachers (Dennison, 1969).

Flanders (1965) studied the effect of teacher behavior on pupil behavior and achievement and found superiority in many ways for what he called "indirect" behaviors of teachers. Indirect influence means that teachers accept pupils' feelings, praise them, use pupils' ideas, and ask them questions. Direct influence consists in lecturing, giving directions, and criticizing. Others have made follow-ups of Flanders' analyses and leads and report much the same result: Pupils of indirect teachers made better achievement scores, produced higher levels of critical thinking, and gave more active manifestations of curiosity than did pupils of direct teachers. Direct teachers, more frequently than indirect ones, have confused and apathetic pupils (Campbell and Barnes, 1969).

Grams (1960) found that teachers play a critical role in the degree to which pupils reveal discrimination toward and acceptance of pupil differences in race, religion, color, and behavior.

What pupils learn, whether academic knowledge, social behavior, or personality traits, is a matter of slow accumulation. In many cases, the impact of teacher personality persists for years. The fact that a whole class does not respond in the same manner does not mean that individuals are not being affected. It has been frequently said that child behavior reflects parental handling. When we consider the number of waking hours the child spends with teachers, it can safely be remarked that *pupil behavior reflects teacher personality*.

The Dynamics of Teacher-Pupil Interaction

Pupil behavior reflects teacher behavior in many ways: Imitation, rejection of the role, and defenses against the teacher's attitude and action are most noticeable. Acting like the teacher is not simply a matter of modeling oneself after an ideal; it is also a matter of identifying with the teacher. The imitation may be of specific mannerisms, modes of speech, or attitudes. Rejection is illustrated in the pupil's determination never to be a teacher. It would be unfortunate if pupils did not reject authoritarianism, discourtesy, and intolerance, but these behaviors are not automatically replaced with positive characteristics. Rejection may go so far as to stimulate repudiation of one's sex role or to repudiate the pursuit of education under more competent teachers. Thus, in experiments on the reduction of dropouts a frequent emphasis is that of accepting pupil differences and trying to make pupils appreciate their own abilities and worth (Levine, 1970). Such acceptance is more a matter of what the teacher is than what he does.

Learning takes place within a total context that is more than the mere sum of the parts. There are qualitative aspects of the school milieu—self-concepts, attitudes toward authorities, perception of areas of psychological safety and adventure—that are to some extent responsive to the teacher's skill. The lives of students may be enriched by the teacher's (1) recognizing individual pupil characteristics, (2) knowing and acknowledging home and family influences, (3) assessing the character (ecology) of the school, and (4) acknowledging the significance of peer relationships (Danskin, Kennedy, and Friesen, 1965).

Not only can teachers be led to see that they are responsible for the learning climate ("The trouble with Philadelphia is us!") but that something can be done about themselves. An example is South Brunswick, N.J., where a new superintendent, James Kimple, liked the idea of the school board that the sleepy schools should be wakened. The notion that teaching and education were processes of human relationships was developed. Studies on how those relationships could be improved were made.

Families from nearby districts pleaded with Superintendent Kimple to allow them to pay extra tuition so their children could attend these schools. Let it also be noted that the students in the Crossroads Middle School, a school involved, equaled or exceeded the national norms on achievement in mathematics, science, reading, and social studies.

Behavior Problems and Teacher Personality

Articles appear frequently in magazines and newspapers about the state of discipline in the school—some assert that it is too lax and contributes to delinquency, whereas others say it is repressive and curbs creativity (Neale, 1969). Many psychologists agree that *methods of discipline must vary with the teacher and the individual pupils concerned*. A few pupils may temporarily need the security of rigid control. Others are restive under such a regime. The usual result of dictatorial control is that pupils ultimately break the boundaries and get into trouble. Their accumulated resentment may cause them to break windows, write on lavatory walls, or deface books and materials.

Much has been learned about the relation of behavior problems and teacher personality from attempts to make education more appealing to the culturally different pupil. What has been learned emphasizes what was previously known: Education is improved by acceptance of pupil differences, tolerance for ambiguity, respect for unique talents, and a broadened view (not just IQ) of human value, all of which are personality characteristics rather than methodological skills. However, a word of warning is pertinent. When the misbehaving pupil encounters an accepting, respectful, tolerant teacher, the pupil often becomes worse. This is because the pupil, having been disappointed so many times previously by adults—parents, teachers, community authorities—wonders if this new person is "for real." Before he will yield to his hope that this new type being does accept and trust him, the pupil puts his teacher to a test by intensifying misbehavior (Axline, 1964; Dennison, 1969).

Some teachers, by virtue of their patience and understanding, motivate pupils constructively. Most of the pupils in such teachers' classes work close to their capacity, even when the lessons are not individually designed. Really knowing pupils' ages, their parents, community, siblings, and past performance and understanding their motives, unique talents, and areas of concern leads to the teacher's acceptance of them and their acceptance of him. Many teachers after gaining such acquaintance will say something like, "My wonder is not why he acts as he does but why he is not much worse." This knowledge enables the teacher to praise or prod appropriately. Rejection, on the other hand, prompts the pupil to "leave the field" either physically (truancy and dropouts) or psychologically (daydreaming or underachievement).

The teacher's knowing what book to recommend, to whom, and when is a stimulus to read. Knowing something about pupils' interests—horses, cars, cycles, football, or music, for example—provides points of contact. Having enough self-confidence to be able to admit ignorance is important. Sometimes the admission stimulates the pupil by making him feel that teacher and pupils are learners together. Thus, learning is stimulated by mutuality and cooperation. Teachers set the pattern for social relationships. Pupil self-confidence is stimulated by teachers who have confidence in themselves and in their pupils.

Characteristics of Effective Teachers

Variable Criteria of Teacher Effectiveness

Your own initial impressions of different people and those with whom you ultimately form friendships indicate that the effectiveness of a person is in part dependent upon others' perceptions of him. A teacher does not impress school administrators and pupils in the same way. Teachers may have many combinations of personal qualities, and what appeals to one student and is effective provokes a negative response from other students (Biddle and Ellena, 1964). Teachers who are effective at one level may not be similarly effective at another because pupils are at different stages in their mental and emotional development. One outgoing teacher welcomes the young people who flock around her to talk and ask questions. She is level-headed, professionally well-prepared, and an energetic worker. Most of the youngsters openly assert that she is wonderful. Her roommate and fellow teacher presents a marked contrast. She dresses well, is sincere, and is also well-trained for her job. But she is somewhat shy and is not at all colorful. She does wear well, though it is difficult to become acquainted with her. This teacher has so-called "warm, friendly relations" with only a few pupils. But these pupils are not part of the throng that clusters about the outgoing Miss Blankville. They are pupils who find in the quiet, reserved teacher a kindred spirit and a great stimulus for personal security. Without this teacher, these pupils would receive no help from an understanding adult.

The moral of this example is that you need not try to assume certain personality traits in order to be effective. Pupils have different reactions to the same teacher-behavior patterns (Anderson and Hunka, 1963). Nevertheless, there are characteristics that can serve as a guide to personal improvement. There is a wide range of "good" teachers, but there are also discernible differences between those who are good and those who are poor (Hamachek, 1969).

Criteria Stated for the U.S. Office of Education

The U.S. Office of Education investigators concluded that outstanding teachers could be characterized in the following generalizations:

1. The best teachers are professionally alert. They do not live their lives in the tight confines of the classroom. They are attempting to make the community and the school better places for young people.

2. They are convinced of the worth of their job. Their ambition is to improve constantly in the work to which they have dedicated themselves.

3. They seem not to be irritated by the taboos on personal liberties that are said by some to characterize the teaching profession. Apparently they are so psychologically mature that the irritations are tolerated.

4. They have an artistry in human relations that stems from observing the workings of psychology, biology, and cultural anthropology in the classroom.

5. They are humble about their own need for growth. "They are poignantly aware that under their influence this raw material (human resources) may also change its very destiny" (Rummel, 1948).

This set of criteria makes two things clear. First, good teachers see their goals and work clearly and with conviction. Second, teachers should exemplify the learning habit; good teachers give planned attention and effort to their own continuous growth through learning.

American Council on Education Studies

This organization used the premise that the qualities of good teachers are interacting factors that depend, in part, on educational philosophy, pupil characteristics, and course level, content, and purposes. Various personality-assessment devices, such as the Guilford-Zimmerman, California Psychological Inventory, and the Kuder Preference Record were used in determining teachers' characteristics. The following characteristics were listed for women teachers in the elementary grades:

They frequently give as reason for teaching liking for children and interest in their development.

They express admiration of such qualities as friendliness, permissiveness, definiteness, and fairness in teachers.

They dislike in teachers such qualities as arrogance, intolerance, sarcasm, and partiality.

They typically appear to be "accepting" and generous in appraisals of other persons and see the good points of a person rather than the bad.

They express satisfaction with teaching (and also with teacher salaries) and intend to continue teaching indefinitely.

They frequently engaged in teaching activity as child (e.g., taking charge of class in absence of teacher).

The decision to become a teacher frequently was made prior to college enrollment; i.e., they had planned to be a teacher from relatively early age.

They enjoyed school when they were students themselves.

They showed superior accomplishment when in school.

They report large number of teachers among parents and relatives.

They report participation in religious activities.

They enjoy activities with friends, but prefer small groups.

They frequently are members and officers of clubs.

They are married (85 percent of group).

They are interested and active in literary affairs (e.g., write poetry, have published books, etc.).

They are more emotionally stable than average adult (Guilford-Zimmerman).

They are more friendly than average adult (Guilford-Zimmerman).

They are more cooperative and agreeable than average adult (Guilford-Zimmerman).

They are more restrained than average adult (Guilford-Zimmerman).

They are more objective than average adult (Guilford-Zimmerman).

They are more tolerant than average adult (California Psychological Inventory).

They are more inclined to "try to give a good impression" than average adult (California Psychological Inventory).

They are more interested in social service than average adult (Kuder Preference Record).

They are less interested than average adult in computational and clerical activities (Kuder Preference Record).[1]

Research studies show that pervasive parental attitudes and the overall atmosphere of the home, rather than specific training practices, count most in optimum child development (Bernard, 1970a, p. 216). Study of the characteristics of effective teachers point to a similar conclusion: *The human climate for learning is more important than the specific teaching procedures adopted.*

Pupils' Viewpoints

The consumer in educational institutions is not frequently consulted about his preferences. As a pupil—if one does not become a dropout, or a stayin-and-cop out—one takes what he gets and hopes it will fade or get over with quickly. When pupils are asked [the following combines the results of several studies], there are a few surprises. Pupils often express a liking for teachers who "make us work," who expect and get "acceptable social behavior," or who are "business-like." Otherwise their preferences are about what would be expected. They want teachers who, on a peer level, one would like to have for a friend—ones who are:

Democratic	Consistent
Cooperative	Open-minded
Kindly	Helpful
Patient	Companionable
Fair	

and their preferences are for teachers who have:

A sense of humor	Flexibility
Varied interests	An interest in pupils
Knowledge of subject matter	

and for ones who avoid sarcasm and nagging.

Pupils' reactions differ somewhat depending on age, subject matter, institutional purpose, and pupil purpose. Nevertheless, the characteristics of preferred teachers remain rather stable. Such items as being friendly and cheerful,

---

1   David G. Ryans, 1960, *Characteristics of Teachers: A Research Study*, Washington, D.C.: American Council on Education, pp. 365-366. The titles in parentheses refer to personality and interest inventories.

knowledgeable and poised, and lively and interesting still rank high in pupils' views. They want both firm control and nondirective milieus—with the preference depending on the subject matter being taught more than being a matter of social class or level of maturity (Veldman and Peck, 1969).

Regardless of what parents think constitutes good teaching or what qualities administrators seek when they hire, the youngster is the final judge. To the degree to which pupils like or dislike the teacher and associate that with hard work, books, school, and the pursuit or abandonment of continuous learning the enterprise of formal education must be considered a success or failure.

Excellence in teaching is not inherent—good teachers may be born, but they are also made. Competence in teaching is not a gift from your professor, nor is it a revelation from a textbook. It is the result of a clear goal that you, the future teacher, can help to set (Bryan, 1962). It is the outcome of many hours of work, more hours of reflection, many irritating failures, and a few gratifying successes. Both competence and confidence come from planned and purposeful work, and both are qualities that contribute to success and being a well-liked teacher (Blume, 1971).

Teachers as Helpers

The Helping Relationship

Crowded cities, urban tensions, racial strife, constant warfare, and pollution suggest that it may be a psychological principle that the closer mankind is physically, the greater is his tendency to increase psychological distance (Dubos, 1970). If we have a realistic concern for man's future, scientific discovery cannot be detached from philosophical values—nor can education. Education can serve many ends, and it has been used both to enslave and to free man. It is here assumed that education in the United States is oriented to the freeing of pupils so that each can make his contribution to an evolving society. This society, it is further assumed, should be one in which people can become **self-actualizing**, using the optimum development of their capacities to enhance their own lives and the lives of others.

From psychological investigations, we know that *certain behaviors by helping persons probably will be followed by certain changes in personality and behavior on the part of the helped.* Rogers (1969) has found that if we want persons to become (1) more realistic in self-perceptions, (2) more confident and self-actualizing, (3) more mature and socialized, (4) less prone to be upset and quicker to recover from stress, and (5) more healthy, integrating, and effective, then the helper should have certain attitudes. These attitudes include some of the items cited for effective teachers: (1) They are genuinely and demonstrably sincere in their relationship with those being helped; (2) they accept the person with whom they work as a separate, different, and worthwhile individual; and (3) they are empathic—able to see the person's private world of feelings and attitudes through his eyes. This kind of person, says Combs (1965), does not behave in stereotyped terms by copying the traits of another. The formula for achieving creative answers resides in the unique perceptual field of the helper himself.

Two challenges arise from the concept of the uniqueness of the helper's perceptual field. One is that "good" and "poor" teachers cannot be distinguished on the basis of what they know should be done, but can be distinguished on the basis of how they perceive their pupils. Good teachers believe their pupils are capable of good work and can make them "work like crazy" because they know their pupils can do it. The second challenge is the matter of how one sees himself. In order to see good in others one must see good in himself. Some characteristics of such people are: They see themselves as being adequate rather than inadequate. They are identified with people, not apart from them. They feel that they are trustworthy, likeable and liked, wanted, and accepted. They are sufficiently confident of themselves to be self-revealing rather than self-concealing (Combs, 1961, p. 56).

The Self-concept of the Helper

We can with some accuracy describe the *general* factors that tend to produce a robust self-concept. One's self-concept is significantly related to the attitudes he believes his parents hold toward him—what he believes is apparently more significant than their actual handling of him. In later childhood, many children select some glamorous figure as an ideal. Strength, good figure and features, and skills play a role in peer acceptance, although it is not always a crucial role. Altogether, we can say that acceptance by others, skills and knowledges that allow one to achieve status, and experiences that lead to feelings of security are conducive to a healthy self-concept.

It is, however, somewhat futile to trace the origins of traits of good teachers. The historical approach to personality improvement has some disadvantages (Glasser, 1969). For example, blaming one's parents for self-centeredness or lack of socialization does not predispose one to take steps of remediation. Blaming provides an excuse for not assuming responsibility. It is unnecessary for one to continue to carry the "monkey on his back" of inadequate prior experiences—experiences at home, in the community, or with teachers. This is not to say that one can by an act of will change his personality. He can, however, seek experiences which will exercise a given trait. He can, for instance, attempt to see good in a pupil who irritates him.

Pierson (1965, p. 39) postulated that the counselor who is unable to accept help is likely to fail the challenge of helping others. This would seem to be no less true of the teacher—who in order to be most effective should receive help from principals, supervisors, secretaries, fellow teachers, parents, and pupils. But many teachers are so insecure that they wish to conceal their feeling of inadequacy. They bristle at the suggestion of assistance from the principal. They resent visits from supervisors. They question the wisdom of one who is "just a plain secretary." Some are irritated when a bright pupil corrects their mispronunciation of a word.

Fortunately, such persons can be taught how to be helped, by their peers and by professional counselors, if they will make an initial gesture. Jersild (1963) reported that over 90 percent of those teachers who sought help believed that they profited from the counsel of psychiatrists, counselors, and consultants and would repeat the experience. It is worth noting that these were frequently people who were not sick, and did not have their job security threatened. They simply wanted to become better persons.

Some forward-looking teacher-education institutions are examining the processes of teacher self-evaluation as one of the promising avenues pointed toward educational improvement (Blume, 1971). Some schools use **interpersonal process groups** as a part of in-service education for teachers (Cottle, 1969*a*; Harrison, 1970).

Basic Encounter Groups

A popular approach to understanding self and others is an activity variously called "sensitivity training," "basic encounter groups," "interpersonal process groups," "T-group training," or "intensive group experience." It has been used in nurses' training, with business executives, in ministerial preparation, in drug therapy, and in in- and outpatient psychiatric clinics. The power and distinctiveness of the intensive group experience has led to a wave of popularity so high that unprepared or ill-prepared leaders, or "facilitators," are numerous. With such inept leaders unfortunate episodes have occurred that have frightened some people away and made others skeptical even while they venture participation. The potential for accelerating human understanding is so great that, just as the delinquent adolescent colors his whole generation, the spectacular incident is accepted as the typical.

Birnbaum (1969), Rogers (no date), and Shostrom (1969) have all issued warnings about the dangers involved. At the same time they advise caution, they agree that the potential value of interpersonal process groups is great—under qualified leadership. Rogers (1968) calls it the great social invention of the century. Some of the dangers are

Encouraging persons to reveal things about themselves that others do not know how to handle or keep confidential

Opening problems which are not subsequently dealt with by competent counselors

Permitting anyone to participate without study of their prior emotional stability or capacity to handle stress

Making the process so attractive that the necessity for content learning is by-passed

Precipitating a psychotic break on the part of a troubled person—often the very one who invests readily because of his urgent need for help

Forcing some people to move too fast in self-revelation and too far in behavioral change

Becoming an advocate of a single particular process and denying the value of other approaches

There are advantages which offset the hazards created by the occasional inept or casual leader: Emotions do exist in our lives—attractions, aversions, aspirations and disappointments, jealousies, and hostilities—and ignoring their existence does not make them go away. In fact, trying to disguise our less admirable proclivities tends to lead to the creation of elaborate **defense mechanisms** which actually hamper one's effectiveness and magnify his problem. Understanding the normality of our own peculiarities leads to a more sturdy self-concept, which in turn makes it easier to accept others. Process groups help to crack personality facades—one learns that others see through him much more readily than either viewer or viewee realizes. The realization makes it easier to abandon the facade; one may become more "real," and others find it easier to deal with such open and genuine persons. Participants receive honest feedback on how they perceive and are perceived, and their perception is thus sharpened. They are *confronted* with "how they are doing." They can therefore be more **purposeful** in their efforts to improve than when they have to guess about the impressions they make.

One important discovery of encounter groups is that negative thoughts are easier to express than positive ones. It is not thought to be odd that we should express our disdain, contempt, or dislike for another. But, open admiration for others may lead to unfortunate and misleading conclusions in the minds of others. Admiration expressed for a member of the same sex may be misconstrued as an abnormal form of behavior; and admiration for one of the other sex may be misinterpreted as a crude or insulting attempt at conquest. One is left without defenses when he expresses something positive. Negative feelings are often expressed during initial group stages—each must protect himself. In later meetings admiration and liking are more readily expressed, and one learns that the positive can be uttered without any real danger.

For teachers and prospective teachers there need be no emphasis on chronic situations, disrupted family situations, or past failures. There is no need to reveal the secrets of one's past. The aim is that of learning how one "comes across" in a group. One may learn what others think of him and why. And this in itself is not a description of what one *is*. There may be a real difference in *what one is* and how he is seen by another. The beholder reveals himself in the verbalization of *his* impression.

An interpersonal process group provides a laboratory situation in which one may practice interpersonal relations. One can learn something about the accuracy of his self-perceptions and his perceptions of others. The group provides an arena in which to test one's values, views, and visions. Interpersonal process groups can be made to focus meaningfully on interpersonal relations if certain emphases are made. Discussion should be personal. It should deal with feelings. It should concern only those people present (discussion of one's first grade teacher—or others who are not present and cannot express their side—is wasted time; it is "academic"). It should concern the present time. The group is not a lesson, it is an experience.

The implications of this section on interpersonal process groups are: Interpersonal reactions are a part of classroom life and merit study in a teacher preparation program. Feelings exist whether we acknowledge them or not. Self-disclosure may involve discomfort or pain; but, growth often involves pain and effort as the comfort of the habitual is abandoned. However, the dull ache of defeat and bare sufficiency is also painful. Perhaps some must choose between sharp and passing pain and chronic and disabling discomfort. Because pupils also have feelings, the teacher's study of his own feelings—with the aid of trained facilitators—may enhance his understanding of pupils. It may make him better able to use the assets he has. Understanding one's own defenses, facades, and behavior patterns may enhance the process of self-actualization.

Summary

The personality of the teacher has direct and cumulative impact on the lives and learning habits of pupils. It is neither expected nor desired that some ideal model of a teacher be established. Each teacher has his unique combination of experiences, interests, perceptions, and attitudes, and he must use them in ways most appropriate to him. Differences are desirable too from the standpoint of pupils.

Although differences among teachers are to be valued, common traits characterize the more effective ones. It is to be expected that desirable traits would differ for elementary and secondary teachers, but they are surprisingly alike. Educators and pupils both see good teachers as people who are energetic, objective, fair-minded, cooperative, stable, flexible, and considerate. It is well worth special note that good teachers *all* have the habit of continuous learning.

The trait approach to describing good teachers has defects, as research has frequently indicated. Attention has recently been focused upon the dynamics of the life patterns of those engaged in the helping professions. Here the object is to describe the attitudes that underlie the behaviors of successful teachers. The basic attitudes thus far discerned are acceptance of self and others, enabling teachers to inspire confidence in pupils because of their own self-confidence.

The traits of effective teachers can be directly cultivated through purposefully pursued developmental activities—study, reading, travel, experimenting. The rate of such growth can be accelerated by interpersonal process groups (led by trained facilitators) which provide immediate feedback on how one is perceived and how he is doing.

Suggested Additional Reading

BERNARD, HAROLD W., 1970, *Mental Health in the Classroom*, New York: McGraw-Hill Book Company.
>Chapters 2, 6, and 20 deal with the impact of teacher personality on pupil learning. Steps that teachers have made for personal and professional improvement are described.

COTTLE, THOMAS J., 1969, "Bristol Township Schools: Strategy for Change," *Saturday Review*, vol. 52, no. 38, pp. 70-71+, Sept. 20.

HARRISON, CHARLES H., 1970, "South Brunswick, N.J.: Schools Put a Town on the Map," *Saturday Review*, vol. 53, no. 8, pp. 66-68+, Feb. 21.
>The above two articles describe how interpersonal process groups constituted a major factor in the rehabilitation of schools.

DENNISON, GEORGE, 1969, *The Lives of Children*, New York: Random House, Inc.
>The lives of children are transformed by teachers who sought to distinguish between what were pupil needs and what were teacher needs. Placing the needs of teachers in second place becomes easier as they come to know children.

ROGERS, CARL R., 1969, *Freedom to Learn*, Columbus, Ohio: Charles E. Merrill Books, Inc.
>The major part of the book describes some of the qualities and interrelationships which are deemed to be desirable in teacher-pupil relations. The last chapter deals with how the intensive group experience may contribute to the qualities needed.

2

Developmental Processes and Lifelong Learning

Today's student and tomorrow's teacher will find few problems as basic, pervasive, and recurrent as that dealing with development. The student's task is to seek his own optimum development and self-realization. The teacher's task is to provide the milieu for such development in pupils.

The study of development is important for many reasons. Effective instructional practices are based upon the development, or **readiness**, of the pupil. Because human beings have little, if any, predetermined conduct—which has been called "instinct"—they must develop the kinds of behavior that will facilitate adjustment in their particular milieu. Because of ignoring developmental principles, some widely extant educational practices are futile or even inhibiting. Education itself is both a product and a process of development. Full-living and self-realization is, for everyone, a developmental process.

The Nature of Development

Basic Concepts

Growth may be thought of narrowly as sheer increase in size, but in educational and psychological literature the term frequently includes also maturation, development, and learning. "Maturation" refers to the **intrinsic** process of coming to maturity or reaching stages of development. The nerves, without perceptible increase in size, change in the process of myelinization and, without exercise or experience, become more efficient in message transmission. Maturation is a biological rather than a psychological or learning phenomenon. "Development" refers to progressive changes in the organism and embraces not only physical change (e.g., altered body proportions) but also change in function (e.g., strength and coordination). "Learning" is the aspect of development that connotes the modification of behavior (usually we think of improvement) that results from practice and experience.

The relationships of all these concepts may be illustrated by the way a child learns to read. An initial level of growth and development is requisite so that he will have achieved eye coordination and the ability to concentrate. His experience must be wide enough so that the words, which are abstractions, have meaning for him. There should be a milieu—books, oral reading, and feedback— favorable to encouragement and success. There should be a secure self-concept which makes the child feel that he is capable of task mastery. Thus, the individual, the physical surroundings, and the human environment are simultaneously bound to reading development.

Development—A Creative Process

Inasmuch as development involves organization and reorganization, it is a creative process. Every act of an organism alters its possible and probable future behavior. A baby's first steps represent progress toward his ultimate ability to run. Each word he says is progress toward his ability to converse. Development is a creative process in that the individual chooses the aspects of the environment to which he responds. For example, as you read the morning newspaper, you— your intelligence, your previous experiences, your mood—create your own response. If you all read the same news item, some of you will be discouraged, others will be challenged, and still others will find nothing of importance. Newspapers and books are more than words placed in a certain order. For the reader, a book includes the meaning which he brings to the printed page.

If development is to be optimally creative it must involve guidance of the less-experienced by the more-experienced. Creative persons ". . . need recognition and rewards in order to continue producing their best work. Similarly, they tend to learn most from those who are demanding yet fair. A typical creative scientist comes from a home where parental authority, although somewhat impersonal, was consistent, predictable, fair, and psychologically supportive."[1] Teachers who appreciate the idiosyncratic nature of development will be able to give the encouragement and permit the freedom which will enhance optimum development of pupils.

1   Harold K. Hughes, 1969, "The Enhancement of Creativity," *Journal of Creative Behavior*, vol. 3, pp. 76-77.

The Inclusive Nature of Personality Development

Children are born with varying potentialities for developing social personalities. Mental and physical predispositions incline the child to be optimistic and cheerful or pessimistic and doleful, lethargic and stoical or active and responsive. Some authorities postulate that personality types are related to body build. One's perceptual acuity, rate of learning, endocrine balance, strength, and stature all contribute to the effect he produces on others (Williams, 1971). These personal attributes are quickly and continuously modified by his experiences. The pedagogic theory which does not consider the political, economic, and social setting of the educational process, as well as physical and mental data, will be superficial and deserves to be ignored (Bruner, 1968*a*).

Three major factors influence the growing individual's characteristics and behavior. *Biological factors*, such as genetic structure, physical build and appearance, and rate of maturation, all bear on how the individual acts and how others perceive him. The human influences on him and the way others perceive him are conditioned by his *cultural milieu*. Specific variations within the culture— the way he is raised, the values, ideals, and goals he is taught—have a strong impact on his personality. His *personal history*, his experiences with things and people, also influences his personality development.

The limits of what one may do or become are set by biological factors. Whether one becomes a star athlete or an honors scholar is influenced by biology, but one's values and motivations are the result of various interacting influences. One's success in any occupational activity depends to a large extent on his ability to adapt his behavior to various situations and people. The important and complicated lesson of social adaptation can best be learned in the school, where contacts are wider and more impersonal than they are in the home. Moreover, some control can be exercised in choosing the experiences the pupil will have. There is much concern about children's attending de facto segregated schools in the slums and in middle class suburbia because their contacts with others is so restricted as to lead to bigotry, provincialism, and prejudice (Meyer, 1969).

Principles of Development and Some Implications

Some of the tendencies and probabilities of developmental processes can be epitomized by stating them as principles.

Development as a Function of the Interaction of the Organism with the Environment

Some believe heredity to be the important factor in development (Jensen, 1969*b*); others consider the environment to be the significant factor (Cron-

College Newsphoto Alliance

bach, 1969; Hunt, 1969; Kagan, 1969). The question is highly important to teachers. If heredity is believed to be the important factor, then it is logical to wait and see what nature has given to the individual.

Most authorities today would be counted as interactionists. They believe that heredity provides the potential, which is acted upon by a dynamic environment (R. Williams, 1971). Therefore, an attempt should be made to provide for each child a stimulating environment. If 90 percent of the personality is due to environment, so much the better. Even if only 10 percent is due to environment, it is still the only factor that can be influenced by educators.

Heredity can never be sharply differentiated from environment; the two operate concurrently and cooperatively. It would be best to regard heredity as providing potential for development and setting the bounds beyond which environmental stimulation cannot cause the individual to develop.

Some characteristics seem to be predominantly a matter of heredity, including color of hair, facial features, and stature—though stature, within limits, is subject to environmental influences. Orientals reared on the West Coast of the United States are, on the average, slightly heavier and taller than their brothers who were raised in their native lands, although they have maintained their Oriental facial characteristics. On the other hand, language, specific interests, and social behavior are determined by environmental influences. A Japanese born and raised in the American culture speaks and behaves as do his fellow Americans.

The nature-nurture, or heredity-environment, controversy has perhaps nowhere become more lively than in the study of intelligence. Thirty years ago the postulation that the IQ was constant (that is, that the rate of mental development for a given person was constant) was rarely questioned. Experimental evidence now points to the conclusion that under certain conditions there is a possibility that the IQ may be markedly changed by environmental and personality factors (Stinchcombe, 1969). Although work with slow learners and socially different children has not been uniformly successful in raising IQ, results indicate that continued study and work in this area are amply justified (Hunt, 1969; Tannenbaum, 1967).

Testing instruments and techniques currently in use are too inadequate to prove that actual changes are extensive (Wesman, 1968), but there are limitations to the IQ changes that a salutary environment can produce. The environment determines, to a marked extent, the degree to which innate potentialities are realized and the way in which they are utilized (Bronfenbrenner, 1963, p. 532). The more stimulating the environment, short of pressure, the greater will be the realization of the child's capacity. For one person, however, an environment may be stimulating; for another, it may be boring, and for still another, it may be overwhelming. Stimulation is a matter of what an individual can stand in terms of his present status and capacity.

There is increasing evidence that we have but small conception of what the upper limits of intelligence might be (Boyer, 1971). Improved prenatal care, better birth conditions and diet, more immediate and intimate mothering, reduction of emotional stress in the home, and the development of stronger self-concepts, better teachers, and more appropriate teaching techniques all might contribute not only to the more rapid acquisition of knowledge, but also to the development of vastly increased potential for learning and adaptation.

Certainly, there is evidence that intellectual development, as in other areas of personality, may be retarded or accelerated by environmental factors. It is a matter of the individual's interaction with those aspects of the total surrounding stimuli to which he (the organism) will respond. The teacher who accepts this view will be inclined to study the pupil to determine his present status, how it was achieved, and how to provide him with situations that will be personally stimulating and meaningful.

Educational Implications of Heredity-Environment Interaction

Teachers have two guides in deciding what kind of school environment will be most effective for individual pupils. One is data derived from intelligence tests (which assess potential and accumulated experience), achievement batteries, interest inventories, diagnostic schedules, and readiness scales. If such data are wisely used, the teacher improves his chance of *starting with the student where he is*. In many schools, teachers plan individual programs, and one child is given a reading readiness program while some of his classmates are tackling the first reading books; others, who have learned to read before coming to school, may be reading independently for fun or information or pursuing some other project. Test results may mean that a freshman is offered the choice between general mathematics or algebra. The trend toward differentiated independent work seems to be accelerating.

The other guide is observation. Teachers know that routine school pursuits are not stimulating to a particular child when they observe that he is inattentive or idle, teases his classmates, or devotes his time to unapproved activities. Teachers may challenge such pupils by giving them appropriate work to do, by assigning them special reports, and by encouraging them to undertake leadership responsibilities.

Pupils whose test data place them in lower categories are often irritable, excessively quiet, or easily discouraged. They may refuse to try the work placed before them and are frequently inattentive and idle. Teachers must learn to experiment boldly and repeatedly until a feasible approach is found. Giving the pupil an easier book to read, praising him for less-than-average accomplishment, delegating to him some simple responsibility (even though he seems not to have earned it), and making sure that tasks are understood are approaches which are sometimes successful. One teacher gave a large, overage, and slow-learning bully self-confidence by making him responsible for playground materials. It was up to him to see that everyone had a chance with bats and balls. He earned status by taking particular care of the smaller pupils. Each pupil needs the experience of success, but unless tasks of varying degrees of difficulty are devised, the inevitable result is continuing easy success for some and repeated frustration and failure for others. Each child needs direction—to be steered into areas where he can have the degree of success that will merit commendation. He needs to experiment; to participate in field trips and visit museums, industrial plants, and the like; to report on independent travels; and to read and ask questions. All pupils need to learn to be good followers, and many of them need experience as leaders in appropriate undertakings. *It is in adapting learning experiences to the needs of individual pupils that a teacher capitalizes on the interaction between genetic potential and school environment.*

Rapidity of Development in the Early Years

In a brief period of nine months, from the time of the fertilization of the ovum, the human organism develops from an almost weightless cell to a body weighing about 7 or 8 pounds—increasing in weight 500 million times. In fact, by the end of the embryonic period (the end of the tenth week after fertilization) there has been an increase in mass of some 2 million percent. Just as remarkable is the growth in terms of differentiation. Body parts have become 95 percent differentiated (legs, arms, eyes, ears, etc.) by the end of the embryonic period. The neural system and the brain have already grown rapidly, and at the time of birth, the brain will contain 95 percent of the number of cells it will ever have. Body proportions change markedly during the prenatal period. Thus prenatal growth is characterized by vast increase in size, gross changes in proportion, and increased differentiation of body parts.

Although growth does slow down in the postnatal period, it continues at an amazing pace. The infant is expected to triple his birth weight in his first year. By his second birthday, he is approximately half as tall as he will be as an adult. Just as noticeable as his growth in size is his growth in independence.

Psychological development during the preschool period also continues apace. There is a remarkable improvement in coordination, perception, differentiation of behavior, and acquisition of skills. The preschool child learns to feed himself; he develops regular patterns of sleep and can put himself to bed; he learns to dress himself—although buttons, hooks, and zippers may cause some difficulty. He acquires control over the processes of elimination. Language development continues for years, but the preschool child can make himself understood and can control others through language. He is rapidly acquiring the ability to get along with his brothers and sisters and other children in the community. He is learning to get along with adults, though frequently they thwart his desire for independence. He gains some understanding of time and numbers. His fundamental personality traits (cheerfulness, friendliness, volubility, perseverance, etc.) are becoming crystallized.

Grade-school children continue to grow rapidly, and the most noticeable growth is in further development of skills. A new and complicated skill, reading—a fundamental tool in our civilization—is acquired. Personality traits are further consolidated. Skills in social adaptation are improved.

Development takes place most rapidly in the early years, *but* it is important to realize that it continues *throughout life*. Although it is probable that broad patterns of personality are established before school age, *the manifestation of personality traits is subject to modification during the entire life span* (Smith and Smith, 1966, p. 359). Intelligence, in terms of modifiability, plasticity, and retentiveness of the brain, may have reached its maximum development during the first twenty-five years, but the use made of that intelligence is a matter of personal responsibility for those who have reached maturity or middle or old age.

Educational Implications of Early Rapid Development

Various authorities state that it is in the first five, six, or eight years that the broad fundamental patterns of behavior are developed. This does not mean that responses are solidified in these early years and that little change will take place thereafter, but it is important to recognize the tendency and to make the early school years as enjoyable as possible. It is probable that the first years in school do much to shape the child's liking for, or aversion to, subsequent formal learning.

Increasing recognition of the school's responsibility for emotional adjustment and social development of its pupils is evident (Pileggi, 1969). Appropriately prepared teachers are first concerned with their pupils' habits of adjustment and then with the acquisition of academic skills. They recognize that some children cannot or will not learn until inhibiting emotions have been reduced. Others will learn more efficiently when their social and emotional needs are well on the way to being met. They feel that the interests, ambitions, attitudes, and ideals that the child is formulating are as important as his academic learning. For such sensitive teaching, well-qualified and highly trained teachers are sorely needed (Moustakas, 1966).

The rapid developmental rate of children should be recognized but not forced. Thus, for example, the wisdom of beginning school at an early age is questioned by some authorities. On the other hand some maintain that, because of the rapidity of early growth, social experiences on a wider scale than that provided in the home should be begun at the age of three or four years. Many who work with disadvantaged children assert that the preschool years are crucial ones for later academic achievement (Bereiter and Englemann, 1966, p. 19). Others believe that the child should stay at home longer in order to develop feelings of security and of being loved. Wide experience would probably be fruitful if teachers were careful not to try to make the immature child fit a pattern of behavior more appropriate to a child who had matured more rapidly. Opportunity without rigid prescription is the recommendation that accords with this principle of growth.

Rapid early development necessitates concern for the child's health during the early school years. Although children seem to be ceaselessly active, they tire easily because of the immaturity of body tissues and because rapid growth involves large expenditure of energy. Fatigue may result in loss of appetite, low resistance to disease, restlessness and irritability, listlessness, and inattentiveness, and it contributes to slowness and perhaps difficulty in learning. The child suffering from fatigue comes to believe he cannot learn so well as others, and his reputation is that of a slow learner. One should expect and perhaps encourage frequent absences for minor illnesses during this period of rapid growth.

Teachers sometimes feel that their efforts are fruitless because so much has taken place in a child's life before he enters the classroom and because his attitudes toward learning seem already to be set. Even if the rate of growth is slowing by the time the child enters school, however, there is a steadily increasing ability (not capacity) to learn as age increases. It is fallacious to believe that capacity for learning is dependent solely upon rate of growth or mental agility. There remains, far into the adult years, an enormous capacity to learn that is based on native ability *plus* accumulated experience. Early learning is important, but mental development and learning, unlike height, do not have a definite terminal growth point (Bloom, 1964, p. 81). The matter of experience should not be underestimated—the adult might well feel sympathy for the young learner with his limited experience.

Influence of Maturation on Training Results

Before training, instruction, and teaching can be productive, appropriate inner growth must take place; the muscles, nerves, and brain must have developed to a proper degree. The importance of maturation has been noted in toilet training. Parents who wait until the baby has developed sufficiently discover that the child acquires the ability to keep clean and dry almost overnight. Studies of preschool children indicate that the more mature acquire skills in buttoning, cutting with scissors, and climbing more easily than the less mature. Primary children are not only unable, but they do not want, to learn economic theory or the calculus (Bigge and Hunt, 1968, p. 456). This does not mean that maturation determines teaching entirely and that we just wait for it to occur. Bruner (1963a, p. 47) asserts that almost any subject, in some form, might possibly be taught to any child.

Experiments, observations, and measurements have established the fact that trying to teach a child to read before he has reached a given degree of maturity is relatively fruitless. There are times of readiness for learning a second language (Penfield, 1967). Montessori preschool and primary school methods are based on the proposition of handling materials and liberty within limits that will stimulate development of readiness for more academic pursuits (Goldberg, 1967).

There are many kinds of readiness—probably many more than can be appreciated. Piaget's (1969) theory of stages of mental development involves the matter of readiness for various kinds of thought. Ennis (1967) has been concerned with readiness to master a principle. A forward thrust in teaching-learning may be made when various readinesses are recognized, their statuses can be evaluated, and the results are directed to making more adequate provisions for differences in readiness.

Educational Implications of Readiness

The principle of readiness is frequently ignored in school learning situations. If a pupil is too immature, insecure, and unacquainted with reading materials to permit success, then exerting pressure to make him read or comparing his progress with that of pupils who are ready may instill negative attitudes that persist even beyond the time when physiological readiness has been achieved. Because of required, traditional, and standardized curricula, teachers try to teach reading, arithmetic, algebra, and social abstractions when the child reaches a prescribed chronological age. The consequence is that much teaching is done at or near the frustration level of many pupils. The **nongraded** school, by increasing the age range within an instructional group, tries to avoid the rigidity that makes it difficult to acknowledge differences in the time a pupil achieves readiness for a particular kind of learning experience (Beggs and Buffie, 1967).

Recognition of the necessity for maturation has been given in the primary grades in the form of reading readiness programs. Readiness is achieved by allowing time for the maturation of mental abilities *and* by stimulating it through experience. A readiness program must generate interest, stimulate eagerness, and cultivate desire. Field trips, visual aids, storytelling (by both teacher and pupils), listening games, and experience charts (records made by the teacher of events that the children relate) are used in readiness programs. An effective readiness program allows for intrinsic growth and, through experiences, develops conceptual background.

It should not be inferred that readiness to learn occurs at a precise point on a scale. It might be better to think of several types of reading readiness—a time to begin reading, a time to read about things the pupil has not himself experienced, a time to evaluate what is read, a time to appreciate the chronology of history, and a time to draw inferences. It takes time and experience, not merely a mental age of 6-1/2 years, for full comprehension. This leads to the further conclusion that readiness for one teacher's method of teaching may not be readiness for another teacher's method.

Readiness is related to methods of instruction. At the University of Illinois, investigations into arithmetic teaching have shown that the act of pupil **discovery** is important. Sixth graders in a Harvard experiment learned geography better when they themselves developed theories about the location of cities. Recent studies reaffirm the value of knowing principles and weaving facts into them; and intellectual excitement is more likely if it is worth the individual's knowing—useful beyond the learner's immediate need (Bruner, 1963*a*, pp. 21-31). The new mathematics, science, and economic programs which are based on discovery, understanding, and relationships which are commensurate with the pupils' maturation are means of recognizing the phenomenon of readiness (Shulman and Keislar, 1966, p. 28). In short, the way learning is structured influences the condition of readiness. The teacher cannot evade his own responsibility by citing the child's immaturity.

Children must progress through certain developmental stages before they can be expected to participate successfully in number work. A child is not yet ready to do real addition if he counts objects to get a sum. If he must add in order to find the product of two numbers, he is not ready for multiplication. For teachers, this suggests that if the child cannot meet the traditional standards, the standards and methods should be altered to correspond to the developmental stage of the pupil.

Maturation probably plays a less important part in learning as the individual approaches his adult level of intelligence. However, an example of the role of maturation in later learning can be seen in the study of algebra. Experiments indicate that among high school students of equivalent IQs there are fewer failures in algebra when it is studied in the junior year than in the traditional freshman year. In addition to special selection on the basis of mental ability, attention must also be given to students' understandings of meanings, mastery of basic skills, vocabulary, concepts of causal relations, and to their interests (Gibb, Mayer, and Truenfels, 1960).

It is likely that there is such a thing as overreadiness—having passed beyond the time to "strike while the iron is hot." Schools are programmed to learning certain things at certain times. Retarded readers in the intermediate grades often complain that the materials provided them are too babyish, for example. And the same may be said of emotional learnings. It has been postulated that if normal heterosexual attitudes are not developed during adolescence, psychological or psychiatric intervention may be required to assist in their later achievement. Older persons who are determined to get a college education may be able to deal successfully with their overreadiness through strong motivation. However, they may have already lost some of their readiness for learning easily that which is entirely novel (Penfield, 1967). The learning of school subjects is a developmental task, and our culture demands that these tasks be learned at or about a certain time—failure to do so increases the likelihood of encountering difficulty. Effective teachers must be concerned about the timing of their efforts—Havighurst (1953, p. 5) refers to the "teachable moment."

Sequential Patterns of Behavior

Development is a regular step-by-step process rather than a random one. Any skill, trait, or knowledge must have its antecedents; in turn, these form the foundation for the next level of growth. The baby creeps before he crawls and crawls before he walks, and the growing child walks before he runs and runs before he dances. He babbles before he says words, says single words before he constructs sentences, communicates orally before he writes, and writes simply before he composes learned dissertations.

The regular and sequential appearance of behavior patterns makes it possible to judge the maturity of a given individual. Not all persons of the same chronological age have matured at the same rate: Some are at one level in the general sequence of behavior patterns, while others may be markedly lower or higher on the developmental scale. Edgar A. Doll has devised a scale for evaluating the social maturity of an individual—an example of growth sequences.[2] Representative items in the scale are:

Table 1-1

Behavior Item	Age, Years
Grasps objects within reach	0-1
Drinks from cup or glass unassisted	1-2
Puts on coat or dress unassisted	2-3
Buttons coat or dress	3-4
Goes about neighborhood unattended	4-5
Prints simple words	5-6
Uses table knife for spreading	6-7
Tells time to quarter of an hour	7-8
Reads on own initiative	8-9
Makes minor purchases	9-10
Makes telephone calls	10-11
Is left to care for self or others	11-12
Performs responsible routine chores	12-15
Follows current events	15-18
Has a job or continues schooling	18-20
Uses money providently	20-25
Promotes civic progress	25-+

The complete Vineland Social Maturity Scale has several items for each year, and the composite score is indicative of a given level of maturity. Some children, for example, make telephone calls before they make minor purchases, but nevertheless, the general sequence tends to hold true.

2   A manual of instructions and explanations of theory and use of the scale is Edgar A. Doll, 1953, *Measurement of Social Competence*, Philadelphia: Educational Test Bureau. This manual makes the scale a more usable tool for teachers who wish to understand their pupils better.

     This regular sequential appearance of behavior patterns is one basis for constructing intelligence tests. The Stanford revision of the Binet-Simon Scale, which has been the standard reference for many intelligence tests for some years, uses certain developmental items to determine the mental development of an individual. Some of the items and the years in which they are usually accomplished are cited below:

Table 1-2

Item	*Year*	*Month*
Identifies body parts: hair, mouth, ear, nose, hands, eye	2	
Names objects: chair, automobile, box, key, fork	2	6
Compares size of balls	3	
Sorts black and white buttons	3	6
Names opposites: "Brother is a boy, sister is a . . . ."	4	
Identifies use of materials: "What is a house made of?"	4	6
Forms triangle from square piece of paper	5	
Tells what part of a picture is missing	6	
Points out similarities: wood and coal, etc.	7	
Remembers details from a story	8	
Copies design from memory	9	
Repeats six digits	10	
Repeats sentence from memory (15-16 words)	11	
Understands abstract words: pity, curiosity, etc.	12	
Unscrambles a sentence	13	
Solves oral problem of determined difficulty	14	
Differentiates abstractions: laziness and idleness	Average adult	
Repeats six digits in reverse of order presented	Superior adult I	
Explains meaning of proverbs	Superior adult II	
Repeats thought of orally presented passage	Superior adult III	

Source: Lewis M. Terman and Maud A. Merrill, 1960, *Stanford-Binet Intelligence Scale: Manual for Third Revision, Form L-M,* Boston: Houghton Mifflin Company, *passim.* Used by permission.

     In this scale, there are six items for each half-year through age four; beginning with the fifth year, there are six items for each full year, and the individual taking the test is credited with two months' mental age for each item successfully accomplished. Frequently, the subject fails all the items for a given year and accomplishes one item among those for the next year. But in spite of such variations, behavior development is generally sequential.

Educational Implications of Sequential Development

School curricula should be, and to a large extent are, based on the sequential nature of pupil development patterns. It is recognized, for instance, that appropriate activities for children in the primary grades should utilize the large muscles of the body because children are not ready for fine coordination. Large blocks, crates, oversize crayons, and large pieces of heavy paper are being used to supplement the cutting, weaving, and writing activities used in primary grades in earlier days. As development proceeds, differences between individual children become more pronounced, and the variety of interests and abilities must be recognized if some pupils are not to be frustrated. Children in the upper grades are expanding their horizons in many ways, especially in social activities. They are interested in people and imitate others with sincerity and persistence. As they become more socially conscious, they can make use of adult guidance, and many will like, and profit from, drill in the hope of becoming more competent. Although this is the age when propositional operations (Piaget, 1969) become a characteristic, many may still have difficulty in working abstract problems.

The expanding social horizons of adolescents make adaptations to their peers increasingly important. Teachers and parents might well recognize this factor and be less concerned about adolescents' conforming to adult standards of dress and grooming. Both adults and adolescents, through reflection and discussion, should realize the normality *and necessity* of passing through stages in heterosexual adjustment. The normal stages are boy-girl indifference, dating, falling in love, and marriage. The significance of sequential development is illustrated in studies of marriage which show that unless one has dated different persons and fallen *seriously* in love about four times, the chances for satisfactory and durable marriage are considerably reduced (Burchinal, 1972).

Teen-agers have been helped to perceive stages of development by having them observe younger groups—kindergarten, primary, and intermediate pupils—and then discussing the behavior they saw. After having supplementary skits, films, and discussion panels, the young people came to a better understanding—as revealed by their discussions and behavior—of the meaning and implications of maturity (Kaiser and Timmer, 1964). Thus in a class in government, the teacher might start with local government and the way it affects young people, with visits to community political divisions, or even with problems of class or schoolwide government. Study of state and national government may be undertaken after matters that most intimately concern the student have been discussed. Learning that is abstract and remote from the student's experience is likely to result in mere verbalization, devoid of real understanding and manifested by parroting of statements made in a book.

Individuality of Growth Rates

Some children reach maturity at an early age, and some never become "adults" in the broad sense of the word. It is as if some traveled by ox cart and some by jet plane. Some achieve prominence in their teens, others in their twenties, and a few achieve prominence after they have become sexagenarians.

Different parts of the organism grow at various rates. A child has many ages: a chronological age, a mental age, an educational age, a grip age, a carpal age, a dental age, a social age, and an organismic age, to mention only a few of the distinguishable phases of growth that have been measured. A given child will show much variation in these ages, and the older he is, the greater will be the variation. Moreover, growth in some one area may proceed unevenly. That is, though a child has learned to feed himself, to tie his shoes, or to say "Please," he may not give consistent evidence of it.

Educational Implications of Idiosyncratic Developmental Rates

Some pupil differences, which are evident in pupils' reaction patterns, result from socioeconomic backgrounds—differences in family behavior habits, diet, cultural opportunities, ideals, attitudes, and adjustive actions. Other differences are still more obvious—differences in energy output, learning ability, interests, background information, body build, height and weight, resistance to disease, temperament, and physical attractiveness (Williams, 1971). Dropouts may be accounted for, in part, by the school's failure to solve the problem of dealing with individual differences, but emotional disturbances at home, lack of a family tradition of education, low income, and lack of skill in making peer relationships must also be taken into account. There has been a failure to reach the goal of providing each child with the type of training and education best suited to him as an individual and to his expected needs as an adult. Often a teacher is able to select reading materials at several grade levels, schedule arithmetic classes of varied difficulty and types, and scale requirements for groups of pupils of somewhat similar interests and mental development. Teaching machines and programmed studies are being used to provide some of this needed individuality.

Because developmental patterns are unique, individual, and distinctive, prescriptions for recognizing the divergency are not possible. It can be said that, to date, not enough has been done to capitalize on pupil uniqueness. Independent study, for instance, has not really been tried. Some progress has been made by way of IPI (Individually Prescribed Instruction). In those instances where real independent study has been tried the results in terms of student responsibility, subject mastery, initiative, and enthusiasm have been gratifying to students and teachers (Plunkett, 1969). Some schools have gone as far as quest activities, in which pupils have a block of time in which they may study what, when, where, and how they wish. The heart of much current innovation in education is to individualize instruction.

The uniqueness of individual rates of growth throws much doubt on the value of periodic examinations as a basis for grades. Experimentation on how to modify or extirpate the time-honored practices of grading and examinations for all students will require teachers who have unconditional positive regard for pupils and who have faith enough to trust them.

Constancy of Individual Developmental Rates

A child who is tall for his age at two years will *probably* be tall as an adult. A child who has an IQ of 80 at four years will be *likely* to have an IQ within 5 or 10 points of 80 when he is fifteen, and one who has an IQ of 120 will *tend* to maintain that IQ in later years. When growth curves of several children for any one trait are superimposed, they tend to follow the same general pattern, and there is little crossing of the curves of different individuals.

Ability to predict individual rates and patterns of growth—mental, physical, and social—is helpful in establishing educational objectives, and it helps teachers to avoid expecting too much of some and too little of others, thus reducing the possibility of frustration. Vocational, academic, and avocational suggestions of guidance programs are based on the relative constancy of individual growth rates and patterns. In general, the dull tend to remain dull, and giftedness shows itself relatively early. Delinquency has its warning signs in predelinquent behavior (evidence of social and personal maladjustment). The bright second grader has a better chance of election to Phi Beta Kappa than a pupil who spends two years in second grade. But these are tendencies; marked environmental changes may effect a change in developmental rate. Children who have been inspired by a teacher, or some momentous event, may markedly alter the use made of their potentials. In addition, some children mature later.

Continuity and Gradualness of Growth

The principle of continuity and gradualness of growth can be either encouraging or discouraging. No magical transformations of personality or intellectual development can realistically be expected. However, if one will take the time, exert the effort, and work with persistence, even very difficult goals may be achieved.

If we were to visualize growth as taking place on an inclined plane rather than in sharply demarcated stages or levels, we would comprehend the process better. Childish conduct develops gradually from infancy; adolescent conduct is the result of continuous growth from childhood. There are clear differences between the midpoints of the various levels, but the borderlines are vague. It is wiser to think in terms of expansion and emergence of traits and abilities than in terms of sudden transformations and distinct levels.

Developmental tasks (see Chapter 9, Developmental Tasks of Middle Childhood) are described in terms of broad age spans, but actually those tasks merge and overlap (Bernard, 1970*a*). For instance, the baby's task of learning to care for himself merges into the child's task of learning skills in games, and that in turn is a component of the adolescent's task of achieving assurance of economic independence. Preschool children have small competence in problem solving, but this ability increases with age and experience. The continuousness of development is a major reason why psychologists and educators are concerned with the early years (Hunt, 1968; Kagan, 1968).

Educational Implications of Continuous and Gradual Development

Hurry, impatience, discouragement, and prodding are not in accord with this principle. Teachers must know and accept the fact that sudden transformations of personality cannot realistically be expected. On the other hand, they may be assured that the expenditure of effort and the passage of time will inevitably show results. If it were possible to see, on the same day, a pupil as he is on the first day of the term and as he is at the end of the term, the gain would be apparent. The bewildered freshman presents a sharp contrast to the confident senior; yet the point of change cannot be allocated. **Equivalent tests** given at the beginning and at the end of the term serve to verify the continuity of growth.

Students need the help of teachers to understand that by enlarging knowledge and establishing daily habits, they lay the foundations for later competence. Their haste to leave school, to take a job, to become famous, and to establish families must not interfere with their taking advantage of continued, directed, and purposeful steps.

Differentiation and Integration in Development

Prenatal physical growth provides an excellent illustration of differentiation. During the initial days of development (known as the period of the ovum), the baby to be is merely a rounded mass of cells. During the following period, up to about nine weeks (period of the embryo), the body parts are clearly distinguishable, or differentiated. During the next phase (fetal period), growth is largely concerned with increase in size of already differentiated parts. Shortly after birth, some teeth have become differentiated; as age increases, certain tissues become more clearly distinguished as bone. The wristbones of a five-month-old child are much farther apart than those of a five-year-old child, and those of a five-year-old are farther apart than those of a sixteen-year-old. Differentiation is also seen in physical action. A six-month-old baby grasps a small object with a sweeping motion of the entire hand. Soon after his first birthday, the child is able to pick the object up by his thumb and forefinger.

Language development during the life span involves differentiation. At first, the child refers to all toy animals as "doggie" or "kitty," then toy ducks and bears are eliminated from the dog concept. The word "dog" is later attached to live dogs. As perception is further differentiated, dogs are seen more precisely. Dalmatians, Airedales, pointers, and Pekingese are recognized as specific kinds of dogs.

Complex behaviors, such as catching a baseball, are not built from the separate acts of reaching, grasping, and decreasing muscular tension. The total act is involved at the beginning; only later are the parts of the act analyzed. Pupils learn school subjects in a similar manner. Writing the story or telling about an incident should take precedence over diction, pronunciation, sentence structure, spelling, and capitalization (Kohl, 1967). These details are important, but they would come better as the outcome of integrated, purposeful effort rather than as isolated entities. *The development of skills, concepts, and knowledge are matters of differentiation and specificity.*

Integration—coordinated, harmonious, and efficient behavior—takes place concurrently with differentiation. The phenomenon can readily be seen by comparing an eighth-grade second baseman with a big-league ball player. The eighth grader is tense, he runs hard, he plunges for an easy bounder, he throws with a mighty effort—into the ground or over the first baseman's head. The big-leaguer relaxes in position. A sizzling liner over the pitcher's head hits in front of second base and bounces over the base. Somehow, the second baseman is there at precisely the right moment. He dips his glove and, all in the same series of movements, turns, steps, throws, and the runner is out. Integration means that all parts are working harmoniously and efficiently toward a planned and specific objective.

Integration is also well illustrated in speech. The baby has difficulty saying a single word—he purses his lips, opens his mouth wide, sticks his tongue out— and perhaps says something understandable. Increasing integration over the years may result in his becoming a skilled actor or speaker, whose words are accompanied by integrated inflection, gestures, and facial expressions.

Personality integration, the harmonious and effective working together of abilities, energies, aspirations, and motives, is frequently mentioned by psychologists and educators as a concern for all. Actually, conflicts between abilities, desires, and social demands are normal, and inconsistency of behavior is quite normal. However, the tendency toward integration is regarded by some as a driving force in life that is never quite completely achieved. (Bonner, 1956, pp. 99ff; Combs and Snygg, 1959, p. 46). From the teacher's standpoint, it might be advantageous to think of integrating as a process rather than integration as an achievable goal.

Educational Implications of Learning as Differentiation and Integration

Communication is such an important aspect of total living that precise and selective use of words (differentiation) should be emphasized by every teacher. The differences between "cat" and "dog" and "boy" and "girl" are problems for preschool children. The differences between "surprise" and "astonish," "infer" and "imply," and "healthy" and "healthful" are problems for high school and college students, in whom the process of differentiation is still incomplete. Integration is involved in combining words into incisive and economical sentences; in addition, the inflections, pauses, and combinations of sentences that make meaning most clear and forceful must be used.

The breakdown of schoolwork into subjects facilitates differentiation. However, curriculum makers warn that this breakdown may go so far that the student fails to see the interrelations between subjects and life outside of school. The plea of educators and the demand of students is that of relevance (Schrag, 1969b).

Integration is the process of synthesizing the various aspects of physical, environmental, and personality attributes and of becoming a functioning part of social groups. One way to achieve integration in education is to emphasize the relationships that exist between various school subjects—such emphasis may very well be an advantage of having one teacher for all subjects in the elementary grades. It may be one of the profitable outcomes of team teaching. Teachers may show that data from other subject areas can be used in solving current problems, for example, by approaching subject matter with "Last week we discussed . . ." or "That should remind you of . . . ." Integration may also be facilitated by using problems and projects as points of departure rather than ends in themselves. All school subjects may be related, for instance, to the theme "How children can become involved [well within the comprehension of even primary pupils in today's milieu] in neighborhood activities."

One of the major emphases in "emerging" schools for contemporary society is a shift from teachers' telling to pupils' active involvement in learning processes (Goodlad, 1967). In this shift from teaching to learning, personality integration is of focal importance. The teacher is obliged to watch for evidences of lack of integration, such as (1) inconsistency between professed knowledge and action; (2) failure to apply knowledge in reactive responses; (3) verbalization of facts but failure to apply them; (4) lack of readiness to revise hypotheses, opinions, and beliefs; (5) statements made without corroborative evidence; and (6) condemnation of others for doing what the individual does himself.

The development of socially integrated people, able and interested in cooperating in the improvement of society, has been a goal of our educational system during our entire national history. The school, where experiences can be selected and guided, provides time and place to develop such individuals. Because one of the major problems of the nation and the world is understanding, the study of semantics, or the meanings of language, is a requisite of fundamental education (Passow, 1967*b*). Students at all levels must be given opportunities to exchange opinions through conversation, discussion, and debate. Listening and recitation are not enough; there must also be a revelation of feelings (Rogers, 1968). Problem and project methods may be utilized. It is essential that pupils be provided opportunities to become increasingly self-directive. Working cooperatively on common problems of the operation of the school also will constitute steps in the direction of personal and social integration.

Correlation of Traits in Individuals

"Unto every one that hath shall be given" is nowhere more clearly shown than in the field of psychology. Despite what we might wish to be the case, and contrary to what is sometimes believed, deficiency in one aspect of the organism or personality is not compensated for by giftedness or strength in another. Although the relationship is not sufficiently uniform to warrant prediction in individual cases, there is evidence revealing a low but positive correspondence among the traits or abilities possessed by any one person. Slightly more often than not the child who has a high IQ will have greater physical strength, more skill in physical activities, fewer sensory handicaps, be taller, heavier, more resistant to disease, better looking, and more socially adaptable than his peer of the same age whose IQ is markedly lower. Such remarks as "beautiful but dumb" and "strong back, weak mind" are based on insufficient data. Gallagher (1964, p. 10) warns that children do not arrive in the classroom as averages, hence teachers must not be misled by the slight alleged differences.

Correlation holds for both personality assets and liabilities. Just as the gifted child has fewer sensory defects than do other children, so the handicapped child often has multiple handicaps. Crippling is often accompanied by visual and auditory handicaps or endocrine dysfunction, which may cause low vitality or mentality. However, personality defects that seem to accompany handicaps may be a function of treatment and perception rather than being the inevitable accompaniment of physical handicap (Lipton, Steinschneider, and Richmond, 1966).

These remarks do not hold for another kind of compensation. A person may compensate for a shortcoming by spending more time in developing that area or by abandoning his ambitions in one area and substituting others. But there is nothing innate or intrinsic in such compensation; it is the exception rather than the rule. For every Edison, Roosevelt, or Einstein, there are hundreds of individuals with similar handicaps whose accomplishments are inferior or mediocre. A person does not necessarily have great drive or a high level of aspiration *because* he has a handicap.

The principle of correlation can be observed in a visit to any school. The child who is best in arithmetic is frequently near the top in spelling, is popular with his classmates, and plays vigorously and well.

Educational Implications of Trait Correlations

There is ample evidence that many teachers think erroneously in terms of compensation. Such teachers recommend industrial art or physical education classes for the pupil who has difficulty in academic work. The pupil who is slow in academic work *may* do well in industrial art but rarely because he has outstanding talent for manual work. His good work is due to the extra time he spends on it.

The practical import of the principle has to do with pupil understanding, teaching methods, and curriculum. Teachers should avoid the temptation to steer a child into physical activities, construction exercises, or repetitive art productions *because* he is slow in academic pursuits. The time has arrived when we should emphasize the *slow* learners, rather than think of them as nonlearners.

Many, perhaps even *most*, children have special talents. Taylor (1968) asserts that we are "dumping" valuable human talents by having too narrow emphases in schools. Although it is likely that traits and abilities will be positively correlated, there is some possibility that slow learners may have special talents— leadership qualities, athletic prowess,* or skills as magicians or singers. Pupils with artistic talent do sometimes experience difficulty in the traditional subjects. When these talents are noted, they can be used to build ego strength that prompts the individual to try for goals at more difficult levels.

---

*Studies indicate that athletes have, on the average, higher intelligence than their nonathletic classmates. When their time is not taken by training and practice, their marks are slightly superior to those who are regularly nonparticipants.

Lifelong Development: A Challenge to Educational Psychology

The Cultural Demand for Change

One certainty that everyone must face is that things will be much different in the next decade. A few data will illustrate this fact. It has been estimated that half the children now in elementary schools will, as adults, work in jobs which do not yet exist (McCully; 1969, p. 10). Rapidity of change is also illustrated in the "knowledge explosion." McGraw-Hill Book Company, in an advertisement, congratulated freshman engineering students for selection of a career but warned them that a substantial part of what they learned as undergraduates would be obsolete by the time they were graduated. Moreover, the rate of knowledge change and cumulation is accelerating. It has been postulated that if all extant knowledge could have been compressed into one volume in the year 1, it would have taken until the year 1750 to develop enough knowledge to require two volumes. With that as a base, subsequent changes in knowledge accumulation could be summarized as follows:

Year	*Volumes*
1	1
1750	2
1900	4
1950	8
1960	16
1967	32

Another way of stating this explosive rate of knowledge accumulation is to say that half of the scientists the world has ever known are alive today. However, this may be less startling when population explosion is taken into consideration. Population in the United States has been increasing at a rate of 20 percent per decade since 1910.

Changes in the work world are also taking place at a rate which will challenge the ingenuity of teachers and test the adaptability of educational institutions. Ours is an overdeveloped society, i.e., one in which there is decreasing demand for lower-level skills and accelerating demand for high-level skills (McCully, 1969, p. 64). The working man of the 1900s is considered by some already to be obsolete. Meanwhile the demand for professional workers steadily increases, tripling since 1900 and having almost doubled between 1950 and 1966 (*Statistical Abstracts, 1967, p. 231*). This means that the traditional function of the school as a selecting and sorting agency (Havighurst and Neugarten, 1967, pp.

69ff) will have to be changed to one in which talent is nursed and developed. Encouragement of individuality in rate and direction of development is the task without precedent of schools for the 1970s. Weaknesses currently are frequent points of unfavorable comparison and ego deflation.

Rapid Change and Continuous Learning

The rapidity of change, including knowledge and population explosion, imposes new burdens on educators. At an earlier time it may have been plausible to place primary emphasis on the content of education. This premise must be questioned in view of explosive change. The emphasis must currently be on the process of education. *Learning how to learn is now of primary importance.* There are also some corollaries which merit consideration. Pupils must not only learn how to learn but they must also develop a positive regard—perhaps the word "love" might not be too strong—for continuous learning. An aim of education at all levels must be to develop a "self-renewing" mechanism that will have reference to both the present and the future (Goodlad, 1967). This, in turn, implies that teachers respect different learning styles. The hoped-for result will be encouragement of an independent pursuit of knowledge after the period of formal schooling has been conventionally terminated.[3]

Many of the developmental principles dealt with in this chapter—importance of the early years, sequential development, uniqueness of rate, uniqueness of pattern, gradualness, and continuousness—are involved in the development of love for, and habit of, continuous learning. There are many (Goodman, Goodlad, Friedenberg, Glasser, Rogers, etc.) who believe that unless this educational aim is accomplished, our schools must be considered to be failures.

Teachers must themselves be involved in the process of continuous learning and in individual self-renewal, if only to constitute models for pupils. In addition, research evidence continues to accumulate which indicates that teachers' attitudes toward children show in classroom behavior. Pupils who are the subjects of affection, concern, indifference, or rejection are aware of it, and other pupils in the class can also discern the teachers' attitudes and behaviors (Silberman, 1969). The press of classroom activities—several pupils' asking questions, raising hands, seeking guidance, demanding limits—means that the teacher cannot *logically deliberate* each teacher-pupil interchange. Mead (1970) asserts that the knowledge explosion and social revolution require that in addition to the older generation's teaching youngsters and the older generation's learning *with* young-

---

3   Learning styles are dealt with more extensively in Chapter 6. Independent study is considered in Chapter 16. The words "conventionally terminated" are used in recognition of the fact that already a substantial portion of the population engages in short courses, extension classes, seminars, and institutes.

sters, still another stance is needed: that of oldsters' learning *from* youngsters. All this demands that teachers be engaged in the process of learning new attitudes toward self and others.

A Developing Ego Concept

The pupil's ego concept is an integral aspect of the cultural demand for continuous learning. The pupil must come to think of himself as a person capable of learning, a person tenacious enough to deal with current demands. There are many things, such as teacher feedback, comparison of the pupil's earlier work with what is done today, guidance toward new challenges, and enthusiasm for his creativity, that nurture such an ego concept. There are other practices—competitive grading, rigid curricular requirements, absence of (or limited) independent study, grade achievement standards, unwise use of test results—which undermine the kind of ego concept which fosters the process and habit of continuous learning (Glasser, 1969, p. 77). The ego concept will continue to be a major concern of psychology of learning and teaching.

Summary

Development results from the interaction of the organism with its environment. Hence, it is a function of the individual's perception of himself and his milieu, as well as being a function of genetic potential and of opportunity. Teachers have the task of helping to alter perceptions and of managing the school environment so that developmental principles are recognized.

Development takes place most rapidly in the early years, so primary teachers have much impact on establishing attitudes toward continued learning as well as the tools for learning. It is important not to place sole emphasis on the words "early years" because development continues to take place, and the later years must not be discounted.

The effect of teaching is dependent on the stage of maturation. Readiness, a concomitant of maturation, can be fostered by experiences in number concepts, social contacts, and acquaintance with the physical world.

Patterns of behavior appear in an orderly sequence and thus enable teachers to predict, from present status, what the individual will probably be like later in terms of intellectual ability, social adaptability, and personality and character.

Each individual has his own growth rate, or pattern, which means that education will be most effective when differences between pupils are given functional recognition. For the individual, these rates *tend* to remain constant except for marked changes in the environment or pupil.

Development is gradual and continuous. This principle suggests that teacher may avoid hurry, impatience, and discouragement by trusting the paired phenomena of slowness and persistence in developmental processes.

Development is a matter of both differentiation and integration. Teachers should point out significant differences in the concepts they teach and show how these are related in the total pattern of living. Applications, examples, illustrations, and emphasis on problem solving capitalize on this principle.

Correlation rather than compensation is the general rule for the distribution of traits and abilities. Hence, teachers can expect much in many areas from able pupils but must scale down most expectations for the less able.

The concept of developmental tasks provides a sound rationale for varying procedures according to individual pupil needs. This, in turn, enhances the probability of promoting age concepts which will lead to lifelong learning.

Suggested Additional Reading

BRUNER, JEROME S., 1967, "Education as Social Invention," in H. W. Bernard and W. C. Huckins (eds.), *Readings in Educational Psychology*, Scranton, Pa.: International Textbook Company. From J. S. Bruner, *Toward a Theory of Instruction*, 1966, Cambridge, Mass.: Harvard University Press.

   The author shows how education is itself in a process of development, and he makes some predictions in regard to changes. These predicted changes would bring into focus developmental characteristics of individuals and the nature of society.

WILLIAMS, ROGER J., 1971, "The Biology of Behavior," *Saturday Review*, vol. 54, no. 5, pp. 17-19+, Jan. 30.

   Psychologists will increase their emphasis on recognition of individuality as they learn to appreciate the large differences there are in biological makeup.

STINCHCOMBE, ARTHUR L., 1969, "Environment: The Cumulation of Effects Is Yet to Be Understood," *Harvard Educational Review*, vol. 39, pp. 511-522.

   "Early" education programs for the disadvantaged are not enough. Culture, school, and social conditions must function consistently and sequentially in order to achieve optimum impact.

THORSELL, BERNARD A., 1968, "Discovering Human Abilities," *Journal of Creative Behavior*, vol. 2, pp. 77-82.

   The author asserts that there are many more talents that can be identified and tested than is recognized in typical school practice. When a greater variety of talents are tested, more pupils will find themselves in the gratifying "above average" group in some talent.

3

Children as Learners

The most important elements in teaching-learning transactions are the learners. This book began with a discussion of teachers because the greatest power a person exerts, his maximum influence, is on his own course of action. What he is and does, in terms of human relations, is the teacher's most effective weapon. Presumably, however, his primary concern is the development of pupils.

Developments in learning theory are swinging away from single and simple explanations; e.g., stimulus-response (S→R) or stimulus acting on organism leads to response (S→O→R). Instead attention is given to larger situational and peripheral contributing factors. The study of teaching-learning processes has moved from "educational psychology" to an interdisciplinary approach. As students of educational psychology, readers are concerned with personal values and aspirations.

Autonomy as a Process and an Achievement

Children and Choice

Conflicting evidence may lead to different conclusions about the nature and needs of children. The content orientation of such books as A. S. Neill, *Summerhill* (1960), John Holt, *How Children Fail* (1964), and George Dennison, *The Lives of Children* (1969) suggests that it is fundamental that children be given freedom. It is asserted that adult strictures conflict with the basic needs of children. On the other hand, the failure of progressive education (Goodlad, 1968) and current student unrest suggest that the absence, or minimal use, of adult guidance poses hazards for optimum development (Meyer, 1969; Pileggi, 1969). Because there are conflicting views, students of teaching-learning transactions might consider the proposition that children want and need adults who act as adults; they need teachers who have some positive views about influencing the learning processes.

Freedom, it is here postulated, is a process *and* an achievement. It cannot be granted to the very young and inexperienced. This does not mean adult domination. It means that children need positive guidance. The proposition refers exclusively to children—dealing with adolescents is another matter.

To permit children freedom to do just as they want is, to them, bewildering and disappointing. The awful burden of choice is too great a responsibility when one does not have the maturity of experience to choose with a relative degree of safety. Normal adolescents, by way of contrast, wish to exercise their autonomy, make their own choices, and commit their own errors. The guidance which provided a feeling of safety in childhood has become, to the adolescent, the confining bonds which restrict the burgeoning self. But without the preparatory experience of adult guidance, handling the desired freedom may be unnecessarily perplexing and burdensome.

Children and Learning Theory

Increasingly, it is recognized that children as individuals are unique in terms of rate and style of learning and living and in terms of needs and need satisfaction (Woodring, 1970). No longer are they regarded as being delicate and as "unfolding" into maturity. Instead their marvelous toughness, pliability, and teachability is appreciated. Rather than unfolding, they undergo development which is progressive and dependent on experience.

It is the teachers of elementary pupils who, to such a considerable extent, will provide the milieu which makes the process of learning an enjoyable and anticipated one. It is they who will encourage the desire for continued and continuous learning. Dubious practices such as punishment of the reluctant learner, retention after school of those who are inattentive, and discipline of the mind by rigorous adherence to requirements gradually are being eliminated. However, basic insights—impact of teacher-pupil relationships, pupils as teachers, autonomy and involvement, and processes of inquiry—are suffering from "educational lag" and are not consistently applied.

Perhaps because today school attendance is at an all-time high, both in terms of percent of school-age children attending and in absolute figures, the need for school improvements is highly evident. Criticism has also reached its highest point with dilemmas involving adult guidance-child autonomy; structure-freedom;content-process. Some predict an utter collapse and predict at least partial abandonment of the school system (Stinnett, 1970). Others see this decade as an ideal time to bring about change—a new generation of teachers and a time for significant reform (Fischer, 1970). Agreement as to what is needed is not unanimous. There are certain basic considerations regarding the teaching-learning transaction which may become the guide for sound operation.

Psychological Characteristics of Children

Interest in Process

Young persons do not have the foresight and experience to enable them wholeheartedly to accept the purposes formulated by adults. Parents and teachers, having read books on child psychology, patiently answer questions in terms a child can understand, and he does understand. Presently, the child's lack of experience shows itself when he runs out of questions. He then repeats the same questions, which are again answered, and finally the adult says, "I answered that. You tell me." And the child can give the answer. He enjoys and is interested in the process of talking—his goal is the activity of talking. This is not to deny that many questions are asked for information; but information seeking does not explain the repetitive question. Similarly, children run, shout, tussle, paint, and perhaps even read because of the joy they receive from sensory experience. They relish movement, pressure, taste, sound, and odor. The evolving insight is that children as learners are self-propelling and creative. They require guidance and direction rather than dictation and coercion (Torrance, 1969). They are more interested in the process of learning than in the answers to questions they are not even ready to ask.

Pupils are interested in learning, if it elicits feedback. The joyful news "I can read!" "I can write my name!" are indications of their interest in performance. Children do not need to be stimulated by gold stars, or A's, or S's as symbols of their learning. The development of control over things and people is the child's underlying purpose. At a very early age, Kagan (1968) reports from studies using controlled observation, children realize that their actions tend to control others. A smile, crying, verbalization, temper tantrums are used in terms of what results these behaviors have previously obtained. The child is not just curious—about monkeys or seashells—Kagan has observed; rather his curiosity is an outcome of how teachers and others respond to his curiosity, and what his total culture has told him is important.

It is hoped, of course, that interest in process will merge into interest in results and long-range objectives. The shift will be facilitated if teachers move

Ellen Levine/College Newsphoto Alliance

from process to product slowly and progressively. One should be careful not to ask young children too frequently, "Why are you doing that?" "What is it you are painting?" "Where are you going?" If we do not get too anxious about reading, the time may come when children will read because it is fun to find answers, not because they can, or are expected to, read. It is worth noting that feelings of success occur during the process of achieving and disappear after attainment. Hence, the least teachers can do is to manifest interest in what is going on instead of stressing the end product so heavily.

"Activity" need not mean physical activity at any level of education. But in the early elementary grades, activity should frequently involve muscular and bodily movement. In the early grades, children must have a chance to touch, manipulate, act, play, imitate, and move about freely. But it is a mistake to believe that children are always on the move, that they are never still—there are many times when they sit quietly and pensively. Curricula and teaching methods must allow for and capitalize upon children's basic predisposition to alternate between rest and activity. Teachers who exert pressure, lecture, and try to control the child's spontaneity discourage the processes which are so important to children. Hart (1969) recommends a triple "A" approach—acceptance, applause, and attention.

Need for Immediate Goals

The *now* generation is really early childhood. To the young pupil, "this afternoon" and "tomorrow" are more important than "next week" and the "end of the term." For example, primary teachers have noted that if several weeks are devoted to preparing a Christmas program, interest wanes before the actual performance. Consequently, they stress "finishing the decorations today, sending the invitations this afternoon, and completing the costumes tomorrow."

The need for immediate goals is explained by the young pupil's short attention span and his lack of an accurate concept of time. The teacher should be on the alert for evidences of fatigue, such as restlessness and wandering attention, and shift to another activity as soon as practicable. The duration of the attention span varies greatly with age and still more with the importance of the task. A nine-year-old may spend all morning with his mechanical building set but find twenty minutes' drill in arithmetic boring beyond endurance.

Every teacher has the responsibility of telling his pupils what they will get out of the subject he teaches—**purposeful** activity is preferable, in the classroom, to **purposive** behavior. Although the pupil's ability to comprehend the significance of the future will grow steadily from the first grade, the elementary teacher should study the reactions of pupils to see how effective reference to the future is.

Need for Success

A feeling of success or failure need not stem from an absolute standard of performance. What is success for one person may be failure for another (McNeil and Phillips, 1969). Experiments show that the appropriateness of a child's goals depends on the kinds of experiences he has had, his self-concept, and the expectations taught by his subculture. "Successful" pupils tend to have aspirations that are in line with their previous performance. What an individual aspires to is dependent on what he perceives to be possible of achievement by him (Smith, 1967). If pupils frequently fail (receive disapproval from teachers or feel they could have done better), they lose self-esteem and tend to set levels of aspiration that are below their indicated ability. Pupils in the latter group may hope for too much—they are visionary dreamers, perhaps hoping to receive approbation for high ambition—or they may simply cease trying. When goals are not designed for children in general and individuals in specific, the result is an attempt to fit children to the Procrustean bed of predetermined curriculum.

. . . As time and energy and determination allow, the teacher tries to patch up the situation by helping or pushing those who lag, and quite possibly holding back those who go too fast. It becomes clear, then, that no *one* program can fit more than a very few of the children in the class. To search for a *sequence* that will "fit better" is futile—one might as well hunt for a single garment that will "fit better" on all the children.[1]

Need for Routines and Consistency

The bewildered children who have had too much permissiveness in their lives have been teaching the parent generation a lesson. Autonomy and recognition of individuality, yes; but absence of parental guidance is quite another thing. Maslow (1954, p. 86) was one of the first to clarify, in psychological terms, the reason· why children need adults who provide direction and limits. In his Hierarchical Needs theory, he lists safety needs after physiological needs in their order of precedence. This means that in order to strive for the next higher level of needs—the love needs—the individual requires satisfaction of safety needs. Children need protection from the overwhelming and threatening. Threat is reduced by the safety provided in routines, regularity, and regulations, of law and order. An orderly, predictable, organized world satisfies this level of need.

Leaders, fathers, mothers, teachers are, says Cottle (1969b), by definition not peers; and children are bewildered by the adult's abandonment of these roles. While the young may challenge authority, they are devastated by adult capitulation to their probings and forays. Teacher's schedule is subject to, if not determined by, what children whimsically deem to be of interest. And the result has been that children have become contemptuous of adults. Self-determination is flattering to the ego, but it may also contribute to capricious self-indulgence (Aldridge, 1969). The demands of children, adolescents, and youth increase, in part, because they are looking for the safety of limits. Meyer (1969) writes that today's youngsters of the middle class of suburbia often exhibit disturbing character defects—sexual libertarianism, rejection of adult authority, and disposition to experiment with drugs. They need genuine contact with reality—laws, rules, and all kinds of people—in order to grow toward wholesome personal development.

The desire for routine shows itself in reactions to the environment. Abrupt changes often cause emotional disturbances, and transient family habits are recognized as factors contributing to problem behavior. To the extent consistent with flexible goals of education, teachers should provide for schedules and uniformity in methods and approaches. Conflicting values in the home and the school cause other difficulties in adjustment. Children with problems are frequently those who have discovered that the procedures and aims of the teachers do not parallel those of their parents. Although attempts should be made to estab-

---

1   Leslie A. Hart, 1969, "Learning at Random," *Saturday Review*, vol. 52, no. 16, p. 62, April 19.

lish communication with parents, and modify any unnecessary contrasts, it should be made clear to the child that it is normal and permissible to live different roles and use different routines in various situations (Liddle and Rockwell, 1966). Condemnation, by word or action, of home regimes will arouse ambivalence in the child.

As far as possible, the teacher should be consistent in his moods, routines, and disciplinary attitudes and approaches. Several factors support the desirability of consistency:

1. Consistency tends to reduce anxiety. Some anxiety, especially that connected with the realization of goals, facilitates learning; but too much anxiety and anxiety that is not goal-connected are incompatible with efficient learning (Atkinson, 1965).
2. Consistency of approval for some acts and disapproval for others gives the pupil a clear-cut goal. Children do need and seek the approval of others, including teachers.
3. When habits that are to be cognitively based are strengthened by having a consistent model, the acquisition of those habits is facilitated.

There are many good reasons for interrupting a routine. Teachers should not, however, allow pupils to interrupt each other on one day and condemn such behavior the next. Questions should not be received courteously from some and be regarded as impertinent from others. Horseplay should not be accepted on one occasion and criticized on another.

Need for Play

Mental health workers recommend that all persons round out their lives by regularly participating in some form of recreation or play, and child psychologists stress play as the important business of a child. In the child's eyes play is a natural and significant activity. It gives him an opportunity to come in close contact with his environment. It builds muscle and fosters physical endurance and provides an opportunity to practice the physical skills of balance, timing, and coordination. It provides for the acquisition and exercise of social skills—cooperation, conversation, mutual respect, friendliness, and courtesy. It provides emotional satisfaction in that it fills the need for companionship, achievement, recognition, and freedom. Play is also helpful in releasing negative emotions, such as fear and anger, thus providing for emotional catharsis. Piaget regards play as an introduction to, and arena for, exercise of symbolic thinking and problem-solving behavior (Baldwin, 1967, p. 233).

The child takes his play seriously because it is a way of pursuing his goals. If adults are to be instrumental in building healthy ego concepts, they must avoid belittling the child by making disparaging remarks about the silliness or futility of play. Further, just as an adult dislikes interruptions when he is engrossed in work, the child reacts strongly to interruptions of his play activities. Teachers should look at the educational potentials of play and seek to enhance them by encouragement, by occasional participation, by providing variety, and by supplying appropriate materials.

Capitalizing on the importance of play in the classroom is by no means a matter of watering down the curriculum. Rather, encouraging play—a great deal of it—recognizes a basic psychological characteristic of childhood (the thrust for social and physical competence). There is good reason to agree with the child-guidance experts when they say that depriving children of sufficient opportunity to play may impose handicaps that they may never completely overcome. Because play is such an integral part of the child's life, observation of his play and even structured games are used as an approach to diagnosis of children's anxieties and problems (Hill and Luckey, 1969, p. 222).

Play may be a source of motivation for learning as well as an avenue by which one learns. Playing store or playing at being mayor calls for application of knowledge. Making a game of spelling or arithmetic in no way diminishes the need for accuracy or for exact knowledge. In one of the most interesting class sessions the author has observed, two girls in a social studies class recounted a make-believe journey they had taken to Bolivia. Their account of a descent from high altitudes via narrow-gauge railroads, their experiences in the market, and their observation of schools and artisans at work revealed a background of patient and detailed research.

Certainly not all exciting and lasting learning activities need be considered as being play. Nevertheless, fun, freedom, and friendliness, which are associated with play, should be used in effective teaching. A courteous, relaxed, active classroom atmosphere certainly does not connote drudgery and compulsion. The more closely teachers can make their schoolwork resemble play, the greater the likelihood that work will become a vital, welcome activity.

One further advantage of play activities in the classroom is that teachers can observe and better understand pupils as they express themselves in nonverbal language. Dominant personality trends may be noted in members of the group— the child who characteristically stands doubtfully on the fringe; the one who frequently shoves, bumps, hits, and snatches; the one who subtly manipulates others; the one who confidently provides the ideas and assigns the roles; the one who talks much and does little. Observation of such traits often simultaneously suggests some steps for improvement.

Observation of children while they are playing may be the beginning of a challenging task. The wise teacher does not simply step in to force participation, to curb the garrulous, to put down aggression, or to slow the manipulator and idea man. Rather, *he seeks to understand the motivations and basic needs* being revealed to see if there are more constructive ways in which the needs may be met.

Need for Acceptance and Approval

The need for acceptance and approval may be seen even while the infant is in his crib.

> . . . unless infants are provided with some sort of stimulating environment at home, they are likely to grow apathetic and develop a lack of motivation that could plague them for the rest of their lives. "We've actually seen cases where children who have literally been left alone showed evidence of cultural retardation as early as seven months," Hunt says with feeling. "Among children raised in less-than-desirable circumstances these symptoms are quite common by the time they're a year old."[2]

Children need to face the *necessity* of their learning to use the tools for gaining knowledge. It is unfortunate that this need has resulted in the establishment of rigid school standards that cannot be met, *on a uniform schedule*, by all pupils. Their failure to conform to a uniform developmental pattern has led to their frustration and development of feelings of being unworthy and incompetent. The pupil's reaction is to strike back. *Children defend themselves by behaviors that disrupt school routines and threaten the teacher's prestige.* Yet it is these pupils who are most in need of understanding and acceptance and approval. The teacher's tone of voice, his willingness to give assistance, his deemphasis on grades, and his emphasis on individual progress can reduce the likelihood of the child's feeling unaccepted.

Slightly more than half our children come from the lower social classes. Not only do they have the task of learning subject matter, but their load is doubled by having to adapt to a new culture—the middle-class culture of the school. Disapproval of lack of cleanliness, language, disdain for school—all of which are more frequently met in lower-class pupils than among those of the middle class—is not easy to express without permitting a pupil to infer disapproval for himself. It is accomplished by teachers who can give appropriate words of praise, "How clean your hands are today," "You said that quite correctly," "This is much better than yesterday's paper." Approval can be expressed by a brief hug or a pat on the shoulder when a child is told to keep clean or stop using certain words or when he says "I hate school."

2   Patricia Pine, 1968, "Where Education Begins," An interview with J. McVicker Hunt, *American Education*, vol. 4, no. 9, p. 15, October.

Acceptance is difficult when a child is chronically aggressive, disobedi-ent, or impudent. Circumstances must dictate the advisability of condemning the behavior and accepting the child or accepting both behavior and child. Much de-pends on the teacher's attitude toward himself and his perception of his role as teacher. If a teacher can see that misbehavior is not just a challenge to his prestige and authority, he can accept more of it. If he is insecure, his defenses must be put into action—ordering "Stop," banishing the child, or sending him to the office. It will be very helpful if he can perceive misbehavior as the child's way of saying, "I'm hurting," "I need help," "The pressure is too great," "My needs are not being met" (Thomas, 1967, p. 21ff). Thus, *showing acceptance and ap-proval is facilitated by knowledge of the child's abilities and backgrounds—to know is to understand.* All of us would readily stop to bandage the crushed finger, but first aid for the crushed spirit, which shows no bright flow of blood, is less readily offered.

Need for Nurtural Parents

In a certain sense, the child's whole family comes to school. His self-confidence, his willingness to converse with others, his interest in school tasks, and his masculinity, are measurably related to home treatment and parental attitudes (Lynn, 1968). Many of the child's attitudes—toward work, toward discipline, toward honesty, and toward cooperation—have had their genesis in what he has heard and experienced in his family group. Even a boy's scholastic aptitudes are related to the pattern of relationships he has had with his father (Sontag and Kagan, 1968).

Some parents have achieved sufficient maturity that they can accept the child's being himself. Others want to know that their child is progressing as rapid-ly or performing as well, *or better*, than others in the class. Despite knowing bet-ter and despite individual differences, teachers at times try to secure this end in an attempt to please themselves and the parents. As one teacher said,

> Of course I urged and encouraged constantly—aided and abetted by par-ents who urged, threatened, and no doubt bribed. Small wonder that the reading did not improve. I took away the third-grade readers and, from the discards in the basement, dug up some old primers and first readers. The children in the slow group could read these, and our reading class became the happy experience it should always have been. My pupils were pleased with their success and enjoyed the stories. I am a happier teacher, too.

The obstacle to using differentiated methods and materials seems to be a lack of courage on the part of administrators and teachers. As one teacher ve-hemently put it, "Teachers and administrators are afraid to tell a parent that his son or daughter cannot compete with other individuals in the class. Subterfuge, underhandedness, and subtle segregation all combine to make one realize that when a teacher or administrator yaps about treating each child as an individual, they are really mouthing 'flapdoodles.' They are giving lip service to something they don't really mean." Parents are concerned with the welfare of their children, and when the case is clearly and fairly presented, many of them are quite capable of perceiving the merit of individualized plans. They too are interested in facilitating development (Ginott, 1965).

Another way in which the child brings his family to school is in his worry about family welfare. Illness at home, family quarrels, or financial problems may make it difficult for the child to concentrate on school activities. The teacher can become aware of such problems by talking with the pupil, visiting his home, or reading the reports of other teachers who do so.

Psychological Factors in Teaching-Learning Transactions

Basic Considerations

The essence of a salubrious teaching-learning milieu is the feeling which exists between teacher and pupil—the synergy[3] which prevails in the classroom. Considerations conducive to facile teacher-pupil transactions are at least tentatively definable.

1. Acceptance
Acceptance begins with a teacher who has faith in himself and his professional competence. It involves a working recognition of the pupil's mental, emotional, social, and physical limitations. Acceptance also means that the teacher has patience with the slow process of growth (Rothbart et al., 1971).

2. Security
A feeling of being liked and accepted is partly responsible for the child's sense of security, but feelings of security are also dependent upon the child's knowing what he can do and accomplish. Therefore, it is incumbent upon the teacher to see that tasks are scaled to the level of the child's ability and that every child has some experience of success. Feelings of security will be enhanced when classroom duties are so distributed that all may feel that they are contributors.

---

3   Unpredictable behaviors arising from interaction between component parts (Parnes, 1971).

3. Yielding to Differences

Balance should be struck between authoritarianism and lack of direction. The child's tendency to shyness should not be met with firm determination to make him participate and be congenial. One child's belief that it is all right to help another should not be branded as cheating, nor should another child's refusal to help others be viewed as selfish. There are children in the normal range who play at the expense of schoolwork, and there are also those who do their schoolwork at the expense of play. Each should be permitted to approach his learning tasks as he desires—but with guidance and support.

4. Democratic Procedures

Democracy implies mutual respect, cooperative planning, shared responsibility, and delegated authority. The voice of the pupils should be considered in formulating aims and in planning activities. Programs of education are needed that will provide input for children that will emphasize self-worth, having autonomy, and being a cause. The child must be heard if he is to believe that he counts. It is a characteristic of Americans to believe they can solve their own problems—and this attitude should receive exercise in the school (I. Gordon, 1969).

5. Friendliness

Teacher-pupil relationships cannot be of the most salutary kind unless the teacher genuinely likes the pupils. To this end, the teacher can do two things: He can become so familiar with the characteristics of children that he knows what can be expected of them, and he can become acquainted with each child, with his abilities, his interests, his neighborhood, his home background, and his record of past performance. The teacher can show friendliness by being consistently courteous, taking time to listen, and avoiding situations that undermine a sturdy self-concept (Hart, 1969).

A child is suddenly thrust into the strange world of school with a surrogate parent in charge. He must learn to sit still for what seems to him long periods of time. He must learn to suppress the desire to speak until it is proper to do so. He must adapt his physical needs to a new schedule. He must no longer kick and scream when he does not get his way. And in all this, the strange adult moves with absolute authority and omniscience. In such a world, a kind word, a pat on the head, a friendly smile, or an expression of praise makes a tremendous difference—to upper-grade and high school pupils as well as the primary pupil. Research on the relationship of learning to human relationships is as yet rudimentary; but current data suggest strongly that teacher-pupil interaction—human behavior in general—is a vital component in school learning (Goodlad, 1969a).

The Teacher's View of Divergent Behavior

If a recalcitrant child disturbs the teacher's equilibrium by challenging authority, the teacher is typically not inclined to take time to search for causes when the symptom is being so obviously flaunted before the eyes of twenty or thirty other pupils; he is likely to feel that his prestige is being diminished.

Yet there is another view; misbehavior is a nonverbal way of saying that something is wrong. Unless something is done to remove or mitigate the fundamental cause, correction of the symptom is temporary at best. Suppressing a child's desire to talk loudly, at length, and frequently may only result in his destroying property or picking on other children. Similarly, insisting that the excessively quiet child recite more often may only force him to retreat further from the group. Permanent improvement in his behavior and attitude will result only from improving his self-confidence and helping him become aware that he has something to contribute. Rogers (1968) believes that the ability of young pupils to discuss behavior, feelings, attitudes, and the effect one has on others is greatly underestimated. Such studies, he believes, will be a part of future elementary curricula.

Misbehaving children are frequently children who fundamentally dislike themselves—a reflection of the low opinion that others have of them. They misbehave to confirm the low evaluation of others and because they are convinced that they deserve the punishment or blame which results from their misbehavior. Getting at the roots of this type of misbehavior would mean helping the child to build a different concept of himself. The teacher could point out the things (however few they might be) that are likable, the skills that are commendable, the achievement that others do appreciate and make these the focus of attention. Some will say, "But this is unrealistic." The answer is that, thus far, we have found nothing else (punishment, incarceration, failing grades, retention in a grade) that will work. Getting the pupil to like and value himself is the first step in positive behavior modification.

There are often contrasts in the perception of what constitutes problem behavior. Typically, teachers view such things as disobedience, fighting, profanity, and masturbation as evidences of maladjustment; they are relatively unconcerned about shyness, fearfulness, dreaminess—in fact, it is rather comfortable to have quiet, obedient children in class, and they are often regarded as model pupils. On the other hand, child specialists, psychologists and psychiatrists, are typically concerned about shy, recessive behavior and are less disturbed by aggressive manifestations. No doubt the teacher has some justification for his view—aggressive behavior does upset classroom routine. But to the psychologist, the withdrawn child has been defeated in his battle for recognition and security—he has quit struggling. The modern teacher must realize that such a child also has real problems. Shyness may have back of it such handicapping feelings as guilt, overdependency, and a sense of inferiority or rejection—all of which tend to bind one to a cycle of defeat. Shyness and withdrawal tend to keep the pupil from gaining knowledge and skills which improve self-confidence and enhance the probability of future success. Yet the only true security available to human beings is the ability to face and anticipate change (I. Gordon, 1966, p. 70).

When teachers become aware of pupils' problems and seek to find solutions to them, scholastic work improves. In a study of fourth to sixth graders, teachers used the Wishing Well Test and the Ohio Social Acceptance Scale to locate pupils' needs. Teachers who had studied the nature of pupil needs in formal classes used these data effectively. Those who did not know the theory of children's needs were less successful (Burrell, 1951). With older students, simply providing them feedback consisting of information about test scores, personality inventories, and psychometric ratings seems to act as an incentive for improved academic performance (Flook and Saggar, 1968). In a study of pupils in the upper grades it was found that positive attitudes toward school grow during the year when pupils believe that success or failure is self-determined and when teachers use praise and encouragement. Attitudes toward school were eroded during the year if pupils thought external forces controlled success and failure and when teachers used little praise and encouragement. Of the two factors, the teachers' use of praise and feedback was more powerful in a positive view of school than was pupil attitude regarding the source of success or failure (Flanders, Morrison, and Brode, 1968).

Experience as a Learning Avenue

There are at least three reasons why the young child's learning experience should be more physical than verbal-symbolic: (1) As discussed earlier, the child is interested in process; (2) he is not used to sitting for long periods; he has a strong drive toward physical activity—too much sedentary work bores him; (3) his experience is still too limited to allow him to derive much meaning from verbal abstractions.

These factors provide the basis for such teaching procedures as the experience chart in reading and the experience unit in other studies. The experience chart is simply a book that the teacher writes for the pupils—large enough for all to see clearly. The teacher records what the youngsters tell him in their own words—what they have seen, felt, and done.

Another approach to vitalizing instruction in terms of the real and meaningful experience of the child is the experience unit. This is a series of lessons centered about some integral part of the pupils' lives. The experience unit is not planned in detail in writing. It develops as the teacher leads his pupils through progressive learning experiences. Much time would be required for direct experience, and the school day is not long enough to provide many opportunities for first-hand contact. Hence, audio aids should be used as supplements—recordings, radio programs, and brief talks that are related to what the pupils have directly experienced are invaluable in expanding their world. Visual aids, such as motion pictures, filmstrips, models, replicas, and samples can be used to supplement personal adventures and observations. Transition from the specific and the concrete to the general and the abstract should be gradual.

> There is Melvin, crooning a rock tune softly into a tape recorder, ready with earphones to listen to the playback. Learning? "He was here only three days," says assistant director Phyllis Jones, "when he started teaching me how to use the audiovisual equipment. He has the most incredible grasp of mechanics and electronics." But he also learned fractions in the [learning] center—something he had successfully avoided for years. He did it virtually alone, with film tapes and an occasional pat from a staff member. "That's what I like about this place," Melvin says. "No teacher to make a fuss and bother you."[4]

A child who has a home in which there are many books and magazines is better prepared for learning to read than the one who lacks such resources. The youngster who has worked with his father's tools has an advantage in the wood or the metal shop. The pupil who has traveled extensively has an advantage in geography and social studies over the one who has not ranged so widely. Sometimes the school staff makes an extra effort to expand the experience of pupils by providing contacts outside the school; this was done on a large scale and with gratifying results in the higher-horizons program in New York City. Many programs in schools for the disadvantaged make much use of direct experience in and beyond the classroom. Storefront schools are highly effective in reaching some pupils because the action is where they live (Dennison, 1969).

Pupil Participation in Planning

Pupil participation in planning makes their learning more purposeful. It capitalizes upon the need for personal involvement in learning and the learning process. It gives the child a chance to satisfy his need for independence and his curiosity. It provides him with valuable experience in social intercourse.

Pupil participation does not mean that school activities are determined by the fortuitous interests of children. There is still a place for the teacher's guidance and counsel. However, the pupil should have an increasingly large part in

---

4   Lois Wille, 1969, "Room for Miracles," *American Education*, vol. 5, no. 7, pp. 8-9, August-September.

planning as he matures because experience adds to his effectiveness as a participant and because we hope that, ultimately, he will assume total responsibility for continued learning.

A national panel, working for the U.S. Commissioner of Education, reported that a most promising lead for improved education was a **contingent relationship** between teacher and pupil. This means a teaching-learning situation in which the learner has some control over the pacing of information he is getting. He has some choice of the kind and amount of information he gets. There is dialogue between the learner and the wise and informed tutor (*Innovation*, 1964, p. 13).

Kelley (1962, pp. 83-85) has described a vocational school in which there was a disproportionate number of academic and social misfits; student participation in government was tried in this school, and the results far exceeded both hopes and expectations. Destruction of school property and open conflicts with teachers were reduced, attendance improved, and dropouts diminished. In addition, both curricular and extracurricular activities functioned more smoothly than was the case when the school was run by adults alone.

Too often we tend to think that opportunities for self-direction and participation in student government should be reserved for the more mature students. The author observed student participation in a third grade, where the day's concern was for a boy whose noon movies ticket had been confiscated by upper-class monitors because he was misbehaving there. The third graders were discussing what should be done by their class representative in the next council meeting. Some felt that because the ticket had been paid for, it should not be taken away. Others felt that the upper-class monitors should have referred the case to the principal. Some stated that a warning should be sufficient. The boy himself said that he had been warned earlier, and he believed that one or two days away from the movies would be enough. The meeting closed. It was decided to let the matter drop, when a little girl said, with a lisp, "Well, when he goes to a movie and goofs off, it's like he was taking a lot of kids' tickets away from them when they can't enjoy the movie."

Democratic practice probably should not be justified in terms of the teacher's advantage. Because democracy depends on participation of the individual in the solution of common problems, it should be a function of the school to provide such experience.

One of the distinguishing features of various learning theories relates to the matter of purpose, or goals, versus stimulus or input. Those psychologists who are referred to as "purposivists" maintain that it is only when one's goals are clear-cut and personally significant that learning becomes meaningful (Kuethe, 1968, p. 30). Participation in planning is one way for pupils to clarify their goals.

Teacher-Pupil Evaluation

There has long been dissatisfaction with the process of grading pupils simply on the basis of subject-matter achievement, because educational objectives include much more than factual knowledge. Increasingly, educators are beginning to appreciate that the judging role required in grading is antithetical to developing the contingent relationship essential to a positive teaching-learning relationship (Raths, 1966). One approach to the improvement of evaluation is to make it a cooperative, cumulative, and continuous process. The shift from grading to cooperative evaluation is an attempt to help the pupil perceive his goals more clearly, to stress his personal growth rather than his competitive status, to make his purposes specific and tangible, and to encourage his growth toward greater independence. The task is perceived as helping all pupils realize their unique potential as contrasted to identifying and rewarding a favored few (Tyler, 1969). As is the case with pupil participation in planning, teacher-pupil evaluation can be instituted by degrees as pupils gain in experience.

Such evaluations can serve to make the pupil's academic learning more meaningful. When he keeps his own scores on spelling tests and arithmetic exercises, he begins to see that the scores have a personal reference. Graphs of progress drawn by the pupil will motivate him. But more than that, evaluation should emphasize the pupil's doing something unique.

Perhaps one of the greatest values of pupil participation in evaluation lies in its influence in improving rapport between home and school. If pupils evaluate themselves in terms of cooperatively determined objectives, they are not going to go home and report, "Oh, we just played today" or be so likely to criticize the teacher for being unfair.

Ability Grouping

Ability grouping means selecting and placing pupils so that the range of differences in learning speed and background within a class is lessened. It may be thought of in terms of whole classes, i.e., in a school with five fifth grades, one contains the one-fifth of all pupils with top-ranking scores on the criteria for grouping, another class contains the fifth of the pupils who have the lowest criteria scores, etc. Ability grouping may also mean that, from a class whose total membership is constituted at random, the four or five top-ranking students in reading are placed in a small group with different books and expectations. Another small group is organized by the half-dozen who are making the most progress in arithmetic. The whole class selected in terms of ability is sometimes referred to as segregation, **tracking**, or **streaming**. The grouping within a class is less objectionable to critics because in different subjects, such as art, music, or leadership, different pupils compose the group.

The arguments in favor of ability grouping (the streaming variety) are about as follows: By reducing the range of differences within a class the teacher tends to have a more homogeneous audience. Grouping by ability provides an approach to adapting instruction to meet the needs of more pupils than does class organization by age or grade placement alone. It is recognized that slow learners may need more repetition in skill subjects, more frequent concrete illustrations, and a slower pace than do other pupils. Rapid learners need less repetition and drill, can grasp abstractions, and are eager to move rapidly to new challenges. The effects of ability grouping are readily seen in discussion: In heterogeneous groups, a few individuals are likely to dominate; in ability groups, discussion includes more pupils because fewer feel they can dominate, and no one feels that he need be timorous in making comments. Conant (1959, p. 49), while admitting that ability grouping is highly controversial, recommends that it be used for required courses and that the very slow learners have special teachers. He endorses ability grouping for each class, not across-the-board grouping, which tends to segregate the bright, average, and slow for all activities. Special classes, led by special teachers, for retarded or otherwise handicapped children are regarded as a special consideration, not subject to the same pro and con arguments. Let it be noted, however, that getting handicapped pupils back into regular classes as soon as possible is an aim of such teachers.

Arguments against the whole-class grouping (streaming) include such as the following: *Grouping does not solve the problems of individual differences* but tends to delude teachers into thinking it has solved the problem. The difference in MA (mental age) of the highest and next highest pupil is typically much greater than the difference between pupil 15 and 16—in a group of thirty. Leadership, artistic ability, athletic skill, and musical talent are not necessarily distributed among the pupils who have mathematical aptitude or reading skills, and the groups will and should be different for mathematics, football, chorus, and class officials. Grouping tends to minimize and obscure differences rather than to make teachers face up to the challenge of encouraging and developing those differences. Grouping tends to diminish the opportunities teachers have to capitalize on the fact that pupils are often very effective teachers of other pupils. A wide range of differences within a class makes the teacher acknowledge that the emphasis should be on learning rather than on teaching. Grouping may lead to bigotry, justifiable and avoidable feelings of superiority or inferiority, and lack of true social sophistication (Meyer, 1969).

Research does not resolve the questions. Data on academic achievement are equivocal. Some slow learners seem to learn best in heterogeneous classes. Their self-concepts are higher in heterogeneous groups, but their attitude toward school learning is more positive with ability grouping. Ability grouping challenges the superior pupil, and although the advantages are consistent, they are not large. Average pupils gained academically in ability groups, but their self-concepts were less favorable than those in heterogeneous groups. Such equivocal data on 4,000 junior high school pupils led one investigator to conclude that ability grouping will have no dire consequences but that its use does not solve any academic problems—despite small advantages for the slow learner (Borg, 1966).

Some people feel that ability grouping is undemocratic, whereas others say it is democratic because it provides the best chance for each to develop his potential. It may be that the real question is not one relating to a technique— such as ability grouping—but the way a technique is used by individual teachers. Team teaching and nongraded organization are successful to the extent that they aid teachers in knowing the students. Similarly, ability grouping, when used to improve such understanding rather than as a mass production technique, may be advantageous. There can be little doubt that some grouping has merit—college students do not have the same educational needs as elementary pupils. Grouping or not grouping must not be allowed to obscure the realization that education is a human transaction (Clark, 1967, p. 140).

Emphases in the Facilitation of Children's Learning

Some aspects of learning—relevance, success, **feedback**—are common for all learners, be they children, adolescents, or adults. Some considerations, as cited earlier, have special pertinence for the teaching of children—structure, guidance, concreteness, immediate goals. Children are more interested in processes than in ultimate results; they are more interested in the immediate, concrete, and personal than in the remote, abstract, and impersonal (Piaget, 1969). Despite a cult of freedom for children, there is sound evidence that children want and need guidance, order, routine, and consistency.

Because their self-concepts are in the process of formation, children need acceptance and approval more than do older students. The essential element in any formal learning, but particularly for children, is the quality of teacher-pupil relationships including **dialogue**, mutual esteem, age-appropriate tasks, and recognition of individual differences. Because direct experience is such an effective learning approach for children, participation in planning, teacher-pupil evaluation, and pupil-pupil interaction are assets to optimum learning. Evaluation that emphasizes individual growth rather than competitive status is needed. Techniques, such as ability grouping, need to be used as approaches to appreciation of the human aspects of school learning.

The big push in the early 1960s was for high standards, achievement, and educational rigor. But in the late 1960s the human aspects of education were again called to attention by critics such as Friedenberg, Goodman, Holt,

Kozol, and others. It appears that the educational problem of the 1970s may be to balance formal learning and standards against the human factors (Woodring, 1970). It seems highly likely that these two aims are not mutually exclusive; in fact, they may be quite complementary.

> . . . we do not have to throw out all sequence—we merely have to regard sequence as pretty meaningless in itself and subject to change for any good education reason.
>
> We *do* have to throw out practically all of the administrative garbage that has been accumulating for a century; and that includes the class, the classroom, grades, annual promotions, fixed groups, marks, most examinations, report cards as they now exist, subjects, courses, and a good deal else that has little to do with education needs.[5]

Just as there is no need for emphasizing conflict between content and process, guidance versus autonomy, dialogue versus research, or academia versus relevance, there is no real need for abandoning standards to emphasize humanistic orientations. Mass media make the youngest school child aware of the fact that the pressing problems of today are overpopulation, pollution, racial discrimination, employment (technology), distribution of wealth, and human communication. Resolution of these problems calls for exacting standards of research, problem-solving processes, and continuous learning pursued through an observance of pupil differences and pupils' ego health. The question for school personnel concerns the kind of education—both content and process—most beneficial to the individual and society during these early, impressive, formative years.

The fact is that the institution of education resists change, but nevertheless does so. The agents of change are the teachers who mediate the teaching-learning transaction—who are the key persons between the structure and children as learners.

Summary

Study of teaching-learning transactions has moved from a heavy emphasis on stimulus (curriculum, achievement, reward, materials) to a position which also includes the sociological milieu and persons involved. It has been postulated that children as learners need direction and guidance more than they need freedom—freedom being something learned through maturing and experiencing. Children's basic safety needs call for structure, regulations, routines, and dependence on older, experienced persons. The burden of choice is too great for the novitiate. Children are interested in process; activity and doing are more likely to be motivators than many of the "goals" which are established by adults. Play is serious

5   Leslie A. Hart, 1969, "Learning at Random," *Saturday Review*, vol. 52, no. 16, p. 63, April 19.

business in childhood not just because it calls for activity but because it is a social and physical laboratory where children can test their freshly acquired knowledge.

Children have needs which, when satisfied or on the way to being satisfied, make them better learners than they would be otherwise. Among these needs are acceptance and approval, autonomy, and room to exercise curiosity. They need recognition as causal and significant agents in their learning milieu (they need to be seen *and* heard).

Children need teachers who are wise and mature enough to recognize that misbehavior is a child's way of saying that he is hurt or bewildered. They need teachers who perceive children's learning as transcending teachers' teaching.

Some conventional school practices must be viewed critically to determine their impact on the young learner's ego. Examples of questionable practices are grading, ability grouping, uniform curriculum, age-grade stratification, report cards, and frequent subject examinations.

Many data indicate that teachers are needed who respect pupils enough to use genuine dialogue, who know the needs and interests of individual pupils, and who are sufficiently self-assured that they can allow pupils to range widely and explore uniquely.

Suggested Additional Reading

CLARK, DONALD, ARLENE GOLDSMITH, AND CLEMENTINE PUGH, 1970, *Those Children*, Belmont, Calif.: Wadsworth Publishing Company, Inc.

 Case studies (from the inner-city school) of eight boys and girls provide an opdividuals. There is no one successful method; there is the key called understanding.

CRAIG, ROBERT, 1966, *Psychology of Learning in the Classroom*, New York: The Macmillan Company.

 This 85-page paperback provides a brief explanation of various viewpoints of learning. Contiguity, reinforcement, and cognitive theories are presented and related to classroom practice.

GUINAGH, BARRY J., 1971, "An Experimental Study of Basic Learning Ability and Intelligence in Low-socioeconomic-status Children," *Child Development*, vol. 42, pp. 27-36.

 The study was designed to test Jensen's (see 1969 citations in bibliography) major emphasis on hereditary determination of intelligence. The author's conclusion is that certain kinds of planned experiences are capable of raising young children's intellectual level.

HENTOFF, NAT, AND MARGOT HENTOFF, 1970, "The Schools We Want: A Family Dialogue," *Saturday Review*, vol. 53, no. 38, pp. 74-77, Sept. 19.

 Proponents of "open" schools emphasize that it is the teacher, not the organization or philosophy, which gives life to the classroom. An exacting, sincere teacher may achieve much and exhilarate his pupils because he respects them and expects much of them.

4

Adolescents
as Learners

Explanations of learning based on stimulus-response, conditioning, reward, feedback, competition, and the like hold true for some learning situations. Nevertheless, unless teachers also understand the uniqueness of individual students and the general characteristics of categories of learners (children, adolescents, slow learners, etc.), the teaching-learning transaction will be impeded.

Probably the most perceptible aspect of the adolescent's uniqueness as a learner resides in his need to be autonomous, to be his own person. School policies, teachers' attitudes, standard requirements, and methodological approaches which cast him in the role of "nigger" will lead to learnings which are not those hoped for by school personnel. Another aspect of the adolescent's distinctiveness is his need for identity. The need for autonomy and independence is counterbalanced by the need for belonging—belonging to "the group" and having a recognized place therein. Adolescents need, simultaneously, to be a-part-of and apart from.

The study of adolescents as learners is further complicated by adolescents' growing away from the family and encountering the broader culture. Many of the adolescent's dilemmas are culturally induced, and study of the adolescent must be paralleled by study of the culture. In fact, the phase of development called "adolescence" is predominantly a cultural rather than a physiological or growth phenomenon.

The Meaning of Adolescence

A Concept of Adolescence

The basic meaning of the term "adolescence" is simply growth toward maturity. It is the period between the onset of puberty and maturity—*roughly* ages fourteen to twenty-five years for males and about twelve to twenty-one years for females. Many books on education and psychology embellish the definition by referring to it as a period of stress and strain, a time of rapid growth and perplexity, or a period during which the individual is neither one thing nor another. Generalizations about adolescents have limited applicability. Not all are undergoing stress and strain; many are strained beyond endurable limits. There is a "Now" generation, but there is also a generation which does not deviate far from parental expectations. There are differences in the values, behaviors, and perceptions of adolescents. There are differences of opinion between them and their parents, depending on whether they are ghetto or suburbanite, rural or urban, black or white, upper class or lower class, indulged by parents or expected to contribute, or whether their parents are relatively educated or uneducated. In short, about anything that is said of adolescents will be accurate. And a contrary respondent will also accurately say, "But I know an instance which is the exact opposite." The psychological orientations and manner of behaviors of adolescents are ambiguous and unpredictable (Gaier, 1969).

In a world of rapid change, it is inevitable that the behavior of some adolescents would be uncertain as they search for status, relevance, and identity. The adolescent is not a child, but neither is he accepted as an adult. He tends to be rather sensitive because his role is not clearly defined; he encounters conflicting values and expectations that further complicate his dealing with his emerging role. The adolescent is an individual undergoing a special set of developmental tasks.

Uniqueness of Adolescence

One major reason why adolescents are misunderstood stems from the erroneous belief that they are a unique breed. Objective psychology, however, continues to stress that growth is continuous and gradual. An individual does not suddenly become a different person because the sex organs mature, because the hairline on the forehead alters, because hair grows in the pubic area and under the arms, because the angular lines of the girl change gradually to curves, or because the boy's voice changes.

Although adolescents are not unique as adolescents, they are unique as individuals. Adolescents in the same family are different in size, intelligence, interests, and social personalities. Twins are different despite the identity or similarity of their inherited potential. Adolescents from different social classes differ in their attitudes and ideals. In short, some of the uniqueness of adolescents lies in their individuality rather than in their adolescence. A major protest, of those adolescents who protest, is that they resent being a number in a computerized educational mill—yet many slavishly follow fads in dress and grooming.

Fallacies about Adolescence

Many of the current ideas about the nature of adolescence stem from beliefs that have been largely disproved. Unfortunately, for the sake of straight-thinking, almost anything that can be said is correct for some adolescents. One can minimize or exaggerate, be specific or speculate, and still have some background support (Bauer, 1969).

Pubertal Changes Explain Adolescence

It has been thought that the onset of puberty marked a unique period in the life of the individual. Actually, fewer changes take place during adolescence than during an equal number of years beginning with birth. Much of the psychology of adolescence, when based on physical, endocrinological, and mental changes—that is, internal changes—needs to be corroborated and supplemented with a sociology of adolescence.

The cumulative effects of growth, increase in physical strength and mental development, bring the adolescent closer to maturity. In an earlier day boys and girls were valued economic assets as the result of this increased power. Today they are not economic assets and their increased power is wasted and becomes a source of frustration. Thus, the intrinsic factors of growth have their impact in terms of the cultural milieu.

Adolescents Are Awkward

It is difficult to determine the origin of this popular misconception. Perhaps it arose from the fact that some adolescents are as large as adults, and because of their size observers expect them to be as graceful and well coordinated as the adult. Generally, they are not so well coordinated as adults, but they are better coordinated than younger persons. Observation will confirm this state-

Jan Lukas/College Newsphoto Alliance

ment. Adolescents are less stiff when dancing than their younger schoolmates or siblings, they skate better, they play games with more skill, they fall less frequently. Thus there is little reason to think of this period as the "awkward age." Such lack of coordination as does exist is, in some measure, due to the misconception rather than to innate growth factors or tendencies; that is, the adolescent is made awkward by misinformed individuals who allude to "typical awkwardness" when a young person stumbles. Such comments make the adolescent self-conscious and likely to appear more awkward than he need be. Blair and Jones (1964, p. 53) have suggested that attribution of awkwardness might be due to the envy of the older generation which sees its youth slipping away. Some practical implications may be derived from the hypothesis.

It has been theorized that movement and posture are clues to one's personality orientation. Feelings of inferiority or inadequacy may be reflected in stooped posture or slouching movement or in a cocky, swaggering attitude. A healthy, well-adjusted individual often has poise, good posture, and graceful, coordinated movement. There is some specificity in motor skills, i.e., superiority in some, mediocrity or inferiority in others, rather than a general status.

There is a relationship—either cause or result—between personal adjustment measures and measures of physical growth and skills. Larger boys and those who mature earlier are more frequently chosen for, or appointed to, positions of leadership. Because of the relation of self-concepts to body size, timing and duration of the processes of maturing, and normal variations between individuals, it is recommended that a course dealing with growth changes, variations in timing, and the wide range of normality be given in junior high schools (Dwyer and Mayer, 1968/69). Much of the physical education work in high schools of the posture and correctional type is not beneficial, says Keeve (1969), because it emphasizes differences which are not functionally important.

Closely allied to the concept of awkwardness is the fallacy that adolescents are socially inept. Again, the matter is one of experience and training rather than a matter of "adolescence." When they are given the opportunity to express themselves in class, they develop the skill to express themselves in public. One adult observer came from a city council meeting on the civil rights which was also being studied in school and remarked, "I was amazed at the ability of high school youngsters to get up and straightforwardly express a fair and sensible point of view. When I was in school, neither my classmates nor I would have thought of such a thing."

There are at least some who see the criticism and disparagement of young people—an example of which is the allegation of awkwardness and ineptness—as a defense mechanism for the older generation and the status quo, and one of the reasons for the vehement defense is that adult status quo deserves criticism (Friedenberg, 1969*a*; T. Gordon, 1969).

Because awkwardness and social ineptness relate to the self-concept, some propositions merit consideration: Teachers need to take a look at their own dispositions when tempted to make disparaging remarks. Pupils should be encouraged to develop their strengths so there is a basis for feelings of worth rather than for adults to emphasize remediation of weakness. Competition between unequals in both physical and mental realms should be avoided. The range of activities in a school should be broadened so the distribution of success can be more equitable.

Adolescents Are Rebellious and Negativistic

When adolescents are given freedom by parents and teachers to exercise their need for independence, they often cease to be resistant and negativistic. Negativistic traits are a healthy indication that the individual wants to become self-directing. However, negativism does not always prevail, and the degree of rebellion varies from one individual to another. Some investigators regard the rebelliousness of youth as a myth (Bealer, Willits, and Maida, 1969). Others regard it as a normal—especially at this time in history—worldwide phenomenon (Musgrove, 1969).

The problems involved in the matter of independence and self-direction are difficult for both the adolescent and his parents. The adolescent justifiably feels that with increasing age and experience he should be allowed more freedom of choice in activities. The parent feels justified in thinking that as long as he is providing food, shelter, and an allowance, he has a right to regulate the young person's life. Teachers can help simply by showing the parents and the young person that there is a dilemma.

Throughout Western culture, many of the problems of adolescents arise primarily from the uncertainty of adults regarding the role that should be given to youth. Their uncertainty leaves young people confused and ambivalent about their own present status. And at school, many adolescents are unable to accept the goals for the future that formal education sets for them because of their social backgrounds or physical or mental limitations, or because of the impersonality and authoritarianism of the school (Pileggi, 1969). They are anxious to achieve independence from adult prescription, but they are uncertain and often negativistic.

The majority of adolescents do not show negativism to the extent of joining revolutionary movements and engaging in student strikes and protests. However, to dismiss the protest on the grounds that it is a minority is to miss the significance of the current episodes (*Children of Change*, 1969). This is more than the typical, and historically persistent, difference between the younger and older generation. It is a result of rapid change and particularly of change to technological production. The emergent value is that man is esteemed as a human being rather than as a factor in a production unit, and it requires new thinking.

There is no easy solution to this problem because it stems from the wider culture, from school practices, and from family traditions. An approach, timid and partial though it may be, is to encourage discussion groups. Participation of parents could be sought; and the temptation of teachers to "teach" in such groups must not be yielded to. However, if the idea that a period of long dependency and prolonged education is a worthwhile investment for adolescents, for parents, and for society is ever mentioned, it should be endorsed and further discussion of the theme should be encouraged. The verbal-symbolic approach to the resolution of tension should not be underrated. Although it is meant to be derogatory, the remark, "All they ever do is talk," may be a constructive approach.

There are two reasons why the teacher needs to examine his own perception of the extent and meanings of adolescent rebellion. The first is that by and large we tend to see what we look for; the second is that adolescents—like others—tend to behave in ways expected of them.

Adolescents Are Growing Rapidly

It is erroneous to think of "an adolescent spurt" in growth. There is some acceleration of rates of growth but it occurs during the preadolescent years, and then it is nothing like the rapidity of growth—either in a relative or absolute sense—which characterizes the first year or two of postnatal life. The growth status of the preadolescent and adolescent, as of the present, is more important to teachers than is the rate of growth. Two significant points may be noted. One is that the differences cannot be accounted for by a one- or two-year growth spurt; the differences have been increasing over a number of years. The other is that the problems of adjustment for the individual, if any, *stem from the perception* of differences in gross size rather than from a period of accelerated growth.

How to arrange suitable heterosexual experiences becomes a problem for adolescents, parents, and teachers. The difference in individual growth patterns sometimes creates problems when boys and girls perceive themselves to be out of step with their peers. Feelings of inferiority or oddity hamper their free movement in social experiences and adjustments. Because growth changes can present psychological problems, the understanding of a mature adult can be helpful (Garrison, 1968).

The truth is that changes in the nature of growth occur not only in childhood and adolescence but also in the later years. Some aspects of growth are *predominant* in some periods, but basic needs remain fundamentally the same. There is orderliness and regularity in human growth, though individual rates vary. Each period in the individual's life is an outcome of what has previously occurred and a preparation for what will happen next.

Using delinquent behavior as an example, it may be noted that there are no cataclysmic changes in one's pattern of development. Before the adolescent engages in sex delinquency, stealing, destruction of property, or violent crimes, there are danger signals. For example, the youth typically becomes surly at home and in school, defies conventions, and in other ways indicates that he is becoming maladjusted. It is believed that many shocking crimes might be avoided if attention were devoted to the fulfillment of needs or to the treatment of personality when these first symptoms of dangerous tensions occur. Predelinquent behavior often takes the form of disliking school, teachers, and principal; it is not confined to academic difficulty. It has been said that when a child is most unlovable, he is most in need of love. Teachers who can view misbehavior as a symptom of unmet needs of the individual are in a strategic position to lend assistance (Count, 1967).

Research has repeatedly shown that those pupils who engage in norm-violating behavior have experienced grade failure or persistently low grades. Their failure leads to low self-concepts and the temptation to get even (Amos, 1967). Commendable adolescent behaviors show similar patterns of step-by-step development, and this fact again points to the necessity for providing a variety of ways in which one may be perceived as being worthy and successful.

Adolescents Are Bothered by Sex Maturation

It appears to be likely that this belief is a carry-over from previous generations. Parents of today's teen-agers report that they had little or no instruction and consequently tended to worry about certain aspects of their development, particularly if it were very different from that of their peers. Maturation did bother many adolescents. These reactions generally occur when adolescents are unprepared for the manifestations of maturation.

Today's adolescents are better informed than the parent generation. Television, newspapers, and magazines frequently have discussions of adolescent concerns, which are about social rather than about the physical phenomenon. For example, boys and girls today seem to adults to be in too much hurry to grow up, and the steadily lowering age of marriage and the disquieting number of high school marriages contribute to that viewpoint. The increasingly high rate of illegitimate births is an additional worry and certainly offers no consolation to those concerned with our present methods of dealing with sex maturation (Osofsky et al., 1968).

When teachers and parents have given adolescents objective instruction about the meaning and onset of puberty, its outward manifestations will cause less perplexity. They will regard the changes as indications that they are coming into their own as men and women. The fact that many uninformed boys and girls ultimately developed into normal adults should not constitute an endorsement for failing to instruct today. The focal factor in good adjustment is love and acceptance by one's family. Love and acceptance are the primary means of sound sex education. Confidential talks, questions freely answered, and sex education are simply a bonus in a salutary situation.

Teachers can contribute to a sound environment by studying and evaluating their own response to sex, their discussion of sex, and their sexual behavior. Many case studies illustrate the fact that what occurs in childhood is of importance during adolescence. For example, if a child's questions about sex are answered frankly and freely, he will be well prepared to accept the changes of puberty. If, on the other hand, adults are reluctant to answer such questions, he is likely to develop an abnormal curiosity about what seems to be so secret. Parents have frequently been surprised to find how nonchalantly a youngster accepts information that is emotionally very difficult for them to impart.

The matter of sex education and sex information is another of those areas where broad generalizations are hazardous. Because of this Elias and Gebhard (1969) of the Institute for Sex Research at Indiana University emphasize that it is extremely important for teachers to know the wide variety of information and misinformation about sex that will exist within a high school class. Parents and teachers, through the technique of discussion, might deal with sex as (1) a drive to action and accomplishment—in dress, companionship, work, in general—not just to sexual gratification; (2) a social urge that attracts men and women and boys and girls; (3) an emotion that involves other emotions, i.e., love, understanding, mutual interests, and loyalty; and (4) a cultural as well as an individual matter. And this latter is a tricky matter in this day of emphasis on "doing one's own thing."

There are still those who believe the task of the schools is to teach cognitive matters. Progressive education in the first half of the twentieth century placed emphasis on personal needs and interests of pupils. Presumably, progressive education atrophied and died, and perhaps quite fortunately, because some of its practitioners overdid pupil interest to the neglect of systematic, sequential learning. However, much of progressive education has now been absorbed into conventional wisdom, and interest in life adjustment, pupil interest, and unique need is again becoming an urgent curricular concern (Goodlad, 1968). Sex maturity will be a less crucial concern when the pupil's total development and life adjustment—his feelings, social skills, self-concept as well as his academic pursuits—constitute a systematic focus of teachers. Rogers (1968) predicts that this day is on the immediate horizon.

Facts about Adolescence

Adolescence Is a Cultural Phenomenon

Many of the problems of adolescence are related to culture, particularly Western culture. Puberty is not necessarily accompanied by the problems. In primitive societies, agrarian societies, and among less extensively educated populations, pubertal ceremonies constituted the step from childhood to adulthood. In contemporary society, the period of dependence is prolonged by child labor laws (Goldberg, 1964). Industrialization in our society has resulted in strong competition, except during periods of war, in the labor market. Laborers protect themselves from the competition of youth by supporting extended compulsory education and sponsoring child labor laws. Rapid technological and ideological change creates a gap between the generations larger than that existing in less rapidly changing societies. Women's predominance in child rearing virtually excludes men's participation, and although this is unchosen and undesired, it is a factor in adolescent behavior. The uncertainty of military service and the threat of annihilation are among the factors that make the adolescent's world unprecedentedly complex. Finally, the uncertainty of adults themselves and the conflict between professed ideals and daily living disturb adolescents (Wyzanski, 1969). Prolonged education, extending into the late twenties for some professions, extends the period of "adolescent" dependency. All these factors complicate and intensify the adolescent's transition to autonomy and adulthood.

More youth-adult effort must be directed to devising curricula and methods that suit various objectives. This does not imply that present high school methods and curricula are totally wrong. Many pupils find the structure of established curricula quite comfortable. They gain satisfaction, recognition, identity, and a sense of achievement from getting good grades—but this satisfaction must of necessity be limited to small numbers (Meyer, 1969). The broadening of objectives means that curricula, techniques, instructional media, *and* processes of evaluation must be broadened so that the needs of more young people can approach satisfaction. Furthermore, each adolescent must perceive that methods and curricula meet *his* needs. Vocational emphases are of value, but such problems as consumer education, preparation for marriage, functional citizenship, the maintenance of health, and the use of leisure time should also receive attention.

If adolescence is, in part, a cultural phenomenon, then it is obvious that the school alone cannot solve the problem. However, the school can enlist the aid and support of other community organizations. Business and industry can and, in some communities, do help to solve the problems of youth by cooperating in school work-study projects. These projects permit coordination of the pupil's work in school with on-the-job training experiences (Venn, 1969). Citizens' advisory councils have been formed to study ways of meeting the needs of youth in community and leisure time activities. Youth councils in which youth are encouraged to find the answers to their own problems have been found effective. Park bureaus, city-planning commissions, juvenile correctional authorities, and public health departments all have a part to play that should be correlated with the work of the school.

Behavior Is Influenced by Adolescent Culture

There are some who believe there exists a distinct and clear-cut peer culture (Coleman, 1965). Others believe that, despite some extremists, most adolescents have one foot in a youth culture and the other firmly in the adult world (Bealer, Willits, and Maida, 1965, 1969).

Due to the abnormally high birth rates following World War II, only slightly less than half of the population is now under twenty-five years of age. Out of a total national population of about 196 million, about 71 million were under the age of eighteen, about 107 million were eighteen to sixty-four, and the remainder were over age sixty-five (*200 Million Americans*, 1967, p. 7). This is much different from the demographic distribution before the baby boom of World War II. The depression years of the 1930s resulted in a low birth rate which was reflected in an unusually small number of teen-agers in the 1950s. The population in the 1950s was "old," but in the 1970s it is "young."

Thus, the adolescent, when he was one of a minority group, in a demographic sense, could be ignored. But the number of persons reaching the age of eighteen jumped from 2.6 million in 1964 to 3.6 million in 1965. Today the adolescent is a threat and suffers the suspicion, hostility, prejudice, innuendos, and stereotyping that so often characterizes treatment of a prominent minority group. Adolescents are a major consideration on the money markets (Luce, 1966). They are introducing new sex mores and lowering the age of first marriage (Freedman, 1966), and the long hair that was, and often still is, protested by school authorities is being emulated by the well-dressed business executive (*Children of Change*, 1969).

The adolescents' numbers has been a factor in the creation of a so-called "peer culture." Peer culture is fostered by their employment status. It is the potential worker below age twenty who is, with the highest frequency, unemployed. And the black teen-ager (a further compounding of the minority matter) is about twice as likely as the white teen-ager to be unemployed (*Manpower Report . . .*, 1969, p. 43). This forces them, defensively, into hostility with and withdrawal from dominant society. Coleman (1961), although emphasizing a peer culture, shows in his research more adult-adolescent community of values than do the more readily observed matters of dress, morals, and employment patterns reveal a generation disparity. He found that the high school culture—the in-group—placed emphasis on getting good grades, good citizenship, and for boys, athletic prowess. Thus, while emphasizing the differences between parental and student values, he (Coleman, 1961, p. 32, p. 288) cites figures which show that students actually do listen and conform.

The existence of a peer culture as distinct from dominant culture, is at least in part, a matter of perception. If differences are sought, they can be found. If community and continuity is sought, that too can be found. And, as far as teaching is concerned, the search for continuity of culture may be productive in establishing communication. The latter search may also result in a more tolerant view of the discrepancies; e.g., perhaps the professed adolescent value of emphasis on person rather than things merits serious consideration by parents and teachers. Glasser (1970) asserts that we need to understand that the adult is primarily goal-oriented whereas the adolescent is primarily role-oriented. For the adolescent, *being* precedes gaining.

Some of the foregoing notions mix fact and fallacy; that is, there is enough truth in the complex data that they may give rise to a fallacious belief but not sufficient to establish an unequivocal generalization.

Teachers Have a Role in Adolescent Transition

As the adolescent grows older and begins to outgrow his family, there is an intensification of the desire to be like his peers, but varied cultural backgrounds, different rates of growth, and varied inherent potentials result in an increasing differentiation of individuals. Therefore, because the youth is moving into new and unknown roles, uncertainty about himself grows.

The counsel of adults can be of some help, but probably the young person's greatest help in accepting individual differences will come from discussions with other adolescents. One youth bemoans the fact that he has moles on his face, that he has bowlegs, or that he is short or tall. Another reveals his unhappiness about his unsightly acne, his inability to buy clothes similar to those of others, his difficulties with his parents, and his dissatisfaction with school. As these problems are discussed, each comes to realize that his feeling of difference is shared by others of his age group—even though the feelings are generated by different problems.

Feelings of identity with the group evolve from behavior, speech patterns, manner of dress, *and* from braggadocio. Because of the latter, even the youth themselves do not know what the real situation is. Riesman (1969*b*) indicated that they are captives of each other. In visiting a college campus he talked with thirty students about drugs, one of whom suggested that "Of course, all of them had tried pot." Riesman said that such an approach made it difficult for those who had not tried it to say so. When he asked who had not tried it, shyly and slowly hands went up, and 40 percent of them admitted they had not tried it. Teachers may help young people avoid the error of accepting the opinion of an aggressive or vociferous minority by encouraging frank discussion. Self-direction, self-maintenance, and respect for peers are more likely to occur when the stage is set for candid expression of individual beliefs, goals, and interests.

Both teachers and pupils need to know that behavior patterns and ideals differ in various socioeconomic strata. It is not an inborn tendency that makes adolescents question or even spurn the counsel of teachers. When they disagree, it may be simply an indication their background has influenced thinking in another direction. Some may not see the value of continuing education. Their concept of what is moral or immoral, ethical or unethical, may differ from that of the teacher. Good rapport with adolescents is partially contingent upon our recognizing and respecting these differences.

The teacher who desires to influence the conduct of the adolescent must exemplify the behavior, attitudes, and ideals that he would have the young person emulate. There is no choice in this matter. Whether we wish it or not, our conduct does influence that of the adolescent. One of the most difficult problems in this area is that all too frequently the adolescent has not had an adult model which helped him to establish goals which accorded with adult beliefs.

Basic Needs of Adolescents

Common Human Needs

As is the case with children and adults, adolescents need to love and be loved, to have new experiences, to achieve recognition, to be independent, and to satisfy physical needs. However, some of these needs may be intensified during adolescence. The adolescent's search for new experiences will take him beyond the school and the neighborhood that were his world as a child. He still needs recognition by parents and teachers, but recognition by his peers now becomes a much more dominating influence. As he grows to adult size and proportion, he asserts his need to be independent more aggressively. This latter need is the cause of some difficulty with *some* adolescents as they try to outgrow dependence on parents. Parents often cause some difficulty because in living with the adolescent daily, the slowly emergent competency for autonomy is not perceived.

The Need for Identity

Erikson (1964, p. 90) and others (Eisenberg, 1969; Glasser, 1970; Mead, 1970; Shore and Massimo, 1969) emphasize **identity** as *the great need* of adolescents—they need to belong, to make a difference, to be recognized, and to have their presence felt. Providing some feedback in terms of recognizing such identity is a common behavior of successful high school teachers.

It has been shown that competition on the labor market, sentiment against early marriage, and extended education have served to prolong the period between the achievement of physical maturity and the achievement of functional maturity. Much of the feeling of uselessness that adolescents sometimes develop can be avoided if they can be given responsibilities which they feel are important. There is a cry for relevance in education. Unfortunately, the specifics of relevance cannot be identified for all pupils in all situations. The search for relevance may begin with the teacher's self-examination: How much does *he* need structure? How much must he depend on authority? How relevant are his contributions? How willing is he to change? And the last question is particularly crucial.

> . . . Changes are made historically because older ways are no longer relevant; value changes take place because of the apparent irrelevance of previous values, or at least the degree of relevance found in past values; roles change as it becomes apparent that new or broader goals cannot be

served by the roles as previously conceived; and alienation, taking several forms, is a result of some manner of irrelevance.[1]

Some quit school to work or join the armed services to establish their identity. For others identity can be supplied by the school. Revisions of the curriculum that recognize varying backgrounds, abilities, and ambitions of youth will help. Leisure time pursuits, boy-girl relationships, family life, relationships with adults, community services, part-time employment, and consumer economics are problems of basic importance. Genuine participation in student government and a place on scheduling and curriculum committees may be, in part, a way to give youth a feeling of significance. School-sponsored community clean-ups and area redevelopment have been successfully used in some school systems. Working with the disadvantaged as tutors and pals, providing companionship for shut-ins of all ages, and supplying human contact for handicapped children are other ways in which youth have come to feel that they are significant.

An identity for youth demands coordination of home, school, and community. Parents must recognize the necessity for a progressive unloosening of the apron strings. Business and industry must come to realize that their participation in work-study programs is an economic advantage as well as a social service. The Peace Corps can provide for a few the responsibility of an adult and a socially contributing role. It can give physical release to those who feel confined by the lack of opportunity in their own community. Churches can institute programs that will be of aid in the daily life and problems of youth. And in all this, *the participation and counsel of youth themselves must be enlisted.*

All the psychology of learning points to man's responsiveness to his milieu. In the right atmosphere, there is no reason why education cannot be prolonged, or why the young person must begin work at an early age (witness the progressively shorter work week with no decrease in production). But youth need to know why life is so different for them than for their parents, why education is important, and why leisure needs to be planned. Moreover, they need the opportunity to discuss it, debate it, and challenge the ideas rather than arbitrarily to be told. Youth can be helped to take advantage of delayed emancipation when they, and those in the helping professions, understand and deal with the cultural nature of adolescence.

Parsons (1964) and Porter (1969) are among those who have emphasized that youth in a rapidly changing society have a difficult time stabilizing their values. There is bound to be some discontent and much search for far higher attainments. They feel, however, that youth are eager to learn and are ready to accept responsibility. This view—realistic and optimistic—is one which teachers might well adopt as they evaluate and work with adolescents.

---

1   Carlton E. Beck, Normand R. Bernier, James B. MacDonald, Thomas W. Walton, and Jack C. Willers, 1968, *Education for Relevance*, Boston: Houghton Mifflin Company, p. 237.

Youth Need the Help of Understanding Adults

Growth is characterized by both progressions and regressions. The young person will staunchly defend his right to make his own decisions at one moment and request advice and counsel at the next. "Please give me credit for knowing when to come in at night" is soon followed by "Do you think I should wear a white or a colored shirt?" Some parents have learned to be patient with this apparent inconsistency. Teachers will more readily avoid dogmatism and authoritarianism when they realize that the inconsistency of youth is a normal aspect of maturing.

One of the persistent and highly admirable needs of a young person is to outgrow adult domination, particularly parental domination. Because the other adult with whom he is best acquainted is his teacher, he turns to the teacher in the attempt to free himself from parental domination. Should the teacher assume a substitute-parent role (by being dogmatic and authoritarian), adolescents will tune him out. If, on the other hand, the teacher will listen, talk with the youth, and act as a coworker, the young person will consider the adult viewpoint.

In some cases, a great deal can be gained by teachers' *avoiding* contact with parents. This idea runs counter to the advice most frequently given, but it does work in many instances. The youth and the teacher can work out approaches to difficult problems; but when the parent is called in, some youths feel that teachers and parents are in league against them.

Many youth programs have failed before they began because they were planned and organized by "experts" and imposed upon youth. Autonomy is as important to adolescents as it is to adults. In the educational field, guidance programs, curriculum revisions, and improved grading techniques have failed not because they were faulty, but because they were imposed.

The ability to exercise wise self-direction and socially oriented autonomy grows with practice. It must be realized that youth's decisions will not always accord with the adult view (Kelley, 1962, pp. 136-140). Specific issues and decisions must be weighed against the processes of achieving those decisions. Teachers and parents need to realize the pervasiveness of the antithesis of self-direction—authoritarianism—in our society and seek its reduction. The probability is that youth are much more capable of self-direction than some parents and teachers think.

Because youth need an identity (to counteract the "neither fish nor fowl" concept), educational programs will be more effective when they are individually tailored in pace, quality, and interest appeal. The teacher's protest of "not enough time" and "numbers are too great" is invalid because, no matter what, the way pupils really learn is an individual matter. In order to achieve this there must be much greater dependence on the techniques of individually prescribed instruction and independent study. Flexible modular scheduling provides an administrative device for implementing such independence and autonomy.

In a survey of 654 adolescents, Horrocks (1962, p. 516) found that they need (1) to conform to the approved behavior, values, and standards expressed by parents, teacher, and peers, whom they consider important; (2) to receive affection that is sincere and unqualified; and (3) most importantly, they need to "work hard, endeavor, and attain worthy goals." There are some who would question the idea, in terms of the "generation gap," but teenagers do seek conformity to parental expectations.

Adults can best help adolescents by understanding the sources of their perplexities. Specifically, adults can help meet needs by talking (not preaching) with them about behavior and its long-term consequences, giving them affection that stems from understanding and helping them establish vocational goals and find part-time jobs. The developmental task of achieving assurance of economic independence is highly significant in a society which prizes one's productivity; but this task is made difficult for those adolescents who have been raised in relative affluence. Not having had to do hard physical work to satisfy their wants, they focus on their wants, *now*, rather than on processes of acquisition (*Children of Change*, 1969).

Adolescents in the Teaching-Learning Milieu

Mental Growth and Assessment of Potential

It is inappropriate to condemn adolescents to certain low levels of school expectation or occupations because of the fallacy that intelligence stops growing at age sixteen—or some other such alleged age. So little of our brainpower is used that the issue is use rather than possession (Otto, 1969). However, hope is further bolstered by recent discoveries about the nature and development of adolescents' intelligence.

The notion that intelligence reached its highest level at about age sixteen was formulated when the average individual terminated his schooling at about the eighth grade. Terman and Merrill (1960, p. 26) in revising the manual for the Stanford-Binet Intelligence Scale adjusted the age tables on the assumption that mental growth, according to recent findings, extends beyond age sixteen. Average educational achievement for the population being studied was by 1960 closer to completion of twelve grades. Thorndike (1948) studied 1,000 students who were tested from ages thirteen to twenty, using the American Council on Education Psychological Examination and reported an average gain of 35.5 standard score points. GIs attending college after military service made distinctly better records when compared with college students having comparable test scores and school records who entered college immediately out of high school. Of course, this may have been emotional maturation (motivation) more than intelligence; but it still indicates that the notion must be questioned that after age twenty-two or so a gradual decline occurs.

Increasingly the evidence seems to point to the conclusion that intelligence continues, or ceases, to grow in terms of whether or not the individual's capacity for mental development is exercised—and this extends up to age fifty or better (Owens, 1966).

A study with important implications for teachers and which bears, perhaps only distantly, on the matter of the cessation of intellectual growth is that reported by Strauss (1957, 1969). Of eighty-nine men who received Ph.D. degrees in physics, chemistry, and engineering at Ohio State, and California and Cornell Universities, 3 percent had high school IQs of 96 through 100, 6 percent had high school IQs of 101 to 110, and 29 percent scored from 111 through 120. In short, about one-tenth of the particular group studied would ordinarily be considered only of dubious high school caliber. Strauss suggests that perhaps more important than finding and defining the ability of a high school student is the matter of having teachers who express faith and interest in their pupils. The study further suggests that instead of the notion that only 10 or 20 percent of our population might "profit from college," perhaps the figure—even at a time when much of the talent from the lower classes encounters neglect or even discouragement—is closer to 50 percent.

There are two considerations which are related to the notion that a mental ability test indicates potential. First, there is the idea that intelligence is not a sort of "global" or single thing that can be probed or evaluated with a single **psychometric** device. Rather it seems that individuals have intelligences. Guilford (1967b) postulates that there are at least 120 different kinds of intelligence and possibly even more. Most psychologists agree that one intelligence test, yielding a global score, does not give a fair estimate of the individual's potential. They further agree that although the conventional intelligence test does **correlate** positively with school achievement, there are other kinds of intelligence which should be recognized in school than the more strictly academic; e.g., creative, artistic, social, leadership, divergent.

The notion of a variety of intelligences fits with a theory postulated twenty years ago which received little attention. Certainly it merits attention because it has such important bearing on our beliefs about adolescent intelligence and because it continues to be corroborated. Segel (1948, 1969) administered tests which showed that subabilities (which, when combined, constitute general intelligence) emerge more sharply as distinct and separate entities beginning about age thirteen. That is, when such things as vocabulary, arithmetic, form board, and digit span were compared, the coefficients of correlation got smaller and smaller between ages twelve and fifteen. Each of these subabilities became, with age, more distinct as a subability of "general intelligence." The same thing occurs with such subabilities as perception, number, verbal, spatial, memory, and induction—their coefficients of correlation become smaller with the subject's passage through adolescence.

The implication and challenge to school personnel is to abandon the course, that has been followed for so long, of sorting and classifying pupils (Havighurst and Neugarten, 1967, pp. 69ff) and placing them in college-bound, terminal, and vocational courses. The task is to find an adolescent's strength or emergent strength and use it as a fulcrum to develop his ego and those nascent potentials which society demands. Fulfillment of society's need for specialized and technical personnel may be approached by capitalizing on the adolescent's unique strengths instead of attempting to level off uniqueness by "bringing all of them up to average." Categorical grouping hampers rather than promotes uniqueness, particularly because school personnel are deluded into thinking something has been done by grouping.

> Educators should encourage every student to develop his native talents to the fullest so that he may later put them to the most effective use. They should apply tests devised to measure potential rather than the tests that have been applied to measure intelligence. They should give each student the individual care, attention, and guidance he needs.[2]

Facilitating the Learning of Adolescents

The structured, conventional school program has worked quite well for the middle class pupil. For pupils with a different background and motivation, the conventional program has produced alienation. For those who have caught the spirit of the time—rapid change, innovation, being one's self, and emphasis on persons rather than things—the school has frequently produced **ambivalence**. Therefore, from the abundant literature on the psychology and sociology of adolescence, and from the study of their needs and developmental tasks, some propositions on the facilitation of the adolescent's formal learning are proposed. The following propositions on learning emerge, in part from the study of adolescence as a cultural and biological phenomenon. They derive, in part, from conventional and innovative practices in secondary schools.

1. Learning is facilitated when there is a balance between limits and responsibility and autonomy and freedom.

   Because adolescents are only growing toward adulthood—they have not reached it—their safety needs require that limits and structure should be recognized. This means that administrative policies and teacher guidance need not be abandoned when the cry for autonomy is heard. It does mean that youth should be called into council on the evaluation and implementation of policies and curricular patterns and that their

---

2   Barbara H. Kemp, 1966, *The Youth We Haven't Served*, Office of Education, U.S. Department of Health, Education, and Welfare, p. 9.

voices are heard (Kelley, 1962; Schrag, 1969*b*). Learning will be facilitated when adults know they are adults and act like it. Parnes (1971), summarizing research concerning the realization of potential, asserts that we need imagination developed and then disciplined; discipline *with* freedom, not discipline *versus* freedom is the keynote.

2. School learnings will be facilitated when pupils are treated as persons rather than as things.

    Because adolescents need feedback, much greater use must be made of dialogue. The author watched a popular high school instructor teaching the ideas of major philosophers. She questioned, challenged, and she listened; and the pupils obviously had read widely and divergently. Because she listened, she was talking only a small part of the time. She was listened to when she did speak. Dialogue not only helps one get his ideas and concepts straightened out, but it also is an approach to establishing, clarifying, and displaying his identity.

3. Learning will be facilitated when the adolescent knows that his voice is heard and that his vote is really being counted.

    With crowded populations and the shrinking of job opportunities, youth—more than ever before—need to have an identity, to be a cause, to have a degree of autonomy. They should have a voice in school policy, curricula, activities. Their "having a voice" does not mean that conventional wisdom will quixotically be set aside. It does mean that dialogue between adults and adolescents should be cultivated—perhaps with trained group facilitators who know the hazards and assets of group dynamics—so that learning may proceed most economically.

4. Learning is facilitated when one knows that he is accepted, recognized, and that his presence makes a difference.

    Because adolescents need affection and esteem, chances to be important to other people should be incorporated into the school program. In some schools this is done with students interested in becoming teachers. A mother (not a teacher) in Boston inadvertently made her home a youth center because she did not know the answers! She listened. In Baltimore, delinquent high school boys and girls became tutors of those needing special help in elementary classes. In the process they developed their own purposes and academic skills and became dependable persons. The frequent evaluation was "He (or she) needs me!" (Pfeil, 1969).

5. Learning will be facilitated and symmetrical personality development will be enhanced when a variety of intelligences and learning styles is recognized by school personnel.

    Because growth processes and the emergence of logical thought processes produce continuously greater individual differences (Piaget, 1969), the content of the school program must be greatly broadened. In the current program, academic superiority, which at best can be achieved by but a few (Meyer, 1969), is the major, if not the sole, criterion of success. Even athletics—the most visible competitor of the academic—is tied to academic success in the form of eligibility.

In addition to recognizing a variety of intelligences, learning will be positively reinforced by recognizing a variety of styles of learning. Some pupils enjoy reading, others learn by listening *or* talking. Some prefer to work alone, others enjoy group activity. Some prefer the comfort of structure and convention, and others enjoy autonomy and responsibility (Gordon, 1971). Preferences can be determined by teacher observation and teacher-pupil dialogue; and the implications of the analyses can be cooperatively determined.

6. Learning will be facilitated, for many but not all, when the adolescent's capacity for self-reliance is acknowledged and encouraged.

Because protest, rebellion, and negativism are healthy parts of the process of becoming independent from parents, and of becoming independent learners, resistance and arguments should be regarded as symptoms of health. It is presumed that we really do not want heel-clicking obedience.

7. Learning school-selected concepts and healthy self-concepts will be facilitated when adolescents understand themselves and the "adolescent culture."

For example, because sex development is taking place and because a universally acceptable approach to sex education has not been developed, parents, teachers, and pupils should meet together to make decisions for local school systems. Content (facts or facts plus feelings), approach (separate courses or correlated with other courses), and class composition (boys and girls in the same or different classes) should be among the items considered.

Because personality orientations (e.g., predelinquent behavior or creative production) do become patterned behaviors, adolescents should come to appreciate what is happening to them by means of help of individual and group counseling (Glasser, 1969).

Opportunities for young people to interact and to analyze such matters as prejudice, cliquishness, crowd behavior, and socioeconomic isolation should be provided. Wide hallways and small tables in the cafeteria (open at all hours) should be provided. Opportunities for contacting culturally different people might be sought, including tutoring, visiting the home- or hospital-bound, playground supervision, or teaching music, riding, or swimming to the culturally disadvantaged.

8. Learning will be facilitated when grades are eliminated and continuous evaluation, through dialogue and tests of progress (rather than status), is substituted (see Chapter 17).

Because rates and patterns of physical development differ so widely, competitive grading in physical education should be abandoned. Evaluation should be in terms of teacher-pupil assessment of individual growth and needed next steps. Because specific aptitudes, mental status, patterns of development, and interest also differ widely, competitive grading should also be abandoned in the academic area. Teacher-pupil assessment of individual growth and next steps should be a continuing aspect of a program involving independent study and teacher-pupil dialogue.

Simon (1970) epitomizes many of the indictments of grading in stating five reasons why "Grades Must Go." (*a*) Grades separate pupils and teachers into two antagonistic groups. (*b*) Grades overreward the pupils who are intrinsically motivated and punish those who are in greatest need of support and acceptance. (*c*) Grades tend to keep pupils from developing their own interests and pursuing them in supplementary excursions. (*d*) Grades emphasize the "archaic notion" of competition when our society needs more cooperation. (*e*) "Of all the destructive things grades do, probably the ugliest is that they contribute to debasing a student's estimation of his own worth." (p. 400).

9. The teaching-learning milieu for adolescents will be improved when teachers know and accept the burden and challenge of their own centrality as a person and as a model.

Because the self-concept is important in physical posture, health, motivation, socialization, and **levels of aspiration**, a guiding concept for teachers must be "What effect will my behaviors, attitudes, assignments, personal remarks, evaluations, techniques, or responses have on my pupils' self-concepts?" Learning will be facilitated when teachers recognize their responsibility, although it is not the sole factor in adolescent development. In addition, because adolescence is a cultural phenomenon, teachers should study the nature of adolescence in contemporary society and should deal with the personal implications which are indicated.

Summary

Adolescence is a phase of development which occurs just preceding maturity, and in various individuals at different rates. The period has been prolonged by technological and social changes which delay work and increase the need for education. Although extended adolescence creates some difficulties for society and the individual, it is realistic and optimistic to believe that the chances of becoming more fully human are enhanced by the lengthening span of adolescence.

Certain fallacies, because they are rooted in occasional instances and because the instances are exaggerated in the telling, are difficult to dispel. Until they are dispelled, they constitute hazards to development. Some of the fallacies, when stated as pervasive generalizations, are adolescents are awkward, they are socially inept, they are rebellious, and they are confused by sexual maturation. Objective adults know so many exceptions to the myths that it is puzzling to witness the tenacity of the misconceptions.

The facts are that most adolescents are steadily and pridefully (to parents and themselves) moving toward a maturity that surpasses the adult generation. In this development, teachers who have confidence in adolescents, respect their individuality and wisdom, and who are themselves mature enough so they need not be defensive about professional status have a significant role to play. And the role is inescapable—good, bad, or no consequence—teachers are models.

Adolescents have a need, in the midst of rapid change, expanding technology, and shifting values to establish an identity. They must know what they are, what they can do, and what they might become. The alternative to establishing an identity is to risk alienation or anonymity.

It is postulated herein that certain procedures in teaching can aid adolescents in the processes of becoming. These procedures include such things as balance between limits and freedom; the adolescents' knowing that their voices are heard, that their presence is desired, and that it makes a difference; pupil differences really making the basis for varied school tasks; adolescents developing autonomy; and adolescents being helped to understand themselves. Implementation of these postulations depends on teachers who see evaluation and teaching as contemporaneous processes and who are themselves psychologically mature enough to enjoy a stern challenge.

Suggested Additional Readings

BERNARD, HAROLD W., 1971, *Adolescent Development*, Scranton, Pa.: International Textbook Company.
> Chapter 4 expands the idea of adolescence as a cultural phenomenon. In addition to delay of work, rapid change, and prolonged schooling, control by women, voting age, draft and war, mass communication, demographic features, and authoritarianism are discussed.

BLAIR, GLENN M., AND R. STEWART JONES, 1964, *Psychology of Adolescence for Teachers*, New York: The Macmillan Company.
> This paperback condenses much of our current knowledge about adolescence. Delinquency, discipline, social development, peer groups, and various aspects of development are considered.

BURKHART, ROBERT C., AND HUGH M. NEIL, 1968, *Identity and Teacher Learning*, Scranton, Pa.: International Textbook Company.
> The authors emphasize the need for teachers to understand themselves in order to become significant factors in the pupils' learning. Dialogue, evaluation, and pupil self-direction are presented in case-study form.

DIVOSKY, DIANNE, 1970, "Vermont Schools: Young Ideas in an Old State," *Saturday Review*, vol. 53, no. 14, pp. 62-65+, April 18.
> The emphasis in Burlington, Vt. is on how pupils learn. Student strikes, dress codes, and integration are problems one just does not leave to discussion—something is done about them. If one thing does not work, then another is tried. The whole community is *involved*: school personnel, pupils, businessmen, parents, and citizens.

5
Cultural Influences on Learning

A practical aspect of the study of the psychology of learning and teaching cannot afford to ignore the organic equipment of the pupil—his mental potential, his sensory acuity, his health, and his vitality. Neither can practical educational psychology treat the pupil as a sort of disembodied intellect, giving attention only to the cognitive aspects of learning. Certainly those who guide the school learnings of pupils must consider attitudes, beliefs, and aspirations as an integral part of the learning milieu. In short, cultural conditioning of pupils and their teachers is a significant aspect of teaching-learning transactions.

Bruner (1968a) asserts that psychologists and educators who ignore the economic and social setting of educational processes deserve to be ignored in the classroom and in the community. The readiness of the pupil to learn, the manner in which he learns, and the persistence with which he pursues learning are influenced by the cultural forces to which he has been exposed. The pupil's socio-economic status has an intimate influence on his ego concept. The teacher's view of curriculum, behavior, and values is similarly conditioned by the segment of culture in which he has lived. The purpose of this chapter is to define and clarify the impact which socioeconomic status has on learning processes.

Contrasting Cultures

The Meaning of Social Class

Quite bluntly, social class means that people are differentiated—categorized—in terms of privilege, prestige, power, and opportunity. Some have these conditions, whereas others experience restriction, feel anomie, lack power, and have severely limited opportunity. It is difficult in our democratically oriented United States to accept the notion of social classes. Ideals of equality, justice, fraternity, and freedom and opportunity to develop one's potentials are deeply ingrained by our culture. Nevertheless, the facts that have been derived from numerous and continuing community case studies show that privilege for some and deprivation (of needs and opportunities) for others is a concomitant of socio-economic status (Havighurst and Neugarten, 1967, pp. 3ff). When one reads in the newspaper the opinion of an Oregon beet farmer to the effect that the Office of Economic Opportunity is destroying a paradise because "good Mexican workers are being taken off the farm and put into school" (Guernsey, 1971), he realizes that social class is real; it is deeply rooted. Within the statement one can see the conviction of personal superiority-inferiority. He can see the profit motive as transcending human values; and he can see a reason for Heilbroner's (1970) placing values among the top priority of concerns for the 1970s.

The criteria by which social class is determined, or approximated, include amount of education, occupation, amount of income, source of income (wages, salaries, rents, or royalties), place of residence (high on the hill, suburban, or "across the tracks"), kind of residence, *and* behavior. In the higher-status ranks there is at least some tendency to protect and perpetuate one's position in the prestige hierarchy (Edwards and Scannell, 1968, p. 466). Behavior, including dress, is perhaps one of the more obvious criteria of social class. Social class influences the language and grammar one uses, the interests he has, the regard and relationships he has with his immediate and remote associates, his regard for social amenities, and his hopes and aspirations—what he sees as being possible.

The phenomenon of social **mobility** indicates that, in the United States, social class lines are neither rigid nor impenetrable. There is much shifting (studies indicate 25 to 50 percent) of individual status during a lifetime. It is possible, by developing special talent (art, music, athletic), to rise to a higher class. Education is a means (not always readily available) by which one may rise on the social scale. One may marry into a higher or lower social group, but he or she must practice the proper behaviors of that class before being accepted. Social classes are not sharply differentiated from one another. If, for instance, research workers were to decide on six major criteria for judging one's social status, a given person might have three criteria which place him in the lower and three which indicate that he is middle class. Hence, many people are on the borderlines of categories.

In some communities, a three- or four-group system fits the situation quite well because of the virtual absence of people at either the high or low status. For instance, there may be an insignificant number of lower-class persons in a new village of suburbia, but on the other hand, there is no one from the upper class in a mining community. *Statistically*, the population of the United States is predominantly lower class (see Figure 5-1). *Culturally*, our population is predominantly middle class—this is the one referred to in magazines as "typically American."

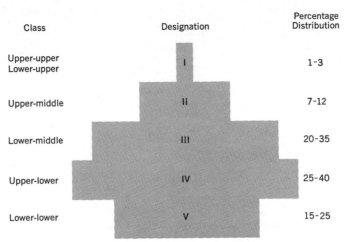

Class	Designation	Percentage Distribution
Upper-upper Lower-upper	I	1-3
Upper-middle	II	7-12
Lower-middle	III	20-35
Upper-lower	IV	25-40
Lower-lower	V	15-25

Figure 5-1 Distribution of population by social class status, Source: Robert J. Havighurst and Bernice L. Neugarten, 1967, Society and Education, 3d ed., Boston: Allyn and Bacon, Inc., p. 19.

Socioeconomic Status in the United States

The highest social class, class I,* is based on the combination of economic, legal (inheritance), and family factors. One must be born into this class, which comprises less than 3 percent of the total population. Families are small, usually consisting of the parents and one or two children, and divorce is firmly condemned. Some individual family incomes may be very high, but the average is somewhat less than in class II. Sources of income are rents, royalties, and dividends from stock rather than salaries. There are two or three expensive cars in the family. Extensive ownership entails heavy taxes, so there is a desire for low assessments and tax rates, which is pursued through control of political organizations. Because their children go to private schools, they may not be particularly interested in bond issues to fund new local schools. Most adults have attended college for at least a year or two, but there is no "education compulsion" as in the middle class. There is no problem of "keeping up with the Joneses"—they are the Joneses. The majority of young persons attend college but are likely to be in liberal arts rather than in curricula leading to the professions. Few enter teach-

*A five class categorization is used in this book.
Class I = upper-upper and lower-upper classes
Class II = upper-middle class
Class III = lower-middle class
Class IV = upper-lower class
Class V = lower-lower class

Columbia Daily Spectator/College Newsphoto Alliance

ing, a great many become lawyers. Fewer class I than class II students complete college. Because this is a relatively small group and because children are sent to exclusive private schools, public school teachers do not see pupils from this class.

Those in class II have achieved their positions largely by virtue of their own efforts. They live in the best residential communities and virtually all own their homes. Law, medicine, dentistry, and engineering, privately owned businesses, and salaried positions provide the means by which this group attains top rank in income. Marriages are stable, and there are typically two or three children in the family. *Education is vital.* The class as a whole is better educated than is class I. The occupational aim of boys is business or a profession. Girls are educated for a "desirable" marriage, though there is no attempt to "marry them off." Parents and children are striving and competitive. Hopes for maintaining or improving status are high because such hopes have been fulfilled in the past. Children's "achievement motivation" is high. On the other hand, their superficial sophistication may be upsetting to the school staff (Meyer, 1969).

Class III, lower-middle class, members are much aware of class lines. They see class I as superior, but class II as much like themselves. They look down upon class IV, but do not scorn its members. They believe class IV persons simply do not have quite the ability to do better, but they attribute their own inferiority to the efforts of class I and II to hold them down. Incomes from wages and salaries are moderate with about a third of wives working as teachers, bookkeepers, and secretaries. Despite some overlapping, lines indicating the status of residents can be drawn on a city map (Havighurst et al., 1962, p. 8). Marriages are contracted at somewhat younger ages than in class II, and the number of children per family is somewhat higher. Marriages are comparatively stable. Relatively few fathers have been graduated from college, and only a few mothers hold a college degree. They are typical joiners of clubs, lodges, and societies. A few belong to the country club. The striving for upward mobility in this class is perhaps somewhat more apparent than in the classes above and below.

The lower-middle-class person—between the slums and the suburbs—has been called the forgotten man of America. He and his wife work hard, often the man will "moonlight" a second job, either blue- or white-collar. Despite the striving, travel, vacations, and education for children constitute difficulties which are not consistently overcome. The resultant feeling is one of anger rather than futility. There is the feeling that they are overtaxed and that those in the lower ranks are rewarded for indolence and dependency (Schrag, 1969a).

Upper-lower-class persons, class IV, are cognizant of their inferior prestige. They resent the attitudes of the upper classes and avoid contact with the class below. They are regarded as poor but honest—hardworking persons who never seem to get ahead financially. Dependence on relief is common during hard times and not unknown at other times. Families are unstable, with one-third of them being broken by separation, divorce, or death. Young people marry at an earlier age than those from the classes above, and the average number of children per family is higher. A third of the mothers work at nonprestige jobs outside the home and, in addition, bear heavy household burdens. The educational achievement of parents is below the national average, and the example set for children, though not verbalized, is to leave school as soon as possible. Leisure time is consumed by radio, movies, and television. There seems to be an attempt on the part of men to get away from the tired, irritable, and frustrated wife, whose task is somewhat too difficult for her.

Lower-lower-class persons, class V, include a number of diverse groups—migrant workers, slum dwellers, and the poverty-stricken inhabitants of rural regions such as Appalachia. As the truly disinherited and alienated members of society, they are regarded as being delinquent, immoral, slovenly, lazy, and cantankerous. Where such manifestations of behavior do exist, they should be regarded as symptoms of slum-shock. The view that these behaviors are congenital and the cause of status is an unproductive orientation. Boyer and Walsh (1968) discount the postulation of survival of the fittest and the genetic determination of traits in asserting that America was settled by, and its citizens originated from, the lower classes of Europe. If brains and strength to compete and survive are inherited and are characteristics of the elite, then America is doomed to mediocrity by virtue of its lower-class origins. How much of one's behavior is due to ancestry and how much to environment is a futile controversy. Schools today have the idealistic task of preventing every individual from becoming apathetic about his potential.

Until lower-class pupils encounter someone who can inspire in them hope and faith in themselves, there is danger of becoming apathetic. Lower-class people have often seen the futility of serious effort. Slight prospect for better- ment is perceived. There is little apparent reward for developing the capacity for delayed gratification of impulses. This is seen in the incidence of early marriages, high rates of illegitimacy, early school dropout, and frequent job changes. Find- ing employment is difficult because of lack of job skills and lack of basic educa- tion, and these same lacks intensify adapting to new jobs imposed by rapid tech- nological change.

In rural areas homes are run-down boxlike structures with coal or wood stoves and worn-out furniture, and closets consisting of nails in the wall. Homes are near the railroad tracks or the swampy river bank, not on the bluffs. In the city slums housing is run-down and rat-infested, utilities are irregularly supplied, and garbage disposal and street clean-up are, to say the least, irregular. In Detroit, Chicago, San Francisco, etc., the areas can be clearly identified by the accumu- lated street litter. Because parents, relatives, and children live in two or three rooms, privacy is almost unknown—a factor which is regarded by psychologists as being inimical to healthy ego development. Divorce is rare, but separation and desertion are frequent, and over half the homes are "broken." The marital pat- tern has been referred to as "serial monogamy" or "tandem marriages." Few of the parents have graduated from elementary school. Leisure activities consist of gambling, gossip, attendance at cheap theaters, and drinking, none of which is pursued by the family as a unit.

Schools and Social Class

The Early Impact of Deprivation

The neglect of developmental opportunity begins with the rapid suc- cession of births to mothers who begin child-bearing prior to the optimum age. Neglect is evidenced in limited prenatal and postnatal clinics and instruction. Mothers at the poverty level have a higher-than-normal incidence of syphilis, rubella, and infections of the reproductive system. They more frequently than the average have anemia, malnutrition, vitamin deficiency, vascular disease, con- tracted pelvises, and premature labor (Hurley, 1969, pp. 54-66).

Babies born in such conditions have lower average test intelligence than those in the higher classes. They are brutalized by neglected injuries, by frus- trated parents who project their frustrations in the "battered babies" syndrome. Although the latter is not a social class characteristic, battered babies are more frequent in those situations where frustration and hostility are high (Wasserman, 1967).

The brains of babies of poverty are less well nourished, their cortexes are not so heavy, there are fewer cells than in the generality (Hurley, *passim*, 1969). The story does not cease at organic starvation—Krech (1969) has found that, at least in rats, those in rich environments (many playthings, opportunities to explore, and freedom) have heavier and thicker cortexes, larger brain cells, and greater activity of brain enzymes than do those whose lives are less varied. Krech, of course, says this does not necessarily apply to children; but he "guesses" that there are some parallels.

> Lack of money directly affects the disadvantaged child's opportunity in the classroom. The inability of impoverished parents to buy new clothes and shoes means that the child will not even be able to dress as well or in the same fashion as the wealthier child. All children are conscious of material symbols of affluence and power and the lack of proper clothing certainly affects the wealthier child's attitude toward the impoverished child and affects negatively the poor child's attitude toward himself . . . . Extra money for dating, parties, transportation by taxi and other such expenses is simply out of the question.[1]

Readiness for School

Children of the middle class have been well indoctrinated with the obligation to be "good" and do what the teachers tell them to do. Lower class children may enter school with the same initial orientation of others.

> Such children [from the ghetto] come to school prepared to be active, vigorous, perhaps much more outgoing on an average than middle-class children. But they are quick to lose patience, sulk, feel wrong and wronged and cheated by a world they have already learned to be impossible, uncertain, and contradictory.[2]

On the other hand, the slum may already have reduced the child to apathy, listlessness, and suspicion (Dodson, 1963).

Middle-class pupils have many advantages. Even before they were born, it is probable that their mothers had adequate prenatal care and during parturition had obstetrical assistance. Well-baby care was routine, and any sensory defect was identified and corrected. At home the small number of siblings and relatively large available space permitted the child to be talked to, given individual attention, and given the beginnings of a healthy ego. Picture books and educational toys supplied an introduction to the literary tasks which are a focus in the

---

1   Rodger Hurley, 1969, *Poverty and Mental Retardation: A Causal Relationship*, New York: Vintage Books (A Division of Random House), pp. 107, 108.
2   Robert Coles, 1967, "Violence in Ghetto Children," *Children*, vol. 14, p. 103.

schools. Interest in books and reading was further stimulated by being read to and having available for exploration a supply of adult books and magazines. Many children will have had experience in Sunday School, preschool, and kindergarten.

Hunt (1968) has postulated that the effects of the child's being left on his own can be detected as early as seven months. On the other hand, being talked to, played with, and provided with variety will probably accelerate mental development. One marked advantage of the middle-class home is the provision of an adequate language model—one which is similar to that which prevails in schools. In addition to the verbal endorsement of the importance of education, the middle-class child has a model to emulate. Both his parents probably have completed high school and many will have had some college. Research shows that there is a measurable tendency for children to attend school only a little more than did their parents.

Even though both middle-class parents may work, and the father may "moonlight," there is opportunity to travel, visit museums and zoos, and take music, dancing, or riding lessons. When such things are mentioned in elementary textbooks, which have a middle-class orientation, they have some significant meaning to the pupil. The teacher's response to such eager, bright, and cooperative pupils can hardly help but be one of gratification and endorsement. This is shown in the fact that grades tend to be assigned along class lines (Sexton, 1961, p. 82). Moreover, the social class bias of grades persists even in some instances in which standardized test data show the lower class child to be equally competent. Thus, the teacher himself becomes a part of the problem of social class influence on learning.

Some of the contrasts in readiness for school between the middle- and lower-class pupil are marked, and others are quite subtle. Certainly the lower-class pupil is not devoid of language facility, but it is different from the middle-class model. There is a tendency to regard this as a deficiency, and it is spoken of as a language handicap. A poor place to start, if we wish to maintain or improve motivation for school, is to criticize the child's language (Calitri, 1968). McDavid (1970, pp. 105-107) tersely summarizes the view teachers should have of language differences: Varieties of language, dialect or standard, are learned by contacts with other speakers. Dialect can and should be used as a source of curriculum enrichment. To condemn one's language is to belittle his family, associates, and him. It is specious to verbalize acceptance of differences if one fails to receive opportunities because of linguistic differences. McDavid concludes by asserting that English teachers need not be sadists in order to teach a standard idiom. The fact is that to the extent that the child can be made proud of what he brings to school, he will be able to take away more that is positive—in this case becoming bilingual instead of becoming noncommunicative and sullen.

The language of the ghetto child is understood very well and communicates effectively in his milieu. A way to avoid the language barrier and the typical criticism of dialect is to regard the child as having a second language, as being bilingual. He can then be admired for his versatility in the same way that German- or Japanese-speaking pupils, who speak English with an accent, can be respected for linguistic skills. The importance of the point is that when one's language is criticized, he is being criticized as a person. Not only is a word spoken differently in the ghetto or rural slum, the sentence structure is different. The slum child is spoken to in short sentences, "Come here," "Get out," "Shut up," "Pipe down." When the sympathetic teacher patiently explains some matter in lengthy detail, the child becomes lost in a mass of verbiage.

As will be shown later in the chapter, culturally different children have some strengths which merit recognition. One of these is that young children who might not be able to read might nevertheless be quite competent tenders of other children. There is a strong in-group feeling which comes from being responsible for siblings while mother works or because father is away from home (McCreary, 1967). Many have achieved a degree of independence and autonomy which is disturbing to the teacher. Their readiness to help others and their habit of communicating with peers may irritate the teacher, who reprimands them, causing both anger and bewilderment. This resentment is, through the defense mechanism of **irradiation**, manifested in a dislike for school. What might be regarded as a sign of maturity (independence) is, in some circumstances, regarded as a lack of social readiness for school.

A tangible evidence of the lack of readiness for school on the part of the lower-class youngster is his comparative score on various tests. The slum child ranks comparatively low. Even though rank on a readiness test is temporary, he is placed in a special enrichment, opportunity, or remedial class. The situation is ripe for the child to get the idea that he is dumb, he is different, he is deficient and inept. Where intelligence tests are used, the results are similar (Jensen, 1969*b*). Even if the child is not told of the results, the teacher knows. The teacher forms some kind of an expectancy which the pupil then tends to confirm (Rist, 1970). Some teachers, knowing how difficult it is not to form such expectancies, even while they reiterate the words, "Tests are only approximations and indications," refuse to look at the roster of scores when it arrives from the office.

Attitudes toward School

A given pupil's **attitude** toward school does not have a one-to-one relationship with his being from the lower or higher social status ranks. There are lower-class pupils who have been read to, whose parents have talked with them about travel, social experiences, and who have visited parks and museums. There are upper- and middle-class pupils who have been neglected by their parents and who have developed a resentment toward, or contempt for, adults and toward authority (Meyer, 1969). Exceptions to the contrary, lower-class children begin to lose their enthusiasm for school at an early age (Dennison, 1969). The average differences in attitudes toward school become increasingly clear as students reach high school age. The hope for breaking the cycle of poverty begins to turn to apathy, despair, or hostility, or some other symptom of **alienation**. Schreiber, by quoting in part from 1 of the 700,000 annual dropout victims, reveals the attitude.

> At first you don't realize that you are going to fail. You sit in class while the teacher is explaining things and you just don't understand what she is talking about. You ask a question or two and the teacher gives you the answer, but you still don't understand. So you think you will find out from some of your friends what it's all about, *because you feel kind of ashamed to keep on asking questions.* It makes you feel like you're kind of dumb. I remember the first time I asked the kid next to me a question about the work, the teacher became angry and said I should stop fooling around and pay attention. You know there ought to be one time in school when you could get together with the other kids in your class and talk about the things you would be afraid or ashamed to ask a teacher . . . [Schreiber]: He then goes on to describe his reaction to the first big test in that class: how he wrote answers to questions he made up because he was ashamed to hand in an empty paper and how he slouched in his seat so that he would be as inconspicuous as possible. Finally the papers were returned, charitably his was placed face down. Without looking at it, he folded it and placed it in his pocket. Let him tell what he did next. "I felt so upset I couldn't go to my next class right away. I went to the boys' room. I went into the john and took the paper out of my pocket to look at it . . . It didn't have a mark." Failure bred more failure, followed by class cutting and truancy, and finally the realization that there was no hope. "By April my parents had accepted the idea that I was going to fail and they couldn't do anything about it; the teacher knew I was going to fail, and she couldn't do anything about it; I knew I was going to fail and couldn't do anything about it. Somehow I found myself going around more with other kids in the class who were also failing."[3]

The School's Holding Power

Prior beliefs that dropouts result from the desire to get a job, desire to get married, dislike for teachers, lack of ability to do schoolwork, and inappro-

---

3   Daniel Schreiber, 1968, "700,000 Dropouts," *American Education*, vol. 4, no. 6, pp. 6-7, June.

priateness of the curriculum are shown to be excuses for what is more basically a function of socioeconomic status. Going to work at an early age and getting married at an early age are social class characteristics of the lower half of the population. They are manifestations of the need for immediate gratification—an understandable result of the marginal living, the constant frustration, and the chronic disappointment that are normal in these classes.

The belief that intelligence determines the length of one's stay in school does not hold up. Upper- and upper-middle-class children in the lower quartiles of intelligence stay in school, while those of the lower classes tend to show high dropout rates. There is little difference in the intelligence ratings of lower-class boys who drop out and those who stay (Havighurst and Neugarten, 1967, pp. 74ff). Girls stay in school or drop out somewhat more in relation to intelligence than boys; boys are more likely to stay in or drop out in relation to their position on the social status scale.

School withdrawals follow the family pattern—the number of years children attend school tends to be only a little higher than that established by their parents. Dropouts have significantly lower scholarship and attendance records than do those who remain in school. Scholarship and attendance seem, however, to be more a manifestation of orientation toward the value of an education, level of aspiration, degree of participation in school activities, and whether or not the individual finds an adult in school with whom he can identify (Herriott, 1963) than they do of test intelligence. Dropouts are correlated with economic pressures, peer relationships, appropriateness of curriculum, participation in school life, and treatment by the teacher—in short, a function of social class. The financial strain of buying books and clothes that make the pupil comfortable, having money for dates, dues, and admissions, as well as the necessity for helping out at home are all difficult problems of lower-class youngsters. They feel the pain of being isolated from student groups and activities. The sentiment is often expressed by teachers that withdrawal is good riddance—get rid of the "bad apples." To all these factors may be added the difference in value systems of teachers.

Less than 2 percent of class I pupils, aged 16 and 17 years, are not attending school. In the lower classes the nonattendance figure is closer to 33 percent. The self-perpetuating nature of low status—the cycle of poverty—is suggested in Figure 5-2. The crucial role of the school in one's being included or excluded in the wider culture is also reflected in Figure 5-2 and in the following:

> About 77 percent of the young people currently finish high school, and about 45 percent of them (or close to 60 percent of the high school graduates) can be expected to enter a degree-credit program in a college or university. If present trends continue, about 22 percent of the persons in their late teens today can be expected to earn a bachelor's degree; 7 percent, a master's degree; and 1 percent, a doctorate.*

*W. Vance Grant, 1970, "A Statistical Look at Education in the United States," *American Education*, vol. 6, no. 8, p. 15, October.

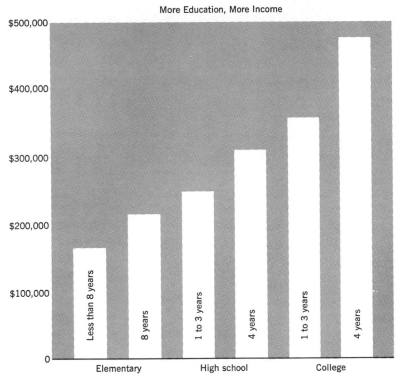

Figure 5-2 Lifetime earnings of males by years in school. Source: 200 Million Americans, *Washington, D.C.: U.S. Department of Commerce, Bureau of the Census, November 1967, p. 55*

For whatever combination of reasons, lower-class pupils constitute the bulk of school dropouts (Greer, 1969). Although complete solution of the problem would require changes in the total culture, there are steps toward remediation which can be taken in the schools.

Schools as a Sorting Agency

In spite of the myth that schools are a melting pot in which children of immigrants, the poor, and the Negro may take steps toward being assimilated into the total culture, the sorting and classification function of schools is a reality.

Public schooling cannot be understood, nor the current problems manifest in it, apart from a consideration of the predominant influence of social and economic class. For at least the last eighty years, socioeconomic class, as signified by employment rates and levels, has determined scholastic achievement, as measured by dropout and failure rates.

From 1890, at least, the schools failed to perform according to their own as well as the popular definition of their role. In virtually every study undertaken since that of Chicago schools made in 1898, more children have failed in school than have succeeded, both in absolute and in relative numbers.[4]

Dropping out of school, in terms of one's status on the prestige hierarchy, is not a malicious, or perhaps even consciously recognized, phenomenon created by teachers. The sorting function is facilitated by society as a whole, implemented by school personnel, and abetted by the students themselves.

Society plays a role in the sorting process. The school's competitor for youth's time is employment opportunity. When day laborers and farmers were needed, schools tended to have little attraction for those whose prospects were for such employment. Working fathers "begat" working sons, not because of inherited ability but because of social association. As the need for laborers decreased and the employment of clerical help and sales workers increased, the young stayed in school longer, and high school curricula were adapted—very slowly—to the changed need. Adaptation to current employment needs is far from being accomplished; in fact, the change is not even widely appreciated. The ratio of professional and technical workers grew by 50 percent between 1950 and 1960, and the rise in percentage of professional and technical employment continues (*Statistical Abstracts*, 1967, p. 231). Although schools and students have responded to society's technological needs (see Figure 5-3), shortages of qualified workers in the higher echelons continue.

Society, in the form of the federal government, is stepping in to *treat the symptom* by providing adult education and reemployment job training. To a limited extent society *is attacking the cause* by providing college loans for those lower-class youth who have survived the sorting process through high school, and even for some who did not survive.

The school's role in the sorting process begins with the administration of reading readiness and intelligence tests. Obviously, the child who is not read to, has seen few books, and who has a different linguistic pattern, is comparatively handicapped on the readiness test. He does not fare well on intelligence tests. These tests, with an exception or two, are recognized as having a cultural bias which favors the linguistically facile middle-class child (Pine, 1969). The big dangers in the use of intelligence tests are probably not in the cultural bias but in some misconceptions. One danger is contained in the fallacious belief that such tests are measures of innate or congenital intelligence. Another resides in the belief that one score (IQ, percentile rank standard score) provides a measure of how one will do in school and life. The fact is that intelligence tests might better be called "scholastic aptitude tests" (Wesman, 1968). Even here, though, motiva-

---

4   Colin Greer, 1969, "Public School: The Myth of the Melting Pot," *Saturday Review*, vol. 52, no. 46, p. 84, Nov. 15.

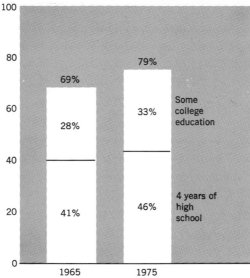

Figure 5-3 Workers in the age group 25-34 will be better educated in the 1970s than workers 25-34 in the 1960s. Source: U.S. Department of Labor, U.S. Manpower in the 1970s: Opportunity and Challenge, Washington, D.C.: Government Printing Office, 1970.

tion, family background, identification with some valued person, ego concept, and specificity of interests also condition school success. Still another hazard of tests is that users might believe that scholastic aptitude is indicative of the many other types of intelligence—not necessarily prized in school—which one might have (Taylor, 1968). Tests are a part of the process by which pupils are routed into slow, average, and bright groups in the elementary school. In the high school the process continues with sorting into college preparatory, commercial, and general curricula.

School marks follow class lines, with a disproportionate number of the high grades going to middle-class children (especially upper-middle) and a disproportionate number of the low grades going to the lower-class pupils. The unbalanced distribution persists despite standardized test scores which place the lower-class pupil on a level in both mental ability and scholastic achievement with his higher-class peer who nevertheless gets higher marks (Havighurst and Neugarten, 1967, p. 244; Sexton, 1961, p. 82ff). There are some understandable reasons for this. Lower-class children do not verbally endorse education, and their behavior in school is more often of the nonappreciated variety than is the case among those from the "better homes." It is natural for teachers to see pupils most like themselves in a favorable light and to want to help them. In addition, experience with police and investigating social workers has made the children suspicious of adults with authority and teachers do not readily "win their hearts."

Pupils sort themselves. They conform to the expectancies of school personnel. Those in the higher socioeconomic strata, despite comparative ability, choose the college preparatory curriculum. Those from the lower strata tend to choose the general curriculum where science and mathematics are at minimal levels—pupils begin to see themselves as belonging to the slow group and perform accordingly. Of course there are exceptions. Kahl (1953) gives credit to early parental pressure and early school success for the occasional high educational ambitions on the part of lower-class boys. Herriott (1963) attributes the high educational ambitions of those who attend college, despite low income, low status, and the repudiation of college by high-ability upper-class youth, to (1) the assessment of self in comparison to others, and (2) the level of expectations that the individual perceives as important people in his life (parents, teachers, friends) have for him. These self and other evaluations are important variables in the relationship of class and school attendance.

As the sorting process continues through the college years not all the dropouts are prompted by low grades. Jencks (1968) calls attention to the fact that the students are eased out rather than flunked out. The pressures of a competitive, unsupportive, and unfriendly institution is so oppressive that pupils would rather drop out "than to soldier on."

Teachers' Attitudes and Social Class

Teachers are influenced by test data—both achievement and aptitude. Other factors such as dress, grooming, speed of learning, and attitudes toward adults and authority may also cause teacher to prefer middle-class pupils. It might all be summed up with the simple thing that often accounts for racial, political, nationality, or linguistic preference: "They are more like we are."

Rist (1970) found that teacher differences were at least as crucial in children's assignment to ability groups as were the pupils' measured abilities. He found that once a child was placed in a group, he would continue in successive grades to be placed in that level group despite ability and performance. The error is intensified by the pupil's internalizing the concept established for him.

It should be apparent, of course, that if one desires this society to retain its present social class configuration and the disproportional access to wealth, power, social and economic mobility, medical care, and choice of life styles, one should not disturb the methods of education as presented in this study [seating arrangements, grouping, and grading]. This contention is made because what develops a "caste" within the class-room appears to emerge in the larger society as "class." The low-income children segregated as a caste of "unclean and intellectually inferior" persons may very well be those who in their adult years become the car washers, dishwashers, welfare recipients, and participants in numerous other un- or underemployed roles within this society. The question may quite honestly be asked, "Given the treatment of low-income children from the beginning of their kindergarten experience, for what class strata are they being prepared other than that of the lower class?" It appears that the public school system not only mirrors the configuration of the larger society, but also significantly contributes to maintaining them. Thus the system of public education in reality perpetuates what it is ideologically committed to eradicate—class barriers which result in inequality in the social and economic life of the citizenry.[5]

Teacher-pupil influence is not a one-way street. Jenkins and Deno (1969) found that pupils' behavior influenced teachers' self-evaluation as teachers. Pupils who were coached to act interested and excited caused teachers to feel that they were effective and to feel that teaching was enjoyable. Pupils who were coached to act uninterested and unexcited caused their teachers to rate themselves as ineffective and to predict that they would not enjoy teaching. This being the case, it would seem that beginning teachers, who have yet to find themselves, probably had better not start their careers in the ghetto schools where problems of motivation, interest, and inadequate background loom large and where adherence to school routines is not a family tradition or conviction. Rivlin (1965) shares with many others the belief that teachers in big city schools, where there are cultural minorities and migrants, need special training. They must learn their skills in schools, not in colleges. They must learn on the job. Teachers must avoid the temptation to overgeneralize. Many children from the upper classes do poorly, have negative attitudes toward school, and drop out—at least psychologically. Many children from the lower classes get high marks, are amenable to guidance, and enjoy both their teachers and school success. Miller (1970) confirms such conclusions and reports that the environmental conditions which influence school success are widely distributed across social class boundaries. He recommends that teachers give less attention, in the future, to social class per se and learn more about the pupils' backgrounds, especially the quality of parent-child relationships.

---

5   Ray C. Rist, 1970, "Student Social Class and Teacher Expectations: The Self-fulfilling Prophecy in Ghetto Education," *Harvard Educational Review*, vol. 40, pp. 448-449.

Contrasting Schools

Community Schools and Comprehensive High Schools

Probably the majority of schools are so situated that they draw from a representative cross-section of the population. The percentage of pupils from various social classes, especially in the early elementary years, would rather closely approximate the percentage figures shown in Figure 5-1. It is in such schools that the melting pot function might operate. But ability grouping and **tracking**, designed with the best of intentions, has extensive ill effects on teacher expectancy and pupil self-evaluation. Intelligence tests, the maintenance of schedules for learning, and competitive grading serve to make schools a sorting machine instead of a melting pot (Greer, 1969). Grouping pupils channels and limits the experiences of pupils and undermines the egos of those in the slow groups. Even those in the top groups get some unfortunate and distorted ideas about their ability and destiny (Aldridge, 1969).

> We could afford failure in the schools as long as the economy had room for unskilled workers and as long as the lower classes accepted without protest what appeared to be their inevitable place. Now, however, there are practically no jobs left for the unskilled, and even if there were, the black lower class no longer is willing to accept only that kind of opportunity—not in a society in which real wealth is increasing so fast.
>
> What this means, in effect, is that in a variety of different ways we have increased demands on the schools. Thirty years ago the purpose of public education was culturally defined as little more than baby-sitting for all the children. Now neither corporations, government, suburban parents, nor the black community are willing to accept the school as a mere custodian. Its purpose has been redefined by society: Not only must it serve all children, but it must graduate them all with salable skills.[6]

If schools are to serve all pupils, one of the practices which must be questioned is ability grouping. Several criticisms of ability grouping are weighed against the possible advantages. Some of the advantages are thought to be:

> Avoiding embarrassment of the slow learner
> Removing the indulgence of average expectancy from the bright pupil
> Grouping is lifelike—in life out of school one competes and associates with his kind
> The teacher's job is made easier by reducing the range of differences within a class

---

6   Colin Greer, 1969, "Public Schools: The Myth of the Melting Pot," *Saturday Review*, vol. 52, no. 46, p. 102.

Criticisms of ability grouping include such things as:

> Failing to provide pupils contact with the variety of people who constitute society
>
> Heterogeneous groups show the need to use and exploit the advantages which may accrue for independent study
>
> Grouping distorts ego development—slow learners have their inferiority emphasized and bright pupils suffer from inflated ideas about their importance. (Proponents of grouping argue that pupils will develop superiority feelings when they see how easily they surpass classmates in heterogeneous groups.)

At least some research suggests that the classroom climate which is perceived as being unstratified and democratic is advantageous in some subjects (physics) and in terms of motivation (Walberg and Anderson, 1968). It appears that heterogeneous classes might be considering the pupil as the primary focus whereas the "ability group" plan is looking mainly toward the mastery of content. In terms of the needed promotion of independent study (as a prologue to lifelong, self-directed, learning) and in terms of human rights and dignity, the practice of ability grouping would seem to be due for some rigorous reexamination.

There is some evidence that where courses are general, vocational, and college preparatory, the social class lines are distinct, even though not necessarily dominant (Havighurst et al., 1962). The formation of cliques tends to follow class lines. The belief that pupil groups, at least in high school, are formed on the basis of age, intelligence, and interest is not supported. Should two girls from different classes become friendly, it is not uncommon for the other clique members to show their disapproval. Dominant factors in being in the in-group are personality, athletics, scholarship, and having a car (Coleman, 1961). Whether cliques and dating in terms of class lines would be less marked where pupils chose courses without regard to general, vocational, or college preparatory is an open question.

Boys in all classes participate in sports in about equal proportions. Other than this, the lower-class pupils are likely not to be a very significant part of school life. The fact must be faced that pupils from the lower class have twice the adjustment problem of other children when they go to school. The school is a middle-class institution in terms of behavior, values, and language. *Not only must the lower-class pupil adjust to curricular demands, but he must also adjust to a different kind of culture.* Some youngsters are kept out of school affairs on the basis of costs—uniforms, football shoes, musical instruments, club dues, and even the cost of books. Lower-class pupils are made to realize that they come from the wrong side of the tracks (Havighurst et al., 1962, p. 72). One girl, asked if she cared for the school dances, replied that she did not know they were held (Havighurst et al., 1962, p. 62). The proportion of membership in student activities is almost 100 percent in the higher classes but is almost negligible (except for athletics) in the lower classes.

Slum Schools

Because communities do not publicize the worst aspects of school facilities, it is difficult to say what a typical slum school is like. Some, certainly, have adequate equipment, ample supplies, and skilled, experienced, and dedicated teachers. Some of the slum schools are distinctly otherwise. The buildings themselves are old, and despite remodeling and repair—when available at all—it is difficult for pupils to take pride in the plant. However, pride is not a function of age of physical plant. In an Oregon town with three high schools the pupils contested their parents' moving to another part of town where they would have to switch to a new school. They debated the administration's zoning which would also occasion change from the old to the new plant.

Often teachers who lack experience begin their work in these physically run-down, low-morale schools because it is a way to get started in the profession. They look forward to the time when they will have served their "apprenticeship" and be promoted to schools in the better city districts or in suburbia. Much educational theory seems to have little pertinence to the problems of pupil indifference, antagonism toward adults and authority, inadequate background for academic achievement, underlying hostilities, weak feelings of worth, and lack of relevance of school subjects. Simon (1966) asserts that disdain for education courses is created in those teachers who see the gulf between theory and what is seen in the slum school. He perceives the slum school as being a harsh test for new students—hard, often unrewarding, work which challenges the teacher's sense of his own worth.

Rivlin (1965) has somewhat the same view, but he places more emphasis on what the teacher should do: study social class, anthropology, cultural change, and pursue these studies through in-service as well as preparatory courses. He suggests extra pay for service in the slum schools. Movement on the part of experienced teachers to, instead of from, the slum school should be encouraged. Many young teachers are today coming to believe that service and significance are more important than the amount of money earned. The accuracy of this statement is reflected in the fact that some do serve willingly, efficiently, and persistently in the Peace Corps and the Domestic Peace Corps (Lunstrum, 1966). However, guidance by the old hand is needed in order to maintain perspective in the Peace Corps. Some young teachers, however, seek to teach in the slums precisely because precedents have not been set. They can be pioneers. They see the possibility of a more immediate solution to the problems of teaching in slum schools by tackling the job themselves.

The Schools of Suburbia

A few years ago the schools of suburbia were looked upon as constituting models for teaching methods, up-to-date curricula, and adequate school plants. In such schools one saw the exciting possibility of team teaching, independent study, computer-assisted instruction, programmed study, and continuous progress. The success of the schools was reflected in courses which differed little from those traditionally offered in college. Success was, presumably, reflected in the large ratio of suburbia's students who attended college.

There are, on the other hand, those who take the view that all is not well in the schools of suburbia. Some of the characteristics may be interpreted as symptoms of failure rather than success. Pine (1966) has called attention to the phenomenon of delinquency among the affluent students. Although there has probably always been delinquency among the well-to-do, it is becoming increasingly hard to conceal. Factors in the rise of delinquency rates include both school and communitywide items. Examples of the broader causes are the country's economic growth, social mobility, prevalence of female-dominated homes, and weakening of middle-class social and ethical values. Factors related to the school's role in "affluent delinquency" are the matters of educational compulsion or "sheepskin psychosis" of the upper-middle- and upper-class, and the adoption of lower-class values by middle-class children.

Discontent in the schools of suburbia is shown in student strikes and protests. Disdain for the school is not confined to slum areas. Radical political activity has become a part of school life. Pupils are finding, even without teachers' or parents' consent (which they often have), enough support from their peers that their resolve for reform persists (Pileggi, 1969). Different views are taken of this protest and the repudiation of the establishment.

Friedenberg (1969*b*) approves the student movement and endorses their fight for change, representation, and participation. He says that there is too widespread a feeling that the protests, rather than the grievances being protested, are the problem. Havighurst (1969) predicts that citizens, newspapers, and civic organizations will regard the protests as being the work of immature students. He recommends that (1) students be used more in active supervisory roles; (2) courses be made relevant by dealing with problems of war, poverty, and urban adjustment; (3) students and staff join in formulating rules for conduct and discussion; and (4) that greater variety of opportunity be developed. Others are not so inclined to endorse the manifestations of alienation and see less justification for youths' protestations.

At first glance most of our suburban youth share a common background of comfortable homes, loving parents, "good schools," high intelligence, excellent health, and almost unlimited opportunities for self-development. They have almost all the advantages that many of their mothers and fathers growing up during the Great Depression and World War II were denied. Yet many of today's middle-class suburban youngsters exhibit disturbing character qualities—sexual libertarianism, vehement rejection of adult authority, and a widespread disposition to experiment with drugs . . . . Our nation's suburbias are evidently becoming so segregated that children can grow up without genuine contact with others of different racial, religious, or social backgrounds. The result is a growing provincialism in spite of ease of travel and communication. Suburbia's children are living and learning in a land of distorted values and faulty perceptions.[7]

The mother of the suburban youngster has been forced by wide space and suburban structural design to be the instantly ready chauffeur of the family station wagon. Her schedule fits the child's schedule for music, dancing, and swimming lessons, and for Cub Scout, Bluebird, and Scout meetings. In addition to this availability of adult service children have been brought up on a psychology of child-rearing which emphasized permissiveness. It is easy for these children to develop the idea that adults exist for the convenience of the young. Their tolerance for frustration has been underdeveloped. The father's absence from the home, due to travel and work, has further distorted the children's ego balance. Ample finances have not given reality to the concept of delayed gratification.

> . . . It is possible to sympathize with any student who wishes to have some control over the content of his education, particularly if he suspects, often quite rightly, that his education is in the hands of cretins. But one ought also to be aware that the notion of educational self-determination is a perfectly logical outcome of a childhood experience in which few or no restrictions were placed on the child, and parents habitually made it a point, in moments of choice, to let the child cast the deciding vote. Such delegation of authority occurring at an early age is hugely flattering to the young ego and is conducive to either megalomania or a wonderful independence of mind. Unfortunately, very few children are gifted enough to derive high intellectual strength from this sort of freedom. The great majority are conditioned by it to become capricious, self-indulgent, and drunk with the glory of their incontestable omnipotence. Thus, they enter the universities convinced that whatever is required is wrong. Any exercise of authority and imposition of laws, is a violation of their civil liberties as well as their divine rights as members of the new royal family of adolescence. It is also a violation of

---

7   James A. Meyer, 1969, "Suburbia: A Wasteland of Disadvantaged Youth and Negligent Schools?" *Phi Delta Kappan*, vol. 50, p. 575.

the rules of the game they have been playing all their lives, the particular variety of checkers in which they were always given the first move and allowed to jump backwards and forwards on the board long before they had earned any kings.[8]

Knowledge of the problems, attitudes, and characteristics of the pupils of suburbia is as essential as is knowledge about the "educational psychology" of slum pupils. At some points the behavior of the teacher might be the same toward both groups: acceptance of the pupil (but not necessarily of his behavior), respect for differences, provision of time for listening, and providing, in decreasing degrees as pupils grow older, adult direction and authority. Generally, the challenge will be to build the ego of the slum pupil to the point where he has some confidence in himself and some faith in his future. Generally, the problem will be to reduce the ego of the suburban pupil to size so that he can be respected rather than merely tolerated by others.

Middle-class Orientation and the Schools

Middle-class Curriculum

There has long been a protest against the middle-class bias of textbooks in primary and elementary grades. It is recognized that many of the things studied in those books are not vitally interesting to lower-class pupils. The language spoken, and until recently, the clothes worn, in school were middle-class, all of which means that the lower-class pupil has two major adjustments to make when he comes to school: an academic adjustment as well as a cultural one—a way of life.

There are five determinants of curriculum which must be considered (Beck et al., 1968, pp. 182ff):

It is believed that basic knowledge must be presented as organized, systematically presented disciplines.

Regardless of courses of study, institutional plans, or cultural pressures, it is the teacher who determines, in the final analysis, what is taught.

The individual uniqueness of pupils requires that their values, aspirations, and perceptions be considered in curricular emphases.

Long-prevailing tradition indicates that the school system—the school board and local tradition—determines curricular offerings.

Whatever the curricular emphasis of the school, as manifested through the above, it is society at large which determines what needs to be taught.

---

8   John W. Aldridge, 1969, "In the Country of the Young," *Harper's Magazine*, vol. 239, no. 1433, p. 63, October.

It can be seen that each of the above could result in a different kind of curriculum if a particular determinant were to hold sway. Benjamin (1939) has summarized the need for educational aims and the need for *change* in aims and methods in a satirical book, *The Sabre-tooth Curriculum*. By taking a small primitive society as a case he shows how futile some of our educational activities are today. An agent of a foreign tribe after an "inspection" tour makes a report and the following exchange occurs:

> ... "They have plenty of meat to eat and skins to wear, but they are so uneducated that they don't know how to distribute food and covering, and consequently many of them are wretchedly fed and clothed. They have a tremendous amount of work to do, yet they are so uneducated that they force many of their people to be idle all the time. They are forever blocked in attempts to better their lives by reason of having only mis-education, pseudo education, in place of real education."
>
> The great ruler's scowl deepened. "Good" he muttered. "Such people need to be taken over by a superior race. We march at dawn. See that the necessary orders are given now."[9]

In these few sentences Benjamin summarizes the challenge of curriculum—relevance to life, work, war, and social justice. To the psychologist, curriculum must take cognizance of such things as individual differences, encouragement of healthy ego processes, actualization of one's potential, and involvement in the continuous process of education. What is taught is less important (but not unimportant) than how it is taught and the effect it has on individual pupils.

Despite the alleged disinterest of the disadvantaged in literature and science and other abstract and symbolic academic disciplines, it seems possible that with (1) enthusiastic teachers, (2) attention to individual interests, and (3) the elimination of comparative and necessarily invidious school marks, the culturally different pupil might share enthusiastically in the wisdom of mankind. Support for the contention is to be found in teachers who have encouraged reading (Fader and Shaevitz, 1966). Respect for the individuality of the pupil and for his language can result not only in interest in literature but in its production (Kohl, 1967). Former dropouts have learned the academic disciplines when it became a matter of their choice and they were able to see the importance of those disciplines (Kelley, 1962). It is not subject matter, per se, that educates but the spirit in which it is pursued (Holt, 1964). The essence of education is the transaction which takes place between the teacher and the learner (Bruner, 1968a; Goodman, 1968; Moustakas, 1966).

Curriculums comprised of answers to questions of fact and value will not satisfy those who are either disturbed by the disintegration of social

---

9   Abner Peddiwell, foreword by Harold Benjamin, 1939, *The Sabre-tooth Curriculum*, New York: McGraw-Hill Book Company, p. 136.

norms or stirred by the increasing prospects of directing the course of human history and reordering the conditions of human society. *The relevance of education is its capacity to help students learn how to influence their own futures instead of resigning themselves to supposed inevitabilities.*[10]

The teacher is a part of the curriculum. The student who is interested in facilitation of the teaching-learning process, without ignoring the importance of structured curriculum, can begin by placing less emphasis on the question, "Why don't *they* decide what should be taught?" Instead the question which has immediate and practical significance is, "What can *I do* to enhance the teaching-learning process?"

Teachers as Representatives of the Middle Class

Learning the problems, attitudes, values, and behavioral meanings of slum and suburban pupils is an especially difficult task for the great bulk of teachers whose own social status origins were lower-middle class. Their own backgrounds do not provide experience from which to generalize. Study of community organization and social status, plus discussion in in-service classes and interschool visitation, may help to provide the perspective which may avert "disadvantage."

If the process of education is to be enjoyable for pupils from all socioeconomic strata and if maximum self-realization is to be effected, then teachers must begin by looking at themselves and the impact their own backgrounds, attitudes, biases, and prejudices have on pupils.

The majority of teachers belong to the middle class (Webster, 1966, p. 454). Some start in the middle class and stay there; a few start in the middle class and move upward; and some start from the lower class and move upward. The last group have a struggle to (1) overcome the barriers of peer and teacher attitudes and (2) resist the tendency to place them in terminal school curricula. To stay in college, they must have learned middle-class values to some extent. When they become teachers, it is only natural that they should reflect middle-class ideology and attitudes. Consciously or unconsciously, they seek to maintain or consolidate their status. Some teachers are helpful to pupils from the lower classes. A principal stated that "teachers who were raised in the middle class tend to offer much help to lower class youngsters. Teachers who came from the lower class steer clear of implicating themselves" (M. Bassett, 1962). Conversely, Webster (1966, p. 458) hypothesizes that socioeconomic divergence be-

---

10   Carlton E. Beck, Normand R. Bernier, James B. Macdonald, Thomas W. Walton, and Jack C. Willers, 1968, *Education for Relevance: The Schools and Social Change*, Boston: Houghton Mifflin Company, p. 172.

tween pupil and teacher is disadvantageous. Some teachers recognize the struggle and are very strict and demanding because they want pupils to develop the attitudes and skills that will facilitate the climb. Others treat children protectively because they do not want to add disadvantages to what the children have already experienced.

Attempts to improve the viewpoints of children from the lower classes, to accept them in spite of their behavior and attitudes, and to view them objectively despite soiled clothing, body odors, and dirty faces and hands are not always rewarding. A considerable degree of hostility is sometimes expressed by members of the lower class who have not achieved the symbols of success in school. Gratitude for assistance is not a typical response. Hostility toward those to whom one might seem to be indebted is about as likely to occur as is thankfulness (Davenport, 1968; Riesman, 1969a). There is also the possibility that some in the middle class will look askance upon the teacher's efforts. Thus the teacher will find his own security threatened. In addition, the protective shell of the lower classes is likely to cause pupils and parents to resent the well-meaning advances of the teachers. The teacher, on inviting the parent for an evaluative conference, may be greeted with "What trouble has Johnny been getting into now?"

Teaching tends to attract those who are inclined to be sympathetic, tolerant, and understanding and to adopt the ideal of social equality. It seems probable that, once having recognized the existence of the problem, teachers are likely to take firm action in helping the less fortunate. Continued professional study, particularly of psychology, cultural anthropology, and sociology, will aid in broader orientation. Programs along this line have been initiated with considerable emphasis on teacher self-analysis (Cottle, 1969), follow-up programs emphasizing in-service teacher education (White, 1969, p. 88), and institutes emphasizing teaching of the disadvantaged (Klopf and Bowman, 1966).

The Need for Educational Reform

In view of rapid change, the process of education—making it a likable and lifelong pursuit—is a central concern. The nation needs the developed potentiality of all individuals to fulfill the existing need for technical and professional competence. The population explosion plus the rise in unemployment creates social dynamite in the form of alienated and purposeless young people. Hence, schools need reformation because of changed purposes and the difficulty of reaching diverse populations.

Summary

It is an unpleasant thing to have to acknowledge that being born into a given socioeconomic class confers on one certain privileges and opportunities and on others certain deprivations and discriminations. Membership in these classes is determined by birth but is continued by acquiring certain characteristic behaviors and material possessions. Middle-class children typically have a well-indoctrinated attitude of pleasing teachers and doing the work assigned. Lower-class children, surrounded by defeat and despair, are less amenable to working for the delayed satisfactions which education promises. These attitudes, plus traditions built into our society, have resulted in the school's becoming a selecting and sorting agency.

Schools contrast sharply from one another. But none is without pressing problems in motivating all children to maximize their potential. Even the children of suburbia are seen by some to suffer from premature sophistication and prejudices stemming from lack of vital contact with wider culture.

Teaching the disadvantaged should begin with appreciating their strengths and capitalizing on them. In addition, involvement of parents, local organizations, and the children themselves in the teaching process seems to have resulted in educational progress. The shunting of lower-class children into vocational courses has borne positive results, but there are aspects of the emphasis which merit careful and continued consideration.

Reform in curriculum, in methods, in pupil involvement is needed. The focal emphasis must, however, be on personality orientations and action patterns that each teacher can produce in himself.

Suggested Additional Reading

ALDRIDGE, JOHN W., 1969, "In the Country of the Young," *Harper's Magazine*, vol. 239, no. 1433, pp. 149-164.
> We hear and read much about the rapidity of social change. In this article, the author makes each of us a part of that change by revealing the reasons for the much different viewpoints of youth today. He explains how and why those changes occurred.

BRONFENBRENNER, URIE, 1969, "Dampening the Unemployability Explosion," *Saturday Review*, vol. 52, no. 1, pp. 108-110, Jan. 4.
> The author presents the view that education, from the nursery school on, must change markedly in order to meet the employment demands of a technology which has changed rapidly in the past two decades and continues to change.

LOCKE, ROBERT W., 1971, "Has the Education Industry Lost Its Nerve?" *Saturday Review*, vol. 54, no. 3, pp. 42-44+, Jan. 16.
> After a few years of enthusiastic effort it has become apparent that machines and educational technology will not solve all the problems of schooling. Education, as "the most humanistic activity in our society," must depend on teachers who will use the potential of hardware to individualize instruction.

MEYER, JAMES A., 1969, "Suburbia: A Wasteland of Disadvantaged Youth and Negligent Schools?" *Phi Delta Kappan*, vol. 50, pp. 575-578.
> Much is heard about the poor teaching and facilities of the slum schools. Recently some questions have been asked about the effectiveness of the schools of suburbia. Isolation from the mainstream of life, chauvinism, and egotism are some of the disadvantages being experienced.

Part two

Factors in the Learning Process

Learning is what educational psychology, schools, culture, becoming human, and utilizing one's potential is all about.

In this section we examine the (1) meaning of learning, (2) conditions under which it best occurs, and (3) established and emergent theories of how and why learning occurs. Various types of learning are used to illustrate the conditions and theories.

The uniqueness of man is sometimes explained in terms of his being able to talk, having opposable thumb-finger action, and having ball-and-socket rather than bladed shoulders. These, together with his most remarkable potential—intelligence—enable him to be a tool-using being and infinitely increase his power. What intelligence is and how the potential for its development can be maximized are aspects of the theme of Part 2.

Some of the things we think about intelligence are just not so! The nature, limitations, and valid uses of intellectual assessment are an integral part of how we view and use our potential to effect the learning which, in one short lifetime, makes us so different from our equally well-endowed ancestors—Cro-Magnon man. Assessment may be a help or hazard in developing intelligence or in the facilitation of learning processes.

6
The Nature of Learning

Marked changes are being experienced in educational thought and theory. In some schools the beginnings of changing emphases have been initiated, and in others the seeds of thought have not sprouted.

Conventionally teachers have taught the things which society deems to be necessary or advisable. Teachers have been responsible for seeing to it that curriculum has been "covered," and if the pupil has not learned what has been taught, then teachers withhold the rewards. Pupils are given low or failing grades and are not promoted, or are promoted only as a matter of courtesy or humanitarianism. The teacher is held to be responsible for learning and has the enforcement tools of curricular requirements such as grades, credits, certificates, and diplomas. For many the system has worked. For many others the system has failed.

The about-face is that *pupils, not teachers, are responsible* for their own learning. The role of the teacher as "instructor" is being diminished, and the evolving role is "learning resource consultant." Teachers are to guide learning activities of pupils instead of "laying it on the line" for those willing and able and condemning others with the stigma of failure and inferiority. This emerging role is not the idle dream of theoreticians—already in some schools and colleges the learning centers of the future are taking shape.

The Nature of the Learning Process

A Concept of Learning

Learning includes not only the acquisition of subject matter but also that of habits, attitudes, perceptions, preferences, interests, social adjustments, skills of many types, and ideals. Even such seemingly simple things as learning to spell and add involve varied forms of learning. Because of this complexity, it is desirable that some embracing explanation be made that will account for the various modes and nuances of learning. Helpful statements that are somewhat inclusive, but definitely not conclusive, have been postulated. More is being discovered daily, and the frontiers appear to be wide open—as witness the surge in programmed learning, group involvement, independent study, and emphasis on unique styles of learning.

It is quite likely that we are coming closer to knowing what chemical, electrical, biological, and neurological changes occur during the process of learning (Krech, 1969). We do not know so much about those changes as is desirable, but much is known about the conditions under which learning takes place most effectively. These conditions and the ways in which they may be improved are, at least in part, subject to the control of teachers. In part, conditions affecting learning, such as cultural deprivation and physical and physiological handicaps, are beyond control by teachers. Even so, those factors are part of the psychological field with which teachers must be concerned.

Learning involves the modification of perception and behavior. Improvement of behavior, i.e., the more complete satisfaction of the needs of society and self, is usually implied. Even when behavior is maladaptive in the eyes of society, the individual perceives that his behavior will satisfy his own needs. Learning means that behavioral modifications occur in meeting changed conditions so that obstacles are overcome or so that homeostasis may be maintained or heterostasis may be experienced.

Not all behavior change is learning. A child may eat more because his stomach enlarges and because his energy needs increase, but the changed behavior is not learning. He may, however, *learn* to eat more because of parental example or because of psychological needs that appear to be satisfied through food. The loss of an arm through accident modifies behavior, but the loss itself is not learning. The person may, though, learn to compensate for the loss of his arm by learning new skills.

Modification does not necessarily result in improvement—at least in terms of social values. Pupils may learn to dislike school, but their adjustment is not improved thereby. Criminals learn to violate legal and moral codes and may become experts at it, but their behavior, from a social viewpoint, is not improved.

With these and many other considerations, we may define learning as change in performance through conditions of activity, practice, and experience (Hilgard and Bower, 1966, p. 5). This is an operational definition, and it is derived in part from scientific investigations. In the classroom, the activities and experiences that lead to change in performance involve telling and listening, judging, reading, reciting, observation of demonstrations, experimenting, pupils' interacting, and individual learning quests and activities. It is hoped that both sporadic practice and formal drill in reading, writing, computing, and speaking will carry over to performance in daily life. Living and working with others, supplementing the feedback that comes from reflecting and discussing while engulfed in classroom learning, will, we hope, lead to continued learning beyond the school years.

Learning begins with the organism. We, for instance, may listen to the speaker's word; we may shut out that sound and reflect on last night's discussion; or we may respond to the warm sunshine and plan this afternoon's golf game. Our learning may be conditioned by our ability to see what is written on the board, by the fact that the battery to our hearing aid has run down, or by the misery of a cold we have just caught. Hearing may be influenced by the physiology of one's emotions (being angry or in love does not enhance learning the results of Mycenaean excavations). There can be no doubt that pupils' learning abilities are affected by the speed with which nerve messages move and are sorted and combined and by the degree of permanence of the impression they make. These physical bases may be hereditary, congenital, or developmental in origin, but they do influence the nature and speed of learning. Learning depends on the inclination and ability to receive and respond to stimulation.

Physical Aspects of Learning

There are physical aspects of learning that cannot be ignored by the teacher, e.g., vision and hearing. Biochemical factors influence the amount of energy that can be brought to bear on learning, and they also affect the comfort and satisfaction that an individual derives from the pursuit of learning (Eichorn, 1963). Such influences bear heavily on personality orientation and, whether we like it or not, on teaching-learning processes.

Learning depends on the retentiveness and plasticity of the central nervous system. Recent findings in psychological laboratories suggest that mental ability and retentiveness are functions of enzymes, the action of ribonucleic acid (RNA), and the nourishment of brain cells.

The scientist as well as the man on the street recognizes that differences exist among individuals in innate ability to learn. A cretin, a mongoloid, or a microcephalic does not learn with the facility of a normal individual. Less obvious, but nonetheless certain, is the fact that among children who appear to be normal, there are also enormous differences in degrees of aptitude for learning.

Jan Lukas/College Newsphoto Alliance

Unless basic differences in learning style and ability are recognized, teachers may try (and have tried) to force all children to learn at a uniform rate and berate youngsters who do not keep up with the class. On the other hand, a child who learns more rapidly than the group may become a troublemaker to offset his boredom. Hence teachers should become aware of symptoms (indifference, failure, boredom, inattention, tantrums, and the like) which indicate that they are expecting too much or too little of their pupils. Pressure can mean trying to make a pupil go more rapidly or more slowly than is comfortable for him.

The teacher should be on guard for symptoms that indicate the need for medical examinations. For example, visual difficulty may be evidenced by squinting, rubbing the eyes, leaning forward to see the board, tilting the head, brushing material off the printed page, holding a book very close to the eyes, reddened or watering eyes, or frowning. Hearing difficulty may be manifested by turning the head to one side, asking that questions be repeated, failing to respond or responding belatedly to questions or remarks, speech defects, difficulty in group discussions, inattention, and listlessness.

It is estimated that 50 percent of the schoolchildren in the United States who have physical disabilities are not receiving the necessary attention (Voelker and Mullen, 1963). Add to these the environmentally handicapped, and the need for education which is relevant is magnified (Barbe, 1967). There is the conviction on the part of many that physical and environmental handicaps can be compensated for, prevented, or remedied.

There are many limitations imposed on learning by virtue of glandular dysfunction and dietary deficiency. Hypofunctioning (underactivity) of the thyroid is accompanied by listlessness, lethargy, and varying degrees of dullness. A certain teacher noticed that one pupil had a tendency to be somewhat pudgy, appeared to be sleepy much of the time, and had some difficulty in learning. He suggested that the child be given a metabolism test. A slight thyroid deficiency was found, and appropriate treatment was instituted. Of course, not all learning difficulties will be removed by glandular treatment. The physical disorder which has caused maximum frustration for teachers is the one which is not visible—in fact, it is hard to detect by test—namely, **dyslexia**. This disorder, which causes distortions of visual perception and spatial orientation, is an excellent example of the inseparability of education and physiology.

The Learner's Response

Heredity and environment constitute only two of the major facets of the learning process. An important third is the individual's response—the "processing" which the learner conducts (Gagné, 1970a). Pupils respond with varying degrees of vigor and purposefulness. This vigor derives only in part from physical conditions; it also comes from perceptions and motivations. One pupil may perceive that succeeding academically will place him in positions of prestige or leadership. Another may perceive academic success as constituting submission to authority figures whom he resists. Just how one perceives any situation is itself subject to change through instruction. Effective teaching of the culturally different must include skill in seeing the world and its people through the eyes of pupils. Some of the disadvantages pupils encounter reside in the rigidity of the school itself (Elkins, 1969).

Fortunately, most youngsters wish to please authority figures, they cherish the prestige of leadership, and they are willing to try to achieve the academic task—not because they see it as serving their personal needs directly but because they wish to get along with others and win approval. Should these pupils not meet the experience of failure too frequently or too consistently, they will continue to give vigorous application to their school learnings.

One's response is partially dependent on the nature of his social relationships with his peers, parents, siblings, and teachers. Response is also influenced by interest, goals, abilities, and social expectation. At all school levels, from kindergarten to college, the conventional attitude of "Here it is, you learn it" has been shifting to one of responsibility for trying to make the learner receptive. If the teacher is cognizant of the ways in which different pupils respond to ostensibly the same situation, he can change the nature or pattern of physical stimulation; e.g., present material through a demonstration rather than via printed description. Another approach is to attempt to alter the pupil's perception. This can be done through explanation in class, but success is more probable if the pupil is approached in a person-to-person conversation (not a lecture). Success is still more likely if the attempt is made through peer-group discussion.

The point here is that the teacher's job is much greater than the mere presenting of materials. The real teaching will occur when both teacher and pupil are actively involved in the fluid process of learning. Variations in learning styles are due, in some measure, to the way the pupil sees himself and his world.

The Learning Milieu

The creation of a favorable environment for learning is the basic problem, and the most amenable to modification, of our system of formal education. At the national level pressing problems are racial integration, equalization of educational opportunity, and better schools and teachers in inner-city and rural slums (*The People* . . ., 1969). The problems are being tackled through Head Start by starting children to school earlier than the conventional age; by VISTA programs in which adults become involved with pupils; by street academies in which the immediate environment serves as the curriculum.

Because full employment and continued technological progress depend heavily on educated citizens, much attention has been given to occupation-related education. In work experience programs and in cooperative education students spend some school time in stores or industrial plants and get first-hand contact with the environment outside the school. In some places evening classes are made available to those who must work but have not finished high school or who seek upgrading of their occupational skills. Some young people get credit in their hometown school for a term or year which was spent abroad. The extended school year—twelve months instead of nine—is being tentatively tried. As important and as exciting as these organizational modifications are, it may be that they are only instrumental to the most significant part of the educational environment—teacher-pupil transaction.

Adults-people-peers and dialogue-communication are key concerns in the enhancement of the learning environment. Goodman (1968) recommends adult guidance, as contrasted to institutional prescription, as the essential aspect of education. Bruner (1968) emphasizes the matter of contact and conversation with older people as being a major stimulus to facile learning. Coleman (1961) has shown how strongly peers influence the aspirations and activities of adoles-

75591

cents. Rogers (1968) has repeatedly shown how essential dialogue is to mental health and efficient learning. Krech (1969) suggests that the really *human* aspect of education might very well be language and communication. Hence, a persistent theme in this book is that the pivotal factor in the educational milieu is the adults—teachers, teacher aides, parent assistants—who constitute the human environment of the school.

Categories of Learning

Although the following forms are not mutually exclusive, they may serve to show the complexity of the problems with which the teacher must deal.

Sensorimotor Skills

One category of learning is that called "sensorimotor skills." These are actions which become so automatic that other learned activities may be carried on simultaneously without interference. Walking, riding a bicycle, using eating utensils, getting dressed (except when choice is involved), dancing, and for some persons, such things as plain knitting are examples. The stimulus for these acts comes from pressures and impulses from joints and muscles, and outside stimulation may actually interfere—as for example, when a person tries to analyze or explain just how he performs a certain dance step or ties his shoelace. The teacher's contribution to the learning of sensorimotor skills resides in the early detection of gross errors (such as posture, or holding a pencil), in setting a good example and in providing encouragement.

Associational Learning

Another category of learning is that called "associational." Vocabulary is a good example—certain sequences of letters become so related to given objects, concepts, or situations that one tends to recall the other. When we speak of "meaning" in a teaching-learning setting, we refer to the power of words to recall real, tangible situations or objects to the learner. Facilitation of associational learning is accomplished by preliminary surveys, classifications, relating the new to the known, review emphasizing the new associations, and explanations accompanied by models, pictures, and demonstrations.

Perceptual Motor Skills

Perceptual motor skills are a category which combines sensorimotor skills with associated learning. In typing, for example, the same finger is used consistently to strike a given letter, but the sequence of letters and spacing depends on what is being typed. These skills, therefore, depend on association. Teachers aid in the learning of perceptual motor skills by watching the form of sensorimotor skills, by clarifying understanding of the associations to be formed, by acting calmly and slowly so that there is no unnecessary interference with early acts, by providing drill in various situations, and by providing alternate periods of drill and rest or change. As in other learnings, it is important that the learner think well of himself. This for the teacher means minimizing criticism and being sensitive to pupil progress and then letting the pupil know he *was* there and *is now* here.

"Percepts" are the mental modifications that come into existence when one perceives; they must not be mistaken for the physical thing that is objectively present. Perception depends, too, on what the individual has been conditioned to perceive. A radiologist, for example, can perceive accurately and derive meaning from shadows on an x-ray; an outdoorsman can readily see forms in grass and brush that are birds or animals. The uninitiated would have to have these pointed out specifically and would probably miss them on the next trial. Similarly, experiments indicate that potentiality for learning a language declines after the age of nine because perceptual ability has not been exercised when the neural connections are ready (Penfield, 1967); after that the capacity for developing nuances in pronunciation becomes more limited. The "foreigner" simply does not hear the shadings of pronunciation that are meaningful to the person using the "foreign" language. Moreover, the muscles of the throat and tongue that are needed to pronounce the "foreign" word correctly have not been exercised with the appropriate coordination and quite possibly have atrophied or lost their plasticity. Perceptual ability depends on exposure to patterned stimulations in the early environment as well as upon the general intellectual aptitude of the learner (Hunt, 1968).

How one perceives a situation is influenced by how he perceives himself. Kathy may anticipate that the tasks suggested are too difficult for her to perform; she approaches them hesitantly and interprets the first difficulty as an insurmountable obstacle. Rick seems to believe that nothing is too difficult and sees failure (which is frequent, in view of his numerous ventures) as only a temporarily inadequate approach that needs some modification. Many authorities, be they psychoanalytically, behavioristically, or humanistically oriented, view the concept of self as being the core of personality (Buhler, 1967).

Conceptual Learning

Conceptual learnings are general or abstract mental representations of situations or conditions. Although simple associations are a one-to-one affair, concepts involve many interrelationships and conditions; several percepts are combined in terms of some cogent relationship or common theme to form a concept. Democracy may be used as an example—others are motherhood, communism, Negro, salesman, etc. The concept of democracy, for example, goes beyond the idea of equality. It includes the notion of the supreme importance of the individual, but it also recognizes the delegation of authority and responsibility to the unusually able person. Democracy emphasizes responsibility for one's own conduct and regards institutions as the servants of man, at least in theory. Common consent, voluntary cooperation, devotion to truth, brotherhood, and freedom to develop individuality are aspects of the concept of democracy that evolve throughout a lifetime.

Attempts to provide education for the culturally different have demonstrated that a common error is the teacher's assumption that one child has the same conceptual grasp of a situation as another and that both are similar to his own:

> Some Indian children have been taught directly as well as unintentionally that being "better than" is not socially acceptable to the tribe. Children so taught will strive to be "as good as" but then will diminish their effort. Hence, when they get in school and the teachers attempt to motivate them through the promise of high grades they are unimpressed —they want such grades only if their classmates also get them. Contests to "see who can finish first" are embarrassing. Instructions to seven pupils at the chalkboard such as "Turn around as soon as you finish" find all seven still facing the board, glancing sidewise, and wondering how they can ever get away. To be an athlete for individual excellence is not exciting; but contributing to the prestige of the school and the satisfaction of teammates and fellow students is quite another matter (Clements, 1970).

Briefly, the teacher's role is to provide a wide variety of experiences, call attention to details that initially escaped attention, reiterate the most essential features of a situation, encourage discussion, and lead in the discovery of characteristics that are common and pervasive. He must give attention to the individual pupil's ability to act as an individual or as part of a group, his tolerance for stress and strain, the quality of his interpersonal relations, and the recognition of his competencies and limitations. The teacher must be concerned with knowing his pupils and strengthening their self-concepts. All this might seem impossible if the teacher must be in control, but becomes possible if the teacher's primary concern is to provide freedom to develop pupil responsibility for learning—in accord with his unique style (Hart, 1969).

Ideals and Attitudes

The learning of ideals and attitudes is currently being examined with fresh interest. A major world problem is the difficulty that people from different cultures have in really understanding one another. To some, pork and chicken are delightful foods; to others, the thought of eating them is nauseating. In some cultures, women with large buttocks are admirable; in others, such development is equivalent to deformity. One is not born with tastes and preferences—they are acquired through learning processes.

Some men do prefer "overweight" women, but others wonder why in the world there is such preference. Some persons "turn green" at the sight of pork. Tracing back their personal histories, it is usually found that the first contact, or first series of contacts, with large women or with pork was in a distinctly pleasant or unpleasant situation. If the first contact were pleasant, the response was liking, accepting, seeking to prolong contact. The reason why there are national likes and dislikes is that any society tends to create emotional atmospheres around given situations.

One is tempted to say that the learning of tastes, preferences, ideals, and attitudes is the most important outcome of education because they are so likely to inhibit or foster the continued learning that is essential for growth and development beyond the school years. If literature is presented by a gruff taskmaster with the aim of covering so many pages or getting through the syllabus or course of study, then the probable results will be dislike and avoidance. On the other hand, a teacher who can communicate his own liking and interest, who takes the time to prepare an attractive physical setting and to maintain a pleasant atmosphere, and who relates the literature to events in the pupils' lives is most likely to get the immediate lesson across and, in addition, is more likely to create an attitude that will lead to the continued pursuit of reading. The student seeks to recapture the pleasant associations.

Problem Solving

Problem solving is considered by some authorities to be the highest type of learning because responses are not dependent simply on past associations and conditionings; rather response is dependent upon the ability to manipulate abstract ideas, to use aspects and modifications of previous learnings, to perceive small differences, and to project oneself into the future. Problem solving demands the creation, not the repetition, of responses when a situation arises that is of such complexity that initiative and mental synthesis are required to adjust to it.

Teachers may facilitate problem-solving behavior in many ways. The provision of broad experiences is one of them. Certainly, because the first step in problem solving is recognition of the problem, problems must be suited to the maturity level of pupils. This involves taking the problem from the life experiences of children. When students are encouraged to participate in the life of the school and community, they are being provided with excellent opportunities for exercising problem-solving ability. Time must be allotted for exploration, discussion, and experimentation. A teacher who feels that a certain number of pages should be covered in the textbook or who is afraid to "get off the subject" is not likely to foster problem-solving ability. He must avoid the temptation to believe that his own conclusions are necessarily the right ones. He must avoid haste so that the pupil will have time to explore possibilities and "incubate" ideas. It takes time to think.

Theories of Learning

Significance of Theory

"Practical" solutions to teaching-learning dilemmas, drawn from teachers' experiences, often work on one pupil but not another. In the eyes of some teachers, practical means giving an encompassing answer—a panacea. The pervasive answer does not work because a given symptom, aggressiveness for example, does not have the same meaning for all children (Cohen, 1971). On the other hand, theory provides bases for a teacher's devising a specific solution for an individual case. Although theory will not tell us, figuratively, why little boys steal apples, it may suggest why *a boy* steals an apple. Theory does not provide recipes for motivation, classroom control, or the continued pursuit of knowledge, but it does provide clues for resolving a pupil's problem. There are those, for instance, who recommend putting the child outside the room when he fails to conform. Some have suggested, and have assigned, more work for the bright child. There are those who believe boys should start school at a later age than girls. These are practical answers—and are wrong as often as they are correct. The really applicable teaching-learning theory will say, it depends on (1) the learner and his style of learning, (2) the teacher and his personality, (3) the outcomes desired, (4) the situation which prevails at the moment, and (5) what culture and technology demand. These constitute the criteria by which teaching-learning effectiveness may be evaluated.

Various theories, or viewpoints, of learning have been evolved. These theories differ largely in the relative emphasis that is made in each theoretical formulation; i.e., one emphasizes the relationship between and repetition of stimulus and response, emphasizes success and/or reward, while another emphasizes perception, insight, and understanding. Bigge (1966) has summarized ten theories and pointed out some educational implications. Bruce (1966) emphasizes three forces, and Gagné simply describes new concepts of learning. In the shorter listings the authors have included in one category what others have included in longer lists. Four viewpoints are described below—simple conditioning, reinforcement, insight, and phenomenology or humanistic psychology.

Conditioning

Simple conditioning, or contiguity theory, emphasizes that learning consists of eliciting a response by means of a previously neutral or inadequate stimulus. Through contiguity of stimulus and response, a stimulus that was inadequate to arousing a response becomes capable of doing so.

The pioneer in the field was Ivan Pavlov (1927), a Russian physiologist, who provided some of the basic terms that are commonly used in conditioning theory. His basic experiments consisted of cutting small holes in the cheeks of dogs so that secreted saliva could be collected and measured. A tuning fork was sounded, and seconds later meat powder was presented to the subject dog. Originally, the tuning fork did not cause the flow of saliva, but the meat powder—the "unconditioned stimulus"—did. As the experiment was repeated, the tuning fork —the "conditioned stimulus"—did cause the flow of saliva. The flow of saliva, when caused by meat, was called the "unconditioned response"; but when caused by the tuning fork, it was called the "conditioned response." If, after conditioning, the tuning fork was sounded and reinforcement with meat did not occur, the amount of saliva progressively lessened—this process was called "extinction."

Conditioning includes two main types: *classical* and *instrumental*. The classical type can be illustrated by Pavlov's pioneering experiment. When the sound of a bell causes a dog to salivate, the iris of a human eye to contract, or a chicken to turn twice to the right—all of which have been accomplished—we say that an inadequate, or unconditioned, stimulus has become adequate because it now elicits the response. Basically, conditioning may be defined as the automatization of a response by repetition of a stimulus that *accompanies* a given response and ultimately becomes a cause for behavior that formerly it merely accomplished.

A prominent part of simple conditioning is association. This means that patterns of stimuli functioning and being given some attention *at the time* of a response tend to give rise to that same response when the stimuli recur. Association is facilitated by contiguity, that is, proximity in space and time strengthen association.

Simple conditioning is an important means of learning in childhood. Babies learn through "No, no" to avoid touching the hot stove, to keep away from kitchen knives, or to stay on the curb. Some school learning comes through conditioning, and repetition, drill, and practice are important learning avenues. It is essential that the pupil be led to do what he is to learn; examples are spelling and learning number combinations, chemical symbols and formulas, foreign vocabulary, etc. The fundamental implication of contiguity conditioning for education is that pupils learn by making, doing, repeating, and responding. However, if we do not want pupils to be mere automatons, mere carbon copies of their teachers and parents, then some additional dimensions of learning psychology are needed. The challenge of individuality and the complexity of creativity call for additional psychological perspectives.

Instrumental conditioning involves the *active* participation of the organism to a much greater extent than does classical conditioning. Reward, or reinforcement, is an integral part of instrumental conditioning; need satisfaction and relief from tension, or avoidance of punishment, are all part of the total process.

A dog in a box is given an electric shock in his foot, upon which he yelps, moves his foot, puts his tail between his legs, or snaps at some object. If each time, just before the shock is applied, the dog hears a bell, he will soon react diffusely to the bell alone; but as the process continues, the useless parts of the diffuse response are dropped, and he simply lifts his foot at the sound of the bell and avoids the shock and is rewarded, or reinforced, by avoiding it.

There is much evidence that the organism does not respond mechanically solely on the basis of association or contiguity. Response is partially dependent upon the state of the organism. Pavlov's dog might have reacted differently if he had been so sick that meat would not cause him to salivate. If a child feels that the multiplication tables have no significance, he will learn them slowly, if at all. There must be some ability, however, small, to respond to the task at hand. Further, stimuli are usually not purely mechanical because there is a cumulative effect. A schoolgirl standing in line may not respond to the tug given her hair by the boy behind her the first five times, but one more tug may have the cumulative effect of causing her to turn and give a resounding slap to her tormentor. Learning theorists are currently supplementing the idea of conditioning with the concept of "information processing" (Gagné, 1970).

It can be seen that responses are not purely mechanical when one considers the phenomenon of forgetting, which may be explained in terms of the weakening of old responses or by the learning of new ones. New associations destroy, weaken, or overlap the connection between original stimuli and responses. Forgetting is thus not necessarily the loss of a function but may be due to the addition of more recent ones.

There are several ways in which teachers may gain from conditioning theory. First it is well to realize that pupils will learn what they do—what they enact. Their diligence and sincere efforts carry over into habit patterns. This does not mean that work need be so rigorous as to be burdensome. Rather, the teacher should encourage application, industry, and studiousness by seeing that the material fits the child's needs or wants; thus, study will bring him the reinforcement of personal satisfaction.

Admittedly, mere repetition is not all there is to learning. Pupils may understand a poem, the multiplication tables, or formulas in algebra or chemistry without knowing them well enough to repeat them. Nevertheless, practice, drill, or repetition is necessary to consolidate such knowledge. Drill should involve practice in various settings and orders. For instance, drill should be sufficiently effective so that a pupil can give the product of 7 x 8 without having to repeat 7 x 5, 7 x 6, and 7 x 7 before he arrives at 56. Moreover, the drill should be motivated and meaningful, varied and periodic.

Closely allied to drill is review. Review will prevent the initially rapid forgetting that often accompanies learning. The word "review" means "taking another view"—placing the material in a different perspective, relating the facts learned to another problem, and attaching them to the present lessons. Review should serve the purposes not only of sustaining learning but of attaching new meanings to what has been learned and of providing a transition to new subject matter.

Finally, the teacher must be aware of the existence of conflicting and competing stimuli in the classroom situation. For example, a child may scarcely be aware of a clear, colorful, and impressive situation that the teacher has attempted to create because he is concerned about the illness of his mother or because his father is unnecessarily strict. High school pupils may be concerned about making the basketball team, getting a part in the class play, holding a part-time job, or solving some problem in peer relationships. Some teachers take the attitude that the pupil's inattentiveness is a personal insult and reprimand him accordingly. Thus, the child may be conditioned to respond to 7 x 8 correctly but also be conditioned to dislike the teacher, arithmetic, and school in general.

Connectionism

Stimulus-response, or reinforcement theory, has been elucidated by E. L. Thorndike, who held that learning consists of forming bond or connections between stimuli and responses. New bonds form through experience, and the formation of these bonds is influenced by frequency, recency, intensity, and vividness of the experience, mood and capacity of the subject, similarity of situations, *and resulting satisfaction*, or reinforcement, which is basic in conditioning theory. These conditions are summarized in the "laws of learning," which are very much in use in daily classroom practice:

1. The Law of Effect
Thorndike's early formulation of the law of effect was that when a modifiable connection between a stimulus and a response has been made, it was

strengthened if it resulted in satisfaction and was weakened if it led to annoyance. This statement was criticized, and his own experiments indicated that annoyance did not seem to be an adequate explanation for weakening responses. Thorndike modified his position in 1932 (pp. 267, 311). Satisfaction, according to his later statement, strengthens the bond between stimulus and response, but annoyance does not weaken it. A child may be reinforced by the recognition of inappropriate acts.

Some classroom implications of this law are that a pupil should have (*a*) a teacher who enjoys his work and his pupils and who has good mental health; (*b*) schoolwork and activities that are understandable and meaningful in terms of his personal life; (*c*) schoolwork and activities in which he can have some degree of success; (*d*) schoolwork that is progressive in nature and builds on earlier work, thereby giving him an awareness of growth; (*e*) presentation of material with varied approaches so that novelty is provided; (*f*) guidance, praise, and encouragement that bring him the satisfaction of knowing that he is on the right path.

2. The Law of Exercise

This law is made up of two parts: use and disuse. The law of use asserts that, other things being equal, the more frequently a modifiable connection between a situation and a response is made, the stronger that connection will be. The law of disuse asserts that, other things being equal, when a modifiable connection between a situation and a response is not made over a period of time, the strength of that connection is weakened.

This "law" has a number of implications, such as the following: Pupils should be given opportunities to use what they know. Examinations have their place in providing exercise—though they should not be regarded as the sole objective of classroom instruction. Oral quizzes can serve to diagnose weaknesses in teaching procedures and at the same time provide pupils with an opportunity to display their knowledge. Review provides an opportunity for repetition (exercise) and at the same time places knowledge in new settings. Provided understanding accompanies repetition, the law of exercise justifies the use of drill in various forms. But drill must lead somewhere. Instead of rote recitation, discussions should encourage pupils to bring their own experiences to class for interpretation in terms of the content being presented. Recent professional literature places much emphasis on discussion, pupil contributions, and the conversational method (Bruner, 1968*b*; Goodman, 1968). Mathematics instruction, for example, is more effective when discussion immediately follows the assignment of exercises. Even at the college level, where the lecture method is most firmly entrenched, it is estimated that dependence on lectures during the past few years has decreased from about 90 percent to slightly over 50 percent. Increasing emphasis has been placed on student reports, individual research, group projects, and class participation. It is considered important that all pupils have a chance to contribute; therefore, physical and intellectual freedom have been encouraged (Jackson,

1969). Memorization of facts has given way to the use, cross-use, and interpretation of those facts. This practice accords with the findings of research, which indicate that the ability to recall memorized items is lost much more rapidly than is the ability to apply principles or interpret new experiments.

3. The Law of Readiness

When a modifiable connection is ready to act, to do so is satisfying; when it is not ready, to do so is unsatisfying. Readiness is dependent upon both maturation and experience. This statement may be clarified by reference to the concept of reading readiness. It has been found that if, among other requisites, a child has reached the mental age of 6-1/2 years, he is mentally capable of learning to read. If he does not have the requisite maturation, the experience of trying to learn to read may be annoying and frustrating. But *he must also have* the mental set, the desire, to learn to read. The more or less permanent condition of readiness should not be confused with the temporary condition of mental set, which is dependent upon interest, pertinency, or timeliness. Readiness is influenced by the organization of the material. Bruner (1963*a*, p. 12) has indicated that the foundations of any subject may be taught to pupils of any age in some form. Primary teachers of reading have found that pupils can master some beginning books in reading but not others.

The classroom implications of readiness are often overlooked. This is demonstrated by teachers who ask, "How can I teach numbers (or spelling, algebra, or history) to pupils who have low IQs?" "How can I bring slow learners up to the class average?" At least part of the answer is to be found in the concept of readiness. Teachers must either wait for readiness, accept the present level of readiness and be satisfied with a slower learning rate, or provide experiences that will enhance readiness.

Educators are today strongly advising that a child not be forced "beyond his depth" in reading, arithmetic, or social activities. With good reason, in terms of readiness, there is much current concern with relevance (Goodlad, 1969*b*). No doubt some children are taught to swim by being tossed into the deep end—but frequently at the expense of their desire to swim. A pupil who is forced to read before the elements of readiness converge may acquire some degree of reading skill, but he may also decide that he will read only when forced to do so. Very recently an experienced teacher said, "But I just can't let him go on this way in reading any longer—he's eight years old." This nonreading lad had a mental age of about five years on a group test of intelligence—eighteen months below the mental age considered necessary for reading.

Preparatory experience that will hasten the growth of readiness can be provided. Thus the primary teacher reads and tells stories to his pupils, encourages them to look at picture books and tell stories about what they see, and takes them on excursions and records the results on experience charts. Because readiness for reading consists of more than book experiences, he encourages group play and the exercise of independence and praises emotional control. A major function of preschool education for the disadvantaged is to compensate for the lack of contact with books by reading aloud, telling stories, and conversing (Bereiter and Engelmann, 1966, p. 5).

Aptitude tests in various subjects can be helpful to teachers in determining the thoroughness of pupils' preparation for those subjects. For example, there are mathematics, English, chemistry, language, and mechanical aptitude tests and, of course, general intelligence tests. Correctly used, such tests should help the teacher avoid the bewilderment and frustration that result from starting students in various subject areas simply because they have reached a certain grade or chronological age. Such tests are inappropriately used when they become the excuse for sorting, classifying, and stigmatizing.

Five supplementary principles, in addition to the three above-mentioned primary laws of learning, are included in Thorndike's formulation of stimulus-response, reinforcement theory.

1. The Principle of Multiple Response

This principle emphasizes that many trial-and-error responses may be tried before a satisfying one is hit upon. As learning takes place, useless parts of an act are dropped. There are several factors involved in trial-and-error learning: a need or motive; a difficulty (problematic situation) or obstacle; random, experimental, sometimes almost aimless attempts to achieve the goal; a successful trial; elimination of unproductive responses and consolidation of successful (reinforced) ones; and finally, the coordination of selected activities into large, unified patterns of behavior.

The significance of trial-and-error learning for education is that it allows pupils an opportunity for wide experience, a chance to experiment for themselves, to learn from their own errors. Help is provided when it is requested or when a pupil makes chronic errors, but there is an increasing realization that experience, including the making of errors, is educative. Art teachers, for example, are moving away from stereotyped methods and encouraging children to select their own art media, to choose their own subjects, and to experiment with their own techniques. Art is regarded as a means of opening ways to experimental views of the world (Keel, 1965).

2. The Principle of Mental Set

Mental set is the more or less temporary condition of one's attitudes, feelings, and interests. A pupil may be *ready* in terms of maturation for the experience of reading, but not have the *anticipatory adjustment* that causes him to seek the learning goal. "Mental set" refers to the predisposition to act in a given way. When pupils are not conditioned to expect to learn to read and write, to accept the teacher in his role, and to adopt school behavior, both the pupils' and the teacher's tasks would be most difficult. Mental set is seen to operate in a negative and alarming manner in school dropouts. The youngsters do not participate in school activities; they are discouraged with their past performance; and, even when they have the requisite ability, they are not predisposed to apply themselves to school tasks (Schrieber and Kaplan, 1964).

Teachers can capitalize on school events, anniversaries, and outstanding community events to orient students to the daily lesson or new unit. Many high school pupils read at least the newspaper headlines, and virtually all of them are exposed to televised news. Events thus encountered and often discussed in the home can provide a convenient orientation point for learning activities. For example, one elementary school teacher used the community dairy as a point of departure in teaching geography and social studies. The meaningfulness of the schoolwork is a powerful determinant of mental set.

It has been shown that the emotional atmosphere of the classroom is an important factor in mental set. If the teacher is happy and congenial, the attitude of his pupils is likely to be positive. An attempt should be made to encourage congenial attitudes and cooperative relationships between pupils. An important aspect of mental set is the extent to which pupils feel they have some control over their own destiny (Glasser, 1969, p. 123).

The temporary disappointments that every individual suffers have a negative effect upon the mental set for learning. A junior high school girl with an IQ that placed her in the superior classification was failing in part of her work and causing disturbances by fighting with boys. The teacher, in talking with the girl, discovered that she was embarrassed by the lack of one front tooth and a protruding abdomen. Help was secured from a charitable organization to defray the cost of a new tooth, better clothes were obtained, and the teacher taught the girl some pertinent aspects of personal grooming. The girl was objective and accepted the teacher's explanation that a protruding abdomen was normal during early adolescence. Her attitude change seemed to be miraculous. The girl's grades quickly improved; she was able to laugh at the boys who made fun of her; and soon she had a substantial group of friends. Pupils have been known to develop favorable attitudes toward learning merely on the basis of knowing that the teacher is concerned about them and that the teacher desires to be of assistance.

3. The Principle of Partial Activity

A response is made only to parts or aspects of a total rather than to the totality, according to this principle. Part of a total situation may be prepotent in the determination of a response. For example, a baby will respond to its mother whether she is in night clothes or evening dress, whether she is at home, on the street, or visiting with friends. A pupil will respond to the number combination 3 x 4—if he has learned it—whether he sees it in a book or is asked for the product by his teacher or his father. Words are perhaps the most widespread means by which part of a situation serves to recall a larger total.

4. The Principle of Analogy, or Assimilation

This means that when an individual is faced with a new situation for which he has no natural or learned response, the response he makes will resemble an earlier response to a similar situation.

Classroom implications of the principle of analogy include the need for pointing out similarities between the new and the old, the importance of leading from the known to the unknown, and the usefulness of bringing textbook abstractions to life by relating them to the experiences of the learner. Schools cannot hope to prepare pupils for all future experiences, but they can provide some basis for assimilating later experiences if equivalents, similarities, and parallels are indicated in the course of instruction. Recent emphases on the "structure of learning" and the "discovery" orientation have much similarity to the principle of analogy. The establishment of relationships, such as is involved in these approaches, facilitates learning and improves retention (Bruner, 1963b; 1970a). Teachers who point out similarities between historical events and present-day happenings are helping to produce understanding and responsible citizens. Work-study programs (Jaffe, 1969), whether intentionally based on the principle of analogy or not, are illustrations of the principle.

The unit approach in organizing school studies gains support from the principle of analogy. This is the focusing of subject matter on a central theme, for instance, in social studies, concentrating on transportation or food production as the unit theme (Bigge and Hunt, 1968, p. 572). The purpose of the unit is to draw related knowledge from various fields. The unifying factor may be a problem, an era of history, or a trend in scientific development. The unit generates a large, related body of subject matter that cannot be covered in a day or in one lesson. It is therefore of increasing importance that relationships be perceived by the pupils. There is a dual need for seeing a situation in its larger perspective and studying the contributions that can be made by separate subjects. The principle of analogy is simply the psychological explanation of what has been pragmatically tested. It has been shown, for instance, that pupils learn to make wise choices, render decisions, evaluate consequences, and in general, become better citizens when they participate in student activities and government. School personnel need to learn that pupils need, and gain from, a voice in the running of their own school (Kelley, 1962).

The experience unit illustrates the principle of analogy. The basic notion, in this instance, is that reality for each individual resides in his perceptions. Objects have different meanings for different persons. It is recognized that superior learning takes place when the task contributes to ends that have value for the learner. And finally, from the democratic point of view, personal growth, i.e., an individual's pursuit of his own goals, is synonymous with social progress. The experience unit, then, is psychologically sound—from the standpoints of learning efficiency, appeal to the individual (motivation), and productiveness of social values. By promoting perception of cross relationships, encouraging the observation of parallels, and capitalizing on individual experiences, the unit approach capitalizes on the principle of analogy. The reader's own study of educational psychology, for example, will be more interesting and meaningful if he traces parallels between his own school experiences and the textbook and class discussions. Good teachers characteristically seek to relate school experience and the pupil's perceptions (Hamachek, 1969).

5. The Principle of Associative Shifting

This means that any response of which a learner is capable may be attached to any stimulation to which he is sensitive. A common school example would be reading, where certain combinations of letters—through practice, repetition, and reinforcement—call to mind highly specific things. The letters h, o, r, s, e, in that sequence, are attached to a large solid-hoofed grass-eating animal. Associative shifting may then cause these same letters to mean a device on which wood may be held while it is being sawed, to move an object by brute power, or to engage in tomfoolery.

The habits, attitudes, and interests that children develop in the school inevitably form the working equipment with which they will perform their functions as adults in society. Everything the teacher can do to make learning both successful and gratifying will contribute to this desirable type of associative shifting. A respect for objective viewpoints, the search for reliable data, systematic methods of problem solving, concern for others, and effective work habits will more readily become part of adult behavior patterns if they have been practiced in school, and these behaviors, rather than answers in the form of information, must be the objectives of education today. Learning how to learn is the basic function of formal education (Lee, 1966, p. 22).

Associative shifting does not operate independently of other principles of learning. Some of the factors that work together to produce effective learning and desirable conditioning are pleasurable aftereffects, consistency in the program, recognition of the necessity for readiness, guided activity, attention to temporary mental set, knowledge of the most compelling aspects of a situation, and indication of similarities.

It can be seen that stimulus-response, reinforcement theory has very practical implications for teaching. Whether or not teachers are acquainted with the term "connectionism," which identifies Thorndike's interpretations, this viewpoint has played a dominant part in our educational practice for the first half of the twentieth century. Refinements of the theory are still being developed, but currently much attention is given to a more global approach (White, 1969).

Conditioning Theory and Learning

Several theorists have made contributions to our understanding of learning by conditioning. Guthrie (1952) is noted for his emphasis on contiguity—the importance of proximity in time or space if stimuli and responses are to be associated. Thorndike is noted for his formulation of principles which are applicable in the classroom. Hull (1943) has emphasized the importance of acquired drives and acquired rewards as contrasted to the primary drives such as those emphasized in classical conditioning. Inasmuch as rewards and punishments are administered by people, social learnings are better understood if culture and society are recognized as providing the locus of acquired drives (Bruner, 1968*b*). This emphasis receives particular attention in the study of adolescence as adolescence increasingly becomes recognized as a cultural phenomenon. Grades, marks, credits, and the like have been tried as acquired drives to learning. Unfortunately they do not work for some and for some they become ends in and of themselves.

Skinner is noted for his explanation and endorsement of operant conditioning. He has described and taken motion pictures of the way in which rats, chickens, pigeons, and other creatures were trained to do some rather amazing things—bowl, play table tennis, shoot baskets. This is done by reinforcing immediately actions which are already in operation as they more and more closely approximate the response sought by the experimenter. Skinner admits that we do not know nearly enough about human learning—that we have pictured the results but not the process of learning. For instance, behavior is almost never invariably reinforced in natural situations, yet new patterns of behavior are constantly being acquired. We must therefore consider that intermittent reinforcement is effective. Witness the fisherman who only occasionally catches a fish yet keeps at it and will return after failure—provided he is reinforced now and then by landing a fish.

Skinner (1967) suggests that considerable teaching-learning effort has been disappointing because it was based on aversive and punitive methods, or because reinforcement came so infrequently or at the wrong point. Attractive classrooms reinforce school attendance. But these motivate the preliminaries rather than the consequences of learning. What is lacking is positive reinforcement after the learning. Positive reinforcement occurs when the student learns in order to satisfy his own curiosity. To a limited extent reinforcement occurs when the teacher takes notes of learning and praises the result.

The slowly growing popularity of programmed learning and teaching machines dates from Skinner's (1954) article, "The Science of Learning and the Art of Teaching." Programmed learning and teaching machines provide the immediate, frequent, and rather regular reinforcement which encourages optimum learning of structured material. Computer-assisted instruction provides the immediate reinforcement which encourages the continued expenditure of effort toward educational objectives. There has been considerable resistance to automated instruction because it appeared to some alarmists that the human aspect of teaching would be neglected. Others take the view that it is futile for teachers to do that which can be better done by a machine. Thus machines can teach step-by-step processes in mathematics, science, language, and many other subjects. There is still plenty left for teachers to do in encouraging creativity, studying and helping pupils use varied learning styles, and in planning with the pupils next steps in education: be they with machines, or independent study, or group participation. There are many still unanswered questions about how best to use Skinner's suggestions about operant conditioning (MacGinite and Ball, 1968, p. 3).

Mowrer (1947) has developed a two-factor theory that includes both classical (associational) and reinforcement conditioning. He emphasizes significant differences between the two learning processes instead of trying to consolidate them. He regards them as two distinctly different avenues of learning. One involves the central nervous system and skeletal muscles: it is a process of need reduction, and thus reinforcement, through successful action.

The other takes place at the level of the automatic nervous system and involves visceral and vascular changes. Rather than solving problems these visceral (or emotional) changes are problem creating. These unconscious arousals of love, fear, anxiety, etc., are usually neither pleasant nor need-satisfying, and they cannot, according to Mowrer, be acquired in the same way (through reinforcement) as the responses that successfully reduce tension. What the organism learns is not a response, but the anticipation of a response, a motivation that predisposes it to an action (Travers, 1963, p. 13). Thus in a conditioning experiment, the immediate learning is that the bell is cause for fear, which then becomes the drive for the avoidance behavior of raising the foot to avoid shock.

Mowrer's theory explains some classroom phenomena that were difficult to interpret prior to his presentation; namely, why children learn in unenjoyable classrooms or when the need for security or recognition has not been satisfied. Many attempts have been made to make learning pleasant, need-satisfying, or nonthreatening because of the assumption that learning demands reinforcement. Yet we know that many pupils have learned, and learned effectively, under threat. The threat that it will be hard to find and easy to lose a job if scores are low provides impetus for schoolwork—as a means of avoidance of the unpleasant—for some pupils.

Learning, from the conditioning viewpoint, may be summarized by stating that it involves (1) drive, the stimuli that impel action, the motivation to achieve a goal, including both primary and secondary, (2) cues that elicit responses and determine if, when, where, and how a response will be made, including the physical classroom, classmates, the teacher, and the learning media as they provide the setting for a response; (3) the response, which must be made before it can be rewarded; and (4) reward for the individual's correct response, or reinforcement.

In the classroom, reinforcement frequently comes from unplanned and unexpected sources and, from the teacher's viewpoint, for the wrong behaviors. Thus, a slow reader might receive reinforcement from the attention he gets from being able to be with the "special" reading teacher. He knows that if he learns to read at grade level, he will no longer be sent to these enjoyable sessions. The misbehaving girl might be getting reinforcement from her peers as well as from the teacher's obvious displeasure.

Field Theories and Learning — The Molar Emphasis

Field theories have been formulated in reaction to what is sometimes considered to be the atomistic (i.e., concerned with supposedly isolated details) nature of so-called "molecular view" of conditioning and reinforcement theory. Field theories endorse the molar view, which maintains that all parts are intimately interrelated and interdependent. Emphasis is placed on the total organization of the "field," which is made up of (1) the occurrence of many stimuli, (2) these stimuli assembled into a meaningful pattern, (3) the reaction of the organism, which alters both the external situation and the organism, and (4) the changing nature of the organism itself (Figure 6-1).

Field theories emphasize the phenomena of perception and organization. They stress the fact that a stimulus never occurs in simple isolation—there are always competing stimuli and shifting conditions. Thus, in Figure 6-1 the double arrows indicate reversible transactions—the organism selects out of the total situation certain stimuli to which it reacts; in turn, what is selected changes the organism; and thus, an action is not only a product of the world but is also a force in altering the environment. Learning, in field theory, is a matter of constant organization and reorganization resulting from many interacting influences in the changing environment of a developing organism.

A prominent field theory is Gestalt psychology. The word "Gestalt" means shape, form, or configuration and is capitalized because it is a German noun. In this context, it implies that a set of stimulating circumstances takes shape according to the relative values of various stimuli acting at the same time. A musical pattern is not dependent upon c, d, e, f, etc., alone, but also upon the relationship in time and sequence that the notes bear to one another. The same notes may be used in "Annie Laurie" and "Yankee Doodle," but the timing and sequence of the notes give each piece its distinction and configuration. Identity resides in the total organization.

Configuration is partially dependent upon the phenomenon of "figure ground." Typically, the figure in a perceptual field is clearly outlined, small, and well shaped, whereas the ground is vague, relatively massive, and amorphous. Figure-ground recognizes that some stimuli are prominent, whereas others constitute the fringe or background. Thus the professor's words regarding operant conditioning, despite their clarity and brilliance, may not be the "figure" for the young man who is concerned about a date for Friday as he eyes the girl with jet-black hair two rows in front.

Field theory places much emphasis on the learner. Action begins with the organism, and pupils must have a desire or need to achieve learning goals. This

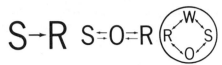

Conditioning   Connectionism Field theory

*Figure 6-1 Schematic representation of
three major learning theo-
ries. (S indicates stimulus;
R, response; O, organism,
learners; and W, world.)*

creates tension that causes action. In diagramming learning, Lewin (1942, pp. 215ff), represents the person as central in the learning configuration and by arrows and cross-hatching shows the existence of tension. After the goal has been achieved, the organism returns to a state of response until a new desire or need creates another condition of tension. In field theory the organism is an important part of the total situation.

"Insight" is a major emphasis in Gestalt theory. It is the mental process by which new and revealing combinations of data are perceived; it is sometimes defined as the sudden perception of the relationships in a total situation, i.e., the relationships between the organism, the goal, and the intervening obstacles. Even though we admit that the moment of insight itself may be sudden, it is important to realize that it is preceded by more or less gradual development, growth, or progression toward a goal. It is necessary in learning to take preparatory steps. Factors which influence this improved perception are the following:

1. Insight depends on capacity. Here the problem of readiness applies. Teachers must recognize age and differences in capacity.
2. Previous experience conditions insight. This indicates the necessity for preliminary steps, for basic vocabulary, for familiarity with cause-effect relationships (Gagné, 1970a, p. 63).
3. The structure of the elements in the situation conditions insight. In general, this means that teachers should study pupil reactions in order to determine the methods and order of presentation that will prove most helpful (Bruner, 1963b).
4. Fumbling and search are preliminary to insight. This is more than trial-and-error procedure. The teacher should seek to overcome the temptation to hurry because the amount of insight is unpredictable.

Insight is a restructuring of the perceptual field—previously unseen relationships are perceived, and all elements of the situation appear to be unified in some way. The student who has been laboring over an algebra problem expresses insight when he says that he "sees" the answer. In fact, insight is the factor that distinguishes the student who perceives the principle or pattern in geometry from the one who, having memorized the theorem, is upset because the teacher places a new set of letters at the corners of the geometrical shapes. Learning to repeat a set of figures, such as 6, 7, 9, 12, 16, 21, 27, 34, etc., or 8, 7, 9, 6, 10, 5, 11, 4, is more readily accomplished when the pupil sees the pattern or relationship of the numbers. If insight is achieved immediately, there is no need for repetition.

1. The teacher must help the pupil to perceive, at least partially, the goal and the intervening obstacles.
2. If the goal is too difficult in terms of the pupil's present development, it must be made easier or its pursuit must be delayed. Otherwise, the pupil will develop symptoms of recessiveness or aggressiveness.
3. Teachers should not be disturbed because all problems are not solved. It is stimulating to the pupil to know that some progress has been made and that there are approaches to the remaining problems.

The major classroom implications of the phenomenon of insight focus about ways of contributing to understanding. One of these relates to the necessity of building step by step—be it in history, geometry, or skill in playing a musical instrument. Some insight is sudden—like the moment at which the mountain climber achieves the peak and sees before him a vast panorama of other peaks, valleys, rivers, fields, and forests. But he has had partial glimpses of the scene before he reached the peak. So too, the learner has partial insights of the total. The culminating step toward total insight may take place suddenly, but there are many preparatory steps.

The figure-ground concept stresses the importance of clear explanation and demonstration to make the most significant points stand out. Distinctive, understandable vocabulary, pictorial and auditory aids, and direct experience are necessary. Broad generalities have their place in an introduction to the subject area, but out of them should come preciseness and exactitude of description. The figure-ground concept shows the need for seeing the whole, but also for observing the details. In reading, word analysis and phonetics are subordinate to getting the idea. Experienced teachers know that there are many pupils who can read the words but fail to grasp the meaning.

One of the more significant contributions of field theory is the idea that school tasks should be appropriate to the pupil's experience and understanding. Some failures in school suggest that (1) the work is too difficult for pupils to achieve insight or (2) explanations by the teacher are not sufficiently clear to foster insight.

The teacher who trusts in the slow processes of growth will not despair when pupils state or otherwise indicate that they do not understand a particular problem. In such cases, smaller steps may be taken or more immediate goals may be pursued. Experiments on laboratory animals show that they initially require much time to solve problems. After being exposed to a number of situations and solving some problems, they solve new problems more readily (Krech, 1969).

Typically, insights require study and work—they do not come "out of the blue." Teachers use the concept of insight when they realize that insights are partial, when they acknowledge the experience and developmental level of the learner, and when they realize that goals tend to consolidate energy. Even the attempt to solve a problem, though it may not really be answered, may be educative.

Classroom implications of field theory as a whole include the importance of seeing the total situation at the beginning. Questions that will be answered during the study of the subject should be raised. The teacher should preview the activities involved and the problems to be encountered. However, details should not be ignored; they are important as *aspects* of the larger problem. For example, in primary reading, the teacher will tell briefly what the story is about, describe the characters, and relate the story to the pupils' experience. At the high school level the teacher might well discuss how chemistry functions in our daily life or in the industry of the community.

The pupil, the teacher, the school, and the peer group are all parts of the total situation. We may summarize by saying that learning is characterized by changed perception, improved reactions, differentiation of stimuli and response, integration of stimuli and response, and achievement of understanding, or insight. Factors that condition learning are the state of the organism, the appropriateness of stimulation, and the existence of goals.

Phenomenology and Humanistic Psychology

The psychological viewpoints mentioned in the foregoing primarily emphasize the external conditions of learning. Phenomenology and humanistic psychology call attention to the conditions existing within the organism—the psychological state of the learner. Other viewpoints do not ignore this, but humanistic psychology assigns the star role to the learner as a person. Effective teachers have used the humanistic orientation, as the concept is not new. The challenge of developing creativity, of reaching the culturally different pupil more effectively, and of reducing still further the incidence of dropouts serves to validate the significance of the humanistic viewpoint.

Combs and Snygg (1959, p. 11) refer to phenomenological psychology as that approach which focuses on the individual and his personal and unique perceptions. Behavior is not merely the result of external causes, it is the *response* of the individual to the way he perceives those external events. Humanistic psychology is that orientation which is more interested in the human attributes of behavior than in those things that compare him to experimental animals in the laboratory, i.e., more interested in man as a talking, concept-forming, thinking, and feeling person than in responding to the physical here-and-now (Bugenthal, 1967).

Humanistic psychology is concerned not only with what one has been and is but with what he may become. The subjective aspects of behavior, such as feelings, attitudes, desires, self-concepts, are given priority in interpreting behavior. This psychology is sometimes called **"proactive"** psychology to emphasize the forward-looking aspects of dreaming, aspiring, goal-forming, choosing actions of man. Proactive psychology may be contrasted to reactive psychology in which man responds to environment and circumstances—reacting to stimuli (Bonner, 1965, p. 182). Proponents of humanistic psychology have claimed that other psychologies have a deterministic outlook. The "third force" psychologists emphasize the uniqueness of the individual and what he puts into the situation. The emphasis is on what man may become as well as on what he was and is (Bruce, 1966). The proactive orientation is certainly not new. It has recently emerged, however, as a powerful force in psychology and education when people conclude that we do not have to be victims of the past. Humanists emphasize man's freedom rather than his captivity. It is not necessary for one to carry, for a lifetime, the monkey-on-his-back of trauma, neglect, and deprivation experienced in childhood. Man can come to see himself as being in control of his destiny (Kelly, 1955, p. 127). Proactive psychology perceives man to be in a constant process of becoming. The belief of Erikson ("The Stages . . ., 1970) that man, throughout his lifetime, is capable of growing and achieving ever more self-actualization is also suggested by the works of Bonner, Maslow, and Rogers. If Henley had been a psychologist, he would have been of the proactive-humanistic orientation:

> It matters not how strait the gate,
> How charged with punishments the scroll,
> I am the master of my fate:
> I am the captain of my soul.
>
> William Ernest Henley, Invictis.

Many teachers, regardless of the orientation of the psychology they studied in college, do much that is recommended by humanistic psychologists. They are concerned with the self-concept of the pupil. They try to avoid the things—sarcasm, ignoring the pupil, assigning failing marks, making invidious comparisons—which will push him toward being a diminished person. They realize that confidence precedes successful effort. They give recognition to the self-fulfilling prophecy and maintain faith in the worth of the pupil. Because man is a choice-making creature, they permit the pupil choices of activities, with guidance, and encourage independence. They try to assume the role of guiding learning activities rather than being instructors of subject matter. They seek ways to make the motivation of learning come from aspirations, curiosity, the urge for self-realization rather than from the external compulsions of grades, credits, and diplomas. They try to give the pupils a voice in the running of their own affairs in democratically oriented classrooms. The accent in the classroom based on humanistic psychology is on individual success and achievement in terms of one's own capacity, perception, and goals.

Reconciliation of the Viewpoints of Learning

Teachers often express the desire for a "practical" course in the psychology of learning and teaching. By this they seem to mean being given answers to questions such as "What do you do when . . . ?" The charlatan would give answers—but the answers would not fit. The pupil, the situation in the school, the social context, and the personality of the teacher differ with time, place, and person.

The practical psychology is one which promotes understandings and insights which will aid the teacher in making his own choices of action to fit the pupil, problem, and the orientation of the learning resource manager (Goddu and Ducharme, 1971). Many views of the nature and emphases of the psychology of learning and teaching are advisable. The purpose of presenting representative viewpoints of learning is to emphasize that there are various and multiple explanations for the highly complex nature and conditions of learning. No one theory presents all the answers, but each has a contribution to make in terms of understanding the total field of learning and teaching.

The fact that psychologists have not reached a common agreement disturbs some people. Others feel that the disagreement is healthy and serves to bring attention to various important aspects. Both viewpoints have merit. It is unfortunate that we do not have enough precise information to be able to discard doubtful theories. Yet it is fortunate that such stimulation by disagreement keeps psychological knowledge growing. McDonald (1964) gives emphasis to the fact that each viewpoint calls to attention some significant aspect of learning that is relatively neglected by other views. Actually, there is considerable consensus, and such arguments as there are concern *relative* importance rather than unimportance of given issues. All viewpoints, for example, see man as being highly educable, as being responsive to culture, and see children as needing warm, accepting adult association and guidance. Certainly, most educators and psychologists today are not disciples of any one or another of the major viewpoints (Hilgard and Bower, 1966). Most scholars can find merit in the outstanding contributions of the various orientations. Finally, it must be remembered that much of our knowledge about the psychology of learning and teaching is independent of any particular viewpoint.

The nature of learning and its various theoretical explanations can be utilized to make the work of the teacher more effective. It is up to the teacher to use all available knowledge in attempting to solve specific classroom problems.

Summary

Learning is an extremely complex phenomenon, and it is not surprising that new discoveries as to its nature are being gained constantly. We do know that learning depends on biochemical factors, on opportunity, and on the individual's response to his physical makeup and opportunity.

Learning occurs in many ways and has many types of outcome. These may conveniently be classified as sensorimotor skills, perceptual motor skills, associational learning, conceptual learning, perceptual learning, the learning of attitudes and ideals, and problem-solving skill.

Learning is so varied and complex and occurs in so many forms that inclusive and conclusive theoretical descriptions are extremely difficult. In fact, no such uniformly acceptable formulation has been yet accomplished. Four viewpoints have been described in this chapter; another author might describe five or ten or even omit any "naming" of a viewpoint.

Simple conditioning or contiguity theory emphasizes the virtually simultaneous occurrence of a stimulus and response. Repeated occurrences result in the organism's responding to stimuli that really have no natural or inherent connection. Drill, practice, repetition, and consistency in the classroom can be justified in terms of conditioning theory.

Reinforcement theory involves the participation of the learner in a vigorous and vital manner. Simple repetition must be supplemented by reinforcement—in fact, in the presence of reinforcement, the number of repetitions can be reduced to almost the point of disappearance. Thorndike has elucidated reinforcement theory with his primary and secondary laws of learning; these laws have for almost half a century been used to justify much current practice. Skinner's emphasis on reinforcement lends support to the appropriate use of programmed learning and automated instruction.

Field theory places emphasis upon the unity rather than the units of a learning situation. All parts of the total pattern—the nature, size, and structure of figure-ground, the learner's perception, and the learner's insight—are important focuses in field theory.

Humanistic, or proactive, psychology deals with what has been but still more with what may be. The matter of more complete realization of existing potential is a focal emphasis. One's perceptions, goals, self-concept, aspirations, choice-making, and assumption of personal responsibility for becoming are of deep concern.

The various viewpoints on learning have values in that each stresses some factor that another viewpoint either overlooks, takes for granted, or includes as a minor emphasis. Together, they provide a basis that enables teachers to adapt to the unique problems of their own classroom situations rather than depend on a prescription derived from a learning situation that is inevitably and invariably unique.

Suggested Additional Readings

BONNER, HUBERT, 1965, *On Being Mindful of Man*, Boston: Houghton Mifflin Company.
    This book is not designed exclusively for classroom teachers. It portrays for the serious reader, the meaning and significance of proactive psychology. The book is only a little over 200 pages long, but if time is limited chapters 2 and 10 are particularly pertinent to teachers.

CAMPBELL, ROALD F., 1969, "Teaching and Teachers—Today and Tomorrow," in *The Schools and the Challenge of Innovation*, New York: McGraw-Hill Book Company.
    Future educators will not only have to accommodate themselves to programmed learning, educational television, and computer-assisted instruction but will also have to recognize the affective phases of education. In-service education will be a continuous need.

GAGNE, ROBERT M., 1970, *The Conditions of Learning*, 2d ed., New York: Holt, Rinehart and Winston, Inc.
    Such things as the organization and structure of materials, the matters of reinforcement and sequencing, and perception and problem solving are related to programmed learning and conventional classroom instruction.

KRECH, DAVID, 1969, "Psychoneurobiochemeducation," *Phi Delta Kappan*, vol. 50, pp. 370-375.
    The physical basis for learning has been discovered. Learning or experience causes changes in enzymes and RNA molecules in the brain. This knowledge about the chemistry of learning does not yet mean that teachers will be replaced by medical injection.

7

The Nature and Nurture of Intelligence

         The human individual has several points of uniqueness and superiority over other animals. One of these is thumb-finger opposition, which enables him to grip and handle tools. Another is the facile use of language, which helps him to describe, remember, and communicate ideas. Tool using and language are dependent for their optimum use on man's intelligence. The ability to remember, to make analogies, to discern relations, to condense experience into symbols, and to think abstractly are mankind's great advantages.

    The basic problem of education is without doubt a matter of directing intelligence to the understanding and control of perplexing situations. There are some who say that emotional control and direction are the big tasks of education, yet if emotion is to be wisely controlled, it must be through applying intelligence.

    A number of scholars—William James, Kubie, Maslow, Mead, Otto, and Rogers—have speculated that man uses only a small fraction of the intellectual potential with which he is endowed (Kubie, 1956; Otto, 1969). The reasons for this waste and neglect are that we do not understand sufficiently well the nature of intelligence and we do not take into account the social and internal conflicts and impasses which the individual encounters in the course of development.

The Concept of Intelligence

Definitions of Intelligence

Terman (1960, p. 6) stated that intelligence is the ability to do abstract thinking.[1] That is, through the manipulation of symbols (largely words), the intelligent person is able to think about and deal with things and ideas without their material presence. Intelligence in action involves direction, adaptation, and self-criticism in mental adaptation.

Thorndike (1927, p. 22) believed that intelligence is the ability to make good responses and is demonstrated by the capacity to deal effectively with novel situations. Just as there are different kinds of situations, there are also different patterns of intelligence—abstract, mechanical, or social. For example, the skilled leader of people may be quite inept in mechanical matters; the skilled mathematician may evidence bewilderment in political groups.

Stoddard (1941) postulated that intelligence is the ability to understand problems that are characterized by (1) difficulty, (2) complexity, (3) abstractness, (4) economy, (5) adaptiveness to a goal, (6) social value, and (7) encouragement of originality (inventiveness).

Wechsler defined intelligence as "the aggregate or global capacity of the individual to act purposefully, to think rationally and to deal effectively with his environment."[2]

Guilford (1967b) has postulated a concept of intelligence which, if accepted, could result in gigantic changes in educational procedures. Instead of thinking of intelligence as a unitary function (such as learning ability) or as a binary function (such as general, "g," and "s" or specific factors), Guilford proposes that intelligence is composed of interlocking factors that compose a "structure of intelligence." There are three major parameters in this concept, each with a number of subdivisions, as shown in Figure 7-1. By multiplying these subdivisions it turns out that there are 120 intellectual factors. It may be that more will have to be added as research continues, but forty of these have now been demonstrated, and Taylor (1968) states that the number of discovered talents is over eighty.

Taylor indicates the implications of Guilford's theory: Typical intelligence tests cover only about nine-tenths of the possible intellectual factors known today. When more tests are given in schools, different pupils will appear in the

1   Most of the widely used intelligence tests (both individual and group) resemble to some degree the Stanford revision of the Binet-Simon tests. The revision reflects Terman's concept of the nature of intelligence.

2   David Wechsler, 1944, *Measurement of Adult Intelligence*, 3d ed., Baltimore: The Williams & Wilkins Company, p. 3.

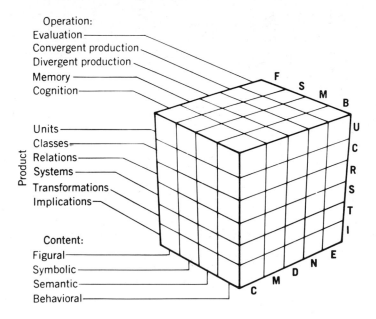

*Figure 7-1 The structure of intellect model, with three param-
eters (other parameters may need to be added).
From J. P. Guilford, 1967,* The Nature of Intelligence, *New York: McGraw-Hill Book Company,
p. 63.*

upper 10 percent—or the upper 50 percent. But as each pupil is given confidence
in his worth by appearing near the top or being above average, he concomitantly
gains in the prospect of using his latent talents with confidence. As schools capitalize on strengths, rather than emphasizing weakness through remedial programs,
the possibility of better-focused development of potential is further enhanced.

Such definitions of intelligence as cited above may be roughly summarized by stating that *intelligence is the ability to make facile and appropriate adjustments to, and alterations of, the various facets of one's total environment.*

It has been said, somewhat facetiously, that intelligence is what intelligence tests measure. The statement is not absurd. Each designer of an intelligence
test has started with a concept of what intelligence is and has formulated problems and questions that probe into the facets of the governing concept. Intelligence test ratings often correlate positively with demonstrated ability to do a job,
to do academic work, to solve problems, and with the judgment of experts who
have observed the behavior of the testees. Intelligence test items are not merely
arbitrary questions but representative samples designed to test the individual's
total performance. On the other hand, intelligence tests do not uniformly corre-

Jan Lukas/College Newsphoto Alliance

late with, or predict, success in life or even academic success. Intelligence has not yet been adequately defined or its components sufficiently well identified.

The Function of Intelligence

It will be noted that all the definitions of intelligence given above directly state or imply the matter of adjustment. In this connection, one further concept may be given: Intelligence is a congeries of abilities to learn in varied situations, to understand and collate broad, subtle, and abstract facts with speed and accuracy, to focus mental processes on problems, and to display flexibility and ingenuity in the search for solutions.

Correlates of Intelligence

Age*

The ability to adjust to one's environment increases as he grows older. Infants have less capacity for adjustment than do six-year-olds, and six-year-olds have less adjustive ability than do normal twenty-year-olds. The youngster with the highest IQ in the class may not always be the most intelligent. A child who is two years older chronologically than a child whose IQ is points higher might actually be more intelligent in terms of adjustive ability (**mental age**). Teachers must be careful to note the age of children with respect to their intellectual development, particularly in the primary grades.

> A parent asked a first-grade teacher how her young son was getting along in school. The teacher said, "Just fine," and mentioned some of the good habits and attitudes he had developed, but she placed little stress on his reading progress. However, his reading was what concerned the mother. "He did not get as good a grade as his brother did in the first grade." The teacher knew the answer: "But there's a year's difference in their ages. Your older boy was born in January and could not enter school until he was almost seven. Your younger boy was born in December and entered school before his sixth birthday."

Theoretically, it appears that intellectual growth ceases at the age of twenty or twenty-five years. Growth is more rapid and continues for a longer time for more intelligent persons, whereas the person of less intelligence grows more slowly and ceases to grow at an earlier age. However, the important consideration again is the definition of intelligence. Is intelligence largely a matter of learning ability as such or of learning ability with respect to *new* things? It is conceivable that a person of eighteen may be better able to learn something that is *entirely new* because of greater mental retentivity and adaptability. Past experience in seeing relationships, discovering meanings, and perceiving implications is a factor in learning that is no less important than mental retentivity and adaptability. The fifteen-year-old has a limited background of experience to which he can attach new meanings. The twenty-five-year-old with approximately the same IQ has almost half again as much experience. Thus, just as the child of two will learn less than a child of six with the same IQ, the person of thirty or forty years should learn more readily than the fifteen-year-old. The older person, despite somewhat lessened powers in terms of mental adaptability, can still learn.

The records of military veterans who have taken advantage of educational assistance by federal or state governments give support to the idea that age

---

| *See the principle dealing with "maturation" in Chapter 2.

increases learning efficiency. The veterans scored higher on intelligence tests in college than recent high school graduates even when they made like mental test scores during their high school years. Longitudinal studies covering a period of thirty-one years after college showed gains more often than declines. The gain was particularly marked in verbal subtests while other subtests showed neither marked gain nor decline (Guilford, 1967, p. 447). Wechsler (1955) found increase in mental ability up to age thirty with a slight dropping off up to age sixty. Many studies indicate that adult subjects continue to develop verbally. Understanding that builds on previous knowledge and experience continues to increase until the senile years.

The pertinent conclusions to be drawn from age and intelligence studies are: (1) Doubt has arisen that there is necessarily a psychological decline that parallels or is concomitant to degeneration of biological function. Unlike physical functions, intelligence does not have a terminal growth point. (2) There is a growing belief that lack of motivation is as important a factor in low intelligence test scores of older persons as is the phenomenon of organic involution. (3) There is a steady growth in scores on vocabulary subtests, a constancy in mathematical subtests, and a decline in subtests involving performance. (4) There is some consensus that the mind atrophies through disuse rather than through disability.

There is, with age, a loss in reaction time but an increase in dependability of judgment. There is a loss in sensory acuity but an increased proficiency in tasks demanding accuracy. Older professors are not uniformly inferior to younger professors in learning. Older persons often test lower on some subtests of intelligence tests, but higher in vocabulary, opposites, and disarranged sentences. Kaplan (1952) concludes that when a mental function is used, it does not atrophy.

The implications of this discussion are twofold. First, all teachers have the professional opportunity and obligation of infusing into their pupils a desire for learning that will last a lifetime—of helping pupils build the habit of continuous learning. Second, there is the personal challenge of nurturing one's own habit of continuous learning so that his rate of decline (if inevitable) can be retarded.

Heredity

The potential for the development of intelligence is inherited *through* one's parents. This basic principle is accepted by those who champion the importance of environment as well as by those who warn that there are limits as to how much IQ can be raised by salubrious environments. Studies running back to the early 1920s indicate that although parents who are in the professional class constitute only a small portion of the population (5 to 10 percent, depending on the decade in which the study was made), their offspring comprise about one-third of the gifted child population. Almost half of those persons who are prominent today had fathers who were eminent. Conversely, the parents of slow learners are typically below average in intelligence. There are some who argue that intelligent, eminent, and well-educated parents provide an early and continuous environment that is conducive to the development of potential, whatever it may be.

Another consideration that further complicates the question of heredity is Galton's principle of hereditary regression. This theory postulates that a child receives only one-half of his heredity from his immediate parents, one-fourth from his grandparents, one-eighth from his great-grandparents, etc. Sooner or later the ancestry of gifted children and those less richly endowed in intelligence becomes common stock. The principle of hereditary regression suggests that children of intelligent parents will not be similarly intelligent—or that dull parents will not have children who are equally dull. Children tend to regress toward the *average*. Children whose parents have a midparent IQ of 135 will *tend* to have a somewhat lower IQ—between 100 and 135. Children whose parents have a midparent IQ of 64 will tend to have a somewhat higher IQ—between 64 and 100.

Studies of twins who have been reared apart provide data pertinent to the effects of heredity. Many studies show that identical twins, after years of living in different localities, still tested about the same. However, when twins were reared in environments which were not only located away from each other but were judged to be different in intellectual stimulation value, much variation was found in test scores. Jensen (1969*a*), on the basis of analysis and reanalysis of many twin studies, plus data from race and socioeconomic class studies, concluded that about 80 percent of variation in IQ scores is due to genetic factors. His studies and conclusions aroused much interest in the heredity-environment problem when he stated that race differences in intelligence were largely genetic. This conclusion was unpalatable to those who had been theorizing that the differences in black-white test intelligence were due to differential opportunity.

It is widely conceded that blacks, on the average, do make lower intelligence test scores than do their white peers. This is not, it is often maintained, due to hereditary factors but may be attributed to limitations of the tests themselves. In short, the test, being designed to test understanding of, and adaptation to, the dominant culture, demands that those who are, in varying degrees, outside the culture make responses to items which are quite unfamiliar. In addition, where test administrators were given instructions to make sure lower-class children understood the nature of the test and felt comfortable with the tester before the test was begun the subjects' scores were eight to ten IQ points higher than those not so prepared (Cazden, 1970).

No doubt the heredity-environment question is scientifically important. In practical application it is merely interesting. Averages do not tell much about individual potential. If blacks have, on the average, lower IQs than whites, we can also say that 35 or 40 percent *are above* the average white pupil. Moreover, no matter whether IQ is 50 percent, 20 percent, or only 10 percent attributable to environment that is the part—after biological conception—that we have to work on, and no matter how small or large, should be exploited. And still further, even if and when heredity is known for an individual, the IQ does not provide data on how rigorously one pupil will pursue the development of his potential. The practical problem is how, for each individual, the optimum environment can be devised to develop whatever hereditary potential each child and pupil has.

> How much *can* we boost IQ and scholastic achievement by deliberately altering the ecological niche of infants and young children, from birth to age five, through early childhood education? Who knows? As I read the evidence, the odds are strong that we can boost both IQ and scholastic achievement substantially, but we cannot know how much for at least two decades. Moreover, we shall never find out if we destroy support for the investigation of how to foster early psychological development, for the development of educational technology, and for the deployment of that technology.[3]

Environment

Investigations have pointed for a long time to the thesis that *individuals evidently develop only the portion of their potential that is required by their environment.* Many children living in areas of low cultural status are average in intelligence at the younger ages (indicating average potential), but as they grow older they have lower IQs in proportion to their ages. Intelligence tests were given to children from four isolated communities, each characterized by a different degree of isolation. Communities in which the family stock was much the same—English and Scotch-Irish—were selected. The IQs of six- to eight-year-old children were much the same in the different areas, but the greater the isolation, the lower the IQs at ages above eight. The lower IQs of the older children were also related to the amount of schooling. The children of the community that had sixty-six months of school in the twelve preceding years had higher IQs than the children of the community that had thirty months of school in the same period. It was concluded that children develop only as the environment demands (Sherman and Key, 1932).

Studies of children reared in city slums also show that their IQs are, on the average, lower than their age-mates of middle-class communities. At least in part, these differences can be attributed to tests that are unfair to those in a minority culture, comparative lack of exposure to verbal complexity, a high noise level which leads to "tuning out," limited exposure to environmental contrast (travel), and unfamiliarity with test situations.

There appears to be a need for early and continued stimulation if one is to realize his potential. Children who score high on initial tests of intelligence

---

3   J. McV. Hunt, 1969, "Has Compensatory Education Failed? Or Has It Been Attempted?" *Harvard Educational Review*, vol. 39, p. 297.

show less improvement on subsequent tests than do those who score lower on initial tests. This suggests that typically the bright child has been stimulated to achieve more of his potential and has less room for improvement. Conversely, the slower child has achieved less of his potential and responds more readily to what, for him, is a markedly more stimulating environment. Children from orphanages sometimes improve their test ratings after being placed in good foster homes. Nevertheless, the fact remains that foster children more closely resemble their true parents in intelligence than they do their foster parents (Heber, Dever, and Conry, 1968; Jensen, 1969b)—there are limits to what environment can do in the stimulation of potential.

Factors which are conducive to optimum intellectual development may be inferred from various studies:

> Parents who take an interest in their children and who have the time and inclination to talk to them and answer their questions have a higher proportion of children who score high on tests and do well in school.

> The same factors of love, acceptance, and consistency of treatment that are conducive to mental health appear to have a salutary effect on intellectual development. Here we can refer to Maslow's theory that higher needs (self-actualization) become predominant only after the lower (physiological and safety) needs are well on the way to being met (Chapter 9).

> Parents who encourage emotional dependence in their children tend to retard their offsprings' mental development. Aggressiveness, self-initiation, and competitiveness are personality attributes that accompany intellectual growth.

> If we can take language development and reading skill as evidence of intellectual development (and both are prominent in tests of intelligence), then homes in which there are books to read and an adult example of interest in reading are positive influences.

> Studies by Gordon (1923) and by Sherman and Key (1932) suggest that communities and homes in which there is contact with the mainstream of life are helpful. Contacts that can be made through travel—visits to museums, zoos, libraries, concerts, theaters, parks—are an intellectual stimulant (Passow, 1967b).

> It may be inferred from Krech's (1969) studies on rats [he does not so imply] that freedom to explore widely and an environment which contains much to explore are conducive to brain development.

There are many questions which remain unanswered: Do brighter persons tend to leave the isolated community and the slums, leaving in such communities parental stock of lower potential? Were equivalent tests used on repeated evaluations? Are typical intelligence tests fair to children in various cultural milieus? While these questions are being answered, it should be kept in mind that although average scores differ by socioeconomic class, many of the higher scores of lower socioeconomic class pupils exceed the scores of individuals from the higher levels.

Sex

Boys, as a group, show greater variability than girls in the range of intelligence; that is, more boys than girls are defective in intelligence, but also more boys than girls are markedly superior. Boys, as individuals, show greater stability of IQ on successive tests administered in connection with changed environments (Levine, 1966). It is pointless, however, to speak of superiority or inferiority of one sex or the other. At least during the ages of seven to sixteen there is little justification for separate analyses of boys and girls on intelligence test data (Bloom, 1964, p. 55).

On the average, males demonstrate *slight* superiority over females in general reasoning, arithmetic reasoning, ability to detect similarities, and certain aspects of general information. They tend to excel girls in speed and coordination of large body movements, spatial perception, and mechanical aptitude. Boys seem to have a stronger motivation for achievement than do girls; but achievement motivation for either sex is more explicable in terms of maternal child-rearing practices than in terms of sex. Girls *tend* to have *slight* superiority in memory, language usage, manual dexterity, numerical computation, and perceptual speed. Boys are not inferior to girls in learning to read *after* autoinstructional devices have provided them with frequent and equal opportunities to respond (McNeil, 1964).

Culture plays a part in sex differences, and boys, in accordance with expectations, are superior in mathematical reasoning and science. Boys are expected, culturally, to be aggressive, independent, and rebellious; but these traits are not *expected* in school. It seems that teachers expect boys to conform to feminine role expectations. When the boys do not conform, then one of the methods of coercion is to receive low grades. Despite standardized achievement test scores which show the inequity of grades, girls get the bulk of high grades and boys get the majority of low grades.

It has been recommended by some persons that boys start school at a later age than girls because of their lesser facility in language usage and reading. Such broad recommendations blithely disregard individual differences within a sex, different subabilities in intelligence, cultural expectations, and varied motivation. Any differences in intelligence between boys and girls, as a group, are so slight as to have no practical significance for educational design. It has also been suggested that boys and girls be placed in separate classes so that unequals will not be competing (Peltier, 1968). Such a procedure, in the author's view,

would mean that we are trying to legislate, or organize, differences out of exis-
ence. It is here maintained that boys and girls should start school at the same
time and be kept in the same classes. Perhaps then the differences which will inevitably continue to exist among boys, among girls, and between and among
boys and girls will receive more prompt attention and action.

The significant conclusion to be drawn is that *differences between the
sexes are smaller and much less significant than the differences within the sex.*
Even though girls *generally* are more verbal than boys, and boys are *generally*
more mathematically apt, there are enough boys who are superior to girls linguistically and enough girls who are superior to boys mathematically so that no
general curricular provisions should be made on the basis of sex.

Race

Widespread notions about differences in intelligence between races are
also based on tenuous assumptions. Research studies reach the same conclusion
as to sex differences: *Differences between the races in matters of intelligence
are much less significant than the differences within the race.* Many studies indicate that when a group of blacks, Indians, or Mexicans is given an intelligence
test, the average score may be somewhat lower (five to ten IQ points) than the
average of a group of white children. Such data, acquired in the earlier days of
mental testing, have been taken at face value. It is presently considered necessary
not only to interpret test data in terms of many concomitant variables (motivation, opportunity, prejudiced perception, social-class expectations), but also to
realize that tests do not have widespread validity when used with groups other
than the **standardizing population**. For educational purposes, race differences
are negligible when the groups being studied have similar cultural and experimental environments.

Jensen (1969*b*), basing his conclusions on studies made by numerous
scholars, reported that whites exceeded blacks by about one **standard deviation**, or
about fifteen IQ points, even when the sample populations were controlled for
gross socioeconomic level. This he attributed not only to basic genetic differences
but also to the matter of selective breeding; i.e., the reproduction rate for lower-
class blacks is greater than for upper-class blacks. Numerous scholars have objected to the conclusion that average test differences are due to racial differences.
They point to the fact that there are great differences in the opportunity to develop minority group potential. Jensen regards the matter of the genetic determination of racial intelligence as being just as open a question as is cultural or environmental determination. He and those who have argued for cultural causation
agree on many points:

At least 15 percent of the blacks population exceeds the average of the
white population.

The important distinction between the individual and the average population must be kept in mind in discussions of race and intelligence.

The factors of race, socioeconomic status, and national origin are so poorly correlated with criteria of intelligence that they are irrelevant as a basis for dealing with individuals.

If a society believed in and practiced the ideal of dealing with individuals, the question of race would be extraneous.

It is unfair to base treatment of individuals in the educational process in terms of the irrelevant criteria of race, skin color, or national origins.

Teachers must be just as aware of the potentialities that reside within individual members of a minority group as they are of the potentialities of children of majority groups.

Emotional Factors

The dean of a prominent college of education told of a man who wanted to study there for his doctor's degree.

> M took the required qualification tests but his score on the mental ability test disqualified him. He went to another school with an equally good academic program where different criteria of admission were used. The student obtained his degree with honors and later became one of the outstanding men in his field. The dean of the school which had disqualified him said, "I am sure that the test gave a good indication of his ability but there is one thing it did not show—his determination and drive to use what he had to good effect."

It is a common occurrence for teachers to become well acquainted with a given pupil, judge him to be average, superior, or dull on the basis of his work, and then discover that the recorded intelligence score of the pupil is at wide variance with their otherwise *justified* judgment. They note frequently that the child with an IQ of 100 is accomplishing just as much as is one with an IQ of 120, despite the fact that the latter is living up to reasonable expectation. Strauss (1969), in a rather startling study, found that among eighty-nine men who earned Ph.D.s in the physical sciences from Ohio State, University of California, and Cornell there were 3 percent who had high school IQs below 100 and another 6 percent whose high school IQs were 101 through 110. The success of those at the lower test levels was attributed to "challenging the inner drives" of those concerned.

Experimental studies show that when babies are cuddled, talked to, and cared for affectionately and individually they respond by being more active and alert, talking more, or trying to talk, and playing more constructively (Hunt, 1968). Children attending preschool have made gains in intelligence test ratings during the year, and some of these gains are attributed to the fact that they have become better adjusted. For this reason, intelligence tests are not administered during the opening days of school, but only after the children have become somewhat adjusted to the situation in which they find themselves (Blank, 1970).

For teachers, the importance of the reciprocal role of intelligence and emotion lies mainly in helping the pupil make effective use of his abilities. Interpersonal dislike and even hatred among students must be avoided by shunning autocratic and highly competitive situations. Anger and frustration should be reduced by seeing to it that the tasks assigned are appropriate to each child's ability. Constructive emotions must be employed by seeing that each pupil gets some satisfaction from achievement. Cooperative activities should be encouraged so that friendliness and sympathy will be generated. Pupils should see clearly the goals toward which they are working. Democratic methods should be employed so that each child has a feeling of personal worth. Provisions for individual differences are inherent in all these suggestions. Differentiated assignments enhance feelings of security, provide the thrill of accomplishment, and make the pupil feel that both his limitations and his abilities are recognized by others.

Health and Physique

Gifted children are, on the average, slightly taller, heavier, have fewer sensory defects, and have a lower incidence of illness than those with lower IQs. The relationship is slight, however, and the basic concern must be for the individual. Empirical evidence indicates that when one is in good health, he tends to have greater drive to participate vigorously in difficult situations.

There is some evidence that diet plays a part in the growth and development of intelligence. Diet, especially during infancy, is a factor in mental retardation (Read, 1969). Moreover, inadequate diet is associated with susceptibility to infection and disease which may also limit mental development (Birch and Cravioto, 1968).

Oxygen is needed for the brain to function efficiently. Oxygen deprivation at birth, called "anoxia," is associated with IQs lower than the generality, but some of these differences diminish over the years (Corah and others, 1965). The brain is sometimes damaged when a person has been resuscitated after heart stoppage has occurred. Experiments with persons at high altitudes where oxygen is rarefied show defective functioning of memory, attention, and judgment. The thyroid glands, those regulating oxygen metabolisms, if defective, are often associated with markedly lowered mental efficiency.

In a study of the effects of alcohol, amounts equivalent to two martinis were found to have little effect on mental functioning. Larger amounts impair memory, associative ability, and perception (Nash, 1962). Caffeine has been found to increase spontaneity, ideational abundance, and word fluency. The belief that LSD is a mind-expanding drug is not supported by experimental evidence. Significant losses in total IQ and marked losses in some subtests have been noted in connection with the use of LSD (Guilford, 1967*b*, p. 384).

Vitamins of the B complex, especially thiamine, and vitamin C (ascorbic acid) have had the effect of raising the level of mental performance. Two groups of children, one high and the other low in blood plasma ascorbic acid concentration, were given a supplement of orange juice over a period of time. The group that was high in ascorbic acid had higher IQs to begin with, but the other group (lower in both ascorbic acid and IQ) gained in IQ. It was concluded that changes in ascorbic acid concentration were closely paralleled by changes in average IQ (Kubala and Katz, 1960). Numerous studies attest to the value of adequate amounts of milk in increasing children's height and weight. Of particular interest to teachers are data indicating that giving children milk in addition to the usual allowances has the effect not only of improving general health but also of increasing mental alertness.

In such studies as these it should be noted that changes occur when the subject has a dietary deficiency that is remedied by the special diet. Additional thiamine, ascorbic acid, or milk will not aid the child who already has an adequate diet. It follows that not all the teacher's problems will be solved by improved diets. But increased learning ability comes from many small improvements.

There is a more widespread recognition of school responsibility for health factors in the matter of sensory acuity than in the matter of diet. When a child is cut off from intimate contact with his environment by a visual or auditory handicap, his intellectual development suffers. Defective vision or hearing is an insufficient basis upon which to judge that a given child will have less than average intelligence. But when hundreds of children with such defects are considered, a tendency is noted for those with sensory defects to have slightly lower than average intelligence in proportion to the seriousness of the defect. A child who does not see and hear closely has a poorer operational environment than the child who has normal sensory acuity.

There is, of course, the possibility that the hearing defect or visual handicap cannot be corrected. In such cases, it is desirable that the regular program of work be adapted to the child. Recognition of the importance of such procedures is growing, but at the present time it is estimated that only about 10 percent of the pupils in need of special work programs are receiving them. In recent years there has been a trend toward keeping exceptional children, both slow learners and gifted, in regular classes. It is believed that such advantages as better socializing, avoidance of stigmatization, and help and inspiration from one's peers are more likely to occur in regular classes. Even though special classes are needed for the blind child to learn to read braille and for a deaf child to learn lipreading, as soon as possible they are returned to regular classes.

Teachers should be aware of the importance of health factors and sensory defects. Symptoms such as restlessness, drowsiness, inattentiveness, frequent illnesses, unexplained nosebleed, decreasing accomplishment in school, pallor, pains in muscles and joints, and excessive irritability may be signals to the teacher that the pupil needs some medical help.

IQ Change: Clues and Conditions

The Phenomenon of IQ Variability

Intelligence is a function of natural processes of growth and development and is therefore presumed to have a steady progression. The difficulty of test items is gauged so the succession of items confirms the postulation of steady development (see Figure 7-2). This has been accomplished in terms of averages so that developmental curves for groups of test subjects are smooth and show continuous progress. Individuals refuse to conform to these averages; and acceleration and deceleration of developmental rates are typical; the developmental curves for individuals are wavy. Originally, variations in the rate of mental development were attributed to test inadequacy, lack of comparable tests for various ages, and errors in administration and interpretation. Today it is an accepted fact that the IQ changes do occur which are beyond the area of variability of the test itself.

Several hypotheses for IQ variability have been offered: Tests for various age levels are not comparable. For instance, infant tests depend largely on motor function, whereas later tests probe cognitive function. Marked changes in the intellectual stimulation value of the environment probably explain some individual variability. Intrinsic factors may underly the timing of thrusts of mental development. Changes in the pervasive emotional climate—change of foster home, change in financial stability of the home, death of a parent—may influence the subject's response to the environment.

The Extent of Change

A representative study of IQ change concluded that 62 percent of the subjects tested changed more than 15 IQ points, in either direction, over a period of three to ten years (Sontag, Baker, and Nelson, 1958). The fact of IQ change does not necessarily mean that a changed comparative level of functioning has developed. Jensen (1969*b*) recommends that the belief in "fixed" intelligence—determination at the time of conception—be retained as a research hypothesis. He warns educators to keep their dreams from soaring about the extent of change possible. He then postulates that although it may not be possible to make pro-

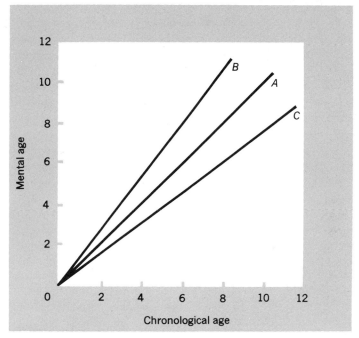

Figure 7-2 Schematic portrayal of constant IQ. Subject A grows
at the rate of two years mentally for each two years
of chronological age. According to the formula
MA/CA x 100 = IQ, his IQ is 100 at two, four, six,
etc., years. Subject B grows at the rate of twelve
months mentally for each chronological period of
nine months (four years mentally in three calendar
years, etc.) and, according to the formula, has an
IQ of 133 at any given age. Subject C grows at the
rate of nine months mentally for each calendar year
(three years' mental growth on his fourth birthday)
and has an IQ of 75.

fessionally competent persons out of the bulk of students, it is quite possible that
much of the talent pool at the level of typical citizen has not been so fully developed as is possible.

Because identical twins have the same hereditary potential, their ultimate
mental ability would serve as clues regarding the amount of change that might be
expected as the result of differential environmental stimulation. In a pioneer
study it was found that among identical twins reared apart, about half of the
nineteen pairs had little difference in IQ after a varying number of years. In eight

cases the IQ varied by 10 to 24 points. In five of these cases—those who showed the greatest difference in IQ—there was a difference in schooling of four to fourteen years. The estimated educational advantage of the environment was rated much higher for the twin with the higher IQ, and the social advantages were superior, though not consistently so. The greatest difference was 24 IQ points. The twin with the superior rating had been graduated from college and had become a teacher, while her twin had only two years of regular schooling. In the five cases in which differences in schooling were four to fourteen years, the IQ differences were 7, 12, 19, and 24 points (Newman, Freeman, and Holzinger, 1937). Gottesman (1968) in another twin study found that the extent of change depended on what measures were used. Twins reared apart had an average IQ difference of 14 points; in one-quarter of the group, the IQ differences were more than 16 points. Vocabulary tests showed the greatest differences, while nonverbal tests showed smaller differences. Gottesman sheds more light on the extent of change in indicating that twins reared together have an average IQ difference of 9 points.

In one study it was found that, on the average, children attending preschool made gains in accordance with length of time and regularity of their attendance. Gains of up to 40 IQ points were recorded in some instances. Children who attended preschool for three years made an average gain of 10.5 points. Children who originally tested average made greater gains than those who originally tested superior, with an average gain of 18.9 for average children attending over three years and of 11.5 points for superior children being reported (Wellman, 1940, pp. 377ff). Blank (1970) reports average gains of 14.5 IQ points for three-year-olds attending a school emphasizing individual tutoring five days a week for three months. Those who attended three days a week gained 7.0 IQ points.

For several reasons (lack of similarity between tests for various ages, rapid growth, circumstances at the time of testing, motivation of the test subject), it is generally recognized that early childhood tests are not sufficiently reliable for long-term predictions of later intellectual status—an old test score should not be regarded as proof of the individual's present rate of mental development.

Studies of the changing IQ have been critically examined by various authorities, and doubts have been raised as to whether or not the results are genuinely encouraging. There are questions about the statistical treatment of data, possible bias of examiners, the effects of practice on the pupils who take the tests, and the shortcomings in the tests themselves. Few of the questions have been answered, and certainly *the avenue* to early mental development—when change is taking place at its highest rate—is yet to be discovered. The results of compensatory early childhood education have not, to date, been highly encouraging in regard to accelerated mental development. Some programs have reported beneficial results in terms of IQ change, but in other studies gains have been offset by losses so that the average gain is near zero.

Sometimes faith in the power of the environment to effect IQ changes has become too great. There are children whose potential is such that any additional stimulation beyond what they receive in a relatively easy environment will only produce frustration. A good working hypothesis is that appropriately stimulating environments do *in some cases* have the effect of raising test intelligence. But intelligence tests do not invariably tell how bright or capable of learning an individual is; we know only that he has at least as much intellectual potential as the test indicates, but how much more he has is still an unknown.

Factors Associated with Changing IQ

Several conclusions may be tentatively drawn from changing IQ studies. One is that changes that accompany upward shift in test scores should take place early in life—much earlier than has typically been thought to be the case. Hunt (1968) recommends that such education should begin during the cradle days. The habits of response and the attitudes toward self progressively become more stable; thus, the earlier attempts to affect them are made, the more effective those efforts will be. This does not imply that later efforts will be futile. Changes in the rate of development are still occurring in adolescence, and for some individuals, especially those pursuing education rigorously, changes continue to occur into the college years. Piaget (1969) has postulated that different aspects of intelligence bloom at various ages; moreover, experience is a necessary correlate of such differential development.

Changes in environment must be rather large and be continuous in order to effect change. Most children do not experience a shift from cultural impoverishment to a culturally enriched milieu. This fact probably explains why IQs do not change significantly and consistently more than they do. Moreover, relatively few children are provided with the stimulating environments provided in the experimental situations in which the largest changes have been noted. Too often the cumulative effect of environment has been overlooked. Certainly, in individual cases there are times when the intellectual stimulation values of the broad environment change because of altered circumstances in the home (Stinchcombe, 1969).

It appears from research available that the optimum environment for the preschool child's intellectual development is one in which adults play a very active role. Dialogue between parent and child, affection, warmth and nurture, and planned variety of input are aspects of such a milieu (Caldwell, 1967). It is easy to think of a stimulating environment as one in which there is an opportunity for free and varied play; one in which there are books, records, and musical instruments to attract the child's interests; and one in which adults are responsive to children and are themselves vocal, interested in a variety of pursuits, and seeking self-improvement. Emotional dependence on parents is inimical to optimal mental development. Children who are competitive, curious, and highest in need achievement more frequently make upward movement on tests than do those who are lower in these variables (Kagan and Moss, 1962).

The data on conditions of IQ change suggest that there be balance between pessimism and optimism. Such a balanced view is indicated in the following:

> Equality of opportunity is a worthy and attainable goal. Equality of performance is a misguided hope. The important thing for the welfare of children and of society in general would seem to be to try and create conditions that will maximize the proportion of the population that can learn and work successfully and rewardingly in the diverse occupational roles that the society provides. It is clear that various peoples and societies in the past and in the present have approached this realistic goal to quite different degrees, and it would seem worthwhile to inquire into the social, biological, and educational conditions which have either hindered or promoted the realization of this goal. I should hypothesize that among the relevant conditions would be at least two prominent factors: (a) the working of eugenic pressures, either consciously and directly, or indirectly through the value system, social structure, socially conditioned mating patterns, and the like, and (b) a wide diversity of educational options, paths, and goals.[4]

Adaptations to Intellectual Differences

The "Overdeveloped" Society

Mankind's uniqueness resides, in some measure, in his tool-using and problem-solving ability. Increasingly, man has become less of a work animal and more of a manager of machines. In fact, it is said that "Today the working man is obsolete." The number of persons classed as professionals increased 50 percent from 1950 to 1960 and gained another 50 percent from 1960 to 1970; no decrease in the rate of change is anticipated. There are temporary shortages and oversupplies in certain professional fields, e.g., teacher surplus in the late 1940s, short supply in the late 1960s, and oversupply again in the early 1970s. The situation has been temporarily similar in the field of engineering and business administration. However, generally there are serious shortages of manpower at the professional levels. Developing the intellectual potential that is available is rightly considered to be a crucial problem of national survival. We can no longer say, as was claimed in previous decades, that there was a place for the "school misfit" in the role of laborer.

---

4   Arthur R. Jensen, 1969, "Reducing the Heredity-Environment Uncertainty," *Harvard Educational Review*, vol. 39, p. 467.

The Challenge of Differences

Students of educational psychology may recite proven facts about differences in intelligence—how many pupils cluster about the average, what the range of differences is, and how many pupils are at the extremes of the distribution. We are sometimes told that the difference between a pupil with an IQ of 130 and one of 80 is a matter of degree. We are told that there are various styles of learning through which intelligence may be manifested. But this information remains theoretical until the teacher sees these differences in the classroom.

The differences between Johnny with his IQ of 130 and Tommy with his IQ of 80 seem to be much more than a matter of degree. Johnny quickly covers the material that is assigned and asks penetrating questions about what he has read. These questions suggest to the teacher that extra reading and research be found that will be of interest to Johnny. Johnny shortly comes back with suggestions of his own for additional research, which the teacher readily endorses. The teacher's job here is to provide encouragement and to suggest directions for independent research and experiment. Tommy, on the other hand, after repeated explanation, varied approaches, and concrete explanations comes up with absurd answers. Tommy is a well-behaved, likable boy, but he just does not seem to understand geometry. Explanation, drill, and demonstration seem to have no effect. Finally, while he is studying parallel chords intersecting a circle, Tommy is asked why angle A is equal to angle B. He replies, "The square on the hypotenuse of a right-angle triangle is equal to the sum of the squares of the other two sides." This gives rather clear evidence that the subject is over Tommy's head, so the teacher tells him to "study" *National Geographic* when he comes to the geometry class and he will receive a passing grade. This is not a good solution, but when other course choices are not available, it is better than continuing to humiliate Tommy.

The study of intelligence will have little meaning unless it suggests ways for dealing with the differences that one inevitably encounters in his teaching career. It can be admitted that the aims of education are the same for every individual; but the approach to achieving these ends must of necessity be varied. Gagné (1970, pp. 26ff) suggests that the first step is to translate educational aims into specifics by unambiguous communication among educators, students, parents, and the public. The word "specifics" means that pupil behaviors are described, definition of the conditions for developing them are postulated, and approaches to their assessment are designed. It is certain that the classroom methods and organizations for achieving effective recognition of differences have not yet been designed. However, it would not be realistic to claim that substantial steps have not been taken.

Learning Style

One of the characteristics of school pupils and their differences that has been mentioned occasionally, yet one on which there are few research data, is the matter of learning style. Whether learning styles are characteristics of intelligence, or kinds of intelligences, as is suggested by Guilford's hypothesis, or whether they are congenital or acquired makes little practical difference. Unfortunately, the styles which are recognized as being acceptable in the classroom are quite limited, and for a pupil to use divergent styles often results in teacher's criticism and pupils' lowered ego concepts.

Riessman (1966a) asserts that some pupils learn most readily by reading; others by listening, and others by means of physical doing. It seems that to his list should be added talking. Certainly many people clarify, organize, and collate conceptual materials by talking. Riessman also postulates that these styles are used in a variety of ways. Some pupils like a leisurely pace and others do their best work under the pressure of deadlines. Some like to pace the floor. Others concentrate best when sticking tightly to a chair. Hence, reading quietly may be suitable for one child but singing and dancing to the words of a story may be the preferred style for another. Some people seem to prefer peace and quiet, but others can work quite efficiently in the midst of noise and turmoil.

Nations (1967) perceives learning styles as a combination of sensory orientation, responsive mode, and thinking pattern. (1) "Sensory orientation" describes whether the learner depends primarily on visual, auditory, or tactile contact with his environment. Sensory orientation influences whether one sees, hears, or feels the cues and sensations which provide information and perception. (2) "Responsive mode" determines whether one works best alone or in a group. It is manifested in one's being, most typically, an active participant or an observer. It suggests that given students are inclined to depend on the teacher or to act autonomously. Responsive mode influences whether one will more typically support or challenge a conclusion, assignment, suggestion, or directive. (3) "Thinking pattern" refers to whether one learns best by first getting many details and then organizing them into a pattern or by getting an overall picture and then gathering information to support the notion. Thinking pattern refers to whether one prefers a deliberate, methodical gathering of information or whether he is comfortable making giant intuitive leaps.

Guilford (1967b, pp. 138, 171) and others speak of convergent and divergent thinking. The convergent style is characterized by naming, classifying, ordering, and systematizing. The convergent thinker uses logic and seeks to find a known answer to a problem; he tries to obtain the "right answer." In divergent thinking the individual moves away from facts and known solutions to processing novel and unknown products (Parnes, 1971). Divergent thought patterns are revealed in fluency, flexibility, and elaboration in thinking.

Students in the author's classes sought to improve their appreciation, as prospective teachers, of the learning styles which existed among elementary and high school pupils. Among the many items which they gathered (from observation, reading questionnaires, and pupil self-ratings) such things as the following were deemed to be aspects of style:

Studying alone or with others
Needing quiet or finding noise a comfort
Preferring to read, discuss, observe, or theorize
Preferring teachers who "know their stuff" or ones who know their pupils
Preferring teachers who are factual or friendly

Some of the elements of style may prove disappointing because they seem to suggest resignation, apathy, or at best, tolerance for learning activities rather than involvement and autonomy. It seems that learning is for many an obligation rather than a response to heterostatic urges. A six-year-old, reporting to his mother, suggests the sad condition in which some pupils find themselves, "The teacher sent me out on the playground to get some gravel—and, you know, I could have escaped." In the following continuation of the list, most pupils checked the first of the alternative elements of style:

Accept facts or improve on them
Concentrate on listing of facts or relating them
Regard teachers as authorities or learning resources
Accept unpleasant things or talk to the teacher about them
Study further or just do the assignment (Surprise)
Prefer to do own scheduling over having the teacher do it. (Even college students typically endorse freedom until they get the opportunity to exercise choice).

One group studying the question of learning styles after a preliminary administration of a questionnaire redesigned it to correspond to the following categories:

1. *Seeing*
   Reading
   Observing
   Visual aids
   Programmed learning

2. *Hearing*
   Lectures
   Listening to discussion
   Repetition

3. *Reflecting*
   Thinking
   Testing
   Associating
   Researching

4. *Speaking*
   Discussing
   Arguing
   Asking questions
   Telling

5. *Writing*
   Taking notes
   Organizing ideas
   Creative writing
   Drawing

6. *Doing*
   Mimicking
   Touching
   Participating
   Memorizing

7. *Formulating*
   Imagining
   Exploring
   Trying and testing
   Discovering

If a pupil's learning style could be defined or described, it would not mean that teachers should present material to that pupil via his preferred style, but it would mean that credit could be given for his strength (e.g., listening) while he worked to overcome his weakness (e.g., reading). If a pupil received positive feedback for his skill in listening, it might increase his desire to explore another avenue of learning. Acknowledgment of styles of learning might cause the teacher to evaluate the pupil more accurately when he discovers that the pupil scores well on a test (because his learning style is observing) despite the fact that he has not read (the teacher's own preferred style being reading) the text. Above all, the matter of learning style should make the teacher aware that equal levels of intelligence are not equivalent to equal time intervals being required to complete a journey (finish the course). In addition, the course may be finished in the same time but in a different manner.

The matter of style must be considered in relation to the personality— or learning style—of the teacher. Strom (1969, p. 407) asserts that it would be foolish to suggest to a teacher who has high need for structure that ambiguity and freedom be cultivated. Asking a teacher with low measured creative potential to invite pupil speculation would be threatening. But, he continues, with help teachers can learn to accommodate to divergent pupil responses. Drews (1961) found that of three groups of students the creative students received the lowest grades from teachers.

Underachievement and Alienation

The complex structure of intelligence, the variety of factors that influence congenital potential, and the patterns of factors which foster optimum mental development simultaneously cast light on such phenomena as underachievement and alienation.

Underachievement (doing less than ability assessments indicate as being possible and probable) may cause the teacher to think of motivation, social class, pupil personality development, teaching methods and materials, or his own personality orientation. These are pertinent but another factor may be added. It may be that identifying and acknowledging learning styles is also a step toward the pupil's better use of intellectual potential.

Alienation refers to the process by which one becomes an outsider, a stranger, in the society in which he should belong. The alienated person is lacking roots for a sense of dignity and attachment (Erikson, 1964, p. 101). Certainly, it would not be accurate to attribute the feeling of alienation which some young people experience to failure to recognize different kinds of intelligence in the schools; it would, however, be inaccurate to ignore the fact that the range of acceptable learning styles within schools today is narrow. Schools do act as a sorting and classifying agent. Many schools persist in practices (competitive grading, homework, uniform pacing, "maintenance of standards," etc.) which contribute to the feeling of alienation.

Providing for Intellectual Nourishment

Krech (1969) identifies himself as being a "rat brain" psychologist and warns against drawing hasty inferences for children from his work. He states that the important thing in making rat cortexes heavier, thicker, and having bigger cells, more glia cells, and being comparatively more active was the freedom of the rat to roam about in a large object-filled space. Such nourishment was not the simple result of exercise, varied visual stimulation, handling, presence of brother rats, or teaching. These things helped, but the really crucial factor was freedom.

Without condemning structure, prescription, and requirement-fulfilling as being an unproductive learning milieu, flexibility can be recommended. There is a need for convergent thinking, for those who will methodically collect and collate materials from the past and who logically arrive at well-documented conclusions. There is also need for the accommodation of those whose preferred learning style is divergent, for those who are creative.

Hallman (1967) has made recommendations on how to stamp out creativity and how to encourage it. He says that if the creative orientation is to be diminished, then teachers should exert pressure to conform, maintain an authoritarian stance, use ridicule to lower the student's ego, keep one's facades intact, emphasize grades, fulfill the student's quest for certainty, emphasize success, reveal hostility toward divergent personalities, and be intolerant of playful attitudes. With the exception of ridicule, hostility, and intolerance, such behaviors may actually be comfortable and salutary for the convergent learning style. Creativity will, says Hallman, be enhanced by such actions or traits on the part of the teacher as making provisions for self-initiated learning, being nonauthoritarian, encouraging over-learning, stimulating discussion, giving deliberative responses, deferring judgment, asking pupils to shift their judgmental positions, asking questions, and encouraging students to evaluate themselves and to live with ambiguity.

Ability grouping has been one of the ways in which intellectual differences have been handled. It is true that such grouping reduces the range of differences; but it does not eliminate them. Hence, grouping is regarded by some as being a hazardous administrative device that compounds the problem of differences by contributing to the delusion that allowances have been made for them. Remedial classes constitute another approach to those on the low side of the "difference" scale. Such classes in the hands of specially trained teachers are typically quite effective because the teacher knows that work with the partially sighted, the hard-of-hearing, or the slow-learner cannot be generalized—it must be individualized. The great hazard—and the most important point if pupils rather than subject matter mastery are paramount—is that the pupil's ego concept is diminished by such categorization. He internalizes the idea that he is a remedial case.

Work with exceptional children and those who are culturally different supports the theory: Classification and grouping are self-defeating approaches. Attention to individual levels of intelligence, individual speeds of learning, and individual styles of learning help to provide a nutritive environment for actualizing individual potential. Such is not an impossibility for teachers who have faith in students to exert a degree of autonomy and who place learning above teaching.

Summary

Universally acceptable definitions of intelligence are difficult to formulate. Intelligence grows at various rates throughout man's lifetime, but the rate is comparatively rapid during the first two decades. Heredity plays a large role in one's ultimate intellectual status, but environmental factors are inextricably woven into intellectual behavior. Moreover, it is the environment—no matter how small or large a share it has—that can be manipulated after birth.

During the first thirty years of the existence of the concept of the IQ it was thought that rates of mental growth were inherent and characteristically steady. For the last thirty years, it has been realized that growth rates are a function of the *interaction* of *hereditary potential and environment.* Cultural deprivation and emotional disturbance are inimical to optimum mental development. Good health, proper diet, rich intellectual opportunity, and environments that produce emotional stability, independence, and self-confidence are productive of optimum developmental rates.

Schools and teachers can capitalize on knowledge of the nature and nurture of intelligence when appropriate provisions for differences, in presently indicated levels of intellectual functioning, are recognized. Such differences are particularly noticeable in the concept of learning style. Although each child does not have to learn exclusively through his preferred style, it would be well, from the standpoint of motivation and ego nurture, to start from and emphasize strength.

Underachievement, dropping out, and alienation are evidences of the need for school personnel to be concerned about developing intellectual potential by capitalizing on uniqueness of style. Teacher personality, pupil individuality, and neighborhood milieu are among the factors which must be considered in intellectual actualization, but freedom to explore has received special emphasis. Such freedom cannot be legislated or programmed—it must be individual.

Suggested Additional Readings

BROPHY, JERE E., AND THOMAS L. GOOD, 1970, "Teachers' Communication of Differential Expectations for Children's Classroom Performance," *Journal of Educational Psychology*, vol. 61, pp. 365-374.

> However their expectations are communicated, pupils from whom teachers expect much are better performers than those from whom teachers expect little. Teachers are likely to praise the performance of pupils from whom they expect much but neglect to praise the good work of those from whom less is expected.

FLEMING, ELYSE S., AND RALPH G. ANTTONEN, 1971, "Teacher Expectancy or My Fair Lady," *American Educational Research Journal*, vol. 8, pp. 241-252.

ROTHBART, MYRON, SUSAN DALFEN, AND ROBERT BARRETT, 1971, "Effects of Teachers' Expectancy on Student-Teacher Interaction," *Journal of Educational Psychology*, vol. 62, pp. 49-54.

> Rosenthal and Jacobson (1968) postulated the exciting idea that teachers' expectancies have a strong influence on pupils' intelligence and school achievement. The two articles cited above indicate that more than expectation must be included in the dynamics of teacher-pupil relationships.

HUNT, J. McVICKER, 1968, interviewed by Patricia Pine, "Where Education Begins," *American Education*, vol. 4 no. 4, pp. 15-19, October.

> One of America's most prominent authorities on early intellectual development describes the conditions and stimulations which are likely to promote optimum use of potential.

JENSEN, ARTHUR R., 1969, "How Much Can We Boost IQ and Scholastic Achievement?" *Harvard Educational Review*, vol. 39, pp. 1-123.

> This article has stimulated many negative responses in regard to his well-documented assertion that there are racial differences in intellectual development. He does not deny the influence of environment, but he says it is relatively small compared to genetic factors. (In the same volume, next issue, pp. 449-483, he responds to some of his critics.)

PIAGET, JEAN, 1969, *The Theory of Stages in Cognitive Structure*, New York: McGraw-Hill Book Company (Pamphlet). Also in H. W. Bernard and W. C. Huckins (eds.), *Exploring Human Development: Interdisciplinary Readings*, Boston: Allyn and Bacon, Inc., 1972.

> The much-studied and frequently translated theory of cognitive function as postulated by Jean Piaget is discussed by the originator. He responds to the more frequently asked questions and speculations about his theory in an address given in Monterey, Calif.

8

Assessment of Pupil Differences

There is much talk about pupil differences in motivation, intelligence, interests, and personal and social adjustment. Strangely enough, in schools, differences are largely a matter of talk, and little is done about them. This is not a catastrophe because pupils—all people—are, in most ways, more alike than they are different. If this were not so, the study of the psychology of learning and teaching would have little point. However, our inability to detect and make use of differences does keep schools from being optimally effective.

It is important that the last fifty years of talk about differences in pupil development be translated into action. Emphasis on differences is needed for the sake of the pupil, his ego status, and his motivation to make the best use of his talents. Emphasis on developing differences is vital for a society which needs diversified and cultivated talent.

Whether a class is composed of first graders, fifth graders, or high school seniors, the pupils will by no means be alike. If there are thirty pupils in the class, there are many more than thirty problems to solve if the teacher's work is to be effective. Words of advice will be listened to attentively by some; others may not even know the teacher is speaking. Some will quickly and eagerly do the tasks assigned; others will do them reluctantly and laboriously. A teacher's success will largely depend on understanding such pupil differences and capitalizing on them.

Some Basic Considerations

The Function of Testing

There are many purposes of testing, such as statistical surveys, sociological studies, predicting probable success, and college screening. From the standpoint of educational psychology, the reigning purpose is the guidance and improvement of the teaching-learning transaction for the benefit of individual pupils. Tests (mental, special aptitudes, achievement, diagnostic, readiness, adjustment inventories, and classroom quizzes) should be regarded as a part of the process of instruction. Tests provide clues to, and verification of, the pupil differences which when recognized may individualize and vitalize education.

> Researchers in human learning agree that individuals differ markedly in the ways they learn, in the speed at which they learn, in their motivation to learn, and in what they desire to learn. But educational institutions cater only fractionally to these individual differences. Even in the best schools, where students' achievements in the three R's and the standard subjects are well above grade, and resounding percentages graduate from high school to enter college, many thoughtful educators and outside observers believe that institutions have lost touch with the individual student.
>
> Most schools and colleges are still locked into conventional patterns of grade structure, time span, and subject matter division that fail to exploit each student's individual capacities, interests, and personality. Conventional practice is geared to some abstract "average" or "norm" that penalizes both the unusually gifted and the seemingly backward student as well as the spectrum that lie between.[1]

The educational purpose of testing is to spotlight the pupil. To the extent that tests cause us to lose touch with the individual (as suggested above), they constitute hazards rather than helps in the teaching-learning processes.

The Normal Curve of Distribution

This curve is a graphic representation of the similarity and differences found when a large group is measured for any one trait, such as height, weight,

---

1   *To Improve Learning*, 1970, A report to the President and the Congress of the United States by the Commission on Instructional Technology, Committee on Education and Labor, House of Representatives, Washington, D.C.: U.S. Government Printing Office, p. 15.

intelligence, knowledge, or other (e.g., fathers' income) items that might be quantitatively expressed. The IQs of the great majority of children range between 90 and 110 (68+ percent as shown by the bottom line of Figure 8-1). A flat curve would show a greater overall range in IQ, e.g., from 60 to 140, with fewer falling between the points of major cluster (90 through 110). A normal curve might also show the range and cluster of a specific trait of personality. Data for such evaluations might come from a combination of pupils' ratings of their peers, teacher judgments, and personality inventories. A curve might indicate differences in typical fifth graders' reading ability and range from second-grade level to average high school level. Even if the group plotted were a so-called "homogeneous group" (members selected on the basis of similar IQ, similar physical and social maturity, and similar academic achievements, etc.) there would still be marked differences in other, and *significant*, traits.

Some of you have as much knowledge about educational psychology now as others will have at the end of the term—in spite of the fact that you are all in one class and that a process of selection has been going on since the beginning of your school careers. All this indicates the futility of attempting to teach all pupils as though they were "average." Although well over one-half of a typical fifth-grade class reads at just about fifth-grade level, another curve drawn to plot interest and competence in other subjects would probably assume a different shape.

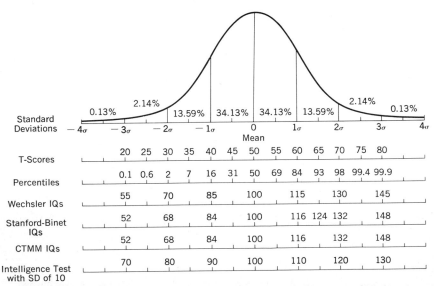

Figure 8-1 Normal curve of distribution. Source: A Glossary of Measurement Terms, *Monterey, Calif.: CTB/McGraw-Hill.*

Marion Bernstein/College Newsphoto Alliance

The Fallacy of Distinct Types

There are fat people and there are thin ones. Some people are introverts more of the time than they are extroverts; some people are bright in most things, and others are rather consistently dull. But the notion that these extremes of distribution constitute sharply demarcated types has been repeatedly refuted by scientific investigation. There are not just two types of students in an educational psychology class or just three types of pupils in a fifth-grade class. Yet the terms "fifth graders," "good readers," "cooperative pupils," and "ten-year-olds" are used as if there were clearly defined types. In a recently published book, we read that seven-year-olds "are sensitive to the feelings of those about them and desire approval"; the interests of boys and girls are growing apart; they are full of energy but tire easily. Such information about seven-year-olds may be helpful to teachers if it is understood that many of these things can also be safely said of five-year-olds. *Some* of these characteristics will not appear until age nine in *some* individuals. In short, defining by characteristics must not blind teachers and parents to the fact that there are individual differences. Types exist only as *hypothetical* averages (fifth graders) or as extremes of a continuous distribution (fat and lean). Categorization into types is more misleading than it is helpful.

Because, however, our mental processes work by reducing the complexities of the world to simple schemes, type descriptions will be with us in popular thought for a long time. And as surely as they will be with us, they will lead to oversimplification and error in the description of human personality. Once you have, for example, characterized a person as extroverted, it is easier to remember those things that conform to the type than those that do not. Hence, your picture of that individual may be a very different one from his, and, to the degree that your original characterization was wrong, a very unreal one. For these reasons as well as others, contemporary psychologists have been skeptical of type descriptions.[2]

The popularity of ability grouping has waned somewhat in recent years because implications of the type fallacy—slow, bright; college bound, non-college bound—have been perceived. We are not yet ready to have elementary pupils attend college classes, but when ability grouping causes teachers to think they have such pupil homogeneity that pupils can be taught as a group, then "typing" imposes limitations. A great deal of instructional effort will be futile unless the teacher appreciates the fact that in the plotting of any set of test scores there will still be pupils who are at the extreme ends of a newly drawn curve. He must also realize that those in the center of the curve on one measurement may be at the extreme ends when another characteristic is measured. For example, motivation cannot be plotted simultaneously with intelligence on a distribution curve.

The Value of Differences

Individual differences are of immeasurable value to society, even though they are a constant challenge and sometimes a source of irritation to teachers. In primitive groups, when each family provided its own food, built its own shelter, and made its own clothes, it was probably advantageous for everyone to possess the same skills and knowledge. But in our complex and highly integrated society, specialization and uniqueness are necessary for our continued existence. One man makes his contribution to the welfare of society as a whole by becoming a scientist (and in a specialized area). Another becomes a teacher, another a house builder, and still another a distributor of goods. The contributing citizen and educated person must be a high-grade specialist who has a sound and continuing education (Harrington, 1967, p. 129).

Earning esteem and being important enough to make a difference are functions of individuality and are thus important to the individual. One may have below-average finger dexterity but be gifted as a social facilitator. Another may

| 2   James Deese, 1967, *General Psychology*, Boston: Allyn and Bacon, Inc., p. 430.

be gifted in mathematics. This, of course, does not mean that any individual will always be able to do the things he is most able to do, nor does it mean that pupils in school should do only the things that they like to do. The individual will frequently have to do the kind of work that society needs to have done (*Manpower Report* . . ., 1970, pp. 161-185). Only a few will be able to make their choices on the basis of interest and aptitude, and they will be able to do so largely because extended education keeps open the avenues of choice. Recognition of differences in school helps to provide the ego strength that makes one capable of yielding readily and graciously to the demands of society and technology.

The orientation point in democratic education should be the uniqueness of each child (Taylor, 1968). Although mass education has merits in disseminating knowledge, education that recognizes the individual holds forth the promise of self-realization for pupils and improvement for society. A major criticism of contemporary schools is that its workers try to solve learning problems by organizational schemes and new curricula instead of recognizing individuality by expanding opportunities for independent and diversified study.

Tangibles and Intangibles in Education

It seems that controversy over the purposes and processes of education is an enduring concomitant of formal learning. One issue is concerned about the tangibles (content measurable by tests) and intangibles (attitudes, aversions, and preferences which are less amenable to testing). Sometimes the issue is referred to as the cognitive versus the affective aims of education. And at still other times as the content versus persons controversy. What we teach for determines what we will test for. However, it seems that the matter is complicated by the possibility that what we teach for is influenced by what things we are able to measure.

The debate is illustrated in the "National Assessment" project. Some oppose it because the assessment concentrates on content rather than considering why and how much pupils like themselves, schools, and the learning process. The need for national assessment is expressed in terms of **accountability**. The public spends a large part of its tax money on schools and deserves to have an accounting of what kind of results are being obtained. Plans were formulated in 1963, and the first tests were given in 1969 in one-third of the areas ultimately to be tested, with another third to be tested in 1970 and the final third in 1971. The ten areas of subject matter being probed are science, writing (composition), citizenship, mathematics, music, literature, social studies, art, reading, and career and occupational development.

Sampling is used not only in any given test itself (see number 6 under Criteria Involved in the Adequacy of Tests) but in the administration of the national assessment. Ten to twelve students are tested at a time, with up to seventy-five students being selected to take the test in most school districts and up to one hundred fifty students in large districts. Children from large cities, urban fringes, small cities, and rural towns are tested in preplanned numbers so the sampling will be representative of the total population. Care is taken to see that sex, race, and socioeconomic strata are also proportionately represented. Age is also taken into account on the sampling, and in order to get comparable results, nine-, thirteen-, and seventeen-year olds and adults of ages 25-35 are included in the sample populations. Data are finally presented for the nation as a whole, for the various regions, and by type of community, sex, socioeconomic status, and race (Norris, 1969).

There are many who oppose national assessment because they believe that attitudes, beliefs, likings and aversions, values, and aspirations might be forced from positions of important focus by emphasis on quantitative scores on subject matter. The author's view[3] is that there is no irreconcilable dichotomy involved in learning for content and focus on the affective goals of education. When the pupil's attitude includes acceptance of self and others and perceives the school as a good place to be, his mastery of content will be improved. When a student sees himself making progress (which can be assessed by tests) in a given subject, he will accept progressively higher aspirations for himself. The real danger of content (or cognitive) versus affective aspects of education lies in the fact that tests are available to assess content but that parallel measures in the affective realm are newer and less well established and accepted, in which case the measurable tends to overshadow the intangible.

A principle of effective teaching methods is that the teacher should have objectives. Recently the statement of behavioral objectives for courses taught has become an almost obsessive but purely academic interest. Few teachers have stated behavioral objectives except as a class activity for some evening class or seminar course in education.

> Teaching is purposeful activity. Part of a teacher's effectiveness depends on his having the right purposes. Hence it is important for the curriculum builder, the textbook writer, the teacher, and the student to think hard about their purposes, about the objectives they seek to achieve.
> These considerations support the belief that objectives are important. They do not suggest that objectives need to be stated explicitly or in detail. The pedagogical issues that divide teachers, the inadequacies that limit their effectiveness, cannot be disposed of by statements of objectives. Little that is wrong with any teacher's educational efforts today can be cured by getting him to define his objectives more fully and precisely. We ought not to ask teachers to spend much of their limited time in writing elaborate statements of their objectives.

---

3   It will be profitable for students of educational psychology to debate or discuss the issue in an effort to improve perspective.

Nor should we insist that the statements be in behavioral terms. Our main business as teachers is developing the cognitive resources of our pupils, not shaping their behavior. The great majority of teachers at all levels who feel no urgent need to write out their objectives in detail, and in terms of behavior, are probably wiser on this matter than those who have exhorted them to change their ways. Too much of the current reverence for behavioral objectives is a consequence of not looking closely enough at their limitations.[4]

One may infer from Ebel's remarks that the results of education need not always be measurable, discernible, and palpable. Before being carried away with the—quite admirable—aspects of education which are obvious, tangible, and testable, the teacher must give thought to such matters as, for instance, the pupil's enthusiasm for learning and the school.

Measurement of Individual Differences

Limits of Measurement

Human traits are so complex, so interrelated, that precise measurement is difficult—if not impossible—for most of them. Devices are available to measure height, weight, blood pressure, white corpuscles, albumin, bone ossification, and the like, but no tool is available to measure intelligence, drive, honesty, social adjustment, etc., with like precision. Data obtained from tests yield valuable approximations of traits, abilities, and qualities, but it is important to remember that intelligence, personality, and social maturity are so complex that single measures are subject to much doubt (Guilford, 1967, p. 27). Despite their limitations, psychological tests yield much valuable information from which inferences may be drawn. Teachers should regard intelligence tests, personality inventories, and rating scales as instruments that provide data for evaluation rather than exact measures.

A test is a sample—of blood, behavior, or perhaps, of one's total knowledge. Several samples enable the investigator to make a more accurate guess about the total. For example, a diamond drill is bored into a mountain from different positions and at different angles. This enables the engineer to determine the length, breadth, and depth of an ore-bearing fault. The assayer then analyzes different sections of the core taken by the diamond drill and determines the richness of the ore in terms of the amount of worthless rock, copper, silver, and lead for each section of the core. But the final judgment about the amount and quality

---

4   Robert L. Ebel, 1970, "Behavioral Objectives: A Close Look" *Phi Delta Kappan*, vol. 52, p. 173, November.

of the ore can only be determined by driving a tunnel, taking out the ore, and having it milled. Do the mine owners or stockholders get rich? It depends on the efficiency of the mining, the market value of the ore at the time it is shipped, the distance and availability of transportation, and the honesty of the bookkeeper. Tests have reduced the possibility of error, but they have not covered the entire situation.

In psychological testing, samples of intelligent behavior are taken by sampling the individual's ability to comprehend and handle numbers, to perceive and interpret symbols, to understand words, to solve problems. Developing the individual (driving the tunnel) is the responsibility of teachers, who seek to perform their work with the least waste. Predictions can be made about the ultimate adjustment of the individual, but the environment (market conditions) that greets him at the time of graduation will influence the subsequent source of his life. Tests provide clues for making more accurate estimations, they assist the teacher in answering specific questions about particular pupils. In the final analysis, tests must be interpreted in terms of corroborative evidence: other teachers' reports, the pupil's past record, and the teacher's own judgment of what he sees in the pupil's daily behavior.

Makers of tests have not presumed to measure *innate* (whatever that might be) intelligence.

> Instead of measuring a mystical force called intelligence, the tests actually attempt to predict how well a child will do in school—that is, if he chooses to work up to his capacity. The first intelligence scales were developed in the early 1900's by Alfred Binet, in cooperation with Thomas Simon, as a means of identifying children in the Paris schools who would not be able to do the work their classes would demand. From the outset, Binet had to prove his test was valid: Would a poor score actually predict low academic performance? To check, he compared children's test scores with the grades they later made. If a test item did not help predict grades accurately, Binet dropped or revised it, a procedure testmakers have, more or less, followed ever since.
>
> Thus, to a large degree, cultural biases that affect school grades are quite frankly built into the tests, which attempt to assess "entry skills" that academic work requires. If a child's home experiences have not prepared him to meet school demands his test score will very likely be affected, too. No test score should be interpreted as a final, irrevocable judgment of a child, Thorndike cautions, especially during the early school years. "A test—any test," he explains, "is a sample of an individual's performance here and now, and usually just a 30-minute sample at that. Any further significance attached to the score is an inference, and

both sound and unsound inferences have been made from aptitude test scores.[5]

Criteria Involved in the Adequacy of Tests

Certain expectations have been evolved for judging the value of tests:

1. A Test Should Be Standardized[6]

If a test is to be of maximum usefulness, it should be applicable to more than a small group. Standardization involves several considerations. Directions must be carefully and uniformly worded, and exact timing must be observed. When the test is being developed, it should be given to children in various localities to see whether there are regional differences that must be taken into account. The norms are often stated in terms of pupils' ages, sex, socioeconomic conditions, or grade achievements. The results are often treated statistically to lend additional meaning to them (Tyler, 1963, p. 35). When the test has been administered experimentally to hundreds of subjects in various localities, a given score is often expressed in terms of IQ, **mental age**, **grade equivalent**, or **percentile rank**.

2. A Test Should Be Objective

The feelings, hopes, likes, and dislikes of the person administering and scoring the test should be largely eliminated. Objectivity implies that a given answer is either right or wrong. There should be wide agreement on the correct answers and upon the meaning of those answers. Objectivity is easier to maintain in group testing than in individual testing. Hence, individual tests must be administered *only by specially trained technicians*. However, in the hands of a trained worker, the individual test is superior because it allows for interpretation of intention, motivation, and application and thus yields data beyond the test score alone.

3. The Test Should Be Easy to Administer

The teacher should be able to administer the test with the facilities that are ordinarily available in the classroom. The directions should be understand-

---

5   Patricia Pine, 1969, "What's the IQ of the IQ Test?" *American Education*, vol. 5, no. 9, p. 3, November.

6   Teacher-made tests, of value for use in local situations and specific learning situations, need not meet this criterion. They should, however, approach satisfaction of the remaining criteria.

able and easily followed by the examinee. Simplicity of scoring and interpretation also come under the heading of ease of administration.

4. A Test Should Have Validity

The items in the test should actually sample what the test is designed to measure. An achievement test that requires a great deal of reading during the examination may be invalid because the score depends more on reading ability than on knowledge of the subject matter, as for example, an arithmetic test in which much reading is involved.

The test data should agree with other assessments. This quite frequently involves computing correlations (see Appendix) between test scores and other *quantitatively* expressed measures. Classroom grades may be correlated with intelligence tests to see that the measures of achievement accord with the measure of intellect. The judgments of experts, expressed on a numerical scale, may be used to compute the validity coefficient of intelligence tests.

5. A Test Should Be Reliable

A test is reliable when the results of one administration agree with the results of another administration to a like group, or when two administrations of equivalent forms of the test give the same general results for the same person. **Reliability** thus indicates accuracy and consistency of measurement; it is determined by experimentation and experience.

It is difficult to construct a reliable test. In consequence, tests have "equivalent forms" that very rarely are actually of the same degree of difficulty. For example, two teachers were using form A and form B of a given reading test. The one who gave form B first found that her pupils made a very gratifying gain. The other, who used form A first, found that the class average was practically the same at the end of the year as it was at the beginning. Some pupils had apparently retrogressed.

A test may be reliable without being valid. The arithmetic test referred to above, which contained much reading, gave consistent measurements. Successive administration of equivalent forms to the same individual yielded scores that were much alike. Yet it did not measure ability in arithmetic and therefore was not valid. On the other hand, if a test is to be valid, it must also be reliable.

6. A Test Should Sample Widely

Test questions should be varied. In arithmetic tests, the problems should embrace all the processes. In reading tests, poetry, directions, stories, and technical passages should be included. In intelligence tests, numbers, vocabulary, problems, abstract materials, and memory tests should be included. One of the major objections to theme-type tests, which are often used in classrooms, is that the sampling is too limited. For instance, one pupil might know twenty incidents in

American history but not know one of two called for on a two-question test; another might know only the one incident out of a possible twenty but get as high a score on the two-item test as the pupil who knew much more.

7. A Test Should Be Economical

Economy involves both time and money. Simple equipment, a relatively limited number of carefully selected items that obtain wide sampling, and ease of scoring are essential. An inexpensive test that is easily administered may contribute so little to understanding and guidance that any cost is excessive. Moreover, the tests must be valid and reliable, or the price tag will have little meaning. When selecting tests, test manuals, published reviews of the tests,[7] and the advice of specialists can be helpful.

The Assessment of Intelligence

As is the case with other kinds of psychological and educational assessment (achievement, motivation, personality), intelligence is "measured" indirectly by means of what the individual knows and does. In short, intelligence is inferred from samples.

The unit for evaluating intelligence is the **mental age**, which is obtained by testing. Typically, the mental age of the subject is divided by his chronological age and multiplied by 100 to give the IQ. When the child's mental age is the same as his chronological age, he has an IQ of 100 and is considered "average." Actually, it is worth noting that "average" in intelligence is a **band** of scores, not a point; i.e., average IQ varies from 85 to 115, or from 90 to 110. (Some authorities make the average band wider than others do.) Growth in mental age, as in other aspects of growth, tends to slow down as maturity is approached. When children reach about sixteen years, it is helpful to replace the IQ as the numerical expression of intellectual status with **percentile**, **decile**, or **standard score**, which are ways of indicating one's relative standing in a criterion group.

The mental age unit is not an equal distance between levels of difficulty of performance, as are inches on a yardstick; i.e., the difference between a MA of one year and a MA of two years is different from a MA of fourteen and one of fifteen years. The unit for each year is determined by studying a large number of individuals of various chronological ages. Tasks that are performed by the majority of three-, seven-, or fourteen-year-olds are, on the basis of this *average* performance, assigned a mental age value of three, seven, or fourteen years. This may be clarified by citing some examples:

7   The *Mental Measurements Yearbook*, published periodically by the Rutgers University Press and more recently by the Gryphon Press, Highland Park, N.J., should be consulted by teachers and by others responsible for selecting tests.

Year III-6 months
Compares size of balls
Assembles "patience pictures"
Discriminates animal pictures
Identifies objects or names action shown in pictures
Sorts black and white buttons
Comprehends and answers simple questions
> (The subject is given one month's MA credit for each correct response as identified in the manual.)

Year VII
Identifies absurdities in pictures
Describes similarities (wood, coal, etc.)
Copies a diamond
Solves a social problem
Recognizes appropriate opposites
Repeats five digits
> (The subject is given two months' MA credit for each correct response at years V and above.)

Year XIV
Scores seventeen on Stanford-Binet vocabulary list
Formulates principles from observed occurrence
Solves verbal problem
Solves a problem requiring ingenuity—getting one pint of water with three-pint and eight-pint measures
Retains directional orientation as turns are described
Tells how things usually thought of as opposites can be considered alike
—winter, summer.[8]

Other test items have similar mental age values. If the sum of these values equals the chronological age of the subject being tested, the resulting IQ is approximately 100. But if a seven-year-old answers all the items on the Year VI level, four on the Year VII level and, in addition, two items on the Year VIII level, two on the Year IX level, one on the Year X level, and one on the XI level, but misses all on the next level, his total mental age is ninety-two months (two months' credit for each answer at these levels).

Ninety-two months, or seven years, eight months, is found on the tables in the manual and, for age seven years, yields a "deviation IQ" of 109.[9] If a subject were not to answer the number of items that is average for his chronological age, his IQ would be less than 100.

8   Lewis M. Terman and Maud A. Merrill, 1960, *Stanford-Binet Intelligence Scale, Manual for Third Revision, Form L-M*, Boston: Houghton Mifflin Company.

Table 8-1

Number of Items	MA Equivalent, Months
Up to 6-year level, all items correct	72
Seven-year level, 4	8
Eight-year level, 2	4
Nine-year level, 2	4
Ten-year level, 1	2
Eleven-year level, 1	2
Total	92

Although intelligence test makers are attempting to assess the same thing, there is typically variation in items and tasks from one test to another depending on what the particular authors believe to be the most important components of intelligence. Moreover, as has previously been indicated, a subject will earn somewhat variant scores on equivalent forms of tests bearing the same title because he may feel better on one day than another. This indicates the fallacy of saying that a child has an IQ of precisely 92, 107, or 132. Tests are so variable that they should be identified by name. Thus, instead of saying, "Bill has an IQ of 98," it would be more indicative of the teacher's knowledge of the nature and purpose of the test if he were to say, "Bill has an IQ of about 100 on the Blank Test." (Incidentally, it is erroneous to speak of an IQ test; it is an "intelligence test.")

At the high school and college levels, students' mental ages are increasing less rapidly than their chronological ages. Hence, it becomes convenient to use some indication other than IQ to express test intelligence. One example is percentile rank, which indicates one's relative position in a theoretical group of 100. If his rank were thirty-fifth percentile, his score exceeded those of 65 percent of the group. Assume that a test containing 100 items was given to 100 subjects. The top score was 75, the lowest score was 25, and 12 students in the middle of the distribution received 52 (44 students received more than 52, and 44 received less than 52). The student receiving 75 would have a percentile score of 99, the one receiving 25 would have a percentile score of 1, and the middle 12 students would be in the 50th percentile.

The IQ can be translated into percentile rank, which indicates the pu-

---

9   A measure of intelligence based on the extent to which an individual's score deviates from a score that is normal for the subject's chronological age. In the above example, the IQ based on the formula MA/CA x 100 would be 110. (The difference of one IQ point is well within allowable limits of accuracy.)

pil's comparative standing in the class. Thus, on one widely used group intelligence test, representative IQs and their meaning in percentiles are as follows:

Table 8-2

Score	IQ (at age 12)	Percentile
5	82	6
17	94	30
29	106	70
35	112	84
44	121	96
56	140	99

An individual scoring over 140 IQ on this test would still be ranked in the ninety-ninth percentile, and theoretically no pupil would exceed him in a group of 100. In general, an IQ of 140 would occur only once in 200 to 250 cases, depending on the test used.

Evaluation of Personality

The assessment of personality is under much the same handicap as is intelligence testing. There is no way to measure it directly—it must be inferred from verbal or overt behavior. Among the techniques for evaluating aspects of personality are (1) rating scales, (2) attitude scales, (3) interest inventories, (4) adjustment inventories, (5) projective techniques, (6) observations, and (7) encounter groups. Each of these approaches gives a picture of the individual and—if the teacher observes the inherent limitations of each method—provides a supplement to a more objective view than could be achieved by personal observation alone. Much research is being devoted to personality assessment, but success to date has been limited (Tyler, 1963, p. 71).

1. A rating scale asks one to evaluate another person or may call for self-rating. A pupil, for instance, may be asked to indicate the five individuals with whom he would most like to work, to play, to talk, etc., in the order of his choice. Or five names may be given, and the respondent is asked to relist them in the order of his preference. Two features of the rating scale are significant: (*a*) There must be a rather intimate acquain-

tance between the rater and the subject, and (*b*) the technique is obviously subjective; i.e., even as one is called on to rate others he is, in fact, making disclosures about himself. Subjectivity is not a shortcoming, because part of the definition of **personality** concerns the impact that a person has on others.

2. An attitude scale asks the subject to tell how he feels about certain propositions or situations. The scale may be based on from two to five degrees of attitude: simply "like" or "dislike"; or "like very much," "like mildly," "no feeling," "dislike mildly," or "dislike intensely." Attitudes regarding peer relationships, family life, school responsibilities, community activities, racial questions, or religious attitudes may be investigated. The value of such a scale is limited, because the subject may tend to give answers that he feels will please the teacher. The scale is artificial in that some of the situations may not have been encountered by the subject, and while he may answer the questions honestly, his conduct in the actual situation may vary from his answer.

3. The interest inventory is an approach to discovering a pupil's interests. Interest inventories, used in occupational counseling, indicate whether or not the pupil's interests are similar to those of people who are satisfied in various occupations. They can also be used to guide the selection of study units, extra reading, hobby development, and special reports. A point worth considering is whether schoolwork should follow a pupil's presently indicated interests or whether he should be "motivated" by incentives or pressure to develop additional interests.

4. The adjustment inventory consists of questions that delve into the emotional, social, and school life of the individual. The following questions are similar to those used in adjustment inventories:

   Do you get angry easily?
   Do you have frequent headaches?
   Does making an oral report in class bother you?
   Do you often find it difficult to sleep?

   Students find words such as frequent, often, and sometimes difficult to interpret—once a week, once a month, once a year? They sometimes regard the test as a joke. If the results are to be used in a screening process, the answers may readily be "doctored" or, at least, slanted. Thus, tenuous clues to, not conclusions about, pupils' behavior in various areas (home, school, community health,, etc.) may be supplied by inventories, and the clues should be supplemented by interviews and observation. Probably the inventory's greatest value is the possibility of using the subject's atypical answers as *the starting point for an interview*.

5. Projective techniques include a wide variety of approaches to the study of personality. When a **projective technique** is used, the respondent adds

structure to an unstructured situation. Persons giving "average" responses are adjudged normal, whereas those giving unique reports are considered deviants from the normal. Study of both typical and atypical responses permits an expert to get a view of the "private life" of the subject.

Play techniques are used in a similar manner. A child is given some toys. What he does with them and what he makes them do enable the analyst to extrapolate or infer motivations, interests, and biases that the subject would be unable to verbalize. The play situation is undirected (unstructured) and any structure which results is provided by the child. In a similar way, the ending that a child gives to an incomplete story or the meaning that he attaches to a picture provides clues to his personality orientation.

Teachers can also use play therapy principles to advantage. Observing the way a child plays spontaneously, the recurrent themes expressed in his paintings and drawings, and the kinds of stories he writes give teachers valuable clues to his problems of adjustment (Bernard, 1970*b*, Chapter 17). However, it must be emphasized that definitive interpretation is only for the expert. Teachers should seek to corroborate what *might be* with evidence gleaned from other sources—inventories, other teachers' reports, other children's reports, and his own observations.

6. Teacher observation is an important aspect of evaluating pupil personality—it is the most continuously employed evaluation technique. Observation, to be most reliable, should be supplemented by formal instruments, such as sociometry, anecdotal records, the behavioral journal, and teacher-made and standardized tests. But the informal day-to-day glimpses of pupils in action should not be discounted as a significant source of data. Asking why a pupil behaves as he does aids in maintaining objectivity, and examining his own reaction to behavior should become a habitual part of the teacher's observation. Because most psychological tests—especially personality tests—are fallible, the teacher should question such data when they conflict with his own observation.

7. A field test of personality, but one which does not yield a numerical score, is the **basic encounter group**. The term is not copyrighted or patented and has come to mean many things—some of highly dubious psychological merit (Paris, 1968). As a technique for examining one's feelings, perceptions, aspirations, and how one "comes across" in social situations it seems to have considerable merit. It is, thus far, used more in business and religious organizations than in education, but its popularity in teacher and counselor education is growing. Dangers of inept leadership and attempts at therapy by novices must be avoided, but the promises are considerable (Shostrom, 1969). To date basic encounter groups have been used only by adults, but Rogers (1968) has predicted

that within a few years it will be considered to be an essential classroom technique and a basic part of school curriculum. A competently led basic encounter group has an advantage over test and inventory approaches to the assessment of personality. Such groups look at a real process of social interaction while it is taking place.

Measurement of Achievement

Achievement tests indicate with reasonable accuracy where the pupil stands in reading, arithmetic, language, algebra, history, science, etc., without contamination by socioeconomic status, motivation, or intellectual potential. But they have limitations—they do not tell why a pupil is having difficulty with arithmetic or why he is below (or above) grade norms in particular subjects. Such tests, adequately standardized, objective, reliable, and valid, enable us to assert that pupils in the third grade vary from first grade to eighth grade in reading ability, for example. When the teacher has objective instruments for evaluating pupil differences, there is little excuse for his treating pupils as though they were alike.

Achievement tests are frequently designed to indicate status in one subject. Others, known as achievement batteries, are divided into parts that yield separate scores in such subjects as language, reading, arithmetic, spelling, science, and social studies. The raw scores are easily translated into meaningful data: grade norms, age norms, or percentile ranks for various ages and grades.

One of the best uses to which teachers can put these instruments is to give one form of the test at the beginning of the term and an equivalent form at the end of the term. This procedure has two very significant advantages: (1) The teacher can see the progress a given pupil has made, even if he is below class average on both tests, and thus the test prevents uncalled-for discouragement on the teacher's part; and (2) both the superior and the slow pupil can profit from seeing objective evidence of their own growth. The superior pupil will probably feel encouraged only when he has maintained his relative advantage. The slow pupil can see that, in terms of where he was at the beginning of the year, he *is* growing, even though slowly.

If standardized tests are to have maximum value, they must be administered and scored strictly in accordance with directions. Because they are standardized on the basis of the procedures indicated in the directions, any deviation will warp the results, and an erroneous "measurement" will result. Some teachers have "shaved the time" on the first administration and allowed a minute or two extra on the second, or they follow advice on the first test and give no help, but ignore the directions and give a little help on the second.

Aptitude and Diagnostic Tests

An aptitude test is designed to estimate probable future performance. An intelligence test might justifiably be considered an aptitude test—one that indicates an important part of capacity to perform in certain areas, especially academic areas. There are, in fact, intelligence tests called "Differential Aptitude Tests," "The General Aptitude Test Battery," and "The Factored Aptitude Tests," for example.

An aptitude test may also be considered a prognostic test; it is designed to predict the future performance of the individual in a specific area. Thus there are reading readiness tests that predict the probable course of the pupil's acquisition of reading skills. There are musical ability, or aptitude, tests that predict the individual's probable success in carrying a tune or playing some musical instrument. Aptitude tests have also been formulated to predict success in mechanical pursuits, foreign languages, and various branches of mathematics.

There are loose-leaf publications, known as "college profiles," or "freshman profiles," that indicate the probability of a student's success in college in terms of the typical entrance examination scores made by college freshmen at given colleges in previous years. Subject selection or college selection is "safe" when the scores of the subject are extremely high or low, but difficulty is encountered with pupils on the borderline between superiority and normality and normality and inferiority. In such cases, other factors should be considered—past performance, application and tenacity, and expressed desire of the pupil. If the case is still doubtful, there remains the pragmatic test, namely, a "trial run" in the area concerned.[10]

Diagnostic tests further illustrate the range and variety of differences in the classroom. A diagnostic test deals with specific subdivisions of a subject and consequently suggests some specific remedial procedures for the teacher. (Actually, no test is diagnostic or remedial—the teacher makes the diagnosis and prescribes the remedial work on the basis of all data available.) A diagnostic test in arithmetic may indicate that a particular number combination is giving difficulty (for example, a persistent answer that $8 \times 7 = 54$) or that a particular process (addition, subtraction, multiplication) is inadequately understood. A diagnostic test in reading may indicate the need for vocabulary drill, the need for attention to details, or failure to comprehend meaning. But the teacher himself makes the particular diagnosis.

Both aptitude tests and diagnostic tests illustrate the desirability and advantage of specificity in testing. Knowledge of human differences becomes

10 Examining a college profile would be helpful to teachers in seeing test scores as approximations. Some students who are in the upper ranges of scores fail *and* a proportion of those who are below the cited range of scores succeed.

more helpful as it becomes more precise. As test users, teachers need to understand that ability tests are not tests of potential.

Use and Misuse of "Measurement"

The Purpose of Testing

Much of the criticism of currently used intelligence tests is based on the idea that an entirely inadequate variety of intelligences are assessed. Although academic intelligence may be adequately probed, very little is known about assessment of social intelligence, the synthesis of concepts, or wisdom in processes of physical and cultural survival. Some religious groups are opposed to the assessment of personality on the grounds that such devices constitute an invasion of privacy. These groups have been joined by those who do not admit the value of the teacher's knowing as much about his pupils as is possible.

The purpose of testing should be that of improving teaching-learning milieus; testing should form part of the basis for designing individualized instruction. Instead, testing is too frequently used to promote a function of the schools which we are hesitant to admit; i.e., the sorting and classification—indeed, the elimination—of pupils.

> The American educational system provides opportunity for social and economic mobility by selecting and training the most able and industrious youth for the higher-status positions in society. Insofar as the school system does this job efficiently and fairly, it equips youth to be qualified for career opportunities and contributes to the success of democracy. . . .
>
> One may ask whether or not the educational system does an efficient and fair job of selecting able and industrious youth. This is not an easy question to answer, because it is not easy to determine who are the ablest and most industrious youth. The ablest in terms of intellectual ability (at least in terms of IQ) can be discovered more easily than the most industrious. Intelligence tests are fairly good measures of intellectual ability, even though they do not measure artistic, music, or social leadership ability. Furthermore, the ordinary paper-and-pencil test of intelligence probably underestimates the abilities of lower-class youth. . . .

11   Robert J. Havighurst and Bernice L. Neugarten, 1967, *Society and Education*, 3d ed., Boston: Allyn and Bacon, Inc., pp. 71, 72-73.

Another passage which expresses similar concern about the purpose of much school testing contains considerably more affective overtones:

In 1965 the passage of the far-reaching Elementary and Secondary Education Act gave the public schools of America a clear new mandate and some of the funds to carry it out. It was a mandate not just for equality of educational opportunity but for equity in results as well. In place of the old screening, sorting, and reject system that put students somewhere on a bell shaped curve stretching from A to F, the schools were asked to bring educational benefits to every young person to prepare him for a productive life. Under the new mandate the schools were expected to give every pupil the basic competence he needed, regardless of his so-called ability, interest, background, home, or income. After all, said a concerned Nation, what's the purpose of grading a basic skill like reading with A, B, C, D, or F when you can't make it at all today if you can't read?[12]

Because tests are so frequently used to close doors of opportunity, for screening rather than to provide guidance regarding which doors to enter, pupils occasionally develop phobias about tests. Some pupils become nauseated, develop headaches, and form mental blocks as their experiences accumulate in classification and exclusion processes.

Susan participated willingly and with sagacity in class projects and discussions. Yet on the final examination her responses were illogical and random, when the item was responded to at all. The teacher was so surprised at the disappointing result that he kept Susan after school to talk with her. Because she was poised and logical in the discussion the teacher asked two or three questions from the test and got correct and complete answers. Ultimately he ran through most of the items on the test and found that Susan had a comprehension of the course which was quite laudable.

Susan's difficulty was not a fault of tests but the fault of usage to which prior tests had been put. Teachers may sometimes use tests punitively. If the pupils have misbehaved or been neglectful of homework, a test may be sprung that will provide an excuse for giving low marks. Tests which are used to classify, compare, close doors, and punish can justly be regarded with fear. The purposes of tests are to guide next steps, to provide feedback on correctness of information, and to indicate growth from there to here.

12   Leon M. Lessinger, 1969, "Accountability for Results," *American Education*, vol. 5, no. 6, p. 3, June-July.

Effective Use of Tests

Some of the critics of school testing take the view that the remedy for misuse is to discard them. They want all tests abolished. Sophisticated users recognize hazards but are unwilling to "throw out the baby with the bath." Tests have limitations but, when used with due respect for what they do and do not do, there is a proper place for them. The all-inclusive aim of psychological measurement in the school is to understand pupils better and to improve instruction. These aims are reflected in the following list of values of testing:

1. Tests help in evaluating progress toward goals. By giving tests at the beginning and end of the term, the teacher has an objective aid in evaluating pupil growth in specific areas and can then more wisely plan the next steps.
2. Tests may show where emphasis has been placed. Achievement and diagnostic tests can show the teacher whether or not balance has been maintained in the instructional program. For instance, they may show that insufficient attention has been devoted to vocabulary or use of reference materials in the reading program. They may show that problem solving has been emphasized to the exclusion of drill in the arithmetic program.
3. Tests can help to determine effective methods. By comparing the progress of pupils of apparently similar ability the teacher may decide that somewhat different approaches should be used with certain pupils. The tests do not show what approaches should be made—they show only that one approach is comparatively ineffective for at least some pupils.
4. Tests can help to motivate pupils. Knowledge of progress is an effective means of motivation for individual pupils, and perhaps on occasion, for the entire class. If an initial, midpoint, and end test is given, each pupil can see where he is, where he was, and how much (in terms of score) he has grown.
5. Tests give training in thinking and using language. In taking a test, the pupil has an opportunity to use what he knows in a different context from that which occurs in daily classwork or in his out-of-school life. The more such opportunities are provided, the more firmly consolidated learning will be.
6. Tests can be used in pupil guidance. The data supplied by tests can be effectively used to help pupils select future courses. The data may also be used to help the pupil select the curriculum from which he will probably profit the most. Of course, such a choice is not automatic. The pupils' interests, their demands for what they regard as being relevant, and the relation of courses to long-range objectives and aspirations must be considered (Ebel, 1970*b*).

7. Test data may be valuable parts of pupil records. Such data are widely understood; and when they are entered on a pupil's permanent record, they provide clues by which later teachers may approach an understanding of the pupil. Two precautions must be observed: The name of the test, the form used, and the date of administration should be entered along with the results; and the teacher should use such data as *background information*, not as a measure of status.

8. Tests can be used by supervisors to help teachers. The supervisor who appreciates the values and limitations of tests may use the data as clues for suggesting changes in teaching procedures. However, if test results are used as the major criterion for evaluating teacher effectiveness the results are being *misused*.

The possible harmful consequences of tests have been summarized as follows: (1) They may place a rather permanent stamp on the pupil's intellectual status; (2) they may lead to a narrow interpretation of ability; (3) they may place test makers and publishers in a position to control education; and (4) they may encourage an impersonal, rigid, and mechanistic process of evaluation of pupil ability and development (Ebel, 1970*b*).

The value of tests in determining individual differences will be greatly enhanced if the user is fully aware of the things that tests do *not* do. It cannot be stated too emphatically that present psychological and educational tests do not measure with the accuracy of a yardstick or a laboratory balance. Psychological tests yield only approximations, estimations, and indications, which are extremely valuable if used with due regard to the limitations.

Tests do not measure motivation. An intelligence test does not indicate the determination of a pupil to use effectively the intelligence that is indicated on the test. There is, in fact, a growing interest in the proposition that what the teacher expects—whether based on test data, observation, or deliberate misinformation by experimenters—is a focal aspect of pupil performance (Claiborn, 1969). A reading readiness test does not measure the willingness of a child to keep trying to master reading skills. A reading achievement test does not measure the quality of books that pupils voluntarily select for leisure time reading.

Tests do not provide answers. Scores on a variety of tests do not tell the teacher how to bring about better adjustment on the part of the pupil, but they do help him to determine the area of need.

Tests do not provide a valid basis for assigning marks. Even though the progress indicated by initial and end-of-term tests is used in grading, home background, illnesses, absences, and distracting (and sometimes valuable) interests must also be considered.

The wise teacher will accept tests for their limited worth, not as perfect instruments. The warning in the old cliché, "The clumsy carpenter blames his tools," should be heeded by the teacher. The imperfections inherent in educational and psychological tests impose serious obligations upon those who use them because they are dealing with human beings—their self-regard and their futures.

Summary

Teachers are sometimes disturbed and frequently bewildered by the range of differences perceived in a fifth grade or a class in geometry or English composition. Measurements of individual differences serve, however, to warn that grouping on one measure does not serve as an index of homogeneity in another measure. Further, the distribution of differences provides warning against classification of individuals into "type" categorizations—third graders, athletes, scholars, adolescents—with meaningful accuracy. Fortunately, the philosophy, if not the practice, of American public education emphasizes the value of human differences and adjures the teacher to capitalize upon them.

Much research work has been and is being devoted to the more accurate assessment of differences. Many valuable instruments have been devised, such as intelligence, achievement, aptitude, and diagnostic tests. These, when used with due precautions for their inherent limitations, provide valuable clues to the understanding of individual pupils and, consequently, to the improvement of instruction. In order to be of greatest value, standardized tests should satisfy such criteria as objectivity, ease of administration, validity, reliability, breadth of sampling, and economy.

Tests should be viewed as clues, samples, and indications rather than precise measurements of traits and potentials. Tests should serve as supplementary data to the teacher's observations. As such, the teacher's judgment and evaluation should be a large factor in the assessment of differences. In the final analysis, it is the teacher's skill in understanding and dealing with differences that provides effective education.

Suggested Additional Readings

BEATTY, WALCOTT H. (Chrm. & Ed.), 1969, *Improving Educational Assessment and an Inventory of Measures of Affective Behavior*, Washington, D.C.: Association for Supervision and Curriculum Development, NEA.

   The purposes, concepts, problems, and challenges of educational assessment are considered. About half the booklet consists of a list of instruments for assessing attitudes, creativity, motivation, personality, self-concept, and other noncognitive aspects of education.

DE CECCO, JOHN P. (ed.), 1963, *Human Learning in the School,* New York: Holt, Rinehart and Winston, Inc., pp. 416-501.

   The editor has brought together in these pages what might be called the "classics" in the area of mental and personality assessment. Articles are by Sir Cyril Burt, J. P. Guilford, Nancy Bayley, and Philip Vernon—names well known to scholars in the area of assessment.

GRONLUND, NORMAN E., 1971 *Measurement and Evaluation in Teaching*, 2d ed., New York: The Macmillan Company.

This text gives somewhat more attention to the construction of teacher-made tests than is typical. Measurement terms, aptitude tests, and achievement tests are considered.

PINNEAU, SAMUEL R., 1961, *Changes in Intelligence Quotient*, Boston: Houghton Mifflin Company.

The author describes research studies on the changing IQ with both conceptual and statistical interpretations. Among other things, the use and value of the deviation IQ is considered.

SHERTZER, BRUCE, AND SHELLEY C. STONE (eds.), 1970, *Introduction to Guidance: Selected Readings*, Boston: Houghton Mifflin Company, pp. 223-300.

In addition to dealing with uses and misuses of tests, articles in this section expand the scope of the foregoing chapter by discussing sociometry, sentence completion tests, and meaningful student records.

Part three

Classroom Teaching-
Learning
Transactions

How to put together some of the things we know about teaching-learning transactions is the burden of Part 3.

Motivation and emotions determine how vigorously and in what direction one will develop and apply his intellectual potential. It has been postulated that we use only a small fraction of the potential we have. Motivation and emotions are vital in establishing the size of that fraction.

Personality constitutes another perspective on motivation. Just as knowledge is indivisible (arithmetic, language, social studies, etc., cannot be sequestered into periods), personality is not divisible into mind, body, endocrine glands, and spirit. In the chapter on personality we look at how the total being (student or man) got that way and at what he might become.

Problem solving and creativity are presented as the readily available avenues to facilitating the journey toward self-realization. Socialization versus individualization, freedom versus structure, permissiveness versus responsibility are some of the dilemmas considered.

Nevertheless, the problems of motivation, personality development, and creative problem solving are not insurmountable. This is demonstrated in what has been done by creative teachers for those who are, to a degree, shut off from the prerequisites and privileges of dominant society; i.e., the different pupil.

9

Motivation:
The Facilitation
of Learning

Within the classroom, the big problem
for teachers and learners is that of motivation. Teachers hope to get each pupil
to make use of his talents and time while in school so that maximum learning of
certain objectives occurs. Learners, whether they realize it or not, hope to make
use of their potential—to grow most rapidly toward developing their latent talents. Unfortunately, teachers' goals are often different from those internalized
by pupils and instead of motivation there is disinterest or even alienation.

It was believed, until quite recently, that whippings were an effective
means of motivation. Huxley (1956) has observed that whether by carrot in
front or stick behind, the important thing is to induce children to make some
slight intellectual effort toward learning.

The question of how to induce children to exert that slight effort is not
easily answered. The cliché "You can lead a horse to water, but you can't make
him drink" is readily appreciated by parents who have tried to make a baby eat
something he did not want and by teachers who have tried to elicit pupil effort.
Teachers can lead pupils to the fountain of knowledge but that does not mean
that they come there with thirst. Pupils often learn to hate school, to avoid serious reading, to think of themselves as academic dolts and literary morons. Conversely, some learn to like school. They get sufficiently involved in learning to
pursue it themselves, even outside the school. They think of themselves as curious people quite capable of learning new answers to both new and old dilemmas.

The Basic Role of Motivation

Meaning and Import of Motivation

"Motivation" refers to all those phenomena which are involved in the stimulation of action toward particular objectives where previously there was little or no movement toward those goals. Motivation considers basic or internal drives as well as external incentives or rewards. As a classroom problem, motivation is the process of arousing, maintaining, and controlling interest. Boys often prefer playing football to solving problems in arithmetic. Girls frequently engage in gossip with greater enthusiasm than they display in searching for data on the Mayan empire. Although these statements are generally true, there are boys who prefer to work problems in arithmetic, and there are girls who enjoy reading history.

A basic principle of behavior is that an individual always takes what he perceives to be the shortest route toward a goal. If sweethearts take the long way home it is because getting home is not the immediate objective. Adults may perceive that pupils in school should devote themselves to mastering the curriculum, but pupils do not always see school tasks as the best way to independence, productivity, adulthood, or whatever they may consider desirable development. The basic task for the teacher then becomes learning how to help pupils to choose topics, activities, and goals that have long-term significance as well as immediate appeal. For example, a pupil may be motivated to memorize a long list of Latin words by being given an A by the teacher and a dollar for the A by his father. But the emphasis on the A and on the dollar tends to obscure the long-term value of his study.

Motivation should take one beyond the problems of the classroom to such questions as: How does one use his talents after being graduated from school? Does he believe in himself and in society? What books does he voluntarily read? What kind of ideals guide his choices? How does he spend his spare time? What kind of model does one provide for his own and others' children? How does he regard civic obligations and duties? One's spontaneous likes and dislikes, his interests and ideals, his longings and ambitions are really the determiners of what kind of person he will be. Thus, motivation involves consideration of how current school pursuits can contribute to the continued pursuit of knowledge in the next years and decades.

Motivation in Education

The author postulates that much of the teacher's concern about motivation is uncalled for. What is needed more than "motivating" the pupil is to get out of his way by aligning our concerns with his ongoing interests and activities. There is an inborn, natural impulse to grow and become. It does not have to be taught; but the desire to satisfy curiosity, to explore, to try out, to adventure can be so coerced that its manifestation in school is obliterated. Bonner (1965) refers to the urge to grow as the proactive aspects of behavior—the tendency to dream, hope, aspire, plan. These proactive aspects supplement the reactive aspects—the past and present causes of behavior. Maslow (1968b) refers to this inner urge to become as the processes of actualization. Menninger (1963, p. 84) calls this impulse to become and grow the **heterostatic** urge. Rogers (1961) calls the self-determining aspects of behavior directional growth.

Conventionally, motivation has been thought of in terms of what and how pupils learn about subject matter. A concomitant of education for the disadvantaged, the handicapped, the underachiever, and the emphasis on continuous learning beyond the formal school years is concern about what and how pupils learn about themselves (Strom, 1969b; Rogers, no date). It may be that the distinction between self and things is slender and theoretical; but how the pupil sees himself, the degree of self-esteem he possesses, the sense of worth he has will to a marked extent determine how well he uses and exploits his potentials.

> Steve is a good-looking, cheerful, socially-at-ease boy who is well liked by teachers and his classmates. His parents are proud of the A's he earns and are not concerned with the predominance of B's and the occasional C. They are proud that he is continuing school beyond the point they had achieved. Steve works summers and weekends in a local garage-service station. The owner has offered Steve a guaranteed job with a minimum salary and 10 percent partnership in the company when Steve has been graduated from high school. Because of his easily earning A's in science and mathematics courses and because of his 145 IQ on the Wechsler-Bellevue, Steve's teachers have urged him to attend the four-year state technical college. The prospects of a job, a part in the business, and of "getting on with the business of life" have the greater appeal to Steve and his parents.

The causes that underlie behavior are always multiple and complex rather than single and simple. There are no nostrums, panaceas, or formulas that the teacher can use in reaching all pupils. Actually, considerations of intelligence, social class, developmental status of pupils, growth patterns, and principles of learning all have implications for motivation. This chapter funnels some of these considerations into some suggestions for the teacher.

Motivation and the Teacher

As a successful engineer of learning activities, the teacher must plan strategies and tactics, assemble materials, guide pupils' assumption of responsi-

Marion Bernstein/College Newsphoto Alliance

bilities, and oversee activities to the end of arousing pupils and encouraging them to maintain effective pursuit of the learning goals. Often pupils enter the school with certain learning goals (perhaps somewhat vague ones) in mind, and little arousal is required. Others are reluctant, resistant, or less perceptive and require more assistance (Miller, 1970). If the teacher attempts to motivate all these pupils by means of the same technique, some will be helped and others will be turned off. It is as though these pupils were running with different motors. They not only require different kinds of fuel (high octane, regular, diesel, or kerosene) but also need different kinds of spark for igniting the fuel.

The truly educated person is one who continues to study after his formal schooling has been completed. Teachers who "motivate" by means of demands and threats may get a degree of conformity that is temporarily satisfactory. An example is the literature teacher who assigned thirty pages a day in a book on contemporary American literature and then gave daily tests. The test consisted of citing one line; for this line, the student was to supply the name of the poem or story, author, period, and message carried by the piece as a whole. The students were motivated to do the reading; but even some of the successful students vowed never to read "literature" again.

Another teacher of literature worked with individuals in interpreting stories and poems. All pupils were given a chance to participate. Much time was devoted to relating the characters and incidents of literature to the problems and events in the pupils' own lives. Some discussion was held with individuals or small groups who had been previously guided into reading selections that accorded with their interests and would encourage further reading (Kohl, 1967).

It is safe to assume that if the students in the two groups were of equal ability, more from the latter group developed a continuing interest in literature.

Practical Approaches to Motivation

Many books and pamphlets approach motivation on the "how to" basis. Thus, first graders are encouraged to learn to read and to continue to read by the use of praise. The teacher encourages the third grader to learn to spell by pinning his better papers on the bulletin board. He motivates the fifth grader to study history by planning and producing a dramatic program. He encourages the eighth grader to study civics by taking the entire class for a day's visit to the city hall. High school pupils are stimulated in their efforts to write by working on the school paper. Other high school youngsters work hard to get on the honor roll. These practices have worked and deserve the attention of the prospective teacher. However, it is more practical to know *why* praise stimulates effort, *why* symbols, honor rolls, and activities are effective motivators—when the "why" is understood, greater versatility in teachers is probable. A beginning can be made by emphasizing the principle: *All behavior is caused, and understanding pupils entails comprehending some of the causes.*

A fifth-grade boy, who was considered to be the teacher's "boy with problems" sat mumbling to himself. By edging his chair close to the boy, the observer could hear the boy saying to himself, "What'll I do? If I go I'll have to buy a present. I'll miss the next *Wagon Train* show on TV, but maybe that won't matter." These remarks were occasioned by his reading an invitation to a birthday party. He was rocking back and forth in his chair, kicking the desk in front. There was real danger of his falling backward on a pupil who was working at a floor-level bookshelf. The teacher finally took hold of his chair and asked him to help a slow-learning girl with her arithmetic. He protested audibly and was then told to get busy on his own work. The incident illustrates the necessity for understanding causes. The boy's problem needed to be understood, and the teacher was working on it. She already had much useful information (one of the major factors was parental pressure on him to be the best pupil in the class); but she also had the problem of immediately stopping his disturbing other pupils and interrupting classroom routines.

Two motivational implications are clear: (1) Pupils can be motivated by applying routine, tested, techniques. The theory is that successful motivation in the schools should *stem from meeting the fundamental needs of children.* When specific motivators fail (such as getting good grades, helping others, or recognition), then the teacher must ask, (2) "What fundamental need has been neglected or is temporarily satiated?" Theory provides guidelines and suggests solutions. A youngster is not "instinctively" desirous of displeasing adults. He simply takes what he perceives to be the shortest route to his goal.

Basic Needs as Motivators

Some Concepts of Needs

The discussion of motivation through an analysis of needs is a theoretical approach. It is difficult to state basic needs to the satisfaction of all concerned, and various authorities have conceptualized them in somewhat different terms. The basic idea is that unfulfilled needs result in maladjustment, but there are exceptions: one child who apparently is not loved deeply by his parents may be well adjusted, but another who is apparently loved lavishly may be poorly adjusted. However, the exceptions are understandable *when other needs are considered.* The following list presents varied basic human drives or needs as quoted by various authors:

Thomas[1]
New experiences
Security

Response
Recognition

Symonds[2]
Be with others
For approval
Be a cause
Mastery
Maintain self

Gain attention
Security
Affection
Curiosity

Maslow[3]
Physiological
Safety
Belongingness or love

Esteem
Need for self-actualization
Aesthetic needs

1   W. I. Thomas, 1923, *The Unadjusted Girl*, Boston: Little, Brown and Company.
2   Percival M. Symonds, 1934, "Human Drives," *Journal of Educational Psychology*, vol. 25, p. 694.
3   Abraham H. Maslow, 1954, *Motivation and Personality*, New York: Harper & Row, Publishers, Inc.

Carroll[4]

Physical security	Mastery
Emotional security	Status

Murray[5]

Achievement — accomplish, manipulate, excel

Abasement — submit to external force or pain

Aggression — overcome, belittle, or ridicule

Exhibition — excite or amaze others

Deference — admire and support a superior

Autonomy — be free of restraint,

resist influence

Dominance — control one's environment, influence others

Affiliation — remain loyal, please and win affection

Succorance — have needs gratified by help of others

Nurturance — give sympathy and help to others

Sentience — seek and enjoy sensuous experience

An Hierarchical Order for Needs

It is apparent that there is considerable duplication in the lists and that the longer lists break down items in the shorter lists. It is not so apparent where basic needs, in the sense of being essential to life, begin to merge into needs that are learned or acquired from the individual's cultural milieu. It is important that teachers realize that the way tissue or biological needs are met is dependent on parents and other key people. Hence, one's early life and school experiences shape his current and emerging needs and motivations.

The explanation of needs as postulated by Maslow (1954, pp. 80ff) is particularly helpful because it explains why some needs are, at a particular time or developmental stage, predominant. Maslow suggests that when needs are satisfied at one level, the next higher order of needs become prepotent. Thus, the satisfying (not necessarily 100 percent) of low-level needs predisposes the individual to seek goals at a higher and more productive level.

1. Physiological Needs

These needs are not usually powerful in well-fed, adequately housed Americans. They are, in our culture, emergency needs that occur infrequently but are likely to be prepotent when unsatisfied. The needs are for food, water,

---

4   Herbert A. Carroll, 1955, "Motivation and Learning: Their Significance in a Mental-health Program for Education," in National Society for the Study of Education, 54th Yearbook, part II, *Mental Health in Modern Education*, Chicago: University of Chicago Press.

5   James Deese, 1967, *General Psychology*, Boston: Allyn and Bacon, Inc., p. 123, citing and interpreting H. A. Murray.

oxygen, sleep, activity, sex, and sensory satisfaction. Up to 15 percent of children of poverty families are sufficiently malnourished or undernourished that mental development may be impaired (Read, 1969). And it is estimated that 10 percent of white families and 35 percent of black families live in poverty (Heilbroner, 1970).

> Those who have worked with undernourished or hungry children know that they exhibit behavioral alterations. These include apathy, lethargy, inability to pay attention, and perhaps, overconcern about food to such a degree that responses to classroom stimuli do not occur. . . .
>
> Learning is increasingly recognized as progressing in stages, each stage becoming a foundation for the next. By not responding to early stimulation, the child gradually becomes unable to benefit from "normal" experiences at a later period. He fails to learn, not because the genetic potential or neurological structures are absent, but because he lacks the experiential foundation. Improved nutrition alone will not correct this deficit. Neither will improved educational opportunities by themselves. Both must be provided in a coordinated program to develop the child's potential.[6]

Physiological needs go further than food. Such considerations also include being tired or fresh, availability of energy, health or illnesses, effectiveness of sensory function, growth rates and status, and acceptability of facial and bodily characteristics and conformation.

> Paul J., whose family was in difficult financial circumstances, was causing some trouble in the sixth grade. He was only a fair reader, and his arithmetic was poorer than aptitude tests predicted. He displayed a resentment toward the teacher and had a few physical clashes with classmates. His work was sporadic, and in general he manifested an "I-don't-care" attitude. Praise, bestowal of responsibilities, careful selection of books, and individual attention did not change the situation. One day the teacher noticed that he squinted and twisted his head when looking at the chalkboard. The teacher began to suspect poor vision and later noticed other symptoms. A visual examination confirmed the suspicion. With his astigmatism, Paul probably saw only a blur from the back of the room, the opthalmologist reported. Paul's behavior changed markedly when the Lions Club obtained glasses for him.

Teachers of children with sensory handicaps stress the importance of giving these pupils as close a contact with their visual or auditory defect and then reducing that difficulty to a minimum. Often children are not dressed warmly

---

6   Merrill S. Read, 1969, "Malnutrition and Learning," *American Education*, vol. 5, no. 10, p. 14, December.

enough for comfort. Others may not have had an adequate breakfast. The beauty of *Thanatopsis* will probably not compete with physical discomfort as a "motivator."

Proper room temperature, circulation of fresh air, and adequate lighting are important. If the need for glasses can make one child difficult in school, it is quite possible that glare or dingy lighting will have a negative effect upon several children. Many schools do not have regular recess periods in the elementary grades; instead, the teacher watches for signs of restlessness after a period of quiet work and, when they appear, announces a play period.

Some of these considerations can be turned over to pupils. One pupil can be responsible for seeing that windows are opened after a play period and that the room is warm during quiet periods. Another can see that shades are properly drawn. A "captain of recess" can be named to see that rubbers and coats are worn outside. The pupils will profit by sharing responsibility, and the teacher's burden will be lighter. It is the teacher's responsibility, however, to check periodically to be sure that chairs, desks, and tables are the proper size. This is particularly important in the lower grades, when pupils are growing rapidly. "The mind can absorb no more than the seat can endure."

> Matt B. regularly fell asleep in class, and the teacher finally became impatient and told him to stay awake or stay away. It appeared that Matt was not greatly motivated in the direction of ancient history. The teacher later discovered that Matt was greatly motivated, but that physiological needs took priority. Matt's father did not approve of education and told his son that going to school would not excuse him from farm chores—nor would there be any money for "fancy clothes." Matt got up at 5 A.M. to do his chores and after school held two jobs, firing a bakery furnace and acting as bellboy at a small hotel until midnight. The next time this teacher had a sleepy student, he first sought for understanding—and with the next student the cause was an underactive thyroid gland.

One principle of motivation which emerges from the foregoing considerations is: *Physiological needs must be met or on the way to being met before the next higher order of motivators become predominant.* Teachers have not always been concerned about the bodily needs of children. However, recognition of the desirability of such concern is increasing as more work is done with disadvantaged and handicapped children. It is being realized that *the determiners of behavior are always multiple, and intellectual activities are conditioned by bodily processes and attendant feelings and emotions.*

2. Safety Needs

An individual seeks safety. Neglected children appear to be dominated by safety-seeking behavior if their physiological needs are satisfied. Children prefer care during illness, routines, dependable parents, and an orderly world because of the need for safety. They need the feeling of security that comes from structure, discipline, and consistency. Permissiveness *within limits* rather than unrestricted freedom is needed by children so that they can perceive their world as being organized and dependable rather than unstructured and unpredictable. The discipline of self-direction must come *after* the external discipline provided by wiser, more experienced persons. Expecting a young child to be self-disciplined is to ignore his safety needs.

Pupils need and appreciate routine and regularity. This was demonstrated to the author, visiting a seventh grade, by a girl who asked for attention and stated with concern, "We did not put arithmetic on the board today." Each morning, the teacher listed the day's activities on the board. This day, because they were to watch a television broadcast of the President's Inaugural Address, there just was not time enough to schedule all subjects even in shortened periods. No doubt, students who had stronger feelings of security would welcome a change in schedule, but for some, adhering to a schedule was important.

Safety needs also tend to be filled when the teacher's behavior is consistent. Whether his tone is optimistic and cheerful or stern and demanding, the students can work more effectively if they can depend upon his mood. The more clearly and specifically educational objectives are stated, the greater is the motivation and the more efficient is the learning (Carroll, 1965, p. 257). Consistency is helpful, especially to the pupil who tends to be insecure. Written work to be handed in should not be demanded on one day and excused on another. Similarly, grading should not be based partially on conduct and attitude at one time if it is to be based entirely on achievement on other occasions. When a test is announced, it should be given on schedule. It follows that assignments made on a punitive basis are more likely to harm class morale than to be effective motivators.

Children need discipline within the limits of understanding and respect for differences rather than **authoritarian** control—where the primary focus is on the source of power. **Authoritative** control is another matter. Choosing the more advantageous behaviors is too much of a burden for the immature, inexperienced individual. *Children need discipline in order to perceive an orderly, organized world.* Observance of group welfare, conformity to legal requirements, respect for authority and learning, and temporarily postponing one's own immediate wishes are lessons that must be learned.

The ultimate goal of discipline is to help the individual become independent, self-directing, and able to function in a democratic society. This implies that discipline must be reasonable and cooperative rather than arbitrary and autocratic. Such discipline should be characterized by four basic considerations: It should (1) recognize the inherent rights and dignity of the individual, (2) be based on the humanitarian ideals of freedom, justice, and equality, (3) aim at self-direction and self-discipline rather than unquestioning obedience, and (4) entail a clear understanding of the goals at which discipline is directed.

3. Belongingness and Love Needs

When physiological and safety needs are fairly well met, the need to give and receive love emerges as the next order of priority. Hunger for affectionate relations is, when unsatisfied, a basic factor in psychopathology.

> Art K. had again fought with a classmate. The fourth-grade teacher had pleaded with him not to pick on others. She had punished him and had sent him to the principal. But there were still periodic fights. Praising him on days when there were no fisticuffs was no solution. But the remark "Art, some of the big boys in the upper grades are picking on our boys. You are a big, strong fighter and you can protect the little boys" did work. Art was big and strong. He was big because, as a slow learner, he was behind a grade. The cause and the remedy for his difficulties could be stated in terms of belongingness needs.

The words "a warm, responsive personality" are frequently encountered in the literature dealing with teachers, counselors, and others in the helping professions. This is the first characteristic of those deemed to be *good* teachers (Hamachek, 1969). Being warm and responsive requires a person who feels secure and can radiate security in establishing contact with others. Characteristically, one who has not had the opportunity to give and to receive affection presents a hostile front. He is often defensive and, being afraid, assumes the attitude of not caring or of not wanting affection. The situation is aggravated because the pupil's need for affection causes him to act in such a way that it is difficult for others to be affectionate. *When one is most unlovable, he is most in need of love.* There are many such emotionally wounded children in school. The teacher must be genuine when he says to the child, "I like you," and he must show it in actions. Well-integrated teachers are effective with all types of pupils. Weakly integrated teachers are ineffective with all but the "strivers" (Sears and Hilgard, 1967).

One of the frequent concomitants of **underachievement**, which is a symptom of inadequate motivation, is the pupil's frequent change of residence—perhaps the safety needs of routine, regularity, and the familiar are in short supply. However, if the home is stable and the pupil is psychologically secure, physical change of residence is of little consequence. When the home is not stable, the child encounters school difficulties. For a period of time, transient youngsters do not *belong* in the new social group, and special efforts must be exerted to make them feel welcome. Teachers have approached the problem in three ways, by (1) using group and individual counseling to encourage pupils to make their classmates feel at home, (2) designating duties and responsibilities in such a way that *all pupils* become functioning members of the group, and (3) grouping pupils **sociometrically** so there is mutual attraction and support within the group.

In some primary schools the importance of belongingness is recognized by having teachers "pass along" with pupils; i.e., one teacher stays with a class through both the first and second grades.

The relationship of belongingness and motivation is probably best shown in studies of school dropouts. For a long time dropping out of school was thought to be a function of intelligence or the lack of it; but it becomes increasingly clear that ability to do schoolwork is not of the highest importance. Much more significant is the fact that dropouts have not become an integral part of the school. They have not participated in school activities such as parties, sports, club activities, band, orchestra, choruses, or offices (Schreiber, 1969). There is no open sesame for this phase of motivation, but the concept of **identity** is a key one (Burkhart and Neil, 1968). Teachers need to know who and what they are before they can genuinely accept pupils. It has been amply demonstrated that *when pupils feel that they are part of the group, desirable and purposeful learning activities are facilitated.*

4. Esteem Needs

All people need a "stable, firmly based high evaluation of themselves" (Maslow, 1954, p. 90). This entails a self-respect and esteem from others that is rooted in achievement relative to capacity. The need is satisfied by (*a*) confidence and independence and (*b*) recognition, attention, and appreciation from others.

Schoolwork does not have to be easy, neither does it have to be fun in order to motivate pupils. Challenge, a task "worthy of one's steel" will tend to enlist pupil effort. It seems unwise for teachers to say, "Oh, that's easy." It may not be easy for the pupil, but if he does do it, those words mean he really has not done much, and if he fails he is a "nincompoop" for sure. It would be better for the teacher to be able to say, "This one is a real challenge—but I think you can do it." Many teachers do voice this effective principle, *"Find something the pupil can do—something that makes him feel important."* One evidence of inadequate motivation is dropping out of school, and a lack of status looms large in explaining dropouts. Major characteristics of dropouts are shunning extracurricular activities, which causes difficulty in maintaining status, and lack of esteem of teachers and peers. Walberg and Anderson (1968) reported more concerted work and better accomplishment in a physics class when the classroom climate was one characterized by "synergism," i.e., one in which interpersonal relations were intimate and gratifying because each member was a significant, valued member of a democratic group. One's ego concept is directly and intimately related to his school success. Those whose self-concept is strong are more likely to achieve academic success (Kubiniec, 1970).

The teacher's effectiveness in motivation can be increased by (1) recognizing the importance of status and (2) realizing that children of different socioeconomic backgrounds achieve status in different ways. Each human being wants to be recognized as a worthy person in the group in which he lives (Densham, 1971). If he cannot get approval, he may have to be satisfied with forcing recognition. Though the need for status is the same everywhere, the way in which it is achieved is not. Children from the lower class may achieve status by being pugnacious and aggressive. Children from the middle classes achieve status by being well behaved: Parents praise them for avoiding battle. The lower-class boy who earns status with the teacher by avoiding battle loses prestige in the eyes of his playmates for being a softy, but the middle-class boy, by the same behavior, is successful. An emphasis on grades and marks will be a source of strong motivation to the middle-class child, whose parents believe in the monetary and cultural value of an education. Grades are often less important to the lower-class child. In order to motivate these lower-class children, the teacher should recognize their view of life; they have a relatively high reality orientation that makes the practical and immediate of value. Deferring gratification to earn diplomas and degrees is less important than learning something that will get the individual a job and give him independence. Thus the abstract curriculum (college preparatory) is less appealing than the vocational and commercial curriculum (Havighurst and Neugarten, 1967, pp. 87ff).

Some teachers and administrators want the age minimum for compulsory school attendance reduced because many of these unmotivated youths are troublesome, but the fault is not entirely that of the eighteen-year-olds. Since their grade school days, teachers have probably tried to motivate them with the threat of poor grades or the promise of good ones. When this motivation proved relatively meaningless, teachers became disgusted with the stubbornness of pupils who would not learn despite ability and incentives. In consequence, these pupils felt that school had nothing for them. But another generation of eighteen-year-olds under another teacher orientation could be different. Teachers should recognize that there are different ways of achieving status; consequently, there are different methods for using status as a motivator. Taylor (1968) has suggested that the intelligence test criteria by which superiority is determined be expanded from the five or six conventionally recognized to include a greater number of the 120 components of intelligence which have been postulated by Guilford. In this way perhaps up to half the pupils could be judged to be in the upper 10 percent in some esteemed area. This broadened base for recognition would tend to cause the student to be esteemed for his strengths instead of being stigmatized for his weaknesses. Shuell and Keppel (1970) seem to be lending support to this hypothesis when they report that slow learners remember just as well as their faster learning peers.

Physiological, safety, belongingness, and esteem needs should not be too sharply differentiated. The child whose uncorrected vision prevents his taking part in ball games is denied satisfaction of both physical and social needs, and his emotional turmoil may keep him from being motivated to work hard on arithmetic, algebra, or literature. The girl who is concerned about protruding or missing teeth has a physical difficulty that has its greatest impact in terms of esteem and belongingness needs.

5. The Need for Self-actualization

Self-actualization means that what a person can be, he must be—his potentialities tend to be actualized. Before this level of need is reached, the other needs must be satisfied; when achieved, the result is a healthy individual who reaches more complete realization of his potential. Emphasis on self-actualization[7] is a means of recognizing the **heterostatic** tendencies of the human organism—the urge to grow, to become, to learn.

Because "one must be what he can be" (Maslow, 1954, p. 91), the pupil with athletic ability will train and drill; the pupil with musical talent will practice eagerly; the pupil with mathematical aptitude will work assigned *and* unassigned problems; the pupil with linguistic ability will study without being forced. It should be noted that self-actualization need not entail unusual talent. A run-of-the-mill athlete, a thorough workman, and a good mother may be self-actualizing. At the highest level, self-actualizers are those rare creative individuals who are more frequently found among the intellectually gifted. Most persons are satisfied with lower-order motivations. Much depends on the **level of aspiration** adopted by the individual (Marx and Tombaugh, 1967, p. 97).

Some pupils work as a matter of compliance to authority, others strive for approval of nurturant teachers, some seek to satisfy curiosity, others respond to challenge, others work to prove their superiority, and still others work because the immediate task is seen as a step toward a long-range goal (Atkinson, 1965, p. 25). Hence, varied curricula, provision for choice of activity by individual pupils, plans for independent study, and availability of guidance and counseling workers all have a place in providing opportunities for and challenges to self-actualization. *Students should be able to choose the type of knowledge or skills desired, with flexibility as to the time they will devote to developing that knowledge or skill.* "Lockstep" education (annual promotions and uniform curricula), which is so strongly condemned by philosophers and educators, can also be criticized by psychologists.

Random learning lets the individual child take the prime responsibility for his own learning. He should because the younger children are, the less they can tell us about "where they are" in the process of learning. No teacher, even one who has time and tries, can divine more than a glimpse of the state of the child's digested and undigested input of what he knows, what he thinks he knows, and what he knows that's wrong or garbled. The skeleton, the supporting structure of learning, is *concepts* as they mesh and connect and interweave. The grasp of concepts depends on the moment of insight—that sudden, thrilling flash of un-

---

7   Maslow believes that actually to fulfill self-actualization needs one would probably have to be at least in his late thirties or early forties. Hence, as self-actualization is referred to in the following the thought is "steps toward self-actualization."

derstanding. When it will occur, and why no one can say. A sequential approach, producing anxiety and desire to appease the teacher by "right answers," may block it and usually does. A random approach, without pressure, without timetable, will achieve a desired understanding far more certainly, and probably sooner.[8]

The urge for self-actualization becomes prepotent *after* other more basic needs have been satisfied, at least in part. There must have been some success in achieving goals that are real and important to the individual. There must have been parent, peer, and teacher approval of behavior and accomplishments. There must have been considerable evidence of faith in the individual so that he can feel free to act on his own and assume responsibility.

Craig asked his counselor for suggestions for a college where he could combine the study of mathematics and science with the opportunity for participation in college symphonic music. The counselor asked what his father, a teacher, thought about college choice, and Craig said, "We just talk about it, but my dad rarely expresses opinions on my major decisions. He will refuse permission for me to go out if I've been on the go too much, but choosing a college is my job. That's why I come to you." The boy indicated that he had applied for an American Field Service Scholarship. He had not yet told his parents about this application.

It was later learned that Craig did go to Germany for part of his senior year. While in Germany, he was elected president of his class (he returned before his term of office started). Besides participating in school politics, he was active in musical activities and publications and maintained his honor-roll status.

Much later, the author talked with the parents about Craig and discovered the following: They planned *not* to make decisions for him. He readily got the clarinet and saxophone he decided he wanted, and he used them effectively. The parents regularly attended the school activities in which he engaged when they were open to the public. It was also learned that the summer before Craig went to Germany, he conducted his own symphony orchestra composed of about twenty classmates and chosen instrumentalists from other high schools. Playing was the sole objective. The following summer, he led a group of eight students who met weekly to give, listen to, and react to book reviews. Craig had the nerve to apply at only one college (Harvard)—he was selected and made the Dean's list his first semester.

Studies of achievement motivation show many factors at work—success, special aptitudes, anxiety and fear of failure, external incentives, etc.,—and among

---

8   Leslie A. Hart, 1969, "Learning at Random," *Saturday Review*, vol. 52, no. 16, p. 63, April 19.

them are parental attitudes. Achievement motivation tends to be high when parents have high aspirations for themselves and when they stress independence and excellence from their children. Dominant and demanding parents, however, tend to overwhelm the pupil to the point where he shuns involvement (Ausubel, 1968, p. 398).

Alfred was called to attention by a college admissions officer who wanted to know whether the boy could be accepted as a risk or a challenge. Alfred's reports showed that he had made a fair record in high school but had flunked out of two Western colleges and one in the East. His aptitude tests were encouraging. A call to his former high school principal offered a clue to his ineptitude. The mother was a constant source of irritation to his high school teachers. She selected Alfred's courses, she determined the amount of homework he was to do, she approved or disapproved (generally disapproved) his choice of girl friends, and she selected his school activity program. She had frequent conferences with college professors and deans about how Alfred could be helped. This had involved two plane trips in one semester for conferences in the East. The case was a challenge. The admissions officer made an appointment with the boy, who came *with his mother*. An interview was held with the mother alone; at this time she was told, "Perhaps something can be done. But Alfred must make up his mind for himself. He must freely choose to make this fourth try at college. If *he does not so choose*, it will be best to forget it. The courses, the hours of study, the activities he pursues must be his own choices." It was not counseling, it was brutally frank advice, and the mother was told, "It is your fault." The mother verbally agreed, but as she departed she said, "Well, I'll talk with him and see if I can't get him to settle down."

From the very beginning of their school experiences, pupils should make *some* of their own choices. It should be realized that self-chosen pursuits are more powerful motivators than those imposed or selected by the teacher. It has been found, for instance, that children resist being interrupted when doing self-selected tasks while they will readily abandon those selected by the teacher. One teacher intentionally interrupted children when their drawing of a picture was partially completed. She found that while the pupils were disturbed by arbitrary interruptions at any time, they were more disturbed and more determined to go ahead with what they were doing when they were drawing what they had chosen than when they had been told what to draw. "Do your own thing" is a motto and policy for many of today's adolescents. They want to establish their autonomy, and they disavow relationships with the "establishment." Many encounter difficulty because of their search for identity and the need to be in style with their peers (Halleck, 1969). The problem of these adolescents and their teachers is to become aware of the difficult lesson that life is not always (or even frequently) easy; and that ease and self-actualization are not synonymous.

As pupils make thrusts for self-actualization they must learn, through consistent discipline and firm direction, the boundaries of their activities and the penalties for exceeding them. It must be realized that motivation is an individual matter. This means that *a numberless variety of experiences must be provided in the school if an appeal is to be made to individuals.*

Fundamental needs constitute one theoretical basis for motivation. This has been at least partially validated by experimental evidence, clinical experience, and observation, which indicate five basic drives: physiological needs, safety needs, belongingness needs, esteem needs, and the need for self-actualization. Some of the practical and time-honored approaches to motivation will now be examined to see whether they accord with theory.

Motivational Techniques in Terms of Needs Theory

Some Basic Considerations

Theoretically, if an individual had no needs, he would have reached a state of homeostasis. No such state is known to exist for human beings. Maslow's theory avoids this issue by suggesting that need satisfaction at one level merely makes possible need pursuit at a higher level. It seems that human beings are by nature perverse—as soon as current wants are satisfied, a new order of wants emerges. The practical aim for educators is to approach the satisfaction of needs or to ensure that needs are on the way to being satisfied. If the child feels that progress is not being made toward need satisfaction, he will fight or flee, either psychologically (symbolically) or actually. If progress is being made toward need satisfaction, he will be motivated to exert effort in the expansion of knowledge and development of potential.

Some motivational techniques will be successful because they are in close accord with natural growth tendencies; others will be successful because they accord with needs that have emerged as a result of cultural accommodation. Some approaches to motivation will fail because they are inappropriate in terms of the individual's experiences and to the level at which his needs are functioning.

Rewards

Motivational techniques may be considered to be successful when the outcome is the development of pupil interest. **Interest** is the feeling that what one studies or does has some personal significance. A widespread misconception among those preparing to teach as well as among experienced teachers is that ideally pupils should study only those things in which they are interested. This misconception contributed to the downfall of progressive education (Goodlad, 1968). The fact is that interests are built as the *result* of contact, experience, success, information, and familiarity. Teachers have the job of setting the stage for the *development* of interests as well as capitalizing on those which exist. But it is clear that an educational program cannot function entirely upon the existence of intrinsic motivations (Smith, 1967, p. 66).

Rewards may be either symbolic (gold stars, medals, or honor rolls), material (a piece of candy, a sum of money, or the right to participate in student activities or to hold office), or psychological (knowledge of progress, recognition of adequacy or growth toward adequacy). Rewards, by ensuring safety, indicating esteem, and leading to belongingness, have their place in motivating the pupil in his *initial* contacts with an area of knowledge. Because contact is required to build an interest in an activity, idea, or person, rewards are commendable in the role of making introductions. Some psychologists and educators frown on rewards because *they too frequently become ends in themselves.* The hazard of confusing reward and knowledge is illustrated in the conversation of a father and son. The father had suggested to his mathematically capable son that he study a college text in trigonometry along with his high school text and got the response, "Well, Dad, you can't do any better than an A." Bruner (1961), Goodlad (1967), and Glasser (1969) are among a growing number of authorities who believe that rewards in the form of grades tend to encourage conformity, stifle creativity, and to confuse the symbols of education with the products and process of education.

If there is no motivation for continued activity after the reward has been won, we are stopping short of motivation for self-actualization. Extrinsic motivation arises from factors outside the individual, whereas intrinsic motivation relates to the general personality of the individual and his **identification** with an activity. It is possible that extrinsic rewards (high marks, parental approbation, helping the class or school gain a good reputation) may lead to intrinsic motivation. That is, the knowledge gained may become of interest (intrinsic) to the individual, and further knowledge may be pursued after the extrinsic motivators have waned or ceased to exist. We hope that this generation of functional autonomy will occur routinely, but too often effort wanes as soon as the lure of the extrinsic reward is removed.

Rewards for learning should be so engineered that, after serving their introductory roles, they lead pupils to independent learning and to learning activities beyond the classroom. The teacher must be careful to emphasize to the pupil his newly gained competence, his increased knowledge, and his improved social skills and status. The reward of saying "I can do it" is more important than the symbolic status of a good grade or a certificate of completion.

Grades and Marks

When grades are based on interpersonal comparisons of academic achievement, some pupils will inevitably earn a "respectable" grade too easily and develop habits of superficiality, conformity, and dilatoriness; others will develop feelings of inferiority and discouragement toward their schoolwork. Because about 25 percent of pupils in elementary and secondary schools receive 75 percent of the failing grades, the stage is set for their becoming dropouts (Goodlad, 1967).

> I believe that the kind of education offered (relevance and thinking) and the way it is offered (involvement) have much more to do with incentive than grades. When school offers little material that is relevant and requires little more than memorization, grades provide incentive for some students who get A's and B's; for those who do not get B or better, however, grades are a signal to give up. Those who get C or below consider themselves failures and stop working. They become part of the large group (in my estimate, over 50 percent in an average secondary school) who are learning very little.
>
> Because grades emphasize failure much more than success and because failure is the basis of almost all school problems, I recommend a system of reporting a student's progress that totally eliminates failure. That is, *I suggest that no student ever at any time be labeled a failure or led to believe he is a failure through the use of the grading system.* As stated above, a student who believes he is a failure usually refuses to work in school. Because failure is never motivating, when we eliminate failure we cannot harm a child who is failing under the present grading system. Although he may not suddenly start learning when we stop labeling him a failure, at least we leave the door open for a change of heart later on when he may wish to start working and learning. If we label him a failure, often even once, there is less chance that he will ever start to learn.[9]

There are those who, frankly admitting that grades have no psychologically sound basis in terms of motivation, believe that grades serve the purpose of assessing progress, especially for those who will go to college. The fact is that high school grades do correlate rather highly with college grades (Monday, 1970). Critics of the grading system would say, "Of course." The same factors of halo effect, pleasing teachers, conformity of the students, skills in memorization, unreliability, and teacher bias work in college as well as high school. The important thing is that grades in high school and college do *not* correlate nearly so well with

---

9   William Glasser, 1969, *Schools without Failure*, New York: Harper and Row, Publishers, pp. 95-96.

success in life as they do in predicting more success in academic pursuits. It is also interesting to note that where grades have been eliminated in college, including work in medical schools, the students have learned as well as those who work in grading milieus. In addition, they look back at their medical preparation with satisfaction instead of loathing (Glasser, 1969, p. 68).

The prosthetic devices for the extirpation of grades are already *at hand and in use* in the better classrooms. These include such things as a feeling of belongingness, mutual esteem of teachers and pupils, and exercise of one's heterostatic impulses in growth toward self-actualization. Immediate feedback provides the kind of sustaining motivation that grades, as a terminal assessment, never can. This feedback may take the form of (1) progress in daily work, (2) suggested next steps, (3) how to improve this report, (4) what error was made, (5) display of the pupil's work, (6) pupils' helping one another, and (7) employment of varied learning avenues to provide for different learning styles.

Success and Levels of Aspiration

The term **level of aspiration** refers to the level of performance to which one aspires in the future because of his success or failure in preceding tasks. It is closely related to the concept which an individual has about himself and his prowess. *What an individual aspires to do next is dependent on what he perceives to be possible for him* (Smith, 1967, p. 68). The teacher is largely responsible for designing the level of difficulty, but only the pupil can determine how vigorously he will tackle the task. Level of aspiration is somewhat dependent upon intelligence, socioeconomic status (Borow, 1966), and on parental relationships and expectations; but the dominating factor seems to be a relatively greater proportion of success over failure experience. An appropriate level of aspiration is one which keeps the individual striving but which is such as to give some promise of goal attainment. Some pupils fail and then refuse to try again. Others fail and set high goals—apparently they do not hope to gain the goal but hope that teachers will give them credit for having heart. Pupils who succeed typically will set next goals that call for exertion but which promise victory as the result of that effort. There are ways in which teachers can implement the principle that *goals should be attainable and pupils should feel that they are able to achieve them:*

> Test data help the teacher to form a valid estimate of the pupil's potential and the appropriate goals.
> The pupil's behavior provides clues: If the goal is too high, he will be tense or show withdrawal tendencies; if the goal is appropriate, he will proceed cheerfully and confidently to the job at hand.
> A study of the child's past record (results of standardized achievement tests and samples of past work in cumulative folders) provides information that helps the teacher to synchronize ability and aspiration.

The pupil should be allowed to voice his feelings about the appropriateness of the tasks.

A succession of developmental lessons that will stimulate each child to work close to his *presently indicated* level of ability should be planned. Teachers should make special efforts to prevent above-average and gifted children from being satisfied with mediocrity. Appropriate praise, personally significant goals, the equitable distribution of success, and teacher-pupil evaluations can help in the establishment of appropriate levels of aspiration and urge pupils toward self-actualization. Strom (1969) places emphasis on (1) pupil responsibility, (2) guidance, (3) peer pressure, and (4) community influences in raising youth's aspirations.

Explanations for the motivational character of learned drives include conditioning, tension reduction as the result of goal achievement, and the power of verbal stimuli to evoke muscular and emotional response. *Schoolwork must be sufficiently varied and paced so that every pupil has a chance to succeed at his level.* Success may come through a variety of experiences—not just the academic—if the pupil and key adults set a high value on them. Providing these varied opportunities for success thus accords with the needs for esteem, belonging, and for a degree of self-actualization.

School success, dropouts, population explosion, unemployment and obsolescence of laboring jobs, and educational relevance are all parts of one package. Dropouts are fewer today than they have been in any previous year or decade, yet concern about them is higher than ever. It is, among other things, a matter of so many teen-agers (3.8 million reaching the age of eighteen in 1965 as against 2.8 million reaching that age in 1964—and the high number continues). It is a matter of high unemployment among those below the age of twenty-one and the fact that those with nothing to do and without significance become "social dynamite." School has not been hospitable to all youth (Kirp, 1968), and the challenge to psychology, education, and politics is clear: Schools must provide opportunity for success for all who are reasonably to be expected to remain in school and profit from the experiences available. The historical alternate routes—going to work, going West—have been rapidly and markedly diminished.

Curriculum changes will help. Understanding teachers are essential. Varied opportunities and materials are helpful. But the main ingredient is success. The pupil needs the success of being part of the school, i.e., being in school activities. He needs the success of human acceptance, and he needs to have nonpromotion and failure eliminated as a means of curriculum adjustment. He needs the success of making progress which is discernible and commended.

Praise

The ability to praise is largely a matter of a personal orientation that causes one to see others clearly and to understand them. As soon as the teacher is able to perceive—in addition to academic achievement—humor, leadership, curiosity, independence, artistic aptitudes, a ready smile, the ability to "bounce back," and other valuable human traits, he can begin to answer the needs for esteem, belongingness, and self-actualization. Some teachers chronically find occasions for criticism, while others take such joy in contacts with pupils that praise is almost second nature. Thus it is not surprising to find that the effectiveness of praise depends upon the person giving it as well as upon the person receiving it. As might be expected from examination of the hierarchical needs of safety and esteem, anxious and dependent pupils are most likely to respond to praise (Marx and Tombaugh, 1967, p. 214). Teachers should note the effect of praise and blame on individual pupils. Some can be commended for relatively minor accomplishments because of their limited ability, but others will be motivated only by praise for genuinely noteworthy accomplishments related to their high ability. It should be noted that praise (or approval) can be indicated nonverbally—a nod, a smile, placing one's hand on the pupil's shoulders, or merely stopping long enough to take a good look at what is being done may express the sentiment. Intermittent or occasional comments are as likely to effect favorable action as those given frequently.

Censure

Experimental evidence indicates that blame or reproof is a positive incentive in some cases. It is best to use it sparingly and when it is deserved, which involves knowing the individual upon whom it is used. Blame, when used on retiring students, appears to reinforce existing feelings of inadequacy and therefore threatens safety and dampens motivation. Extroverts, on the other hand, accomplish less when praised than when they are blamed.

The successful use of praise or blame depends upon the student and his needs and prior experiences. The implication for teachers is that they should watch the effects of praise or blame on the individual student, the frequency with which each can be used, and their own feelings when each type of **verbal reinforcement** is employed. Being ignored provides less motivation than either praise or blame. The need for recognition is active in most pupils.

Competition and Cooperation

Rivalry is a potent incentive under certain conditions but can be destructive under others. It is not stimulating to either the winner or the loser to compete out of his class. Competitors should have some chance of winning; *competition should involve a degree of equality among contestants.* Even when there is some equality of competitors, teachers should stress friendly rivalry rather than rivalry that breeds interpersonal antagonism. There are three kinds of effective rivalry:

1. Interpersonal competition among peers often encourages spirited rivalry.
2. Group competition where each member can make a contribution and is involved in the group's success is a strong motivator.
3. Competition with oneself, with one's previous record, can be effective and is recommended.

The needs for self-actualization, for approval, for belongingness, and for safety indicate that cooperation, at least as a learned response, is as strong an incentive as is competition. There are many who believe that society is "fiercely competitive" and that children must learn to compete ruthlessly in order to survive. Others point out that no society can afford indiscriminate competition because cooperation is the main function and most basic form of intergroup relationships (Lowry and Rankin, 1969, p. 179).

Depending somewhat on how it is managed by teachers, competition may stimulate effort on the part of those who seek esteem and see in competition a chance to get it. Competitors who are weak in the area concerned will have both their safety and esteem needs denied. It has been found that gaining high scores on tests may be stimulated by both competition and cooperation. Competition provides excellent opportunities for learning to adjust to social realities and hence to the gaining of esteem and belongingness. Cooperation, involving skills from many pupils, merits more frequent emphasis because the outcomes are more closely in accord with the stated purposes of education and our dominant social philosophy.

Knowledge of Progress (Feedback)

The factor of feedback is so important in motivation that a whole system of teaching is based on it; namely, machine teaching or computer-assisted instruction (CAI) in which the learner has immediate knowledge of how he is doing. He knows whether he is right or wrong because the machine provides immediate feedback. Skinner (1969) has been a leader among those who have espoused this approach to learning. He contends that speaking of traits, virtues, abilities, and the like tends to make the nature of man inexplicable; but recording the results of reinforcement or feedback causes behavior to be understandable. Continuous reinforcement means that every correct response is rewarded. Schedules of reinforcement mean that periodically (say every tenth time or after the elapse of a certain period of time) correct responses are rewarded. The effectiveness of CAI is, among other things, dependent on feedback. CAI is not the panacea for all problems of education, but it does provide an approach to the needs of some individual learners (Stolurow, 1969, pp. 270ff).

Teachers provide feedback in touching a child's shoulder, smiling approval, or using such words as "Good," "Fine," "How about *that*?" They may also provide a confusing kind of feedback when their remarks about pupils and behavior are predominately adverse.

Goals may be used as feedback, especially when pupils help formulate them. If the goals are stated by committees, feedback is involved in discussing the extent to which pupils clearly understand and accept them. A corollary to the value of clear goals is that *pupils' knowledge of their progress toward those goals is an extremely effective form of motivation.* Knowledge of results, in some form, has been shown experimentally to facilitate motivation and improve content mastery. Criticism is better than being ignored. Remarks from a teacher are more beneficial than from someone less intimately concerned with the learning process. Feedback provides additional insights into the meaning of goals. Delayed feedback is, in some instances, better than immediate knowledge of results (Sassenrath and Yonge, 1968).

A revealing incident regarding knowledge of progress concerns the work of a teacher who enjoyed a sound reputation in the community. She had been hired as a replacement for another teacher who, in the principal's estimate, was excellent—the pupils did well on standardized tests, behaved well, and seemed to enjoy school. But parents complained that pupils were not learning. The replacement teacher seemed no more effective than the former, but parents were enthusiastic. Asked what the key to her success was, she answered, "I wonder if it is because the last few minutes each day I ask the pupils to discuss what we have learned today."

Praise is the most readily available technique for keeping pupils informed of their progress. Teacher-pupil conferences have been found to be particularly effective, especially at the upper-grade and secondary levels. Charts of progress can be used in many subjects. Workbooks, if not used too steadily and as busy work, tend to keep the student informed of his progress. Such techniques are advantageous because the time intervals between evaluations are short and tend to stress continuous evaluation rather than an end-of-term grade.

Novelty

The drive toward self-actualization leads pupils to relish the new and the different. Their need for safety causes them to appreciate routine and regularity. Hence, novelty must be introduced in the context of the familiar. The motivation derived from visiting an industrial plant will be greater if the pupils are subject to familiar rules of order and courtesy or if the visit is made in company with their classmates and regular teacher. Novelty has merit when the teacher points out the relationship between the new and the already known, uses familiar procedures, and himself shows enthusiasm for the expansion of knowledge into new areas. Many previously indifferent pupils have been spurred to activity when the teacher says, "I don't know the answer and we should know. Kathy, will you look it up for us, please?" Interest is often sustained or revived by variation in the teacher's technique. Novelty may explain many instances in which an experimental technique seems superior to the older method—the variety, rather than the technique, is the motivator of extra effort. The **Hawthorne effect** is in part due to the factor of novelty.

Other Motivational Techniques

Such factors as are mentioned above, novelty, feedback, competition, success, for example, are conventionally dealt with in the discussion of motivation. There are numerous other factors that have motivational effects. Peer groups, especially in the adolescent years, do much to influence the degree of application to, or disdain for, school-designated tasks. Team teaching, which exposes pupils to different teacher personalities, tends to prevent the alienation of those students who are involved in a specific teacher-pupil conflict. Nongraded organization, which provides a framework for eliminating the worst aspects of unfair competition, merits consideration. Audiovisual aids are a source of motivation, especially for those whose preferred learning style is observing, imitation, and accepting.

The Challenge of Developmental Tasks

Inevitably, the concerns and approaches to education must spring from the cultural, economic, political, and seasonal situation of the time. But educators must extend their concerns about the past and present to include what should desirably happen in the future. Schools and colleges should be responsible for the initiation of change (Heilbroner, 1970). *Effective educational programs are those that meet the current and probable future needs of children and youth.* Another perspective is supplied in the concept of developmental tasks.

The Concept of Developmental Tasks

Robert J. Havighurst, of the University of Chicago Committee on Human Development, is among those who have promoted the idea of **developmental tasks**. These tasks have their roots partly in basic and learned needs and partly in the demands of culture. The concept checks the tendency to study the individual apart from his environment and takes functional cognizance of the fact that one must live in a social world. A developmental task is a responsibility imposed by society and by growth phenomena. Instead of saying "Life is just one darn thing after another," it would be more accurate to say "Life is just one developmental task after another." That is, more and different things are required of a child than of a baby, more of an adolescent than of a child—even in one's declining years, new developmental tasks must be faced.

Developmental tasks are obligations that arise during a broadly defined period of life. The successful performance of these tasks leads to happiness and subsequent successful achievement; failure leads to personal unhappiness and disapproval by society, as well as to difficulty with later tasks. This concept indicates the age at which particular demands become most insistent, and it draws attention to the requirements of society.

Developmental Tasks as Motivation

It is easy to conceive of motivation as something that propels or pushes an individual in a given direction. But it must also be thought of as a force within the individual that prompts him to strive for goals or a force which predisposes him to be pulled toward certain objects and actions. Affects—feelings, excitement, desire—rather than drives are the primary motives (Tomkins, 1967, p. 55). In fact, drives without affects lose much of their potency. Just as a plant growing in a partially darkened room will send its shoots toward the sources of light, a human being is drawn toward a particular objective or activity. This phenomenon has been referred to by various authorities who use such words as hormic, teleological, heterostatic, directional growth, and becoming.

When considering *basic human needs* it is sometimes easy to forget pupil differences. The concept of developmental tasks helps to maintain perspective. For example, in the materials below, it appears that developmental tasks differ somewhat in the various social classes of the overall American culture. The readiness of a pupil to undertake his next developmental tasks depends upon his previous experiences, including his social contacts; thus motivation will be easier for the teacher if he takes note of differences in native endowment, personal experience, and cultural pressures.

Developmental Tasks of School Pupils

The completion of developmental tasks may be thought of as forward thrusts in growth. As each task is completed, the person may coast along rather easily on a plateau until his growth brings him to the next rise (or task) in his development (Havighurst, 1952, p. 120). In general it can be said that *the problem of motivation is simplified when the methods and approaches of the teacher accord with the biological, psychological, and cultural bases of the tasks.* The concept of developmental tasks is illustrated below by listing those of middle childhood and adolescence and indicating the detail with which all tasks may be considered by citing one example from childhood and one from adolescence.[11]

---

11   For important details and additional significant educational implications, see Robert J. Havighurst, 1952, *Developmental Tasks and Education*, London: Longmans, Green & Co., Ltd. Data for this presentation are used with permission of the publisher.

Developmental Tasks of Middle Childhood (About 6 to 12 Years)

Learning physical skills for games
Building wholesome attitudes toward self
Learning to get along with peers
Learning an appropriate sex role
Biological basis: There is little sex difference in the early part of middle childhood, but the later part shows clear distinctions.
Psychological basis: Parents, other key adults, and siblings have taught boys to behave as boys and girls to behave as girls. Parental identification is an important conditioning factor.
Cultural basis: A fighter is admired in lower social classes, but the middle-class boy is expected to fight only in self-defense.
Curricular import: The function of the school is probably that of providing models. To this end, teachers' basic encounter groups will help teachers understand how they come across to others; because, like it or not, they are models—to be imitated or repudiated. A greater portion of men teachers in the early grades would seem to be desirable.
Learning to read, write, and calculate
Developing concepts necessary for everyday living
Developing a scale of values

Developmental Tasks of Adolescence (About 12 to 18 Years)

Accepting physique and sex role
Learning to become men and women—new relations with peers of both sexes
Developing emotional independence from parents
Achieving assurance of economic independence
Selecting and preparing for an occupation
Biological basis: The achievement of adult size and strength in the latter part of the period prepares the individual for the task.
Psychological basis: Social expectations and the adolescent's interests predispose him to occupational study and planning.
Cultural basis: The working role is most important in American society. The choice of a career is difficult in the upper and middle classes, but simply getting a job suffices in the lower class.
Curricular import: The school should (1) take responsibility for vocational guidance, (2) provide general education in a vocational setting, and (3) help those with academic talents and nascent academic talents set individual goals which demand effort, reaching and stretching—where the goal is self-realization rather than competitive superiority.

Developing skills and concepts for civic competence
Desiring and achieving socially responsible behavior
Preparing for marriage and for family life
Building values and ethics harmonious with science

It is difficult but not impossible to give attention to the individuality of developmental tasks. Mouly (1968, p. 152) suggests that pupils typically do not need to be pushed over every hurdle—an occasional bit of guidance and human support will suffice. Teachers need to develop enough faith in pupils so that pupils are allowed "some rope"—autonomy, in good pedagese—to experiment, improvise, and explore. Independent study, small group work, programmed lessons *for individual needs*, are ways in which individuality has been recognized by teachers who believe in their pupils.

The Role of Interest

The Nature of Interest

Interest may be defined as the focusing of the sense organs on, or giving attention to, some person, activity, situation, or object. It may be a temporary or permanent feeling in which a preference is present. It is an outcome of experience—not a gift—and is at one time both result and cause of motivation. Too many teachers look only for the presence or absence of interest and condemn the student whose interest is low or lacking. Equally extreme is the view that pupils should study only those things in which they are "interested." When teachers recognize that interest stems from personally challenging tasks and some degree of success in their pursuit, they will assume some responsibility for its creation and development (Maccoby, 1971). Strong interest creates a drive that will lead to organization of efforts in the consistent seeking of a goal. The strength of such drive is partly dependent upon endocrine functioning, physical stamina, and endurance, but it is also dependent on experiences that have resulted in some need satisfaction. Interest is conditioned by groups, such as family and peers, in which the pupil functions in his out-of-school life (Gilliom, 1969). When teachers "make a subject interesting," they present the study in terms of the pupils' perceptions.

Miss Argyll brought to her seventh grade a record of Chinese music, some trinkets, a jewel, a brass bell, some lanterns, and a silk robe. After her oral presentation, the pupils were allowed to look at and handle the materials. Many questions were asked, some of which were answered by other pupils and some by the teacher with "We'll see." Pupils told about Chinese objects they had at home—some had been sent or brought back by older siblings or relatives who had traveled overseas. Plans for developing the unit were discussed (personal involvement), and various projects were suggested. Some of the projects would require considerable reading and research. The difficult projects held the possibility of high grades and were to be presented before the class as a whole. Not all the pupils undertook to do the more difficult tasks. Some were quite content to work on foil facsimiles of jewel boxes. Others made lanterns. The more ambitious pupils read encyclopedias and advanced reference books in preparing reports on the economic and social conditions of coastal China. All the students participated in some way in the final project, which consisted of a Chinese dinner to which parents and friends were invited and at which the local Chinese consul was the speaker. Reference materials for the unit ranged from books that could be read by average second graders to books that would have been respectable sources for a college student. On three visits, the author noticed one boy copying a wall chart. According to the teacher, the boy had still not learned to read, but found satisfaction in his responsibility for copying a sign that was to be placed over one of the displays at the dinner.

The Influence of Goals

Without goals, man can and often does wander aimlessly. Many diversions and temporarily attractive activities interfere with self-actualization. Because goals give direction to action, they must be of genuine concern to educational psychology. Pupils' perceptions and acceptance of goals are thus central problems in education.

To bring into being responsible citizenship, five goals will still remain important for each of those six and one-half million babies expected to be born in 1980 as contrasted with the four million born during 1966: (1) to learn about self and seek self-realization; (2) to learn about others and the art of human relations; (3) to learn about economic life, so one may be fed, clothed, and sheltered; (4) to learn about organized man and his civic responsibility because organized resources—government, if you please—make it more certain that self-preservation becomes possible; and finally, (5) to learn to battle the elements with attendant successes and failures, and thus to become a philosopher to contemplate the purpose of things.

As a human constant, man's biology in the upcoming period may be tinkered with, hopefully for his benefit. However, along with Poor Richard, he will learn that "Dame Experience keeps a dear school, but a fool will learn in no other." His basic urges will be the same as those of his forebears as well as of his peers. He will need adventure, love, security, motivation, and success. He will be confronted, as have all those who went before him, with three big decisions—marriage, jobs, and leisure. [12]

Other statements of goals for education will differ in wording and minor details; the main thing is for pupils and teachers to realize that education should be designed to facilitate the achievement of these or similar goals. Maslow (1969) emphasizes the fact that goals rather than external pressures determine the course of one's life. It is futile, he says, to claim that one becomes a good physician by chance and fortuitous circumstances. It is futile to believe that overpopulation, pollution, and racial animosity are anything other than a revelation of man's reluctance to set these as goals of his behaviors.

Much of the teacher's effectiveness depends on his own perception of educational goals and his ability to clarify them for pupils. *There should be less emphasis on the child's pleasing the teacher and adapting himself to the system and more emphasis on the formulation of goals that accord with individual children's needs and each one's place on the continuum of developmental tasks.* This involves the teacher's knowing himself, his perception of the nature of man, and his perception of the worth and status of pupils. To implement these notions requires some drastic innovations in education—and the starting point for such applied innovations is teacher self-examination in basic encounter groups ("Carl Rogers Joins . . .," 1970).

Goals increase the probability that one will navigate rather than drift. Goals influence the degree to which one will pursue individual aims and values and the extent to which he will be responsive to group needs and wishes. Goals help in evaluating the relative importance or unimportance of alternative activities. They lend power to ongoing activities. But the goals must be clear and individualized to be most effective. Teacher-pupil planning is relatively ineffective if the plans are filed away only to be brought out when the supervisor visits. *There must be periodic reexamination of the extent to which goals are being realized, and there must be plans for the next steps toward their achievement.* Should any teacher feel that this is a time-consuming process, let him answer the question, "How much time is wasted in trying to force pupils to reach teacher goals that are neither understood nor accepted?" (see the example of Pedro, Chapter 14). Establishing and keeping in mind a number of goals is not easy, but it is a wild delusion to believe that an orderly class of thirty pupils are learning the same thing or even learning *about* the things the teacher has in mind. The things we know best about motivation are the differences between students. If the teacher understands such differences, uses materials that are appropriate to these differences, and permits each child some freedom for growth toward his unique self-

12   Paul A. Miller, 1967, "Major Implications for Education of Prospective Changes in Society: One Perspective," in E. L. Morphet and C. O. Ryan (eds.), *Implications for Education of Prospective Changes in Society*, Denver: Designing Education for the Future, p. 4.

actualization, he is providing the basis for immediate and effective motivation. More important still, he will be providing the kind of motivation that leads the pupil repeatedly to the fountain of knowledge.

Summary

Evidence continuously accumulates indicating that human beings have potentials far greater than are used. Failure to fulfill promises is attributed, in large measure, to inadequate or improper motivation. Basic needs, developmental tasks, pursuit of personal interests or unique heterostatic urges have been used as theoretical bases for contriving teaching-learning situations which are "motivated."

Of many lists of needs, one postulated by Maslow is particularly helpful because it provides an explanation for the relative importance of a specific need, at a certain time, for an individual person. That is, as low-order needs approach fulfillment, a higher-order need assumes priority. The low-order physiological needs, when fulfilled, lead next to safety needs, to belongingness and love, to esteem, and finally to the high-order need of self-actualization.

Implications for classroom teachers are somewhat as follows:

Arithmetic or reading tends not to be an important activity to the child who is hungry, who suffers an untreated sensory handicap, who is cold, whose clothes do not fit, or who suffers from chronic illness.

Arithmetic or reading for pupils functioning at the safety level can be more effectively pursued when there is the order of routine, regulations, system and sequence, and disciplined activity.

Pupils at the higher levels may be able to handle independence and freedom and pursue individually contrived lessons in reading and arithmetic because they are accepted and trusted.

Pupils functioning at the esteem level need still more trust so they can develop their unique talents and achieve their kudos and respect for their distinctive products or contributions.

Respect for the individual, the teacher's study of his interests, and encouragement will help him on the first steps toward self-actualization.

The concept of developmental tasks also provides a point of reference. By studying the individual child and the developmental tasks typically facing children of his age, clues may be discovered as to what he is striving to achieve in his peer relations, in his home life, and in adapting to the broader culture.

The individual is not endowed with interests; they develop as the result of contact, familiarity, personal challenge, and the experience of success. The teacher can implement the growth of interest by being enthusiastic, clarifying goals, and developing his own trust in the pupil's urge to learn. The big challenge in using interest as an approach to motivation is for teachers to achieve enough faith in themselves that they can trust pupils to learn significant things which are not necessarily prescribed in a syllabus—things which prompt learning to continue in and beyond the school years.

Suggested Additional Readings

CRONBACH, LEE J., 1967, "How Can Instruction Be Adapted to Individual Differences?" in Robert M. Gagné (ed.), *Learning and Individual Differences*, Columbus, Ohio: Charles E. Merrill Books, Inc.

> Most school tactics ". . . are intended to minimize the nuisance of individual differences . . ." It is time we thought enough of individual differences to seek them out and use them as points of departure for instruction.

MACCOBY, MICHAEL, 1971, "The Three C's and Discipline for Freedom," *School Review*, vol. 79, pp. 227-242.

> There is an indivisibility of knowledge—hence the objection to breaking the school day into periods. Maccoby shows that motivation and teaching-learning processes are also indivisible. He recommends concentration (hard work), communication (dialogue), and criticism (questioning stereotypes) as ways to enliven education.

MARX, MELVIN H., AND TOM N. TOMBAUGH, 1967, *Motivation*, San Francisco: Chandler Publishing Company.

> This paperback reviews research but builds interest by citing frequent classroom implications. The student might page through the book to see if a particular chapter appeals to him. But stop at the last chapter to read about progressive education, Montessori System programmed learning, "teaching typewriters," and creativity.

MASLOW, A. H., 1969, "Toward a Humanistic Biology," *American Psychologist*, vol. 24, pp. 724-735.

> The reader will have to work at keeping in mind that this article is about biology rather than psychology. Perhaps the author intended to show that the aims of biology and psychology are the same: A better, value-oriented, person.

10

Emotions in
the Classroom

Some people carry the emotional over-
burdens of childhood throughout their life; some children certainly carry similar
overburdens from home to school. Others "trip lightly" through life and school
buoyed up by another congeries of emotions. It may be that the teacher's and
pupils' ability to understand, control, and direct emotions would be the single
most productive factor in vastly improving learning efficiency. The anonymous
individual who said that "the intellect is a mere speck afloat upon a sea of feeling" was a wise psychologist. We should like to believe that man's action is
directed by thought processes, but an examination of the evidence leads inevitably to the conclusion that emotion is a dominating factor. Otto (1969), along
with several other life scientists, presents the intriguing challenge that man's
brain is grossly underused in terms of creating new things and solving old problems. The reason no better use is made of latent capacity is we are continuously
blocked by conflict, negative emotional conditions, and pathological concerns.
Teachers who recognize the partnership of emotion and intellectual development and social facilitation have taken a large step toward accomplishing the
basic objectives of education—pupil self-realization and the continuous search for
knowledge. Such teachers will aim at greater emotional maturity for schoolchildren, consisting of (1) inhibition of emotions that deter development, (2) cultivation of higher tolerance for disagreeable circumstance and conflict, and (3) enhancement of the emotions that facilitate social and intellectual efficiency.

The Nature of Emotions

Emotion—An Elusive Concept

The word "emotion" is so vague and inclusive that some psychologists would like to eliminate its use. Emotion has been defined as an upset state of the organism. Emotions may range from hate, terror, and despair, which result in fight, flight, or behavior immobility, to mild positive emotions such as affection and attention. In between are such "stirred up" conditions as interest, romantic love, ambition, and zeal. Physiological functioning in these emotions leads to a feeling of euphoria, which in turn may lead to the improved welfare of self and others. "Emotion" may mean a rather transitory state, such as brief attention, or an enduring interest that drives an individual toward a difficult goal. It may mean a relatively mild feeling, such as friendliness toward a peer; an intense feeling, such as a paralyzing fear during a riot or bombing; or even the chronic anxiety produced by threat of school failure.

Emotions are much more inclusive than overt behavior. The important factor is the inner feeling that stimulates a certain activity or creates a predisposition to engage in the activity. There is a frequently cited, though oversimplifed, definition: Emotion is a feeling state (affective experience) accompanying an upset condition of the organism. It is a stirred-up state of the mental and physical aspects of the individual.

The broad implications of the above are that pupils should be helped to control emotions that are detrimental to progress and enhance emotions that are constructive. Teachers are important members of the "health professions" as they seek to develop high-level "wellness." The common aim of teachers, physicians, and those in the mental health professions is more than bringing about a freedom from illness; it is to promote ways of living that will maximize the chances for the individual to achieve his potential (Maslow, 1968*a*).

Physiological Aspects of Emotion

W. B. Cannon (1929) formulated what is sometimes known as the emergency theory of emotions. He theorized that emotion has certain physiological aspects which prepare the individual to meet an emergency. These physiological responses include the release of **epinephrine** into the bloodstream. This causes an increased rate in heartbeat, raises the blood pressure, causes more rapid respiration and constriction of the blood vessels on the surface of the body, and makes possible the more rapid coagulation of blood if there is a cut or wound. The flow and function of digestive juices is inhibited. These reactions prepare one for fight or flight to cope with the emergency.

Physiological changes do not cause the emotion, though they are a part of the emotion. Researchers have injected epinephrine into the bloodstream of experimental subjects and reported that some subjects experienced a variety of emotions, others felt no emotion at all, and the remainder said they felt that they were about to have an emotional experience (Cantril, 1932). Thus it becomes evident that a situation is necessary to precipitate the emotion.

Such physiological responses aided ancient man's quest for survival by preparing him for vigorous action, but it is doubtful that these responses are such an advantage to man in civilized society. For instance, when one becomes angry and cannot burn up the extra energy made available to him because present-day custom does not permit getting rid of emotions through violent conflict, a kind of poison is created in his system. Teachers must act upon the knowledge that fear and anger are handicaps to effective learning. Thus we see the physiological justification for avoiding anger-producing shaming and sarcasm. Fear of crucial examinations or punishment should be replaced by more positive means of motivation. Anxiety about status generated by discrimination or by failure to live up to expectations may compound learning problems.

> Earl T. was an upper-grade student who came to the principal's office during a noon hour—he was not sent there. He related how there was nothing he could do to please his teacher. If he spoke up in class, he was answered with sarcasm or scolding. If he kept quiet, he publicly was accused of being stupid. If there were a scuffle, he, the black boy, was immediately to blame and was kept in at recess. Earl ended by saying, "I just ain't learning nuthin'." It would be gratifying if this were the case. However, this unusually insightful and verbal boy was learning something: emotional attitudes toward color, distrust of adults, dislike for school, and over the year, these would become erosive of positive feelings about self.

The teacher who becomes concerned about emotions will need to involve himself in learning about the child's home and community. He will need to practice the difficult art of really listening. If the pupil is worried about family problems, his emotional state will inhibit learning; he may appear to be mentally slow or seem to lack motivation to do the work of which he is capable. The teacher may be helpful by showing the pupil another way of looking at the problems or handicaps. He may arrange a conference with parents to explain the emotional burdens placed on the child. In the past, emphasis in the school has been placed on acquiring knowledge and skill. At present, attention is given to the development of the "whole child." Guidance in the recognition and acknowledgement of feelings, when made an integral part of the teaching-learning transaction will improve the pupil's adjustment and his academic progress (Beatty, 1969a, p. 74).

Marion Bernstein/College Newsphoto Alliance

Cumulative Effects of Stimuli

Stimuli that produce emotion have a cumulative effect. The ebullient energy of children may be gratifying to the teacher early in the day, but the energetic child may be a source of irritation in the afternoon. Similarly, children may be only slightly bothered at first by the insistence of the teacher that they accomplish more in reading, arithmetic, or algebra, but as the pressure continues, their resentment and hostility mount. Pupils may at first be able to cope with the strident demands of an autocratic teacher, but they often find it increasingly difficult to contain their emotion as the demands continue. In counseling sessions when the pupil recalls all the unpleasant things in school, at home, or with peers, this piling up is called the "accumulation of negative experiences."

Minor, cumulative, irritations can be detected by "feedback." This may be accomplished by periodic questionnaires that allow students to check the things they like or dislike about a class or teacher. Typically, these are anonymous. This will not work in the primary grades, but intermediate- and upper-grade pupils make surprisingly incisive evaluations. Brief diaries submitted periodically may focus upon feelings aroused in class activities. Oral gripe sessions may pinpoint some irritations if the teacher can avoid becoming defensive or punitive because of pupils' frankness. Teachers may help pupils take a different attitude toward the disturbing influences through group discussions and individual conferences. School practices that deserve consideration in this connection include overemphasis on grades, competition that involves unequally matched contestants, class sessions requiring pupils to sit still for prolonged periods, class sessions in which there is distracting noise or inadequate lighting, demand for immediate and strict obedience, and the teacher's doing too much of the talking.

The cumulative effect of emotional stimuli also has a positive side. Small, daily satisfactions that derive from accomplishment may serve to establish enduring interests. Much of the success of programmed learning, in which the pupil gets "reward" for correct answers on brief bits of material, is attributed to this piling up of small satisfactions (Suppes, 1964). The assurance that one is accepted by the group can fortify him for meeting instances in which he encounters hostility. Daily acts of kindness on the part of the teacher will help pupils to accept firm handling of undesirable behavior.

"Classroom climate" is an instance, detrimental or beneficial, of the piling up of stimuli. It has been found that this climate is measurable when defined as the synergism of the class—degree of personal intimacy, absence of friction, and the satisfaction which the pupil gets from membership. Moreover, achievement in the subject (physics) is related to classes which are unstratified, democratic in policy making, and have clear goals (Walberg and Anderson, 1968). Beatty (1969a) reports that the productive classroom is one in which the experiences and the learning of pupils center around:

Worth—the pupil is able to perceive himself as being valued by others.

Coping—the pupil is able to do things, himself, that are accepted and valued (Beatty postulates that the fusing of worth and coping is such that competitive grading is used at "high psychic cost.")

Expressing—the reality of affective tones is not only recognized; but such recognition is emphasized in learning processes: How do you feel now, gay or sad? How does that music (story, picture, film) make you feel?

Autonomy—a pupil learns that he has alternatives—that he has some freedom to make a choice.

The Genesis of Disruptive Emotions

A disruptive emotion is that which an unwell child brings to school. Irritability may stem from a headache that results from defective and uncorrected vision or may be a symptom of incipient mumps. Some children are inadequately fed before coming to school and are disposed to temper tantrums—and nutrition and amount of food are not synonymous (Simms, 1970). Children are prone to anger when they are tired, ill, sleepy, or hungry.

Pupils may be irritable because of tension between their parents. Their uncertainty at home may make them less confident at school, with the result that they are less competent than they might be otherwise. An autocratic father or mother may have made difficult demands at home. The tension is released by a tirade against a classmate who the child knows will not fight back, or perhaps he has found that he can vent hostility upon the teacher. The good teacher is aware of these factors in the development of disruptive emotions, and instead of demanding the respect that is "due his position," he begins to wonder what is behind the pupil's hair-trigger emotions.

The delicate child may have more difficulty in achieving emotional control than those who are physically robust. Children with a sensory defect or glandular imbalance may have a lower tolerance for upsetting stimuli than those who are free from such handicaps. It has recently been proposed that predispositions toward maladjustive behaviors are accompanied by supernumerary Y chromosome in the sex determining gene (Montagu, 1968). But glands, genes, and diet have little direct import for the teacher. Whatever the reasons, the teacher's task is that of perceiving and dealing with each pupil's peculiar threshold of tolerance.

School conditions may be factors in the genesis of disruptive emotions. Children who are enrolling in a particular school for the first time are under emotional strain. The frequent rigidity of curricular demands is mentioned in educational and psychological literature. The practice of threatening school failure is gradually disappearing as a result of experimental findings of mental hygiene and psychology, but the frustrating threat does exist for some pupils. Some anxiety may be a source of motivation to some pupils (Shrable and Sassenrath, 1970).

The Genesis of Constructive Emotions

Interest, affection, friendliness, respect for individuality, and humor bring about constructive emotions. Although the roles of the home, and glands, and community are acknowledged, such recognition is self-defeating if it becomes an excuse for teachers' failing to do what they can. Marx and Tombaugh (1967, p. 203) assert that the emotional conditions of a school constitute a "hidden curriculum." They see the nurturing of the elementary school child's natural curiosity and interest and nurturing of the adolescent's independence and divergence as the primary tasks of the school—and ones in which the teacher's personality is focal.

Dealing with Disruptive Emotions

In terms of the physiological processes involved, it is not possible to distinguish sharply between salutary and handicapping emotions, but there is a difference in their effect. Fear produces the same endocrine effects as love; but extreme fear inhibits action, interferes with digestion, and makes the person feel ill, whereas love stimulates activity, aids digestion, and produces a feeling of well-being.

Anxiety

It is probable that the negative, handicapping emotion most often present in the classroom is extreme anxiety. However, there is no clear-cut evidence that all degrees or forms of anxiety should be eliminated, even if it were possible to do so. The problem is to achieve some balance between anxieties that have positive motivational value and anxieties that render the individual incapable or less capable of achieving.

Anxiety may be close to fear in intensity and thus tend to prompt over-reaction—fighting or psychic or physical withdrawal. Anxiety may be chronic, diffuse, and general or it may refer to an anticipatory apprehension of a rather immediate but vague situation. Furthermore, the effects on different persons are similarly variable. As used here, anxiety refers to a painful unrest of the mind involving apprehension or foreboding in relation to what is impending or anticipated. Anxiety is the response to a vague, subjective danger, whereas fear is a response to objective danger (Goldenson, 1970, p. 90). This differentiation is related to the idea that anxiety is produced by one's perception of a threat to the ego, by something seen as limiting one's self-realization. Finally, anxiety is a response (fearful in nature) that is out of proportion to reality. Thus one pupil may become handicappingly anxious about a given test and others will realize that the result will constitute only a part of the final evaluation.

Freud (1936) suggests that anxiety is generated if the child, who is dependent on his parents for care and protection, is separated from them, if they are separated from each other, or if they quarrel or fight, which seems to him to presage separation. Anxiety also may arise when the child's need for instinctual gratification conflicts with environmental demands (cultural expectations), according to Freud. Chronic anxiety, according to Horney (1945), stems from an environment that is inconsistent, unjust, or harsh—one in which there is a limitation of opportunity to grow in self-reliance. Any of three "strategies" may be used as a defense. One may move *with* people by being meek and self-effacing, he may move *against* people by being aggressive and competitive, or he may move *away* from others by becoming withdrawn or aloof. These behaviors, of course, often compound his problems of adjustment. Most theories about the origins of anxiety make reference to parents: their own anxieties are communicated to the child, parental incompatibility tends to make children anxious, parental doubts about adequacy, dissatisfaction with accomplishments and potentials influence child development.

Mowrer (1960) stresses the idea of a distinction between overt, instrumental responses that help the individual control his environment and emotional responses that cause him to expect or prepare for response. Anxiety is included in the latter group, because the anxious individual is alerted and sensitive to stimulations. *Mild anxiety thus facilitates the acquisition of new responses, but intense anxiety narrows the perceptual field and impairs constructive responses.*

Anxiety in the classroom may have the paradoxical effects indicated above. Mild anxiety functions in a facilitative manner for some learning, but severe or very low anxiety seems to retard learning. Shrable and Sassenrath (1970) illustrate the variable effect of anxiety by reporting that programmed instruction should have relatively easy steps for students with low achievement motivation and high failure anxiety. Items should be harder for those with high achievement motivation. Weiner and Potepan (1970), studying the relationship of personality characteristics to scholarship in college, found that low test anxiety and achievement motivation were related to success for men. These characteristics did not predict success for women. They concluded that different "psychologies of motivation" were needed for males and females. The discriminating teacher would, however, want to go still further. Because some girls are more like boys than they are like other girls, the problem of anxiety—or motivation—must be individual.

Grossman (1968), reviewing the progress which has been made in teaching birds, animals, and children things which seem to be "beyond" their capacity —children's learning to read at age three, disadvantaged children's making great academic strides—recommends a hard look at what is being done. Tense, anxious, striving little preschoolers may be submerging their own talents, diminishing their own self-concepts, and incubating a desire to drop out by responding to adult pressure. It might be better, Grossman suggests, to have the desire to learn derive from self-esteem and successes achieved at their own speed rather than from anxieties about what might happen if one fails. Heffernan (1966) also endorses, from the standpoint of both achievement and personality stability, the idea that teachers should focus on challenge rather than pressure.

As an important interpreter of an achievement-oriented culture, the teacher should set a good example by being aware of and controlling apprehensions of his own that have dubious bases. Further, group counseling shows that it is possible to reduce anxieties through discussion (Hoffnung and Mills, 1970; Winder and Savenko, 1970). Anxiety about examinations might be allayed by giving them frequently enough and assigning them a proper place in the total evaluation scheme so that no one examination becomes crucial. In fact, examinations can be used as a learning device if the papers are returned immediately and the answers discussed. These steps, plus not permitting too much to hang on one score, can help to overcome "test neuroses." Guidance in developing study skills, as well as social and personal guidance, can enhance an individual's confidence that he can meet the problems of life as they are encountered. Certainly, the acquisition of knowledge will be facilitated by keeping anxiety at an individually productive level.

As a general statement it might be well to consider that mild anxiety would typically be more useful than very low or very high anxiety. Giving reassuring instructions to highly anxious pupils would be helpful, but reassurance to the low-anxiety pupils might result in their withholding any strenuous effort. In dealing with new material the generation of anxiety would seem to be inadvisable. A teacher might wish to produce a little anxiety when dealing with that which is easy and familiar.

To the extent that anxiety is a generalized trait, confidence in one area gives the individual a sense of self-sufficiency that will spread to other activities. One teacher had noted that an academically inept sixth grader did not show hesitancy about reciting. One day he asked the boy how it happened that he had so much assurance in class. The boy's answer was "I know that I'm not very good in arithmetic and language, but I can always win the other kids' marbles."

Fear

Fear—the tendency to run away from or avoid certain situations—is closely related to anxiety but is more intense and specific. There is less likelihood that the individual can cope adequately with fear than with anxiety. Many fears are irrational—fear of certain classmates or of examinations—but they cannot be explained away. Ignoring fear, ridiculing the pupil for being afraid, and forcing him into the fear-producing situation (swimming or reciting before an audience) will do more harm than good. The confidence and support of the teacher, the development of skills, and the enhancement of feelings of worth are all small steps in the right direction. The positive steps are finding the cause of fear, setting a good example in the presence of the feared situation, providing some enjoyable accompaniments parallel to the fear-inducing situation (emphasize the personal or class achievement of a public recitation), praising the willingness to try despite fear, and providing practice in the skills designed to cope with the fear, e.g., role playing. Techniques employed to enhance ego concepts will diminish both fear and anxiety.

It might appear from the foregoing that external factors control the manifestation of fear and anxiety. Such is not entirely true. A high concentration of lactate in the blood is related to neuroses. Normal adults can be made to have fear reactions by the administration of lactates. A drug—proprandol—blocks the metabolism of epinephrine and lactate, and use of the drug makes susceptible persons less responsive to fear and anxiety situations (Pitts, 1969). Despite the fact that early behaviors of children are persistent, the reports of schools and communities in which large numbers of school children are on tranquilizers are alarming. Even though there is a predisposition to behaviors indicative of fear, not until a doctor has evaluated the hormones and a team has assessed the living climate should drugs become a part of intervention.

The stimulants and depressants have legitimate medical uses. But even when they are being used under the supervision of a physician, they have the capacity to change the mood and behavior of the user. When they are misused through self-medication, the capacity may create problems.

Some persons who seek a change in mood or behavior turn to these drugs as a way to achieve the change. They withdraw into a world where some of their needs are satisfied only by drugs. Participating in the normal activities of family, classroom, and job becomes difficult for the drug abuser.[1]

The usable aspect of the study of fears is that teachers must seek solutions in terms of the environment. A major factor is that environment, for the child, is his teacher.

Aggression

Another emotion which is common in the classroom is aggression. Typically this behavior is a concomitant of frustration which is caused by the thwarting of a motive (Cohen, 1971). It is related to conflict (a normal clash between incompatible aims or desires) but, as the term is used here, frustration stems from opposition of impulses more formidable than is the case in normal, surmountable, ongoing conflict; it is the underlying threat or frustration that makes conflict stressful. The reaction to frustration varies: In some cases the individual retreats, withdraws, ceases to struggle. Crying is regarded as a passive response to frustration (Nash, 1970, p. 190). In other cases the frustrated individual attacks people or things about him. The problem presented to teachers is either to reduce the chronic conflict situations that can be influenced or to aid the pupil in finding healthful ways of expressing aggression.

Aggressiveness may be perceived in attacks on persons (especially on children so small that the aggressor is "safe") or property, swearing, talking back

1   Food and Drug Administration, Life Protection Series, 1968, *The Use and Misuse of Drugs*, Washington, D.C.: U.S. Department of Health, Education, and Welfare, p. 9.

to teachers, asking persistent bothersome questions, blaming others for difficulties. We should also recognize displaced aggression—venting hostility on objects or persons other than the cause of the frustration; destruction of school property is the obvious example. Little is accomplished by the teacher's taking direct action. The immediate situation may be controlled, but the underlying feeling, which may not be an outcome of the immediate situation, remains to break out at another time or place.

A school situation contributing to the origin of aggression is maintenance of grading standards that place unrealistic demands for achievement on pupils with less-than-average intelligence—competition (for grades) between those who are unequal. Also, many pupils become aggressive when their home backgrounds are such that the school's social demands (courtesies, dress, behaviors) conflict with what they have previously learned (White, 1969, p. 45). Punitive parents, especially mothers, tend to arouse the aggressions which predispose to delinquency. It must however be emphasized that parents do not *cause* delinquency (Jeffery and Jeffery, 1967).

Teachers can bring their own frustrations—from marital discord, thwarted ambitions, indebtedness, and illness—into the classroom and be guilty of aggression toward pupils. Some have learned to displace aggressive tendencies in hobbies or leisure time pursuits.

Finally, we should not minimize the fact that, despite the expressed ideal to the contrary, discrimination against various ethnic groups is all too common; it tends to arouse feelings of hostility and aggression and at the same time makes the victim feel guilty and unworthy.

Play has been employed to relieve aggressions of disturbed children. In such play they may throw, step on, smash, squeeze, and twist toys and dolls. There is no "Tsk, tsk. Nice children don't do such things." It is realized that such aggressive responses and releases precede more constructive behavior. Play therapy is not a classroom technique, but substitutes are available. Children can be encouraged to express their hostilities in themes and stories of violence. One seventh-grade boy was preoccupied with drawing scenes of death and destruction—shooting, knifing, bombing, and car and train wrecks. The teacher masked her concern with the persistence of this theme, and toward the end of the school year, the pictures of violence became less frequent and greatly subdued. It was fortunate that the teacher had recognized the need for him to work off hostilities before emphasizing academic tasks. Working off tensions through play or punching a "Bozo" clown are not approaches which are uniformly endorsed by child specialists. Some experimenters have found that, rather than to drain off the emotion, the activities of aggression tend to persist for a longer time when physically expressed (White, 1969, p. 46).

Much can be accomplished in a counseling situation. Some teachers take time after school to let the aggressive child talk out his difficulties. It should be understood that the purpose is to let the pupil vent his feelings. The pupil will stop telling how he perceived the provocation or will cease describing his feelings if the teachers say, "You shouldn't feel that way." Help can be given in the *ventilation process* by really listening—caring and trying to understand instead of interrupting. In dealing with aggression and with symptoms of other problems, the teacher should admit that some cases are puzzling and seek the counsel of other teachers, counselors, and supervisors and administrators (Myrick, 1970). Attempts to conceal one's own bafflement (frustration) run the risk of projecting one's aggression upon pupils.

Group counseling also provides an avenue for the release of aggression:

> Six underachieving high school boys were being observed by counselor trainees. They were in their fifth session when one lad became particularly obnoxious—he interrupted others, snorted at the observations of the counselor, made sarcastic and belittling remarks to the other boys, and criticized teachers. Two trainees later remarked that they would have "straightened him out." The counselor, however, ignored the disrupter. At the close of the session he asked for a summary. Two or three boys said, "Let Steve do it." At the next session, Steve was a much more constructive participant.

We cannot be sure, but it can be guessed that Steve had worked off some of his hostilities and that his peers controlled him much better than an authority person could have. This appears likely because it is often that it is adult authority which generates the frustration of adolescents.

Athletic participation, especially in contact sports such as football, wrestling, and boxing, is regarded as an acceptable avenue for working off aggressions. For this reason, strong emphasis upon varsity teams at the cost of extensive, inclusive, intramural programs is questioned. In intramural athletics, those who are otherwise programmed for failure are given a chance to displace their aggressions. The emphasis on intramural programs and classification of competitors by size, age, and competency might be better, from the standpoint of sound psychology. The more one has experienced success, the more he has realized his potential, the less he is compelled toward hostility and aggression (Strom, 1969*a*, p. 375).

Art classes and art activities can provide the opportunity for release through painting and drawing. The stories and themes written in English classes can serve the double purpose of learning self-expression and providing for the verbal release of aggression. Pounding and molding clay or whittling and carving wood—both calling for muscular energy—can be used in much the same manner as play therapy. Some feel that reading provides a release for many emotions, including aggression. The extent to which readers project themselves into the reading material is still being investigated; but tentative data suggest that such projection—variable in terms of the personality of the reader—is probable (White, 1969, p. 172).

Anger

The procedures involved in teaching control of anger are quite similar to those suggested for dealing with aggression. The example set by others is important. The development of skills will lead to fewer thwarting circumstances and experiences.

Trying to reason with an angry person is difficult because neither party can stay reasonable for long, so ideas, suggestions, and admonitions about controlling temper should be brought out after the storm has passed. Yet all too frequently, the angry individual is dealt with immediately; he is banished from the room, sent to the principal's office, or otherwise punished at once. This does not mean that pupils should rule the roost, but the teacher's insistence on reasonable conformity can take place after a time for cooling off (Prescott, 1957, p. 75). The value of punishment must be questioned as a correction for strong emotion and the punisher might well examine his own motives (Menninger, 1968). But discipline which is related to the transgression—removal for violence, going without for destruction of materials—is quite another matter (Glasser, 1969).

Prejudice

Substantial numbers of pupils, though still only a small percent, are blacks, Mexicans, Puerto Ricans, or Jews, and there is no denying that they are too frequently the recipients of prejudicial treatment not only by other pupils but also by teachers. Factors outside the school may originate or encourage the attitudes underlying such treatment. For example, for the past decade newspapers have headlined various incidents that have attended various school incidents, street riots, protests, and clashes between minority groups and law officers. Such concerns have also been the focus in book-length presentations (Hersey, 1968; Knebel, 1969). Even pupils who have had favorable experiences with a minority group may still develop antiblack or anti-Mexican bias because to do otherwise would be to risk ostracism by the dominant group. The issue is complicated by the fact that the person who is the subject of biased views tends to become defensive. He takes umbrage easily and perceives slighting intent in the teacher's innocuous remarks. His apprehensiveness leads him to read into the teacher's routine behaviors an element of threat and damage to self-esteem. Thus a gap begun by factors outside the school is widened by the psychology of expectancy (Gephart and Antonoplos, 1969).

The salient factor in constructive approaches is the teacher's attitude (Hogan and Green, 1971). It has been found that one person who is supportive can be of substantial value in reducing anxieties and feelings of inadequacy. In dealing with individual children it seems wise to avoid, or be cautious about, references to personal, national, racial, or religious background. In the current scene, it becomes necessary to avoid stereotypes in dramatic productions—the black maid, the stubborn Swede, the innocent Mexican, or to have an all-black chorus. There are some hazards in asking Orientals or Mexicans to put on dances in which native costumes are worn, but some observers say it is advantageous because in admitting their racial origins pupils bolster their individual identity. A few teachers deal with prejudice and stereotyping by role playing or by establishing a permissive atmosphere in which feelings can be discussed. Rogers (1968) has expressed the hope that by the year 2000 we will be able to deal with personal feelings as openly and with the same degree of regularity as we now deal with history of mathematics. Pupils can be led to discuss how they might feel if others made fun of them or called them names. Such discussion lets pupils know that others too can hurt, feel angry, or be afraid—the humanness of everyone is emphasized. Group discussions dealing directly with real problems that arise in the school should be a part of the program of studies. Feelings are contagious, so a teacher's first step is to examine and control his own prejudices.

Lewin (1948, pp. 169ff) advises that there is no use ignoring the fact that a child belongs to a minority group. In fact, those who later have the most difficulty are frequently the ones who experienced the least prejudice in childhood. They should be instructed that membership in two or more groups is natural and normal and that they can and must function in several groups. It is a matter of how to behave in various groups. Conversely, there are children growing up through the schools of exclusive, single-class suburbias who are unaware of prejudice except as a subject for academic discussion. Wise parents are alarmed. To these parents the chauvinistic school and community is handicapping their children (Meyer, 1969; Roberts, 1970).

The impact of prejudice on the part of the giver, as contrasted to the receiver, deserves consideration in class discussions. The prejudiced person hurts himself by limiting his perspective, by twisting his thinking with stereotypes. Logic is destroyed by preconceived notions and by jumping to conclusions. It is also worth bringing out that often the prejudiced person is fundamentally weak and trying to build ego and disguise his weakness by scapegoating.

Because goals are more readily achieved when they are clearly defined, it is obvious that the teacher should not leave to chance the basic attitudes that are being formed and re-formed. Along with the conception that the school is concerned with the whole child must go the responsibility for conscious attention to attitudes. A beginning point for such open consideration is to examine the proposition that our schools have never been really available to children of all social classes; that they are a selecting and sorting agency (Greer, 1969; Havighurst and Neugarten, 1967, pp. 67ff).

Values of Disturbing Emotions

It is generally desirable to reduce upsetting emotions. However, dogmatic judgment about them is complicated by the fact that some positive values may accrue from anxiety, anger, and prejudice. Fear has the value of helping to keep individuals out of danger. Anxiety about examinations may cause the pupil to apply himself more assiduously to his work.

Certain kinds of anger may be advantageous. Anger with oneself for doing less than he is capable, anger about unjust situations, and anger with obviously unfair individuals may serve to motivate an otherwise complacent person. It is pertinent to suggest that the treatment of anger in the classroom should avoid involving a conflict of wills between teacher and pupil.

Prejudice might well be encouraged in the upper grades and in high school. Dislike for war, for inequitable opportunity, for unfair treatment based on skin color or national origins, or for international unselfishness may serve to motivate individuals to become a counteracting influence. This kind of prejudice is, however, directed against practices rather than persons, impersonal rather than personal, general rather than specific, and directed rather than uncontrolled.

Dealing with Constructive Emotions

The study of health rather than sickness or the study of constructive as against destructive emotions is an emphasis which is currently being highlighted by humanists and existentialists (Maslow, 1968b). What is done to reduce anxiety and aggression will also enhance such emotions as sympathy and affection. The positive approach to emotional control will be studied in this section by dealing with affection, sympathy, pleasure, humor, and openness.

Affection

For educational purposes, "affection" may be defined as a mild emotion characterized by a feeling of fondness, tenderness, or attachment to others. It is an emotional response rather than being a matter of cognition or volition (Chaplin, 1968).

Studies of best-liked teachers show that pupils respond positively to qualities that underlie affection—sympathy, kindliness, patience, courtesy, and interest in others (Hamachek, 1968, p. 187ff). On the negative side, it has been shown that delinquency can be paralleled, in part, with the lack of affection or a feeling of the pupil that others have no affection for him (Amos, 1967). As an element in the classroom climate, affection must not be forced, because children are quick to detect sham. Genuine affection arises from a sincere interest in children and a knowledge of their abilities, problems, and limitations.

The other aspect is the growth of affection in children. The example set by the teacher is important. Not only must the teacher use patience in dealing with pupils, he must also notice and praise its manifestation in his pupils. Many primary teachers have found that keeping small pets in the classroom can be a means of encouraging gentleness in children. Group work, committees, group discussions, and classroom projects are all means of providing opportunities for children to develop the familiarity and understanding that leads to affection.

Sociometric grouping can be used to help a social isolate become better oriented or to increase the productiveness or motivation of individuals. The technique can also be used to nourish any nascent affection. The starting point is for the teacher to ask, "With whom would you like to work in preparing a panel discussion?" or "Which pupil would you like best as a substitute?" or "By whom would you like to sit?" (See Figure 10-1.)

Because affection must be built upon existing foundations, certain principles should be observed in sociometric grouping:

1. Mutual choices should be placed together.
2. Isolates (unchosen or rarely chosen pupils) should be given their first choice.
3. A minimum number of isolates should be placed in a group.
4. Stars (much chosen pupils) need not be given any of their choices (though no effort should be made to avoid giving them one of their choices). Their position as stars is probably indicative of their ability to adjust to many different personalities.
5. Natural groupings should be maintained to as great an extent as possible. (Thus, in Figure 10-1, 2, 3, 5, and 7 would form a group; however, since 2 and 7 are both stars, it might be well to make each the nucleus of a different group.)
6. The more difficult it is to follow the foregoing principles, the smaller the groups formed should be.

It should be noted that groups should be re-formed from time to time for various purposes. If a different question were used as the basis for the sociogram, different formation would undoubtedly result. Moreover, as pupils extend their intimate knowledge of one another, they will tend to make different choices.

Empathy

Empathy is a feeling of oneness, identity, a mature sharing. It goes beyond having sympathy for another and wanting to help—it is sensing and experiencing the feeling states of another. When one has sympathy (feels sorry for

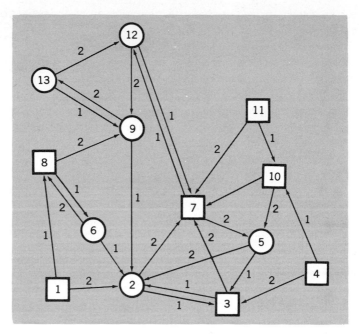

Figure 10-1 Sociogram in which squares represent boys and circles represent girls. The number by the line indicates first or second choice. Numbers 7 and 2 are "stars," or much-chosen individuals. Numbers 1, 4, 11 are isolates — not having been chosen by anyone so far as the particular question was concerned. Numbers 2 and 3, 12 and 7, 13 and 9, and 6 and 8 are mutual choices.

another) he need have no sense of experiencing the perceptions of the miserable person; but the empathic person shares the perception *and* the feeling. Arbuckle (1967, p. 192) places warmth, positive regard, and acceptance high on the criteria of empathy. The ability to be genuine is a necessary precondition of empathy— one cannot be accepted and "feel as" if he has fenced himself off from others by playing a role or wearing a facade.

    Empathy is a desirable quality in human relations but is, unfortunately, too often lacking. Our culture does not encourage the display of emotions— they receive little overt exercise. We are supposed to remain calm, stoic, and objective, which tends to inhibit their development. Men, for example *and especially*, are not supposed to cry or to show "maudlin sympathy." People backed by the western frontier tradition are expected to be strong, autonomous, and to solve their own problems rather than to show weakness by seeking help. At least on the professional level, this concept is being challenged. The man in the street goes to the next town for psychological help, if he is mature enough to accept help. He understands that seeking help is wise but others do not. There also may be a gradual social endorsement of men's showing grief and having empathy. Society has not yet accepted the fact that men might have enough fatherly "instinct" to be able primary teachers.

Another factor which might explain the infrequent manifestation of empathy is that such emotions as sympathy, affection, love, and empathy leave one vulnerable. One invests in others when he has empathy, and then there is a danger of loss, a turning of the tables, an act of traitorousness.

For a teacher a rudimentary step toward empathy is the practice of courtesy in himself and his pupils. He could steel himself to engage in active listening; i.e., hearing, reflecting on, trying to hear beyond that which is uttered and that which is yet unsaid. He could take advantage of those emotional moments by pausing to let affect be felt—the response to a moving story, a significant film, a moving bit of music. Although talking about these feelings tends to make them disappear, they can and should be talked about occasionally. Discussions may be planned—about how it feels to be black in a predominantly white school, about how it feels to be dressed less well than others, about how it feels to speak a language not readily understood by others. Pupils may be asked to try putting themselves in another's place. Role playing may provide such experience. The most important role is that of the teacher. The simple question is, is he a mechanic in human relations or an artist? The one treats human beings as things and the other treats them as people.

A setting in which empathy and other positively oriented attitudes may develop is one's group of peers. Adolescents value traits that promote facile group functioning. This is also true of younger children, but their attitudes are developing quixotically. Again, discussions in which adolescents can talk about how they see themselves, accept themselves, can talk about their loves and hopes are preliminary steps to accepting and empathizing with others (Moore, 1970). Scholars working in the area of racial understanding point out that much intolerance is attributable to ignorance. When one becomes acquainted with those of another race, instead of depending on clichés and the opinions of prejudiced people, he tends to become tolerant. The study of children of other lands in grade school and social living and sociology in high school has the same effect.

Pleasure

A state or feeling of gratification or satisfaction may be considered a definition of the term "pleasure." The pleasure may be very mild, as the enjoyment of rest after activity, or it may be intense, as the stimulation one feels upon hearing a masterful artist sing. Pleasures derive mainly from two sources: (1) the satisfaction of basic needs and (2) the exercise of one's capacities. Children enjoy running, jumping, and romping because of their capacity for physical activity. By and large, competent pianists or golfers find pleasure in the exercise of their skills.

Children will achieve pleasure from their school activities if those activities are designed to satisfy such basic needs as security, accomplishment, adventure, belonging, and physical satisfaction. The relationship of need satisfaction to pleasure further emphasizes the child's need to be accepted for what he is by both pupils and teacher. The necessity for designing schoolwork appropriate to individual capacity is especially important as the value of pleasure is considered. Failure imposed by others' demands, grade requirements, and uniform progress denies pleasure from learning—denies satisfaction from perceived progress—and has no place in schools designed for children (Dennison, 1969; Glasser, 1969). Failure to achieve tasks which are self-selected, which results from having one's power limits tested, is quite another matter.

Relative to pleasure, schools have two responsibilities. One is to provide a variety of school activities in order to exercise a variety of pupil potentials (Taylor, 1968). This may mean exacting academic requirements for some; recognition of athletic prowess for others; the opportunity to participate in musical productions for others; and leadership challenges, manual arts, and homemaking for still others. The second responsibility is to encourage the development of skills. This may apply to skills in arithmetic, writing, and science. Research studies have repeatedly indicated the value of social skills as a source of satisfaction for children and adolescents (Feldman, 1969).

Humor

Because humor adds to the enjoyment of life, opportunities to exercise it in the classroom should be sought. This requires more than a good-humored teacher; it involves the need for insight into the cause of humor. In the primary grades, humor is occasioned by what seems to the adult crude showing off and perceiving the unexpected. Young children find humor in surprise, defeated expectation, relief from strain, and sudden feelings of superiority or embarrassment (Jersild, 1960, p. 251). Thus, first graders think that making faces is extremely funny or find the spilling of paint or a box of crayons quite humorous. An adult's stumbling or falling is very funny. Teachers should recognize that what an adult would often consider as cruel sense of humor is simply a developmental stage in children.

At a somewhat later stage, children find humor in incongruities. Pupils in the intermediate and upper grades find humor in crude (to the adult) play on words or in practical jokes, and these forms of humor may be found at the high school level. Another stage of development is represented by an increase in amusement at jokes about sex (probably arising from embarrassment) that are perhaps only partially understood. These developmental stages prepare for the basic element of adult humor—the occurrence of the unexpected in the place of an event for which set has been established.

Teachers should make an effort to laugh with students rather than at them. Teachers are known to use sarcastic witticisms that are anything but humorous to the pupils. Because laughter fosters a healthy functioning of the body and increases the enjoyment of living, there should be an attempt to make schools less solemn than they often are. This is accomplished by relaxed and confident teachers.

Openness

When one feels insecure, unsure of his worth, and doubts his future, he tends to be defensive—to withdraw, rationalize, or attack. Such a defensive person is apt to rely on bias, stereotypes, and preconceptions—he places persons in boxes before he meets them. Conversely, when one feels confident, knows he is valued by others, and has faith that he can cope with the future, he is said to be open. Openness means that he is curious and has a high tolerance for surprises (Moore, 1970). The open person finds it unnecessary to arrange for "prepackaging" of people or experiences. Landsman (1961) emphasizes the matter of wanting to know and be known as the essential quality of openness. This consists of a willingness to disclose or reveal oneself. Obviously, preconditions are feelings of worth, security, and trust in others.

Classroom conditions which foster openness consist essentially of honesty. Wearing a facade of cheerfulness, pretending to be satisfied with mediocrity from one capable of being superior, hiding one's displeasure at injustice are, patently, not manifestations of honesty. In short, the open person can be himself.

Because it is so important that teachers lead the way and because openness is much less typical than defensiveness, teachers may need help. And at this point the individual encounters a paradox. In order to be more of oneself, growth is essential; and growth is often accompanied by uncertainty, vacillation, and turmoil. Psychological growth is frequently traumatic. Yet the outcome of such growth is the pleasure of becoming more fully functioning (Rogers, 1969, p. 290). Teachers who have pursued the matter of personal development through various forms of psychotherapeutic intervention have almost—but not quite—uniformly reported long-range satisfaction and appreciation for their experience. The great majority who have made the investment would do it again (Jersild and Lazar with Brodkin, 1962).

Projective Techniques and Emotional Release

The Definition and Purpose of Projective Techniques

The concept of **projective techniques** may be clarified by describing the pioneer technique—the Rorschach blots. These symmetrical blots of ink might have been made by dropping ink on a piece of paper and folding the paper to produce two symmetrical halves. The subject is then asked to tell what he sees in the blot—just as we use our imaginations to see various animals, objects, and characters in clouds. The individual "puts himself into" the blot in order to give meaning to what is in reality meaningless, and thus what one sees is a revelation of himself (Rorschach, 1937). Murray's Thematic Apperception Test consists of a series of pictures about which the subject is asked to tell a story. Because the picture might tell any number of stories, what he does tell is a revelation or projection of the individual (Murray, 1938).

Projective techniques can also be used as a means of emotional release, and it is felt that one experiences catharsis from some kinds of projective techniques. A child who senses that it is wrong to repudiate a parent (for either a felt or a justifiable reason) may be unwilling to kick or curse that parent. However, under the guidance and encouragement of a therapist, he will play with dolls in such a manner that the doll child injures the doll parent. It has been experimentally confirmed that such play enables many children who are experiencing difficulties to exercise their negative feelings more wholesomely (Axline, 1964; Moustakas, 1966, p. 39).

Play therapy, Rorschach blots, and the Thematic Apperception Test are not classroom techniques and should not be used by untrained teachers. However, modification of projective techniques is quite feasible. Some pupils find release in creative writing. Upper-grade-school and secondary school pupils release their feelings and perhaps get a better perspective of their problems through writing that places the author in the role of a hero. The following was by a junior high school boy:

Pretty Anna May Malone
Had a heart as hard as stone;
Every year since she was eight
She has been my best playmate.

I half loved that Irish kid
'Till she said just what she did,
Said for me her love was through
'Cause she'd heard I'm half a Jew.

She doesn't need to feel high-toned
'Cause her dad kissed the blarney stone.
I don't think I know it all
'Cause my dad had a wailing wall.

Time will show you, Anna May,
The big mistake you made today.
It's the truth I'm half a Jew
But that's the half that cared for you.

Finger and brush painting, crayon and pencil drawing, and clay modeling have also been used as projective techniques for both emotional release and—if cautiously and tentatively interpreted by the teacher—improved understanding. "Cautiously and tentatively" mean that such data should be corroborated and supplemented by tests, academic assignments, peer relations, work habits, *and* the teacher's openness to continued on-the-spot observation.

Using Projective Techniques in the Classroom

The underlying conception of projective techniques suggests that the manner in which an individual does his work, the frequency of speech and the tone of voice, the manner in which he meets and deals with his peers, as well as the way he paints and plays in experimental situations, reveal his inner self. (Incidentally, this has a rather revealing implication for the teacher: The way in which he describes the personality of his pupils is indicative of his own personality traits.)

Awareness of behavior as a symptom will help teachers see the futility of trying to alter established modes of pupil conduct without first determining the causes. When the teacher takes the view that such behavior is symptomatic, he can help pupils get therapeutic release from play activities if he guards against showing shock. When a child builds something in clay and seems to take delight in destroying what he has created, the teacher should avoid saying, "Why, Bill, that's an awful thing to do!" It will do boys no great harm to make dire threats about murder and mayhem when they are playing Dick Tracy and gangsters. It is a part of the wisdom of the organism to attempt to effect an equilibrium in the face of disturbing influences. Spontaneous play of children tends to effect such equilibrium if there is not too much adult domination and moralizing. Nondirective play therapy has been used successfully in dealing with retarded readers (Bills, 1969).

There are opportunities to approximate projective methods in formal curricular pursuits. Art, language study, literature, physical education, and practical arts may provide the pupil who has problems with an opportunity for release. Teachers should encourage spontaneous creation in writing and drawing. Giving advice on the proper techniques for handling materials does not violate this principle of freedom.

Several aspects of the curriculum require rather rigid conformity. Words must be spelled in a certain manner, and the solution of algebra and arithmetic problems is rather stereotyped. The names of objects and persons must be pronounced in certain ways. Without questioning the great advantages of conformity, we can say that these situations sometimes produce stress for children (Doll and Fleming, 1966, pp. 89ff). Some of the pressure may be reduced by permitting freedom where conformity is relatively unimportant. Art, music, and dancing have for ages been avenues for emotional expression and for building interpersonal unity. However, even such avenues for expression as these may become stilted and formal if the emphasis is on the outcome.

Projective techniques may be utilized in many areas to release disturbing emotions in routine activities. A manual arts teacher, concerned because his shop was becoming the "dumping ground" for pupils who were unable to adjust satisfactorily to academic work, decided to see what he could do to help pupils. Instead of emphasizing craftsmanship, he encouraged boys to do what they wished in the shop. He discovered that it was possible to help many boys merely by providing an opportunity for creativity and accomplishment. He also found that in the atmosphere of freedom, the boys slowly began to reveal to him some of their felt difficulties.

Teachers of English have found that they can help pupils put up with some of the negative conditions in which they find themselves by encouraging them to write themes on "My Pet Peeve," "My Favorite Sport," or "My Ideal Teacher." Poems that express secret feelings are often given to teachers who have the confidence of their pupils with the request that they should not be shown or read to other people. Sound precautions are to (1) avoid moralizing about the activity, (2) permit and encourage the feeling of freedom, (3) seek to develop a high degree of rapport with the student, (4) accept the child and his activities as objectively as possible, (5) provide as great a variety of free and creative activities as is feasible, and (6) remember that constructive emotional development is at least as important as academic accomplishment.

Emotional Maturity

The Relative Nature of Maturity

Although the word "mature" means ripeness, or full development, the psychological meaning is more flexible. A child may be mature in the sense that he has reached the development typical for his age. A four-year-old who has a temper tantrum only once every three or four weeks may be considered mature. A six-year-old who dawdles on Saturdays is mature. An adolescent who quickly recovers from a broken heart is mature for his age. It appears, therefore, that maturity is not an absolute—it is a process.

Emotional maturity is the process of acting one's age. The teacher should not expect children to reach a stability of interest beyond their years. He should not expect the adolescent boy consistently to be a gentleman. He should not consider it odd that freshman girls develop a crush on him. He will consider it normal for a senior girl to be "madly in love" once, twice, or thrice.

Self-acceptance is an important aspect of emotional maturity. Many authorities agree that one's self-concept is a crucial factor in learning. I. Gordon (1969) presents data which show this to be particularly important in primary education because subsequent education is so profoundly influenced. Intervention is essential in behalf of those whose self-concept is weak. One's self-acceptance must be preceded by acceptance from others; to push pupils through developmental stages too rapidly is to imply dissatisfaction with them. Sometimes what appears to be objectionable behavior is in reality a developmental stage *and* a valuable experience.

Some Criteria of Emotional Maturity

Man's capacity for development and adaptation to changing conditions is probably his outstanding characteristic. Today's children continue to prove the validity of belief in man's adaptability. Children are bombarded with information, and they absorb it with astonishing ease. Even preschool youngsters, perhaps largely because of television, but also because of radio broadcasts and parental conversations, know something about atomic energy, rockets, cataclysmic events across the world, racial minorities, and social struggles on other continents (Wann, Dorn, and Liddle, 1962, p. 6). This information and the wide variety of their daily experiences contribute to both emotional turmoil and rapid emotional maturing (Glasser, 1970). The problem for parents and educators is to establish goals of emotional maturity and work for their achievement. A suggested list of criteria, or goals, follows:

1. *Inhibition of direct expression of negative emotions.* This does not mean that feelings of anger or fear should or could be suppressed. It does mean that direct attack and flight should take place less often. The school can help by providing substitute activities that permit the release of tensions.
2. *Cultivation of positive, upbuilding emotions.* Emotional maturity is not so much eliminating disruptive emotions as it is providing commendable substitutes. This can be fostered by experiences of success—in social contacts, physical activities, subject matter mastery, and the development of skills.

3. *Development of high tolerance for disagreeable circumstances.* This, too, is the result of successful experience, which provides compensations for the inevitable failures and the disagreeable experiences. Classroom discussions can play a small, but not negligible, part in the evaluation of one's tolerance level.

4. *Increasing satisfaction from socially approved responses.* Growth from the natural egocentricity of childhood to the sociocentric ideal of adulthood is the result of personal success, plus close association with individuals who are trusting and trustworthy.

5. *Increasing independence of action.* Socially oriented independence is the result of guided experience that provides degrees of freedom commensurate with the ability to exercise judgment. Teachers must be mature enough to believe that sound judgment does not necessarily have to concur with their judgment.

6. *Ability to make a choice and not brood about other choices.* This is probably best accomplished by permitting children to make choices when the stakes are not great. Heavy responsibility placed on youth may be a contributing factor to chronic worry.

7. *Freedom from unreasonable fear.* Concern and forethought should not be confused with fear. The experience of success and contact with confident adults foster this goal.

8. *Understanding and action in accord with limitations.* No one can be the top man in everything. Acceptance of limitations may be fostered by widening the range of activities that are functionally recognized and praised in the school.

9. *Awareness of the ability and achievement of others.* Stress on group accomplishment can be a powerful source of motivation as well as a source of gratification.

10. *Ability to err without feeling disgraced.* This will be fostered by parents and teachers who realize that errors are educative.

11. *Ability to carry victory and prestige with grace.* This will grow from the more equitable distribution of the experiences of success and failure. Stress on cooperative activities and team and school victories will be steps in the right direction.

12. *Ability to bounce back from disappointing experiences.* Experience is the great teacher. But the experience must be scaled to the developmental level.

13. *Ability to delay the gratification of impulses.* This is one of the distinct differences in pupils from the lower social classes, who present many problems in school, and those of higher socioeconomic origins. Many adults fail to achieve this goal.

14. *Capacity to be open, and accept openness, in interpersonal relationships.*
    Normal children have the capacity to reveal their beliefs, attitudes, and
    perceptions of people to a remarkable degree. Society teaches that it is
    desirable to conceal one's emotions and to wear the facades of social ex-
    pectancy. Psychologists then talk of identity and being one's own self in
    order really to be mature.

15. *The enjoyment of daily living.* The opportunity to engage in challenging
    but achievable tasks is the major contributing factor. The exercise of
    mental, physical, emotional, and spiritual aspects of the human person-
    ality provides the avenues to the enjoyment of living.

Assessment of Emotional Maturity

Historically teachers have been only incidentally interested in emotional
maturity. Currently, concern focuses around the relationship of emotional balance and maturity to the optimum functioning of cognitive behavior. However,
there are those who regard the emotional aspect of education as being highly significant, in and of itself, and say emotions should not be placed in a position
subsidiary to achievement (Travers, 1970, p. 119).

Attempts have been made to develop questionnaires, scales, and inventories as devices for assessing emotional status and development, but the matters
of quantitative and qualitative emphases emerge. There is some doubt that emotions can be evaluated by the quantitative measures which are so widely used in
assessing educational achievement. Indeed, some say that because the predictive
level of school grades for success in college and life is so low that there should be
more of the qualitative emphasis in evaluating achievement; e.g., categorizations,
comparison scores, and predictive postulations might better, at this stage of research, be ignored.

Many scales have been devised to evaluate emotional maturity, using
such criteria as those listed above, but there is much doubt concerning their validity and reliability. Consequently, they should be interpreted and used with genuine caution. Some of the scales are designed for self-rating and may serve to provide guidance for the individual, without regard to scores. Responses to individual items on the inventories might serve as the basis for discussion in small, sociometrically designed, groups. The objective would be exercise in openness and self-
evaluation rather than concern about a score.

Probably the best use of such scales is in teacher-pupil conferences and
as the basis for group discussions. Drawing conclusions from the comparative
scores is hazardous because phases of development for various individuals are
difficult to standardize (Wesman, 1968). However, the maturity levels suggested
by the criteria listed above and maturity rating scales are achievable to some de-

gree. It has been postulated that the next steps in man's evolution will not be biological, but that there exists infinite potentialities for increasing individual accomplishment and for increasing psychosocial understanding.

Summary

The concept of emotions is an elusive one because the word embraces mildly pleasant and unpleasant ones, ones that are violent and constructive and violent and destructive, and ones that begin mildly and progress through harmful extremes. Furthermore, both external events and internal mental and physical states influence the feeling of, and expression of, emotions; e.g., anxiety has different effects on different pupils. The complexity of emotions does not prevent their being either a helpful or harmful aspect of educational processes.

Some tentative, greatly abbreviated, and representative suggestions for dealing with disruptive emotions are: Anxiety, a vague fear of unknown phenomena, may be approached by acceptance and respect and by providing a nonanxious model. Fear may be diminished by developing skills and by verbal-linguistic methods. Forcing familiarity may do harm. Aggression may be approached by seeking to understand insecurity and resentment. Prejudice has been dealt with through familiarity, discussion, and role playing. Anger may be reduced by lessening conflict and frustration. Aggression and anger may, on occasion, be handled through removal or by allowing one to suffer the consequences of his own acts. And each of these suggestions may be quite appropriately applicable to another of the named symptoms.

Developing affection calls first for teachers' acceptance and then understanding—which in turn may be gained from active listening. Empathy may be enhanced by trial, practice, and discussion. Respect is basic to the feeling of empathy. Pleasure is gained in many ways—achievement, new experiences, success—but mainly it comes through vigorous exercise of one's capacities. Humor is a difficult matter because the nature of humor changes with maturing—and teachers and pupils are probably tuned to different stations. Openness—to growth, experience, learning, social development—is a pivotal factor in developing an active interest in continued learning. It should be pursued as a directed activity under the guidance of an "open" teacher.

Projective techniques, ways of assessing motivation, are not classroom techniques; but the principles of these methods may be used by teachers to draw tentative conclusions about pupils' motivations and to serve as a means of catharsis. Manner of dress, one's voice, posture, typical behaviors, and socialization are among the items that may be used as projective techniques. Paint, clay, toys may be used to draw tentative postulations and emotional release.

Personality assessment inventories and questionnaires have not reached the stage where the scores are useful as pupil data. They may have merit as research tools in assessing groups and as **clues** to possible sources of pupil difficulty.

In few other topics of educational psychology is the study of what the teacher is and does as vital as it is in the matter of "Emotions in the Classroom."

Suggested Additional Readings

ANDERSON, GARY J., 1970, "Effects of Social Climate on Individual Learning," *American Educational Research Journal*, vol. 7, pp. 135-152.

    Various classes have distinct "personalities." The author identifies some of the attitudes and behaviors which compose those distinguishable class identities.

BERNARD, HAROLD W., 1970, "Adult Mental Health–The Teacher as a Person," in H. W. Bernard, *Mental Health in the Classroom*, New York: McGraw-Hill Book Company.

    Some of the factors which condition personal and professional maturity are considered.

GROSSMAN, BRUCE, 1968, "The Academic Grind at Age Three," *The Record*, vol. 70, pp. 227-231, December.

    The fact that children can be taught to read at age three does not mean that they should. Nor does the foregoing sentence imply that they should not. The opportunity to discover one's self, to learn to think, to exercise one's creativity should also receive the scrutiny of teachers of "preschoolers" who are going to school.

HOGAN, ERMON O., AND ROBERT L. GREEN, 1971, "Can Teachers Modify Children's Self-Concepts?" *Teachers College Record*, vol. 72, pp. 423-426.

    Preservice and in-service workshops for teachers have seemed to produce statistically significant improvement in terms of effect on pupils. Although the authors feel that further study is desirable, results to date indicate that teacher education programs should incorporate the study of pupil self-concepts and what teachers do to them.

MOUSTAKAS, CLARK, 1966, *The Authentic Teacher*, Cambridge, Mass.: Howard A. Doyle Printing Company.

    Teachers have to accept and be themselves before they can be most effective agents in the development of emotions in children. This book describes how some teachers have approached the matter of acceptance, authenticity, and affect.

THOMAS, R. MURRAY, 1967, *Aiding the Maladjusted Child*, New York: David McKay Company, Inc.

    Even in those schools where there are special classes for maladjusted children, the classroom teacher will find that all such pupils have not been identified. Thomas presents some bases for understanding so that it will not be so necessary to act by rule and prescription.

11

Personality--
Self-realization

Because the word "personality" is vague
and variable, there are some who predict its demise as a psychological construct.
In everyday usage, personality refers to "it"—the impression one makes on others.
As a psychological term, personality is a more complex concept, and there is not
complete agreement as to what is innate, what is acquired, and why personality
develops as it does. Every chapter of this book is immediately or ultimately concerned with some significant phase of personality. However, basic educational implications can more easily be postulated and comprehended by specific reference
to some of the more salient features of personality.

The Meaning of Personality

A General Concept

Personality is the total configuration of individual characteristics and
modes of behavior that shape one's adjustments to his environment, especially
traits that influence his getting along with others and himself. Deese (1967,
p. 424) states that because it is impossible to deal with a man in totality, the
word personality must be restricted to those aspects which are functionally important. Physique, temperament, skills, interests, fears, hopes, likes and dislikes,
looks, feelings, habits, and knowledge are included. Personality embraces what
one is, what he can be, and what he hopes to be. Because personality includes

one's adjustment to others, it also includes the reactions of others. Hereditary potential, environmental factors, and personal reaction are involved, along with processes of differentiation and integration. Personality is notably responsive not only to the total culture but to peer contacts, teacher behaviors, and general emotional climate of the school (Clark, Goldsmith, and Pugh, 1970).

Because personality is a social concept, a teacher should note that when he describes the personality of a pupil or a fellow teacher, he is to some extent describing himself. Thus our evaluation of a teacher who characterizes Johnny as an ignorant, dirty, disobedient boy would be quite different from our evaluation of a teacher who describes the same pupil as a slow learner who is handicapped by an impoverished cultural background. The point is illustrated in the following:

> One teacher who read some of the case material said, "She (the child) was certainly unusual because she did not have parents who would sit down and converse with her about school. She never seemed to go anywhere beyond her neighborhood, so she was not given the opportunity to explore and experience new cultural situations." This statement is indicative of the tragic limitations of the cultural experience of most teachers. . . .[1]

Professional-minded teachers will seek to evaluate the social aspect of personality in terms of causative and contributing influences, as well as in terms of the immediate precipitating situation. For example, the newcomer to the school, whose skin color is darker than most of his new peers, and who speaks English with an accent, might react to repeated jostlings quite differently from the popular, sought after, quarterback on the football team.

Aspects of Personality

Personality is an encompassing concept which includes mental, emotional, physical, physiological, social, and perceptual factors. It must be remembered that in one individual a given factor may be comparatively more important than in another.

1. Inherited Factors

Cumulative research data have resulted in a shift in assessing the role of inheritance. Formerly, interest was focused on which traits were inherited and which seemed to be most responsive to environmental influences. Today the conclusion is that *genetic factors produce dispositions or potentials for development rather than directly producing either bodily or behavioral traits* (Mathis, Cotton,

---

1   Donald Clark, Arlene Goldsmith, and Clementine Pugh, 1970, *Those Children,* Belmont, Calif.: Wadsworth Publishing Company, Inc., p. 3.

and Sechrest, 1970, p. 495). It is still believed that heredity sets limits beyond which the individual may not develop, no matter how salutary his environment. It is to be hoped that teachers will realize the existence of these limits and cease acting as though pupils could be or do anything if they would just work hard enough. Belief in this erroneous idea is manifest in our use of age-grade standards, in which we seem to be indicating that if we fail or shame pupils they can be forced to grow and learn at prescribed rates.

Recognition of inherited limits need not lead to resignation to the status quo in development. The truth is that we do not know—nor is there any way of knowing—what those limits are. For example, an intelligence test does not measure inherited potential; it merely indicates the present degree of development of that potential. If we accept the idea of limits, then we shall be on the watch for indications that the pupil is being pushed and prompted beyond his potential (Thomas, 1967, p. 36). These indications may reveal themselves in various ways: sleepiness, nail-biting, inattentiveness, frequent throat clearing, restlessness, or outbursts of anger.

The role of heredity seems larger in intellectual development than in physical characteristics—which are least responsive to environmental variables. Social personality (barring clinical types of defectiveness) is less limited by heredity than either physique or intelligence and appears to be most responsive to environmental variables. It is comparatively easy to see hereditary limits in the size of children; it is less easy to perceive limits in terms of ultimate intellectual development (Jensen, 1969a). However, what often appears to be relatively superior intelligence is merely the possession of much and accurate information of a simple sort. It is comparatively difficult to perceive or determine experimentally how heredity has influenced social personality.

The interaction between heredity and environment is clearly illustrated by the view that is currently taken of the famous study of the Jukes family made in 1874 (Dugdale, 1877). Of 1,200 descendants from a given marriage (exact information was available for 709), most were criminals, paupers, and dependents. The large majority also revealed low physical standards. At first this degeneracy was attributed to heredity, but it is now considered important than these people, besides having poor heredity, lived in a poor cultural environment. A similar study of the descendants of Martin Kallikak (a fictitious name), a Revolutionary soldier who had children by a feebleminded barmaid, was also believed to indicate the role of heredity. Of 480 descendants, 143 were feebleminded, and many were sexually immoral, intemperate, delinquent, or criminal. It is today deemed important that the role of environment be considered along with the role played by heredity. Certainly, this is a highly important concept in current educational programs for culturally different pupils (Zigler, 1970).

Studies of gifted individuals follow much the same line. The descendants of Jonathan Edwards and Sarah Pierpont were, over a period of 200 years, college presidents, professors, authors, lawyers, judges, and statesmen to a greater extent

Jan Lukas/College Newsphoto Alliance

than could be attributed to chance (Carroll, 1940, p. 27). In addition to heredity, these individuals had the advantages of stable homes, financial security, and superior educational opportunities.

Sontag (1963), using **longitudinal studies**, reported that unusual activity in the last two months of fetal life was associated with hyperactivity and timidity and anxiety at the age of two and one-half years. At this age toddlers tended to avoid conflict situations; and these same children, in their early twenties, continued to be socially apprehensive. It would be tempting to believe that such tendencies were inherited, but it is possible that nervous, tense mothers provided an intrauterine environment conducive to hyperactivity. Such mothers might continue to supply an anxiety-provoking milieu throughout childhood and adolescence (Mathis, Cotton, and Sechrest, 1970, p. 500).

Chromosomal abnormality provides an interesting case of the possibility of a close relationship between heredity and personality. There is a higher than normal frequency of abnormal chromosomal combinations among criminals. That is, instead of the normal female XX chromosome or the normal male XY chromosome there are supernumerary Y's such as XYY, XYYY, or XYY/XYYY. Adult male prisoners who have the XYY chromosome are unusually tall, are below normal in intelligence, and have had excessive acne during adolescence. By way of contrast, a study of thirty-six tall, college-basketball players revealed none who had the abnormal chromosome. But an abnormal chromosome does not make a criminal—some who are not criminal have the abnormal chromosome and vice versa (Montagu, 1968). If chromosome abnormality and crime are functionally related, the best that can be said is that the XYY type predisposes one to crime but does not cause it. The possible relationship is doubly unfortunate if it seems to provide an excuse, as was the case of Richard Speck, who had the abnormal chromosome, who claimed that he was "born to kill," and who was convicted of slaying eight nurses in Chicago. The discovery of chromosomal abnormality as being related to criminal tendencies is fortunate if society is warned to provide an especially healthful environment for the unfortunates—but then such should be the birthright of all children.

2. Hormones and Personality

The glands of internal secretion, the endocrines, such as the thyroid, pituitary, pancreas, gonads, and adrenals, influence personality traits to a marked degree. Each of these glands pours secretions known as hormones directly into the bloodstream. Unless these secretions are available in delicately balanced proportions, the whole system is affected, and marked deviations in appearance, growth processes, emotional control, intelligence, and behavior may result (Eckstein, 1969, pp. 257ff).

The use of such knowledge of the endocrine glands as we have has resulted in momentous transformations of personality. Glandular therapy is, of course, a medical problem. The teacher's role is to recognize that glands play an important part in pupil behavior. A teacher would not be likely to label a child "lazy" if he were aware of the medical diagnosis of hypoactive thyroid. One teacher, typically tolerant of questionable pupil behavior, nevertheless was somewhat insulted by a high school girl's regularly sleeping or dozing in class. One day the girl, perhaps noticing the irritation, said to her, "You may have noted my sleepiness. I have a hypoactive thyroid. I'm taking thyroxin and I'm really much better than I used to be." A hyperactive thyroid may result in quite different problems. The pupil may fidget, seem unable to stay in his place, or insistently demand attention by raising his hand to recite. His overactivity can be better tolerated when one appreciates that the glands are exercising some control of personality manifestations. Hyperthyroidism is rare before the age of ten, but it occurs more frequently after that, especially among girls, and is accompanied by instability, moodiness, restlessness, and excessive activity.

Some endocrine imbalances involve changes in blood sugar and blood calcium. Children who have this problem are often negativistic, inattentive, lacking in initiative, and antisocial, along with having physical symptoms. Other endocrine glandular imbalances have less-readily identifiable influences on behavior. The gonads, pituitary, pancreas, and adrenals are known to have certain effects on growth, but the psychological impact is paradoxical; i.e., the same defect may cause one child to be meek and retiring but urge another to be aggressive. Thus, geneticists generally agree that what an individual inherits is a range of capacities to respond to a variety of environments. Influencing factors in a response may be the age of onset of a glandular imbalance, *plus* the type of practices used by parents and teachers. Because pupils suffering from glandular imbalance are more vulnerable than others to stress of any kind, teachers may play a vital part in influencing the child's response to his handicap.

In many cases, glandular influences are simply particular kinds of inherited influences. In other instances, they may be due to congenital or environmental factors. *Glands, like heredity, provide a potential for reaction—what that reaction will be depends partially on how the child is treated in school and how he responds to that treatment.*

3. Physique and Personality

A problem of interest even before psychology was recognized as a scientific study is the relationship between physical build and personality. E. Kretschmer postulated the theory that the thickset, round person (pyknic body type) is gay, good-humored, and happy. The lean, underdeveloped person (asthenic body type) is polite, sensitive, and cold. The athletic, strong, symmetrically, and well-developed individual has a personality midway between those of the pyknic and asthenic types. Still another body type, the dysplastic, fits none of the foregoing categories because of asymmetrical development, i.e., thickset upper body and either lean and slight or muscular lower body. He is a mixed type. Research supports this body-type theory to a limited extent, but objections are made to it because it tends to place human beings in fixed categories and ignores the molding influence of environment.

Physique is, no doubt, related to personality but not so consistently as to allow definite personality predictions for individuals. Endocrine disturbances may be evidenced by physique and social behavior, as is demonstrated in mongoloids and cretins. There may be other relationships. The fat boy may be good-humored because he cannot fight, not because he is fat. One's perception of his own physique must not be discounted.

William H. Sheldon has postulated three major body builds: the endomorph (the obese person with abdominal predominance), the ectomorph (the lean, delicate individual with large surface in relation to weight), and the mesomorph (the athletic type with a predominance of bone and muscle). Briefly, the personality typical of the extremes of each of these types is described as follows:

   a.   The endomorph is inclined to physical gratification, is a pleasure-lover, and enjoys association with others.
   b.   The ectomorph is self-sufficient, enjoys intellectual pursuits, and has a sensitive nature.
   c.   The mesomorph enjoys physical exertion, is energetic, and loves competition.

An interesting feature of Sheldon's theory is that he provides for continuous variation in type rather than postulating a trimodal distribution of body types and personality. A given individual is considered to have one or more characteristics of each type; for example, an extreme endomorph is a 7-1-1, a 1 being assigned for minimum mesomorphic and ectomorphic qualities and a 7 for maximum endomorphic features. An extreme mesomorph would be a 1-7-1, and an extreme ectomorph, a 1-1-7. The total is not always 9; a person might be a 2-7-1, a 3-4-3, or some other index combination of less than extreme proportion or a rather balanced distribution of morphological measurements (Sheldon and Stevens, 1942).

An interesting and unanswered question is whether or not the development of a personality, at variance with bodily predisposition, has not been purchased at the cost of stability and sound integration. Does the endomorph become a scholar at some psychic cost? Does a mesomorph become a researcher at the cost of some ego disintegration? It seems, however, that even with the continuity of types for which Sheldon provides, the best that could be hoped for in the way of predicting personality from morphology would reside in guesses only slightly better than pure chance. There are many exceptions—scholars who are endomorphs, social isolates who are endomorphs, and ectomorphs who are gregarious. Moreover, there is an unknown factor in the psychology of expectancy, i.e., the tendency of persons to live up to what others expect them to be (Gephart and Antonoplos, 1969).

In summary, the many unanswered questions about the relationship between body build and personality make it imperative that *teachers should take care not to categorize pupils on the basis of superficial observation of their physical characterstic.*

4. Environment and Personality

In addition to heredity, glandular balance, and body build, the environment helps determine personality development. Modern advances in medicine and hygiene have influenced personality by making the physiological and safety needs less demanding and thus releasing man to seek the higher-level needs of love and self-actualization. Governmental, community, and religious institutions as well as local customs and mores play dynamic roles in forming personality. From the standpoint of the teacher, the more insistent influences are probably the pupil's home, his socioeconomic status, and the community's educational institutions.

Environment may counteract much of heredity's influence. One study shows that, depending on the environment, children may either be like their parents or develop diametrically opposed characteristics (Crandall, 1963, p. 427). For instance, children reared in homes where parents are exceedingly dominating tend either to be excessively submissive or to develop patterns of behavior quite like those of their parents. An accepting and emotionally stable home builds into children a toughness which enables them to meet and cope with obstacles and conflicts. It is especially important, if lives are to be salvaged, if optimal development of potential is to occur, that schools compensate for deficiencies in love, security, acceptance, and respect when such are in short supply in the home (Clark, Goldsmith, and Pugh, 1970).

It is easy for teachers to believe that a "typical" home is much like their own, but there are no typical homes. There are, for instance, different vocational goals and different attitudes toward education; some parents do not consider a college education for their children, and others tacitly assume that college is an integral part of their lives. There are different attitudes toward such problems as drinking, morality, religion, and racial relations. Achievement motivation—to earn grades and achieve excellence—is intimately related to husband-wife-child relationships and interaction (McCandless, 1967, p. 528).

One's life course is not irrevocably directed by the time he enters high school (Strauss, 1969); but his social class has gone a long way in determining the "path of life" he will choose. A teacher can present the same material to all pupils, but the pupils will not learn the same things. What one learns is certainly influenced though not determined solely by his status in society (Herriott, 1963).

When cultural conditions tend to limit the likelihood of an individual's developing his latent talents, there are ways to interrupt the self-perpetuating nature of those limitations. Some individuals who get a glimpse of a better life can generate the initiative to overcome environmental handicaps. Teachers can, through personal creativeness, provide the hope and stimulation for pupils to rise above the restrictions of their social status. This has been demonstrated by numerous programs such as Higher Horizons, Upward Bound, Head Start, and IN (Interested Negroes).

The development of talent—or personality development—requires more than grants and scholarships. It also requires teachers and counselors like Sam Johnson, Henrine Carter, Paul Rucker, and Jasper Browder who devote extra hours to detecting and encouraging elementary and high school pupils in the Mississippi Delta. They measure their success in terms of the number of scholarships the pupils win and then in the number who achieve their educational goals (Mulligan, 1970). The notable study made by James S. Coleman in 1966, *Equality of Educational Opportunity*, proved again what is already known:

> ... teachers can and do make a difference in human development. But the research also indicates that the influence of the school is limited by a variety of outside factors. Obviously, public schooling can never become a panacea for all the ills and shortcomings of society.[2]

2 John Chaffee, Jr., and Patricia Wagner, 1970, "Teachers DO Make a Difference," *American Education*, vol. 6, no. 4, p. 25, May.

The power of teachers to change the course of life for pupils is not a recent discovery. Teachers have been known to improve nutritional standards in their communities, to persuade citizens to beautify homes and yards, and to encourage sanitation projects. But the school influence does not stop at change in the physical environment—personality may also be changed. In one city where a dark prognosis had been made for intellectually handicapped children, a resurvey after seventeen years revealed that most were self-supporting and adequately adjusted. Fewer of them than of the normal population had run afoul of the law or had come to rely upon welfare agencies. The director of the study gave credit to the teachers for transforming the personalities of the pupils from social liabilities into positive assets for self and community.

> Here, again, we find the effect of contacts in those early years with teachers who were not convictionless, but aggressively determined not to lose an opportunity to inculcate good old-fashioned morality, embodying principles of decency and respect for individual personality and clean-mindedness. The most striking result of this survey is to be found in the lasting impression made on these people in childhood by one of the teachers who came in closest contact with them. Science has no tests to evaluate the influence of personality, but the tests of life on growth and development tell the story.[3]

It seems that for teachers the important conclusion to draw on the matter of personality and environment is what psychologists have recently been emphasizing: *We really do not know how great human potential is until consistent effort is made to develop it* (McClelland, 1971).

5. Personal Response

Two individuals perceive the same stimuli in different ways; they react to the same handicaps or opportunities in different manners. The concept of personal response has been incorporated into the so-called "triangle of life" (see Figure 11-1).

It would be easy and logical to argue that the three aspects of personality, as presented in the figure, are in reality only two; that is, one's response is an outcome of one's potential as acted upon by environment. The fact remains that even if this be correct, responses do differ. *Heredity and environment are welded together as interdependent influences by the way one reacts to what he is and has.* Humanistic psychologists object to the concept of man as a mere recipient and passive respondent to stimuli. Bugenthal (1967, p. 7) calls such a view a restricting, mechanomorph concept. Humanistic psychologists emphasize man's response by saying that his dreams, visions, ambitions, and aspirations, which pro-

---

3   Ruth E. Fairbank, 1933, "The Subnormal Child—Seventeen Years After," *Mental Hygiene*, vol. 17, p. 207.

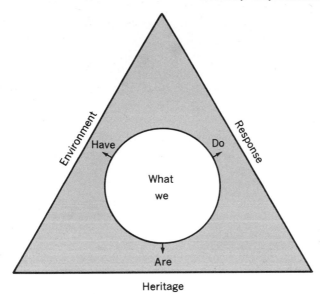

Figure 11-1 The triangle of life. The circle represents the individual whose course of development is influenced by what he has (his environment), what he is (his inherited potential), and what he does (his response to his environment and potentiality). Source: H. E. Walter, 1938, Genetics, 2d ed., New York: The Macmillan Company, p. 280. Courtesy, Estate of H. E. Walter.

ject the future, are as important in determining life style as what one is (heredity) and what one has (environment). Man is, in this view, his own maker (Bonner, 1965, p. 80).

The role of response has been demonstrated in the Fels Research Institute in investigations of IQ changes. Boys and girls tested annually for four years between the ages of four and twelve were grouped into the 25 percent who gained most in IQ (upper quartile of changes) and the 25 percent whose IQ changed least (lower quartile). Those who gained were found to be aggressive, independent, and competitive. Being overly dependent was found to be detrimental to optimal intellectual development (Sontag, Baker, and Nelson, 1958). Nevertheless, we must be sure to avoid ascribing a one-to-one relationship to aggressiveness and IQ. Other factors (potential, opportunity, perception of one's world) must also be considered in intellectual growth. The practical import for teachers is that the following can be recommended as means of fostering improved individual responses:

Faith in the ability of pupils to accomplish can be shown by establishing high, but realistic, expectations. Those teachers who really believe it can say, "I know it's hard, but I believe you can do it."

Freedom to experiment, to find out for himself, and to make mistakes should prevail over the pupil's anxiety to provide the correct answers to problems immediately.

Situations can be devised so that competition, if it is used at all, occurs between peers—where *all* pupils have a chance for victory.

Counseling and individual conferences should encourage pupils to make maximum use of what they have and to view discouraging environmental conditions as a challenge to growth.

Variations in pupils' responses *must* be admitted and *should* be encouraged as a part of developing pride in one's individuality.

Assessment of Personality

Because personality is such a complex entity and because it is responsive to environmental, hereditary, and perceptual factors, its assessment is extremely difficult, and necessarily as vague as our understanding of personality. Just as one who describes another is revealing himself, so the personality assessment device reflects what the maker of the instrument conceptualizes personality to be (Travers, 1970, p. 451). Actually, everything that one does is indicative of his personality; thus any formal evaluation is limited to the range of response allowed by the particular instrument or technique being used.

Personality Inventories

Intelligence and achievement tests must be included in gaining understanding of pupils. Though the areas probed by such tests are certainly aspects of personality, they are dealt with elsewhere in this volume; here we consider only tests that are called "personality inventories."

Our very great need to understand individuals has led to much experimentation on means of standardizing measurement of personality. To date, the degree of success is quite disappointing to those who desire easy and accurate evaluation. Some authors assert that most personality tests—and there are scores of them—lack comprehensiveness and validity and have only limited value for special purposes (Baughman and Welsh, 1962). Others assert that it is psychometric innocence, naïveté, mistaken faith in statistical measures, and a desire to keep up with others that lead to the use and popularity of personality inventories (Rothney, Danielson, and Heimann, 1959, p. 283). Certainly, no one test should be regarded as capable of assessing personality or of doing more than providing some tentative clues to understanding (Ahmann and Glock, 1967, p. 458).

There are several reasons why the use of a static instrument cannot capture the essence of an individual's dynamic pattern of behavior, mood, and temperament. Different aspects of personality are shown in the home, at school, and at play and work; one's answer to items would depend upon how he interpreted the question to which he is responding. In addition, we learn early in life that many of our ideas, aspirations, and fantasies are strictly private, to the degree that we often hide them even from ourselves; it sometimes takes years of therapeutic treatment for us to begin to get an honest portrayal of them. Moreover, the instruments are subject to faking. Rapport with the examiner is vital. If one has little confidence in the tester or wonders how the test might be used, he is likely to ask, "What business is it of his?" One's mood varies from day to day. A happy or unhappy experience a short time before taking the inventory might color many of an individual's responses and lead to an atypical final score. A pupil who comes to the teacher or counselor for personal help will probably be inclined to reveal more of himself than the one who is presenting himself as a candidate for a job.

Some authorities believe that personality inventories may provide limited means of evaluating self-perceptions—an important concept in motivation and learning. If the inventory is used carefully and if results are corroborated by other data, this is a valid contention. However, these instruments should be used as indications or clues—not conclusions. Any standardized test requires some expertise for interpretation; in the case of personality inventories the help of one specially trained in psychometry is essential. Classroom teachers might well turn to other techniques for personality assessment.

Projective Techniques

Projective techniques allow the subject to "project" himself into an amorphous situation and to give it unique meaning. What the individual sees in the meaningless situation is deemed to be a reflection of himself (McClelland, 1971). An example is the Rorschach test: Ink blots of various designs and sometimes colors are shown to the subject, who tells what he sees in them (Rorschach, 1937). Another example is the Murray Thematic Apperception Test (TAT): A number of drawings are presented to the subject, who is asked to tell what is portrayed (Morgan and Murray, 1935). Because the blots and pictures may be considered to have various meanings, what the subject reports seeing in them is considered to be a portrayal (projection) of himself. These and similar instruments, such as doll play, when used by well-qualified psychiatrists and psychologists, provide clues for understanding motives and behaviors of individuals.

Rating Scales

Because the data are obviously tentative and pertinent to limited situations, self-rating scales, such as the Sarbin Adjective Check List (1955), Problem Check List, and the Schrammel-Garbutt Personal Adjustment Scale, can be helpful to the classroom teacher. If the teacher remembers that the results may not be an accurate picture of the personality *as perceived by others*, the view the individual takes of himself may be helpful. For example, clues may be afforded that this individual is hesitant, lacking justified self-confidence, and may need a little more support and encouragement than most of his peers.

An interesting rating scale is the "Guess Who" scale, which has peers rate each other. They are asked to guess who talks a lot, laughs rarely, waits for others to speak, is friendly, etc. The scale has particular value in that the teacher will often see that he perceives a certain pupil in a way that is different from the ways in which the pupil's peers perceive the subject. It is helpful, too, to get some tentative insight into what impression a pupil is making on others.

The teacher can form a tentative opinion as to whether a pupil is justified in having the view of himself that is indicated or whether the view of others is warranted. If the views do not seem to be justified, pointing out contrary evidence over a period of time may help to change opinions. If the views do seem to be justified, the teacher can help the students concerned to develop skills, knowledges, and habits that warrant an upward revision of self-concepts.

Ahmann and Glock (1967, p. 433) indicate that there are several types of errors which affect the **reliability** and **validity** of ratings:

> Personal bias—rating pupils too high or too low
> Rating all pupils near a central point
> Inaccuracies due to ambiguity of the scale
> The "halo effect"—allowing one's general impression of a pupil to influence the scale rating
> Validity is particularly questionable because of the probability of human error on the part of the rater

Rating scales may be somewhat improved if they are used as research instruments to assess group tendencies; if they are used in conjunction with other evaluative devices; and if their tentative and conjectural nature is kept in mind.

Sociometry

Sociometry is a readily available technique for evaluating social personality. Discussion is omitted here because the details are cited in Chapter 10.

Observation of Pupils

This is the most readily available means of understanding pupils, and its use merits deliberate cultivation by teachers. A potential shortcoming of observation is that the overactive and sometimes obstreperous child will be noticed and the meek and quiet one overlooked. There is also a danger that the unusual activity rather than the typical, routine, characteristic behavior will be noticed, or on the other hand, the teacher may be so used to routine behavior that only transitory notice is given to the unusual act or accomplishment. As a teacher, curbing one's tendency to talk and encouraging the participation and activity of pupils by observing their needs and tendencies is a first step toward an integrative classroom. In such a setting creativity, spontaneity, and initiative tend to be high (Flanders, 1965, p. 4).

One way to come to know the pupils and to counteract the tendency to teach by routine and prescription is to make use of anecdotal records. These are brief, periodic, descriptions of typical pupil behaviors. Anecdotes are factual descriptions in behavioral terms (rather than being interpretative) of children's behaviors, development, or social interaction. Anecdotal records require time because they must be done periodically in order to obtain continuity and because adequate **sampling** is essential (Wilson, Robeck, and Michael, 1969, p. 493). Characteristics of a good anecdote are:

1. It gives the date, the place, and the situation in which the action occurred.
2. It describes the actions of the child, the reactions of the other people involved, and the response of the child to these reactions.
3. It quotes what is said to the child and by the child during the action.
4. It describes "mood cues"—postures, gestures, voice qualities, and facial expressions that give cues to how the child felt. It does not provide interpretations of his feelings, only the cues by which a reader may judge what they were.
5. The description is extensive enough to cover the episode. The action or conversation is not left incomplete and unfinished but is followed through to the point where a little vignette of a behavioral moment in the life of the child is supplied.[4]

An example of an anecdote that meets the suggested criteria is the following:

November 1
    Scotty punched Dick today and Dick told me about it. I hadn't seen Scotty do it but Dick said, "Every time he goes by my desk he punches me." I called Scotty up to the desk and asked him about it.

---

4   Daniel A. Prescott, 1957, *The Child in the Educative Process*, New York: McGraw-Hill Book Company, pp. 153-154.

"Sure, I punched him." said Scotty. "Every time he goes by my desk he says, 'Wise guy!' under his breath, so I just let him have it. If he stops calling me a wise guy I'll stop punching him, but he's not going to call me names and get away with it!"

I looked at Dick, Dick said, "Yeah, I call him 'wise guy' because he thinks he is one. He acts like a big shot."

Scotty said, "Who acts like a big shot? Me or You? What did I ever do to you?"

Dick hung his head and mumbled, "Nothing, but I think you act like a big shot."

Scotty looked at me and smiled, "See? I don't know why he calls me a wise guy and I don't think he knows either, but every time he says it I'm going to punch him."

I talked to them both and then told them to return to their seats. As Dick sat down he looked at Scotty and said, "Wise guy!" Scotty punched him.

Dick looked at me and I said, "You asked for it." He said no more.[5]

Although preparing good anecdotes on a number of pupils is time consuming, it takes only a few moments a day when done as it should be done—periodically. The time used may be compensated for by improved pupil understanding, time saved from disciplinary problems, and the salvaging of wasted teaching effort.

The School and Pupil Personality

Next to home influences, the school is probably the most powerful factor in shaping the development of personality. In school the growing individual continues to develop his potential in a planned social context. Here is a laboratory in which he may practice control and direct the display of his basic temperament. If the personality lessons we learn are to be most beneficial in pushing the student toward the pursuit of higher-level needs, *he must not only be understood as an individual, but his environment must be such as to foster the desired kinds of behavior.* Whether or not the aims of school are stated in terms of academic knowledge of behavioral patterns, personality is being changed as the aims are achieved. Too often, emphasis has been primarily on the correction of academic deficiencies. Although such correction is necessary, the more recent emphasis on self-realization, the expansion of the positive, is commendable (Maccoby, 1971). Working to change personality may be pursued (1) by alteration of specific as-

5   Hugh V. Perkins, 1969, *Human Development and Learning*, Belmont, Calif.: Wadsworth Publishing Company, Inc., pp. 27-28.

pects of the environment and (2) by giving attention to the total school atmosphere.

Personality and Child-rearing Practices

Numerous experiments and controlled observations have verified the plasticity and modifiability of the child's personality. Consistency of personality is largely a matter of consistency of environment—having the same parents, home, school milieu, and neighborhood.

It has been found, for instance, that boys who reveal high levels of responsibility had parents who were warm, accepting, and nurturing—especially the mother—and who used moderately strong discipline. Irresponsibility was associated with rejection, neglect, and lack of discipline—especially on the part of the father (Becker, 1964). Many studies point to the fact that parental restrictiveness and hostility tend to foster resentment which may be turned inward against oneself in neurotic anxiety or outward in antisocial behavior (Rosenthal et al., 1962).

Achievement motivation is a phenomenon which shows the complexity of personality. The desire and need to achieve is associated with parental attitudes and behavior. The achiever tends to see his parents as being strong (physically, socially, or economically), dependable, and loving. They reward more than they punish and they let the child know that his success is important to them (McCandless, 1967, p. 541). However, the desire to succeed and earn good marks in school is almost synonymous with anxiety and fear of failure; in addition, achievement motivation is also a matter of faith in oneself—belief that one can succeed (Levine, 1966).

A dilemma for teachers may be inferred from studies of parental handling. They must decide whether they wish to prompt their pupils to become achievers—with a little anxiety and neurotic conflict; or whether they wish to foster freedom, independence, and perhaps some creativity. Most teachers will lean, at least on the verbal level, toward independence and pupil autonomy. If, for instance, they wish to encourage a pupil's self-confidence, they may do so by helping him build skills. If a pupil develops feelings of inferiority because of academic difficulties, he should be given a chance to demonstrate the skills he has. Thus, one poor student who declared he hated schoolwork asserted one day that he could write a better song than the one the class was singing. His teacher encouraged him to try it. He did, and the song was good. It was sung by his classmates, and henceforth he took a more confident and aggressive part in classwork. Similar results were obtained by a teacher who gave a high school boy responsibility for arranging stage lighting—his success flowed over into interest and competence in literature. A girl's poems were read in class and published in the school paper—prior to the teacher's discovery of them, the poems had been hidden.

A junior high school girl gained skill in square dancing. The principal took her dance group to other schools for demonstration, and the girl became perceptibly more outgoing personally and more productive academically. Achievement motivation may be explained by faith in oneself as well as by the compulsion to satisfy and gratify others.

The Effect of the Total School Atmosphere

An example of giving attention to the total school atmosphere is afforded in the Higher Horizons program spearheaded by Schreiber (1960). The setting was in New York City's Manhattanville Junior High School No. 43. The objective was to discover, identify, and stimulate academically able students of a culturally different group. Steps in the total process included (1) identifying "college-able" students through tests, teachers' ratings, and counseling interviews; (2) stimulating them to think of college by pointing to examples of persons with similar backgrounds who made good (thus emphasizing that avenues are open); (3) creating college aspirations by taking them to research centers, libraries, professional schools, and hospitals and by seeking scholarship support; (4) educating the community and parents to accept the worthwhileness of college by personal interviews (parents were found to be not so much uncooperative as busy making a living); (5) educating the faculty through in-service training programs, teacher conferences, and having teachers accompany pupils on planned trips; (6) guiding pupils and parents in individual and group conferences, some of which took place before or after regular school hours, thus requiring an extended school day; (7) providing remedial work to bring pupils to and beyond grade level; and (8) raising the cultural level of pupils by taking them to concerts, operas, theaters, and local college campuses and by securing books for them at wholesale prices.

The results of the Higher Horizons program are encouraging. Of the pupils, 80 percent planned to finish high school, and three-fourths felt that their ambitions had been raised. The year before the project was started, 42 percent of the pupils were graduated from high school; in contrast, 80 percent were still in the project after three years, and others had transferred to other curricula and schools. Students made an average gain of 4 points on the Otis Mental Ability Test.[6] Some pupils from the project became delinquent, but the incidence of delinquency from Manhattanville Junior High School was smaller than that from other comparable schools and did not show the increase that was being noticed citywide.

---

6   A gain of four points would be insignificant for an individual, but such a gain for a group may be regarded as indicative of real progress. When a whole group is tested, both gains and losses will occur as a result of the variability of test results, so a net group gain has a good chance of being real.

Coleman (1968) has shown that schools generate pervasive atmospheres—dependent not only on teachers and their qualifications but also upon the physical plant itself, the neighborhood, and the mental set which the pupils bring to school. In some schools the graduates almost uniformly look forward to continuation of their academic education. In others—and this is not only a function of slum or suburbia—the pupils in large numbers are apathetic toward school or seeking to escape. The major ingredients of a synergetic classroom climate are personal intimacy, lack of friction, personal and social satisfaction, and status (Walberg and Anderson, 1968).

Curriculum and Personality

Those who define curriculum as all the experiences which compose the school would not equate curriculum with course outlines and content. There is a growing number of educational theorists who believe that the curriculum really does not make much difference. The essential emphasis should be upon what is happening to the pupil (Allen, 1971). If he is experiencing wholesome relations with the teacher and his peers, then the content of what he is learning is unimportant, or at least secondary. If the pupil is excited by, or at least not repelled by, the activity of learning, then content is not a great concern.

This author believes that learning the tools of learning—reading, writing, talking, and calculating—are necessary, and some drill, drudgery, and discipline might be in order. Hopefully, pride in achievement, the desire to please others, and a sense of identity will compensate for the hard work necessary to master to tools of learning. After that, developing a love of learning and the habit of learning are the important objectives of the school. Planned, sequential, structured content (including typical classes and programmed studies) is appropriate for some, but others, even in the early grades, do not need imposed structure and can exercise autonomy with mature efficiency. Those who aspire to the skilled occupations and professions—and, in view of changing employment trends, a much greater proportion should be guided toward such aspiration—should be induced (by pressure or temptation) to pursue the systematic study of the sciences and mathematics. Educational theorists and constructive critics view the question of curriculum and teaching-learning transactions in various ways: Brameld (1970) reflects the judgment of many when he says that the curriculum is both outworn and atomistic. In order to provide for relevance and relatedness, the in-school experience should be supplemented by the students' spending half their time outside the school with people and institutions.

Bruner (1968a), who is less outspoken about doing away with curriculum than some of those mentioned immediately below, believes that curriculum should reflect society's needs. And society needs creativity, inventiveness, and exploration. The curriculum also needs to improve human relations and peer-group living.

Hence, the challenge of the school is not so much to answer problems as it is to find them. Curriculum content or structure is useful because appropriate structure can stimulate the process of learning (Bruner, 1963, p. 8).

Dennison (1969) states that the "crisis of the schools" consists of how we are going to deal with the multiple crises in the lives of children. They need to learn to read, write, speak, and calculate, but these learnings can best be accomplished by accepting teachers who look for the teachable moment in the lives of individual children.

Goodlad (1969b) writes that there is too much concern with having a variety of students cover a designated bit of material at a given pace. This necessitates the teacher's doing most of the doing—telling and questioning. The emphasis should be on the development of human beings, on developing individual uniqueness, on fostering a sense of personal worth, and on establishing an identity with mankind.[7]

Goodman (1968) bluntly states that there is no point in having formal studies, a prearranged curriculum, at least until age twelve. He believes that, with guidance to learn a little more, whatever a child learns at an early age will be educational. If Goodman could do as he wished, he would do away with the "machinery" called the public schools. He recommends "incidental education"—the privilege a young child has to poke with interest into whatever goes on and to be able to question, observe, and imitate (Goodman, 1970a).

Hart (1969) discredits the linear plan, in which sequential steps are taken to compel students to learn "the same thing, in the same way, at the same time." Instead pupils should be trusted to handle their own learning at random. The role of teachers is to provide three A's: attention, acceptance, and applause.

Not all critics of education are so desirous of getting rid of the present structure as are such men as Dennison, Goodman, or Hart. Havighurst (1968) voices a widely held view that education has experienced some success and that "the establishment" need not be junked in order to get at some essentials: Teachers who accept pupils, teachers who are models (especially as learners), methods which focus on the enjoyment of the process of learning, and focus on the self-concept of the learner are the matters of basic concern.

Metcalf and Hunt (1970) reflect the burden of this chapter in asserting that the relevant curriculum will deal with personal questions. "Who am I?" "What will I become if my present habits continue?" "What can be done about my conflicts and dilemmas?"

Rogers (1969), trusting in the good which he believes is inherent in every individual, suggests that experiential, self-directed curriculum should be given a trial. He believes that a planned part of whatever curriculum is evolved should

---

7   Such concepts as these are treated in Harold W. Bernard, 1970, *Mental Health in the Classroom*, New York: McGraw-Hill Book Company.

deal with feelings. Dealing with such things as feelings of inadequacy, hatred, desire for power, love, awe, and respect will be an experience in living—not an abstract, verbal preparation for living (Rogers, 1968).

Wright (1970) supports the idea that personality is focal in curriculum in asserting that black studies should illustrate problems of society—identity, humanity, and culture.

Turning from interpretations of what is and speculations on what might be with regard to curriculum and personality development, some data from research investigations provide clues to practical suggestions. The recognition of differences is a continuous and pressing necessity. If the classroom emphasis is on learning content, then slow learners and culturally different pupils are going to suffer blows to their egos in competitive classrooms. If the emphasis is on individual learning, then differences may have positive values: Pupils teach each other about themselves. Hoyt (1964) has reported studies on the nonacademically oriented student indicating that those who appear to be academically inept may give quite another account of themselves when the primary curricular emphasis is on work skills. Kupferman and Ulmer (1964) have also achieved gratifying results with eight- to twelve-year-old boys who had a handicraft program in an industrially oriented school setting. Discipline problems diminished, schoolwork improved, goals were clarified, and boys stuck to projects they would previously have abandoned.

The curriculum is also influential in the motivation of unusually able students. At the present time, about 40 percent of students who are in the upper third in intellectual ability do not enter college. Many factors contribute to this loss of talent—family educational tradition, socioeconomic-class identification, financial resources, local availability of educational opportunity, personality adjustment patterns, and health—but an appropriate, challenging curriculum must also be included.

> Recognizing that the child often does not need drill to learn, he (the teacher) allows the child to discover new relationships, to experiment and explore. He accepts the child as a partner in the exciting search for knowledge. Independent study, creative experiences in science, mathematics, art, and music, and wide contact with the minds of others through books and class visitors are all essential aspects of a challenging program which can stretch the mind and the imagination of the child.[8]

Special classes, independent study, advanced sections of regular classes, individual instruction, research projects, and revised systems of evaluation are used at the elementary and secondary, but particularly at the secondary, levels to assist in providing an appropriate challenge to able students. Whether we con-

---

8   Anna R. Meeks, 1961, in Leonard M. Miller (ed.), *Guidance for the Underachiever with Superior Ability*, Washington, D.C.: U.S. Office of Education, p. 38.

sider the slow learner or the gifted pupil, an important principle is that *curriculum must provide the opportunity for success that derives from exerting one's best efforts.* It should be noted that in all this "the curriculum" is not easily separated from the teacher as a person.

Teaching Methods and Personality

Competitive attitudes are fostered by many aspects of our society, including the highly competitive structure of school life (Meyer, 1969). The easy winner has no challenge to exertion, and the inevitable loser must protect himself by withdrawal or adjust by lowering his self-esteem.

In what has become a classic in the field of experimental method, the late Kurt Lewin and his associates showed how methods of dealing with children can be arranged to produce predictable kinds of behavior. Groups of ten-year-old boys, equated as far as possible, were subjected to autocratic, democratic, and laissez faire leaders. In the authoritarian climate, policy was determined by the leader, steps were dictated one at a time, the leader designated working groups and tasks, and praise and criticism were of a personal nature. In the democratic climate, politics were matters of group decisions, goals were discussed and the leader suggested alternatives, members were free to work with whom they wished, division of tasks was left to the group, and the leader praised or criticized impersonally. In the laissez faire group, there was complete freedom for group or personal decision without leader intervention, the leader said he would help if asked but took no other part—tasks and grouping were determined without the leader's participation. Comments on the work being done were infrequent. After six weeks it was noted that aggressive actions per meeting were thirty-eight for the laissez faire group, thirty for the autocratic group, and twenty for the democratic group. Some of the boys in the autocratic group were apathetic, and others stopped coming. Boys were asked to evaluate the work and declared that they did not like the autocratic group—*but* they directed their hostility to other boys. Boys in the laissez faire group felt they needed more direction and help. They appreciated and liked the democratic leader. Scapegoats were created in the autocratic group, and the products of their labors were ultimately used as weapons of warfare. When the leaders left the room, the autocratic group quickly deteriorated; in the democratic group, there was little difference in the work atmosphere (Lewin, Lippitt, and White, 1939). Repetitions of the experiment in which leaders switched roles indicated that the results were an outcome of the atmosphere rather than the personalities of the leaders.

If children are to develop the quality of independence, they must be given freedom to think, choose, and act on their own, but this must not be confused with lack of direction by the teacher (Bruner, 1968*b*; Hart, 1969). Democracy also demands the ability to delegate responsibility and the development of specialties. In their training and experience, teachers have specialized in order to give responsible direction, and they should not neglect to use their wisdom for the benefit of the pupils. However, as pupils grow and gain experience and knowledge, they should be allowed more freedom in self-direction.

To the extent that the teacher actively recognizes the worth of each child, he will be enhancing the pupil's feeling of personal significance and security. Among other things, this means that a pupil should be commended for the effort he exerts and for the quality of work that is proportionate to his present ability. To say to Sue, "See how neat and well-behaved Sally is," is likely to foster feelings of personal insignificance or resentment toward the teacher or Sally. Giving appropriate praise, taking time to listen to pupils, and showing interest in their comments and activities are classroom essentials.

Teaching methods which neglect group processes and minimize pupil interaction may be criticized on both a developmental and ideological level. In a democracy, perhaps even more than in other political orientations, each individual has a part to play that is significant to others. The belief that there should be no social isolates is based on psychological fact (Fraiberg, 1967) as well as on cultural mores (Bruner, 1968a). Human beings develop by virtue of their associations with one another, and those associations cannot be taken for granted or slighted in teaching methods. Much schoolwork could be better oriented and better motivated if more emphasis were placed on group accomplishment and less upon comparative-competitive grading systems (Glasser, 1969).

The Teacher's View of Personality Problems

Wickman (1928), in a still widely quoted study, showed that teachers were more likely to consider whispering, inattentiveness, carelessness in work, tattling, and disorderliness as serious problems and less likely to be concerned about shyness, withdrawal, and daydreaming. Psychiatrists, on the other hand, were inclined to take another view. They considered that the more serious problems were shyness, withdrawal, and daydreaming. Follow-up studies indicate that in recent years teachers have come to see more clearly the serious implications of such behavior (Hunter, 1957), though there is still much room for improvement. The contemporary view is that behavior, whether it be shyness or bullying, should not be considered too seriously and that the child should be viewed in his total behavior system. Any one trait may be of considerable importance, but its significance cannot be determined in isolation. It is the child, not the trait, that should be watched.

It is acknowledged that the view and role of teachers must, of necessity, differ from that of clinicians. The teacher has a group with which to be concerned —the clinician can view one person at a time (Mathis, Cotton, and Sechrest, 1970, p. 27). Teachers will be in a better position to help personality development when they recognize what is important and significant and what might better be overlooked. They need to know that the child who reveals several atypical behaviors and does so consistently is more in need of attention than one who makes a gross, but rare, misstep. Moreover, they must realize that the behavior is a symptom of difficulty and look for the sources. Knowledge of these source factors will often lead to the identification of basic needs that are not being satisfied; once the needs are recognized, means of satisfying them become evident.

The Teacher's Impact on Pupil Personality

Because education is a human process, the school's most important influence is the teacher (Allen, 1971). He sets the tone of the classroom and establishes the mood of the group. He is the authority figure providing the direction for behavior. If well liked, he is a model and is consciously imitiated; if he is disliked, pupils may still unconsciously absorb his manners and attitudes. A dominating teacher may force an already shy child into further withdrawal. A teacher with social-class prejudice may generate negative attitudes toward learning on the part of those children. Teachers who have colorless, drab personalities may cause pupils to be restive and inattentive.

Flanders (1965), Glidewell and others (1966), Lewin (1939), and Schmuck and Van Egmond (1965), along with many others, have confirmed in experiments what we were pretty sure of anyway—the personality of the teacher (if it could be separated from content and method) is a powerful factor in the learning habits and personality development of pupils. Rosenthal and Jacobson (1968) indicated that even the way teachers viewed elementary pupils in terms of expectancies made measurable differences in the rate and direction of pupil growth. Hogan and Green (1971) found confirmation for the hypothesis, but Claiborn (1969) failed to get similar results with high school seniors. Although not ruling out the possibility of teachers' expectancies having an influence on pupil achievement, Claiborn says the amount of the effect certainly is equivocal at the present time. Silberman (1969) studying four teacher attitudes—attachment, concern, indifference, and rejection—found that not only are children aware of the teacher's attitude toward them but their actions are colored by how they see teachers dealing with their peers.

> It would appear that personally maladjusted teachers may or may not affect the personal and social adjustment of their pupils in an adverse way, depending upon the type of overt behavior through which the teacher resolves her psychological frustrations. The maladjusted teacher who makes her adjustments through *impunitive* (glossing over difficulties) and *intropunitive* (self-blaming) patterns of behavior may be ex-

tremely unhappy herself, but have essentially no negative influence on her pupils' growth and adjustment. However, there is a high probability that the maladjusted teacher who employs *extrapunitive* (blaming others) patterns of behavior to reduce her tensions will have an undesirable effect on the psychological growth and adjustment of her pupils. Children in her classroom will probably suffer intense frustration and pain as she vents her aggressive tendencies through sarcasm, threats, inconsistent episodes of anger, and corporal punishment . . . There seems to be little excuse in a democratic society for *forcing* children to suffer the taunts and gibes of a bitter teacher. This bleak picture of certain teacher-pupil relationships is only partially mitigated by the remarkable resiliency with which children respond to social pressures from all adults.[9]

Fortunately, when teachers are competent and emotionally mature, the total school atmosphere, the curriculum, teaching methods, administrative organization, and, of course, teachers' views of "problems" funnel through the individual teacher. Unfortunately, when the teacher is incompetent and unable to set aside his own conflicts and "hangups," school atmosphere, curriculum, method, administration, and humane philosophy are of little help. In a study of thirty-year-old persons who had been studied as infants, children, and adolescents, Mac-Farlane makes this devastating, or hopeful (depending on what kind of person the teacher is) statement:

You as teachers have a direct impact upon a child for only around 180 days out of his long developmental years. Yet it is surprising how many of our thirty-year-olds remembered all of their teachers and how many recalled teachers who were especially important to them as the ones who simultaneously respected their feelings, excited their interests and elicited a maximum performance from them. At any age, of course, we all like people who add to our earned self-esteem and bring out our best. In this current wave of raucous demand for the teaching of "more hard facts," there is often naïve ignoring of the fact that it is children with all their differences in interests, abilities, temperaments and degree of internal motivation who are to be incited to learning. And this demands of teachers not only knowledge of subject matter but knowledge and appreciation of individual differences of children and flexibility in approach to teaching so necessary to elicit interest and industry. So I urge those of you who enjoy the process of teaching children not to let yourselves be pushed around by these vocal "viewers with alarm." Of course, if you do not enjoy trying to reach this large variety of individuals euphe-

9 George G. Thompson, 1962, *Child Psychology: Growth Trends in Psychological Adjustment*, 2d ed., Boston: Houghton Mifflin Company, p. 670.

mistically known as the "school child," you should not make teaching your profession because variety in profusion you will inevitably meet![10]

Summary

As used in this chapter, personality refers to those aspects of the being which function in interpersonal processes. It refers to the social aspects of living and learning. Although personality consists of inherited, glandular, and morphological aspects and tendencies, it is the environmentally induced aspects in which the educator is functionally most interested. Personality, more than physique or intelligence, is responsive to teaching-learning transactions. Humanistic psychology, more than other psychologies, emphasizes the idea that personality is more than a cumulation from the past—it consists also of what one chooses. One can plan, strive, and rework his personality in terms of what he aspires to be.

Our need to understand personality has led to the development of numerous inventories, questionnaires, and scales, none of which are more than tentatively accepted by teachers and psychologists. When used, they should be for research and be regarded as supplementary and corroborative data. Projective techniques have merit in personality evaluation, as do role playing, observation, and interviewing.

The personality of a child derives in significant part from child-rearing practices and the parents' own emotional status. The school atmosphere, curriculum, teaching methods, and teachers' views of problems all have measurable effect on the developing personality of the pupil. But all these are transferred or communicated to the pupil by and through the teacher; hence, the teacher is the vital factor in the personality development of the child as school pupil.

Suggested Additional Readings

GOODMAN, PAUL, 1970, "High School Is Too Much," *Psychology Today*, vol. 4, no. 5, pp. 25ff, October.

A school critic, who perhaps is the most "far out," tells why he believes the present school system is so obsolete that reform is impossible. The solution is to scrap the system and learn without classrooms.

HAVIGHURST, ROBERT, 1968, "Requirements for a New Valid Criticism," *Phi Delta Kappan*, vol. 50, pp. 20-26.

In presenting some of the things which schools must do in order to be influences for symmetrical personality development, the author evaluates some of the proposals and criticisms of other reformists.

10   Jean Walker MacFarlane, 1963, "From Infancy to Adulthood," *Childhood Education*, vol. 39, p. 89.

MACCOBY, MICHAEL, 1971, "The Three C's and Discipline for Freedom," *School Review*, vol. 79, pp. 227-242.

"Years of schooling have reinforced an abstracted cognitive style which prepares them [pupils] neither to exercise creative talents nor to enjoy their leisure productively." The three C's Maccoby recommends are concentration, criticism, and communication.

MASLOW, ABRAHAM H., 1968, "Some Educational Implications of the Humanistic Psychologies," *Harvard Educational Review*, vol. 38, pp. 685-696.

The first job of each of us is to find ourselves and face up to what we are—or may be. Maslow believes that education can be vastly improved by becoming intrinsically motivated instead of being so largely chosen, directed, and evaluated by others.

ZIGLER, EDWARD F., 1970, "A National Priority: Raising the Quality of Children's Lives," *Children*, vol. 17, no. 5, pp. 166-170.

Improving the quality of children's lives is much more than a school problem; it is a challenge of high priority for the nation. A U.S. Office of Education official presents some of the specific tasks which must be accomplished.

12

Problem Solving
and Creativity

Citizens of contemporary society need to meet and deal with the inevitability of problem solving both as individuals and as group participants. Hence, if education is to be relevant, it must accept the challenge of permitting pupils to solve problems. School experiences cannot duplicate out-of-school situations because those situations are obsolete in a few years. Approaches to problems rather than answers to them should be a serious concern of teachers, for life after school will bring problems that have not been anticipated in the best classrooms. If intelligence is to attain its highest potential, it must be used for more than remembering, imitating, and trial-and-error experimenting. If the individual is to realize his capacity for uniqueness, he must be able to create novel responses. If citizens and statesmen are to keep their government dynamic, healthy tradition and custom must be guides rather than rules. If society is to continue to evolve, individuals must be able to adapt to changing conditions.

Teachers in a democratic society should be acutely aware of the nature of problem solving so that they can give effective guidance to pupils in the development of this significant ability. Uncomfortable as it is to school personnel and government officials in our society, the desirable citizen is the one who questions, criticizes, judges, evaluates, investigates present procedures, and suggests means of improvement.

Creativity is an attribute that leads to solving problems in new ways. Creativity is readily thought of as having artistic or literary connotations. It is that and more. It is the response that is off-beat, odd, and typically uncomfortable to those respectful of tradition (Parnes, 1971). There is much evidence of creativity today in art, music, technology, and social living. However, many feel that creative problem solving does not get much endorsement in schools. Many are convinced that the creativity which is so much needed is stifled in the schools. Creativity survives or is nourished only in the particularly robust individual—the one who enjoys his offbeat, oddball divergence.

The Problem-solving Milieu

Basic Considerations

The words "thinking," "problem solving," and "reasoning" mean much the same thing to some persons, but to others there are shades of difference. Thinking may mean just a fleeting idea such as "I think I'll take a walk." When one says, "I'll think about that," however, he may mean that data will be gathered, weighed, and a deliberate decision reached. He is really engaged in problem solving.

Reasoning means using mental processes and basic principles and the drawing of inferences or parallels. Reasoning is the process involved in working toward the solution of a problem, the answer to which is not immediately supplied by past experience. Three elements in this process deserve particular consideration. The first element is time. Reasoning involves the *delay* of a response while the reasoner assembles, arranges, and rearranges the information needed for the solution of the problem. The second element is the information itself. Reasoning takes place *only* when the facts pertinent to a solution are known. If a solution is stumbled upon, it is only a trial-and-error answer. The third element is the goal toward which reasoning is directed. These elements can be placed together to form a definition of reasoning: A process of delaying responses until data are arranged into a new combination so that a novel solution to a problem is perceived.

Another factor involved in reasoning and problem solving is tentativeness. It is said that the completely logical person is not a man of action. The statement is based on the assumption that the completely logical person requires absolute answers to problems before he is willing to act and on the fact that there are no ultimate, unalterable answers. The logical person knows that not all the data are gathered, not all the situations have been defined, and not all the events in an individual's life have been accounted for. Because *all* the data will never be gathered or *all* the alternatives explored, it is necessary to act on tentative conclusions. These tentative conclusions may be regarded as best current guesses, and because they are based on some data, they will be better than stabs in the dark. We cannot be practical (in the sense of getting something done) and hold action in abeyance until the answers are complete and indisputably correct.

As individuals trying to achieve our own maximum potential and as teachers trying to help pupils toward better adjustment, we must stress the necessity of learning to act on tentative conclusions. It must be realized that there is a need for balance between what *might* be done about a problem and what *is* done about it. Logical and tentative answers must be put into practice. There may be no ultimate solution, but there is, in all probability, a satisfactory one. The classroom implications will be difficult for some teachers to accept. The temptation to give conclusive answers must be avoided. It is wise to leave some unanswered questions at the end of the period or the day. It is necessary to act even when more time would mean more valuable data.

Problems differ in type and degree of difficulty. A young child may assemble jointed sticks to reach an object that is otherwise beyond his reach, but he would find the solution of an algebra problem much too difficult. This difference in ability to solve problems indicates that an important factor in reasoning is maturation. It takes time for the brain and perceptual powers to develop to the point where relationships can be perceived. This, however, does not rule out the possibility of restructuring the material to be learned so that less-mature pupils can comprehend some parts of it. Basic facts of order, cause and effect, and classification can be taught in some form at any age (Bruner, 1963a, p. 12). By encouraging dialogue about these structures, the pupil can come to appreciate their significance in his life in and out of school. Discussion is a crucial aspect in the domain of reasoning, logic, and problem solving (Bruner, 1968a). At this point a psychological principle (see Chapter 2) is illustrated: Growth is a result of the interaction of the learner with a comprehensible environment.

The part played by maturation in problem solving is of much more than academic interest to teachers. In practice, the situations presented to pupils must be appropriate to their developmental level. Adults have concepts which children lack, but those concepts can be learned—and with guidance can be learned economically (Gagné, 1966, p. 149). Problems that are too difficult will result in blind behavior, retreat, or frustration. Children show this blind reaction when their efforts to open a box are futile, and they tearfully beat the box or the cover. Retreat, or "leaving the field," is illustrated by either actually abandoning the situation or retiring within oneself (as the college student does when he daydreams during an incomprehensible lecture). Pupils in school leave the field by engaging in horseplay when they should be working at their arithmetic or algebra problems. Frustration in children is evidenced by such symptoms as withdrawing and temper tantrums. All warn the teacher that more appropriate challenges should be presented. In the past the remedy for the pupil who showed symptoms of frustration w s corporal punishment. Increasingly today, the approach is understanding and studying the appropriateness of school tasks (Emblen, 1969).

Problems appropriate to the pupil's developmental level aid him in acquiring confidence. The teacher, bearing in mind the importance of problem-

Marion Bernstein/College Newsphoto Alliance

solving ability, will (1) show how the problems have some personal meaning, (2) stress the value of *doing* something in addition to knowing something, (3) indicate the relationship of facts to solutions, (4) teach the specific principles involved, and (5) identify the experiences that serve to illustrate those principles. Torrance (1966) suggests that teachers be alert to the effects on the pupils' self-concept of not having their ideas taken seriously and of conveying the idea that there is only one answer to a problem.

It would be gratifying if we could draw up a list of age-graded maturational tasks that would serve as a guide to teachers in various grades. But research in grade placement, acceleration, and retention in a grade shows that maturation is only one factor among many in a pupil's school success. For example, repeating a grade—thus gaining a year's maturation for the pupil—often results in less progress than would going on to the next grade. Success is also dependent on experience and the teacher's skill in making material meaningful or challenging. Normal three-year-olds have learned to read (Pines, 1963), and elementary pupils have learned algebra. Thus no scheme of school organization, however carefully detailed, will provide for the range of differences found at any one school grade. The assumption simply has not worked that students, under compulsion, would learn the same things, in the same way, at the same rate (Hart, 1969).

All reasoning depends on information, as well as on the brain power necessary to utilize that information. People are often considered good thinkers simply because they have experience and information that enable them to deal constructively with a situation. Thus readiness for problem solving is dependent to a very large extent upon a background of experience. The dependence of reasoning on experience suggests four widespread teaching practices that are inimical to reasoning.

Obstacles to Problem Solving

1. Rote learning does not foster the development of powers of reasoning. Teachers and theoreticians speak of rote learning in derisive tones because it inhibits the ability to think. Facts learned in isolation, for the sake of facts, remain isolated and are not called for in variable contexts. Thus, a teacher may be able to recite that frustration tends to increase aggression but then assign further school tasks to the pupil who misbehaves. A pupil may get an A in Latin and then be completely at loss when his teachers ask him to figure out the meaning of the word "agrarian" by examining its roots.

If thinking is to take place, the search for information must not be limited by a course of study or by what the teacher deems to be important. The teacher must, therefore, be patient when pupils seem to wander from the subject. Guidance is needed, certainly, but the school must be a laboratory where experiences pertinent to the particular individual are provided. The role of experience has been summarized in four steps: *(a)* Children should have continuous experience; *(b)* experiences should be discussed and, when appropriate, a record of them made; *(c)* experiences should be related through pupil activity; and *(d)* experiences should have meaning by being related to the pupil's life—insight means relationship.

These remarks should not be misinterpreted as a recommendation that facts should be neglected. Data, facts, and knowledge are the tools for and materials of thinking. But repeating the names of the Presidents in order, listing the classifications of insects, or memorizing the theorems in geometry is learning of a limited type. Unless the facts are learned in terms of the individual's own experience, in terms of his understanding of their meaning and importance, in terms of his problems and needs, they are useless in developing his power to analyze, interpret, and synthesize. Children as young as two can be taught the fundamentals of problem solving; but more important than facts or freedom—being left alone—is the quality of relationship between the child and his mentor.

In a study of 240 two-year-olds, some were systematically taught concepts such as top, open, wet, smooth, far, many, same, different, etc. Children in the "discovery group" had the same experiences, human contacts, and play materials, but the instructors did less labeling and naming. A control group consisted of children who were tested but were not in either experimental group.

> After eight months of training, both experimental groups performed better than those in the control group on 14 of 16 measures, nine of these differences being statistically significant. The experimental groups were superior on such diverse tasks as the Stanford-Binet Intelligence Test, language comprehension and use, perceptual discrimination, motor behavior, delayed reaction, and persistence at a boring task. More important, children of lower socioeconomic background in the experimental group outperformed the middle-class children in the control group on 14 of the measures, on four of which the differences were statistically significant.
>
> However, we were surprised to find that when the two experimental groups were compared [immediately and after a year], the children exposed to the meticulously developed concept training curriculum performed significantly better than the children in the discovery group on four measures only: (1) the concept familiarity index, which is highly loaded with items taught in the curriculum; (2) motor performance; (3) ability to follow instructions in sequence; and (4) simple form discrimination. On all other measures, the children in the discovery group did as well or better. Thus it appears that the concept training did not generalize to other dimensions of behavior any more than did the discovery condition.
>
> We interpret these findings as follows: (1) the two-year-old is highly capable of learning a great deal with only two hours per week of instruction; but (b) what he is taught is not so important as the conditions under which he is taught, specifically the nature of the adult-child relationship.
>
> . . . In the concept training group the child's response to the situation was usually specific to the training materials, and he was guided by the instructor. In the discovery group, the child's response was perhaps less frequently specific to the materials and requirements of the instructor, but he was rewarded by the instructor's voice, gesture, or physical contact when he initiated a response. Thus, both conditions provided the

child with an opportunity to respond and be rewarded in a situation that allowed for a strong affectional bond, and increasingly complex stimuli requiring increasingly complex responses. As the program progressed, most children found it possible to organize the stimulation they received and to respond to the instructor with increasing ease and effectiveness.

We believe that the superior performance of both experimental groups was the result of one or more of the following elements: (1) the regularity of exposure to a structured learning condition; (2) the affective relationship between instructor and child; (3) the uninterrupted nature of the instructor-child interaction; (4) the increasing realization by the child that he could respond to stimulation and be rewarded for his response.[1]

Experience, it must be remembered, is a personal affair. Significant problems and significant learning can be stated only in terms of the individual pupil.

2. In addition to the futility of rote learning, another factor inimical to the development of reasoning is the teacher's excessive dependence on imaginary problems. The study of mental discipline and transfer of training indicates that performance of mental exercises is not necessarily carried over to other situations. Emphasis must be on *real* problems that confront the pupil, and stress must be placed on methods of solutions—the sources of information, the classifying of data, the weighing of relative merits of sources of information. Thus study of any problem should not stop with answers from a textbook; it should include training in the use of encyclopedias and other reference books and emphasize the value of consulting experts. If these methods are stressed, the pupil will be prepared to approach such problems as "How can citizens make their wants known to their elected representatives?" or "How can a hobby be made a source of financial self-sufficiency?" "How can we raise money so the class can make a bus field trip to the state capitol?" These problems are quite different from "How many 1-inch cubes will have three red faces, how many will have two red faces, and how many will have one red face if a 3-inch cube is cut so that there are twenty-seven 1-inch cubes?" The carry-over value of such a problem is negligible. Questions raised by an instructor of the psychology of learning and teaching can be artificial if they are answered in terms of intuitive beliefs or past classroom experiences. The student who reflects on his past experiences *and* consults supplementary references is forming habits of problem solving that have current and future value.

3. The **teacher's complex**—the desire to answer pupils' questions—is another practice detrimental to encouraging reasoning ability. If the teacher feels somewhat insecure, he will be afraid that not answering the question will cause

| 1   Francis H. Palmer, 1969, "Learning at Two," *Children*, vol. 16, no. 2, pp. 55, 56.

the pupil to think less highly of him. Even in the study of mathematics it is preferable to leave the question open rather than to view "authority" with awe. Most scientific questions are, at present, open (Davis, 1966, p. 122). Bright pupils, even in the elementary school, may recognize the bluff of the teacher who fears the unanswered question. A seventh-grade pupil lost respect for a teacher who told his class that meteorology was the study of meteors. If the teacher is sure of himself or has the requisite knowledge to answer the question, he can with confidence say, "That's a good question for you to study. I'd like to know more about it myself. See what the encyclopedia has to say about it and let me know." Another approach might be to say, "I have some very definite ideas about the problem, but before I tell you what they are I wish you'd formulate an answer—then we'll see how well we agree." Certainly, the teacher is nipping a good educational opportunity in the bud if he answers questions in order to prove himself.

4. Problems inappropriate to the pupils' level of experience do not stimulate reasoning. The necessity that the teacher observe his pupils to see that problems are meaningful to them has been exceptionally well stated by William James:

> Let us give the name of *hypothesis* to anything that may be proposed to our belief; and just as the electricians speak of live and dead wires, let us speak of any hypothesis as either *live* or *dead*. A live hypothesis is one which appeals as a real possibility to him to whom it is proposed. If I ask you to believe in the Mahdi, the notion makes no electric connection with your nature—it refuses to scintillate with any credibility at all. As an hypothesis it is completely dead. To an Arab, however (even if he be not one of the Mahdi's followers), the hypothesis is among the mind's possibilities; it is alive. This shows that deadness and liveness in an hypothesis are not intrinsic properties, but relations to the individual thinker. They are measured by his willingness to act.[2]

Facts, data, information are fundamental in problem solving. Students occasionally object to examinations in educational psychology that called for stating facts and principles: "You told us that the important thing was to develop the ability to reason." Theirs would be a valid objection if the facts were treated as isolated bits of information or as words to be memorized. But it must be clearly understood that reasoning—in educational psychology and in all other areas—must always depend on facts; the more pertinent the facts, the more direct and incisive the reasoning. A respect for facts is, of course, an important attitude to be developed in school. When pupils get into discussions and arguments, the teacher should ask them to compare the effectiveness of those who marshal the facts and those who make their emphasis simply by means of loudness. Pupils

---

2   *The Philosophy of William James: Selected from His Chief Works*, New York: Random House, Inc., no date, p. 158. The passage was taken from William James, *The Will to Believe*, 1897.

should learn that in evaluating facts, research articles are superior to popular articles; that newspaper accounts are often slanted; and that first-hand accounts are superior to hearsay and rumor. When teaching methods provide guidance in the search for facts, suggest syntheses of information, pose new interpretations of material, and provisionally tie factual knowledge into new combinations, a problem-solving attitude is fostered (Kuethe, 1968, p. 34).

Scientists emphasize that the solution to problems must necessarily be hidden somewhere in or among the data. If the answer is not discovered, there are only two explanations: (1) The data are as yet insufficient, and (2) the investigator lacks the insight to see the answer. There is an inherent relationship between learning to think and the accumulation of facts which are understood.

If we differentiate between education and training—and it must be admitted that training has a proper place—we could say that the aim of education is to foster problem-solving ability. This broad aim of education can be accomplished if three factors—maturation, personal experience, and the systematic gathering of knowledge—are considered.

Steps in Problem Solving

Dewey (1910) has analyzed the aspects of problem solving into what is now regarded as a classical statement of six steps. These are (1) a felt need, (2) statement of the specific problem, (3) accumulation of data, (4) formulation of a hypothesis, (5) testing the hypothesis, and (6) formulation of a generalization. In the actual process of thinking, the steps do not necessarily follow in the precise order indicated. There is a skipping back and forth. Feelings, partial insights, imagery, and verbal activity are mixed together. The steps are an after-the-fact analysis of what took place (Hardie, 1967). When one reflects on the many inventions, theories, practices, and situations resulting from reasoning, it is quite obvious that problem solving cannot easily be resolved into a series of orderly steps. Certain steps will be discussed in this section, but it must be remembered that in a given reasoning process the steps may be rearranged or two or more steps may be taken simultaneously.

Recognizing the Need

Before the individual projects himself into a problem-solving situation he must feel a need or lack. The difficulty may be felt with sufficient definiteness as to set the mind at once speculating upon its probable solution, or an undefined uneasiness and shock may come first, leading only later to a definite attempt to find out what is the matter.[3]

| 3   John Dewey, 1910, *How We Think*, Boston: D. C. Heath and Company.

Many attempts to teach pupils how to think fail at this initial stage. Problems that pupils do not comprehend and that have no personal meaning are given. Because they do not understand, there can be no felt need. The consequences are superficial performance of the task and dependence upon adult authority for the answer. There is a place for teacher direction and assistance, but the starting point is a problem that pupils can understand and with which they can identify.

Internalizing the Problem

A need may exist but it is not a problem until it is accepted. It may be only implicitly acknowledged, but preferably it will be verbally expressed. External conditions do not necessarily create a problem situation. For example, the payment of income tax may be a problem for an adult. The payment of the tax may actually in some way interfere with the child's easy adjustment, but is not a problem until recognized as such.

Because problems exist only in terms of the experience of the individual, it can be seen why the teacher's eagerness to *give* answers is inimical to thinking. It is not surprising that pupils in permissive classrooms do more hypothesizing than those who learn to depend on authority. Opportunity for flexibility of behavior is an essential of problem solving in the classroom (Harris, 1971). Pupils must be allowed to wrestle with situations before they can see the inherent obstacles. If the teacher gives the solution immediately, the time necessary for the student's understanding of the problem is too short. Many authorities complain that teachers are so much concerned with pouring information into students that little time is left for them to ask questions. Psychologists and teachers who are interested in the future adjustment of pupils as well as in their present behavior must recognize that the questions pupils ask help to develop a lifelong kind of education. Gifted underachievers are too frequently those who resist the conformity demanded by some teachers in "lesson hearing" (Stern, 1962).

Gathering Data

Teachers must respect, if they are to lead pupils to respect, the third step in problem solving—the *accumulation of data.* The tendency to allow prejudice, tradition, slogans, and clichés to interfere with reasoning processes must be avoided. Reasoning cannot begin with a conviction.

Authorities in the field of research state that the "original mind is the informed mind." Competence in research—knowing what is worth investigating, knowing how to select productive methods, and being able to foresee the most likely outcome of study—is the result of being well informed. The accumulation of knowledge in any area contributes to competence.

Although they may recognize the importance of information and its continued acquisition, teachers have apparently grossly neglected the matter of helping pupils record that information. Recognized scholars as a general rule do not depend too heavily on their memories—they "make a note of it." Teachers should begin early to emphasize this important skill. Among the practices involved in gathering and recording data that could be begun as early as the seventh grade and perhaps earlier are the following:

1. Encourage pupils to make a record of sources. Get them to note the writer, the date of the material, and the book or magazine in which the information appeared. Not only will this save time, but it will add impressiveness to their presentation of data.
2. Encourage pupils to develop skill in making brief notes. Too much time spent in recording reduces the time available for research. Too many notes discourage the student from using them.
3. Encourage students to take notes on cards rather than on full sheets of paper. Such notes will require the student to fill in the gaps created by concise notes and to become "active" as he presents his information from his notes.

Forming a Hypothesis

The fourth step in problem solving, *formulation of a hypothesis*, simply means to make a tentative guess about the probable outcome of a particular situation. As a pupil matures and acquires experience that enables him to evaluate his data, his hypothesis will be altered and improved. Thus, it can be expected that the typical high school student will have less difficulty in formulating a valid hypothesis than will younger students, but some elementary pupils can and do form them. It must not, however, be assumed that processes of thinking are alike in the younger and older child. Piaget's idea that children's learning and thinking is *intuitive*—direct and specific experiences—up to about age seven is confirmed by other investigators. From about seven to eleven their thinking is *concrete*—experiences are related and grouped; not until about age eleven, at the stage of *formal* operations, does thinking become abstract and adult (Almy, 1968, p. 74).

It is up to the teacher to stress the point that the hypothesis is a theory to be accepted or rejected. Whether the hypothesis is teacher-stated or brought out by questions such as "What do you think will be the result?" it is something that should be tested and accepted or rejected. It is *not* something that must be supported. This error in reasoning is made by many adults; i.e., they formulate a hypothesis and then seek facts to support it. Pupils should be led to realize that it takes time to formulate a good working hypothesis. This is no less true for elementary pupils who are working on the problem "How playgrounds should be regulated" than it is for high school pupils who are working on the problem "How delinquency can be reduced in our town" or "What is the mathematical formula for timing traffic lights?"

The fact that steps in reasoning do not necessarily follow a sequential order is illustrated in the formulation of the hypothesis. The initial formulation may indicate the need for further data; further data, when gathered, may necessitate a reformulation of the hypothesis. At this step, the biased reasoner will tend to cling to his original theory; the student of superior reasoning ability will keep an open mind.

Group deliberations and decisions have been found to be somewhat more productive of problem-solving skills. The human mind can hold only a minimum amount of data pertaining to any one problem (Bruner, 1968*b*). Hence, the pooling of information and hypotheses can be advantageous, particularly if those who tend to be negatively critical are held somewhat in check. Thus teaching methods—as well as teacher attitudes toward problems—are of consequence in establishing the conditions that may lead pupils to formulating valid hypotheses. In fact, teacher attitude, including respect for pupils' contributions, is probably more important than techniques when it comes to exercising problem solving ability.

Testing the Hypothesis

In order to take step 5—*test the hypothesis*—pupils can be asked to foresee the consequences of their tentative proposal. They can be given an opportunity to put the proposal to a trial run. If conditions permit, both tests may profitably be made.

Group discussions, dealing with situations that are real to the pupils can provide the experience that should accompany the process of maturation. Listening, questioning, and commenting are all helpful in forming a hypothesis. By listening the pupil gets ideas to add to his own. Through questioning, he gets information that he thinks is important. In commenting, he rearranges and alters his own ideas. Furthermore, in group discussion the pupil projects himself more firmly into the situation. The child needs to talk about his problems even more than the adult does. It appears that to the extent to which one can talk about his problems it becomes less necessary for him to act them out. The verbal-symbolic approach to dilemmas works well in many instances (Bernard and Huckins, 1968). In view of those obvious benefits of group work, it seems somewhat odd that it takes so long for teachers to realize that it is so productive. In view of the fact that many problems of citizens must be solved in groups, the motivating factor of social contact, and the advantage of pooled wisdom, the teacher has significant reasons for providing time for group work and group discussion. More and more, educators are accepting the idea that pupils should do more talking, and teachers do less of it, in the classroom (Flanders, 1965).

So-called "experimental work" in the high school sciences may or may not teach pupils how to reason. If the problems have meaning for the students, then excellent training is provided. If the problem is an exercise from a manual, its solution may provide little or no exercise in problem solving. It is necessary for the teacher to stress the probing process, to encourage the pupil to form his own hypotheses and anticipate outcomes. Textbook or manual problems are not necessarily artificial. The point is that the pupil must accept the problem as his own and actively seek the answers, test the hypothesis, and formulate conclusions rather than merely follow each of the steps outlined in a manual.

Testing, whether theoretical or situational, gives additional information or data about the problem. The new information may result in an alteration of the hypothesis or in its confirmation and acceptance. Whatever the outcome, the total process has involved overlapping, repeating, and synthesizing the various steps involved.

Making a Generalization

Testing the hypothesis is too often the final step in the solution of a problem. However, higher forms of reasoning demand still another step—*making a generalization*. The generalization is an attempt to give the discoveries that have been made wider application. Attention may be directed to forming a generalization by such questions as "What other situation would this solution seem to fit?" "How could the procedures used for gathering and evaluating data be used in another problem?" or "How can the results of your inquiry be briefly stated?"

That this final step is often neglected is well illustrated by the fact that children and adults often attack a problem with no apparent reference to previous problem-solving experiences. Groups in permissive classrooms have been found to be particularly effective in the process of generalizing. In fact, groups are particularly beneficial to the discussion and involvement that lead to generalization. Bigge and Hunt (1968, p. 563) suggest four things to foster problem solving, two of which relate to groups: (1) encourage pupils to become group members, (2) reduce threat, (3) employ democratic methods, and (4) encourage group decisions.

Teachers have the responsibility for impressing upon students the value of making sound generalizations. One of the defects of much "thinking" is that people jump to conclusions. We see evidence of this all around us: "I once knew a German who was typically egotistic"; "He's a good example of the stubbornness of the Swede"; or "He's a typical only child." Many prejudices have just this basis—jumping to conclusions on the basis of one or two observations that seem to support some popular belief.

None of these steps in problem solving is beyond the level of ability of school pupils. The power to hold an idea in mind long enough to test it and use, or discard, it is evidenced from the age of two years. By the seventh year, reasoning ability is frequently noticeable.

There is no distinctive qualitative difference in problem-solving ability as age increases, but there is steady improvement in the inclination to use it. The teacher's efforts to promote verbal facility, to grant autonomy, to generate interest, and to describe problems in the pupils' terms will contribute to their ability to generalize. No great results should be hoped for. It must be remembered that adults are also naïve and inconsistent when they are dealing with ideas outside the realm of the familiar.

Pupils who are short on ability, or have tasks assigned to them which are too difficult, come to expect failure of themselves and cease to try (Ziegler, 1966, p. 153). As difficult tasks are tackled, the teacher should admit that they are difficult but remind the pupils of their previous successes. Encouragement plays a vital role.

Psychological experimentation and observation indicate that reasoning does take place, even among very young people, when they are presented with real problems and when they are given encouragement, time, and guidance in solving them. The problem-solving approach reverses the conventional manner of presenting subject matter. Instead of dividing a topic into subtopics and asking questions about each division, pupils may be presented with a question together with a few data. Thus, they might be shown a map without place names on it and be asked to determine where the cities might be located. The teacher would ask himself what he wants the pupils to learn and plan the lesson to include those concepts. Materials, visual aids, further questions, and the sources of data would, at least tentatively, be anticipated (Glogau and Krause, 1969).

An Illustrative Problem

The steps in problem solving in a classroom situation can be illustrated by a case in which the teacher, during the study of a unit on contagious diseases, took advantage of an actual situation in the lives of her pupils. Each of the steps described above was not only apparent but emphasized during the process.

One of the boys in the fifth-grade class had been absent for two or three days. Because he was a leader in both classroom and playground activities, his absence was noteworthy. Pupils asked where he was but no one knew. One boy stated that he lived only two blocks from the absent boy's home and would try to find out where he was. Here was a problem that was felt by the pupils, and guesses about the reasons for his absence were not satisfying. The problem, though vague, was felt, so the teacher decided to use the questions as a means of illustrating the approach to problem solving.

The boy who had volunteered to find the reason for his classmate's absence reported that their classmate had had two teeth pulled. The teeth were too far gone, according to the report relayed from the dentist, to try to save. Reasons for tooth decay were discussed. Fluoridation of water, diet, eating habits, daily dental hygiene, and periodic examinations were among the topics mentioned. The teacher pointed out that here was the beginning of the process of gathering data and sharpening the problem. "How do teeth grow?" "How serious is the loss of a tooth or two?" "Is the loss of teeth equally serious for children and adults?" "What causes tooth decay?" Students volunteered answers, but it was felt that better answers could be obtained. Books were used to supply the answers. One pupil was delegated to ask the school nurse several questions. Another girl said she knew a dentist and would ask him for some pamphlets. Thus data were accumulated and the problem became more specific.

On the basis of the data accumulated, guesses were made about why one pupil had to have teeth extracted and not others. Study and research over a period of several days suggested that perhaps the family had moved from a place where water was not fluoridated; perhaps regular dental check-ups had been neglected; perhaps the family could not afford proper dental care. These guesses seemed to be within the province of the data gathered; in short, the proposed hypotheses were partially confirmed by research results. It remained to test the hypothesis by consulting with the boy who had had the extractions. Water was not fluoridated in the community where he had previously lived. Daily dental care was exercised in the family, but periodic check-ups were unknown. He also added two more points, which were corroborated by other class members: (1) "Chewy" foods are sometimes considered to be a factor in dental health, and (2) decay seems to have at least some hereditary basis. Two generalizations from the study were drawn. One, the solution of a problem is a complex and desirable cooperative affair. Time and accurate data are needed. Two, dental health is governed by some factors which are within the realm of personal control and some which extend beyond the power of the person to influence.

These steps are not too difficult for children at the beginning of their school experience. Tenacity such as that revealed by these fifth graders might not be shown by first graders, but they too can feel and study problems. They can gather data. They can make partially informed guesses. They can test the guesses. And they can make limited generalizations. They can evaluate the knowledge and guesses of individual group members. It is well to reiterate that the correct solution of a specific problem is typically no more important than the processes and interests involved.

Creativity

There has been an acceleration of interest in the phenomenon of creativity in the past decade. The federal government has supported many researches related to it, a journal devoted to creativity was begun in 1967, and those who have long been interested in creativity have accelerated their efforts. Several factors have contributed to this increased interest. Among these forces might be included foreign threat to American leadership in inventiveness, rapid technological changes that increase the need for further innovation, psychological discoveries of the definitive nature of human differences, and better-prepared and more self-reliant and confident teachers. It is probable, too, that the upsurge of humanistic psychology, with its emphasis on self-actualization, has been instrumental in forming a *Zeitgeist* which is favorable to creativity. As our knowledge of creativity progresses, it becomes clear that creativity, like personality as a whole, abounds in intricacies and possibilities.

Stages in the Creative Process

One way of looking at creative thinking is that devised by Wallas (1926) and Patrick (1955). Working independently they have identified four steps in the creative process: Preparation, incubation, illumination, and verification.

1. *Preparation* consists of purposeful study and questioning, experience, and absorption of information that will fill gaps that the creative individual perceives. This is a time-consuming process in which the student steeps himself in the lore of the subject. This involves broad knowledge, because creativity demands new combinations, new relationships, new elaborations, and new implications. The teacher who would encourage creativity can no more depend on inspiration alone than a creative novelist can. He and his pupil must examine purposes, survey available resources, evaluate past experiences, and seek new interpretations. It must be realized that creativity is "ninety-nine per cent perspiration and one per cent inspiration." It is small wonder that a frequently mentioned characteristic of the creative individual is discontent and even unhappiness.

2. *Incubation* in creative thinking is perhaps less susceptible to voluntary control than preparation. The name was probably suggested by the incubation of an egg. Nothing is added to the egg from the outside during this period; it is merely kept warm and "waited upon." In this context, the meaning is that the student is released from the pressure of fact gathering and studying and allowed to wait for the idea to mature. The creative thinker does not completely abandon the idea, but turns it over in

his mind leisurely and periodically, but without trying to force the process. Hence the practical implication is to wait, to turn to other things, but not to forget the matter completely. The process of incubation should include *(a)* time for relaxation—release from the tensions of hurry and compulsion, *(b)* time for assimilation of ideas into the thought processes, *(c)* time for the rearrangement of information into various sequences and contingencies, *(d)* time for various ideas to rise to a central place in thought—or to recede to positions of relative significance. When a plateau of learning seems to have been reached, it would be well to turn temporarily to other subjects and allow time for incubation.

3. *Illumination* is the stage when the hours devoted to study, research, and incubation are rewarded by a clearer conception of the answer to the problem. The school pupil comes to a clear understanding of the situation that was perplexing him. At this time, insight is achieved. The moment at which illumination occurs cannot be stated precisely. But it is certain that preparation and incubation must come first. The only thing that teachers can do about this phase of creativity is to prepare the ground. The teacher should work patiently on the first two steps and then, without letting the problem subject lapse entirely, turn to other things and reduce the pressure to arrive at conclusions.

4. *Verification*, or *revision*, is akin to generalization in problem solving—after the problem is solved, it is extended to other situations. Verification may be considered to be the process of rethinking to improve the solution. It is the attempt to revise and refine the conclusion. Verification in the classroom consists of putting the brilliant idea into practice—polishing the creative work by critical analysis and further trial and examination. The teacher might ask, "How can we improve our mural?" "What ideas might we add to our proposal for better organization of community recreation?" "Are there any points we have overlooked in the personal health program we have formulated?" or "Does our theory of the causes of crime seem to be sufficiently inclusive?" It is constructive to project the illuminating idea beyond the presently achieved answer. Students should be made to feel that even minute additions to present knowledge are valuable. The difference between mediocrity and excellence in creative work is one of degree rather than kind (Patrick, 1935). This also suggests that teachers may reasonably expect all pupils to achieve some success in creative thought and work.

One additional, or supplementary, factor mentioned in one analysis of creativity is the matter of discussion (McPherson, 1968). There is much likelihood that discussion is simply taken for granted in other schemes because such items as communication, questions, possible explanations are specified. Discussion, especially with some brakes on judgments, would be a readily available means by which classroom teachers might encourage creativity.

Creativity is used in connection with the unusual, the "peculiar twist," or the distinctive and novel. MacKinnon (1962) used the following criteria to identify creativity: (1) novelty or at least statistical infrequency, (2) solving a problem or reaching a goal, and (3) developing an initial insight to its full. Torrance (1962, p. 16) endorses the idea that creativity is a matter of sensing gaps of disturbing and missing elements and forming and testing ideas about how those gaps might be filled. Torrance thus includes adventurous, off-the-beaten-track thinking. Creativity involves a search for new meanings and solutions that combine, invent, and synthesize. It is a restructuring of the perceptual field as the result of sensing some kind of deficiency. An example of this is the case of a boy who was failing in school, withdrawing from athletics, and becoming socially isolated. He literally drew himself back into school activities with his drawings, illustrating poetry, depicting football games, and pictures which revealed and released his feelings. Finally, he was achieving satisfactorily; previously, most of his teachers had thought him to be "dumb." Another example is the fascinating classroom account by a high school girl of her travels in Sweden—down to the details of temperature, distances walked, people met, communication problems overcome. The author discovered after class was over that this was simply an assigned report in social studies. But it had been handled in a way that was typical, according to her teacher, of this girl who used both data and imagination.

Creativity and Intelligence

Creativity and high intelligence, although positively correlated, are by no means synonymous (Brunelle, 1971). It is probable that the tendency to link intelligence and creativity has inhibited the development of creativity in many pupils because their teachers categorized them too readily—took a dim view of their potentialities (MacKinnon, 1962). Pupils with quite average IQs, because of special interests and certain personality tendencies, may be quite creative. On the other hand, quite a few youngsters with high intelligence have learned that the way to get along with parents and teachers is to conform; consequently, if they have a drive toward creativity, they keep a tight rein on it so that it eventually atrophies.

Some believe that the urge to creativity is well-nigh universal; others seem to think that—like musical or artistic aptitude—it is a special aptitude. Whether or not the urge to creativity is universal, it can readily be recognized that forces of conformity, expectation, and conservation of the status quo mitigate against the cultivation and flow of the creative impulse. These forces can more readily be understood and constructively dealt with when the divergent nature of creativity is understood. When the characteristics of creative persons (such as prizing aesthetic and theoretical values, as against such values as practical and factual) are identified, the idea takes root that there are gifted, as contrasted to conventional, personality characteristics (Guilford, 1967*a*).

Creative persons have been found to possess some or several of the following characteristics: (1) They tend to talk fluently and to show richness in the flow of ideas and speed in associating apparently disconnected things and ideas; (2) they are flexible and adaptive in permissive atmospheres and restive under the influence of rigid requirements; (3) they are divergent and inventive, rather than convergent and compliant, in their thinking; (4) their good memories and associational thinking cause them to see much that is familiar in the ostensibly new; (5) they tend to reveal humorous and playful attitudes; (6) they have reputations for having silly or wild ideas; (7) their work is characterized by numerous ideas that are off-the-beaten-track; (8) they have good opinions of themselves; and (9) they are open to admission of feelings and emotions.

Some of these characteristics, 1, 3, 5, and 6, for instance, would cause many teachers to be uncomfortable. Fortunately, simply acknowledging the possible origins of nonconformity and its desirable quality is a vigorous first step by the teacher in nourishing creativity. Recognition is not the only concern because the potentially creative become **underachievers** in school rather frequently. They are the ones who are independent, intellectual, highly verbal—"garrulous," when the talk interrupts our own actions and goals—and they are often asocial.

Teachers are justifiably gratified by the more conforming pupil, who is sociable, responsive, responsible, persevering, and respectful of authority. The differences are of degree and frequency and creativity and divergent thinking are not "poles apart" from academic achievement and convergent thinking. Both types of thinking require a long immersion in study, both require the accumulation of data, both demand order and organization, and it is hoped, both will result in illumination and inspiration (Hinton, 1968). The major difference between the two types of students is the tendency for the academic performer to reproduce already established conclusions. The creative person, on the other hand, has a drive to go beyond it. He is particularly responsive to an atmosphere in which he is free to question. He responds to the opportunity to experiment and adventure. His drive is to satisfy the inner compulsion of curiosity rather than the external compulsion of conformity.

Encouraging Creativity

Identifying the Creative Person

The distinctive nature of creative activities and the uniqueness of the creative orientation have stimulated the search for formal techniques of identification. In addition, several factors point to the need for better identification. The temper of the times is to recognize the importance of the existence and the work of the potentially creative. Different environmental influences may deter or stimulate the manifestation and development of creativity. Hence there has been a recently intensified effort to develop tests of creativity.[4]

Testing for creativity must of necessity involve personality assessment. Although Torrance believes that no satisfactory personality instrument suitable for use in guiding creative development has been developed, he lists a number of already well-known instruments that have proved helpful to teachers and counselors of creative children. They include the Strong Vocational Interest Blank, the Allport-Vernon-Lindsey Study of Values, and the Minnesota Multiphasic Personality Inventory (Torrance, 1962, pp. 67ff). On the Strong test, the creative subject rates high on scales as architect, psychologist, and author-journalist, and low on scales as purchasing agent, office man, or policeman. It appears from such scales that creative persons are interested in meanings and implications but not in details of the practical and concrete. On the Vernon instrument, creative subjects rank high on the theoretical and aesthetic scales. On the Minnesota Multiphasic, creative persons are high on masculinity-femininity scales—having high interest and openness to feelings. These scales are not considered entirely adequate for identifying creativity, and attempts are being made to formulate more precise instruments. MacKinnon (1962), however, expresses doubt that tests can be sufficient, for the real test of creativity is production—the work one has done.

Creative Classroom Activities

Not all creative pupils will intrude themselves upon the teacher's attention; but children who test the limits of authority should be studied to see if they do so because of emotional instability or because of curiosity. Those who take risks may be potentially creative. Behaviors showing independence may be indicative of creativity. Asking unusual questions is symptomatic of risk taking and curiosity and will be encouraged by teachers who wish to develop creativity.

Creative children are notable for their having "silly" ideas, their nonconformity to standardized patterns, and being humorous, playful, and relaxed. These behaviors may endear them to some but alienate them from others. The teacher's recognition of the existence of these often irritating traits can constitute a move toward building a creative climate in school (Torrance, 1962, p. 81).

---

4   Many tests have been constructed, but the problem is a difficult one—perhaps more difficult, even, than testing intelligence, because the latter focuses on convergency and creativity focuses on divergency. The complexity and the need for individual assessment is illustrated in Donald W. MacKinnon, 1967, "Assessing Creative Persons," *Journal of Creative Behavior*, vol. 1, pp. 291-304.

It has been noted that homes in which there is safety *and* freedom are frequently the homes of creative persons. Homes which are authoritarian and in which divergence is limited are more often the source of conforming and striving individuals (Wade, 1968). This suggests that classrooms which promote creativity must allow for freedom and individuality but also provide acceptance and applause.

It does not appear, at least to the author, that geometry would be particularly stimulating to creativity. Yet a teacher in Milwaukie, Ore., has shown that it is quite possible. Periodically, he assigns an exercise that must be submitted in some form other than pencil and paper. Pupils have done their assignments on clam shells, baked them in cookies, sewn, woven, or knitted them in aprons, doilies, or pillows. They have been built of wood, tile mosaics, or clay. One was engraved on an old carriage wheel. Each pupil has permission to decorate a piece of the ceiling fiberboard tile—using some concept from geometry. Often the pupil spends hours constructing a mobile, puzzle, or some mechanical device. One boy fixed his tile so it would rotate. It appeared to be blank until the corner was pushed and his futuristic building appeared. Two outcomes of the class are particularly notable. The pupils declare that "We love geometry," and the vice principal declares that some would-be dropouts stay in school so they can be in the class. The second outcome is that two or three times a year some pupil will present a solution to a problem that varies considerably from the textbook solution.

An aspect of creativity is its unpredictability. There is evidence, however, that creativity appears more frequently in some social and cultural contexts than it does in others. Creativity involves adventuresomeness and risk taking. It may be that repression, discouragement, and derogation will stifle creativity in one person, but similar repression will serve merely to stiffen the spine of another. It may be found, too, that overemphasis on creativity will hamper education for well-rounded development in some pupils (Yamamoto, 1964).

A starting point might be for teacher to examine his own orientation. Is he sufficiently professionally and emotionally secure to depart from traditional methods and conclusions? Does he teach children or subject matter? Does he seek new methods of presentation? Is he enthusiastic about his pupils and his specialty? Can he regard his own shortcomings with humor? Is he creative enough to add to this list of questions some concerning the self? What kind of persons would he like to be instrumental in forming—diligent, obedient, conforming, divergent, silly?

One need not wait for the ideal time and place to encourage creativity. There are opportunities within the existing structure, including the current curriculum. Not only does the creative person reveal his interest and aptitude in a wide variety of fields, but perceiving new interrelationships is a mark of his creativity. There is a special need for encouragement *and insistence* that the creative child become acquainted with as many disciplines as possible. While it may be advantageous for many in the class to be exposed to one or two disciplines at a

time, it appears that the creative pupil profits from being bombarded with materials from many fields and by many media (Taylor, 1962).

Some creative persons adjust poorly to others. Their eccentricity alien-
ates others and they claim not to care—but these are the exceptions. Typically,
creativity is accompanied by optimum growth in social interaction. Indeed, the
need to relate to others is a characteristic of most creative individuals; relating
and creating are mutually facilitating (Foster, 1968). Observation and **sociometry**
will provide clues that allow the teacher to give help in socializing when necessary. Team teaching, which exposes the pupil to a variety of subjects and their
interrelationships and to a variety of teachers is recommended as a stimulant to
creativity (Cawelti, 1967).

Brainstorming, a technique that consists of having group members suggest ideas as rapidly as possible, prohibiting criticisms, encouraging speaking out,
and evaluating at a later session, holds possibilities that have not yet been thoroughly tested (Osborn, 1963, p. 203). Much is summarized about the nature,
identification, and encouragement of creativity in the recommendations of Getzels and Jackson. They assert that distinction should be made between:

> . . . intelligence (IQ) and creative thinking
> . . . independence and unruliness and individuality and rebelliousness
> . . . healthy solitude and morbid withdrawal
> . . . tolerance for ambiguity and irresolution and between ability to de-
> lay choice and indecisiveness
> . . . remembering and discovering, between information and knowledge,
> and between the "fact filled quiz kid" and the educated student
> . . . sense perception and intuitive perception
> . . . evaluation and censorship and between judging and forejudging
> . . . organizing the curriculum for information or for knowledge, between
> organizing it for repetition or discovery, and for organizing it for meas-
> uring facts or evaluating wisdom.[5]

What is done to recognize the individuality of creativity also stimulates
endeavor on the part of the comparatively less creative. Taylor (1968) pertinent-
ly suggests that the more aptitude tests that are given, the greater, of course with
some slippage or overlap, the number of pupils there will be who appear at the
top of some list. If teachers capitalize on Guilford's theory of the structure of the
intellect, it will mean that more talents are identified. Hence, teaching the gifted,
the typical pupil, the slow learner, the culturally deprived have much in common;
i.e., the recognition and encouragement of individuality. Acceptance, applause,
and attention are approaches which are well-nigh universally effective (Hart,
1969).

---

5   Adapted from Jacob W. Getzels and Philip W. Jackson, 1962, *Creativity and Intelligence*, New York: John Wiley & Sons, Inc., pp. 124-130.

Summary

In a rapidly changing, dynamic society, problem-solving ability and creative production stand out as important goals of education. Both imply the ability to correlate and integrate facts and to delay, but not indefinitely postpone, action.

A factor in reasoning is maturation. Experience is vital, but an explanation of experiences in terms of problem solving enhances the value of experience. A fund of information is essential. Certain educational practices tend to hamper optimum development of problem-solving ability and should be looked at critically—rote learning, excessive use of workbook problems, the teacher's desire to provide conclusive answers, and problems inappropriate to the pupils' maturation and experience.

Steps in problem solving are having a felt need, recognizing and defining the problem, gathering data, formulating a hypothesis, testing the hypothesis, and—to get maximum benefit—making a generalization.

Creativity is similar in many respects to problem solving, but it goes beyond the data and involves more in the realm of affective response. This is shown in the characteristics of people who are called "creative." They tend to have a rich flow of ideas, are flexible and adaptive, have good memories and associational ability, often have humorous and playful attitudes, and frequently get off the beaten track.

One way of viewing creativity describes a four-step process: preparation, incubation, illumination, and verification or revision. Creativity, in the view of some scholars, goes beyond the processes of thought to include novelty, reaching a goal, and developing an insight fully.

Tests have been derived to identify potential for creativity, but there are so many ways and areas in which creativity may function that such instruments must be supplemented with analytical observation.

Team teaching is thought to be helpful in creativity. Brainstorming has sometimes been productive. But in the final analysis, encouragement of creativity swings back to the personality and resourcefulness of the teacher and his capacity to tolerate ambiguous situations and pupil differences.

Suggested Additional Readings

BRUNER, JEROME S., 1963, *The Process of Education*, Cambridge, Mass.: Harvard University Press.

    This book of fewer than 100 pages is one of the more provocative of the decade. Chapter 3, "Readiness for Learning," contains practical suggestions for fostering problem-solving ability from the earliest school years.

DEWEY, JOHN, 1910, *How We Think*, Boston: D. C. Heath and Company.

    This book has withstood the test of time and is still considered to be an excellent presentation of the nature and procedures of problem solving.

GETZELS, JACOB W., AND PHILIP W. JACKSON, 1962, *Creativity and Intelligence*, New York: John Wiley & Sons, Inc.

    The authors describe the varieties of giftedness and creativeness that exist among pupils. They then present a number of contrasts and similarities between the highly intelligent and the highly creative. Case studies are used to sharpen the reader's insight.

HARRIS, L. DALE, 1971, "Implementing a Problem-Oriented Approach to Learning," *Journal of Creative Behavior*, vol. 5, pp. 60-69.

    The author proposes using an instructional approach which involves a problem relevant to the student, demands imagination, is challenging, and leads to discovery and sometimes to failure to resolve the problem.

MAC KINNON, DONALD W., 1962, "The Nature and Nurture of Creative Talent," *American Psychologist*, vol. 17, pp. 484-495.

    Using architects as subjects, the author examines their life histories, personality characteristics, and suggests what teachers might do to encourage the flowering of creative tendencies. Volumes have been written expanding the issues so tersely set forth in this article.

TORRANCE, E. PAUL, 1966, "Problem-solving Attitudes and Self Concepts of Beginning Junior High School Students," *Guidance Journal*, vol. 4, pp. 74-86. (Also in Bernard and Huckins (eds.), 1967, *Readings in Educational Psychology*.)

    There are peaks and depressions of creative urges at various ages. The author discusses some of the possible explanations for the low point occurring at the time of entering junior high school.

13

Teaching
the Different Pupil

If educators really believed in teaching the "individual pupil" and put the belief into action, there would be no need for a separate chapter on the "different pupil." Indeed, what can be said in this chapter is not substantially different from what the educational psychologist would say about the normal, or typical (if there were such a being), child. Our insights into teaching typical children *and* different children can be epitomized into a few basic principles:

Teaching will be more effective when it is geared to tested status and inferred potential.

Recognition and acknowledgment of pupil differences through implementation of varied styles of learning will facilitate the teaching-learning transaction.

Positive reinforcement, or active feedback, for effort and for achievement will enhance the attainment of educational aims.

Pupils, especially as they grow older, will be more assiduous in learning activities when they feel a degree of power, autonomy, self-direction, and independence.

Whatever the teacher does or says should be evaluated, at least periodically, in terms of what it does to the pupils' ego concepts.

Pupils will be able to marshal their best learning skill and academic energy when they have a feeling of identity, belongingness, and attachment to the school culture.

An important, perhaps the most important, factor in economical learning is the empathic quality of teacher-pupil relationships.

Studying the needs and problems of the culturally different, the handicapped, and the gifted brings into sharper relief the continuous and subtle differences which exist between and among the constituents of an ordinary classroom. Some middle children are more like the pupil from the lower class than they are like some of their middle-class peers. Some partially sighted pupils have sharper perceptions than some of their 20/20 companions. Consideration of "teaching the different pupil" throws into bold relief challenges which the teacher faces in working with the not-so-different pupil.

The Culturally Different Pupil

Characteristics of Culturally Different Pupils

It is advantageous to think of a range of characteristics of culturally different pupils. Such a procedure tells us what to look for and narrows the range for achieving understanding. If the general description causes us to have tunnel vision, then that description may be handicapping rather than helpful; e.g., a teacher said to a high school freshman, "You continually surprise me. You're so well-adjusted for being a girl with divorced parents."

Many pupils from culturally different[1] homes will reveal some, oft-mentioned, characteristics; but the list becomes a hazard to teachers if it leads to an expectancy and self-fulfilling prophecy rather than to an alertness for exceptions.

Those pupils who are outside the mainstream middle-class milieu are known as being "culturally different." Typically, these are persons who are in the lowest ranks in terms of income, prestige, and opportunity. They are those who have most recently sought inclusion into the mainstream culture and who, although in the process, have not yet internalized the identifying values and behaviors. Examples are first-generation Germans, Irish, Swedes, Italians. Skin color is sometimes made the excuse for exclusion, and color diminishes the opportunity to learn the values necessary—Puerto Ricans, Mexicans, Negroes, and others. An Indian consultant, who described his tribe's efforts at establishing identity said, "In population listings, classification categories, we Indians are those 'others.' "

---

1   The words "culturally different" refer to those who are sometimes called "culturally deprived," "disadvantaged," "educationally handicapped." It is hoped that the ideal of "different" contains a seed for understanding and acceptance. The other terms too readily suggest inferiority, trauma, and remediation.

[The connotation: Not worthy of specific mention.] The following summary of characteristics indicates some of the alleged characteristics which constitute disadvantage.

> They have deficient language skills. Children's exposure to books and magazines is limited. Conversations between parents and children occur with considerably less frequency than is the case in middle-class homes.
>
> They, and boys more than girls, tend to act out more than children from the higher socioeconomic strata. Physical prowess is more highly valued than is the development of conceptual approaches.
>
> They are verbally inhibited—they speak with reticence in school and in counseling and employment interviews.
>
> They have little tolerance for deferred gratification and tend to develop a short-term hedonism.
>
> They are person oriented in thinking and dealing with agencies, bureaucracies, and institutions; i.e., they react to structure and system as though the representative were expressing a personal choice (Gordon, 1968).
>
> They tend to develop hostility and aggression as the result of frustration and deprivation.
>
> They tend to have a negative self-concept. They see themselves as being inadequate and powerless.
>
> They tend to resort to the testing of limits. Teachers and counselors are viewed in the ambiguous light of simultaneously accepting and rejecting them.
>
> They show signs of reacting more readily to the concrete, tangible, and immediate and show impoverishment in formal, abstract, and syntactical concepts (Ausubel, 1966).

> [They show] deficiencies in how to connect with the world of things and people: Difficulty in listening, attending, focusing, and sustaining interest or contact; a motoric, staccato, disordered release of energy; difficulty in fitting into a situation that is ordered with respect to time and space; immature ways of dealing with impulses and feelings such as anger, frustration and denial; expectation that the adult will be distant, denying, punishing; vagueness of self-concept; and so forth.[2]

Disadvantage: A Perspective

Disadvantage is, in the eyes of some authorities, at least in part a point of view. Although there is no denying the reality of hunger, inadequate medical

---

2   Barbara Biber, 1970, "Goals and Methods in a Preschool Program for Disadvantaged Children," *Children*, vol. 17, no. 1, p. 15, January-February.

Ellen Levine/College Newsphoto Alliance

care, and poor housing, the view one has of himself and his conditions has some significance. One may be poor and lower class if he is unable to anticipate a distant future. One may be poor and upper class if he is capable of controlling his impulses and conceptualizing a future (Todd, 1970). Fortunately, there have been, and are, many children who grow up not knowing they are disadvantaged. Either their parents do not know they are disadvantaged or they choose not to communicate their status to their children. Instead, these parents communicate their love, envision a brighter future, express their faith in the superiority of their offspring, and view disadvantage as a burden which they would rather be without but which they are capable of carrying.

There is the possibility that teachers may become a part of the disadvantage, or cultural handicap if (1) they accept the characteristics listed in the foregoing section too literally; if (2) they fail to see some of the advantages in differences; or if (3) they accept the statements as being laws rather than tendencies. Let some sample interpretations be cited:

1. Deficient Language Skills

The child's language may be different but hardly deficient for communicating in *his* culture. Russian, French, or Egyptian children speak a different language and are regarded, pridefully, as being bilingual. This view, bolstering his ego concept, might be more stimulating to his learning the language of the school. He may be regarded as though he were in a foreign land, and another language were being used. Indeed, in the eyes of linguists, this is precisely what happens (Bernstein, 1967). Furthermore, the concept of a different language rather than deficient language might help pupils maintain pride in their parents and neighborhoods.

2. Tendency to Act Out

Babies who are inept at making their demands known may scream (act out). Children whose incompetence leads to frustration may have temper tantrums (act out). Husbands who are unable to communicate with their wives may drown their sorrows in alcohol (act out). In short, frustration tends to precipitate acting out. Two teaching-learning implications are apparent. One is to broaden school activities to capitalize more on motoric behaviors; or two, to provide nonpunitive, nonjudgmental milieus in which the conceptual approaches may be practiced.

3. Verbal Inhibition

An Oregonian in an Irish tavern or inn tends to feel verbally inhibited at ale with five or six Irishmen. A group of Mexicans in Mazatlan, discussing their morning's fishing, seem to be something other than verbally inhibited. For the teacher to question the meaning of this truthful assertion (truthful in the sense that strangeness does tend to inhibit, and familiarity tends to prompt, loquaciousness) might mean that he would spend more time listening instead of attempting to fill the communication gap with sound waves.

4. Little Tolerance for Deferred Gratification

This may be explained in terms of the experiences the lower class individual has encountered. However, such an explanation, truthful and objective as it may be, may provide an excuse for not considering the merit of a future oriented assault. Kelly (1955, pp. 1029ff) has emphasized that one of the purposes of psychotherapy is to get rid of the emotional overburdens of childbirth. Teachers may help lighten despair if they will but provide a human association as the pupil formulates his concepts of the future. Positive feedback on what was done today is a step toward envisioning tomorrow.

5. A Negative Self-concept

Pupils from all and any social classes tend to have a negative self-concept unless they find confirmation of themselves from key persons—especially adults—in their lives. Recognition of varied styles of learning, of different starting points in the "academic race," and of a multitude of, as yet untested, and in the school unrecognized, capacities would impede the concentration of negative self-concepts among the culturally different.

6. Tendency to Test Limits

This is a laudable trait for a child of any social class. If the teacher is healthy, he will appreciate this exploratory orientation much more than those pupils who are resigned, defeated, and withdrawn.

Disadvantage inheres partly in the teacher's orientation, and "advantage" inheres in the pupil's being helped to see himself in the process of becoming. To reiterate the Todd (1970) reference, the task of the teacher of the culturally different pupil is to encourage his efforts and bolster his ego to the point that he can conceptualize a brighter future—and thus become advantaged.

Strengths of the Culturally Different

An even better approach to a genuine acceptance and appreciation of the culturally different child than reexamination of the alleged deficiencies is to identify some strengths.

Olsen (1965) refers to the "culturally different" pupil when he speaks of economically poor, or lower-class, persons. He reports to teachers that the child of the lower class grows up quickly. He has more than the typical amount of contact with unemployment, desertion, crime, and alienation. Although lower-class children will compete physically, there is little incentive to compete with peers in a psychological and interpersonal sense. Their lessons of survival have emphasized cooperation and mutual help—sometimes viewed as "cheating" by a culturally naïve teacher. They do value education but not in the sense of the middle class—for schooling itself. They are much interested in the schoolwork which is related to realistic and tangible vocational goals. They do not resist discipline so much as they want clear definitions of what is expected. These are only **some** of the strengths of the culturally different. They, as do the people of all classes, have concern for others, the ability to lend a hand, durability in the face of misfortune, and that highest quality of humanity—compassion.

For the teacher in the slum school, this is probably the major difficulty: keeping discipline. Teachers who succeed learn to set up strict routines from which they do not deviate, establish clear limits from the first day, and make it clear to the students that they are there to learn. The working-class student needs a strong authority figure who can maintain discipline in the class in a climate of informality.

. . . The expectation of the culturally different child is that the authority figure will set up fair rules and enforce them without deviation. At the same time, the teacher lets the students know that he likes and respects them. He knows they can—and will—do the work, because this is why they are in school to begin with: to learn. Above all, the ground rules of classroom routines are not discussed; they are followed.[3]

Our success in dealing with the poor as pupils lies in our understanding more fully their strength, says Olsen. It may be that concentrating on the weaknesses provides both pupils and teachers excuses for not making optimum use of the abundant potential which exists.

Eisenberg (1967), McCreary (1966, 1967), and Tannenbaum (1967) are others who have taken the view that appraisal of strengths would be constructive. Among the strengths they have identified and which they feel teachers should capitalize upon are: Poor children often have developed a capacity for mutual aid and cooperation. They have strong in-group feelings. They develop peer group identity at an early age. Group and family values rank high—one might see here a danger in teacher criticism of the language used. Whereas inner-city children may come from disorganized homes, they may also assume responsibility for important family chores at a comparatively early age. Girls are often quite competent in tending and protecting younger children. They have learned to survive by doing rather than talking and may show some relative superiority in physical skills. They become self-reliant and autonomous at an early age—often to the chagrin and irritation of teachers conducting a field trip. Many are strong and resourceful leaders in gangs and clubs (Sherif and Sherif, 1964).

Inner-city children typically judge people in terms of what they are and do rather than on the basis of titles. Teachers are not automatically respected, as is more typically the case with middle-class pupils. They are sometimes successful in ways that are not appreciated by school personnel—leadership, independence, the tendency to test limits. Their learning styles are, with comparatively high frequency, concrete rather than conceptual; deliberate rather than facile in terms of speed. Their achievement motivation is high in areas where they have experienced some success (music and athletics). They are responsive to immediate and to material rewards.

3   James Olsen, 1965, "Challenge of the POOR to the Schools," *Phi Delta Kappan*, vol. 47, no. 2, pp. 81-82, October.

Teaching Approaches

Taylor (1968), using Guilford's model of the structure of intelligence (see Chapter 7), suggests that a way to reach culturally different pupils is to give them more tests. Instead of giving only one overall and comprehensive test, such as a mental ability test, several tests should be administered. Tests exist which probe such things as creativity, leadership potential, planning talents, decision-making talents, communication skills, social sensitivity, and of course music and arithmetic are considered to be special subabilities. If 100 pupils are given these tests, on each test different pupils will be in the top 10 percent. There will be some slippage, or overlap, so that on two tests 18 or 19 out of the 100 will be in one or the other top 10 percent. These figures would change to 25 or so with three tests, and 30 with four tests of talents. Using still more tests will not mean that ultimately all will be highly gifted in some talent but it is postulated that perhaps a third would be. Nearly all the pupils would be above average in one tested talent.

Sensitive teachers have consistently sought to find ways in which every pupil can be noted for some degree of excellence. *Studied* observation has shown them that it is not always the superior student who is talented athletically, makes a good protector of the young on the playground, can best manage a class meeting in terms of *Robert's Rules of Order*, or can maintain the beat and key in chorus. Tests can supplement such studied observation. In these ways the strengths of the culturally different can be identified and used for the enhancement of the ego.

This is the remark of a fourth grade boy who seemed to enjoy his school and his classmates despite poor work in arithmetic, "Oh, I know I'm not very good at arithmetic, but just wait till we play checkers." His father had taught him how to play by planning moves two or three jumps ahead in response to his opponents' moves.

Principles of Teaching-Learning Transactions for the Different Pupil

McCreary (1967) has proposed a number of principles of learning which are based on his experiences as director of an Upward Bound Special Opportunity Scholarship Program at the University of California. These bear considerable likeness to the principles of learning summarized by Hilgard (1956, pp. 486-487) and to the propositions for the facilitation of learning as postulated by Bernard and Huckins (1968).

Students learn better and enjoy it when they study those things which have relevance to their own circumstances, problems, and personal history.

Because interests, needs, and abilities vary so widely it is necessary that teachers provide maximum diversity of materials and activities.

Culturally different pupils—as is the case with most other pupils—like to be active participants rather than passive receivers.

Students are more likely to enjoy the learning process if they can help others or can associate with them in the learning enterprises. [One of the noted strengths of culturally different pupils was the ability to care responsibly for the young].

Learning tends to be more satisfying when pupils participate in planning what they are to learn and in how it should be evaluated.

Learning tends to be more enjoyable when students can, in a number of ways—physically, verbally, emotionally—express themselves.

Pupils tend to enjoy learning when they are permitted the widest possible choice of material, curricular emphases, and variety of learning subjects—civil rights, delinquency, war, sex.

Satisfaction from learning activities is heightened when the work done is noted by peers and teachers.

Learning becomes most satisfying and efficient when pupils are encouraged to discover for themselves the more significant aspects of the study.

Satisfaction is gained from learning pursuits when the pupil learns that he is wanted and needed—when his presence makes a difference.

Most projects designed to study and facilitate the learning needs and processes of culturally different children perceive letter grades as being antagonistic to such principles as the above. Instead, evaluation is a continuous thing in terms of immediate next steps (progress from where one was) and emphasis on success. Rather than to stimulate one to compete, low grades prompt one to "leave the field."

> Low grades alone were sufficient to convince most students that they were in line for failure, not only in school but in vocational careers. His [Stinchcombe] study focused principally on middle-class youth, but it is significant in illustrating the important, and often baneful, effect of grades on student attitudes and concepts of self.[4]

As long as a healthy ego concept is deemed to be important and as long as independently instigated and pursued continuous study is important, the foregoing principles are likely to be important guides to specific practices.

Community Involvement

In recognition of the fact that motivation for school, problems of tru-

---

| 4   Eugene McCreary, 1967, "Pawns or Players?" *Phi Delta Kappan*, vol. 49, p. 139.

ancy, and becoming a dropout are not solely school problems, the federal government has encouraged projects which encouraged community involvement (Tunley, 1971). Parents, business leaders, church representatives, and "the man in the street" who would give time were encouraged to be in on the planning. It is theorized that such wide involvement would not only reflect community needs more accurately but would tend to lead to viability of the project after removal of federal support.

The PTA is a conventional approach to parent involvement in school learning processes. This, however, is a middle-class institution, and lack of lower-class participation has been interpreted as lack of interest. Some authorities have postulated that it is the feeling of one's not being counted, not having proper clothes to wear to the meeting, and recognition of language differences, rather than lack of interest that accounts for lower-class nonattendance at PTA functions. In instances where parental **involvement** in the schools for the disadvantaged has been actively sought the results have been fruitful.

Through the aid of Ford Foundation funds, Great Cities programs, and federal poverty funds, the theory that the poor have a contribution to make to educational effectiveness has been supported. The poor have a stake in schools and, given the chance, they exert positive influence. Mothers have been hired as paraprofessionals, as family helpers to new families in the community, as library aides, visual-aids assistants, as chaperones on field trips, as nursery school mothers, and particularly as school-community liaison agents—their big contribution. They know the community—its life and dilemmas. They have helped to make curricula relevant, helped pupils retain and improve their school aspirations, and they have been a factor in school morale.

The apprehension that lower-class mothers would not stick to the program was not confirmed in Philadelphia or Pittsburgh. In five years, one helper, who moved away, was lost. The specific duties they competently performed were far beyond either hope or expectation (Saltzman, 1965, pp. 38ff). In a program directed by the author, it was such mothers who helped materially in pupil control and in keeping the teachers on a practical level by saying in staff meetings, "Now wait just a moment. Let's face this fact. . . ."

The achievement of involvement is not an easy thing—something to be accomplished by the application of a nostrum. Cottle (1969a) has described one approach to the laborious process of significant educational change as it occurred in the Bristol Township Schools of Levittown, Pa. The situation was one which might have been called "social dynamite," with enough of the families living at the poverty level to qualify for aid under Title I of the Elementary and Secondary School Act of 1965. Explosion was prevented by the sensitivity on the part of teachers and administrators as they dealt with students, parents, and community leaders. Sensitivity training was instituted for a corp of thirty teachers. Emphasis was on organizational adaptation to change, with particular attention given to human relations. People had a chance to talk, vent feelings, and to be listened to. If prejudice was not eliminated, at least awareness was increased and the problems were out in the open. The report on Levittown is but one bit of accumulating evidence that sound educational psychology must take cognizance of the social and political milieu—and parental involvement is one aspect of such a functional milieu.

Children, too, are a part of the community. It is recognized that their participation in planning, content, material, activities, and evaluation is a factor in motivation and in thoroughness of learning. Not so widely recognized is the fact that pupils are effective teachers of one another. Penn (1969) capitalizes on pupils as teachers by dividing the class into small groups which contain a cross section of ability. Assignments are determined for members of the group, and discussion and evaluation take place within the group. Penn predicts that more and more teachers will shift their emphasis to being guides, with children taking more responsibility for both teaching and learning. This emphasis is particularly significant for the culturally different child. Many, as shown above, enter school somewhat suspicious of adults with authority. Their classmates, particularly in view of the strength of in-group feelings, can more readily be trusted. If criticism for slow learning is involved, it can more readily be taken from one's peers. In addition, the language which the teachers speaks so fluently may be difficult to understand, whereas the pupil's peers speak the same idiom. Finally, one's peers do not hover over the learner with the threat of negative evaluation. Interestingly, the child-teacher does not have to be the brightest or oldest—he simply has acquired a bit of information not yet possessed by the learner—the teacher-pupil roles may be reversed in another activity.

Vocational Education and Job Entry Skills

An approach to the education of culturally different pupils is emphasis on vocational education. There are a few authorities who question the wisdom of such emphasis both in terms of the development of human talent and in terms of realities of the job market.

One of the characteristics of lower-class persons which is conventionally cited is the need for immediate gratification of desires. Allegedly, they are comparatively incapable of denying themselves of some pleasure now, the delay of which would promise greater satisfaction at a later date. In this context, the rigors of education now, without pay, are not worth delaying marriage, not owning a car, or doing without clothes which would be made possible if one quit school and took a job.

It is assumed that this "immediate gratification" tendency stems from living a hand-to-mouth existence. There is simply no chance to put something by for a rainy day because there is no margin. The defeated attitude of parents derives from the reality of past hardships—cumulative experiences are not conducive to optimistic hope for the future. This "immediate gratification" syndrome bears some of the blame for shunting the lower-class pupil into the vocational and commercial courses of the high school, thus continuing the sorting function of the school. This process is **rationalized** with the contention that lower-class pupils will not apply themselves to college-preparatory courses (the academic type of curriculum). The students themselves, teachers say, want to be practical, "I want something I can use now—something that will help me get a job." In view of the facts of unemployment this view is highly questionable. The bulk of unemployment is in the age bracket of sixteen to twenty-four. It is twice as high for this group as for other age brackets.

A part-time job has been part of the culture of teenage boys, but the opportunities are becoming fewer and fewer—girls have joined the part-time and summer workers to a limited extent, but their chances too decline steadily. These part-time jobs, when they are obtainable, compare roughly with their parents' jobs, on a hierarchical level. Those who go to work at an early age are likely to become skeptical about the relationship of education and job performance. This is in accord with the world of reality, if the thesis proposed by Schill (1963) is correct; i.e., education must be in line with the kind of work one performs, or is likely to perform, if it is to serve its maximum mobility function. When youth of higher classes take jobs, they do so as clerks in the better stores or as office workers for professional people.

The myth that every boy may become a millionaire or President or can climb the economic and social ladder to occupational prestige is discredited as studies of the impact of socioeconomic status on youth continue. Except for the few from the lower classes who go to college, prediction of work success can be made on the basis of such factors from childhood as intelligence, social status, personality adjustment, and family stability (Havighurst et al., 1962, p. 137).

Society at large endorses the emphasis on vocational courses and the development of job-entry skills. Recent governors of the state of Oregon have emphasized the need for greater emphasis on vocational courses. The federal government, through the Department of Labor, has developed several programs designed to provide job skills which will prevent youth from being jobless in addition to his being comparatively short on education (*Manpower* . . ., 1969, p. 9):

Neighborhood Youth Corps
Emphasis on part-time jobs while schooling continues

Job Corps
  Residential program which removes young people from their handi-
  capping environment while they develop job skills
New Careers Program
  Emphasis on preparation of paraprofessional personnel
Operation Mainstream
  Retraining for undereducated adults
Special Impact Program
  Emphasis on business training and entrepreneurship opportunities in
  slum areas
Work Incentive Program
  Designed to make all persons over age sixteen employable and pro-
  vide child care for parents while they develop job skills

A booklet published by the U.S. Department of Health, Education, and
Welfare titled, "The Youth We Haven't Served" (Kemp, 1966), emphasizes the
need for extending vocational education. Professional magazines for school personnel emphasize the need for the development of job-entry skills. School counselors and guidance personnel are urged to develop work-study programs, i.e., to
serve a liaison function between business, industry, and schools to provide work
experience programs which correlate jobs and schooling.

Another perspective on the matter of vocational preparation leaves a
big question as to precisely what constitutes a tenable job-entry emphasis. Students and practitioners of the psychology of learning and teaching must ask, "How
are job-entry and vocational students to be selected and prepared?" Instead of preparing pupils for job entry and the prospect of ultimate obsolescence, they wish
to make better use of the potentials which lower-class pupils have for the development of cognitive skills, to broaden their conceptual powers, and to prepare more
of them for the occupations in which there are shortages—technical, professional,
and paraprofessional—shortages which give promise of continuing. In brief, encourage all able pupils to use the college-preparatory, the academic, emphasis regardless of social class.

Barry and Wolf (1962) have already written an *Epitaph for Vocational
Guidance*, postulated on the evidence that school guidance should be personal
rather than vocational. Bronfenbrenner (1969) provocatively suggests the "dampening of the unemployability explosion." He means by the word "unemployability" the continued development of manpower for jobs which are becoming ob-
solescent.

  With continuing technological development, the number of jobs that can
  be filled by persons of limited cognitive capacity will become smaller
  and smaller. Unless present trends are reversed, long before the major
  impact of the population explosion is felt, this nation will have to cope
  with the explosion of the unemployables.

An explosion implies an event both massive and destructive. So the unemployability problem is likely to be. Available evidence indicates that when human beings are brought up in deprivation, experience little humanity at the hands of others, and grow into adults of limited competence—unable to find work, forced to live on leavings while the majority of citizens enjoy prosperity—the impulse to violence is high and hard to control.

But the unemployability explosion need not occur. It is susceptible to control by measures far less costly than its consequences. The weight of scientific evidence, particularly that accumulated in recent years, indicates that much of the incapacity of our citizens is not inborn but manmade during the early years of life.[5]

The challenge for education is one that extends from the time of birth—or even before birth. As a child development specialist and authority on the family, Bronfenbrenner emphasizes that a mother's exposure to malnutrition, illness, fatigue, and emotional turmoil may be far more damaging to the child's learning ability than has formerly been thought. Mental development occurs through interaction with adults in an encouraging atmosphere. He proposes the establishment of a federal "Commission for Children" which would focus the many diverse programs for children and youth. The focal emphasis would be on the development of intellectual and interpersonal skills and on the development of healthy ego concepts capable of dealing with change and challenge.

School personnel cannot, by themselves, solve the problems of unemployment and unemployability. However, they can ask themselves how the creation of a better teaching-learning milieu may evolve so more lower-class individuals will stay in school for longer periods of time to develop their cognitive, linguistic, and social skills and fulfill the nation's need for growing numbers of technical and professional workers.

Upward Bound programs, in which inadequately prepared high school students entered college, were guided in doing work at their level, succeeded—without the threat of grades. They read and discussed, with enthusiasm, things that were pertinent to them. Contrary to the myth that lower-class students must have something practical and of immediate value, the courses for most students in the Upward Bound colleges included English, mathematics, science, and the humanities (Dranov, 1967).

Successes of GI students after World War II destroyed the myth that "college material" existed only in the higher classes. A whole new college-bound generation was created, largely from social classes hitherto without college aspirations or tradition.[6]

Figure 13-1 indicates that great numbers of lower-class pupils, whose ability exceeds that of the average of higher-class persons, are not being developed at the level of college education. Without entering the argument that there are other ways of developing talent, the figures suggest that waste does occur. If lower-class pupils were to be represented in college in proportion to their numbers in the population, the talent pool could be doubled (from inspection of the areas in the curves), with no decrease in test-indicated ability. If the lower class were represented in the same proportion as the upper class is now, college attendance would increase almost fourfold. Because of their greater absolute numbers this would probably mean that about nineteen cases out of twenty of talented lower-class individuals fail to be developed.

The study of the limitations of testing, studies of motivation, reflection on the psychological orientation provided by social class membership, suggest that progress toward better utilization of talent, developed at the cognitive level, for lower-class pupils would merit consideration of the following:

Repudiation of the notion that tests of an entire population reveal the potential of individuals within that population.

Repudiation of a grading system which puts differently prepared pupils into competitive situations.

Repudiation of a classifying and sorting system (so-called "ability grouping") which conveys to some that they are inferior.

Repudiation of one-talent-test approaches to the evaluation of developmental potential.

Repudiation of the idea that pupils must grow at the same rate—one grade per year, two semesters for beginning algebra, etc.

None of the above is meant to suggest that mastery of the tools of learning—reading, writing, computing—should be matters of pupil choice, or be bypassed because the pupil is not "ready," or delayed because the pupils find the work difficult. The above does not imply that schoolwork should be easy. In fact, it is recommended that schoolwork should be difficult so that one can have a feeling of accomplishment when it is done. The above does not mean that pres-

---

6   It should be noted that these GIs have in the past twenty years more than repaid the federal government for the cost of their higher education. In terms of the higher income taxes they have paid concomitant with their increased earning power, they have more than repaid the costs original involved (Emens, 1965). Better education enabled them to get better jobs, to be paid higher salaries, and to get into higher income brackets.

These data should not be relegated to footnote importance by those who formulate school policy. It is no longer necessary to say to the hard-headed business man, "Education is an investment in people." The GI bill has proven that "Education is an investment"—one which pays off in money as well as in people.

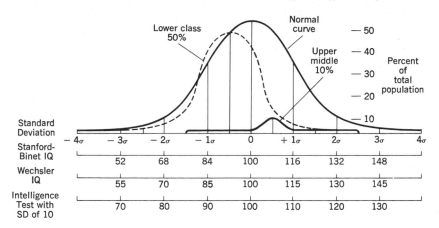

Figure 13-1 Social class, college attendance, and waste of potential.

sure to study formal, systematic, textbook approaches to science, mathematics, and languages cannot be used.

It is being suggested that the emphasis for all pupils be on cognitive development. Job-entry skills should consist of such fundamentals as computation, reading, communication, and effective social interaction, plus a willingness to learn. Job-entry skills should be paralleled or accompanied by study of those subjects which will leave the gates of choice open as long as it is possible.

Slow Learners

The Meaning and Problem of Slow Learners

The term "slow learner" is not altogether satisfactory because it means various things to various people. Some may use the term to refer to pupils such as those just discussed—culturally different pupils who encounter difficulty in the school because they have two challenges to meet—a cultural adaptation and an academic orientation. The term slow learner is used to avoid the stigma of "mental retardation" or "mentally deficient." The term permits the emphasis to be on the pace of learning rather than on the lack of capacity to learn. Often the slow learner is qualitatively different. He comprehends and remembers somewhat less and is less perceptive of relations and contrasts than is the normal pupil.

IQ does not tell the entire story, but when it is a consideration, we generally speak of mental retardation as being below IQ 75, while the slow learner has an IQ of from 75 to 85 or 90. There may be slow learners whose IQs are in the normal range (90 to 110), but most of them will be in the IQ categories below 90. The lower the IQ, the less likely it will be that the child will attend regular public school, and the more likely it is that he will be treated by other agencies. "Trainable" mentally retarded children have IQs between 30 and 50, and the aim is to help them become capable of self-care and socialization. In general, children with IQs between 50 and 75 are regarded as "educable," but it is difficult to keep them in school and interested unless special classes are organized for them. It is also desirable that their teachers be specially trained to provide suitable material and appropriate timing and, consequently, motivation. Interest in slow learners has increased significantly in recent years; one important discovery has been that such pupils are much more capable of learning—at their pace—than was formerly thought to be the case. Moreover, it has been found that in the upper range of the educable, regular school attendance not only produced improved behavior, but tended to help the pupils make greater gains in mental age than did the lower IQ groups and those who stayed at home. Coordinated effort between school, home, and civic agencies should supplement the effective utilization of educational specialists such as counselors, psychologists, and health workers who supplement the work of classroom teachers (Chandler and Bertolaet, 1967).

Below-average intelligence, indicated by mental test results, is the characteristic most readily discernible in slow learners. It is necessary to give an individual test to obtain reasonably reliable results, because physical handicap and emotion problems may mask average intelligence in some slow learners. Slow learners are notable, of course, for their comparative retardation in academic achievement; hence, achievement tests should supplement the data from mental tests. Slow learners need more time and repeated experiences to consolidate learnings that normal and bright pupils somewhat readily acquire. Even with extra time and repetitions, the slow learner often reaches the ceiling of his ability and fails to learn what is expected of his peers in the same classroom. Recent research, however, is undermining many past beliefs about the futility of teaching the mentally retarded. It takes more time, more repetition, and special educational provisions—but they can learn and can become assets rather than liabilities in society (Dunn, 1963, pp. 82ff).

Slowness in academic accomplishment is typically paralleled by slowness in social maturation. The Vineland Social Maturity Test was originally devised by Edgar A. Doll for youngsters in homes for the mentally retarded, and is widely used for validation of the impressions that experienced teachers form. It should be expected that social adjustment will be difficult, and the consequence of frequent and repeated failure is individuals who are insecure, reticent, and recessive. Rejection by peers seems to be based on social ineptness rather than on scholastic deficiency.

Teaching Approaches for Slow Learners

Slow learning may be caused by a large number of, and quite different, factors. There may be actual intellectual inferiority, affective impairment, sensory dysfunction, excessive anxiety, cultural dissonance, physical handicap, *and* poor teaching (Travers, 1970, p. 297). Whatever the cause the basic factor in helping the slow learner to use that potential which he has is to avoid further deflation of his ego. It is important to avoid placing him in a milieu where he is unfavorably compared with comrades who are average and above. In a competitive situation the consistently superior academic performance of the more apt pupil will cause the less apt to withdraw—physically or psychologically. Slowness must be seen, especially by teachers, as another style of learning. Because of the treatment, because of the unfair comparisons, because of the limited number of aptitudes recognized in the schools, the slow learner may become the *poor learner* (Riesman, 1966, p. 259).

The popularity of placing slow learners in special classes has been declining markedly in recent years. It is thought that such placement imposes stigmatization on the pupil that may offset the advantages of the special class. One's being pro or con special classes would probably be influenced by experience, educational philosophy, and anticipation of what the future might bring. There is no doubt that superior academic skills usually result from special class membership, but the negative impact on self-concept is not so measurable but is nonetheless real. If one's philosophy places achievement high, his choice might be special classes; if his philosophy places children first, then the chance to feel "normal" in a regular class would be one's choice. If one thinks that the slow learner must have a special slot in life, he might vote for special classes. If one thinks that other factors than IQ influence the ability to cope with life, then he would probably vote for the normality of the normal classroom.

If the remedial point of view (really making provisions for the individual pupil) and the special skills (knowledge of technical and specific hazards) of the special teachers were used *within* the regular classroom, it seems possible that one might eat his cake and have it too. The following observations will serve to show how knowledge of the psychology of individual differences and the nature of intelligence may be applied to the classroom situation.

The slow learner will be more strongly motivated by praise than by criticism.

Examples, experiences, demonstrations, models, realia, and illustrations serve to make learnings concrete.

Repetition of facts in different contexts and drill on fundamentals (such as numbers and language usage) is essential.

Emphasis should be placed on the development of traits of punctuality, neatness, health, etc., with specific suggestions for practical applications.

Slow developmental rates require patience on the part of the teacher and his showing respect for individuality.

Specific direction and prescription are desirable and gratifying; structure is comforting.

Reading and number work should emphasize everyday situations, such as reading signs and directions, making change. Illustrations should be simple and specific.

Abilities in various areas—music, manual arts, arithmetic, reading—will vary widely, and an attempt must be made to capitalize on pupils' strengths whenever possible.

Promotion must of necessity be largely dependent on social and chronological age. Evaluation must be based on personality growth rather than on academic achievement.

Immediate rewards, short-term goals, praise, and encouragement are effective motivators. The slow learner appreciates being told what to do and receiving feedback on what has been done.

Schoolwork should be closely related to the simple occupations slow learners will probably have as adults.

Slow learners need more, rather than less, schooling than average and superior children. The adolescent years may be profitably devoted to continued schooling with a vocational emphasis.

Gifted and Creative Pupils

Varied Concepts

The heading refers to two categories of pupils because gifted children are not necessarily creative and creative pupils often have quite ordinary intelligence. Several words have been used to designate students who are in the upper portion of a normal curve of distribution for intelligence. "Gifted" is a frequently used designation, with IQ score or percentile rank being an important criterion of identification. Authorities vary somewhat with regard to what this score should be—130, 135, and 140 have all been recommended. All authorities do agree that whatever the score, other criteria (past performance, motivation, special abilities) should desirably be used in conjunction with the scores. One objection to the word "gifted" is that sometimes it is used to indicate special talents—leadership, musical talent, artistic talent—and the importance of the IQ is lessened as an identifying characteristic. "Genius" has been used occasionally, but the term has been largely dropped in professional literature because it so often refers to ability *plus* achievement and is therefore meaningless as far as most gifted children are concerned. "Talent" is sometimes used synonymously with gifted, but talents do exist without being accompanied by high rank in measured intelligence.

"Creative" refers to those pupils who bring together in their associative thinking elements which are novel, useful, or which meet some specified requirement—e.g., respond to the three words "birthday," "line," and "surprise" with one word (answer: party) (Mednick and Andrews, 1967). Such things as imagination, divergent—out of the ordinary—thinking, and offbeat interests and mental associations are characteristic of creative persons (Torrance, 1968). Creative pupils may possess that pattern of emotional and intellectual factors contributory to inventiveness, personal openness, and curiosity which fosters new combinations of ideas. Unfortunately, most classroom teachers are tempted to focus on the fact of rapid learning and only occasionally to encourage creativity and the exercise of special talents. Some characteristics of the gifted pupil which have direct implications for teachers are:

> Gifted pupils find schoolwork rather easy—about half of the group studied by Terman (1925) could read before they entered school. A second grader, truant from school, was found to spend his time reading under the family front porch.

> Gifted pupils frequently are among the youngest in their class. They may have skipped a grade or they may not have been retained in a grade despite missing considerable time because of illness or moving.

> Gifted pupils tend to excel in all their school subjects. However, gifted pupils do not constitute a homogeneous group. The range of their differences in any area other than test IQ is almost as large as the range for unselected pupils (Cronbach, 1963, p. 253).

> Gifted pupils typically have a wide range of interests. Further, these interests tend to be somewhat mature; they tend to lose interest in the games played by their agemates at an earlier age.

> Gifted pupils, *as a group*, are superior in character and personality traits according to tests and the judgment of observers. The misconception that they are queer or asocial constitutes an unnecessary burden for many of them.

Teaching Approaches for Gifted Pupils

The basic challenge of educational psychology of recognizing and making adaptations for individual differences also pertains to those classed as gifted. Nevertheless, some generalizations about groups of individuals will be indicative and pertinent:

Blame and censure will be more effective with the gifted child than with the slow learner—though this should not be interpreted as a blanket recommendation.

Verbal descriptions and generalizations can serve to abbreviate and consolidate learnings.

Repetition is boring, yet many teachers make the mistake of giving these pupils more problems rather than more difficult ones or problems with ramifications. Study beyond that required of the average or slow learner is stimulating and gratifying to the gifted child.

Character traits are important and will be developed through challenge, meaning, and elaboration of school tasks.

An abundant supply of books, laboratory equipment, and illustrative material must be provided. From these, the bright child may select and utilize such materials as are in accord with his personal aims.

Much use of independent study makes it possible to satisfy a wide range of interests and avoids the boredom which accompanies drill on skills and knowledges already acquired.

Reading should expand, clarify, and enrich daily experiences. Numbers can be used as tools for thinking and for consolidating generalizations.

Abilities are more widely distributed among gifted children than among slow learners. For gifted children, emphasis should be placed on well-rounded development and the expansion of interests rather than on existing interests to the exclusion of diversification.

Acceleration (skipping of grades) is recommended up to two years,[7] provided the child is mature enough for the social and interest level of students in the grade to which he is promoted. Acceleration should be based on thorough individual case studies (Cook and Clymer, 1962).

Enrichment, the opportunity for special projects and investigations, is regarded by some as being a better approach than acceleration.

Typically, the gifted pupil has much drive and independence. Permissiveness and challenge are more effective than prescribed work.

Schoolwork can profitably be of a traditional academic nature, particularly for those pupils desiring structure.

Nova High School in Florida was designed and built to capitalize on current knowledge of teaching and learning processes. Mastery of subject matter is basic but many approaches to it are available—independent study, special classes, and ungraded organization are prominent features (Kaufman and Bethune, 1964). Since 1900, Cleveland has had what are called "major work classes" for able ele-

---

7   While there may be individual exceptions, there is no cumulative evidence that acceleration beyond two years is handicapping. It has yet to be proven that acceleration cannot advantageously exceed two years. See Dan C. Shannon, 1957, "What Research Says about Acceleration," *Phi Delta Kappan*, vol. 39, pp. 70-72.

mentary pupils. The range of differences in both the regular and special classes is thus reduced. In classes for the gifted, **enrichment** rather than acceleration is the emphasis. In addition to content, the program aims to develop alertness, initiative, creativity, critical thinking, ability to plan and judge, to share and work cooperatively, and to exercise leadership. It is felt that the advantages outweigh any disadvantages, and the major work classes continue. In some places, whole schools are devoted to the needs of the gifted. Hunter College in New York, which maintains a demonstration school, is an example. The special schools most frequently heard about are those in New York City, which maintains the High School of Music and Art, the High School of Performing Arts, and the High School of Science. These names do not imply specialization to the neglect of a rounded education—each maintains a curriculum that satisfied general educational aims in addition to the professed specialty (Dunn, 1963, pp. 216-219). Nongraded school organization, with decrease in competitiveness and flexibility of course selection for individual pupils, is an approach that has gained increasing popularity in recent years (Beggs and Buffie, 1967).

Dyslexics

The subject of dyslexia is being considered in this context because (1) there are rather large numbers of pupils in typical classrooms who are affected by it; (2) it provides a magnified version of varied learning style; and (3) appreciation of dyslexia provides the insights for dealing with other, more objectively apparent, differences; e.g., partially sighted, hard-of-hearing, crippled, cerebral palsied pupils.

Dyslexia: A Developmental Variation

Dyslexia means impairment of the aptitude for learning to read, which is in part psychological and in part physical dysfunction. Dyslexics have normal intelligence but, ignored, shamed, ridiculed, or otherwise belittled, they may have learned to take on the defense of mental retardation—of being pseudo-feeble-minded. Primary dyslexia is a neurological disorder which makes it impossible, or at best difficult, for the child to perceive and interpret the symbols on a printed page (Ellingson and Cass, 1966).

Notwithstanding the widespread disagreement as to a precise definition of dyslexia, it is generally recognized that the disability appears in two forms. One of these, primary or developmental dyslexia, is endogenous (internally caused) and reflects a neurological malfunction not indicated by any sign or history of brain injury. The other, secondary, reflects

an emotional disturbance, or results of environmental factors, deprivation or distortion in early language experience.[8]

Some believe that, in varying degrees, this difficulty may exist for as many as 10
percent of pupils; others place the figure as high as 20 percent (Pearse, 1969).

Some dyslexics may give no outward clue to the nature of their difficulty in interpreting printed symbols, but others may write p for q, b for p or d,
m for w; they may read *saw* for *was*; or show confusion in the left to right direction required in reading and writing. Some may be hyperactive, squirming, fidgety
pupils or ones who are awkward, stumbling, and out-of-time in rhythmics. Such
symptoms might be evidences of brain damage, but dyslexics do not necessarily,
or even usually, have brain damage. Dyslexics are more often viewed as having
a lag in neurological development. But there is no core factor except learning difficulties (Harris, 1968). These difficulties may be detected by diagnostic approaches which attempt to identify the problem as being a medical or experiential one.

Dyslexia as a Learning Style

The approaches used in clinics vary widely and new tests are being devised, but the urgent need is early detection so the child victim may be understood before frustration, failure, and feelings of inferiority begin to complicate
the perceptual or motoric problem. Delacato (1959) has pioneered in approaching this learning difficulty through physical activity. Because there is a developmental lag, the child is encouraged to crawl, creep, run, skip, and jump. Drawing,
painting, climbing through pipes, placing pegs in holes, assembling puzzles may
be part of the regime designed to provide developmental and corrective exercise
(Pearse, 1969). Such an approach does not uniformly yield encouraging results
(Robbins, 1967).

Children may learn to accept their different developmental rate, as some
must learn to accept their astigmatism, short-sightedness, difficulty in hearing, or
their wearing leg braces, if others do not make a "big thing" of it. Pretending that
the "thing" is not there is also unrealistic.

The import of this section is not to explain or to suggest a regime for
dyslexia so much as it is to make teachers, parents, and pupils aware of the fact
that there are different styles of learning. Dyslexics are not slow learners, in fact
they are often quite bright. They may "keep up" with the class so well that their
inability to read goes undetected for surprisingly long periods of time. They are

---

8   Benjamin H. Pearse, 1969, "Dyslexia," *American Education*, vol. 5, no. 4, p. 11,
April.

different learners. It is here postulated that there are other variations in learning style that are just as real but even less apparent and testable than is dyslexia.

Handicapped Children

There are many kinds of handicap—and an area for teacher specialization in each—such as crippled children, delicate children, hard-of-hearing, partially sighted, slow learners, stutterers, cerebral palsied, epileptics.

Special Classes

In some cases these differences are so great that, at least initially, special classes with special teachers are necessary in order to approach satisfaction of the pupils' developmental needs. Hard-of-hearing children may need special and expert instruction in lip-reading. The difficulties of a speech-handicapped youngster might be severe enough that his needs extend beyond the competence of classroom teachers. Several pupils of various ages will work as a unit making sounds, practicing breath control, using mirrors to become conscious of muscle activity, and then return to their regular classes. Blind children need special teachers in order to learn to read braille. Two decades ago there was a hope that the 5, 10, or 15 percent of such pupils who were markedly different could be placed in special classes with special teachers. Today the goal has been revamped. There is a continuing need for special teachers—not just for remedial teachers but for specialists in specific kinds of handicap (Otto and Koenke, 1969). The well-prepared specialists can work not simply as isolated coaches but as consultants and resource persons for classroom teachers. Some handicaps could be handled by classroom teachers who have understanding and patience, but the sheer press of numbers is discouraging to others. Half a dozen hyperactive, slow speaking, cerebral palsied children might take too much time and energy from the regular teacher.

There seems to be a growing doubt about the too-wide use of special classes. In case of severe handicap they would seem to have a valid function. Even in such cases, many believe that special work should be directed to preparing the pupil to return to the regular classroom as soon as possible or to be in special class for only part of the day. Putting culturally different pupils into special remedial classes is regarded as being a quite different matter. It has been postulated that the grouping of culturally different pupils into special remedial classes because they are, by comparison, below grade level is handicapping to them and to the average pupils who are deprived of a chance to make normal and needed cultural contact (Meyer, 1969).

Handicapped Pupils in Regular Classrooms

Many persons take the position, for a variety of reasons, that special classes should be a last resort, not a readily available "dumping ground." Because the handicapped person must ultimately, in postschool life, do his work and living in a world made of a variety of persons, attitudes, and responsibilities, he needs experiences with across-the-board people (Densham, 1971).

American educators, and the public, have become aware of the discarding of minority groups in the school system, and most localities have attempted to improve the lot of that 10 percent who are culturally different. We have long been aware of another minority, exceptional children, and much talking and writing has been done about them. However, this potential 10 percent of the total school population is, for the most part, not being served and, because of lack of specialized help, is often not even in attendance. In 1969 it was estimated that this 10 percent would amount to over 5 million pupils (about the total of all college enrollments—universities, colleges, and junior colleges—in 1964). These by groups, in decreasing frequency were:

Speech handicapped	Hard of hearing
Mentally retarded	Crippled and delicate
Emotionally disturbed	Visually handicapped
Learning disability (e.g., dyslexics)	Deaf

The unresolved question regarding minority groups, ethnic or handicapped, is whether we wish to spend some money now or wait and assume a continuing burden of unemployment and dependency on welfare. Proof as to the high effectiveness of special classes, both now in terms of school learning, and later for financial security, is abundant and gratifying.

Federal funds for education seem to follow patterns, e.g., vocational education, gifted children, school dropouts, culturally different, etc. The current accelerated emphases are on preschool and exceptional children. Education students might study exceptional children (1) as a possible professional specialty, and (2) for clues to making regular classroom work more effective.

A sharp line cannot be drawn between those pupils who should or should not be in special classes because differences are continuous. In addition, the choice would vary with the preparation and attitude of the classroom teacher and the availability and competence of special help. Being in a regular classroom provides an opportunity for the handicapped person to accept the existence of his handicap without making it an excuse for evading work and responsibility.

There is, in addition, an opportunity to teach the "normal" pupil respect for the handicapped persons. A high school girl, for instance, said after a semester's contact with a cerebral-palsied classmate, "I'm unhappy when I see how little I have accomplished with so much when I see how much George has accom-

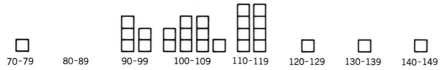

Figure 13-2 IQ scores plotted to show that differences between two pupils at the upper and lower ranges are wider than the differences among 65 to 70 percent of the class at the middle ranges. (Four pupils received a score of 112 and four had a score of 118.)

plished with so little." Some parents are abhorred with the idea that their second grader might witness an epileptic seizure. Other parents see that incident as providing contact with reality, plus the opportunity for their child to learn how to help another in a later similar situation.

It has been found that pupils sometimes can help another who is having some learning difficulty better than a teacher can. The helper does not have to be brighter or even more knowledgeable. Apparently the concept of "teacher" or "adult" inhibits some pupils who relate well to peers. It may be that one slow learner helps another because he appreciates how hard the work is. And then, it might be nothing more than having someone who "is my very own" (Levine, 1970).

Hurley (1969, p. 47) emphatically asserts that placing slow learners, or those with reading difficulties, in special classes amounts to a ghettoization of pupils who are simply starting at different places. Pupils in these classes soon learn, if they did not suspect it at the time of placement in a special class, that they are regarded as being mentally retarded. The blow to their spirit may cause them to internalize the belief that they are "dopes" rather than just being different.

A big argument against special classes is the likelihood of teachers' developing the feeling that the problem of differences has been resolved by such placement. A look at any set of test scores will show that individual differences are still wide, especially in the upper and lower ranges—even when pupils are grouped (see Figure 13-2).

Summary

John Q. Citizen, parents, and school personnel give lip-service to the idea that all pupils are different; then in planning and practice, a contrasting notion prevails: Put pupils in groups in which the members are alike. The quick, and often futile and frustrating, approach is to group the culturally different, slow learners, gifted, and handicapped children into special classes.

Most of the alleged characteristics of culturally different pupils are simply a matter of degree. Middle-class children have the same characteristics with a lesser statistical frequency when we speak of learning difficulties. If differences between groups are important, a sound psychological orientation in the teaching-learning situation would be to emphasize those differences that represent strengths. Principles of sound teaching are the same for culturally different pupils as they are for all other different and "typical" pupils.

There are some special emphases which can be made in class for pupils who are different. Slow learners need protection from the humiliation of competing against those who are markedly superior. They need repeated, concrete, specific, and simple experiences in order to realize their limited potential. Gifted pupils need fewer repetitious experiences. They need the challenge of attacking the ramifications of knowledge; they can generalize and profit from abstractions. They especially need a balance between prescription, wise teacher direction, and freedom. Creative pupils need to be recognized for their individuality. Tolerance for their divergent thoughts and interests is essential. All kinds of learners need the challenge of learning environments and opportunities for the development of self-confidence, which stems from approval, acceptance, the experience of success, a feeling that their presence has some influence.

Dyslexics were considered in this chapter to emphasize the fact that there are different learning styles that merit recognition. In the case of the dyslexic, the difference in learning style is so marked that the importance of unique teaching approaches is vividly demonstrated. Handicapped children also have marked differences and urgent needs. For them, as for others, the special treatment plus membership in regular classrooms possesses many advantages.

Suggested Additional Readings

BLANK, MARION, 1970, "Implicit Assumptions Underlying Preschool Intervention Programs," *Journal of Social Issues*, vol. 26, no. 2, pp. 15-34, spring.
    More individual instruction is needed and less grouping into special classes where the individual is still overlooked.
CHRISTIE, T., 1970, "Environmental Factors in Creativity," *Journal of Creative Behavior*, vol. 4, no. 1, pp. 13-31, winter.
    Home and neighborhood factors are discussed in terms of creative pupils' perceptions and motivations. About half the article is a discussion of the school environment which fosters creativity.
DENSHAM, WILLIAM E., 1971, "The Children Who Had to Be Found," *American Education*, vol. 7, no. 2, pp. 11-14, March.
    This article brings to life some of the work that is being done with handicapped children and illustrates one small way in which youth may perform an emotionally significant task.
HURLEY, RODGER, 1969, *Poverty and Mental Retardation: A Causal Relationship*, New York: Random House (Vintage Books).
    The difficulty of separating physical and mental handicap from socioeconomic class factors is emphasized. Statistics on various facets of retardation are vividly presented.

KEYES, DANIEL, 1966, *Flowers for Algernon*, New York: Harcourt, Brace & World, Inc. (Also a Bantam Book.)

This novel concerns a feeble-minded boy who was transformed by medical treatment into a gifted person. Flashbacks describe the feelings of a feeble-minded boy who tries his best to please but cannot comprehend the task. He *can* comprehend the cruelty which others use in dealing with him.

Part four

Teaching-Learning Problems

Not all the problems of psychology in education can even be discussed, let alone resolved, in a text of limited size. In Part 4, some of the major classroom problems of education (as viewed from the perspective of the author) are considered.

The question of classroom control, more commonly known as discipline, has no "pat" answer. The problem of control is different for a pupil who needs structure than it is for one who seeks identity and the satisfaction of curiosity. The problem of control is different if we want obedient gray-flannel-suit conformists than if we want creative, autonomous, socially considerate adults.

Despite the fact that we live and learn in groups, typically we study more about individual differences than we do about group dynamics. The subject is here treated as an approach to classroom control and a factor in the processes of becoming.

We will never, hopefully, reach the point in education where what we are doing is good enough for young people. Some innovations in education are described with the purpose of encouraging teachers to become habitual innovators. Their own and their pupils' learning and living will thereby become more exciting, desirable, and productive.

Throughout the book there has been an emphasis on the ego-concept. The final chapter emphasizes that evaluative processes are an indivisible part of education. Those evaluative processes which enhance the ego of the learner are those that best prepare him for life outside the school and for the continuous learning which rapid change demands.

14

Classroom Control

There is an ideal, and a myth, existent among teachers and administrators that if the teacher can motivate his pupils, has good rapport with them, and if pupils and teacher accept mutual goals, there will be no discipline problems. As an ideal this concept may be viable—depending on what is meant by discipline problems. Unfortunately the word discipline, as in the case of Alice's friend, Humpty Dumpty, ". . . means just what I choose it to mean—neither more nor less." And unfortunately, no teacher has been able to reach that ideal state where aversive control was unnecessary—though it may not have been used.

In this chapter there is some reformulation of statements previously made regarding the facilitation of learning, because these same suggestions are pertinent to orderly discipline in the classroom. Optimum learning plus disciplined behavior constitute progress in the cultivation and enhancement of mental health.

National leaders place mental health high on the action priority list for our country's strength (*Perspectives* . . ., 1969). Educators are increasingly recognizing questionable mental health as being involved in such persistent problems as underachievement, school dropouts, and personal and social maladjustment. To the extent that teachers accept the idea that pupil self-realization is a viable goal, their involvement in mental health and constructive discipline becomes serious.

The Role of Discipline

Varied Meanings of Discipline

Eleven definitions of discipline are cited in the *Dictionary of Education*. These include such subheads as constructive, corrective, formal, military, preventive, punitive, scholastic, student, and therapeutic (Good, 1959, pp. 176-177). The major concern of this chapter is discipline as an approach to such classroom control as will (1) enhance the teaching-learning milieus and (2) prepare pupils for responsible self-direction in, and beyond, the classroom. There is an immediate dilemma in this two-faceted goal because some procedures which are conducive to classroom control may be inimical to self-discipline in after-school years.

A major issue for educators is that of aversive control of pupils. Because it is possible to achieve immediate conformity without contributing to the long-range goal of self-discipline as adults, aversive control by teachers is condemned by many authorities. Because lack of conformity may also be detrimental to adult self-discipline, the problem of teacher control becomes equivocal, if not controversial.

Historical Roots and Current Problems

In the last 100 years the prime requirement of a schoolteacher was that he be able to "keep discipline." The birch rod and the ruler, and even the oak yardstick, were standard pieces of equipment, freely used, to establish conditions for learning. These may have been mild means of aversive discipline when compared with methods used 150 years ago. One method was to place a 4- to 6-pound log on the fidgety pupil's neck and shoulders so he would have to remain still to keep it balanced. Shackles were also used to keep the "vicious" child from running or skipping. The chronic misbehaver might, as an extreme resort, be placed in a basket or sack and be suspended from the roof of the school as a subject of public disdain. This later was such an effective method that "simply mentioning the device was sufficient." After-school detention was a favorite punishment in "1808 as in 1968" (Emblen, 1969).

When a pupil curses the teacher, it would be comforting to be able to banish him not just to the roof but for all time—and probably to the enhancement of school morale. When a pupil disobeys the request to put materials away with the remark, "You prejudice'," it is difficult, perhaps unrealistic, not to experience some visceral reaction. When a high school boy has a girl up against the hallway wall choking her, it is tempting, despite rules to the contrary, to "clobber" him. In short, one wonders if the teacher with the **permissive** orientation and the "no physical punishment" enthusiast has "been there."

Conversely, aversive methods often become the excuse of the sadist. One does not doubt that there are both men and women teachers who enjoyed the physical and institutional power they had and, on occasion, abused that power and the pupil. On the other hand, the placing of power and responsibility for behavior in the students' hands also seems to have led, despite idealistic hopes, to some abuses and excesses. One hypothesis of student unrest, alienation, and the width of the generation gap is permissiveness in child rearing.

> The Permissive Hypothesis—Perhaps the commonest explanation of student unrest is that it is the result of too much permissiveness in rearing children. The proponents of this view argue that some parents have, through painstaking efforts to avoid creating neuroses in their children, abdicated their responsibility to teach and discipline their children. In so doing they have reared a generation of spoiled, greedy youth who are unable to tolerate the slightest frustration without showing an angry or infantile response.[1]

The Social and Personal Need for Discipline

No society has been able to live without laws and regulations; and, apparently, the more complex the society the greater is the need for detailed description of behaviors which are permitted and those which are proscribed. These social regulations are of different levels of visibility—they are called "mores," "folkways," and "laws." They are designed to make it possible for men to live together harmoniously and thus, in contemporary society, to enhance the living conditions of individuals (Lowry and Rankin, 1969, p. 112). In view of this basic social phenomenon, it is difficult to see why teachers and school patrons should be hesitant to exert coercive influence on children in order to begin teaching them the difference between license and social responsibility.

The arguments for permissiveness are sound ones, but the specific limitations, the borders between "do and don't," are hard to define. It must further be recognized that there are individual differences in teachers both in physical appearance and personality orientation (including tension tolerance) which make a technique effective for some and futile for others. A 110-pound teacher who does not believe she can do it should not try to remove a back-talking halfback on the high school varsity from her math class. But 110-pounders who knew they could do it have done just that—and the delicate and developing personality of the halfback has not been shattered.

The position taken here regarding adult use of authority derives from Maslow's (1954, pp. 80-106) hierarchy of needs theory. He postulated that basic

---

1   S. L. Halleck, 1968, "Hypotheses of Student Unrest," *Phi Delta Kappan*, vol. 50, no. 3, September.

Jan Lukas/College Newsphoto Alliance

needs are motivators in a sequential or hierarchical order—low-order needs must be reasonably or partially satisfied before higher-order needs become sources of motivation (see Chapter 9).

After the needs for food, water, salt, constant temperature, etc., have been relatively well satisfied, *then* a new set of needs emerge—the safety needs. These, for a period of time, become the dominators and organizers of behavior. Family instability threatens the safety of the baby or child, and he brings to school a cowering, withdrawn, defensive, or belligerently seeking-attitude without further equivocation and uncertainty. His need is for certainty and consistency. One who wonders why a child wants to return to a parent who has physically harmed him—the battering parent—may think in terms of safety needs. The child needs not to be abandoned *before* the higher level need for love and belongingness takes priority.

> Another indication of the child's need for safety is his preference for some kind of undisrupted routine or rhythm. He seems to want a predictable, orderly world. For instance, injustice, unfairness, or inconsistency in the parents seems to make a child feel anxious and unsafe. This attitude may be not so much because of the injustice *per se* or any particular pains involved, but rather because this treatment threatens to make the world look unreliable, or unsafe, or unpredictable. Young

children seem to thrive better under a system that has at least a skeletal outline of rigidity, in which there is a schedule of a kind, some sort of routine, something that can be counted upon, not only for the present but also far into the future. Child psychologists, teachers, and psychotherapists have found that permissiveness within limits, rather than unrestricted permissiveness is preferred as well as *needed* by children. Perhaps one could express this more accurately by saying that the child needs an organized world rather than an unorganized or unstructured one.[2]

The author takes no issue with the idea that it is desirable to have teachers who love and accept children. The point has been emphasized throughout this book that even more important than gadgets, innovations, curricula, methods, organization, passing and grading policies is the personality—the acceptance and regard for pupils—of the teacher. However, acceptance and regard are not ruled out by the teacher's respect for reliance on rules, regulations, and requirements. The child is reassured by parents who know they are parents and by teachers who know they are teachers—and act their role.

Parents, by definition, are not peers to their children and to abandon their parental role is to frighten and confuse the child. A child wants his parent to prevail, to assume responsibility (Cottle, 1969*b*). So too, although in a lesser degree, does the adolescent wish to avoid responsibility and the making of decisions in a strange set of circumstances. The situation is no different in the school where teachers are dealing with children and adolescents. Choice is an awesome responsibility, and to thrust it on the primary and intermediate-age children may so intimidate and bewilder them that as they approach adolescence they still shy from decisions and responsibility. If a child has not gone through the developmental stage of having his safety needs satisfied, he may develop neurotic behaviors that render him incapable of assuming responsibility when his more fortunate peers are ready.

Meyer (1969) asserts that this, in the eyes of some persons, is what has happened to the young people of suburbia. They have been pampered and waited on by well-meaning parents. The parents, misled by expert advice on child-rearing practices, have so sought to avoid generating neuroses that they have been caught in backlash. The children are unable to assume responsibility and are childishly frustrated and angry when they encounter any obstacle to their presumed omniscience and omnipotence. Conversely, says Meyer, others see suburbia's children as being so overprotected and dominated by parents that children are not permitted to become self-directing and self-responsible.

The dilemma might, in part, be generated by the fact that no distinction is made between children and adolescents. There should be much direction and

2   Abraham H. Maslow, 1954, *Motivation and Personality*, New York: Harper & Row, Publishers, Incorporated, p. 86.

decision making by the primary teachers whose pupils lack the intellectual and emotional maturity as well as the experience required to make decisions, *but* progressively and purposefully, pupils need to become increasingly involved in decision making as they approach and go through high school. By the time one is in high school, punishment for wrong choices should desirably be the loss of opportunity. This will not resolve the dilemma completely because the adolescents will not permit it. At home when the adolescent demands that he be allowed to drive the family car to the beach (any other issue may also serve the purpose) and the parents say "No" the response is "None of the other kids . . .," and the parent is left with feelings of guilt, cruelty, and unreasonableness. But the parent cannot win. If, in desperation and exhaustion he says, "OK, take the car" the adolescent may weep (or feel like it) and say, "You don't care what happens to me." He really did not want to win, but he had to engage in the contesting process. Because the parent cannot win, he might as well do that which makes him feel comfortable—be a parent.

The Self-defeating Role of Punishment

Control and adult direction does not imply or typically necessitate physical punishment. Deprivation of privilege—being a class officer, having some responsibility, losing a chance to make a special report—will ordinarily suffice. Exclusion from the classroom (loss of a learning opportunity) has been found to be effective. Loss of privilege or removal can result in behavior improvement (better mental health) whereas punishment arouses fear, resentment, hostility (mental illness). Additional school assignments, being forced to stay in at recess, or being kept after school are punishment techniques designed to defeat the goal of developing a liking for the process of systematic learning. It is probable that canings, striking a child, doing school work as punishment were techniques which prevailed when Shakespeare described one of life's stages as:

> And then the whining schoolboy, with his satchel
> And shining morning face, creeping like a snail
> Unwillingly to school.
>
> *As You Like It*

Discipline has a place in school, but a punitive attitude does not. Menninger (1968), speaking as a psychoanalytically oriented psychiatrist, takes the defenses away from the proponent of punishment in asserting that a part of human nature is to conceal our own tendencies toward violence by being harsh to those who transgress mores and laws. Although punishment in prisons has consistently proved to be futile, and often an aggravation to further crime, its use tenaciously persists. Rationalizations to the contrary, it is the sadism of society rather than the curing of the criminal that is being served.

As teachers examine their convictions about the value of punishment some will, if they can be candid, see the roots of vengeance in their own needs. They thus see the flaunting of physical power as their own self-diminution. Punishment may be a need which teachers have as representatives of the society of which Menninger speaks, but it is not listed as a developmental need of children. Some years ago a child psychiatrist, writing on child-rearing practices, included a chapter on "Spank If You Must" (Hohman, 1947). The gist of it was that when a parent can no longer stand it, he should spank the child. But he should know that it is for his own satisfaction, not the good of the child. The remark, "This hurts me more than it does you," in many other situations, and especially in the spanking context, is not accurate.

Glasser (1970) has stated that when a pupil is sent to the office, teachers want blood. If, when the pupil returns and says "Nuthin" when asked what was done, the teacher perceives the principal as being derelict. Glasser's recommendation for treatment of misconduct is to tell the youngster to rest a while. "I'm not tired." "Well, rest anyway. And as soon as you can behave, we'll make a contract, and you may return." His belief is that more speeders are helped by having their driving licenses suspended than they would be if the arresting officer shot them through the accelerator foot—the punitive approach.

Discipline and Mental Health

The Meaning of Mental Health

Today the major mental health emphasis is on health rather than the exclusive emphasis on prevention and cure. Better living conditions and regimes are sought which will cure the afflicted, prevent illness, and bring the healthy to still higher levels of functioning.

Mental health is a way of life which will make it possible for one's potentialities to come to full development. Maslow (1968) endorsed the idea that mental health should embrace the study of the well, the unusually healthy individual. He was interested in the pathway and experiences of the self-actualized individual and thought that such study would provide more clues to effective living than studying the dynamics of illness. Menninger (1953) states that mental health is not *just* efficiency or contentment or complacent abiding by the rules. It is an adjusting process that involves a maximum of effectiveness and happiness. It means an even temper, functional intelligence, and consideration of the social order. Reality is accurately perceived and accepted. Problems are solved when possible and lived with when unsolvable.

Mental health is the practical art of assisting oneself and others to the realization of a fuller, happier, more harmonious, and more effective life.[3] It is a goal toward which to strive rather than a condition that can be achieved. For the classroom teacher mental health is being the kind of person and using the kinds of approaches that will help pupils realize a greater amount of their potential for well-rounded and constant growth and efficient living. It thus becomes increasingly clear that mental health is a particular way of looking at classroom control. It involves the teacher's attitude toward his task and his pupils, his use of methods, his choice of objectives, his use of materials, and his individual influence on the personality development of pupils.

Mental health and discipline are not synonymous, but they are intimately related. Both are central foci in day-to-day classroom procedures. Both call for ego strength and an ever-shifting balance between freedom and responsibility; or, more accurately and realistically, a fusing of freedom and responsibility. Initially discipline may be imposed by an **authoritative** but understanding adult, but increasingly, as the pupil grows older and wiser, the discipline will be inner-directed because one is learning the inseparability of self and society. The mature person does not need structure and stricture because he has accepted responsibility.

The overlapping of education, mental health, and discipline emphasizes the learning principle that we learn what we do. If the school is to teach adults and assume civic responsibility, early steps should be taken in school. Teachers encourage self-realization in their pupils by providing many avenues of development to meet individual needs. They must seek to improve human relationships by providing opportunities for democratic (and "democratic" involves delegation of power to those who are competent) procedures in academic choice and work in student activities. Teachers may develop economic efficiency by stimulating habits of workmanship and economy in the use of equipment and supplies; it involves care of school property and concern about litter. Good citizenship involves practice; such things as passes to go to the lavatory, policing of hallways, mass punishment of individual transgressions must be examined in terms of what the student is learning. Gibb (1965) makes the point that the more rigid the roles, the greater is the time spent by the ruled on how to circumvent the defensive management.

The major concern of the teacher must be maximum welfare of all children. The symptoms of pupil stress and maladjustment—such as shyness, "laziness," frequent absences, lack of application, inability to get along with peers and teachers, withdrawal tendencies, transitory interests not appropriate to age, and failure to work at or near capacity—should not be treated by means of **author-**

---

3   These points are expanded in Harold W. Bernard, 1970, *Mental Health in the Classroom*, New York: McGraw-Hill Book Company, pp. 19-22.

itarian discipline. The feedback should be on the positive. Interest, cooperativeness, adaptability, friendliness, and the ability to bounce back after disappointment should be recognized, periodically acknowledged, and occasionally praised. It is unrealistic to hope that the teacher will be so effective and the school so well organized that repressive discipline will never be needed. But external discipline should be regarded as a passing phase of development rather than a habitual procedure.

Two considerations may help the teacher in the mental health emphasis and in the exercise of constructive discipline. (1) The misbehaving child is saying in nonverbal ways, "I'm in trouble. I hurt. Please notice me." (2) The child is most in need of love and acceptance when he is most unlovable and unacceptable.

Some Fundamentals of Mental Health

When a child disturbs classroom demeanor or flagrantly misuses his talents, it is because he perceives that behavior as filling some need or achieving some task. Those behaviors which are called "self-defeating" are ones which obtain some immediate gain, or apparent gain, but which make later satisfactions more improbable. In this section some needs (and another list might as easily have been used) serve to illustrate the congruity of classroom control and pupil mental health.

Respect for Identity

The need for acceptance is readily appreciated, but Erikson (1970) postulates his theory of lifelong development on the persistence of this need. Man needs affirmation of self by parents, friends, teachers, and the entire culture. To have less is to be alienated and lacking in identity.

The mature teacher will not expect adult behavior and perspective from a pupil; he will know that the pupil's actions are not always synonymous with his intentions. Deviations from desired behavior are recognized as indications that children are encountering growth difficulties. Acceptance means that a person's unique personality, interests, strong points, frailties, disposition, and temperament are uniquely and respectfully evaluated. Accepting a pupil is a difficult task for the immature person who is afraid pupils will not like him. Acceptance is illustrated by the teacher of the slum child who understands the child's attacks on other pupils and sometimes on the teacher himself. It is illustrated by the cheerful encouragement of the pupil who suddenly said, "Dem goddam peaches is burnin' " (Blake, 1964), although previously he had not said anything—certainly not a whole sentence. Genuine acceptance is truly the core of giving functional recognition to pupil differences. Acceptance means seeing through the behavior to the living individual. The idea of "I like you, Johnny, but I do not like what you do" must be conveyed to the child. A high school teacher looked at some discourteous boys and said, "You are too gentlemanly to act like that." The boys knew the teacher liked them and cared about what they did. They knew they were accepted despite their actions, and improvement was soon noted in their behavior.

A particular child needs to be not only with the group but *of* the group. The teacher can help by encouraging class members—as appointed hosts or "big brothers"—to welcome newcomers. Some children misbehave because it is more tolerable to be recognized and punished than it is to be ignored and remain at peace. Teachers must assess the kinds of behavior they reinforce.

> Pedro S., in the fourth grade, was a nonreader who each Tuesday and Thursday at 10 A.M. went to the nearby university reading clinic, where anxious coeds gave him much and varied attention. When other youngsters were getting their assignments, Pedro was marching freely across campus to get some more recognition and understanding. He was bright enough that in three years he had made no appreciable progress in reading.

Child-rearing authorities may recommend removal from the room of the child having a temper tantrum. If he is scolded, shaken, or otherwise given attention, his tantrum is being reinforced. Teachers also find the removal technique effective: "You are welcome back as soon as you can stick to the rules." Glasser (1969, p. 22) recommends that the child who interrupts the class be helped to make a decision and a commitment. And no excuses are acceptable. It is distinctly not a matter of "Why didn't you do it?" This approach stimulates excuses. "When are you going to do it?" or "You didn't do it. Try again" is more likely to be the productive approach.

The Need for Companionship

This need is given particular emphasis by psychiatrists as they stress the seriousness of the symptom of withdrawal. It is of no value to say to the shy pupil, "You should be more friendly." He would be if he knew how. It is necessary to find the causes of the lack of companionship and take steps to correct them. Development of almost any skill will help the pupil build the confidence that will allow him to participate more vigorously in personal contacts.

Not all pupils can be alike in social competence. If a pupil who has few intimate friends seems to be otherwise well adjusted, the teacher should not be too concerned. For example, the teacher should not insist that a high school boy get out on the dance floor with some attractive girl—this might add unnecessary burdens of adjustment, and it could be that he enjoys watching more than participation. If the "loner's" solitary nature is accompanied by other evidences of insecurity and maladjustment, the need for further investigation is indicated.

The possible seriousness of lack of companionship is suggested by the remark of a superintendent of a school for delinquent girls, "These girls are just not joiners—they do not belong to choruses, pep squads, dance teams, or clubs" (McBride, 1963). However, delinquency is not just a matter of not belonging. Appropriate curriculum, the need for success, special help are other factors to be noted. But it is the teacher who perceives the special pattern of needs who represents the school. In the eyes of the community and the pupils the teacher *is* the school; and the school is one of the principal socializing agencies of the culture (Amos, 1967, p. 136).

The Need for New Experiences

Many discipline problems arise from the common reaction of most persons to be bored with routine and monotony. New subject matter, new activities, progressive responsibilities, field trips, and the use of teaching aids and teacher aides can help to satisfy this need. However, the need for new experiences should not dim our view of the comfort of the routine and ordinary. We all like to have conditions upon which we can depend. It is therefore necessary that some of the details of schoolwork be kept much the same from day to day.

Need satisfactions are interdependent. For example, the need to develop feelings of security is dependent upon the pupil's ability to adjust to new situations; hence he needs the opportunity for experience in new areas if he is to develop a versatile competence. Everyone needs to be considered a growing personality and to satisfy curiosity; here again, the need for encountering unique circumstances is apparent. There is also the need for mastery; one needs to have new experiences in order to explore various avenues that may lead to mastery of his particular potentialities.

If the need for new experiences is not satisfied in the school, there is the distinct possibility that satisfaction will be sought by aberrant behavior, including delinquency.

The Need for Success

Success provides affirmation to the individual that he is a worthy, recognized, competent, autonomous individual. Expectation of grade norms in writing, arithmetic, physics, and history is likely to deny genuine success to many— to the slow learner because the pace is too fast and to the able pupil because he has not been challenged. Success is denied to some pupils because their unique talents are not exercised in the academic curriculum. There is, for example, little chance for the budding mechanic, the would-be electrician, and the potential dress designer or dressmaker to be recognized as successful. The chances to satisfy the need for success are particularly limited for that one out of ten who is called an "exceptional" child—the retarded, the gifted, the physically handicapped, the emotionally maladjusted individual, and the culturally different.

It appears, therefore, that *school programs should be arranged for more equitable distribution of the experience of success so that every child may achieve some degree of it.* This means that teacher expectations will be scaled to indicated ability and the records of past performances, that school activities will be so varied as to call for the more extensive exercise of different capacities, and that pupils will judge their own performance on the basis of gain and growth rather than on interpersonal comparisons. This cannot be done when the academic program receives more than its just share of attention. Varied opportunities for emotional, physical, aesthetic, *and* intellectual achievements must be provided. Good teaching, which recognizes differences, illustrates acceptance, and challenges potentials, thus providing every pupil a chance to achieve success in effective learning, is a most positive approach to mental health. More teachers should realize that when they are teaching well, they are applying principles of mental health and diminishing, if not eliminating, problems of discipline. All this depends not so much on new discoveries in teaching as on applying what is already known (Richardson, 1971).

The Need for Responsible Independence

One sees the need for independence asserted very early in the life of the individual. Even before the baby begins to talk, he wants to feed himself. Delicate problems of balance are involved as teachers try to let pupils exercise independence without giving the impressions that "rights" transcend responsibilities. Permissive limits in school are probably much broader than many insecure teachers are able to admit. The limits of adult-imposed discipline are probably narrower than the autocratically inclined teacher will admit.

Children need freedom of opportunity in order to develop. This does not mean a lack of restraint or guidance—as some parents and a few teachers seem to think. It does mean that restrictions should not be arbitrary or imposed for adult convenience. Independence will be developed as the individual is given freedom to cope with his own problems.

A good many of the difficulties of adolescents stem from the desire to act without the prescription and direction of parents and teachers. This striving for independence is a major developmental task of adolescence. Independence contains much of the essence of **identity**. Independence involves curiosity and the desire to test capacities and to make decisions. Wise parents and perceptive teachers recognize in these strivings for independence the seeds of genuine psychological maturity. Because young people of a given age differ in their ability to make wise decisions (those we would make if we were in their place) no rules can be cited but some propositions may be proposed:

> Encourage children to voice their preferences.
>
> Provide variety for exploration of objects and ideas.
>
> Accept children and try to understand undesirable behavior; but accepting socially disruptive behavior is another dilemma.
>
> Be slow to interfere with the inevitable pupil conflicts. Praise youngsters for acts that show evidence of socially considerate independence.
>
> Encourage performances that reveal creativity rather than demanding adherence to formalized patterns (in painting, drawing, and writing).
>
> Challenge some of the statements made in textbooks and thus stimulate pupils to check authority against their own experience.
>
> Assist pupils to organize their own forms of homeroom and schoolwide student government.

Developing Tension Tolerance

There seems to be little danger that too many obstacles may be removed from the developmental path of youngsters. However, we must consider that removal of one barrier (e.g., classroom rules) does not impose another (e.g., making decisions without the maturity or experience). Removing barriers does not mean that schoolwork should be easy. It should be fun—if fun includes the feeling of satisfaction one has from achievement after strenuous effort.

One achieves the feelings of security that may be called "tension tolerance" by overcoming difficulties and enjoying success in physical and social activities. Disappointment and discouragement need not be thrust on growing children. If the individual is oriented toward achievement and growth, as contrasted to motivation toward the avoidance of stress, he can better cope with routine jobs, the routines of life, and other impediments to progress (Freeburg, 1970). The growth-oriented pupil focuses on long-term objectives, whereas the avoidance-oriented one focuses upon transitory comfort, which suggests that school goals should alternate between the immediate (especially for younger pupils) and the more remote.

A balanced program that permits alternation between challenge, success, and occasional defeat (in areas which the pupil has chosen to enter) makes its contribution to tension tolerance. Teachers who provide balance between requirements, directions, guidance, and pupil discovery are lessening the threat of present stress and preparing the pupil for future growth. Some general suggestions are

Teachers must avoid giving too much help, which is so easy to do in arithmetic, spelling, and geometry.

A task that is difficult but not impossible may warrant some help. When the job has been done, words of praise are not necessary, though they may help.

Goals should be attractive, i.e., understandable and important to the child.

Tension tolerance requires balance between help and no help, between freedom and responsibility, between now and later, and between individual and society.

The development of tension tolerance may be likened to the acquisition of resistance to disease. Some resistance is gained through immunization and inoculation; in the area of mental hygiene and education, this might be exposure to planned experiences that are scaled to developmental levels. Some resistance is gained through the development of good health; the mental health parallel is the development of skills and knowledge that will enable the individual to overcome obstacles. The policy of deliberate exposure to disease, which prevailed until recent years is no longer accepted. Neither should the policy of failing students in order to maintain standards, to foster the sorting process, or "to teach pupils the realities of life" be a part of contemporary discipline and mental health (DuPue, 1967; Glasser, 1969; Goodlad, 1967).

Mental Health Hazards in the School

There is much that is good about conventional school practices. The needs of many children are satisfactorily met, and, as adults, they look back at school with satisfaction. The needs of others are not met and the negative in schools then receives much attention. One approach to improving schools is to highlight the psychologically sound, another is to call attention to the defects.

Lack of Friendliness

Teachers use humor more often in a sarcastic manner than in a friendly one. Their own inner hostilities are attributed to others and thus create an unfriendly atmosphere (Jersild and Lazar, 1962). It would be an exaggeration to say that there is a tradition of unfriendliness in the school. Yet the concept of the teacher as a stern disciplinarian and the attitude that "familiarity breeds contempt" tend to prevent a genuinely friendly atmosphere in the school, where mental health is so important (Schrag, 1969b). Silberman (1969) reached the same conclusions as did Ryan (1938) over three decades earlier—although simple friendliness was obviously desirable and seemingly easily obtainable, it was found in shockingly few places.

There are many reasons for the lack of teacher friendliness. Citizens are often critical of the schools and teachers, and consequently teachers hesitate to depart from traditional concepts of the teacher as disciplinarian and undisputed leader. In addition, administrators find it impractical to establish friendly relations with teachers. Both factors are beyond the control of teachers, *except as matters of perception.* A factor within their control is improved understanding of children, professional study and growth, and participation in community affairs. Another factor within their control is improved self-understanding: As much as other individuals, teachers have unresolved problems and conflicts: those with modest talents as well as those with brilliant minds and distinguished careers are subject to anxiety. As long as teachers are security-oriented, any revision of role will be regarded as hazardous (English, 1969).

Emotional maturity is a process rather than an achievement, and individual teachers may pursue the process. Teachers may undertake the gratifying task of continual self-improvement. This was done by a number (over 200) of teachers in a study reported by Jersild and Lazar (1962). A control and an experimental group were questioned as to the nature and resolution of personal problems. The experimental group, whose problems were no more serious than those of the control group, underwent psychotherapy. In surprisingly high proportions, these teachers found that they could take a more realistic view of themselves, their work, and their pupils. They had an inner freedom they did not formerly possess. They were less fiercely competitive, more able to handle anger in themselves and pupils, more spontaneous in their friendships, and more accepting of self and others than they had been prior to therapy.

Self-improvement was also sought in a continuing project conducted by Prescott (1957). Working as a consultant in small groups with teachers in their own schools on real pupil cases, he sought to help them achieve deeper understandings of children's motivations, behavior, adjustment problems, and developmental tasks.

There are other bright spots. Harrison (1970) has described schools in a New Jersey community where Superintendent James Kimple introduced some innovative practices—elimination of grades and grading, abandonment of ability grouping, use of individualized instruction, and the encouragement of teachers to introduce other novel practices. Part of the program dealt with human relations and self-examination. This led teachers to appreciate how pupils see them—and to change their behavior more to what they (the teachers) really wanted to be. Not everybody was happy, but on the national examinations the pupils show up as well or better than comparison groups, and Kimple remarked, "You know, there was a time when every new idea here came from me. Now, there are so many ideas coming from others I can't keep up. I really don't know all that is going on. I think that's probably the way it should be."[4]

Advising the teacher to be friendly is suggesting that he lift himself by his bootstraps—like telling a pupil he should be happier. He would, if he could, and if he knew how. Teachers can help themselves in many ways. Psychotherapy is one way, and it involves self-help. In-service training is another way. Participation in interpersonal process groups will probably soon come to be seen as a powerful and available means by which a whole school staff may move forward (Cottle, 1969a; Fullmer and Bernard, 1972; Harrison, 1970; Rogers, 1968). Through the study of educational psychology, personality theory, motivation, and mental health, teachers may achieve a better understanding of their own childhood and adolescent experiences.

It will be easier for teachers to become friendly as mental health hazards in the school are removed. Subject matter *as a goal* is such a hazard. The "achievement tradition," in which the teacher focuses upon the child's learning certain facts and is irritated by anything that interferes with that goal, makes accomplishment primary and friendliness secondary. Grades and nonpromotion practices are other such hazards. Autocratically imposed discipline, lack of structure, and absence of rules are disturbing to many pupils. Both these extremes seem to ignore the ultimate objective of concerned and participative citizenship.

Competition

Competition should take place between groups and individuals who all have the possibility of success or winning. Competition with one's own previous record is also a desirable source of motivation. Competition should be friendly and cooperative, the kind that minimizes jealousy and suspicion. Scholastic competition that pits slow learners against bright children makes for feelings of insecurity, inferiority, and frustration in some and unwarranted egotism and unjustified feelings of superiority in others. A sense of achievement can be realized by a group, and the teacher who wishes to provide motivation without the hazard of open competition can accent cooperative activities. The impact on pupils depends largely on the emphasis given by teachers (Glanz, 1962, p. 240). The cooperative aspect of American life is just as basic as competition; in fact, it has been said to be our outstanding characteristic.

---

4   Charles H. Harrison, 1970, "South Brunswick, N.J.: Schools Put a Town on the Map," *Saturday Review*, vol. 53, no. 8, p. 90, Feb. 21.

Uniform Grades

If the basis for grading is mastery of content, some youngsters will inevitably receive discouraging grades and others will learn to get by with a minimum expenditure of effort.

Even if there were not wide individual differences among pupils, there would still be valid criticisms of uniform grading. One of these is unreliability. No two teachers give the same grade for work that is equivalent as judged by standardized achievement tests. Experiments show that one paper graded by several teachers will receive scores that vary as much as 50 points on a 100-point scale. Moreover, a teacher may differ in scoring a paper when he grades it a second time. These conditions exist when teachers do not know which student's paper is being scored. When they do know whose paper is being marked, the matter is further complicated by the **halo effect**. In one study, upper-middle-class pupils received 343 A and B grades when their numbers in the total school population would have warranted 216 such marks. Lower-lower-class pupils received 48 A's and B's when their numbers would have indicated 147 such grades. Upper-middle-class pupils received 19 D's and E's when their proportion in the school group was 75. Lower-lower-class pupils received 136 D and E grades when their numbers indicated their share as 51 (Sexton, 1961, p. 83). Even considering the cultural handicap exerted on intelligence test scores, this distribution is out of proportion.

There has not been wide agreement on whether letter grades should mean academic achievement alone, whether they should indicate progress in achievement (personal growth rather than interpersonal comparison), or whether they should also include effort, attitude, social skills, and special interests and abilities.

The few pupils who can get good grades *with reasonable effort* are helped by them. Those who try and repeatedly fail to get recognition through grades do what they must do—adopt the defense mechanism of "I don't care."

Fortunately, the conventional grading systems are undergoing constant examination and evaluation. Increasingly, there is a trend toward reporting in various ways, with letter grades, conferences with parents, and conferences with pupils and parents used in various combinations. There is an attempt to consider individual capacity in relation to achievement, particularly in the elementary schools. More emphasis is being placed on work habits, attitudes, and social and emotional adjustments as items that should supplement academic evaluation.

There are arguments for and against marking; and the debate will probably continue. If the emphasis is on pupil welfare and development of talent, most will agree with Suehr (1968) that letter grades do little to motivate pupils or give others a clear picture of them. Evaluation is necessary, it is an integral part of on-going education, but evaluation as grades must be questioned. As an aspect of discipline, let it be noted that vandalism of school property reaches a high at the time grades are distributed.

Promotion Practices

Prior to the widespread practice of compulsory education, policies of promotion were less perplexing but nonetheless damaging. One either passed, repeated a grade, or quit school. Now the alternative of quitting school has been legally eliminated through compulsory school attendance—though the laws are not strictly and uniformly enforced. The antidote for failing a grade—repetition of that grade—has been found to be almost, but not quite, universally unfruitful.

Many schools practice so-called "block promotion," "nonfailure," or "uniform promotion." It is felt that if a youngster does as well as he can, he should not have the experience of failure forced upon him. Exceptions are made only on the basis of considered judgments involving many factors in the child's life. For example, if a child has started school at a very early age and has not yet attained the social, mental, and emotional age that will allow him to profit from first-grade experience, he may, advantageously, be held back a year. Retentions should be determined in terms of individual cases and then restricted to the primary grades (Travers, 1970, p. 300). Retention in later grades are much less likely to show positive results. It has been found that promoted low-achievers usually do better than their nonpromoted counterparts. After a year, the repeaters showed less gain on achievement tests than did those who had been passed on the next higher grade. Some experiments indicate that as many as 85 percent of trial promotions are successful. Obviously, all who are retained are burdened by the sense of failure.

Nonpromotion runs counter to what is now known about the nature and extent of individual differences, contradicts basic principles of mental health, and aggravates the need for coercive discipline. The practice assumes that education consists of learning facts, but modern psychological and educational theory accent the idea that facts are only part of the educational enterprise. The encouraging outcome is emerging much faster than improved grading systems: Special classes are provided for those whose differences are marked; "streaming," or ability grouping is on the wane because of damage to ego and the arousal of aggression and animosity; individual instruction seeks to correct academic deficiencies that are due to unfortunate school history; and the nongraded primary school helps get many young pupils off to a good start.

No technique will automatically solve the academic problems of all pupils, provide for community demands, or satisfy the aspirations of all teachers. However, the nongraded school makes implementation of philosophical views and psychological insights somewhat easier. In this type of school, grade labels are not applied to students, and a pupil may be assigned to classes according to achievement and maturity. Some pupils may take four years and some only two years to complete what was formerly the first three grades. An effort is made to adapt instruction to individual needs and differences so that all are sure to get the fundamentals. Instead of having one grade and program to which all children must adjust, there is much overlapping—a nine-year-old child may be doing what was previously third, fourth, or fifth-grade work (see Table 14-1).

The major concern of nongradedness is recognition of different learning speeds; and this immediately entails curricular content, grading practices, and most of all, teacher conviction. Nongradedness, any more than any other plan, does not resolve difficult educational problems. Teacher understanding, dedication, and willingness to try are essential ingredients.

> . . . Our schools encompass all the children of all the people. These children represent a range of human capability—and contribution—which, literally, reflects the laws of probability. As this country has reaffirmed its devotion to principles of democracy, and as change of unbelievable magnitude has impinged on accepted practices and values, many of the ways of doing things which have stood the test of time are increasingly coming under searching scrutiny.
>
> The promise of the future for nongraded schools will lie in their potential ability and demonstrated success in two fundamental activities of day-by-day school operation—reorientation of administrative policies and procedures to clear the path for instructional improvement and also a restoration of provision for individual differences in school programs. The achievement of these ends would demonstrate the worth of the nongraded school. If through nongrading our schools we can truly humanize and individualize programs of education for children, we will have made a giant stride.[5]

Regardless of class organization or promotion practices, it is still necessary for teachers to realize that pupil differences will continue to exist. Organization and policy lead to improvement only when teachers use them to promote the significant purpose of individual pupil development.

Acceleration, as the reverse of nonpromotion, has not been so popular as repeating a grade. Research data also produce reverse data. Whereas, nonpromotion generally means less academic progress in the repeated grade than in the next higher grade, plus what it does to the ego concept, acceleration has positive results. Shannon (1957) summarized studies over a period of thirty-four years and found that accelerated pupils as college students two or three years younger than their peers took more scholarship honors, held more offices, took part in more student activities (including athletics), and, in addition, had more lively interest in volunteer activities (concerts, lectures, dramatic productions). His study is corroborated by a more recent study which showed that pupils in the elementary grades made higher scores on achievement tests and took part in as many activities, varsity athletics, and advanced classes as did their equally bright conven-

---

5   Stuart E. Dean, 1967, in D. W. Beggs, III, and E. G. Buffie (eds.), *Nongraded Schools in Action*, Bloomington: Indiana University Press, pp. 114-115.

Table 14-1. One of Several Ways in Which an Ungraded School May Be Organized in Classes

Age of Pupils	Multiage Class
Twelve-year-olds	6-7-8, plus advanced classes
Eleven-year-olds	5-6-7
Ten-year-olds	4-5-6
Nine-year-olds	3-4-5
Eight-year-olds	2-3-4
Seven-year-olds	1-2
Six-year-olds	K-K-1

tionally promoted peers (Klausmeier, Goodwin, and Ronda, 1968). It would appear that a readily available method of recognizing individual differences is chronically neglected.

Homework

There are several reasons why assignment of uniform tasks to be performed at home must be questioned. For one thing the child who already is advanced in relation to his peers is quite likely to have the home advantages (a room in which to study, library resources, and the help of interested adults) that will put him still further ahead. This is fine for him, but the less fortunate become more disheartened in a competitive milieu.

We talk of permitting the child to develop his resources, of encouraging him to enhance his uniqueness, of fostering his creativity. To assign uniform homework is to contradict these aspirations by limiting the free time requisite to their realization. It is not that many pupils will not respond—they do—but the free time needed for exploration of their unique personal interests is reduced. There is at least some probability that overorganization of the child's life, which uniform homework accentuates, has its harmful effects (Bernard, 1970*b*, p. 74). Furthermore, there is no guarantee that additional work improves the quality of performance or knowledge of educational processes. As is the case with the golfer with a discouraging slice, practice makes perfect the errors one commits. The pupils who have poor habits of study and reading at school further consolidate those habits at home—plus providing a concrete issue for pupil-parent contention.

One must consider the effect of uniformly assigned homework on that approximately 50 percent of pupils who come from the lower social classes. When homework is assigned, it is probable that lack of a place to study in a crowded home, household chores or part-time work, lack of interest or example on the part of parents, and unavailability of reference books and materials all contribute to putting the lower-class pupil further behind in comparison with his more fortunate companions. His defense is to quit school as soon as possible and contribute to what is known as social dynamite and the long hot summers.

Strom (1969*a*, p. 66) believes it is contradictory for teachers to sue for shorter hours and longer vacations and then make further encroachments on the pupil's time. He suggests that teachers may not be so impressed with the value of homework for the pupil so much as they are concerned about appearing on the streets without a stack of homework to be corrected. If this observation causes the reader to chuckle, let him consider whether it is from humor or embarrassment. Heffernan (1966, p. 26) also criticizes the anxiety and tension created in the child, and as a participating member of the family, seeing his parents with free time while he goes to school all day and works at school tasks half the night. She wonders how children can learn what to do with leisure, if every moment is prescribed by another person's dictates.

Some agree with the foregoing as far as the elementary school is concerned but believe that homework is desirable in high school and that it is good training for college work. However, the study skills necessary in college can probably be taught better in the school than at home—parents, though they may be expert teachers of other people's children, are among the world's poorest teachers of their own children because they become emotionally involved. In addition, if a student learns to capitalize on his time while he is in high school, he will be able to take on the additional hours of study required for college work when he is surrounded by others who are finding evening study advantageous.

Personally devised homework for those who are absent from school because of an untimely family vacation will not interfere with well-rounded development. Homework may also be desirable for children who are absent because of quarantine or illness, in which case a slow return to normal work is desirable. Home assignments for work that cannot be advantageously done in class may enrich school tasks. For example, interviewing a relative or friend who has had a unique experience or traveled in an unfamiliar land may have its place; building a model or setting up an experiment may enrich schoolwork for other class members; preparing a set of 35-mm slides to illustrate a travel report can help both the individual and his classmates. But these are ways of meeting individual differences, not uniform prescriptions.

Eliminating Mental Health Hazards in the School

If teachers and administrators examine their practices in terms of the fundamental needs of pupils, the stated objectives of education, and the reduction of problems of imposed discipline, many mental health hazards can be eliminated. Correction of any hazard will not cure the entire educational structure.

The correction of any hazard does show an awareness of the priority of the learner as a person.

Improving Mental Health and Discipline

Providing for Individual Differences

Each person, presumably, has a unique part to play in improving the life of all; each has a unique talent to contribute. Some youngsters are interested in sports, and others are devoted to making model planes or doll dresses. Some find adventure in reading, and others are content to sit for hours before the television set. Some like to experiment with home chemistry sets, and others prefer to spend much time with their playmates. Most individuals can perform school-delegated tasks, but the artful teacher will become aware of divergent motivations and suggest books and references that bridge the gap between school and out-of-school interests.

There are differences in motivational milieu. Some parents regard education as a most important aspect of development, whereas others consider it an unnecessary delay to the child's becoming a wage earner. In some communities, it is customary for most youngsters to go to college after high school graduation; in others, only the exceptional youngster is concerned with such a future. Differences in motivation may also stem from the emotional tone of the pupil's home. He can hardly be expected to devote himself wholeheartedly to school tasks if his dominant thoughts are about the turmoil or hostility at home (Westley and Epstein, 1969).

Providing for Creative Expression

Teachers who provide opportunities for creative expression reduce the need for coercive discipline. Free and spontaneous play, writing, painting, and drawing are among the important media for such creative expression. Many teachers at all grade levels and in high school are using such media to enrich academic programs. Jourard (1967) endorses independent study as a readily available stimulus to creativity. It is rather widely believed that spontaneous expression and independent study give pupils and teachers some advantages:

1. The teacher may regard creative expression and unstructured activity as a **projective technique**; that is, what the child freely puts into play and work, his writing and his drawing, what really *is himself*. One plays, writes, draws, and works the way he feels and is sometimes unable to vocalize. The teacher may use the pupil's activities and productions as clues to a better pupil understanding.

2. Creative expression can provide variety in the school program, and creative activities often motivate pupils to do the more academic work. A sophomore boy who had taken little interest in class recitation was permitted to draw pictures of some prehistoric animals on the board to be used in connection with class studies. In order to make authentic pictures, he had to do some reading; he gradually took a more active interest in his academic work as the studies progressed.
3. Students can work off tensions and frustrations through creative expression. A child who is jealous of a sibling may not attack his competitor, but he can with impunity draw a picture in which his brother or sister suffers chagrin or injury. A high school pupil may not wish to reveal feelings of hostility toward a parent or other family member, but he can write a story—presumably about other people. Hostilities and resentment can be aired in role playing that reduces the need for acting out.

Making Schoolwork Meaningful

The things children like, and spontaneously do, and the goals they consider important are different from those of adults. Teachers must be on the alert to make books and courses of study prepared by adults meaningful for children. For example, drill on word selection, sentence composition, and punctuation has been found to be relatively fruitless in terms of the amount of time spent, but if a letter requesting a speaker for the class or some free instructional materials is to be written and the teacher indicates that the best letter will be sent, real effort is usually expended, and good results are obtained. The goal is immediate, related to a need, specific and real.

Democratic Procedures

Some attitudes commonly considered democratic are faith in the worth of *each* child; confidence in the soundness of pooled opinion; belief in the ability of children to face and solve their own problems (especially a belief in their good intentions); delegation of authority to competent persons; and patience with the comparative slowness of democratic procedures. Democratic procedures are not easy, but there are dividends in terms of pupils' steady improvement in socially oriented conduct.

Some of the more common democratic procedures to be used in the classroom are:

Allowing pupils to discuss and decide (under direction) the activities and purposes of the class

Emphasizing freedom and flexibility rather than arbitrariness and indoctrination

Permitting pupils to become increasingly self-directing in their behavior

Helping pupils understand the necessity for certain behavior rather than demanding conformity to imposed regulations—firm but not arbitrary discipline

Providing opportunities in accord with the individual's ability to comprehend and profit from them

Working with pupils on a cooperative and congenial basis

Taking time to talk with and listen to those who wish to participate

Encouraging cooperative group work

Democratic procedures are likely to go far in meeting such fundamental human needs as the desire for independence, the desire for companionship, the need for recognition, the need for security (security being dependent upon safety and the person's ability to meet and solve problems), and the desire for new experiences. Democratic procedures are slow, but so too is growth toward better mental health and self-control.

School-Community Liaison for Mental Health

The most encouraging action for mental health occurs when the school and the wider community join forces. Those who recognize that there are many sources of strain in children's lives are prepared to see that community agencies work together. School workers can and, in some localities, do exchange information with juvenile workers on the police force. Social welfare workers who work intimately with certain families can warn the school of incipient problems and discuss cases with teacher and counselors. Ministers can be enlisted as partners in the work of understanding children and their parents. Recreation leaders can profit from the cooperation of teachers in both program development and utilization of physical resources. (One criticism of the expense of schools arises from the closing of gymnasiums, swimming pools, and playgrounds during vacation periods. Many schools today are encouraging use of these facilities by both children and parents and are even providing supervisory personnel.) Provisions for the handicapped are more effective when the school and community join forces. Some of the greatest gains from communitywide approaches are more widespread assumption of responsibility for mass media (radio, television, newspapers), provisions for the handicapped, and programs for the delinquent and predelinquent.

A concentration of population does not make a community (Srole et al., 1962), and a variety of agencies does not mean effective service (Farnsworth, 1965). It demands a concerned person, who will persist despite criticism, rebuffs, and indifference, to establish and maintain communication. Insecure agency personnel are often territorially defensive and more verbal about a mother's immorality than they are concerned about that mother's babies, children, and adolescents. Yet, accorded the understanding and respect as a human being which we assert pupils need from their teachers, these defensive officials can become part of productive community action.

There are many opportunities for school-community cooperation. The first steps consist of communication—discussions, consultations, critical evaluation of the shortcomings of each agency, and explanations of the functions of each. The problem is often to utilize the existing agencies more effectively rather than to create new ones. Illustrative agencies and a possible way in which each might influence the lives of children are given in Table 14-2. The exchange of information on the extension of "possible function" would enhance the work of the agencies involved.

Mental health work is being done by many individuals and agencies, but the task remains for someone to take initiative and leadership in coordinating and improving action. And in the process of helping to develop these resources, key persons will have to deal with the defense mechanism, "Why don't they . . .?" and get those who are concerned to say, as did the citizens of Philadelphia, "The trouble with Philadelphia is us."

Teachers in Mental Health and Discipline

Excellence of teaching and teacher personality stability will not eliminate problems of discipline or make all pupils mentally healthy. On the other hand, some problems of discipline are precipitated by teaching behaviors, and the precarious emotional balance of some pupils is disturbed by teacher instability.

Table 14-2

Agency	*Possible Function*
Family casework agency	Reduction of family friction
Child guidance clinic	Specific suggestions for guiding children
Boy and Girl Scouts	Development of constructive interests
Church schools	Moral training and social experience
Mental health associations	Provision of literature and lectures
Library association	Guidance of the curious and gifted
Art museum	Development of special talents
Dramatic clubs	Ego enhancement and social contact
Goodwill Industries	Easing of financial pressure on family
Recreation center	Development of skills; building of health
Junior baseball	Promotion of health and leisure interests

Teacher Selection and Development

Teachers range from inadequate through indifferent to excellent and positive influences. For the most part, there is no selection of teacher candidates, except self-selection in terms of identification with a service occupation. Emphases in some teacher-education programs is on content and teaching field, with relative indifference to the teacher as a person. Forward-looking teacher-education institutions do emphasize teacher selection and screen out those who give evidence of future inadequacy, and supplement the selection with developmental emphasis on the teacher as a person.

Once a teacher is on the job, there is variation in the degree to which selection is continued. Probationary periods have the purpose of screening out those whose qualifications are questionable. Probationary periods are sometimes defeated by administrators who recommend the unfit, or doubtfully qualified, teacher for another position. Even this procedure may have merit because with another administrator the teacher may encounter a developmental milieu. The procedure must be questioned if the welfare of the pupil is the uppermost consideration; then the recommendation must admit doubt and specify the area of inadequacy. Once a teacher serves the probationary period and gains tenure, the mental health of many successive classes of pupils may be threatened. For such reasons the Oregon legislature, in 1971, is considering the abolition of teacher tenure.

The problems need not be left entirely to teacher education institutions and administrators. A few school systems have seen fit to activate concern for pupil welfare. With in-service programs for teacher development, (1) the probationary teacher, (2) the tenured teacher, together with (3) the superior teacher seeking further growth work together to examine their own attitudes, techniques, biases, and how they "come across" to colleagues and pupils (Cottle, 1969; Harrison, 1970; Prescott, 1957; Rivlin, 1965; Winick et al., 1969). The great advantage of such in-service development is that teachers gain more satisfaction from their life and profession and pupils gain the models for mental health and self-control.

Classroom Communication

Some problems are caused by ambiguous communication. Many disciplinary dilemmas consist of nothing more than different understandings. Some of these misunderstandings are rooted in cultural variations both in speech and values (Wilson, Robeck, and Michael, 1969, p. 18). Pupils do not always hear that which the teacher said. With no malice aforethought, pupils bring with them a background for perception that allows them to hear some things and tune out others. Thus, the teacher may say, "You are free to do this in your own way." Some hear just the "You are free." Others hear ". . . do this . . ." as a very prescriptive thing; and still others see "in your own way" a responsibility, but one with flexibility. Hence, when the teacher is concerned about varied performance or nonperformance, he might have the pupils rephrase or reiterate what it was they heard. In this process he should be careful not to encourage excuse-making. If the job were not done, it is still to be done. Rationalizations or private interpretations do not change the situation even though they make it understandable.

Inner Tensions

On occasion one's testiness with pupils may readily be perceived to be a residue of worry about financial obligations, husband-wife discord, or having been reprimanded by the principal. At other times it is difficult to own up to the fact of one's own feelings; or to see that the "reprimand" was more a matter of perception than it was a matter of censure. Self-examination, discourse with a wise (and candid) friend, or participation in counseling can help one to deal with these tensions and misperceptions. When one recognizes the existence and nature of tensions, he is then in a position to choose how to deal with them. Such self-examination might have the purpose of detecting evidences of defensiveness (Gibb, 1965) and seeking to achieve openness—a condition so unusual that Rogers (1969, p. 290) says it may be regarded as not normal.

Tolerance for Ambiguity

When teachers are criticized in articles, books, and at education conventions, the critics are applauded because the criticized see the accusations as being leveled against their peers. The Number One person knew these things all the time but others prevent his making modifications. Thus Goodman (1962) notes that instructors agree that grades are injurious to both teaching and learning but they are helpless because registrars, employers, scholarship committees depend on grades for making decisions. And, on the same theme, teachers must deal with ambiguity as they see grades separate pupils and teachers into warring camps (Simon, 1970).

Disciplinary emphases seem to go in waves, cresting and troughing between prescription and pupil license. The teacher who keeps in mind the response, needs, and development of pupils will feel some ambiguity as he contends against the current popular wave. It would be well to note, however, that tolerance for ambiguity is a major requisite or characteristic of mental health.

There is currently considerable emphasis on permissiveness, probably quite rightly so if we expect to produce socially oriented, responsible citizens, but some teachers seem to be puzzled about how permissiveness fits with adult responsibility. Manning (1971, p. 106) suggests that teachers say to pupils something about as follows: I am the adult in charge, the person who is responsible for what goes on. I have experience and I will not abuse my authority. I want you to be a part of the situation, and to do so there are rules and regulations which we will discuss and reform, but to which we will adhere.

The Teacher as a Model

Some would deny it, some hope to avoid it, and others admit that inescapably, as teachers, they become models. There are several reasons why teachers are a focal point in mental health in school. One is that children are with them constantly, and children learn much through imitation. They think more of themselves when a key person in their lives, such as their teacher, accepts them, gives affection, and shows confidence in their potential. Teachers help to remedy children's weaknesses, and they recognize children's strengths; they can help pupils solve troublesome everyday problems; they manipulate the pupils' physical and social environment to reduce mental health hazards. They can do such things as these most effectively when they realize the effect and implications of their classroom decisions. Teachers should not try to mold pupils into some preconceived form; their role is to nurture and prompt growth toward a uniquely creative and self-fulfilling life (Manning, 1971; Rogers, 1969, p. 105).

As mental health influences, teachers must consider not only what they do but what they are—actually, the two are inseparable. This implies that teachers too must be involved in a continuing process of self-improvement; they must and will value objects, experiences, and goals that make for their own survival and growth and for the survival and growth of others. The personal challenge is contained in the bit of wisdom that what one knows determines his role in life but what one is determines his limits of achievement.

Summary

Classroom control, mental health, and effective learning are so inextricably interwoven that suggestions for the improvement of one are pertinent to the others. The bias in this book is that aversive adult control, as a phase of pupil development is congruent with a child's needs, mental health, and learning efficiency.

The idea of permissiveness before one is mature enough to possess the wisdom for making sound choices must be questioned from the standpoint of society, realistic learning milieus, and the mental health of the individual. A child needs the safety of rules, regulations, and the guidance of an emotionally stable authority. Teachers who have a reasonably firm and well-rounded concept of what and how children should learn contribute more to mental health than does the teacher who equivocates and places the burden of important choices on the uninitiated. Discipline and physical punishment are not synonymous or, in the long run, harmonious.

Mental health can be augmented and the need for imposed discipline can be decreased by giving attention to the need for acceptance, for companionship, new experiences, responsible independence, and success. Tension tolerance, as is the case with many other traits, is developed in sequential experiences and achievements; it is not fostered by the accumulation of failure experiences. Barriers to effective classroom control and obstacles to learning the processes of mental health include lack of friendliness, competition between unequals, comparative grades, nonpromotion practices, and homework. These barriers can be lowered through combined and coordinated teacher action and teacher self-examination.

There are many conventional school practices and some on trial that promote discipline and mental health. Really providing for individual differences epitomizes most such practices. Better understanding of pupil uniqueness may be promoted through independent study. Immediate, as well as long-term, goals that are understandable and accepted are essential. Democratic procedures, which imply authority of the expert, contribute to pupils' need for identity, for safety needs, and for approaching contributing citizenship.

Suggested Additional Readings

BERNARD, HAROLD W., 1970, *Human Development in Western Culture*, 3d ed., Boston: Allyn and Bacon, Inc., pp. 552-586.

> The propositions for the facilitation of self-actualization are pertinent to the subject of classroom control and mental health.

BLOCK, JUDITH, 1970, "A Preschool Workshop for Emotionally Disturbed Children," *Children*, vol. 17, no. 1, pp. 10-14, January-February.

> The importance of learning early the steps needed in self-control is emphasized. Although the needs of the individual child are studied, there is also the necessity for teaching him the limits of behavior.

MANNING, DUANE, 1971, *Toward A Humanistic Curriculum*, New York: Harper & Row, Publishers, Incorporated, pp. 96-111.

> The author, as the title suggests, is concerned about children, about love, acceptance, and recognition of differences. He shows that he faces the reality of child violence, depravity, and viciousness. There are sick children and adolescents, and there is a more rational alternative than to turn institutions over to them.

SIMON, SIDNEY B., 1970, "Grades Must Go," *School Review*, vol. 78, pp. 397-402.

> The author cites five reasons why grades must be abolished in college. With certain words being substituted for the "pedagese" of college, the arguments would be pertinent to the public school situation.

15

Group Dynamics
in the Classroom

The study of group processes by teachers is significant for several reasons. One reason derives from the burgeoning population. In 1915 there were 100 million Americans, by 1967 (about fifty years later) the figure had doubled to 200 million; and by the year 2000 (in about another thirty years) it will grow to 300 million. The day of going west or moving to the country in order to relieve the psychological pressure of people is gone. In order to live effectively, one must learn to adjust to groups.

Another reason for studying groups is related to the above. As population grows, there has been a tendency for age groups to form. The decline of the extended family (where grandparents, parents, older siblings, relatives, and younger children lived, worked and played together as a unit) has given way to the nuclear family. In the nuclear family parents and children live together until the older children are ready to move away to school, for marriage, or to a job in another community. This, plus population increase, has made the adolescent peer group a powerful factor in behavior formation.

The idea of "education for all American youth" has, in practice, become the practical goal of mass education. It is deplored by some, but the practical educator views the large numbers of pupils as a factor with which we must deal. Much of the literature on education emphasizes the need and desirability of individual development, individual treatment, and understanding the pupil as an individual. Emphasis on the individual has its justifiable and firm place in our educational scheme. Group processes also have a place in educational practice—a place recognized in fact but less in theory.

This chapter brings to focus some of the phenomena of group behavior that can be used advantageously by the classroom teacher.

Need for the Group Emphasis

The Concept of Groups

In spite of our professed concern for individuals, the teacher deals with groups. It is a seventh grade or second-year mathematics class. Members come from a neighborhood group—sometimes a rather homogeneous socioeconomic group but frequently from quite a diversity of statuses. Within the class group there are cliques and friendship pairs, and groups with varied interests (e.g., in horses or boys). There is a group morale factor in the teaching staff. There is a spirit which characterizes the school, and the school itself is a manifestation of community concerns. All these are subject to better control as their dynamics are appreciated.

Groups are more than collections of things or individuals. A group is a number of individuals bound together by some common factor or factors—age, interests, purposes, or abilities. It is a number of objects (rocks, reptiles, trees) or individuals capable of being regarded as a collective unit because of identifiable common characteristics. Psychologically, a human group is a configuration of persons perceived and functioning as a whole or Gestalt. Members of a group perceive themselves to be alike in significant ways; through social interaction, they depend on other group members to play specific roles in their common pursuits. There are within the group certain regularities of feelings, thoughts, and behaviors which are both institutional and subinstitutional. That is, the home or school or community has certain rules and expectations. In addition, the subinstitutional regularities stem from the rewards of interacting behaviors (Backman and Secord, 1966, p. 167).

Group concepts have long been an emphasis in educational literature, as is evidenced by such well-known terms as "play groups," "ability groups," "control and experimental groups," "normative groups," "peer groups," "cultural groups," "minority groups," "in-groups," "out-groups," "marginal groups," "face-to-face groups," "secondary groups," and the like. Group dynamics involves a number of considerations relating to the interactive psychological relationships by which group members share feelings, aspirations, and ideas and thus achieve some common perceptions and community of action. Such interactive relationships derive in part from the broader culture, but also in part from the immediate and spontaneous mood of the group.

Additional light will be thrown on many complex and perplexing educational problems—discipline, mental health, achievement motivation, staying in (or dropping out of) school—as further understanding of group dynamics is developed.

The Group Emphasis in Daily Living

Many of the major objectives of education, such as self-realization, improved human relationships, civic responsibility, and economic efficiency have a large amount of group components. No matter what line of work one follows, his success is conditioned to a considerable extent by his ability to get along with others. It has frequently been stated that teachers who fail do so because of ineptness in human relations or lack of skill in group functioning, not because of lack of knowledge of subject matter. Because man is a social creature, even the objective of self-realization is at many points dependent upon the functioning of such groups as the family, peer group, socioeconomic class, and various school and class groups.

An individual's behavior in the family is different from that displayed in the classroom. One's reactions at a basketball game are different from reactions in church or at a concert. Individual roles differ in terms of the function and composition of the group; e.g., the same boys behave differently—are different individuals—in the science laboratory and on a street corner watching the girls go by.

Another group situation that parents and teachers are aware of has to do with peer relationships. In the adolescent and preadolescent years, as youngsters are trying to outgrow dependence on parents and establish an identity, they have deep feelings about the vital necessity of peer approval. They feel that they cannot belong to the group unless they wear the right clothes, share the approved goals, talk the same slang. Conflict with parents and emotional conflict within themselves arise when clothes, goals, and language are disapproved by parents.

Some years ago, Prescott expressed, with unusual clarity, the need for understanding group behavior as it related to classroom functioning. After some brief remarks about the influence of physical weather and climate on human behavior, he stated:

> There is another sort of weather to which all human beings are exposed. It is the moods of their fellow men, with whom they work and play and live. Different people tend to create different climates of feeling among their associates; and different groupings of people show prevailing moods as different as the weather of the arctic and the torrid zones. Some groups swelter at their tasks in the heavy, humid oppressiveness of obligatory functioning, like a sea-level metropolis in midsummer. Others buoyantly undertake common responsibilities with the light,

Jan Lukas/College Newsphoto Alliance

stimulating freshness of the autumn in high altitude dryness. The whole odor of life is sweet or sour, fragrant or foul, tangy or stifling, according to the moods we inhale from those around us . . .

The question must be raised, then, whether the emotional climate in the school classrooms of the country is a wholesome climate or not. Is this climate a joyous, buoyant one appropriate to our usual picture of childhood as "happy"? Or is it dull, uninteresting, monotonous, and heavy? Or is it full of tensions, bickerings, repressions, and feelings of failure? Does the child unconsciously absorb the feeling of certainty that he has a significant role in the world and is a valuable person? Or does he get the sense that life is a jungle battle with no holds barred and his own lot a sorry one? Does the child feel that people are "with him" and that as a part of a larger whole he and mankind are moving toward brighter days? Or is he led to feel that other persons are essentially his antagonists, or at best the setters of unimportant and distasteful tasks?[1]

Although we may agree with Prescott that group dynamics influence school behavior, the topic of groups, per se, is rarely considered in educational psychology. However, the role of family, socioeconomic class, peer groups, and school morale are studied in regard to motivation, achievement, and identity.

1   Daniel A. Prescott, 1939, "Emotional Weather," *Educational Record*, vol. 20, pp. 96-97.

Stories of the noninclusion in the class group of school dropouts, individuals who later commit puzzling and violent crimes (Fraiberg, 1967), and those who escape reality in psychological illness and drug and alcohol addiction have caused teachers to be concerned about the matter of group **identity** and **affiliation.** Anthropologists indicate that man is humanized, or socialized by his membership in groups. Psychologists have discovered that group therapy is sometimes more effective than individual treatment.

Factors in Group Dynamics

Acceptance, Competence, and Power

Data from observation, structure investigations, and experiments in classrooms indicate that (1) some pupils and teachers are liked better than others, (2) some are more competent than others, and (3) some have greater influence than others over what takes place (Glidewell et al., 1966, p. 221).

"Guess who" games, questionnaires and themes devoted to "ideal" friends or classmates, and sociometric studies are designed to locate those who are liked or disliked. There is no universal prescription for facilitating acceptance; however, teachers who identify those at the extreme ends of the acceptance scale will have clues for action provided by the processes leading to identification.

Clara seems always to cling to Sheryl at recess and at lunch but avoids others. By seeing to it that Clara had chances to be by Sheryl for various class activities, the teacher helped Clara's self-concept to grow, and by the end of the year Clara had become a more integral part of the group. Bill was another loner who spent considerable time making rather attractive doodles. After two or three other trials, the teacher helped Bill win acceptance by his custody of the art display corner of the bulletin board.

There are many kinds of competencies that have significance for facilitating a pupil's socialization.

Al, in the sixth grade, was quiet to the extent of rarely speaking to others and *never* responding to the teacher. But even putting a wad of paper in the wastebasket involved a leap and an overhead cast—and a score by Al. Picking a flying disk out of the air was a simple task of closing thumb and fingers for Al. His new teacher noticed these things and also that Al stood aside as baseball teams were formed—by volunteering and choosing. The third time Al was about to be overlooked the teacher assigned him to shortstop where he fielded well and during the course of the game hit for extra bases each of three times at bat. Having his physical competencies recognized led Al to more persistent academic application—including one time when he "sweat blood" and chose to stay in at recess to finish his arithmetic. But he wanted his class not to have the school's dummy in mathematics.

Erikson (1968) contends that adolescents must vie with opposing cultural forces in order to establish an identity. One aspect of the adolescent's struggle is to gain some power when there are so many influences which deny it. A condition of mental health, a factor in ego strength, an element in achievement motivation is the feeling that one makes a difference, that his presence is felt.

The Head Start program designed to compensate for some of the cultural differences which handicap the ghetto child in the conventional school is praised, damned, and questioned (Smith and Bissell, 1970; Cicirelli, Evans, and Schiller, 1970). One of the praised features in Head Start has been parental involvement. Where parents perceive that they have some power to affect the educational lives of the children they support the program. They encourage their children's attendance, they attend classes themselves, and they open communication with their children. The same thing is observed when pupils perceive their power in helping make decisions in school policy or discipline. The phenomenon is also seen when teachers are led to participate in policy and administrative decisions (Harrison, 1970). Power is a paradoxical force—teachers can concede it to pupils when they (the teachers) do not fear losing it, and teachers gain power as they are able to concede it (Gibb, 1965).

Individual Goals and Group Goals

Individuals voluntarily join groups because personal goals can be satisfied in the group; often many in the group are seeking the same personal goals. In addition, the group may adopt group goals that are not part of the individuals' initial interest. For example, three young adults may join a charitable group to acquire congenial companions, a fourth may join to be seen in the right places and enhance his prestige as a lawyer. All may join in providing clothing and shelter for itinerant workers and their children.

Before a child enters a classroom group, goals have been formulated by curriculum design. Some individuals may not accept the goals that have served in previous years. Those who do not accept will exclude themselves from the group, be excluded from it, or seek to destroy it. This is what occurs in the cases of problem children, dropouts, and children who are expelled from school. Correctives and punishment have been applied in such cases; but if teachers perceived these behaviors as group phenomena, different approaches might be tried. For example, goals might be modified so that more pupils would accept them; attempts might be made to get pupils to perceive existing goals as having personal meaning; and both approaches could be discussed by the group.

The group approach would call for pupils to formulate their own goals not only because of the matter of group **identification** but also because, if the educational enterprise is to be successful, the teacher is vigorously working to achieve his own obsolescence; i.e., if he is successful he is no longer needed. A progress report of the (then) U.S. Commissioner of Education seemed to suggest raising the pupil from the status of "thing" to that of "person."

> One particularly promising lead came out of the conference's study of various new curricula in mathematics, science, and the social studies. It has to do with the effectiveness of "contingent relationships" between a learner and a tutor, i.e., situations where the learner has some control over the pacing of the information he is getting and over the nature of the information he gets next. The ideal form of such a relation is probably the dialogue between a learner and a wise and informed tutor. But it is encouraging to see the extent to which improvement in performance can be achieved by organizing class discussion into a generalized form of dialogue, using texts and documents as resources to be tapped when needed.[2]

Group goals can be made to complement individual goals. Teachers may aid pupils in the perception of the congruity of group and individual goals. A pupil's desire to write, draw, or practice leadership can be exercised in a class project devoted to a visit-to-Germany program which will be presented to parents. One's need to be a member may transcend the learning goal at least temporarily, but this gives the teacher an opportunity to deal with task-oriented behavior. This emphasis was a powerful factor in the success of a school in an underprivileged area in Detroit in which the staff gave attention to making the school a youth center, with youth participating in planning and policy making (Kelley, 1962, pp. 33-37). Learning as a goal was not forgotten. Learning was simply made to parallel the emphasis on the school as a group that was assembled to serve the many needs of young people.

Participation

One of the limitations to effectiveness in classroom groups is the fact that membership is mandatory. Pupils cannot select those with whom they are supposed to communicate. Often the result is that they are more concerned about the social relationships than about the learning to be achieved or the problems to be solved. Classroom groups are in this way almost unique.

2   *Innovation and Experiment in Education*, 1964, A Progress Report of the Panel on Educational Research and Development to the U.S. Commissioner of Education, the Director of the National Science Foundation, and the Special Assistant to the President for Science and Technology, Washington, D.C.: U.S. Government Printing Office.

Most other groups (military organizations and offenders assigned to traffic school excepted) are voluntary—if not in terms of membership, at least in terms of stated purposes. Sociometry can provide useful clues in forming school groups in which interaction may take place easily despite the mandatory character of the school situation. Because of the **halo effect**, limited personal experiences, rapidly changing social customs, and the generation gap, few teachers have the ability to make accurate assessments regarding those respected by peers, the cliques, and the interpersonal likes and dislikes of pupils. In the lower-elementary grades boys choose boys and girls choose girls as associates; but this changes gradually in the middle grades and choices reflect community patterns. It is then that racial, religious, and socioeconomic factors enter into the formation of subgroups. It has also been found that similar personality traits tend to be factors in group solidarity.

Thus in forming groups, teachers should counteract the compulsory aspects of membership by seating students who like one another together, by choosing for small groups students who express mutual (or at least one-way) attraction. Sex (depending on age) and perceived interest, similarity of traits, similarity of background, and comparable levels of intellectual functioning should be considered. How much weight to be given these factors varies with the nature of the task. It has been found that task-oriented study groups result in greater behavior and personality change than do discussion groups. Friendship, cooperativeness, and general adjustment are better in task-oriented than in discussion groups. Classes which are perceived by students as being difficult have been found to result in achievement; but such a class can also be satisfying in terms of lack of friction, absence of cliques, and the presence of enthusiasm and cohesiveness (Walberg, 1969).

The experience of success or failure conditions the group's acceptance of new members. With a background of failure, the group is more likely to view a newcomer as a resource person who can aid in getting the correct answer or in suggesting a more profitable approach. With a background of success, the group is more inclined to view the newcomer as an unwelcome source of disruption and to rate him lower than the failure group does (Ziller and Behringer, 1960).

Cohesiveness

When a group is bound together tightly by common and cooperatively determined goals, when the backgrounds of members are similar, and when the group remains intact despite changing conditions, it is said to be cohesive. One advantage of a cohesive group is that it is more capable of maintaining forward movement in spite of frustrations. Another advantage is that a cohesive group has greater power to command conformity than one that is less firmly knit. Unhappy or discontented pupils are not allowed to set the overall tone of the cohesive group. This explains, in part, why teachers find some classes easier to work with than others.

A disadvantage of a cohesive group is that individual members may not wish to "rock the boat" by proffering a divergent viewpoint. Assuming that a valid point may not be readily accepted by all causes one to keep the peace by keeping quiet—and thus lowering the problem solving power of the group (Secord and Backman, 1964, p. 386). In contrast, however, it has been found that as students mature they give more credit to group processes and consensus; and, members will tackle more difficult tasks under group than under competitive conditions. Hence, if setting progressively higher goals is an objective of education, then encouragement of peer group influence is a viable emphasis (Kogan and Carlson, 1969).

Group cohesiveness is dependent also upon the effectiveness of subunit communication. Thus, it is to be expected that sociometric groupings (see Chapter 12) increase group solidarity and productiveness—the members feel comfortable with one another. Another factor is the size of the group—it must be large enough to present diversity of views and small enough to allow for the participation of all members. Precisely how many constitute an effective communication group has not been determined because size must be considered in relation to purpose, individual roles, leadership, and in particular, the sensitiveness of the teacher in diagnosing the needs of group members (Thomas and Fink, 1968).

It would seem that commonly accepted goals contribute to cohesiveness, but cohesiveness makes more probable the acceptance of group goals. Starting at the goal-establishing end, self-determined rather than imposed goals are superior for establishing group unity. In the learning of motor tasks (e.g., writing and laboratory skills), those who participated in discussion about the necessity or desirability of change and the nature of the skills sought learned much more, and more rapidly, than those who were simply told what to do. Moreover, there was less aggression and less interpersonal resentment in the discussion-oriented groups. The implications of these phenomena are that teachers might better, on occasion, (1) restructure the group than work more directly on behaviors, and (2) seek to augment the factor of a supportive atmosphere so that each pupil feels accepted (Trow et al., 1966).

There may be circumstances under which group unity is not highly desirable. It has been found, for example, that open groups, in which there is changing membership, are more creative than closed groups, in which new members are not accepted after original formation of the group. Following failure, an open group perceives a greater probability of attainment than does a closed group. Following success, the closed group is more likely to perceive the probability of future success (Ziller and others, 1962).

Competition

There is widespread belief in American culture that the spirit of interpersonal competition should be inculcated into children so that they can meet the exigencies of a competitive life. One hears also that much in American culture demands an ability to cooperate. An overemphasis on competition inhibits effective group action, but there is also the danger that too much group endeavor may inhibit individual initiative. The dilemma should be viewed in terms of broad and varied educational goals. Cooperative effort becomes difficult when group members are competing for their individual goals; there is a disruption of coordinated efforts, of friendliness, and of pride in the group and an inhibition of the ready exchange of ideas. Actually, the evidence that individual pursuit of even strictly academic goals is superior to group pursuit is equivocal. Add the desirability of learning to work with others in various pursuits, and the weight shifts to the desirability of coordinated group action.

Democratic Procedures

The essence of successful group action is a democratic orientation—shared opinions, designated responsibilities, respect for the individual specialist, the reign of group intelligence. We see too much evidence about us that the democratic orientation has not been thoroughly assimilated.

> A democratic relationship requires the educator to be firm and kind. Such a relationship reflects respect for both the educator and the child. The most serious mistake to avoid is spoiling, manifested by overprotection, oversolicitude, and indulgence. This deprives the child of experiencing his own strengths and abilities. Training of the child can be effective in many ways in a democratic setting. Simply stated, it must include a respect for order, avoidance of conflict, and encouragement.[3]

(1) Democratic processes, e.g., group determination of goals; (2) assuming of responsibility in a task-oriented group, and (3) having the teacher act as a group member instead of the voice of authority are factors which condition the success and value of group approaches. It is not surprising that Trow and others designate the teacher's role as "democratic strategist" as one of the three important group roles, along with instructional and therapist roles (Trow et al., 1966).

---

3   Don Dinkmeyer and Rudolf Dreikurs,1963, *Encouraging Children to Learn: The Encouragement Process*, Englewood Cliffs, N.J.: Prentice-Hall, Inc., p. 27.

Knowledge of Group Dynamics

There are several reasons why knowledge of group behavior may be helpful to teachers and pupils. For example, the phenomenon of "behavioral contagion," the spontaneous imitation of behavior initiated by one person, calls for an analysis of interpersonal influences. The fact that deviation from group norms contributes to the exclusion of the offender or the disintegration of the group indicates the desirability of having pupils examine the dynamics of group processes (Sawrey and Telford, 1968). When individuals vary in their needs for achievement or for belonging, the solidarity of the group is threatened. For such reasons, the group should at times focus very specifically upon what is going on, what roles are being played by various members, and how functioning can be improved. The successful group leader will on occasion ask very personal questions such as "How do you feel about that statement?" "Does it seem that Terry is trying to avoid discussion of the central issue?" "You seem restless today—is there some special reason for it?" These questions direct attention to processes rather than the direct solution of the problem. The teacher's knowledge of group dynamics should be shared with pupils. Such sharing makes it appear that the teacher is one of the group and enhances communality of purpose; it also increases the possibility of successfully transferring group functioning to other situations. Participation in groups is not a matter of lessons about living; it is a matter of involvement in the process of living.

Harrison (1970) reported that in the pursuit of faculty development, where interpersonal process groups were used (see Chapter 1), such groups soon began to be used with pupils. In such activities with pupils, teachers found that there were some pupils who were afraid of them or felt that the teacher did not like them. One teacher reported that pupils were less up-tight than they used to be.

The question of power is one which arises in the study of group dynamics. In the era of behavioristic and connectionistic psychology, the teacher's wielding of power was unquestioned. In fact, successful teaching virtually amounted to keeping discipline. With the emergence of humanistic psychology and the emphases on choice, aspirations, and responsibility, an increase in the power of students is deemed to be important. This calls for emphases on autonomy, participation, being a cause, and identity. The issue of power looms large in black riots and protests (Iglitzin, 1970). It also looms large in student riots and protests.

At least some of the difficulty encountered in education for ghetto children and for minority groups stems from the fact that the group experiences of such pupils differs from that of teachers. If the teacher sees his middle-class perceptions and techniques fail to produce, he resorts to reliance on his authority and prestige, and the problem persists (Fischer and Thomas, 1965, p. 227).

Need Satisfaction

Successful group action depends on the existence of common needs. If one is drafted instead of joining voluntarily, he fails to become an integral part of the group until he perceives that the group as constituted can fill either a developmental or deprivation need for him. Friendships that provide a supportive atmosphere are essential to need satisfaction; they must exist or be developed within the group. If showing off or other means of getting attention become prominent, it is an indication that those concerned do not perceive the manner in which the group may satisfy their needs. On the other hand, when participants give help, comment favorably on contributions of others, joke and otherwise show satisfaction, or agree and understand, they lend solidarity to the group and also indicate that needs are being met.

It has been found that comparable age and similarity of intelligence and interests tend to weld groups together. Students, as growing and untested persons, need social approval and the feeling that they can make a contribution to the group. Anything that threatens the prestige they may already have earned will cause them to withdraw from the group or to attempt to destroy or cripple the group itself. Thus the extent to which students reward or coerce one another becomes a prominent factor in the success or failure of the group. Typically, we are much concerned about how we are viewed by our **reference groups**—family, schoolmates, neighbors (Merton and Nisbet, 1966, p. 109).

Varieties of Group Roles

The Teacher's Leadership Role

The role of the teacher as the leader in the classroom is a conventional view. But the perception of how that leadership is to be exercised is shifting from an authoritarian to an authoritative (power-based competence) one, from a dictatorial concept to a participatory one. Indeed, it is difficult to see how school can prepare citizens for effective participation in democracy when the life of the school is characterized by dictatorial teachers. It is difficult to see how respect for economic, cultural, skin color, and other human differences can be taught when the learner's own dignity and autonomy are ignored—if not deliberately diminished (Friedenberg, 1969*b*, Keniston, 1968).

> If one thinks of authority, control, and leadership in political terms, it is clear that the classroom group, at least in its formal aspects, is about as far from democracy as one can get. Not only do the students have no control over the selection of their leader, they normally also have no

recourse from his leadership, no influence on his method of leadership beyond that granted by him, and no power over the tenure of his leadership. There are very few working groups in our society in which these essentially despotic conditions are legitimately so much the rule.[4]

The Teacher's Role as Facilitator

At least in the eyes of some observers, the teacher's role is shifting from that of instructor and director of learning, and from that of disseminator of knowledge to that of one who facilitates the process of learning (Ohanian, 1971). Goodlad (1969a) suggests that more emphasis be given to the processes of inquiry and discovery. Tyler (1967) recommends that teachers should help pupils learn how to learn with a view to the continuation of learning when teachers no longer dominate the scene. Smith (1967) does not diminish the role of structure and teacher guidance, but he sees the problem of motivation, of affect, as being intimately related to the facilitation learning. Hart (1969) asserts that the key to successful teaching resides in acceptance, applause, and attention to children's needs. In each of these references groups played a role—albeit minor.

The teacher's personality is an aspect of his behavior in groups. Teachers can get results by centralizing authority within themselves or by increasing the independence of students (decentralizing authority) and the social access of members. The latter can be accomplished if the teacher talks less and provides more time for and attention to students' comments and questions. By spreading verbal participation and using students' ideas, whether they are pertinent or off the subject, he increases the leadership and prestige of students. This necessitates the differentiation of assignments to accord with ability. It also involves time for student-teacher planning, which clarifies goals and makes them more personal for the pupils. Group action is facilitated when teachers use indirect rather than direct influences. Some of these influences have been presented as contrasts by Flanders (Table 15-1). The import of this table is that analysis of teacher-pupil interaction provides a means of assessing the quality of instruction and improving the teacher's effectiveness. The items may be used as clues in self-evaluation.

The two columns do not necessarily mean a choice between good and bad, salutary and injurious. Group action has its advantages, but so also do strong leadership and informed authority. Teacher-directed learning is an effective approach when a pupil's personality is such that he needs and desires structure, when freedom imposes the necessity for making choices which he would rather

4   Jacob W. Getzels and Herbert A. Thelen, 1960, "The Classroom Group as a Unique Social System," in National Society for the Study of Education, 59th Yearbook, part II, *The Dynamics of Instructional Groups*, Chicago: University of Chicago Press, p. 56.

Table 15-1. Categories of Classroom Activities

A. Planning

R*—	1. Long-range planning, teacher assigns and describes work
E**—	2. Long-range teacher-pupil planning
R—	3. Immediate goal, teacher assigns work
E—	4. Immediate goal, teacher-pupil planning

B. Work

Teacher-Directed

R—	5. Teacher gives directions for current activities
R—	6. Teacher lectures
R—	7. Teacher reads to class
	8. Listening to outside speaker
	9. Listening to tapes or records
	10. Viewing slides, films, pictures
R—	11. Oral reading by turns
R—	12. Prepared oral reading
R—	13. Drill
R—	14. Recitation (teacher questions, pupils answer)
	15. Teacher answers pupils' questions
E—	16. Teacher-led discussion or blackboard work

Pupil-Directed

E—	17. Silent reading of pupil-selected material
	18. Silent reading of assigned material
	19. Individual seatwork or blackboard work
E—	20. Subgroups and individual seatwork
E—	21. Subgroups working
E—	22. Pupil-led discussion

C. Evaluation

Teacher-Directed

23. Test
24. Correcting papers or homework
25. Teacher-led discussion

Pupil-Directed

26. Individual reports
27. Group reports
28. Pupil-led discussion[5]

R* Restricting pupil participation   E** Expanding pupil participation

5   Ned A. Flanders, 1965, *Teacher Influence, Pupil Attitudes, and Achievement*, Cooperative Research Monograph No. 12, Washington, D.C.: U.S. Department of Health, Education, and Welfare, Office of Education, pp. 89-90.

avoid. When a pupil has confidence in his teacher and is functioning in a new area, he is willing to have directions and requirements stated.

Roles in Teacher-centered and Reality-centered Classrooms

Groups in school have distinctive characteristics because of the personalities and motivations of pupils and teachers and the influences stemming from the organization and operation of the group as such. A teacher-centered classroom is one in which the teacher makes the major decisions about content, activities to be pursued, and the individual roles to be performed. He acts as the judge for punishment and rewards and is responsible for the morale of the group. Some pupils are quite content with such an organization. They willingly play the "faithful servant" role and not only try to conform to the teacher's wish, but cultivate his approval and try to anticipate his desires. Other students, however, object to this role; they not only resent the servant role, but try to cut the faithful masters down to size. In effect, they become rivals—they are like children who have older, prettier, or more talented siblings. Still another role in the teacher-centered classroom is that of the rebel who expresses resentment in various ways. Rebels may subject the conformists to scapegoating, criticize the assignments, incite other students to resist the teacher, or question the statements and ideas of the teacher beyond reason.

The reality-centered classroom is characterized by student participation in decisions concerning content, method, and role assignments. Students set the standards of behavior and help to enforce them. The teacher does not abdicate his authority role; neither does he act as dictator. He points out and justifies limits. He expects pupils to act within those limits and encourages response and productivity.

Roles of Pupils

The particular roles played in a group vary according to the task and its stage of development. Benne (1954) has listed the task roles in a problem setting. In the *initiating* role, someone suggests what to do, what to discuss, or what method to use. Data are required to solve a problem, and two roles are significant—the *information-seeking* and the *information-giving* roles. It is interesting for teachers to observe the consistency with which these roles are characteristically assumed by certain pupils. There is a *clarification* role, which is filled by those who restate, cite examples, ask questions, and suggest implications. Finally, it is necessary to collate the various ideas, so a *summarizing* role has its place in effective group action. The teacher should point out the necessity of filling these roles and assist students in assuming them (Taylor, 1961).

Groups, to be effective, must be sustained; threats to solidarity must be eliminated, and communication must be kept open by people who play the *building* and *maintaining* roles. When problems are difficult and failure is imminent, someone must fill an *encouraging* role, giving praise, summarizing progress, and specifying individual contributions: This is not an easy role because progress can be inhibited if praise is not merited, if contributions are not really significant, and if individuals do not actually deserve commendation. Ideas sometimes clash, and someone to play a *harmonizing* role is needed to minimize differences, indicate that each has some points, and recall how much there is in common. Keeping the channels of communication open is a constant challenge, and it may mean asking for opinions from those who have previously been silent, limiting the time for each person's comments, and maintaining order so that everyone has a chance to participate: Benne (1954) calls this the *gate-keeping* role. *Standard setting* is still another role; it becomes operative when there is verbal or tacit agreement that action should be by consensus or by majority rule.

Counteracting negative roles requires rather intimate knowledge of individual motivation. Among the negative roles are *aggressor, blocker, recognition seeker, playboy or show-off, dominator, individual-help seeker* (as contrasted to those oriented to solution of the group problem), and *special-interest pleader*. Still another role is that of the *indifferent acquiescer*, who is not sufficiently involved to make a contribution and thus does not facilitate progression. It might be noted that sometimes the one whom we may designate as "playboy" uses humor not to impede progress—though this is the immediate impression—but because he himself feels or perceives in others a mounting tension that, if unrelieved, will ultimately retard forward movement.

The Integrative Classroom Group

A basic human need, whether inborn or acquired, is that of affiliation—the need to belong, to be a part of a group. As the child leaves his home for lengthening periods of time, the need for membership in groups other than the family increases. As the adolescent continues this process and seeks independence from parental protection and the severance of home ties, the school group or peer group becomes more attractive and important. If the teacher exploits this aspect of group dynamics, he encourages group strength and avoids setting up the teacher-as-leader in one camp with pupils in another. He uses what Flanders (1965) has called "indirect" as contrasted to direct influence. Others have called "join-them or lead-them" proposition the dominative or integrative type of leader.

In addition to dominative behaviors, certain school practices tend to separate teachers from pupils: (1) Expecting pupils to report another who has

Direct or Dominative Teacher	*Indirect or Integrative Teacher*
Lectures, uses rhetorical questions	Asks questions, accepts feelings
	Uses idea of students
Gives direction, commands	Praises or encourages
Criticizes judges acceptability of work	Emphasizes student responsibility
Justifies authority	Talk is with other pupils[6]
Students respond to teacher	

misbehaved or been involved in a classroom mishap; (2) giving letter grades that lead students into a competitive milieu—as is evidenced in cheating, figuring out what the teacher wants, and the increase in running away which attends report card time; (3) requiring hall passes to go to the rest room or slips to visit the library.

A common defense mechanism used to cover one's feelings of inadequacy is **identification**. Children whose scholarship or behavior is questionable take comfort from the achievements and reputation of the class. The teacher may exploit this phenomenon by emphasizing the matter of responsibility. A teacher may capitalize on group function by getting pupils to discuss group weaknesses. For example, Meyer (1969) found that the young people of suburbia, living in homogeneous upper-middle-class neighborhoods, tended to have a superficial sophistication and a socioeconomic prejudice despite their reasoning and linguistic facility in discussions. Aldridge (1969) proposes the thesis that some youth join groups (the hippies for instance) not to achieve, but *to avoid*, identity, responsibility, and confrontation of life. They have no idea what they want to do so they find anonymity in a free-for-all, no-restrictions society. These are at an extreme end of the adolescent behavioral scale, but the antidote to having still more adolescents at this point is dialogue, discussion—in short, integrative teaching or indirect teacher influence.

Groups in Action

Discussion Techniques

There are no sure-fire techniques for generating effective discussion, but class involvement is facilitated when pupils feel that the group is theirs, and they are more likely to feel this when they have been allowed to make some suggestions and decisions. Initially, it is better to deal with problems that are somewhat neutral in tone—study habits, best-liked subjects, future occupations—

6   Adapted from Ned A. Flanders, *op. cit.*, p. 6.

and leave until later topics such as school cliques, racial prejudices, disliked grading systems. It is advisable to engage in metacommunication, i.e., communication about what is going on as communication is sought. Too frequently communication fails because no one paused to consider what was really going on beneath the words as it was going on (Watzlawick et al., 1967, pp. 36ff).

Physical arrangements are significant. Discussion demands freedom of communication, which is facilitated by face-to-face arrangements among other things. Circles, semicircles, or rectangles with the teacher sitting with the group makes communication easier because (1) the consent of the teacher is not deemed vital, and (2) participants can watch to see when others have finished or still have a point to make.

In sophisticated discussion groups, it may be noted that leadership often shifts from one person to another (Secord and Bachman, 1964, p. 310). Desirably the teacher should attempt to shift the leadership about to various students. This may be facilitated by first discussing the roles to be filled—leader, evaluator, etc. (see section above on Group Roles of Pupils)—and asking how these roles might become functional in the present group. Loeffler (1970) has called attention to such group roles as the noncommunicative person (he is unconcerned about his impact on others), the overly logical speaker, the under- or over-talker, the tangential speaker, the helpless speaker (but he would be all right if others in the group would straighten up and fly right).

Pupils as well as teachers should know about group dynamics and the required roles, observe them in operation, evaluate their functioning in the current group, and assume responsibility for filling them. This procedure has the double advantage of making group members aware of their individual roles and facilitating group action—this is making use of metacommunication.

Buzz sessions have been used with varying results. They are formed by breaking up a large group into small discussion groups of five or six persons. Each may discuss the same topic or be assigned a subtopic related to the major concern of the large group. Usually the "buzz" lasts only five to fifteen minutes; after this time, a selected member of the group reports to the larger group. Not all buzz groups are successful. There must be a clearly understood purpose, and a leader, a recorder, and an evaluator may need to be designated. When a group bogs down, someone must redistribute membership so that an effective leader can initiate action.

One of the obstacles to genuine discussion groups is the teacher's difficulty in shifting from the ordinary classroom approach in which he is the authority to an approach that permits others to feel that their voice is of consequence. This may be accomplished by reflecting or mirroring—itself a somewhat difficult technique. Mirroring consists of refraining from giving answers or evaluation and, instead, restating or rephrasing in slightly different words the idea expressed by pupils (Dinkmeyer and Caldwell, 1970, p. 181). Thus when a pupil asserts that thinks he got an undeservedly low grade, the teacher might say, "Paul believes that the grading system needs some improvement." Betty states that she studied hard for the role of a certain character in a class play, but Sue got the part; the teacher may respond, "Is Betty suggesting that the designation of cast members be approached more democratically?" Mirroring is typically needed only at the beginning of group discussion; as the teacher retires from the leadership role, such reflection becomes less important.

Silence can be helpful in improving pupil contributions. Silence can be used to increase the anxiety of pupils (or teachers), and someone hastens to fill the gap. If the silence is uncomfortable and too prolonged, it may inhibit participation. But a silence in which group members are given time to weigh and assimilate ideas is worth cultivating.

The fact that some discussion groups have been successful means that some of the foregoing factors have been operative—whether consciously or inadvertently applied. Because so many experiments show that opinion changes are greater in discussion groups than in ordinary instructional groups, because pupils need to exercise skills in human relations, and because we hope that ultimately students will become self-sufficient, there is sound reason for teachers' persistence in making increasing use of discussion. There is considerable evidence that group methods promote problem-solving skills, consolidate learning, and encourage freedom of thought, a spirit of inquiry, and independence.

Counseling

A considerable amount of concern and controversy has arisen in some circles about teachers or school counselors becoming therapists. The concern stems from a fear of doing the student harm or "pushing him over the brink," but the author knows of no studies that document this possibility. In any case, the teacher is already involved by the mere presence of an emotionally disturbed pupil, and ignoring him has greater potential for pushing him beyond the tolerance level than will talking with him. Glasser (1969, p. 86) encourages teachers to counsel with even the most disruptive pupils on the basis of reality therapy.[7] Proff (1962) asserts that there is evidence that giving the disturbed pupil almost any kind of attention may be helpful. Psychiatrists at the University of Oregon Medical School in Portland are actively seeking to give help to teachers in doing

---

7   Essentially Glasser's reality therapy consists of defining the problem (What's the matter?), describing approaches tried (What are you now doing about it?), making a contract for a new approach and accepting no excuses—not "Why didn't you get it done?" but "When are you going to get it done?" Glasser says that the historical approach—using the past for excusing present failure—is futile in behavioral improvement.

a better job in a situation that is well-nigh unavoidable anyway. There are not sufficient psychiatrists and consulting psychologists to serve all who need help. During periods of delay prior to help by highly trained professionals and after release during readjustment periods, teachers can give substantial help to the mentally ill pupil (Saslow, 1963; Butler, 1962). Arbuckle (1962) contends that it is necessary to work with *all* pupils who are still in school. Whether the process is considered therapy or counseling makes no difference. The helping function of school workers, especially counselors, demands that they do, on occasion, become involved in therapy. Group counseling is a readily available approach to behavioral change—call it therapy, counseling, or teaching—it is learning.

Dinkmeyer and Caldwell (1970, p. 467) indicate that the best way to understand children is through in-depth interviews. In these sessions the child is free to explore his deepest feelings and then encouraged to go deeper. Counseling, psychotherapy, and teaching are all so closely related that it is impossible to build confining fences between them. When a pupil needs help, especially in view of the frequent lack of availability of psychiatric help, it is necessary to do what one can by being there and by listening. One of the methods readily available is group discussion.

Initially, group counseling was to save time and reach more people with the personnel available. It was soon discovered that forward movement was often more rapid in some kinds of problems and for some kinds of people through group therapy than through individual therapy. Several explanations for this have been advanced. One is that the individual is helped by discovering that others suffer from situations similar to his own, which he had hitherto thought to be unique. Advice and suggestions coming from one's peers are sometimes more acceptable or seem more practical than those coming from experts. Apparently, the individual thinks that peers have had actual experience, whereas the expert, with his textbook knowledge, does not *really* understand. One sometimes feels freer to talk candidly with peers than with the professional, who, he fears, might make judgments; thus **catharsis** is more readily achieved through discussion with peers. Counselees may feel threatened by the individual approach, whereas in groups they feel the protection of others who are somewhat like themselves. Group counseling is valuable because it is not a discussion about living; it is an experience in living. Reality testing comes to life in a wisely conducted group. Social skills are learned. Dinkmeyer and Caldwell (1970, p. 154) recommend that the following activities or purposes of a group be given attention: support, reflection (mirroring), clarification, questioning, giving information (good counselors must avoid the teacher stance of telling and must rely more on discovery), interpreting, and then periodically summarizing.

Group counseling was used as an initial contact prior to individual counseling for a group of graduate students. They observed participants who came to the counseling center once a week. In one case, there were four boys and four girls from two high schools; all were referred because the school counselor had data showing that the pupils worked consistently below indicated capacity.

The first session consisted of introductions and speculations by the students as to why they had been sent to the center and what might be accomplished. The counselor did not ask, "Are we on the track?" "Shall we get busy?" but looked at the pupil when he was discussing what might be or was likely to become pertinent and looked away when the pupil took too much time on topics that appeared to have no relevance.

During seemingly casual conversation, words such as "brother," "sister," "mother," "teacher," "principal," "dating," and "school subjects" occurred. Context and degree of intensity with which the words were uttered led the counselor to say, "Tell me more," or "What about your sister (teacher, mother)?" There is enough in common in an area such as underachievement so that a topic on which there is real feeling (e.g., high-achieving older siblings, parental criticism) is readily and widely discussed. When it came to a solution, questions such as "What part do you play?" "How can the situation be improved?" soon begins to confront an individual with his own, his individual, responsibility.

The power of young people to solve their own difficulties is shown in the following case:

A teacher in the seventh grade had five girls who were a constant and irritating problem to her. She had heard about the group counseling sessions at the local graduate school and called for some advice. A graduate student who heard the story volunteered to counsel with the girls. Arrangements were made, and after two sessions the girls really got excited about what was wrong with the school, the administration, and especially their teacher. The group leader had two goals in mind: (1) To get the teacher involved in the solution of her own problem, and (2) to get the girls to see their own responsibility. When the girls were asked how Miss _____ would learn how she was being perceived, the girls were appalled by the idea that she might be there. "Miss K would get even," "She would fail them," "She would kick them out." "How do you know these things?"

Miss _____ was invited in and as the pupils "bored in" on her, they began to see how they themselves were unfair, challenging, testing, and cruel. (Words sound differently when spoken in the presence of the accused from the message they convey in a whispering group of peers). The counselor did no more than give the girl who implied or suggested that some of the difficulty was their own a little more time and an attentive ear. He leaned forward, he asked for clarification. Three years later the teacher is still listening; and when the going gets rough, she invites a colleague in to help her avoid being defensive.

As has been the case in comparable sessions reported in the literature, there were no sharp increases in achievement scores or grades. But subjects reported feeling better about themselves and others, and observers felt that improvement in conduct of the young persons in the group was great enough to be clearly perceptible. Unfortunately, changes in group behavior, although highly important, are not so amenable to measurement as is achievement in subject matter.

Summary

Despite much pious verbalization about individuals, a teacher's effectiveness is very much dependent upon his ability to work with groups. The learning climate of the school is dependent on the congeniality and orientation of the classroom group.

A clear delineation of group goals can enhance the effectiveness of groups. Group goals are sometimes contradictory to individual goals but sometimes they are synonymous. Class groups are not initially voluntary, but the negative aspects of compulsory membership can be offset by applied sociometry, by clarifying purposes, and by recognizing individual needs. Cohesiveness is strengthened by communication, by balance between success and challenge, by using democratic procedures, and by knowing group dynamics and explaining them to pupils.

Teachers may approach capitalizing on groups dynamics by filling such roles as leadership (whether democratic or authoritarian); pupil involvement in class activities, including both goal determination and method of approach; and capitalizing on knowledge of group roles. Pupils may take various roles, such as initiating, information giving, information seeking, clarifying, and summarizing in problem-oriented groups. Roles that appear in both problem-oriented and social groups are building, maintaining, encouraging, harmonizing, gate-keeping, and standard setting. There are also a number of negative group roles; they have been identified as aggressor, blocker, recognition seeker, playboy, dominator, individual-help seeker, and indifferent acquiescer. To the extent that these roles are identified, control of them is enhanced.

The past decade has seen an increase in school counseling services. In the more innovative programs teachers are involved with counselors in both discussion and remedial counseling. Remedial counseling, called therapy or some other name, can be made to function in the classroom when problems of a personal nature are made the business of all groups members—teachers and pupils.

Suggested Additional Readings

BERNARD, HAROLD W., AND DANIEL W., FULLMER, 1970, *Principles of Guidance: A Basic Text*, Scranton, Pa.: International Textbook Company, pp. 155-173.

> Chapter 8, "Teachers and Counselors: Roles and Functions," makes no claim that teachers and counselors perform the same functions. The chapter does say that the roles are complementary, and teachers should work with counselors in the classroom.

HALL, EDWARD T., 1969, "Listening Behavior: Some Cultural Differences," *Phi Delta Kappan*, vol. 50, pp. 379-380.

> Some infrequently recognized behaviors of culturally different children are described. Insight into these different listening patterns will help teachers improve their effectiveness with groups.

JOYCE, BRUCE R., 1971, "The Curriculum Worker of the Future," in National Society for the Study of Education, 70th Yearbook, Part I, *The Curriculum: Retrospect and Prospect*, Chicago: University of Chicago Press, pp. 307-355.

> In the curriculum of the future, which should revitalize humanistic values, the "curricular mode" of group inquiry will have high priority.

SHOSTROM, EVERETT L., 1969, "Group Therapy: Let the Buyer Beware," *Psychology Today*, vol. 2, no. 12, pp. 36-40, May.

> If the author of *Psychology of Learning and Teaching* has seemed, in this chapter, to endorse group counseling too heartily, let it be known that he agrees with Dr. Shostrom regarding his cautious endorsement.

WHITE, WILLIAM F., 1969, *Psychosocial Principles Applied to Classroom Teaching*, New York: McGraw-Hill Book Company, pp. 145-165.

> His chapter on "Group Cohesiveness, Problem Solving by Groups, and Leadership Characteristics," will serve to emphasize some of the points in this chapter but will also add some additional considerations.

16

Educational Innovation

Society and technology are in a state of unprecedentedly rapid change, yet paradoxically, schools are said to be strangely and uniquely resistant to change (Locke, 1971). Some people see schools as being so out of harmony with children's out-of-school exposure to change, technology, and mass media that they predict the abolition of schools as we now know them. Other observers see the need for drastic changes in aim, scope, and methods but also believe that there are sufficient open-minded, flexible, and dedicated personnel that schools, in an improved form, will survive. Few persons believe that schools adequately perform, in any substantial degree, such functions as have been assigned to them.

Schools are big business. They involve the energies of about one-third of the total population as pupils, teachers, administrators, publishers, manufacturers, etc. This statistic is cited to suggest that teachers are engaged in working with a colossus. This is not an excuse. A pervading theme in this book is that teachers are a power even though not all-powerful. Unless there is a ripple effect in education, a transfer factor, that goes beyond the amount of time and energy any teacher spends with one pupil, then education in any form is futile. Teachers cannot drastically change the culture or technology, but their cumulative efforts and their corroborative impact are far from negligible.

The point of view taken in this chapter is that teachers are not solely responsible for the role schools play, or fail to play, but it is psychologically self-defeating to deny *any* responsibility.

The Need for Innovation

Dropouts and the Alienated

When school enrollments are at an all-time percentagewise high, it is gratifying to see teachers concerned about the school's holding power. Teachers need, for their own mental health, to recognize that rapid change, population explosion, communication media, parental attitudes and models, and varied styles of learning are factors in dropout rates.

To some extent, dropout rates are an indication of the school's failure to reach the pupils who are already inclined to feel alienated. Many things have been tried and have met with some success. Further innovation is needed to reach some of the unteachables; some dropouts do rightfully blame the schools. There is no panacea for the problem of dropouts, but one generalization may be made: Whatever we have been doing is not good enough. Further innovation is needed. Another valid generalization is that adaptation to varied learning styles is crucial. Some are dropouts because they have not acquired the rudimentary skills of reading, writing, and computation (Benson, 1969). Yet with new materials, varied approaches, and audiovisual supplementary equipment, these people—even as adults—can be taught to read in remarkably short periods of time (Bergneder, 1971). Others become dropouts because their highly developed learning skills lead to their seeing lock-step methods as being boring, repetitious, and lacking in relevance; and they see themselves as being treated as a punched data card, totally lacking in autonomy. Oddly, a programmed text or a video tape in an individual study carrel may in some instances contradict the feeling that one is a cog in an endlessly turning wheel.

All Children and Pupil Differences

If teachers ever thought, and some did, that innovation was a search for *the method* of education they should reevaluate the complexity of the human being. A decade ago some teachers seriously objected to computer-assisted instruction because they were afraid the pupil would be deprived of human contact in the school, or they were fearful that teachers would be replaced by a machine. Some feared a loss of such flexibility and adaptation to differences as already existed (*Commission* . . ., 1970, p. 25).

New methods and new media are recognized, by scholars in those areas, as being supplementary devices and corroborative material which will facilitate the recognition of pupil differences. If this pervasive purpose is overlooked or forgotten, then innovation becomes part of the problem rather than an approach to its solution. Innovative practices can as readily become routinized and impersonalized as are the conventional practices which have failed to reach some pupils.

The organization of schools and colleges takes little account of even what is now known about the process of human learning, including the range of differences among learners and styles of learning. This condition makes schools particularly unresponsive to the needs of disadvantaged and minority-group students. . . .

Most schools and colleges are still locked into conventional patterns of grade structure, time span, and subject-matter division that fail to exploit each student's individual capacities, interests, and personality. Conventional practice is geared to some abstract "average" or "norm" that penalizes both the unusually gifted and the seemingly backward student as well as the spectrum that lies between.[1]

Thus, the need is for new methods, materials, and equipment and also for teachers who understand pupil differences and varied learning styles. Teachers are an inseparable aspect of innovative practice.

A New Aim: Teaching versus Learning

The need for innovation goes even beyond a new breed of teachers and new material and method. A new aim for education is needed. (1) Rapid change means that pupils cannot learn, in school, the content that is basic for an effective adult lifetime. (2) Reflection on the part of each of us suggests that what we were taught in school does not remain as a highly integral part of our life. Hence, the new aim for education must shift from teaching to learning. The burden and responsibility for learning must be transferred from teachers to pupils. However, it must not be assumed that emphases on learning as against emphases on teaching are incompatible. McMurrin (1969, p. 9) asserts that the "central task of a school is the achievement and dissemination of knowledge, the cultivation of the intellect, and induction into the uses of reason." Emphasis on teaching can and has often achieved the "knowledge" aspect; but emphasis on learning could enhance all three aspects of the task McMurrin mentions.

It is necessary that teachers cease thinking that presentation is equivalent to learning. It is necessary to realize that even when the student learns what is presented (poetic phrases or lists of Presidents, for instance), he may be learning other things as thoroughly—to curb his creativity, to dislike structured learning, or how to beat the system.

Placing some reliance on programmed texts, audio-visual instructional aids, or computer-assisted instruction will provide improved access to children whose learning styles differ from the listening and abstract styles required in

---

1   Commission on Instructional Technology, 1970, *To Improve Learning*, A report to the President and the Congress of the United States, Washington, D.C.: U.S. Government Printing Office, pp. 14, 15.

Ellen Levine/College Newsphoto Alliance

many classrooms (Campbell, 1969, p. 118). Small group discussions give the pupil whose learning style is talking his day in court. Individual or small group projects give the pupils whose learning style is doing their chance to keep pace with those whose style is listening and reading. In short, the teacher's new role becomes less that of instructor and presenter and more that of finding, devising, and then orchestrating a variety of learning activities. The role of the innovative teacher is managerial and supportive (Campbell, 1969)—his behavior is determined by the needs and responses of his pupils.

Another dimension of the teaching versus learning problem is that teachers may be called to work with more adults than is the case at present. Experiments in team teaching and the use of teaching aides are proving themselves of sufficient value that their extension seems probable. Such an extension will probably entail **merit pay** and the abandonment of heavy reliance on a **salary schedule**, which in turn may entail some attack from the inside of the teaching ranks and a defense of the current teaching emphasis.

Educational hardware calls for creativity in devising programs for individual pupils and for teachers' being technicians in the use of equipment.

As teaching machines and individual study booths and televised lectures multiply, what will happen to the school as a stage for the display of intellectual proficiency? As we improve in our ability to individualize instruction will students still be interested in talking to each other about their school experience? Indeed, will they be interested in talking to anyone about their experiences? It is questions such as these that bother some critics of technological progress.

Here then are some of the more realistic hopes and fears aroused by the proponents and the critics of educational technology. On the one hand, there is the promise of improving the quality of education through a greater individualization of instruction and through a greatly enriched library of teaching materials. Furthermore, there is even the possibility of reducing the cost of instruction in the bargain. On the other hand, there lurks the threat of increasing the assembly line aspects of school life, of reducing the professional integrity of the live teacher, and of subtly altering the social character of the learning process. The question of which of these effects predominates depends in part upon the kinds of collaborative relationships that grow up among technologists, manufacturers, school administrators, and classroom teachers. It is entirely possible that the quality of this relationship will not be uniform throughout our schools but will vary from region to region and possibly from one level of education to another.[2]

Nongraded Schools and the Innovative Package

The rationale of nongraded schools is, as discussed in Chapter 14, to provide a vehicle which will implement continuous progress. Here let the emphasis be on the interrelationships of innovative concepts—this has been called the "innovative package," meaning that changing one important feature of the educational program entails some other alterations. Nongraded organization can become a gimmick unless its psychological bases are understood. It can be most effective when accompanied by team teaching, individualized study programs, the elimination of grading, and reliance on pupil initiative and responsibility. The author visited an elementary school, nongraded, in Corte Madeira, Calif. and observed or discussed the following with teachers.

The building was many-sided (octagonal), with all rooms centered on and observable from, a large central learning laboratory. Books, pamphlets, reading accelerators, tape players and recorders, slide projectors, taped lectures, and realia were readily available to groups or individuals at any level in this learning center. Even primary students had to have some reading skill in order to use the file catalogs. Team teaching was used, and twice or more a week teachers met to discuss pupils, programs,

2   Philip W. Jackson, 1969, "Technology and the Teacher," in E. S. Mason (Chm.), *The Schools and the Challenge of Innovation*, New York: McGraw-Hill Book Company, p. 145.

and materials. Five pupils, not above the lower-intermediate level were working all alone in a room for more than an hour. Some were working alone with cassette tapes, and others were reading in easy chairs. No grades were given, but teachers scheduled interviews with parents; and parents were welcome to visit at any time (and two were there at the time we were). Typical-sized groups were six to eight pupils with each teacher working with several groups who were watching a movie. Some use was made of teacher aides, with the hope that there would be more.

From this small sample, it can be seen that nongraded organization may become a vehicle for shifting from the teaching to the learning emphasis, from teacher dominance to pupil responsibility, from interpersonal comparisons to individual progress, from managing pupils to trusting them, and for the implementation of an innovative package.

Educational Vouchers

The idea of using educational vouchers is to accelerate breaking away from some of the practices which are recognized as being ineffective, if not futile, but which are deeply embedded in bureaucracy. The medium for this movement is to issue parents vouchers for their children's elementary school education which may be "cashed" at any school of their choice. Schools which did not conduct schools with the program, facilities, and personnel which attracted customers would not survive. Aside from maintaining minimum standards and observing certain regulations, established by the "Educational Voucher Agency," schools would be free to expand and experiment along lines which parents and pupils deemed to be worthwhile.

The plan was developed by Jencks (1970) under contract with the U.S. Office of Education, and it was anticipated that it would be tried on a limited basis. Forecasts of success are based on the success of the GI Bill which allowed students to pursue their educational careers at multitudes of approved institutions. Some of the problems which must be dealt with in basic regulations are:

Seeing that better-supported schools are not provided by the financially able than are those of low economic status.

Prohibiting parents from supplementing the value of the voucher

Not providing a device by which racists may avoid having their children associate with those of another color

Preventing distance and transportation from becoming a barrier to equal educational opportunity

Preventing religious organizations from using vouchers for purposes of proselyting

There is some apprehension that this untried version of education will destroy public education (Clayton, 1970) or that parents are any better qualified to judge and seek for better schools than are elected school board members (Havighurst, 1970). Nevertheless, "Teaching and learning are subtle processes, and they seem to resist all attempts at improvement by formal regulation. Rule books are seldom subtle enough to prevent the bad things that can happen in schools, and are seldom flexible enough to allow the best things."[3]

Modular Flexible Programming

There are a number of flexible programming plans, but a pioneer one at Marshall High School, Portland, Ore., may serve to illustrate the major features. Instead of the forty-five-minute to one-hour periods which were characteristic of the high school day a few years ago, Marshall has 21 twenty-minute modules. These may be combined to as many as five modules to provide a laboratory meeting or shifted about to provide for daily flexibility. Thus, the lunch period, instead of being from 12 A.M. to 1 P.M. extends from 11 A.M. to 2 P.M., with the possibility of four or five shifts in the cafeteria. In order to provide an individual schedule for 1,800 to 2,000 pupils, the work of a computer was required and was contracted for through Stanford University. The contract included consultative services for staff training, technical assistance, and trouble shooting (Petrequin, 1968, p. 2).

Flexible modular scheduling makes it possible for pupils to have time for quest activities which may include reading, extra time in a laboratory, visiting a class which is reputed to have an exciting program or to be pursuing a unique topic, or to conduct some extramural pursuit; e.g., full-day visits to local colleges and universities. Some pupils independently study learning packages which enterprising teachers have devised and continue to devise; others use programmed texts and can finish a given unit ahead of the usual time allotment. Patterns of independent study range from a skills center where reading and writing are taught to enrichment experiences which only one pupil may be pursuing. The range of activities is suggested in the following list of twenty pursuits which are representative rather than inclusive:

Slide rule	Italic lettering	Lab-technician class
Creative writing	Weight-lifting	Drama festival
Knitting instruction	Clarinet instruction	Automotive program
Conversational Japanese	Creativity class	Office-assistant program

3   Christopher Jencks, 1970, "Giving Parents Money for Schooling: Education Vouchers," *Phi Delta Kappan*, vol. 52, p. 51, September.

Classical Greek	Charm course	Adventure Theatre
Oil painting	Dance band	Librarian's book-
Clothing construction	Literature class	review committee[4]

Flexible-modular scheduling may be used to illustrate the difficulty of educational change because of the need for an innovative package—change of a part involves change of other aspects. Specifically, modular scheduling requires technology for programming and desirably to provide avenues for independent study. Teachers need to be involved, and team teaching was used at Marshall. Independent study, a learning skills center, and interinstitutional cooperation were also factors in implementation.

Storefront Schools

The merit of using the community as a medium for enhancing and giving substance to social science concepts has been recognized by teachers who make field trips, use local realia, and who keep abreast of community affairs. Goodman (1970*b*) believes that schools are so far detached from the realities of the pupils' lives that they had best be abandoned. Incidental education, he believes, will be sufficient to serve the needs of elementary and secondary pupils. There are others who view such abandonment as being impossible if for no other reason than the sheer magnitude of the problem (Fischer, 1970).

A variety of storefront schools for children and adolescents are based on the idea that schools should be only a step from the sidewalk and be just as close to the life of the pupil. Thus, the psychological bases are related to individualization, creativity, relevance, and interpersonal investment. Teacher-pupil ratio is low—three teachers to fifteen to thirty pupils—so human contact can also be close. "A typical social studies lesson slid over Vietnam, Biafra, the French Foreign Legion, the concept of civil war, capitalists in Texas, Indians in Mexico, drugs in Mexico, academy students in Mexico (a summer trip organized by this teacher), American imperialism, white imperialism, etc." (Black, 1969, p. 89). In Chicago, parents and their children attend a storefront school in the evening after work to learn to speak English in addition to their already-acquired competence in Spanish. From the standpoint of the teachers, the emphasis is on "Let's be different." Tardiness is casually accepted, tutoring is available, transfer from class to class is frequent, tapes and records are used (Gaber, 1971). In another storefront school the point of revitalization was a deep personal involvement with kids.

---

4   Lyle K. Meyer, 1968, "Independent Study: Enrichment Experiences," in Gaynor Petrequin, *Individualizing Learning through Modular-Flexible Programming*, New York: McGraw-Hill Book Company, p. 67.

Private grants, community action, donations, and support from the local school board represent the variety of funding. Teachers are often part-time and volunteer. Working in these street-corner, sidewalk, storefront schools is not a seven-hour-a-day job, nor one confined within the walls of whatever store, church, or apartment as may be headquarters. Whatever the variety of success, it has been reflected in pupils who have evolved a trust in themselves and a hope for the future as they have concurrently mastered the tools of learning.

Educational Contractors

The difficulty of transforming the educational system is reflected in the involvement of big business in education, its retreat after trial, and its ambivalence about staying in or getting out. Some business-education partnerships have worked well. Involvement takes the form of on-the-job, work-study sponsorship of special courses taught by industry or business personnel. In other instances, book publishers and manufacturers of educational **hardware** have combined forces. Textbooks have been programmed, lessons have been video-taped, and tachistoscopes, tape recorders and players, and recording-talking-teaching machines have been used in doing a part of the instructional function.

In the early 1970s the business-education partnership was beginning to be seen as (1) unprofitable, (2) only a drop-in-the-bucket, and (3) requiring understanding and receptive personnel rather than a ready-made service. The amount of cash for innovation provided by school board custodians of public funds was not so great as the potential seemed to be in terms of a "third of a nation's population." Moreover, it was hard for profit-minded industrial giants to communicate with education-oriented subsidiary companies (Carlson, 1970). Businessmen overestimated the readiness of education personnel to accept the innovative stance or found educators willing to accept the gadget but lacking the dedicated personnel to breathe life into it (Locke, 1971). The tremendous power of pupils—their ability to turn-off and tune-out—which has been demonstrated in their television viewing, has yet to be appreciated by many teachers and businessmen.

An optimistic view of business in education, and possibly presaging a national trend, is reported on Texarkana's experience. There the plan was no product, no pay. Unless the pupils in a Rapid Learning Center learned in terms of that which they were theoretically expected to learn during the course of a year, payment was withheld in proportion to the deficiency. The concept is performance-contracting-accountability. Preliminary reports indicate such favorable aspects as a teacher fired because of poor pupil performance, numbers of dropouts reduced, vandalism decreased, use of machines which do not laugh at a pupil's mistakes, teachers—No!*Learning managers*—who know each pupil and plan with and for him the films, records, tapes, books to be used the next day (Elam,

1970). Not all the pupils made the hoped-for progress—teaching machines do not fit all learning styles.

A questionable feature of Texarkana's Rapid Learning Center is the use of Green Stamps (literally, not figuratively) and prizes to those who make the greatest gains on the Iowa Tests of Educational Achievement. This takes one back to the possibility of mistaking the symbols of education for education, of leaving no lasting incentive for pursuing learning after the prize has been earned, and of believing that one learns for other people. The lessons of reinforcement have been implemented without consideration of functional autonomy or of habituation. Commendable features are teacher accountability and intensification of the crucial educational concept—programs, rates, and materials devised to attract and motivate the unique pupil in his contemporary milieu.

Curricular Approaches to Innovation

Reorganization is one way to approach the restructuring of education in order better to meet pupils' needs. Another approach is via instructional materials designed to be responsive to pupil curiosity, which enable pupils to be self-pacing and self-propelling, which stimulate several sense modalities, and which free teachers from scoring and record-keeping trivia (Goodlad, 1967).

The psychological principles of programmed instruction are clear and were worked out in advance (many educational practices seem to be justified after the fact). The dominant psychological themes are immediate reinforcement of successful responses, knowledge of progress, avoidance of errors by step-by-step progression, and speed of advance determined by the pupil. There are two major types of programmed instruction: linear and branching. Each is illustrated by its initial creator.

The machine devised by Skinner feeds information in smaller units. The psychological justification for the smaller unit is that the human organism is rewarded (reinforced) by small, simple, and regular gains in performance (Holland and Skinner, 1961, p. vi). Moreover, Skinner contends that errors should be corrected immediately; otherwise, the wrong response has a chance to be retained. Ideally, the program should be so constructed that errors occur rarely, if at all. Another justification for small units employing fill-in questions is that responsibility is placed on the learner for supplying the answer; in contrast, the student merely has to choose (at the recognition level) from among the alternatives presented by the machine in the multiple-choice items.

In the linear program each sentence builds on the previous one. This may be clarified by reproducing a portion of *The Analysis of Behavior*, an introductory psychology text. The first sequence appears originally on page 1; the the next following sequence shown here appears on page 2, etc.

			page 1
Stimulus		Technically speaking, reflex involves an elicit-	
(tap on		ing stimulus in a process called elicitation.	
the knee)	1-7	A stimulus _____ a response.	1-8
			page 2
elicits		To avoid unwanted nuances of meaning in	
		popular words, we do not say that a stimu-	
		lus "triggers," "stimulates," or "causes" a	
	1-8	response, but that it _____ a response.	1-9
			page 3
elicits		In a reflex, the stimulus and the elicited	
		response occur in a given temporal or-	
		der; first the (1) _____, then the	
	1-9	(2) _____.	1-10
			page 4
(1) *stimulus*		A kick of the leg is _____ by a tap on	
(2) *response*		the patellar tendon.	
	1-10		1-11
			page 5
elicited		The time which elapses between the onset of	
		the stimulus and the onset of the response	
		is called the *latency*. Thus the time be-	
		tween tap and kick is the _____ of	
	1-11	the knee-jerk reflex.	1-12
			page 6
latency		The weakest stimulus sufficient to elicit a	
		response marks the *threshold* of the reflex.	
		A tap on the knee will not elicit a kick if	
	1-12	it is below the _____.	1-13
			page 7
threshold		If you blink when something brushes your	
	1-13	eye, the _____ is a response.	1-14
			page 8
blink		A puff of air striking the eye will elicit a blink	
		only if the force exerted by the air exceeds	
	1-14	the _____ value. To p. 1	1-15

		page 1
threshold	The fraction of a second which elapses between "brushing the eye" and "blink" is	
1-15	the ———— of the reflex.	1-16

		page 2
latency	In the patellar-tendon reflex, a forceful tap elicits a strong kick; a tap barely above the threshold elicits a weak kick. Magnitude of responses thus depends on the in-	
1-16	tensity of the ————.	1-17

		page 3
stimulus (tap)	The magnitude of a response corresponds to (is a function of) the ———— of the	
1-17	stimulus which elicits it.[5]	1-18

Note that the answer to an item appears on the next page. This occurs for this program for seven panels of items and responses, when the full set is completed on page 8. After reading page 8, one returns to page 1. The entire set was designed for use in a teaching machine, but it can be used as a programmed textbook, as here. Holland and Skinner point out that it is essential to write the answers before turning the page to check for the correct response. In short, one must commit himself, or he tends to be satisfied with vague and poorly formulated guesses.

In a branching program multiple-choice questions and large units of instruction are involved. If a student makes a correct choice he proceeds normally. If he makes an error, he is shifted from the main line of progress onto a branch where he gets additional instruction, and the specific error is clarified. Still another wrong response directs him to further supplementary material in which that specific error is clarified. If the student gives a series of correct responses, he may be directed to skip a number of frames so that the material to be studied will be somewhat more difficult and challenging.

The following examples illustrate a branching program as devised by Norman A. Crowder and Grace Martin. For lesson 1, "The Power of Numbers" the authors first explain the decimal system and its relationship to computers, then proceed:

---

5   James G. Holland and B. F. Skinner, 1961, *The Analysis of Behavior*, New York: McGraw-Hill Book Company, pp. 1ff.

Now here is a question on the material you have just read. Select what what you believe to be the correct answer and turn to the page number indicated to the right of the answer you choose.

Would you say that the two numbers 492 and .29 are both written in the decimal system?

Answer
Both 492 and .29 are written in the decimal system. page 4
Only .29 is written in the decimal system. page 8[6]

If the student says 492 and .29 are written in the decimal system, he turns to page 4, which tells him:

Your Answer: Both 492 and .29 are written in the decimal system.
You are correct. The word "decimal" refers simply to the fact that our common number system uses only ten different numerals, or digits. With these ten single digits (0, 1, 2 . . . 9), we can count up to 9. Beyond 9 we must use combinations of these numerals, such as 1 and 0 for ten (10), and 1 and 1 for eleven (11), etc.

Do you know, or have you ever heard of, a number system for representing quantities other than our familiar 10-digit decimal system?

Answer
Yes. page 14.
No. page XIV.
I'm not sure, page 1111[7]
If the student's answer is "Only .29 is written in the decimal system," he then goes to page 8, where he gets some "remedial" information:

Your Answer: Only .29 is written in the decimal system.
Well, let's see.
You once learned that . . .

The advantages of programmed study are well illustrated in its use with culturally different pupils. Kliger (1968) asserts that in conventional learning situations the unprepared pupil makes a mistake, others laugh at or chide him, he decides that learning is not for him, and he is off on a self-fulfilling prophecy cycle of defeat. A learning program may provide variety, positive and immediate feedback, perceivable success, gradually improving insights, and a structure which provides a sense of security.

6   From *The Arithmetic of Computers* by Norman A. Crowder and Grace C. Martin. Copyright © 1960 by U.S. Industries, Inc. (Tutor text). Reprinted by permission of Doubleday & Company, Inc., p. 1.
7   *Ibid.*, p. 4.

Audio-visual Instruction

A programmed course, portrayed on video tape, as well as the long-familiar filmstrips, movies, overhead projectors, and language laboratories are among the devices included in the audio-visual category. The rationale for these devices is that much that we learn is from seeing a thing and talking about it; *and* that what we see today is influenced by what we bring to the processes of perception—what we already know. In school, where so much material is contained in abstract words, many pupils do not visualize—see as a real thing—that which is being studied, described, or supposedly conceptualized.

One example of a visual aid is a reading accelerator. This device is highly successful when properly used, i.e., with regularity, with appropriate and varied material, and with continual attention to comprehension. It continues to be a part of the curriculum of some high schools and colleges. A doubling of reading rates, with no loss of comprehension per unit of reading, in a period of eight to ten weeks is typical. The machines are simple. A book is placed in a frame in such a position that a curtain, like a miniature old-fashioned window blind, descends the page, progressively covering more lines of print. The speed of the curtain's descent can be electrically controlled or regulated by graduated spring tension, scaled on a words-per-minute basis. The reader is being gently and constantly urged to improve his speed. Each pupil sets the machine at a few words beyond his present rate. Keeping a record of rate and comprehension provides an incentive to improve—in competition with oneself.

Tachistoscopes, which also may be used in reading, are employed in Ontario, Ore., to teach below-grade level, and especially Mexican-American, pupils to develop functional literacy. Phrases which they can already read are flashed on a screen and as skill is developed they can be played more and more rapidly.

> The author observed a non-English-speaking, Mexican-American primary-level girl teaching herself to speak English with the aid of a machine. A phrase was printed and taped on heavy cardboard, "I am a girl. My name is Teresa." The card, slipped in a slot, fed through the machine and enunciated the phrase while Teresa listened. The card was then slipped in again and Teresa touched the "Off" button for sound and spoke the words herself. During a half-hour to forty-minute time span she worked with about ten cards. It looked like a dull device, but Teresa's face, and the teacher's report, gave a more enthusiastic evaluation.

Allen (1969) opines that there are two barriers to the wider use of audio-visual instruction (1) the rigid curriculum and departmentalized instruction, and (2) the persistent tendency for teachers to control the use of the machines. Some schools, especially those in which learning centers are adjacent to several classrooms, or as in Matzke School, Houston, Texas, where there is just one big room which houses six grades with a learning center as the center of the school, make heavy demands on the audio-visual equipment. Many machines, booths, tapes, programs were available on a small group and individual basis. In the Matzke instance, the winning attraction, judged from the pupils' attention, was the fourth grade teacher's story-reading session!

Computer-assisted Instruction

Although much has been written about computer-assisted instruction, it is only practiced in a couple of dozen locations, e.g., Palo Alto, Calif. and Pittsburgh in connection with university research centers. The idea, despite many variations in theory, is that a school will have a terminal head hooked into a data-storage center, from which programs may be retrieved by individual pupils. The advantage is the great variety of programs available at the press of a button. The disadvantage, at present, is the expense of a sufficiently large number of terminals in schools to make it widely available to pupils. Another difficulty, possibly an even greater one, is a sufficient number of well-designed programs. The cost of well-designed, and constant redesigning of, programs would, of course, be negligible if computer centers were used on a statewide or nationwide basis. Few local systems could afford the groundwork, and the programs might tend to become sterile.

At present computers as educational media are largely confined to administrative scheduling, organization and budgeting, personnel record-keeping, testing, research, and the scoring of papers and examination. It seems possible that this may remain the major function of educational computers (Bratten, 1968).

Instructional Technology

Men have been reassured, if they really needed it, that because men must put programs into them, computers can never "take over." The situation seems similar in instructional technology. Currently, one must predict that technology will not be given an adequate trial in the near future or on a large scale— there will be no technological revolution in the schools. The inflexibility of programs, biases of teachers, and lack of clear evidence of their general effectiveness are factors which will retard implementation (Jackson, 1969, p. 137).

Problems to be faced, in addition to high costs of computers, television, and talking typewriters have been summarized by the Commission on Instructional Technology of the House of Representatives Committee on Education and Labor:

(1) Developing and testing high-quality programs.
(2) Providing time for teachers to gain an understanding of technology, to learn the technical skills necessary, and to plan programs.
(3) Employing media specialists and teacher aides.
(4) Maintaining equipment. . . .

High cost and inadequate costing techniques are clearly a major cause of instructional technology's lack of impact on American schools and colleges. There are other causes. . . . Some are quite tangible, such as insufficient time, talent, and resources to produce effective and imaginative programs; the inaccessibility of whatever good materials exist; lack of specialists in instructional technology; inadequate preparation and inservice training of teachers and administrators; the tendency of some commercial firms to sell educators hardware designed for noninstructional purposes. . . . Too little is known about how human beings learn, still less about how to apply what *is* known to the instructional process. [8]

Instructional Techniques

Dialogue and Small Groups

The importance, for general mental development, of the mother's talking to the infant has been emphasized as a sound child-care practice (Hunt, 1968). The effect of either limited exposure to linguistic variety of bombardment by undifferentiated sound has been mentioned in Chapter 7 in the discussion of the language and intellectual development of mountain children and those from the ghetto. Separation from parents and lack of communication is postulated as being one important explanation for lack of a feeling of identity on the part of adolescents (Halleck, 1968). Bruner suggests that,

> Finally, one of the most crucial ways in which a culture provides aid in intellectual growth is through a dialogue between the more experienced and the less experienced, providing a means for the internalization of dialogue in thought. The courtesy of conversation may be the major ingredient in the courtesy of teaching. [9]

In addition to the better, or at least equivalent, mastery of subject matter there remain such educational gains as feeling that one has an influence, that he

8   Commission on Instructional Technology, 1970, *To Improve Learning*, A report to the President and the Congress of the United States, Washington, D.C.: U.S. Government Printing Office, pp. 23, 24.
9   Jerome S. Bruner, 1968, "Culture, Politics, and Pedagogy," *Saturday Review*, vol. 51, no. 20, p. 90, May 18.

gets and gives feedback, that he has an opportunity to be an overtly active participant in the teaching-learning transaction.

Artful, educational, productive discussion is not achieved just by the teacher's remaining silent a greater portion of the time. A low level of discussion is to ask questions on materials already studied with the idea of obtaining answers from previously considered data. Gagné (1970*a*, p. 372) suggests that when questions are used, they should be on interpretations of and deductions from previously studied materials. But discussion is also low level when all participants are merely vocalizing their ignorance. Hence, a first step in discussion is some preparation—which should be on an agreed-upon subject but most desirably will utilize a variety of references, books, films, or research projects. The variety would depend partly on the pupils' levels of sophistication. A high level of discussion is probable when participants have prepared themselves by self-instructional means. With this kind of preparation, it can be a "great delight" to pupils and teachers because they not only contribute but get new data during the process (Gagné, 1970*a*, p. 374).

A limitation of discussion is that it must depend largely on transfer of knowledge and communication about that which is already known. Discovering new problems and getting learning to occur are not major features of discussion and dialogue.

Discovery

The emphasis in the "discovery" technique is on learning rather than teaching. However, as is the case with discussion, discovery is dependent upon past knowledge and the establishing, or discovery, of the relationships of various existing knowledges. Discovery and inquiry are facilitated by the well-informed mind (Allender, 1970). The essence of discovery is rearranging and transforming evidence in such ways as to produce a new product and new insight (Bruner, 1962).

An oft-cited example of the discovery technique is in geography. Pupils are given maps and learn the location of various rivers, lakes, mountains, plains, and plateaus and are then asked why cities and towns are located where they are. Another example is in a laboratory where pupils are asked to formulate the principle of leverage and fulcrum (Kuethe, 1968, p. 74).

Discovery capitalizes on the phenomenon of **insight** and diminishes the role of drill and memorization, thus reducing the speed and incidence of forgetting. It emphasizes the learn-by-doing postulation by involving pupils in planning, experimenting, and reflecting. Although primarily used as an elementary school technique, discovery would seem to be still more pertinent for adolescents. Children, lacking experience, more readily will take the work of another as proof, whereas healthy adolescents want to assert their autonomy and test their power.

Second, education must concentrate more on the unknown and the speculative, using the known and established as a basis for extrapolation. This will create two problems immediately. One is that the shift in emphasis will shake the traditional role of the teacher as the one who knows, contrasting with the student who does not. The other is that, in any body of men who use their minds at all, one usually gets a sharp division between what my friend Joseph Aggassis calls "knowers" and "seekers." Knowers are valuers of firm declarative statements about the state of things. Seekers regard such statements as invitations to speculation and doubt. The two groups often deplore each other. Just as surely as authority will not easily be given up by teachers, so too will knowers resist the threatening speculations of seekers. Revolution does have difficulties.[10]

The discovery technique is not a single or simple approach. Shulman and Keislar, in *Learning by Discovery: A Critical Appraisal* (1966), show that discovery will not and should not be *the* method of education. On the other hand, there are potentialities in various subject matter disciplines for the functioning of discovery that are only beginning to be probed.

Organic Teaching

Many individuals have written stimulating accounts of the rationale and approaches of their educational innovation—Dennison (1969), Holt (1964), Kelly (1962), Lane (1964), Lewis (1946). Despite glowing accounts, the general practice has not been transformed, though changes here and there have been effected, and perhaps the accounts have had some small cumulative effect on teachers' attitudes. It may be that the innovative approach is always subordinate to the personality of the innovator; e.g., "One man's meat . . ." One description of a rebellious approach is that of "organic teaching" described by Ashton-Warner (1963).

Ashton-Warner (1964) rebels against the encapsulation of the child's mind by the use of stereotyped, adult-written, mass-produced primary school reading books. She feels that this approach suppresses the great potential for creativity with which children enter school. Her recommendation is that the organic approach be used. This means that out of the life and person of the child should come the textual materials. "Simplicity is so safe" she says—in Maori, where she taught, the English-published texts about "See John run. Oh, look and see. See the boats," did not have meaning for her brown-skinned boys and girls. Take, break, fight, be first, were uppermost for boys, and house, Mummy, doll

---

10   Jerome Bruner, 1970, "The Skill of Relevance or the Relevance of Skills," *Saturday Review*, vol. 53, no. 14, p. 78, Apr. 18.

were the thoughts of the girls. So reading materials were made one word at a time by the pupils as captions for pictures they drew. But one word tells a story when it is the child's word.

Reading becomes really creative in the organic technique. Ashton-Warner feels that hostility, aggression, and antisocial behavior wane and disappear as pupils have a chance to replace such behaviors with their own creativity. Reading is fun when it concerns what pupils write about what they live.

The organic approach seems to emphasize the learning aspect of the teaching-learning process. "I reach a hand into the mind of the child, bring out a handfull of the stuff I find there, and use that as our first working material" (Ashton-Warner, 1964, p. 247).

Independent Study

Most of what is called "independent study" throughout the nation would more accurately be called "individually prescribed instruction." Certainly, the psychologically sound approach to pupil differences calls for departure from uniform preparation and presentation. Individually prescribed instruction recognizes differences and is an admirable step away from uniformity. However, prescription is "not all that bad!" There are basic skills which all pupils, indeed, all persons, need. We are not yet ready to say that a pupil may study anything he wants in the elementary and high school and still be prepared later for the pursuit of professional work in engineering, medicine, law, and the behavioral sciences. Experience may be education but not all experiences are equally educative—some are destructive (childhood in the ghetto) and some are a cipher (many television programs).

Howard (1966) suggests four steps which would lead toward the student's taking progressively more responsibility for his own learning. (1) Student options regarding pace, content, time, and materials would involve the pupil, increasingly, in the decision-making processes of his own learning. (2) Content options would allow pupils the choice of materials to be read on a stated subject or permit him to work for extra credit. (3) Time options, of which continuous progress is one type, permit the pupil to choose library, laboratory, or independent project as well as to choose the teachers with whom he will work.

A very few schools have genuine independent study in the form of Quest or Independent Projects. Independent study, according to the *Dictionary of Education* (Good, 1959), means study carried on with a minimum or a complete absence of external guidance. In the school setting the meaning of minimum calls for examination. In one situation it may mean that the pupil is released from a physical setting to carry out an assigned task; in another it may mean that he chooses what, as well as where, to study. Another aspect relates to pace. Ultimately and ideally, independent study probably should be regarded as a situation in which the pupil works at his self-selected task, at his own pace, and with his choice of materials with only occasional teacher guidance. There is a significant difference between guidance and assignment or prescription, even prescription on an individual basis.

The recommendation here is not for an entire program of independent study for any student (Ohanian, 1971). Some proportion of time, more for those who wish it, should be devoted to independent study; but there should also be a part devoted to requirements, assignments, and firm teacher leadership.

> While it is clear to me that some flexibility in teaching and some faith on the part of the young people that they have some control over their path through life may be the difference between a liberal society and a totalitarian one, too much openness in the socialization process is terrifying to the student; it swamps him, saps his energy, and may lead him to search for security in sex, in social movements with "answers," in dependence on shallow personal connections, or in a position which rejects the society altogether.[11]

Fallers (1970), writing as an anthropologist as well as a teacher, also contends that students pampered with the notions of individualization, personally tailored programs, and independent learning are not being prepared for life as it will be met. Safety needs (see Chapter 9), as well as the necessity for learning fundamentals in science, mathematics, and human relations, indicate that independence be judiciously used.

Independent study calls for trust and empathy on the part of teachers. It calls for patience with the pupil who just wants to rest—day after day. It will not work for all—the learning style of some pupils requires imposed structure. It does deserve to be tried, including its examples of defeat, if we are to achieve the objective of a lifetime of continuous learning. Finally, teachers must consider the awesome dilemma: Does the concept of independent study really exist if *after* a program has been agreed upon, we can blow the whistle on those pupils who do not fulfill our expectations?

The Person in the Innovative Process

Interactional Analysis

The foregoing discussions of innovative organization, curricula, and techniques have made at least occasional reference to the ideas that (1) there is no panacea for shortcomings of education—no uniformly successful method, and

11   Margaret Fallers, 1970, "Choice Is Not Enough," *School Review*, vol. 78, p. 234.

(2) teachers as persons are of vital significance in classroom success. It has been reported that despite much research and sincere efforts to improve the quality of teaching, in most schools, methods of teaching, types of teachers, and size of classes make no significant difference in pupil performance (Clements, 1968). Part of this conclusion is not particularly surprising because it is recognized increasingly that pupils differ in learning styles. Not only do they differ from each other but, as they grow older, they differ from themselves; e.g., in the course of normal development, pupils tend to become more autonomous and to develop unique interests; and the specific subaspects of intelligence emerge more distinctly during the early teen years (see Chapter 7). Nor is it surprising that size of class has little impact, because research for years has emphasized the point—an exception being where pupil differences are very great, as in the case of exceptional and/or handicapped.

Teachers do make a difference. If we also include pupil attitudes toward learning and self-curiosity and creativity, and critical thinking as well as factual learning, then the nature of the pupil-teacher transaction makes discernible differences. At least in the early grades, teachers who accept pupils' behaviors, praise them, and capitalize on pupils' ideas get significantly better results than do teachers who lecture, give directions, and criticize (Brown, 1960; Campbell, 1968; Davidson, 1968; Flanders, 1965). These teacher behaviors have been reduced to a number of microelements so that trained observers can, especially with the use of computers, analyze in specific detail just what the teacher does, how pupils respond, and what took place. This process called "interaction analysis" could lead us to an advantageous appreciation of just what it is that effective teachers do (Campbell and Barnes, 1969). In short, the study of classroom behavior *in careful detail* may lead to specific and critical knowledge about teaching.

Team Teaching

There are many varieties of team teaching, and an evaluation of its merit must be tentative. In some instances, team teaching means "Let's combine classes. And while I teach arithmetic you take a coffee break and then I'll have coffee and get caught up with record keeping while you teach social studies." In other instances teachers stay together while each does "his thing." In still other cases several teachers plan together, discuss and diagnose individual pupils, project remedial approaches, try to integrate the subject matter, and then help one another in the execution of plans. On some teams all teachers are equal members, and in other cases there is a lead teacher and a hierarchical distribution of responsibilities; e.g., team leader, master teachers, specialists, apprentices, and aides (Shaplin, 1964).

Many advantages have been cited in support of team teaching. The talents of a gifted teacher are likely to be distributed to a greater number of pupils. Because of specialization a better use of audio-visual aids, library, and technological devices may be effected. It facilitates the use of teacher aides. It makes possible the sharing of varied perceptions of a given pupil's talents, motivations, and progress. It allows teachers to make better preparation in the specific areas of their interests. It enhances the potential for giving some pupils individual guidance and for taking advantage of small group activities. It may be used to implement aspects of nongraded organization (Dean, 1967).

Because of human differences, team teaching would be advantageous for some pupils and teachers because of their social, gregarious nature; others tend to be independent loners. In one school where team teaching, continuous progress, and learning packages were being developed new teachers who were interested in team teaching were employed; but ones who were in the system could, and some did, choose to be in sole charge of the classroom. Following is a paraphrase of how team teaching looked to a team member:

> I have been teaching for seven years and by and large I enjoy it. However, at times I had the feeling that I was going flat—hours a day with children may be emotionally challenging and interesting but the association is not an intellectual challenge. I voted to join the team experiment.
>
> From the beginning it was fun. There was so much more to team teaching than I had imagined. Then it began to be burdensome. We spent long hours after school at least once a week discussing, debating, evaluating, and sharpening our perceptions of pupils. I began to reminisce pleasantly about those good old days when I could close the classroom door and be the ruler in my own kingdom.
>
> Then I began to see some changes in myself. Even without direct reference to my teammates' observations I was different. No feedback was required, just the presence of another adult. Previously as the day drew to an end, I'd become irritable. I spoke crossly to the pupils. Well, I screamed at them. Outside the classroom my behavior had also changed. I used to be able to tell other teachers how stupid, ornery, and uncooperative some of my pupils were. On occasion I went to class unprepared—I could pass out some workbooks. With an adult present, it is just unthinkable to have a temper tantrum or to be sarcastic to pupils. With an adult present, who is seeing the same pupil you see but with another pair of eyes, the stupid, ornery, and uncooperative pupil is seen in another perspective.
>
> Team teaching is hard work. It involves extra hours. It is highly rewarding in terms of my own self-perception. It is rewarding in my growing appreciation of pupil differences. I should not want to go back to the self-contained classroom.

And that, unfortunately, still leaves unanswered the question, "Do pupils learn any better?"

Teacher Aides

A teacher aide is a nonprofessional who assists the teacher in nonteaching activities and thus relieves the teacher for the fuller performance of professional functioning. For the pupil the function is to increase the amount of contact with an adult.

Bowman and Klopf (1968), working in contract with the U.S. Office of Education, reported results of studying fifteen demonstration projects using various levels of paraprofessionals. Most teacher aide programs centered around the ideas that more adults in the classroom would enhance the pupils' education, that the aides' concern for children was significant, that when qualified they could assist individual pupils, they could check papers, help keep track of individual learning packages, and be coaches and conductors on field trips and at recess. The aides function largely on the affective aspects of the teaching-learning transaction:

1. Listener—listens to as many as six children read, tell stories, etc.
2. Trouble-shooter—works with overly active children (up to eight) on learning and behavioral problems, helps them plan learning activities.
3. Relater—works with children who seem isolated, alone a great deal, or have crises at home. Helps new children become adjusted. Done individually or in small groups.
4. Supporter—supports children who get hurt and discouraged in learning activities, especially new tasks.
5. Inspirer—works with children as they show signs of creativity. Takes them away from class for library work and possibly on field trips for observation and research.
6. Linker—visits homes and the community, interprets goals of the school and progress of the children. Communicates community and home information to the teacher.
7. Trainer—helps older children work with younger children in cross-age teaching. Offers support and skill training.[12]

One benefit of teacher aide programs is that involving the parents of low-socioeconomic-level pupils is causing the parents and their neighbors to be

---

12   Garda W. Bowman and Gordon J. Klopf, 1968, *New Careers and Roles in the American School*, New York: Bank Street College of Education, p. 45.

more interested in the education of their children. They become supportive rather than indifferent or skeptical about what schools may mean.

Pupils as Teachers

On occasion, teachers have used pupils as teachers with gratifying results. Sometimes, particularly in communities where children have learned to be afraid of adults in authority (other than their parents) such as policemen, welfare workers, and truant officers, rapport with teachers is not easily established. One youngster can talk to and hear another. As one pupil helps another with less sophistication, the teacher-pupil consolidates his own learning. Pupils do not feel the compulsion to cover ground, so the feeling of hurry is absent. In the summer of 1970 in about 100 communities, high school students, including potential dropouts, were enrolled, with pay, in youth-tutoring-youth programs.

> . . . Most had applied mainly because it was a chance to earn some money. By the time they had been on the job a couple of weeks, however, the idea of helping younger children to learn begun to gain ground as their main motive. In mid-July, one skinny, freckle-faced tutor reported in her most professional voice that her tutees could now tell time, recite the days of the week, and identify months of the year—none of which they could do a few weeks earlier.[13]

The not-too-important question with the pupils as teachers concept is, "Who helps whom?" In one program Will, a long-haired barefoot teenager, has as many problems as his pupil David:

> The rapport between the tutor and his student grew quickly. Will missed a day during the second week of the project. The next day no faculty member reprimanded him or questioned his absence, but David did. "He really gave me the going over," said Will. "At first I thought I could put him off by saying I missed the bus. But then the kid wanted to know why I missed the bus. So I explained that I had been horsing around at home. I guess that took care of him. But, gee, telling that to a little kid. . . ."
> . . . At first many of the tutors had several charges, but as more tutors came into the program, the children were reassigned. Some of the original tutors fought hard to keep all their children: "She needs me," said a tutor, objecting to the transfer of one of her charges.[14]

13   Myrtle Bonn, 1970, "Reading Pays," *American Education*, vol. 6, no. 8, p. 26, October.
14   Mary Pat Pfeil, 1969, "Everybody's Somebody," *American Education*, vol. 5, no. 10, p. 23, December.

The Impact of Innovation

The reduction in the furor over automated instruction and the threatened demise of teachers, the backing away from "business as educator," and increasing appreciation of the value of human transaction may mean that new and fundamental concepts of the nature and needs of students will be developed (Mitzel, 1970). The trend toward individualization of learning experiences is now being countered by expression of the fact that individuals live in a society. There is need for social reaction and interaction and there is need for student choice and for teacher direction (Ohanian, 1971). There is also the possibility that the technological device B O O K will remain the cheapest, most readily available, and most adaptable aid to instruction thus far developed.

Innovation, quite apart from its impact on pupils, merits endorsement because of what it does to teachers. Any innovative practice can add zest to learning, as was the case in the **Hawthorne effect**. In addition, it is possible that many innovations work because teachers and pupils expect them to work. Conversely, innovation can, after the zest wanes, become perfunctory. Routines are psychologically tiring and can be offset by change as readily as by rest.

Reference has been made in this book, and especially in this chapter, to the "innovative package," to the need for systemwide engagement in innovation, and to the need for teamwork in using technology. Innovation, thus, may be the excuse for bringing teachers, specialists, administrators, and parents into a communicative relationship.

Finally, it is worth considering that innovation is not something that happens to and from things. It is something that occurs in people. The real impact of innovation resides in the cumulative effect on the attitudes and behaviors of individual teachers *and* multitudes of teachers.

Summary

The need for innovative approaches to education is evidenced in the failure of schools to reach *all* pupils. Although most pupils do well, and some thrive, on contemporary practices, there are some who become alienated and drop out. Others, it is felt, do not fully exploit their potential for development. There is some conviction that more emphasis on learning and less burden on teaching is a constructive orientation.

One approach to improving the educational milieu is through organization. Nongraded schools, storefront schools, educational vouchers, modular flexible programming, and contracts with business have improved the probability that teaching-learning milieus could become more salutary and stimulating. Without the trained and approving teacher, these organizational changes have little effect on what happens in the classroom.

Curricular approaches—such as programmed courses, computer-assisted instruction, and instructional aids—get somewhat closer to where pupils live than do organizational patterns. Occasionally, and for brief periods, a curricular approach may diminish the need for teachers; but, to gain maximum benefits, the endorsement and assistance of teachers is needed.

Innovative instructional techniques often have a long history. These include dialogue and small groups, the use of discovery and inquiry, deriving the curriculum from the life and experience of the child, and independent study. Each of the above-mentioned techniques runs the danger of compounding, collating, and multiplying ignorance. Teachers have the challenging task of using children's interests and knowledge to develop new interests and expand knowledge. To rely on opinion for discussion, on discovery solely, on personal life wholly, or current interests exclusively raises some crucial issues for teachers.

Suggested Additional Readings

ATKINSON, RICHARD C., AND H. A. WILSON (eds.), 1969, *Computer-assisted Instruction: A Book of Readings*, New York: Academic Press, pp. 3-61.
> Five contributors discuss the theory, possibilities, applications, and future of computer-assisted instruction.

GROSS, RONALD, AND JUDITH MURPHY (eds.), 1964, *The Revolution in the Schools,* New York: Harcourt, Brace & World, Inc.
> Technology, television, programmed study, team teaching, and autotelic responsive environments, and teachers are discussed in this paperback collection of readings.

MASON, EDWARD S., (chm.), 1969, *The Schools and the Challenge of Innovation*, New York: McGraw-Hill Book Company.
> There are chapters on programming, audio-visual aids, computer-assisted instruction, and instructional TV, but pages 110-153, on the teacher's role in innovation, are particularly relevant to the educational psychology student.

OHANIAN, VERA, 1971, "Educational Technology: A Critique," *Elementary School Journal*, vol. 71, pp. 182-197.
> Attempts to individualize instruction strenuously test a teacher's ability to diagnose and prescribe for pupil differences. A balance between individualization and social interaction is essential.

17
Evaluation for Continuing Development

There is some evidence that educational practices are constantly improving. School holding power and pupil competence show superiority when compared with *then* and *now*. It is certain, however, that there is still much to be done in implementing existing knowledge of psychological principles. Rote procedures, uniform curricula, stern disciplinary procedures, and primary emphasis upon subject matter (as contrasted to a pupil-centered emphasis) are being questioned. Grading and evaluation practices are also being modified, but the rate of change is not gratifying in view of the dangers.

It may be predicted that innovations will be superior to conventional practices to the extent that evaluation is a part of the total learning transaction, e.g., feedback, reinforcement, knowledge of progress. To the extent that evaluation can cease being a judgmental, status-ranking, end-of-term practice, conventional practices may be perceived to have values heretofore unappreciated.

In this chapter an attempt is made to show how pupil-evaluation techniques may help to make more effective use of our knowledge of motivation, ego concept, goal seeking, creativity, and principles of learning—all moving toward the implications of evaluation for the future.

Purposes and Concepts of Appraisal

The Multiple Functions of Evaluation

Much of the dissatisfaction with current approaches to evaluation stems from the fact that there is no clear and widely accepted agreement as to the purposes of evaluation and especially as to the purpose of the most widespread vehicle of evaluation, grades. Some of the functions purportedly served are:

Informing the pupil about the progress he is making
Motivating the pupil to work more effectively
Showing the pupil specific faults that need correction
Identifying special individual talents and weaknesses
Informing parents about their child's status and progress
Providing data for teachers and counselors for pupil guidance
Providing data to principals to determine placement of transfer pupils and of pupils in their next year's class
Providing data on which to base educational plans—classes, curricula, choice of college, etc.
Providing data on which to base career plans—manual worker, technical worker, professional career
Aiding employers in the choice of employees
Establishing a school record of the pupil's performance

The above list considers aspects that are known as the **cognitive** area of development. Motivation is an emotional function but, above all, it refers to how one will approach his schoolwork. There is another purpose of evaluation known as the **affective** domain (Krathwohl, Bloom, and Masia, 1964) which is receiving serious current consideration (Beatty, 1969*b*). Such things as the following are objectives considered under the affective domain:

Developing a confident self-concept
Developing persistent interests instead of resting with the acquisition of skills.[1]
Developing a positive attitude toward the process of continuous learning
Developing a tolerance for ambiguity and for the awful burden of choice and responsibility
Preventing the waste of intellect because of the creation of internal blocks (Merwin, 1969)
Practicing the skills of interpersonal communication and transaction
Considering the relative merit of *being* versus *becoming*

It may be possible to quantify such things as the above—as has been

---

1   More than forty years ago F. E. Bolton, in *Adolescent Education* (New York: Macmillan Company, 1931, p. 175), wrote, "On graduation from high school, what a boy loves is vastly more important than what he knows. . . . His attitude toward society and its problems, his attitude toward religion and morals, his attitude toward duties and obligations, are vastly more important than the few items of intellectual knowledge he has gained. His spontaneous likes and dislikes, his loves and his hates, his longings and aversions, will really determine what manner of man he shall be."

done with limited success in achievement tests—but translating them into letter grades is fatuous.

Appraisal by Grades

In the early 1900s evaluation was expressed in terms of numerical grades, with no indication that the grade received was due to percentage of subject matter mastered, comparative standing in a class, being the "teacher's pet," or having a father on the school board. The absurdity of ninety-two and a half in spelling was perceived, and numerical grades have pretty much disappeared as evaluative media. The exception is that letter grades—designed to remove the fallacy of numerical grades—are translated into numerical scores, multiplied by the number of credits in the course, added, divided by the total number of credits, and carried out to three decimal places.

Letter grades have persisted despite criticism by many educational theorists (Bernard, 1952, pp. 232ff; Goodlad, 1967; Holt, 1964; Simon, Kirschenbaum, and Napier, 1970; B. O. Smith, 1967; Strom, 1969a, p. 57; Whitla, 1969). Except for a few elementary schools which have eliminated grades in the past five or ten years, letter grades are used in many elementary schools, secondary schools, colleges, and universities. Glasser (1969, p. 68) cites an example of a medical school which has not used grades for over twenty years, but by and large, grades are a well entrenched, anachronistic, practice.

Appraisal by Evaluation

Only part of the "evaluation" of a house may be made by measuring the floor space, listing the cost of materials and labor, and citing the size and cost of the lot. The buyer's evaluation must also include style; utility of floor plan; age; neighborhood; proximity to schools, markets, and transportation; probably taxes; resale potential; and his own ability to pay. Similarly, many factors must be considered in school evaluation. Emphasis is placed on broad changes in personality, personal needs, and goals and on the achievement of *interrelated* major objectives of education (Beatty, 1969b). It has been said that measurement and grading are *atomistic*, whereas evaluation is *organismic* in scope. Grading focuses attention on minute and often disparate elements of development; evaluation considers many interrelated facts of personality and growth processes. Evaluation is continuous rather than terminal; it is a part of the teaching-learning transaction rather than a judgment of it. Grading is not contemporaneous, rather it is a reflection and ranking of the past. Evaluation provides the immediate feedback that facilitates learning.

Marion Bernstein/College Newsphoto Alliance

Evaluation capitalizes on tests; in addition, data from anecdotal records, interviews, questionnaires, pupil profiles, are needed to obtain a complete view of the child. There is still a need for test results (achievement, ability, diagnostic, etc.), but it becomes clear that *test data must be interpreted*. An IQ score must be viewed in terms of age, sensory acuity, cultural background, emotional stability, type of test used, and recency of administration. An achievement test score must be interpreted in terms of ability, competing interests, past opportunity, and personality trends.

Personality Appraisal

Interviews

Questionnaire data may be used in evaluating the personality adjustment of the child, but it is no less important to know how he feels about the circumstances and conditions which surround him. An interview is helpful in obtaining this information, but the teacher must know what kinds of questions are most likely to bring results. Typically, it is advisable to do more listening than questioning.

Questions that probe into relationships with parents, siblings, and out-of-school playmates may provide data on adjustment. Questions about the pupil's spare time activities, his interests, and his vocational aims (in the upper grades and high school) will provide clues. Building on the interests discovered in interviews tends to make the pupil increasingly independent in his study and investigations.

A teacher who was concerned about the lackadaisical schoolwork of an eighth-grade boy discovered that he was interested in electricity. She made him responsible for the lighting effects in a stage production. He planned the arrangement of footlights, spotlights, and color lighting, and installed the necessary equipment under the supervision of an electrician. His interest spread to the construction of stage sets, and he learned the play thoroughly. Acceptance by the group and his own increased feeling of personal worth enabled him to apply himself more vigorously to academic work.

An interview is more than a verbal questionnaire. One should be aware of a smile, quickened verbal tempo, a change in voice or eyes that indicates a special interest. One should follow up the lead, be it verbal or nonverbal, that suggests something of unusual importance to the individual. Give him time— time to reflect, to form the answer he wants, to elaborate, or to wander. The following contribute to rapport: genuinely wanting to know the pupil, expressing interest in his interests, liking him despite objectionable behavior, avoiding the show of emotional or moral shock at some of his expressions, and seeing to it that he has an opportunity to make a contribution to the interchange. Above all, the teacher must be genuinely friendly and accepting (Rogers, 1969, p. 109).

Interviews should encourage the pupil to solve his own problems. The teacher should encourage the pupil to make his own suggestions for improvement of behavior. The evaluation that a pupil makes of his conduct has proved to be much more productive than the gratuitous advice of teachers. If given a chance to make decisions, the pupil moves toward the assumption of responsibility (Glasser, 1969, p. 22). The word "interview" should be made to live up to its definition—a viewing between two persons.

Observation

Teachers can learn a great deal about pupils if they will take time to observe them carefully.

Remembering the child's deficit in important relationships with people and his sense of distrust toward those who have power over him, the teacher invests energy and imagination in finding ways of making contact with him and building up an image for him of an adult as a giving, supporting, caring person. She not only expresses pleasure in the child's accomplishments, but shows as much affection as the child can accept, often doing so through physical contact, touching, soothing, taking the child on her lap. She listens hard for the meaning the child is trying to convey with his poor speech and protects his early efforts at communication by giving his message back to him in correct form while sparing him the negative impact of correcting his usage.[2]

Observation leading to constructive evaluation is neither incidental nor accidental. Systematic notes on what has been seen serve a double purpose: They make the teacher increasingly aware of what is important, and they provide an inclusive record.

Objective Approaches to Personality Appraisal

One approach to personality appraisal is the inventory or questionnaire. These inventories are mainly designed for the upper grades and beyond, though some can be used from the fourth grade up. Results are typically given in percentile ranks on such items as home adjustment, social adjustment, school adjustment, self-reliance, attitudes, beliefs, feelings of worth, etc. However, it must be observed that the score on such tests is *approximate* and *representative*. Thus interviews, observations, other teachers' reports, and supplementary test data should be used in connection with the formal inventory.

The user of personality inventories must be strongly warned against putting too much credence in them. They may provide a convenient point of orientation for an interview. That is, one might tentatively determine what area of a child's life is causing difficulty, but taking and recording a score or percentile rank from the test is another matter. Actually, inventories have very low objective value, the scores have meaning only within a very limited situational range, and their diagnostic value is highly dependent on the specific training and knowledge of the administrator of the test.

The lack of precision found in the typical personal inventory precludes their satisfactory use in the construction of diagnostic adjustment profiles. If any score is used, the total score would seem to be the wisest choice. Its total reliability and validity are superior to those of the subtests.

Despite the limitations mentioned in the foregoing discussion, adjustment inventories can be helpful if they are used in conjunction with

2 Barbara Biber, 1970, "Goals and Methods in a Preschool Program for Disadvantaged Children," *Children*, vol. 17, no. 1, p. 19, January-February.

other evaluation data. The teacher must understand their weaknesses and under no circumstances, use the scores from these instruments as his sole source of information about the pupil.[3]

Sociometry (see Chapter 10) is an easy and valuable approach to the evaluation of social adjustment. Said one teacher, trying the sociogram for the first time, "I was amazed at the results. I thought I knew my pupils very well, but I learned that some of the ones whom I thought would be frequently chosen were not very popular. Some whom I thought to be rather lonesome individuals were in reality quite attractive to their classmates." Her evaluation of the pupils became more realistic. She was able to reseat and regroup the pupils so that some of the disciplinary problems she had been encountering diminished or disappeared.

Evaluating School Progress

Grading

The absurdity of grading is widely recognized. Experiments have indicated that different teachers grade the same paper with scores ranging from 70 to 95 even in such subjects as algebra and arithmetic. It is reported that on one such experiment, the scoring key was inadvertently mixed in with the papers to be scored. It received grades from below failing to excellent. In addition to being unreliable, grades permit painful and unwarranted traumatic comparisons between unequals.

Grades for course work are undesirable for many reasons: fear of failing or receiving a low grade can produce anxiety, and often hinders students rather than increasing their level of efficiency; grades often come to be perceived as the most important academic goals since honors, scholarships, "classroom fringe benefits" and many kinds of academic recognition seem to depend so much on a student's grade average; the teacher is forced to assign a single letter grade to a student, even though there are often many kinds of achievements that should be separately evaluated and recognized in a single course; and grades can also become the basis for a kind of reverse motivation in which the "gentlemen's grade" of C becomes not only a rationalization for many students, but also the cause of better students' lowering their own level of achieve-

---

3   J. Stanley Ahmann and Marvin D. Glock, 1967, *Evaluating Pupil Growth: Principles of Tests and Measurement*, Boston: Allyn and Bacon, Inc., p. 448.

ment. Grades are considered to be, like heterogeneous groupings, a necessary evil accompanying mass education.[4]

Grades are alleged to tell how well one will succeed in college. Despite heavy dependence on grades and the research of registrars, many institutions find it necessary to disqualify about 25 or 30 percent of its entering freshmen prior to graduation. Grades, despite vigorous teacher protestations, rely heavily on interpersonal comparisons of those who are initially, currently, and will in the future be, different. Grades thus constitute a barrier to the much needed step of individualizing instruction.

Substantial improvement is not discernible, except in the elementary schools where grades have been replaced by teacher-pupil, teacher-parent, and/or teacher-pupil-parent conferences. Improvement in terms of student motivation and enjoyment of learning was noted at Western Reserve University Medical School where grades are not used (Glasser, 1969, p. 68). Improvement may be hoped for if the emphasis is on people, as it is at the Center for Humanistic Study of the University of Massachusetts, in doctoral-level courses (Simon, Kirschenbaum, and Napier, 1970). However, the whole question is complicated by the question of improvement for whom: teachers, administrators, registrars, parents, pupils, or for the responsible citizen of tomorrow?

Standardized Tests

Standardized tests have a valid place in a program of evaluation. They are designed to ensure validity and reliability. Administration and scoring are precisely defined so that all pupils are tested and scored in the same manner—the **halo effect** is diminished, if not eliminated. Norms are available for guidance in the interpretation of scores. These are often expressed in percentile ranks, grade equivalents, age equivalents, or standard scores.

Standard scores must not be used to grade pupils, to judge a teacher's effectiveness, or to test the value of the curriculum. Scores should be considered fallible.

The proper use of standardized instruments should be to give the teacher a more objective view of the child. They should help him to learn the child's present stage of development. Evaluation of the pupil should be *partially* in terms of his growth from a given point (the score on a test at the beginning of a term) to a given point (the score on an equivalent test at the end of the term). The pupil need not be judged in terms of the absolute score (grade equivalent of 5 in reading, etc.) or in comparison with other members of the class. A child who has experienced a prolonged illness, frequent change in residence, or an untoward

---

4   William A. Deterline, 1962, *An Introduction to Programmed Instruction*, Englewood Cliffs, N.J.: Prentice-Hall, Inc., p. 76.

event in his family or a child who is handicapped by some sensory defect should not be "graded down" because of his lack of accomplishment. Standardized tests can be additionally fruitful when they are used as motivating influences. A pupil well below average for his class may receive vigorous stimulation from knowing that he has made notable strides from where he was at a prior time. Because educational growth is characteristically slow, it is invigorating to have some objective indication of improvement.

The following kinds of standardized tests are of particular value in programs of evaluation that look toward the continuing growth of the individual pupil:

1. Intelligence tests give the teacher an *indication* of the potential with which he is working. Tests of mental ability translated into mental ages and grade equivalents, rather than intelligence quotients, provide the teacher with valuable clues. They *help* determine whether or not the pupil should be accomplishing at or near the norms for his grade.
2. Achievement tests are available for single subjects (arithmetic, English, reading, geography, etc.) and also in the form of batteries, in which several subjects are included in one test. They enable the teacher to estimate progress over a period of time.
3. Diagnostic tests are available in such subjects as arithmetic, language, and reading, and aid the teacher in locating specific areas of difficulty within subject areas. They do not tell what should be done by way of remediation. They give indications that narrow the search for difficulties as teachers do the diagnosing.
4. Inventories of interest aid in the discovery of more productive approaches for individual pupils and provide tentative help in choosing the curricula and vocations that will be most stimulating to them. To the extent that an interest test helps a pupil avoid an area where an interest might be developed, the test must be regarded with skepticism.
5. Personality tests may help the pupil and teacher locate specific areas of difficulty in personal and social adjustment, but they make no diagnoses. To the extent that results fall into the hands of those who might misuse or overinterpret the results, personality instruments may be regarded as hazardous.

Teacher-made Tests

The most widely used tests in classrooms are those devised by teachers. Such tests, especially essay tests, have been much, and consistently, criticized because of their typical lack of **validity**, **reliability**, and **objectivity**. Strange tales about scores obtained have made teachers highly skeptical about using classroom tests as the basis of grades, but except in some elementary schools, the skepticism has not been sufficient to lead to the demise and burial of grades. One tale is that one paper scored by several teachers has been graded all the way from F to A. Another is that the same paper, scored unwittingly twice by one teacher received different scores. Because of the widespread knowledge about this lack of reliability and objectivity, there has been a trend away from essay examinations to the so-called objective type test items—T-F, completion, multiple-choice, and matching. The results in terms of inconsistent scores are only somewhat improved over essay examinations.

The use of any examinations, standardized or teacher-made, can be constructive (despite their defects) if they are used for feedback on what is being learned, if they are used tentatively to locate weaknesses and strengths, and if they are used as guidance for next steps. In fact, these are just the kinds of purposes that periodic tests serve in many learning packet programs. The pupil gets his packet, studies the objectives, gathers and uses the reading materials, performs the exercises or experiments, and when he feels that he is ready, he takes the examination. If his score is high enough, he goes on to another packet. If it does not reach a stated standard he works through the difficult points and takes another examination. It is unnecessary for the examinations to be translated into grades.

As soon as the scores on standardized tests or teacher-made tests are used to allocate grades, to place pupils in various tracks, to close doors of opportunity (the technical courses versus college preparatory), or otherwise sort and classify pupils, it becomes essential that objectivity, reliability, and validity become major concerns of the classroom teacher.

Essay examinations have a place in the teaching-learning situation because they call for organizing, integrating, and interpreting material. It is argued that such examinations help pupils to think logically, that pupils will profit from the reflection and organization which an essay test requires. However, writing what the teacher wants under the pressure of time (five questions in fifty minutes) does not do a great deal for reflection, organization, and logical presentation. Elsewhere in this book, it is emphasized that an important ingredient in logical thinking is *time*. Essays written without the pressure of time in minutes or without the threat of grades have much educative merit. Desirably they should be ignored as *the* basis for grades.

The T-F, "objective" type test is so deceptively simple that it is popular with teachers who do a little more than prepare five essay-type questions in their heads on their way to class. It is an appealing item for those who see the world in terms of black and white. But for those who take a discerning look, the simplicity of T-F disappears. For example:

> Educational psychology is the study of classroom conditions which facilitate learning.

It has been found that bright students, who know the material well, do relative poorly on T-F items because they can and do note exceptions and nuances which are overlooked by others—including the testmaker. The test composed of T-F items is criticized because of the 50-percent chance of guessing correctly when one does not know the item. Chances of guessing correctly are increased when the item contains words such as "many," "some," "often," and "several." At least they provide grounds for argument, if the teacher will permit attack of the position he has assumed. Students with test sophistication know that long items tend to be T. Some testmakers use a scoring formula like R—W (right minus wrong) to discourage guessing instead of simply counting the number correct. Adding even this statistical correction cannot improve an item that was unreliable to begin with.

Multiple-choice items are ones which can call for both information and interpretation:

> The IQ is (1) a measure of one's intelligence (2) an indication of one's intellectual status (3) an indication of one's rate of mental development (4) the numerical index of inherent intellectual potential (5) the most dependable index of mental ability.

One is asked to indicate the correct answer or the best answer. With five possible responses, guessing is minimized. Some argue that tests consisting of T-F or multiple-choice items tend to fragment learning—that one learns minutia and is not concerned with learning the overall theme or pervasive message. Knowing definitions, for instance, of specialized words will be helpful in taking multiple-choice questions in most subjects.

Matching questions call for the student to associate items in two columns with each other. Usually, to avoid guessing by elimination, the two columns are of different length. For example:

> Match the word in the second column with the word in the first column by placing the corresponding letter in the space provided.
>
> | _____Evaluation | *a* IQ |
> | | *b* Teacher's complex |
> | _____Motivation | *c* Objectivity |
> | | *d* Guidance |
> | _____Thinking | *e* Cognitive |
> | | *f* Heterostasis |
> | _____Adjustment | *g* Identification |

Completion tests call for the insertion of a word of phrase in a space which best completes an accurate or correct statement.

> A group of questions, or statements to be checked regarding one's behavior and adjustment patterns is called _____.

There are many suggestions which may be made regarding improving the teacher-made test.[5] Herein the suggestions for improving these evaluation devices will be confined to recommending:

Essay-type examinations are easy to prepare but time-consuming to score and are lacking in objectivity due to the **halo effect** and teachers' mental sets.

T-F items are easy to score, hard to make, and tend to militate against the able and well-prepared student.

Matching questions call for judgment, integration of subject matter, and factual knowledge. The items are difficult to make.

Multiple-choice questions are time consuming to make, time saving to score, and call for both knowledge of facts and (depending on how made) may call for judgment and application.

Completion questions are rather easy to make, but the variety of defensible answers which pupils can contrive make it similar to the essay test in subjectivity.

Whatever type of test is used, the teacher should be aware of the fact that pupils will study differently for an essay examination than for a short-answer-type test. Hence, one must choose his test items in terms of the course objectives he has stipulated.

Desirably, the essay-type examination and the various short-answer types should be used both as evaluation and teaching devices. That is, after the test is given the answers should be discussed and improvements in the students' answers should be suggested—without resulting in a grade. To transform the total score into a term grade will result in a defensive attitude on the part of teachers and pupils which impedes learning. Again one must ask, "What are the objectives of the testing program or the educational experience?"

A Technique for Using Test Scores

Many teachers express the aspiration of helping the student work up to his capacity. Too often this means little more than getting him to work a little

5   J. Stanley Ahmann and Marvin D. Glock, 1967, *Evaluating Pupil Growth*, 3d ed., Boston: Allyn and Bacon, Inc., pp. 156-212. Suggestions are made for making and scoring essay and short-answer achievement tests.

Robert L. Ebel, 1965, *Measuring Educational Achievement*, Englewood Cliffs, N.J.: Prentice-Hall, Inc. Several chapters are devoted to improving classroom tests.

William J. Micheels and M. Ray Karnes, 1950, *Measuring Educational Achievement*, New York: McGraw-Hill Book Company. Chapters are devoted to principles of test making, and then separate chapters are devoted to multiple-choice, matching, T-F, and completion-type tests.

Jerome Siedman, 1965, *Readings in Educational Psychology*, 2d ed., Boston: Houghton Mifflin Company, pp. 339-356. Three selections deal with improving essay examinations and short answer type questions.

harder than he did last term or in comparison to his peers. One practical way to relate capacity and achievement is to use the quadrant of expectancy (Figure 17-1). MA scores are plotted on one axis, with the median MA being the center line. Achievement scores are plotted on the other axis, with the median grade score being the center line. Figure 17-1 shows the scores for a fourth grade class at midyear. Each pair of scores is given one tally; thus pupil 1, having an MA of 132 and an achievement equivalent to third grade, is tallied at the intersection of the lines for these two scores.

Pupils above the diagonal, in quadrant I (8 and 14), may well receive some help. Possibly their retardation is due to too much previously applied pressure. Quadrant III indicates that pupils 1, 5, and 11 are "retarded" despite having average or better-than-average ability—special help for them may be quite fruitful. But it is possible that they suffer from some sensory difficulty, emotionally disturbed homes, tense sibling relationships, or lack of a sense of personal worth. Pupil 10 (quadrant II) may profit from some encouragement; although he is above class average, attempts might be made to have him evaluate himself in terms of where he was, is, and might be.

> A seventh grade teacher, exposed to the postulation of the quadrant, saw that one low-ability boy was achieving above class average. She then noted that he came to school early, stayed late, and frequently did not play at recess time. She next noticed that he was a cipher in the classroom. He made no contact with his peers, and they virtually ignored him. A conference with his parents revealed that they were pleased with his studying so much on weekends. The result of conversations between parents, pupil, and teacher resulted in everyone's playing down the academic, which had previously been lauded, and giving the boy encouragement in play and social activities.

This graphic representation of scores makes it easier for the teacher to see those who need special study. In the past, too often the teacher's major attention has been devoted to bringing pupils up to average, regardless of their potential.[6] Further, the child with high ability who was average or better in accomplishment (e.g., pupil 10, Figure 17-1) was neglected, despite the fact that he was not working in accord with his ability.

Teacher-Pupil Evaluative Conferences

One function of evaluation should be to clarify the pupil's responsibility for his educational growth, which can be done in teacher-pupil evaluative con-

---

6   It may help to remember that, by definition, 50 percent of the pupils, in any item of measurement, are below average.

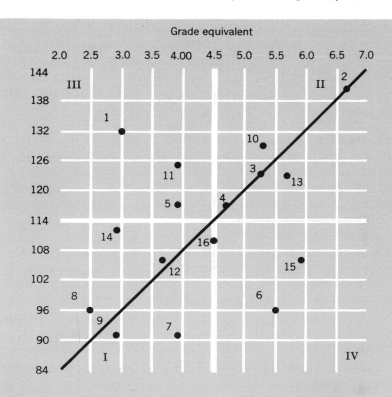

Figure 17-1 Using standardized test scores in pupil education. Source: Courtesy of Victor N. Phelps, Portland State University.

ferences. A first step is to define objectives *in terms that the pupil can understand.* Of necessity, there must be many objectives to fit the many activities of the school and the many variations between individuals—thus, the outcomes of learning are many and varied (Merwin, 1969). A few representative items to be evaluated by the pupil and teacher might include (1) ability to carry out self-directed activities, (2) ability to solve problems in arithmetic appropriate to developmental level, (3) interest in varied pursuits, (4) skill in written expression, (5) skill in oral expression, (6) manifestation of courtesy in dealing with others, (7) execution of assigned or accepted responsibilities, (8) respect for school property and the property of others, and (9) attention to personal appearance. Thus academic subjects, personal interests, social habits, and attitudes toward citizenship are involved. An advantage of teacher-pupil evaluation is that the pupil understands the marking system and what it means exactly.

Teachers find that teacher-pupil conferences are no more time consuming than is the attempt to grade accurately and conscientiously. Of course, if grades are assigned arbitrarily, teacher-pupil evaluation is comparatively time consuming. The element of arbitrariness is reflected in one upper-grade student's remark: "You should not expect to get a good grade the first six weeks. If you did, then you could not show improvement in later periods. Just wait, next time you will have some grades that are higher than the ones you now have."

Four advantages of teacher-pupil conferences are worth considering:

1. Evaluation clarifies the pupil's concept of what he is working for.
2. Evaluation stimulates the child to ask questions that he feels are significant to him.
3. Evaluation makes possible the formulation of progressively higher objectives that are appropriate to the individual's present status and potentiality.
4. Evaluation helps the pupil to focus on growth rather than end-of-activity status.

A sound evaluative process is an integral and continuous part of the teaching-learning process. The daily feedback, affirmation of a completed contract, suggestions as to source material, discussion as to the advisability and direction of supplementary activities, and talking of possible next steps are parts of evaluation (Bloom, 1969, p. 41). These are incidental acts in most classrooms.

Parent-Teacher Conferences

Because the home and family constitute the greatest part of a child's psychological environment, bringing the school and parents together is good procedure, quite apart from evaluation. Three major advantages accrue. First, preparing for the conference helps the teacher obtain a better understanding of the human being with whom he is working. Second, parents can come to a better appreciation of what teachers are attempting to do. Third, the pupil will profit from the positive view that the teacher is encouraged to take; that is, knowing that effective conferences start with remarks about favorable characteristics, the teacher looks more searchingly for the pupil's good points. Finally, there is the possibility that the teacher or the parent has perceived some attitude or pattern of behavior overlooked by the other that can be helpful; e.g., one of them knows that praise causes Craig to "rest on his oars" or that criticism causes Vicki to quit entirely.

Bringing parents and teachers together results in a type of evaluation that fosters optimum pupil development. Some believe that parent-teacher-pupil conferences would be a further improvement. There are, however, inherent shortcomings to the conference plan that makes the search for still better methods necessary. It is, of necessity, time consuming. Unless conferences are a part of the regular teaching load, they impose a burden on teachers.

Manning (1971, pp. 281-289) asserts that evaluation and reporting should serve seven functions. He regards planned teacher-parent conferences as the best, because they are the only approach to evaluation that fulfills all functions:

1. Evaluation should convey information about the pupil's attitude toward school, relationships with others, strengths and deficiencies, status and progress, and ways parents can help.
2. Evaluation should emphasize the uniqueness of the individual pupil. It should be personalized.
3. Evaluation should involve the pupil's assessment of himself. Samples of work, goals worked toward, self concept, special skills, and curiosity are areas which might be included herein.
4. Evaluation should convey information. Grades, scores, and marks cannot communicate status, progress, strengths, specific weaknesses, special needs, or how parents can help; but conferences can transmit such information.
5. Evaluation should promote constructive, cooperative action.
6. Evaluation should be fair. Too many schools fail children because their best is not good enough. Evaluation considers background, starting point, ability, and progress.
7. Evaluation should have reference to standards; but rather than to fail a child because he has not reached fifth-grade standards by the time he is eleven, the achievement he has made is noted, and suggestions for further development are proposed and discussed.

The Essentials of Evaluation

Definition of Goals

The first step in evaluating teaching and learning is to define the purposes of instruction (Mager, 1968). It is necessary to see these broad objectives *in terms of the particular pupil* one is teaching. For example, the objective of citizenship might include such subgoals as being responsible for school property, keeping the school grounds and classroom clean, executing assigned responsibilities, participating in group activities, observing rules and regulations, and voicing one's opinion in group discussion.

If pupils are not invited to define objectives, at least they should be allowed to discuss and modify them. Whatever the technique used in formulation, the following tests should be applied to the statements in order that they may be productive of good learning and helpful evaluation:

1. Can the pupil understand the statement of the goal? This can be easily determined by having pupils tell what the statement means to them.
2. Can the goal be stated in terms of pupil behavior? The objective should be to accomplish some desirable change in the actions of pupils.
3. Is the goal related to the needs of the pupil? If the objective does not have meaning for the individual, the result is likely to be learning only at the low level of memorization and verbalization.
4. Can the goal be achieved by the pupil? This suggests the need for constant evaluation to meet present level of ability.
5. Is it possible to devise techniques for evaluating progress toward the goal? Unless this can be answered affirmatively, the resulting evaluation will be vague.
6. Does the goal have both present and future reference for the pupil? This criterion will help in deciding which school activities are most desirable and least desirable. This is important in a society where the schools are called upon to perform more and more functions.

The Dilemma of Behavioral Goals

It is logical that translating educational activities into definable goals is essential to sound evaluation. Some persons believe that too often in the past goals were somewhat vaguely or even unrealistically stated. In order to make them meaningful and place them in a category where they could be evaluated, it would be helpful to state them in terms of behavior. One of the prominent proponents of behavioral objectives states:

When clearly defined goals are lacking, it is impossible to evaluate a course or program efficiently, and there is no sound basis for selecting appropriate materials, content, or instructional methods. After all, the machinist does not select his materials or specify a schedule for construction until he has his blueprints (objectives) before him. Too often, however, one hears teachers arguing the relative merits of textbooks or other aids of the classroom versus the laboratory, without ever specifying just what goal the aid or method is to assist in achieving. I cannot emphasize too strongly the point that an instructor will function in a fog of his own making until he knows just what he wants his students to be able to do at the end of the instruction. . . .

Unless goals are clearly and firmly fixed in the minds of both parties, tests are at best misleading; at worst, they are irrelevant, unfair, or useless. To be useful they must measure *performance in terms of the goals.*[7]

There is some belief on the part of educational theorists and school practitioners that behavioral objectives are not entirely adequate. They may cause teachers to give too much attention to the trivial, but definable, goals at the cost of sufficient emphasis on more important objectives which are not readily amenable to definition and measurement (Ausubel, 1968, p. 351). Some educators are not sure that behavioral objectives are the really important features of the teaching-learning transaction.

Since the central goal of the school ought to be to develop the ability to think, why have we traditionally treated all goals as if they were equally desirable? The reason is found, I believe, precisely in our defining our goals in terms of behavior, and this we have done under the assumption that the child's education ought to equip him to succeed in the "real" world—that is, in the world in which he will live and act and interact with other human beings. We have been educating him for the world of sense experience. Yet, as we have seen, the world of sense can no longer be looked on as the only world. The worlds of abstract reason may be just as real, or even more real. . . .

I am not trying to say that I hold behavior to be unimportant. It is obviously one of the elements of life which education must affect. But I am saying that to elevate it to the central role is fallacious and leads to considerable mischief. Yet this error appears to be quite characteristic of the times; it might be called the educational fallacy of the twentieth century.[8]

7   Robert F. Mager, 1962, *Preparing Instructional Objectives*, Palo Alto, Calif.: Fearon Publishers, Inc., pp. 3-4.
8   James E. Russell, 1965, *Change and Challenge in American Education*, Boston: Houghton Mifflin Company, pp. 41, 43.

The reader may, by now, be wondering what educational objectives look like. The author (for illustrative purposes but not as a model) would state the objectives for the study of this chapter as follows:

Objectives for the Study of Pupil Evaluation

To develop in the student an appreciation of the thesis that measurement is only a part, but an important part, of evaluation.

To develop in the student an appreciation of the high merit of regarding evaluation as a continuous and ongoing part of education (informal as well as formal)—evaluation is a form of feedback.

To plant the seed of the idea that feelings (e.g., love of learning, curiosity, healthy ego concept) are higher on the scale of objectives than are cognitive learnings—but do not exclude cognition.

To indoctrinate the student with the idea that letter grades cannot embrace all the objectives of education, that they are unfair competitively, and they are often cruel and discouraging when education is symbolized through them.

To help teachers know that standardized tests have value for individual assessment when data are used to provide clues as to starting points and to indicate progress.

To help teachers know that standardized tests have merit when used as part of the program of all-school assessment.

To suggest to teachers some approaches to better pupil evaluation.

If the objectives of this chapter were expressed in behavioral terms they might be about as follows:

Behavioral Objectives of Pupil Evaluation

The teacher can evaluate his pupils continuously, fairly, and individually.

The teacher can use tests and inventories to supplement interviews and observations.

The teacher takes steps to eliminate competitive—comparative grading practices in his school.

The teacher defines the objectives of his class in terms of the philosophy of the school as developed by his colleagues.

The teacher keeps in mind that the overall goal of education in a rapidly changing society demands evaluation of pupils in terms of their enjoying the continuous and continuing process of education.

The foregoing objectives are presented as a point of departure for discussion. This might be followed by some exercises in developing objectives for a course the student will teach at a later time.

Approaches to an Evaluation Program

If our knowledge of educational psychology is brought to bear on evaluative processes, it must first be recognized that neither a single instrument nor a single symbol can suffice (Taylor, 1968).

1. Teachers, together with their pupils and other teachers, should examine the broad statements of education to see which are particularly pertinent in the present situation.
2. Teachers, together with their pupils and other teachers, should translate the broad objectives into definable and achievable behaviors.
3. Intelligence tests should be used to give an indication of the pupil's present level of mental development and should be used to supplement other data.
4. Standardized achievement tests should be used so that one has objective information regarding the pupil's growth in specific subject areas over a given period of time.
5. Diagnostic tests should be used to narrow the range of search for a specific area of difficulty for individual pupils.
6. Personality inventories should be used as clues to pertinent questions.
7. Case studies should be used for pupils who are manifesting unusual difficulties of adjustment.
8. Interviews should always be used in interpreting such data as are listed. *How the child feels* is no less important than the conditions that surround and impinge upon him.
9. **Anecdotal records** are valuable in describing behavior that is difficult to evaluate by means of test scores or case-study data.
10. Sociometry provides a means of evaluating interpersonal relations and gives clues to the grouping of pupils that will lead to more harmonious social relations and to social growth.
11. Home visits by the teacher have the double advantage of helping the teacher see the child in terms of his environment and helping parents arrive at a more objective evaluation of the school.
12. Letters sent to the home by the teacher tend to get away from the stereotype of traditional report cards. Letters necessarily give attention to individual differences.
13. Teacher-made tests have their place in a comprehensive evaluation program. Such tests can be made to fit short units of study or brief periods of school. They can be made to fit the particular objectives that are dictated by the local situation.

14. Pupil diaries or logs can serve as a means of keeping the pupil informed of his progress. Teachers need but to indicate the items that are of educational significance.
15. Rating scales and questionnaires can be used to supplement other bases for evaluation, such as personality inventories, objective test data, and anecdotal records.
16. Cumulative records that summarize all the above data or contain representative samples of the pupil's work should be regarded as essential instruments of the evaluation program (Findley, 1963). Care must be taken so that material is not allowed to accumulate. Test results should be recorded in appropriate places and dates noted. Periodically, the material should be examined to see whether it contributes to an understanding of the child. Too thick a folder discourages the teacher's use of it.

Emphasis on the Total Program

It has been emphasized throughout this book that the child as a learner has emotions, physical characteristics, and social relationships that influence the acquisition of intellectual information. The pupil cannot be separated from his home and family and community influences. Hence, the emphasis in evaluation must be upon the entire program of education—its broadened scope and its innovative thrusts (Tyler, 1969). Evaluation is a *continuing* aspect of the learning process, and it involves the use of *all* the instruments available. If evaluation is made on the basis of one or two instruments, the result is likely to be grading rather than evaluation. The purpose of evaluation is to make specific some precise steps in further and continuing development.

Teachers should include themselves in the evaluative process. Some of this can be self-evaluation, using criteria selected or derived from professional reading. Some of it may be done by supervisors and principals, whose job is made more effective if teachers express interest in the evaluation of themselves. Despite the fallacious belief that personality is formed at an early age, or any age, patterns of behavior undergo steady change. Evaluation by self or others helps that change to become directed instead of being a matter of drifting. Teachers who exemplify the learning process will use evaluation throughout their entire careers to determine where they are weak and how they can improve. Evaluation gives them an incentive to continued professional and personal development; only through such continuous growth can teachers make their maximum contribution to the growth of children.

Summary

One of the more perplexing problems of formal education is that of pupil evaluation. The difficulty probably derives from the fact that evaluation is such an important aspect of so many phases of education. Not only are many items—together with complex interrelationships—to be considered in evaluation, but there are also widely varying purposes of education to be served.

Grading is still widely used, but there is much justifiable dissatisfaction with the attempt to reduce so much to a single letter or number. This is particularly true at the elementary level, where universal education brings such a diverse population together. Even at the professional level (e.g., prospective teachers or doctors), it is doubtful that grades are truly indicative of the global aspects of assessment.

Observations and interviews are viewed with comparatively high regard in personality assessment. Personality inventories and questionnaires are held in low esteem and must, for the most part, be used as points of orientation for further study and as supplementary and corroborative evidence rather than as measuring and diagnostic devices.

The psychologically sound approach to evaluation involves the use and interpretation of standardized test data, supplemented and corroborated by teacher-made tests. The defects and limitations of both standardized and teacher-made tests are lessened when results are not made the bases for grading. Evaluation should be an ongoing and essential aspect of the educative process—not just an end-of-period signing off. It should involve talking with pupils about specific aspects of learning activities. Because parents are important partners in the educational enterprise, teacher-pupil-parent conferences are growing in use and in esteem. Standardized tests are useful in providing objective data, but grades should not depend on their results.

Effective evaluation depends on the precise statement of goals, which can then be translated into definable and achievable—though not always tangible—objectives. These objectives can then be discussed meaningfully with the purpose of indicating next steps in educational development.

Suggested Additional Readings

GLASSER, WILLIAM, 1969, *Schools without Failure*, New York: Harper & Row, Publishers, Incorporated.

   A psychiatrist who serves as a consultant to schools proposes changing the grading system and eliminating the F. If a pupil does get into a course where he is unable to perform satisfactorily, he is allowed to withdraw and move to something else without penalty or being branded.

GUBA, EGAN G., AND JOHN J. HORVAT, 1970, "Evaluation during Development," *Bulletin of the School of Education, Indiana University*, vol. 46, no. 2, pp. 21-45.

   The authors demonstrate that much of the perplexity which accompanies evaluation is neglecting to identify the *kinds* and *stages* of decisions which are to be made as the result of evaluation.

MAGER, ROBERT F., 1968, *Developing Attitude toward Learning*, Palo Alto, Calif.: Fearon Publishers, Inc.

A leader in the area of evaluation may be allowed to introduce himself:
"To rise from a zero [as a teacher]
To Big Campus Hero
To answer these questions you'll strive:
    Where am I going,
    How shall I get there, and
    How will I know I've arrived?"

MANNING, DUANE, 1971, *Toward a Humanistic Curriculum*, New York: Harper & Row, Publishers, Incorporated, pp. 276-300.

The last two chapters in this book present the problem of evaluation as it appears when pupils, rather than information acquisition, is the focus. The author criticizes grades but perceives planned parent conferences as a commendable approach.

TYLER, RALPH W., (ed.), 1969, National Society for the Study of Education, 68th Yearbook, part II, *Educational Evaluation: New Roles, New Means,* Chicago: University of Chicago Press.

Basic issues of evaluation, evaluation for guidance, evaluation in relationship to college admission and scholarships, in terms of individualized instruction, and in terms of innovation and new media are among the things discussed by nineteen experts.

Appendix
The Concept of Correlation

The word "correlation" is a helpful one in psychology and education. It is a statistical term indicating *relationship*.

We frequently want to know whether two things have any connection. We may wish to know what effect a certain kind of home environment has on learning. We should like to have an answer to the question: Are athletes characteristically slow in academic work? Partial answers to such problems are phrased in terms of correlation. Thus the growth principle "Correlation rather than compensation is the general rule" means that there is a tendency for persons who are gifted in one area to be superior in other traits. If exacting measurements of the related traits are available, the degree of relationship may be expressed in terms of a "coefficient of correlation." This is a numerical expression of the amount of relationship between two factors.

If a number of individuals are measured in two things and the relative order, or comparative rank, of each individual is the same in both measures, the measures are said to be perfectly positively correlated. That is, the largest measure of one item (say, IQ) is found in the same person who has the largest measure of another item (say, vocabulary), and the next highest scores in both measures are found in the same person, etc., through the entire list, until the lowest scoring person in IQ has the lowest vocabulary score. This perfect positive correlation would be expressed as +1.00 (read "plus one, point, oh, oh"). This is *not* a percentage score. In some instances, it is conceivable that much of one thing would correspond to a lack (and to a corresponding amount of lack) of another. Thus, if the person scoring highest in IQ had the lowest vocabulary score, the next highest in IQ had the next lowest vocabulary score, etc., the correlation would be expressed as a perfect negative correlation, written as –1.00 (read "minus one, point, oh, oh"). Actually, such perfect correlations exist only in things subject to physical laws—not in terms of psychological measurement of traits now available.

Perfect positive correlation is shown in Charles' law: "The volume of a gas is directly proportional to the temperatures to which it is exposed—pressure remaining equal." That is, the greater the temperature, the greater the volume. There is a definite increase in the volume, which corresponds to each degree of rise in temperature. Perfect negative correlation is illustrated in Boyle's law: "The volume of a gas is inversely proportional to the pressure exerted upon it—temperature remaining constant." That is, the greater the pressure, the less the volume—the more you have of one thing, the less you have of another, and in proportionate amounts.

Human traits are less directly related than can be indicated by either a plus or minus 1.00. The relationship typically falls somewhere between no correlation (0.00) and a high positive, but not a perfect, correlation. Thus, there is no relationship between hair color and IQ. There is a slight positive correlation between size and intelligence (.10 to .25), but it is so slight that prediction for individuals would be foolish. The same thing may be said of correlations of good looks and intelligence—positive, but slight. Measures of school achievement and intelligence may be more highly correlated (.40 or thereabouts), but still one cannot say that the highest pupil in IQ should or will be the highest-ranking pupil on an achievement test. Two different tests of intelligence will correlate still more highly (.70 or so) than do achievement and IQ. Two forms of the same test will correlate still more highly (.85 or more). The meaning of coefficient of correlation may now be summarized roughly as follows:

1.00	Smoke drifts in the direction the wind blows and at the same rate.
.90	Two forms of a reliable test may correlate to this extent.
.80 .70	Different tests of the same trait may agree to this extent. Helpful in predicting probable future of individuals (success in school, etc.)
.60 .50 .40	Various intellectual traits may agree to this extent.
.30 .20	Just enough correlation to disprove stereotyped misconceptions, but of no value in individual prediction. Helpful in indicating a trend or generalization.
.10 0.00 –.10	No connection between the two traits or measures.

Human traits are so fluid that measurement of one trait will differ from day to day for one subject. The sum of the scores of thirty pupils in IQ or arithmetic achievement varies even if the measurements are taken on the same day (though individual fluctuations tend to cancel one another). Hence, a paired set of scores will not consistently show the same relationship. For this reason, the concept of probable error is usually used with the coefficient of correlation. For example, the relationship between a set of reading scores and a set of IQ scores may be .53 ± .12 (read "coefficient of correlation of point five three, plus or minus twelve"). It means that if other correlations were computed with similar tests and subjects, half the correlations could be expected to be between .65 (.53 + .12) and .41 (.53 – .12). The correlation is said to be significant if it is four or more times as large as its probable error.

In educational psychology, correlations are used to indicate the relationships between traits, between the results of two administrations of a test (coefficient of reliability), and between test results and other measures or estimates of the same trait (coefficient of validity).

Glossary

It has been indicated in the text that clarity of meaning in vocabulary usage is an aid to clear thinking. Attention to the terminology of educational psychology is therefore another step to a functional understanding of the subject. Of course, definitions are not enough. The student should try to form a concept of the word or term.

Some of the words in this glossary are familiar ones but may have a slightly different use from, or narrower concept than, the popular usage. Other words will probably be encountered only in educational or psychological literature. Whatever the category of a particular word, an understanding of it will contribute to improved thinking.

Ability. Refers to what can actually be done as contrasted to capacity—which is the potential for developing an ability. Developed capacity is an ability.

Ability grouping. A subdivision of students into groups so that the range of individual differences is narrowed. Ability grouping may be made on the basis of one kind of measure or may consider several correlated measures. Homogeneous grouping is not a good synonym.

Active recall. Remembering or recalling without the use of aids or reminders. Remembering without specific and concrete clues.

Adolescence. A phase of development that follows childhood and precedes maturity. Sometimes referred to as the "teen age." Roughly, the period between twelve and twenty years of age.

Adrenin. One of the hormones secreted by the smooth (endocrine or ductless) glands called the "adrenals." Plays a major part in emotional manifestations.

Affective. Relating to feelings or emotions. Frequently contrasted to "cognitive."

Alienation. The feeling of not belonging, of being in a strange and unfriendly environment. Feeling powerless to affect the direction of one's own life.

Ambivalence. A state in which one contemporaneously has feelings which are polar opposites: love-hate, interest-boredom, self-other, anger-affiliation.

Anecdotal record. A brief and usually periodic recording of typical, characteristic, or significant incidents in the child's school life. The objective is to observe and record facts and then (without judgment) try to understand feelings.

Aptitude. Capacity, plus a probability that the individual will develop an ability. Aptitude usually refers to a rather narrow field of behavior, e.g., musical or mechanical aptitude.

Attention. Focusing of the sense organs upon a particular source of stimulation. Attention may be contrasted to interest, which is long-term or enduring. Attention may be brief.

Attitude. A predisposition to act in a certain way. A state of readiness that influences a person to act in a given manner.

Atypical. Deviation from the "normal" behavior or growth pattern.

Authoritarianism. The attitude that control and power should reside external to the judgment and experience of the individual; the stance that the one in power has the right to make decisions and prescribe behaviors.

Basic encounter group. See *Interpersonal process group.*

Behaviorism. A viewpoint (or school) of psychology in which stress is placed on the primacy of external stimulation. The environment is considered to be prepotent. The phenomenon of "consciousness" is excluded from consideration.

Branching program. The type of programmed study in which one may skip frames if he makes no errors, but if mistakes are made, he is referred to another sequence which deals with the specific error.

Capacity. Potential for development. That which one is potentially capable of doing or being. See also *Ability.*

Catharsis. A process of cleaning out; specifically, a getting rid of unpleasant emotions or tensions through talking, writing, playing, drawing, etc. A means of emotional release.

Chronological age. The actual length of time an individual has lived since birth. Usually expressed in years and months. Synonymous with "life age."

Cognitive. Relating to the conscious life—knowing, remembering, judging, reasoning, etc. The contrasting aspect of "affective."

Compensation. Making up for a real or imagined deficiency by stressing the development of a skill or ability. Indirect compensation is the development of skill other than the one that is weak. Direct compensation is the expenditure of more time and energy to overcome the particular real or felt defect. Also, the erroneous belief that a weakness in one aspect of the personality is offset by a balancing strength.

Concept. The mental image of a thing or class of things formed by generalization from particulars. As used herein, the characterization of an idea that is broader and more inclusive than a definition.

Concomitant learning. Knowledge or skill that is not specifically aimed at but accompanies the learning sought after.

Conditioning. The process of getting the organism to respond to a substitute stimulus as though it were a natural stimulus for that behavior.

Configuration. A Gestalt term referring to the fact that stimuli occur in patterns rather than as isolated phenomena. Also connotes the fact that stimuli are not to be considered apart from the organism that is affected by the patterned stimuli.

Congenital. Existing at the time of birth. A condition not due to heredity but to birth or prenatal conditions.

Constant IQ. The theory that IQ does not change—that apparent changes in IQ are due to deficiencies in the instruments for evaluating intellectual growth.

Contingent relationship. A situation in which what pupils do and say affects what the teacher does, as well as vice versa.

Control group. In an experimental situation, the group with which the experimental group is compared. All factors are held constant in the control group, whereas in the experimental group, one factor is intentionally varied.

Correlation. 1. Numerical: A statistical concept used to indicate the degree of relationship between two sets of paired phenomena. Correlation varies from a −1.00 through 0.0 to a +1.00. 2. Subject matter: Relating what is learned in one subject-matter area to that learned in another area, e.g., mathematics and science, science and social studies, social studies and literature.

Cramming. Attempting to compress into one long learning period the study that should have been done over a period of days, weeks, or months. Cramming contrasts with spaced practice, which is short periods of regular study intermittently distributed over a prolonged period.

Culturally different. Having experienced child-rearing patterns, home, school, and work milieus which differ from those of the mainstream, predominant, middle-class culture and, therefore, having internalized different values.

Decile. One of the nine points that divide a ranked distribution into ten parts, each containing one-tenth of all cases.

Defense mechanism. A kind of evasive behavior in which the individual seeks to avoid, or deny the existence of, conditions that make adjustment difficult.

Development. Change or increase in function due to experience and/or exercise. For *practical* purposes, no sharp line of distinction can be drawn between growth and development.

Developmental task. A specific learning problem that arises at a particular stage of life and that an individual must accomplish to meet the demands of his culture and next developmental tasks. The nature of the task is such that one learning is related to, merges into, and forms the basis for the next *throughout life*.

Deviate. One who departs from the wide band of what is called "normality" in any measured trait. One who would be placed at either extreme end of the normal curve of distribution. See also *Atypical*.

Dialogue. Conversation between two persons in which both are listened to and both are heard.

Differentiation. 1. The process by which body parts and functions become increasingly distinct from other parts and functions. 2. The changed perception of a field of stimulation whereby the observer sees unique parts and values more clearly.

Discovery. The teaching technique by which pupils are encouraged to perceive and formulate on their own, in their own words, relationships and contingencies between and among varied data.

Dyslexia. Extreme difficulty in learning to read, attributed to physiological impairment or dysfunction which contributes to faulty perception.

Education. The processes by which behavior is changed and, ideally, improved through experience; especially, the formal situation in which the experiences are thoughtfully guided by an expert.

Educational psychology. The branch of applied psychology in which the facts, theories, and hypotheses of the science of psychology are studied, with particular reference to their application and implementation in schools.

Emergency theory. The theory which asserts that emotions are a means of preparing the individual for fight or flight. Also known as the "Cannon theory of emotion."

Emotion. A stirred-up state of the organism that involves mental, physical, physiological, situational, and habitual factors. Emotion embraces both strong and mild states and pleasant and unpleasant ones.

Empirical. Based on experience or observation; that which is known on the basis of what has been seen and experienced. Frequently contrasted with experimental evidence.

Endocrines. The glands of internal secretion, such as the thyroid, parathyroids, adrenals, pituitary, thymus, etc.

Enrichment. A means of providing stimulation to children (usually superior ones) by giving them more to do in the same subject matter area in which other pupils of the class are working. May be contrasted with rapid promotion as a means of caring for individual differences.

Equivalent test. A test that is equal to another in terms of length, difficulty, subject matter area, and type of questions, but that is not a duplicate.

Euphoria. A feeling of well-being involving good mood and vitality, as contrasted to the emotional states of fear, anger, pain, etc.

Evaluation. The process of assessing the overall worth of an individual or activity. Many facets are investigated and many measures are employed so that a broad or comprehensive assessment is achieved.

Experimental. Deriving data or conclusions from the controlled conditions existing when factors causing behavior are artificially established.

Experimental group. The group in which one factor in teaching, learning, etc., is intentionally varied in order to evaluate the causal role of that one factor.

Extirpation. Removal of part of the brain, particularly of a laboratory animal. An experiment designed to determine how the brain functions.

Feedback. A situation in which output becomes part of the reinforcement system which influences subsequent action. In machine teaching, the answer or product provides clues suggesting next steps.

Frustration. The act of blocking the needs or desires of the organism or individual. Sometimes means prolonged tension from which no relief is afforded.

Functional autonomy. A condition in which an act is carried on because of its own motivating power—outside incentives are no longer needed. For example, reading voluntarily because one has skill and developed interest, as contrasted to reading because one is required to.

Genetics. 1. The study of genes in inheritance. 2. The phenomenon of growth in general, considering both inherited and environmental factors that influence progress toward more complete maturity.

Genius. An individual who has achieved eminence through unusual accomplishment that is esteemed by his social group. The term should not be used to denote giftedness—which is the potential for the development of genius.

Gestalt. Shape, form, or configuration. More specifically, the name given to a viewpoint in psychology that objects to simple cause-and-effect relations. The Gestalt view criticizes atomistic (fragmented) interpretations.

Gifted child. One who is unusually bright—who has an IQ in excess of 135-140. May also refer to special talents in a person whose intellect is only average. Should not be confused with genius.

Grade equivalent. A score or scale expressed in terms of the school grade and month which indicates the average chronological age, mental age, achievement test score, or other characteristics of pupils classified at the given school grade.

Group test. A test that is administered to several subjects at one time.

Growth. Change and development as the result of the interaction of the organism with its environment. The word is sometimes restricted to mean increase in size as a result of multiplication of cells, i.e., maturation.

Guidance. A process of careful study of the pupil which precedes or accompanies an interview or a series of conferences with a pupil. The study and conferences are aimed at helping the pupil become capable of making his own choices with wisdom.

Halo effect. The influence of one trait or behavior on the evaluation of other traits or behaviors. Any pervasive impression of an individual that causes the rater's estimates of specific traits or abilities to be generally too high or too low, a bias.

Hardware. The physical aspects of technology in education; the televisions, projectors, computers, tape players, reading accelerators, etc., and contrasted to the programs (software) which are used with the machines.

Hawthorne effect. A condition of experimental situations which causes subjects to perform better, not because of experimental variables or external incentives, but because of the attention given them during the experiment.

Hereditary potential. The inborn possibility for development under favorable environmental conditions. The limits for development beyond which additional opportunity would be of no avail.

Homeostasis. The tendency of an organism to remain stable or seek to achieve balance or stability through its own regulatory action, as regards temperature, bodily chemistry, or psychological conditions.

Humanistic psychology. See *Proactive psychology.*

Hypothesis. A tentative conclusion or guess. The basis for testing a particular procedure either by experiment or by observation.

Incentive. An external stimulus to action. Grades are thought by some persons to be a valuable incentive to learning.

Incidental learning. Information or skills acquired during the process of intentional learning, e.g., learning to use the dictionary, bibliographical aids, etc., while writing a paper on literature, psychology, etc.

Identification. Placing oneself in another's position, e.g., getting satisfaction from another's success or prestige. Acceptance of an action or goal as being significant to one's own self.

Identity. Having a face and a place. Identity refers to the need or fact of being an identifiable and recognized person who has a function and status—his roots are established.

Individual test. A test administered by one examiner to one subject at a time.

Insight. The perception of a functional relationship between various factors or phenomena in a problem situation. Often thought to be sudden, but actually the result of a continuous growth and development.

Integration. A process of shaping facets of the personality into a harmoniously functioning whole. Sometimes used to indicate relationships between various subject-matter areas. The latter meaning is more frequently termed "correlation," thus leaving the word "integration" to refer to a condition of the organism in which subject matter has been functionally assimilated.

Intelligence. The developed ability of an individual to cope with his environment. The speed, facility, and appropriateness with which one does schoolwork and copes with the tasks of daily living.

Intelligence quotient (IQ). The ratio of mental age to life age. Specifically, mental age divided by chronological age multiplied by 100.

Interest. A personal attitude or feeling involving identification with or concern about some person, situation, or object. A feeling of oneness between person and object.

Interpersonal process group. Six to ten people who meet, with a trained facilitator, for the specific purpose of learning how they "come across" to others and who seek understanding and control of the affective phases of their lives. Also called "basic encounter groups," "sensitivity groups," "T-groups."

Irradiation. A defense mechanism in which one's feelings are diffused or spread to many other contexts; e.g., anger at one's friend may be spread to other peers, teachers, parents, and people in general.

Isolate. In sociometry, the rarely, if ever, chosen pupil.

Learning. The modification of behavior through activity and experience that alters modes of adjustment to the environment.

Learning style. The particular sense organs or combination of sense organs one employs in mental intake processes designed for, or at least effective in, behavior modification. Some people are listeners, some are readers, some argue, some agree, some observe, and others must participate.

Level of aspiration. The degree of difficulty of response that an individual will attempt to overcome. The quality of goal which an individual desires to achieve.

Longitudinal studies. Investigations of behavior or traits carried on over a span of time, e.g., recording the intelligence test scores of the same individuals in babyhood, childhood, adolescence, and adulthood.

Maladjustment. Inadequate responses to the demands and problems of living in a particular environment.

Maturation. The processes involved in progressive advancement toward maturity. Some references to the word imply growth from within (intrinsic), but increasingly it involves experience factors as well.

Maturity. Used in two senses in psychology: 1. The full development of the individual, achievement of adult behavior and proportion—achievement of maximum growth. 2. Achievement of conduct or growth and development appropriate to one's age. (An immature child is one who acts below his age level—a mature child is still a child but "acts his age.")

Mean. The sum of the scores divided by the number of cases. The average.

Median. The midpoint of a series of scores. The point at which there are an equal number of cases (scores) below and above.

Mental age. A numerical term used to express the level of intellectual ability an individual has achieved to date. A mental age of ten years means an intellectual ability that is equivalent to the average achieved by children who are ten years old chronologically.

Mental discipline. The belief that "faculties" of the mind are stimulated to develop by exercise (usually rigorous). The belief that problem-solving ability in general is fostered by exercise in mathematics, that memory is cultivated by studying Latin, or that perseverance is generated by adversity.

Mental set. A temporary preparedness to act in a certain direction at a given time, e.g., the disposition to study arithmetic at a given time—or resistance to such study. (Mental set is temporary, whereas readiness is a more or less permanent condition. A pupil may have achieved readiness for reading but not have the proper mental set for it.)

Mobility. Movement of persons from one socioeconomic class level to another. One may move up or down the scale, but upward mobility is much the more frequent.

Molar. A comprehensive approach to the study of behavior. The "world view" of a set of phenomena. ("Molar" and "molecular" are relative terms, not points of antagonism.)

Molecular. An atomistic or fragmened approach to the study of behavior. The study of discrete bits of behavior. Analysis.

Morphology. The study of body types or structures in relation to the effect these have on personality development and personality manifestations.

Motivation. The process by which behavior is aroused or accelerated. Stimulation of activity toward a goal when previously there was little or no such behavior.

Need. A lack (or requirement) which unless fulfilled or on the way to fulfillment leads to lack of self-realization, frustration, or maladjustment.

Negative transfer. A condition in which one learning hampers the acquisition of another learning.

Negativism. The personality characteristic in which one chronically opposes reasonable requests and requirements (a normal and desirable phase of development in some circumstances).

Neurosis. A minor mental or emotional disturbance. A condition in which the individual chronically falters and stumbles in the course of his daily living.

Neurotic. One who suffers from minor mental or emotional illness.

Nongraded school. A school which does not have progressive and successive grade levels, but attempts to ignore the concept of grades, instead of having each pupil progress continuously at his own suitable rate.

Norm. An average or typical measure of a trait, level of development, or behavior.

Normal curve. A graphic representation of the distribution of a set of scores made by an unselected group showing a few cases at the extremes of the distribution and a clustering of cases at the center. The normal curve is often called the "bell-shaped" or Gaussian curve.

Objectivity. The characteristic of a test which indicates that it can be scored without danger of personal bias on the part of the scorer. A view in which opinion or wish has been eliminated.

Organismic. Referring to the totality, or inclusiveness, of the individual. A view which considers the individual—his physical, mental, emotional, spiritual past and present status—and the situation in which he functions—his home, school, peer group, national setting, etc.

Overlearning. In memorizing, the repetition of a selection after it has been learned to the point of one successful reproduction. Applying oneself to the acquisition of a skill or knowledge beyond the point at which one can say it has been learned.

Percentile. One of the 99 point scores that divide a ranked distribution into groups, each of which contains 1/100 of the scores. A pupil scoring 75 points out of a possible 100 on a test may have a percentile score of 90, which means that out of a theoretical group of 100 persons, he exceeds 90 of them with his score of 75. The score may also be interpreted to mean that 10 pupils out of 100 would equal or exceed this individual's performance.

Perception. The mental apprehension of that which is physically seen, heard, or felt. Psychological awareness.

Permissiveness. A predisposition on the part of those in power to allow wide latitude in the right of the child to choose freely how he will behave. Permissiveness must be limited to the child's developed ability to act prudently.

Perseveration. 1. The tendency for neural activities, once having been begun, to continue for a time. 2. The momentum one has to continue acting in a given direction. 3. The time, following learning, required for learning to be established.

Personality. The sum total of one's behavior and potential behavior in terms of physical, emotional, moral, social, aesthetic, and spiritual aspects of living as viewed and conditioned by one's fellow human beings.

Plateau. The level part of a learning curve, representing a time during which no measurable progress is being made in terms of the particular item being investigated.

Proactive psychology. That viewpoint of psychology which emphasizes the dynamic, causative role of man in his own behavior. Man is viewed as a thinker and chooser who, in some degree, formulates his own future by virtue of his dreams, hopes, aspirations, imaginings, and self-concept.

Profile. The graphic representation of a set of test scores that shows an individual's comparative strengths and weaknesses in the various measured traits.

Projective technique. Any of a number of means by which inner personality trends are made known and/or released. Fundamentally, projective techniques consist of the subject's adding structure to (or reading structure into) unstructured situations—painting and interpreting pictures or ink blots, playing with toys, finishing a story, etc.

Psychological approach. Introduction of a unit of schoolwork in terms of its meaning or interest to the pupils in a particular class, contrasted with the logical approach, which starts at the beginning and follows a series of events through to their ending.

Psychometrics. Knowledge concerned with the development and application of mathematical and statistical concepts to psychological data; psychological testing.

Puberty. The process during which the adolescent achieves sexual maturity.

Purposeful. Action carried on because it has a definite purpose that is discernible to the behaving person.

Purposive. Action that is directed toward satisfaction of certain needs, e.g., breathing, moving or exercise, the speeding up of heart action during a strong emotion, etc. The subject may be and often is unaware of the purpose of the behavior or action.

Rapport. A feeling of oneness or identity that may exist between two persons. A feeling of mutual concern and warm, friendly regard.

Rationalization. A process of false reasoning in which facts are twisted in order to justify a completed or contemplated act.

Readability. The characteristic of a written selection that describes the ease with which it can be understood. Length and difficulty of words and length of sentence are among the determining factors of readability.

Reading readiness. A stage of growth and development at which reading instruction will probably be effective and before which instruction will be relatively fruitless. Readiness for reading includes such factors as a mental age of 6.5 years, adequate sensory perception, emotional control commensurate with age, desire to read, and appropriate experiences.

Reference groups. Those groups of persons from whom one draws his values, norms, and aspirations.

Regression. A phase of development in which the individual reverts to a less mature level of conduct after having apparently achieved a higher level. This is often a normal phenomenon, but it can become chronic.

Regressive eye movements. Movements of the eyes back over a line of print to fixate upon a spot that is to the left (and on the same line) of a point that had previously been fixated. The eyes go back over material already once *visually* seen.

Reinforcement. The effect of one process of mental excitation or activity in increasing the strength of a second activity. Immediate rewards tend to reinforce (strengthen) preceding behavior.

Reliability. In terms of tests and measurement, the characteristics of a test that indicate that results will be consistent. A second administration of the test (or an equivalent form) on the same subject or group would yield highly similar results.

Retroactive inhibition. The tendency for one experience to inhibit the recall of another; e.g., of two groups who learn a set of nonsense syllables, the one that rests between trials recalls more of the first set than does the group that learns a second set before attempting to recall the first set.

Role playing. Assuming the part, either imitatively or imaginatively, of another in a short dramatic skit. Taking the part of a character other than one's typical self. It is spontaneous rather than being rehearsed.

Saltatory. Progressing suddenly—by leaps and bounds.

Sampling. The degree to which items in a test or inventory touch upon a wide and adequately representative number of traits and behaviors.

Self-actualization. The process of becoming all or most of what one wishes to be and is capable of achieving; living at a level in which lower level needs are no longer dominant; the process of bringing into accord one's concept of self, his ideal self, and his potentialities.

Socialization. The process by which one makes himself an integral part of his living group.

Sociometry. A schematic device for studying human relations or social attractions and/or repulsions. A mapping of interpersonal likes and dislikes.

Specificity. The term refers to the fact that such character traits as honesty, dependability, truthfulness are different in various contexts or situations; that is, honesty is specific to a situation—one is not equally honest in all circumstances.

Standard deviation. A statistic used to express the extent of deviation of a score from the mean of the total distribution. Approximately one-third of the scores are within one standard deviation above the mean and approximately one-third of the scores are within one standard deviation below the mean. Only about 27 percent of the scores are within the next two standard deviations (13+ percent on each side) above and below the first two standard deviations. About 99.7 percent of all cases lie within the limits of three standard deviations above and below the mean.

Streaming. Grouping pupils for classwork in terms of indicated ability and prior achievement.

Subjective. Influenced by personal opinions or wishes. Personal bias.

Standardized test. 1. A test for which norms have been established. (It has been given to large numbers of subjects and scores have definite expectancy values for given groups.) 2. A test for which uniform conditions of administering and scoring must be followed.

Standardizing population. The group or groups used in determining the norms for a test.

Tachistoscope. A device for controlling the illumination and duration of images, words, phrases, etc., that the subject must see in a brief unit of time in reading or in reacting to the stimuli presented.

Teacher's complex. The tendency of a teacher to rephrase the answer to a question in the precise words that were in his mind before the pupil responded. An indication of the teacher's eagerness to answer all the questions that arise.

Teleological. Directed toward a goal or purpose; behavior designed in accord with a definite pattern.

Tension tolerance. The ability of an individual to withstand pressure, disappointment, and frustration. The capacity of an individual to bounce back after a rebuff or defeat.

Test battery. A group or combination of psychometric tests. Several tests rather than one are thought to give a more comprehensive basis for evaluating an individual.

Track. One of several terms used to indicate varying levels of difficulty in school learning tasks. Thus in a given school, pupils in the C track skip general science (unless experience indicates the wisdom of another approach) and take biology during their first year in high school, move into chemistry and physics the following year, and take a second year of chemistry or physics during their senior year.

Transfer of learning. The phenomenon of learning being facilitated in situation B by virtue of common elements, ideals, or generalizations that have been derived from first having been learned in situation A.

Underachiever. A pupil whose academic accomplishment is at a level below that expected in terms of the predictive index yielded by general or specific aptitude tests.

Validity. The characteristic of a test which indicates that it measures that which it is supposed to measure.

Verbal reinforcement. Spoken words which praise or confirm the response of the individual by asserting that he is correct, doing well, can be proud of himself, etc.

Will power. A strengthened resolve resulting from clarified and increased motivation and a better understanding of and more conviction concerning advantages of the proposed course of action.

Worry. The process of turning a problem over and over in one's mind without arriving at a solution or hypothesis. A process of circular, as contrasted to straight-line, thinking.

Bibliography

AHMANN, J. STANLEY, AND MARVIN D. GLOCK, 1967, *Evaluating Pupil Growth*, 3d ed., Boston: Allyn and Bacon, Inc.

ALDRIDGE, JOHN W., 1969, "In the Country of the Young," *Harper's Magazine*, vol. 239, no. 1433, pp. 149–64, October.

ALDRIDGE, JOHN W., 1969, "In the Country of the Young, part II," *Harper's Magazine*, vol. 239, no. 1434, pp. 93–107, November.

ALLEN, DWIGHT, 1971, "The Seven Deadly Myths of Education," *Psychology Today*, vol. 4, no. 10, pp. 70–72+, March.

ALLEN, WILLIAM H., 1969, "Audiovisual Instruction: The State of the Art," in E. S. Mason (chm.), *The Schools and the Challenge of Innovation*, New York: McGraw-Hill Book Company.

ALLENDER, JEROME S., 1970, "Some Determinants of Inquiry Activity in Elementary School Children," *Journal of Educational Psychology*, vol. 61, pp. 220–225.

ALLPORT, GORDON W., 1968, *The Person in Psychology*, Boston: Beacon Press.

ALMY, MILLIE, 1968, "Wishful Thinking about Children's Thinking?" in W. H. MacGinitie and S. Ball (eds.), *Readings in Psychological Foundations of Education*, New York: McGraw-Hill Book Company.

AMOS, WILLIAM E., 1967, "Prevention through the School," in W. E. Amos and C. F. Wellford (eds.), *Delinquency Prevention Theory and Practice*, Englewood Cliffs, N.J.: Prentice-Hall, Inc.

ANDERSON, C. C., AND S. M. HUNKA, 1963, "Teacher Evaluation: Some Problems and a Proposal," *Harvard Educational Review*, vol. 33, pp. 74–79.

ARBUCKLE, DUGALD S., 1967, *Counseling and Psychotherapy: An Overview*, New York: McGraw-Hill Book Company.

ASHTON-WARNER, SYLVIA, 1963, *Teacher*, New York: Simon and Schuster, Inc.

ASHTON-WARNER, SYLVIA, 1964, "Organic Teaching," in R. Gross and J. Murphy (eds.), *The Revolution in the Schools*, New York: Harcourt, Brace & World, Inc.

ATKINSON, JOHN W., 1965, "The Mainspring of Achievement-oriented Activity," in J. D. Krumboltz (ed.), *Learning and the Educational Process*, Chicago: Rand McNally & Company.

AUSUBEL, DAVID P., 1966, "The Effects of Cultural Deprivation on Learning Patterns," in Staten W. Webster (ed.), *The Disadvantaged Learner*, San Francisco: Chandler Publishing Co.

AUSUBEL, DAVID P., 1968, *Educational Psychology: A Cognitive View*, New York: Holt, Rinehart and Winston, Inc.

AXLINE, VIRGINIA, 1964, *Dibs: In Search of Self*, Boston: Houghton Mifflin Company.

BACKMAN, CARL W., AND PAUL F. SECORD (eds.), 1966, *Problems in Social Psychology*, New York: McGraw-Hill Book Company.

BALDWIN, ALFRED L., 1967, *Theories of Child Development*, New York: John Wiley & Sons, Inc.

BARBE, WALTER B., 1967, "Identification and Diagnosis of the Needs of the Educationally Retarded and Disadvantaged," in National Society for the Study of Education, 66th Yearbook, part I, *The Educationally Retarded and Disadvantaged*, Chicago: University of Chicago Press.

BARKER, ROGER G., TAMARA DEMBO, AND KURT LEWIN, 1941, *Frustration and Regression: An Experiment with Young Children*, University of Iowa Studies in Child Welfare, vol. 18, no. 1.

BARRY, RUTH, AND BEVERLY WOLF, 1962, *An Epitaph for Vocational Guidance*, New York: Teachers College Press, Columbia University.

BASSETT, MILDRED, 1962, Vice-principal, Lincoln High School (Portland, Oregon): Personal interview, Nov. 20.

BAUER, FRANCIS C., 1969, "Fact and Folklore about Adolescents," in H. W. Bernard (ed.), *Readings in Adolescent Development*, Scranton, Pa.: International Textbook Company. From the *Bulletin of the National Association of Secondary-School Principals*, vol. 49, pp. 172–182, March, 1965.

BAUGHMAN, E. EARL, AND GEORGE WELSH, 1962, *Personality: A Behavioral Science*, Englewood Cliffs, N.J.: Prentice-Hall, Inc.

BEALER, ROBERT C., FERN K. WILLITS, AND PETER MAIDA, 1969, "The Myth of a Rebellious Adolescent Subculture: Its Detrimental Effects for Understanding Rural Youth," in H. W. Bernard (ed.), *Readings in Adolescent Development*, Scranton, Pa.: International Textbook Company. From

Rural Youth in Crisis: Facts, Myths, and Social Change, Washington, D.C.: U.S. Department of Health, Education, and Welfare.

BEATTY, WALCOTT H., 1969a, "Emotion: The Missing Link in Education," in Walcott H. Beatty (ed.), *Improving Educational Assessment*, Washington, D.C.: Association for Supervision and Curriculum Development, NEA.

BEATTY, WALCOTT H., 1969b, *Improving Educational Assessment and an Inventory of Measures of Affective Behavior*, Washington, D.C.: Association for Supervision and Curriculum Development.

BECK, CARLTON E., NORMAND R. BERNIER, JAMES B. MACDONALD, THOMAS W. WALTON, AND JACK C. WILLERS, 1968, *Education for Relevance, The Schools and Social Change*, Boston: Houghton Mifflin Company.

BECKER, WESLEY C., 1964, "Consequences of Different Kinds of Parental Discipline," in M. L. Hoffman and L. W. Hoffman (eds.), *Review of Child Development Research*, vol. I, New York: Russell Sage Foundation.

BEERS, CLIFFORD, 1917, *A Mind That Found Itself*, New York: Longmans, Green & Co., Inc.

BEGGS, DAVID W., III, AND EDWARD G. BUFFIE (eds.), 1967, *Nongraded Schools in Action*, Bloomington: Indiana University Press.

BENJAMIN, HAROLD (pseudonym, J. Abner Peddiwell), 1939, *The Sabre-Tooth Curriculum*, New York: McGraw-Hill Book Company.

BENNE, KENNETH D., 1954, "More Learning Takes Place When Teacher and Students Understand the Various Roles in the Classroom Group," *NEA Journal*, vol. 42, pp. 205–208.

BENSON, CHARLES S., 1969, "The Efficient Allocation of Educational Resources," in E. S. Mason (chm.), *The Schools and the Challenge of Innovation*, New York: McGraw-Hill Book Company.

BEREITER, CARL, AND SIEGFRIED ENGELMANN, 1966, *Teaching Disadvantaged Children in the Preschool*, Englewood Cliffs, N.J.: Prentice-Hall, Inc.

BERELSON, BERNARD, AND GARY A. STEINER, 1964, *Human Behavior*, New York: Harcourt, Brace & World, Inc.

BERG, IRWIN A., 1967, "Cultural Trends and the Task of Psychology," in H. W. Bernard and W. C. Huckins (eds.), *Readings in Educational Psychology*, Scranton, Pa.: International Textbook Company. From *American Psychologist*, vol. 20, pp. 203–207, 1965.

BERGNEDER, VIRGINIA, 1971, "An Approach to the Functionally Illiterate," personal interview, Oregon City, Ore., Jan. 28.

BERNARD, HAROLD W., 1952, *Mental Hygiene for Classroom Teachers*, New York: McGraw-Hill Book Company.

BERNARD, HAROLD W., 1970a, *Human Development in Western Culture*, 3d ed., Boston: Allyn and Bacon, Inc.

BERNARD, HAROLD W., 1970b, *Mental Health in the Classroom*, New York: McGraw-Hill Book Company.

BERNARD, HAROLD W., AND WESLEY C. HUCKINS, 1968, *A Rationale for Educational Innovation*, typed report, Dayton, Ohio: Institute for Development of Educational Activities (I/D/E/A), Kettering Foundation.

BERNSTEIN, ABRAHAM, 1967, *The Education of Urban Populations*, New York: Random House, Inc.

BIDDLE, B. J., AND W. J. ELLENA, 1964, *Contemporary Research on Teacher Effectiveness*, New York: Holt, Rinehart, and Winston, Inc.

BIGGE, MORRIS L., 1966, "Representative Theories of Learning and Their Implications for Education," *NEA Journal*, vol. 55, no. 3, pp. 15–17, March.

BIGGE, MORRIS L., AND MAURICE P. HUNT, 1968, *Psychological Foundations of Education*, 2d ed., New York: Harper and Row, Publishers, Inc.

BILLS, ROBERT E., 1969, "Nondirective Play Therapy with Retarded Readers," in W. Otto and K. Koenke (eds.), *Remedial Teaching*, Boston: Houghton Mifflin Company. From *Journal of Consulting Psychology*, vol. 14, pp. 140–149, 1950.

BIRCH, HERBERT G., AND JOAQUIN CRAVIOTO, 1968, "Inflection, Nutrition, and Environment in Mental Development," in H. F. Eichenwald (ed.), *The Prevention of Mental Retardation through Control of Infectious Diseases*, Washington, D.C.: U.S. Department of Health, Education, and Welfare.

BIRNBAUM, MAX, 1969, "Sense about Sensitivity Training," *Saturday Review*, vol. 52, no. 46, pp. 82–83+, Nov. 15.

BLACK, JONATHAN, 1969, "Street Academies: One Step Off the Sidewalk," *Saturday Review*, vol. 52, no. 46, pp. 88–89+, Nov. 15.

BLAIR, GLENN M., AND R. STEWART JONES, 1964, *Psychology of Adolescence for Teachers*, New York: The Macmillan Company.

BLAKE, PATRICIA, 1964, "A Big Break for Poverty's Children," *Life*, vol. 56, no. 14, p. 89.

BLANK, MARION, 1970, "Implicit Assumptions Underlying Preschool Intervention Programs," *The Journal of Social Issues*, vol. 26, no. 2, pp. 15–33.

BLOOM, BENJAMIN S., 1964, *Stability and Change in Human Characteristics*, New York: John Wiley & Sons, Inc.

BLOOM, BENJAMIN S., 1969, "Some Theoretical Issues Relating to Educational Evaluation," in National Society for the Study of Education, 68th Yearbook, part II, *Educational Evaluation: New Roles, New Means*, Chicago: University of Chicago Press.

BLUME, ROBERT, 1971, "Humanizing Teacher Education," *Phi Delta Kappan*, vol. 52, pp. 411–415.

BONNER, HUBERT, 1965, *On Being Mindful of Man*, Boston: Houghton Mifflin Company.

BORG, WALTER R., 1966, *Ability Grouping in the Public Schools*, Madison, Wis.: Dembar Educational Research Services, Inc.

BOROW, HENRY, 1966, "Development of Occupational Motives and Roles," in L. W. Hoffman and M. L. Hoffman (eds.), *Review of Child Development Research*, vol. 2, New York: Russell Sage Foundation.

BOWMAN, GARDA W., AND GORDON J. KLOPF, 1968, *New Careers and Roles in the American School*, New York: Bank Street College of Education.

BOYER, WILLIAM H., AND PAUL WALSH, 1968, "Are Children Born Unequal?" *Saturday Review*, vol. 51, no. 42, pp. 61–63+, Oct. 19.

BRAMELD, THEODORE, 1970, "A Cross-Cutting Approach to the Curriculum: The Moving Wheel," *Phi Delta Kappan*, vol. 51, pp. 346–348.

BRATTEN, JACK E., 1968, Personal interview, Los Angeles: Systems Development Corporation, Feb. 1.

BRONFENBRENNER, URIE, 1963, "Developmental Theory in Transition," in National Society for the Study of Education, 62d Yearbook, part I, *Child Psychology*, Chicago: University of Chicago Press.

BRONFENBRENNER, URIE, 1969, "Dampening the Unemployability Explosion," *Saturday Review*, vol. 52, no. 1, pp. 108–110, Jan. 4.

BROWN, G., 1960, "Which Pupil to Which Classroom Climate?" *Elementary School Journal*, vol. 60, pp. 265–269, February.

BRUCE, PAUL, 1966, "Three Forces in Psychology and Their Ethical and Educational Implications," *Educational Forum*, vol. 30, pp. 277–285.

BRUNELLE, EUGENE A., 1971, "Apollo and Dionysius," *Journal of Creative Behavior*, vol. 5, pp. 37–43.

BRUNER, JEROME S., 1961, "The Act of Discovery," *Harvard Educational Review*, vol. 31, pp. 21-32, Winter.

BRUNER, JEROME S., 1962, *On Knowing Essays for the Left Hand*, Cambridge, Mass.: Belknap Press, Harvard University Press.

BRUNER, JEROME S., 1963a, *The Process of Education*, Cambridge, Mass.: Harvard University Press.

BRUNER, JEROME S., 1963b, "Structures in Learning," *NEA Journal*, vol. 52, pp. 26-27, March.

BRUNER, JEROME S., 1968a, "Culture, Politics, and Pedagogy," Saturday Review, vol. 51, no. 20, pp. 69-72+, May 18.

BRUNER, JEROME S., 1968b, "Learning and Thinking," in W. H. MacGinitie and S. Ball (eds.), *Readings in Psychological Foundations of Education*, New York: McGraw-Hill Book Company.

BRUNER, JEROME S., 1970a, "Bad Education—A Conversation with Jerome Bruner," by Elizabeth Hall, *Psychology Today*, vol. 4, no. 7, pp. 50-57+, December.

BRUNER, JEROME, 1970b, "The Skill of Relevance or the Relevance of Skills," *Saturday Review*, vol. 53, no. 14, pp. 66-68+, Apr. 18.

BUGENTHAL, JAMES F. T., 1967, *Challenges of Humanistic Psychology*, New York: McGraw-Hill Book Company.

BUHLER, CHARLOTTE, 1967, "Human Life as a Whole as a Central Subject of Humanistic Psychology," in J. F. T. Bugenthal (ed.), *Challenges of Humanistic Psychology*, New York: McGraw-Hill Book Company.

BURKHART, ROBERT C., AND HUGH M. NEIL, 1968, *Identity and Teacher Learning*, Scranton, Pa.: International Textbook Company.

BURRELL, ANNE P., 1951, "Facilitating Learning through Emphasis on Meeting Children's Basic Needs: An In-service Training Program," *Journal of Educational Sociology*, vol. 24, pp. 381-393.

CALDWELL, BETTYE M., 1967, "What Is the Optimal Learning Environment for the Young Child?" *American Journal of Orthopsychiatry*, vol. 37, pp. 8-21.

CALITRI, CHARLES J., 1968, "On Language and Human Dignity," *High Points*, winter, pp. 3-5.

CAMPBELL, JAMES R., 1968, *Cognitive and Affective Process Development and Its Relation to a Teacher's Interaction Ratio*, Unpublished Ph.D. Thesis, New York University.

CAMPBELL, JAMES R., AND CYRUS W. BARNES, 1969, "Interaction Analysis—A Breakthrough?" *Phi Delta Kappan*, vol. 50, pp. 587-590.

CAMPBELL, ROALD F., 1969, "Teaching and Teachers—Today and Tomorrow," in E. S. Mason (Chm.), *The Schools and the Challenge of Innovation*, New York: McGraw-Hill Book Company.

CANNON, W. B., 1929, *Bodily Changes in Pain, Hunger, Fear, and Rage*, 2d ed., New York: Appleton-Century-Crofts, Inc.

CANTRIL, H., AND W. A. HUNT, 1932, "Emotional Effects Produced by the Injection of Adrenalin," *American Journal of Psychology*, vol. 44, pp. 300-307.

CARLSON, ELLIOT, 1970, "Education and Industry: Troubled Partnership," *Saturday Review*, vol. 53, no. 33, pp. 45-47+, Aug. 15.

CARROLL, JOHN B., 1965, "School Learning Over the Long Haul," in J. D. Krumboltz (ed.), *Learning and the Educational Process*, Chicago: Rand McNally & Company.

CAWELTI, GORDON, 1967, "Innovative Practices in High Schools," Reprinted from *Nation's Schools*, April.

CAZDEN, COURTNEY B., 1970, "The Situation: A Neglected Course of Social Class Differences in Language Use," *Journal of Social Issues*, vol. 26, no. 2, pp. 35-60.

CHAFFEE, JOHN, JR., AND PATRICIA WAGNER, 1970, "Teachers DO Make a Difference," *American Education*, vol. 6, no. 4, pp. 23-25, May.

CHANDLER, B. J., AND FREDERICK BERTOLAET, 1967, "Administrative Problems and Procedures in Compensatory Education," in National Society for the Study of Education, 66th Yearbook, part I, *The Educationally Retarded and Disadvantaged*, Chicago: The University of Chicago Press.

CHAPLIN, J. P., 1968, *Dictionary of Psychology*, New York: Dell Publishing Company, Inc.

"CHILDREN OF CHANGE," 1969, *Kaiser Aluminum News*, vol. 27, no. 1, pp. 1–40, May.

CICIRELLI, VICTOR G., JOHN W. EVANS, AND JEFFRY SCHILLER, 1970, "A Reply to the Report Analysis," *Harvard Educational Review*, vol. 40, pp. 105–129.

CLAIBORN, WILLIAM L., 1969, "Expectancy Effects in the Classroom: A Failure to Replicate," *Journal of Educational Psychology*, vol. 60, pp. 377–383.

CLARK, DONALD H. (ed.), 1967, *The Psychology of Education*, New York: The Free Press.

CLARK, DONALD, ARLENE GOLDSMITH, AND CLEMENTINE PUGH, 1970, *Those Children*, Belmont, Calif.: Wadsworth Publishing Company, Inc.

CLAYTON, A. STAFFORD, 1970, "Vital Questions, Minimal Responses: Education Vouchers," *Phi Delta Kappan*, vol. 52, 53–54.

CLEMENTS, MILLARD, 1968, "Research and Incantation: A Comment," *Phi Delta Kappan*, vol. 50, p. 107, October.

CLEMENTS, WARREN, 1970, "Cultural Differences and Understanding," Lecture, Division of Continuing Education, Portland, Ore., Nov. 24.

COHEN, STEWART, 1971, "The Development of Aggression," *Review of Educational Research*, vol. 41, pp. 71–85.

COLEMAN, JAMES S., 1961, *The Adolescent Society*, New York: The Free Press of Glencoe.

COLEMAN, JAMES S., 1965, *Adolescents and the Schools*, New York: Basic Books, Inc.

COLEMAN, JAMES S., 1968, "The Concept of Equality of Educational Opportunity," *Harvard Educational Review*, vol. 38, pp. 7–22.

COMBS, ARTHUR W., 1961, "A Perceptual View of the Nature of 'Helpers,' " in *Personality Theory and Counseling Practice*, Gainesville, Fla.: University of Florida.

COMBS, A. W., 1965, *The Professional Education of Teachers*, Boston: Allyn and Bacon, Inc.

COMBS, ARTHUR W., AND DONALD SNYGG, 1959, *Individual Behavior*, New York: Harper & Row, Publishers, Incorporated.

COMMISSION ON INSTRUCTIONAL TECHNOLOGY, 1970, *To Improve Learning*, A report to the President and Congress of the United States, Washington, D.C.: Superintendent of Documents.

CONANT, JAMES B., 1959, *The American High School Today*, New York: McGraw-Hill Book Company.

COOK, WALTER W., AND THEODORE CLYMER, 1962, "Acceleration and Retardation," in National Society for the Study of Education, 61st Yearbook, part I, *Individualizing Instruction*, Chicago: University of Chicago Press.

COUNT, JEROME, 1967, "The Conflict Factor in Adolescent Growth," *Adolescence*, vol. 2, pp. 167-182.

COTTLE, THOMAS J., 1969a, "Briston Township Schools: Strategy for Change," *Saturday Review*, vol. 52, no. 38, pp. 70-71+, Sept. 20.

COTTLE, THOMAS J., 1969b, "Parent and Child—The Hazards of Equality," *Saturday Review*, vol. 52, no. 5, pp. 16-19+, Feb. 1.

CRANDALL, VAUGHN J., 1963, "Achievement," in National Society for the Study of Education, 62d Yearbook, part I, *Child Psychology*, Chicago: University of Chicago Press.

CRONBACH, LEE J., 1963, *Educational Psychology*, 2d ed., New York: Harcourt, Brace & World, Inc.

CRONBACH, LEE J., 1969, "Heredity, Environment, and Educational Policy," *Harvard Educational Review*, vol. 39, pp. 338-347.

DANSKIN, DAVID G., C. E. KENNEDY, JR., AND WALTER S. FRIESEN, 1965, "Guidance: The Ecology of Students," *Personnel and Guidance Journal*, vol. 44, pp. 130-135.

DAVENPORT, STEPHEN, 1968, "Farewell to the Old School Tie," *Saturday Review*, vol. 51, no. 42, pp. 66-69+, Oct. 19.

DAVIDSON, R. L., 1968, "The Effects of an Interaction Analysis System on the Development of Critical Reading in Elementary School Children," *Classroom Interaction Newsletter*, May.

DAVIE, JAMES S., 1953, "Social Class Factors and School Attendance," *Harvard Educational Review*, vol. 23, pp. 175-185.

DAVIS, ROBERT B., 1966, "Discovery in the Teaching of Mathematics," in L. S. Shulman and E. R. Keislar (eds.), *Learning by Discovery: A Critical Appraisal*, Chicago: Rand McNally & Company.

DEAN, STUART E., 1967, "The Future of Nongraded Schools," in D. W. Beggs, III and E. G. Buffie (eds.), *Nongraded Schools in Action*, Bloomington: Indiana University Press.

DEESE, JAMES, 1967, *General Psychology*, Boston: Allyn and Bacon, Inc.

DELACATO, CARL H., 1959, *The Treatment and Prevention of Reading Problems*, Springfield, Ill.: Charles C Thomas, Publisher.

DENNISON, GEORGE, 1969, *The Lives of Children*, New York: Random House.

DENSHAM, WILLIAM E., 1971, "The Children Who Had to Be Found," *American Education*, vol. 7, no. 2, pp. 11-14, March.

DEWEY, JOHN, 1910, *How We Think*, Boston: D. C. Heath and Company.

DINKMEYER, DON C., AND CHARLES E. CALDWELL, 1970, *Developmental Counseling and Guidance: A Comprehensive School Approach*, New York: McGraw-Hill Book Company.

DODSON, DAN W., 1963, "Schools in Our Rural Slums," *Saturday Review*, vol. 46, no. 16, p. 75.

DOLL, RONALD C., AND ROBERT S. FLEMING (eds.), 1966, *Children under Pressure*, Columbus, Ohio: Charles E. Merrill Books, Inc.

DRANOV, PAULA, 1967, "A Taste of College," *American Education*, vol. 3, no. 4, pp. 25–27, April.

DREWS, ELIZABETH M., 1961, "A Critical Evaluation of Approaches to the Identification of Gifted Students," in A. Traxler (ed.), *Measurement and Evaluation in Today's Schools*, Washington, D.C.: American Council on Education.

DUBIN, ROBERT, AND THOMAS C. TAVEGGIA, 1968, *The Teaching-Learning Paradox: A Comparative Analysis of College Teaching Methods,* Eugene: Center for Advanced Study of Educational Administration, University of Oregon.

DUBOS, RENE, 1970, "We Can't Buy Our Way Out," *Psychology Today*, vol. 3, no. 10, pp. 20–22+, March.

DUGDALE, R. L., 1877, *The Jukes*, New York: G. P. Putnam's Sons.

DUNN, LLOYD M. (ed.), 1963, *Exceptional Children in the Schools*, New York: Holt, Rinehart and Winston, Inc.

DUPUE, PALMER, 1967, "The Great Faults of School Marks," *Journal of Secondary Education*, vol. 42, pp. 217–222.

DWYER, JOHANNA, AND JEAN MAYER, 1968/69, "Psychological Effects of Variations in Physical Appearance during Adolescence," *Adolescence*, vol. 3, no. 12, pp. 353–380.

EBEL, ROBERT L., 1970*a*, "Behavioral Objectives: A Close Look," *Phi Delta Kappan*, vol. 52, pp. 171–173, November.

EBEL, ROBERT L., 1970*b*, "The Social Consequences of Educational Testing," in B. Shertzer and S. C. Stone (eds.), *Introduction to Guidance: Selected Readings*, Boston: Houghton Mifflin Company. From *Proceedings of the 1963 Invitational Conference on Testing Problems*, Princeton, N.J.: Educational Testing Service, pp. 130–143, 1964.

ECKSTEIN, GUSTAV, 1969, *The Body Has a Head*, New York: Harper & Row, Publishers, Incorporated.

EDWARDS, ALLEN J., AND DALE P. SCANNELL, 1968, *Educational Psychology: The Teaching-Learning Process*, Scranton, Pa.: International Textbook Company.

EICHORN, DOROTHY H., 1963, "Biological Correlates of Behavior," in National Society for the Study of Education, 62d Yearbook, part I, *Child Psychology*, Chicago: University of Chicago Press.

EISENBERG, LEON, 1967, "Strengths of the Inner City Child," in A. H. Passow, M. Goldberg, and A. J. Tannenbaum, *Education of the Disadvantaged*, New York: Holt, Rinehart and Winston, Inc.

EISENBERG, LEON, 1969, "A Developmental Approach to Adolescence," in H. W. Bernard (ed.), *Readings in Adolescence*, Scranton, Pa.: International Textbook Company. From *Children*, vol. 12, no. 4, pp. 131–135, 1965.

ELAM, STANLEY, 1970, "The Age of Accountability Dawns in Texarkana," *Phi Delta Kappan*, vol. 51, pp. 509–514.

ELIAS, JAMES, AND PAUL GEBHARD, 1969, "Sexuality and Sexual Learning in Childhood," *Phi Delta Kappan*, vol. 50, pp. 401–405.

ELLINGSON, CARETH, AND JAMES CASS, 1966, "New Hope for Non-readers," *Saturday Review*, vol. 49, no. 16, pp. 82–83+, April 16.

ELKINS, DEBORAH, 1969, "Instructional Guidelines for Teachers of the Disadvantaged," *The Record*, vol. 70, pp. 593–615.

EMBLEN, DON L., 1969, "For a Disciplinarian's Manual," *Phi Delta Kappan*, vol. 50, no. 6, pp. 339–340.

EMENS, JOHN R., 1965, "Education Begets Education, the GI Bill Twenty Years Later," *American Education*, vol. 1, no. 6, pp. 11–12, September. Also in H. W. Bernard (ed.), 1969, *Readings in Adolescent Development*, Scranton, Pa.: International Textbook Company.

ENGLISH, FENWICK, 1969, "Teacher May I Take Three Giant Steps! The Differentiated Staff," *Phi Delta Kappan,* pp. 211–214.

ENNIS, ROBERT H., 1967, "Readiness to Master a Principle," in B. Paul Komisar and C. J. B. Macmillan (eds.), *Psychological Concepts in Education*, Chicago: Rand McNally & Company.

ERIKSON, ERIK H., 1964, *Insight and Responsibility*, New York: W. W. Norton & Company, Inc.

ERIKSON, ERIK H., 1968, *Identity, Youth and Crisis*, New York: W. W. Norton & Company, Inc.

"ERIKSON, ERIK: The Quest for Identity," Special Report, 1970, *Newsweek*, vol. 75, no. 25, pp. 84–89, Dec. 21.

FADER, DANIEL N., AND MORTON H. SHAEVITZ, 1966, *Hooked on Books*, New York: Berkley Publishing Company.

FAIRBANK, RUTH E., 1933, "The Subnormal Child—Seventeen Years After," *Mental Hygiene*, vol. 17, pp. 177–208.

FALLERS, MARGARET, 1970, "Choice Is Not Enough," *School Review*, vol. 78, p. 239.

FARNSWORTH, DANA L., 1965, "Mental Health Implications for Teachers," in E. P. Torrance and R. D. Strom (eds.), *Mental Health and Achievement*, New York: John Wiley & Sons, Inc.

FELDMAN, RONALD, 1969, "Social Attributes of the Intensely Disliked Position in Children's Groups," *Adolescence*, vol. 4, no. 14, pp. 181–198.

FINDLEY, WARREN G., 1963, "The Complete Testing Program," *Theory into Practice*, vol. 2, pp. 192–198.

FISCHER, JOHN H., 1970, "Who Needs Schools?" *Saturday Review*, vol. 53, no. 38, pp. 78–79+, Sept. 19.

FLANDERS, NED A., 1965, *Teacher Influence, Pupil Attitudes, and Achievement*, Washington, D.C.: Office of Education, U.S. Department of Health, Education, and Welfare.

FLANDERS, NED A., BETTY M. MORRISON, AND E. LELAND BRODE, 1968, "Changes in Pupil Attitudes during the School Year," *Journal of Educational Psychology*, vol. 59, pp. 334-338.

FLOOK, ALFRED J. M., AND USHA SAGGAR, 1968, "Academic Performance With, and Without, Knowledge of Scores on Tests of Intelligence, Aptitude, and Personality," *Journal of Educational Psychology*, vol. 59, pp. 395-401.

FOSTER, FLORENCE P., 1968, "The Human Relationships of Creative Individuals," *Journal of Creative Behavior*, vol. 2, no. 2, pp. 111-118.

FRAIBERG, SELMA, 1967, "The Origin of Human Bonds," *Commentary*, vol. 44, no. 6, pp. 51-57, December.

FREEBURG, NORMAN E., 1970, "Assessment of Disadvantaged Adolescents: A Different Approach to Research and Evaluation Measures," *Journal of Educational Psychology*, vol. 61, pp. 229-240.

FREEDMAN, MERVIN B., 1966, "The New Honesty about Sex on Campus," in Time-Life Special Report, *The Young Americans*, New York: Time, Inc.

FREUD, SIGMUND, 1936, *The Problem of Anxiety*, New York: W. W. Norton & Company, Inc.

FRIEDENBERG, EDGAR Z., 1969a, "Comments" [on "Revolutionaries Who Have to Be Home by 7:30"], *Phi Delta Kappan*, vol. 50, pp. 566-567.

FRIEDENBERG, EDGAR Z., 1969b, "The Generation Gap," *The Annals of the American Academy of Political and Social Science*, vol. 382, pp. 32-42.

FULLMER, DANIEL W., AND HAROLD W. BERNARD, 1964, *Counseling: Contents and Process*, Chicago: Science Research Associates, Inc.

GABER, ALICE, 1971, "Aqui Estoy—Here I Am," *American Education*, vol. 7, no. 1, pp. 18-22, January-February.

GAGNÉ, ROBERT M., 1965, "Educational Objectives and Human Performance," in J. D. Krumboltz (ed.), *Learning and the Educational Process*, Chicago: Rand McNally & Company.

GAGNÉ, ROBERT M., 1966, "Varieties of Learning and the Concept of Discovery," in L. S. Shulman and E. R. Keislar (eds.), *Learning by Discovery: A Critical Appraisal*, Chicago: Rand McNally & Company.

GAGNÉ, ROBERT M., 1970a, *The Conditions of Learning*, 2d ed., New York: Holt, Rinehart and Winston, Inc.

GAGNÉ, ROBERT M., 1970b, "Some New Views of Learning and Instruction," *Phi Delta Kappan*, vol. 51, pp. 468-472.

GAIER, EUGENE L., 1969, "Adolescence: The Current Imbroglio," *Adolescence*, vol. 4, no. 13, pp. 89-110, Spring.

GALLAGHER, JAMES J., 1964, *Teaching the Gifted Child*, Boston: Allyn and Bacon, Inc.

GARRISON, KARL C., 1968, "Physiological Changes in Adolescence," in James F. Adams (ed.), *Understanding Adolescence*, Boston: Allyn and Bacon, Inc.

GEPHART, WILLIAM J., AND DANIEL P. ANTONOPLOS, 1969, "The Effects of Expectancy and Other Research-Biasing Factors," *Phi Delta Kappan*, vol. 50, pp. 579–583.

GIBB, JACK R., 1965, "Fear and Facade: Defensive Management," in R. E. Farson (ed.), *Science and Human Affairs*, Palo Alto, Calif.: Science and Behavior Books, Inc.

GILLIOM, M. EUGENE, 1969, "The High School Culture and Academic Progress," in H. W. Bernard (ed.), *Readings in Adolescent Development*, Scranton, Pa.: International Textbook Company. From *High School Journal*, vol. 47, pp. 153–157, 1964.

GINOTT, HAIM G., 1965, *Between Parent and Child*, New York: Avon Books, The Hearst Corporation.

GLANZ, EDWARD C., 1962, *Groups in Guidance*, Boston: Allyn and Bacon, Inc.

GLASSER, WILLIAM, 1970, "Exploring the World of the Adolescent," Lecture, Portland, Ore., Jan. 17.

GLASSER, WILLIAM, 1969, *Schools without Failure*, New York: Harper & Row, Publishers, Incorporated.

GLIDEWELL, JOHN C., MILDRED B. KANTOR, LOUIS M. SMITH, AND LORENE A. STRINGER, 1966, "Socialization and Social Structure in the Classroom," in L. W. Hoffman and M. L. Hoffman (eds.), *Review of Child Development Research*, vol. 2, New York: Russell Sage Foundation.

GLOGAU, LILLIAN, AND EDMUND KRAUSE, 1969, "What Will Future Man Look Like?" *Grade Teacher*, vol. 86, no. 5, pp. 76–80, January.

GODDU, ROLAND J. B., AND EDWARD R. DUCHARME, 1971, "A Responsive Teacher-Education Program," *Teachers College Record*, vol. 72, pp. 431–441.

GOLDBERG, ARTHUR, 1964, "Juvenatrics: Study of Prolonged Adolescence," *The Clearing House*, vol. 38, pp. 488–492, 1964.

GOLDBERG, MIRIAM L., 1967, "Methods and Materials for Educationally Disadvantaged Youth," in A. Harry Passow and others (eds.), *Education of the Disadvantaged*, New York: Holt, Rinehart and Winston, Inc.

GOLDENSON, ROBERT M., 1970, *The Encyclopedia of Human Behavior*, Garden City, N.Y.: Doubleday & Company, Inc.

GOOD, CARTER V. (ed.), 1959, *Dictionary of Education*, New York: McGraw-Hill Book Company.

GOODLAD, JOHN I., 1968a, "Curriculum: A Janus Look," *Teachers College Record*, vol. 70, pp. 95-107.

GOODLAD, JOHN I., 1967, "The Educational Program to 1980 and Beyond," in E. L. Morphet and C. O. Ryan (eds.), *Implications for Education of Prospective Changes in Society*, Denver: Designing Education for the Future.

GOODLAD, JOHN I., 1969a, "How Do We Learn?" *Saturday Review*, vol. 52, no. 25, pp. 74-75+, June 21.

GOODLAD, JOHN I., 1969*b*, "The Schools *vs.* Education," *Saturday Review*, vol. 52, no. 16, pp. 59–61+, April 19.

GOODMAN, PAUL, 1962, "For a Reactionary Experiment in Education," *Harper's*, vol. 225, no. 1350, pp. 61–72, November.

GOODMAN, PAUL, 1968*b*, "Freedom and Learning: The Need for Choice," *Saturday Review*, vol. 51, no. 20, pp. 73–75, May 18.

GOODMAN, PAUL, 1970*a*, "High School Is Too Much," *Psychology Today*, vol. 4, no. 5, pp. 25–26*ff*, October.

GOODMAN, PAUL, 1970*b*, *New Reformation: Notes of a Neolithic Conservative*, New York: Random House, Inc.

GORDON, IRA J., 1969, "The Beginnings of Self: The Problem of the Nurturing Environment," *Phi Delta Kappan*, vol. 50, pp. 375–378.

GORDON, IRA J., 1966, "New Concepts of Children's Learning and Development," in W. B. Waetjen and R. R. Leeper (eds.), *Learning and Mental Health in the School*, Washington, D.C.: Association for Supervision and Curriculum Development, NEA.

GORDON, JESSE E., 1968, "Counseling the Disadvantaged Boy," in William E. Amos and Jean D. Grambs (eds.), *Counseling the Disadvantaged Youth*, Englewood Cliffs, N.J.: Prentice-Hall, Inc.

GORDON, L. V., 1971, "Weber in the Classroom," *Journal of Educational Psychology*, vol. 62, pp. 60–66.

GORDON, TED, 1969, "Comment," *Phi Delta Kappan*, vol. 50, p. 567.

GOTTESMAN, I. I., 1968, "Biogenetics of Race and Class," in M. Eutsch, I. Katz, and A. R. Jensen (eds.), *Social Class, Race, and Psychological Development*, New York: Holt, Rinehart and Winston.

GRAMBS, JEAN D., 1960, *Understanding Intergroup Relations, What Research Says to the Teacher*, no. 21, Washington, D.C.: National Education Association.

GRAMBS, JEAN D., AND WALTER WAETJEN, 1966, "Being Equally Different: A New Right for Boys and Girls," *National Elementary Principal*, vol. 46, pp. 59–67.

GREER, COLIN, 1969, "Public Schools: Myth of the Melting Pot," *Saturday Review*, vol. 52, no. 46, pp. 84–86+, Nov. 15.

GROSSMAN, BRUCE, 1968, "The Academic Grind at Age Three," *Teachers College Record*, vol. 70, pp. 227-231.

GUERNSEY, JOHN, 1971, "Activist Firings Stir Ontario Chicanos," *The Sunday Oregonian*, vol. 94, no. 6, p. 1, Jan. 10.

GUILFORD, J. P., 1967*a*, "Creativity: Yesterday, Today, Tomorrow," *The Journal of Creative Behavior*, vol. 1, pp. 3-14.

GUILFORD, J. P., 1967*b*, *The Nature of Intelligence*, New York: McGraw-Hill Book Company.

GUTHRIE, E. R., 1952, *Psychology of Learning*, New York: Harper and Row, Publishers, Incorporated.

HALLECK, SEYMOUR L., 1968, "Hypotheses of Student Unrest," *Phi Delta Kappan*, vol. 50, pp. 2–9.

HALLECK, SEYMOUR, 1969, "You Can Go to Hell with Style," *Psychology Today*, vol. 3, no. 6, p. 16+, November.

HALLMAN, RALPH J., 1967, "Techniques of Creative Teaching," *Journal of Creative Behavior*, vol. 11, pp. 325–330.

HAMACHEK, DON E., 1968, "What Research Tells Us about the Characteristics of 'Good' and 'Bad' Teachers," in D. E. Hamachek (ed.), *Human Dynamics in Psychology and Education*, Boston: Allyn and Bacon, Inc.

HAMACHEK, DON E., 1969, "Characteristics of Good Teachers and Implications for Teacher Education," *Phi Delta Kappan*, vol. 50, pp. 341–345.

HANSON, HENRY R., 1969, "Day-of-judgment Examinations," *Phi Delta Kappan*, vol. 51, pp. 81–84.

HARDIE, C. D., 1967, "Thinking," in B. P. Komisar and C. J. B. Macmillan (eds.), *Psychological Concepts in Education*, Chicago: Rand McNally & Company.

HARRINGTON, FRED H., 1967, "Adult and Continuing Education," in E. L. Morphet and C. O. Ryan (eds.), *Implications for Education of Prospective Changes in Society*, Denver: Designing Education for the Future.

HARRIS, ALBERT J., 1968, "Diagnosis and Remedial Instruction in Reading," in National Society for the Study of Education, 67th Yearbook, part II, *Innovation and Change in Reading Instruction*, Chicago: University of Chicago Press.

HARRISON, CHARLES H., 1970, "South Brunswick, N.J.: Schools Put a Town on the Map," *Saturday Review*, vol. 53, no. 8, pp. 66–68+, Feb. 21.

HART, LESLIE A., 1969, "Learning at Random," *Saturday Review*, vol. 52, pp. 62–63, April 19.

HAVIGHURST, ROBERT J., 1953, *Human Development and Education*, New York: Longmans, Green & Co., Inc.

HAVIGHURST, ROBERT, 1968, "Requirements for a New Valid Criticism," *Phi Delta Kappan*, vol. 50, pp. 20–26.

HAVIGHURST, ROBERT J., 1970, "The Unknown Good: Education Vouchers," *Phi Delta Kappan*, vol. 52, pp. 52–53.

HAVIGHURST, ROBERT J., P. H. BOWMAN, G. P. LIDDLE, C. V. MATTHEWS, AND JAMES V. PIERCE, 1962, *Growing Up in River City*, New York: John Wiley & Sons, Inc.

HAVIGHURST, ROBERT J., AND BERNICE L. NEUGARTEN, 1967, *Society and Education*, 3d ed., Boston: Allyn and Bacon, Inc.

HAWKINS, DAVID, 1966, "Learning the Unteachable," in L. S. Shulman and E. R. Keislar (eds.), *Learning by Discovery, A Critical Appraisal*, Chicago: Rand McNally & Company.

HEBER, R., R. DEVER, AND J. CONRY, 1968, "The Influence of Environmental and Genetic Variables on Intellectual Development," in H. J. Prehm,

L. A. Hamerlynck, and J. E. Crosson (eds.), *Behavioral Research in Mental Retardation*, Eugene, Ore.: University of Oregon Press.

HEFFERNAN, HELEN, 1966, "Challenge or Pressure?" in R. C. Doll and R. S. Fleming (eds.), *Children under Pressure*, Columbus, Ohio: Charles E. Merrill Books, Inc.

HEILBRONER, ROBERT L., 1970, "Priorities for the Seventies," *Saturday Review*, vol. 53, no. 1, pp. 17–19+, Jan. 3.

HERRIOTT, ROBERT E., 1963, "Some Social Determinants of Educational Aspiration," *Harvard Educational Review*, vol. 33, pp. 157–177.

HERSEY, JOHN, 1968, *The Algiers Motel Incident*, New York: Alfred A. Knopf, Inc.

HILGARD, ERNEST R., 1956, *Theories of Learning*, 2d ed., New York: Appleton-Century-Crofts, Inc.

HILGARD, ERNEST R., AND GORDON H. BOWER, 1966, *Theories of Learning*, 3d ed., New York: Appleton-Century-Crofts, Inc.

HILL, GEORGE E., AND ELEANORE B. LUCKEY, 1969, *Guidance for Children in Elementary Schools*, New York: Appleton-Century-Crofts, Inc.

HINTON, BERNARD L., 1968, "A Model for the Study of Creative Problem Solving," *The Journal of Creative Behavior*, vol. 2, pp. 133–142.

HOFFNUNG, ROBERT J., AND ROBERT S. MILLS, 1970, "Situational Group Counseling with Disadvantaged Youth," *Personnel and Guidance Journal*, vol. 48, pp. 458–464.

HOGAN, ERMON O., AND ROBERT L. GREEN, 1971, "Can Teachers Modify Children's Self-Concepts?" *Teachers College Record*, vol. 72, pp. 423–426.

HOHMAN, LESLIE, 1947, *As the Twig Is Bent*, New York: The Macmillan Company.

HOLLAND, JAMES G., AND B. F. SKINNER, 1961, *The Analysis of Behavior*, New York: McGraw-Hill Book Company.

HOLT, JOHN, 1964, *How Children Fail*, New York: Pitman Publishing Corporation.

HORNEY, KAREN, 1945, *Our Inner Conflicts*, New York: W. W. Norton & Company, Inc.

HORROCKS, JOHN E., 1962, *The Psychology of Adolescence*, 2d ed., Boston: Houghton Mifflin Company.

HOWARD, EUGENE R., 1966, "Developing Student Responsibility for Learning," *National Association of Secondary-School Principals*, Bulletin, vol. 50, no. 309, pp. 235–246, April.

HOYT, KENNETH, 1964, Guest Lecturer, University of Oregon, Eugene, Ore., May.

HULL, CLARK R., 1943, *Principles of Behavior*, New York: Appleton-Century-Crofts, Inc.

HUNT, J. MCV., 1969, "Has Compensatory Education Failed? Has It Been Attempted?" *Harvard Educational Review*, vol. 39, pp. 278–300.

HUNT, J. MCV., 1968, Interviewed by Patricia Pine, "Where Education Begins," *American Education*, vol. 4, no. 9, pp. 15–19, Oct.

HUNTER, E. C., 1957, "Changes in Teachers' Attitudes toward Children's Behavior over the Last Thirty Years," *Mental Hygiene*, vol. 41, pp. 3–11.

HURLEY, RODGER, 1969, *Poverty and Mental Retardation*, New York: Vintage Books (Random House).

IGLITZIN, LYNNE B., 1970, "Violence and American Democracy," *Journal of Social Issues*, vol. 26, no. 1, pp. 165–186, winter.

INNOVATION AND EXPERIMENT IN EDUCATION, 1964, Panel on Educational Research and Development, Washington, D.C.: U.S. Government Printing Office.

JACKSON, PHILIP W., 1969, "Technology and the Teacher," in E. S. Mason (Chm.), *The Schools and the Challenge of Innovation*, New York: McGraw-Hill Book Company.

JACKSON, PHILIP W., MELVIN L. SILBERMAN, AND BERNICE J. WOLFSON, 1969, "Signs of Personal Involvement in Teachers' Descriptions of Their Students," *Journal of Educational Psychology*, vol. 60, pp. 22–27.

JAFFE, DOROTHEA K., 1969, "Antioch Students Like to 'Co-op'," *Christian Science Monitor*, May 15.

JAMES, H. THOMAS, 1969, "Financing More Effective Education," in Committee for Economic Development, *The Schools and the Challenge of Innovation*, New York: McGraw-Hill Book Company.

JEFFERY, C. RAY, AND INA A. JEFFERY, 1967, "Prevention through the Family," in W. E. Amos and C. F. Wellford (eds.), *Delinquency Prevention: Theory and Practice*, Englewood Cliffs, N.J.: Prentice-Hall, Inc.

JENCKS, CHRISTOPHER, 1970, "Giving Parents Money for Schooling: Education Vouchers," *Phi Delta Kappan*, 52: 49–52.

JENKINS, JOSEPH R., AND STANLEY L. DENO, 1969, "Influence of Student Behavior on Teacher's Self-Evaluation," *Journal of Educational Psychology*, 60: 439–442.

JENSEN, ARTHUR R., 1969a, "Reducing the Heredity-Environment Uncertainty: A Reply," *Harvard Educational Review*, 39: 449–483.

JENSEN, ARTHUR R., 1969b, "How Much Can We Boost IQ and Scholastic Achievement?" *Harvard Educational Review*, 39: 1–123.

JERSILD, ARTHUR T., 1960, *Child Psychology*, 5th ed., Englewood Cliffs, N.J.: Prentice-Hall, Inc.

JERSILD, ARTHUR T., 1963, "What Teachers Say about Psychotherapy," *Phi Delta Kappan*, vol. 44, pp. 313–317.

JERSILD, ARTHUR T., AND EVE ALLINA LAZAR WITH ADELE M. BRODKIN, 1962, *The Meaning of Psychotherapy in the Teacher's Life and Work*, New York: Teachers College Press, Columbia University.

JOURARD, SIDNEY M., 1967, "Fascination: A Phenomenological Perspective on Independent Learning," in G. T. Gleason (ed.), *The Theory and Nature of Independent Learning*, Scranton, Pa.: International Textbook Company.

KAGAN, JEROME, 1968, "The Child: His Struggle for Identity," *Saturday Review*, vol. 51, no. 49, pp. 80–82+, Dec. 7.

KAGAN, JEROME S., 1969, "Inadequate Evidence and Illogical Conclusions," *Harvard Educational Review*, vol. 39, pp. 274-277.

KAGAN, JEROME, AND HOWARD A. MOSS, 1962, *Birth to Maturity: A Study in Psychological Development*, New York: John Wiley & Sons, Inc.

KAISER, GEORGE M., AND JOANN TIMMER, 1964, "Teen-agers with a Looking Glass," *Personnel and Guidance Journal*, vol. 42, pp. 608-609.

KAUFMAN, BURT, AND PAUL BETHUNE, 1964, "Nova High Space Age School," *Phi Delta Kappan*, vol. 46, pp. 9-11.

KEACH, EVERETT T., JR., ROBERT FULTON, AND WILLIAM E. GARDNER (eds.), 1967, *Education and Social Crisis*, New York: John Wiley & Sons, Inc.

KEEL, JOHN S., 1965, "Art Education, 1940-64," in National Society for the Study of Education, 64th Yearbook, part II, *Art Education*, Chicago: University of Chicago Press.

KEEVE, PHILIP, 1969, " 'Fitness,' 'Posture,' and Other Selected School Health Myths," in H. W. Bernard (ed.), *Readings in Adolescent Development*, Scranton, Pa.: International Textbook Company. From *Journal of School Health*, vol. 37, pp. 8-15, 1967.

KELLEY, EARL C., 1962, *In Defense of Youth*, Englewood Cliffs, N.J.: Prentice-Hall, Inc.

KELLY, GEORGE A., 1955, *The Psychology of Personal Constructs*, vol. 1, *A Theory of Personality*, New York: W. W. Norton & Company, Inc.

KEMP, BARBARA H., 1966, *The Youth We Haven't Served*, Washington, D.C.: U.S. Department of Health, Education, and Welfare.

KENISTON, KENNETH, 1968, "Youth, Change and Violence," *The American Scholar*, vol. 37, pp. 227-245.

KIRP, DAVID L., 1968, "The Poor, the Schools, and Equal Protection," *Harvard Educational Review*, vol. 38, pp. 636-668.

KLAUSMEIER, HERBERT J., WILLIAM L. GOODWIN, AND TECKLA RONDA, 1968, "Effects of Accelerating Bright, Older, Elementary Pupils—A Second Follow-up," *Journal of Educational Psychology*, vol. 59, pp. 53-58.

KLIGER, SAMUEL, 1968, "A Strategy of Compensatory Education," *Teachers College Record*, vol. 69, pp. 753-758.

KLOPF, GORDON J., AND GARDA W. BOWMAN, 1966, *Teacher Education in a Social Context*, New York: Bank Street College of Education.

KNEBEL, FLETCHER, 1969, *Trespass*, Garden City, N.Y.: Doubleday & Company, Inc.

KOGAN, NATHAN, AND JULIA CARLSON, 1969, "Difficulty of Problems Attempted under Conditions of Competition and Group Consensus," *Journal of Educational Psychology*, vol. 60, pp. 158-167.

KOHL, HERBERT, 1967, *Teaching the "Unteachable,"* New York: A New York Review Book.

KRATHWOHL, DAVID R., BENJAMIN S. BLOOM, AND BERTRAM B. MASIA, 1964, *Taxonomy of Educational Objectives: The Classification of Educational Goals*, Handbook II: Affective Domain, New York: David McKay, Inc.

KRECH, DAVID, 1969, "Psychoneurobiochemeducation," *Phi Delta Kappan*, vol. 50, pp. 370-375.

KUBALA, ALBERT L., AND M. M. KATZ, 1960, "Nutritional Factors in Psychological Test Behavior," *Journal of Genetic Psychology*, vol. 96, pp. 343-352.

KUBIE, LAWRENCE S., 1956, "Hidden Brain Power," *Saturday Review*, vol. 39, p. 26, Oct. 13.

KUBINIEC, CATHLEEN M., 1970, "The Relative Efficacy of Various Dimensions of the Self-concept in Predicting Academic Achievement," *American Educational Research Journal*, vol. 7, pp. 321-336.

KUETHE, JAMES L., 1968, *The Teaching-Learning Process*, Glenview, Ill.: Scott, Foresman and Company.

KUPFERMAN, SAUL C., AND RAYMOND A. ULMER, 1964, "An Experimental Total Push Program for Emotionally Disturbed Adolescents," *Personnel and Guidance Journal*, vol. 42, pp. 894-898.

LANDSMAN, TED, 1961, "Human Experience and Human Relationship," in *Personality Theory and Counseling Practice*, Gainesville, Fla.: University of Florida.

LANE, HOWARD, 1964, in Mary B. Lane (ed.), *On Educating Human Beings*, Chicago: Follett Publishing Company.

LEE, GORDON C., 1961, "The Changing Role of the Teacher," in National Society for the Study of Education, 65th Yearbook, part II, *The Changing American School*, Chicago: University of Chicago Press.

LEVINE, MURRAY, 1966, "Psychological Testing of Children," in L. W. Hoffman and M. L. Hoffman (eds.), *Review of Child Development Research*, vol. 2, New York: Russell Sage Foundation.

LEVINE, RICHARD H., 1970, "Reaching Out to Danny," *American Education*, vol. 6, no. 6, pp. 10-14, July.

LEWIN, KURT, 1942, "Field Theory and Learning," in National Society for the Study of Education, 41st Yearbook, part II, *The Psychology of Learning*, Chicago: University of Chicago Press.

LEWIN, KURT, 1948, *Resolving Social Conflict*, New York: Harper & Row, Publishers, Incorporated.

LEWIN, KURT, RONALD LIPPITT, AND RALPH K. WHITE, 1939, "Patterns of Aggressive Behavior in Experimentally Created Social Climates," *Journal of Social Psychology*, vol. 10, pp. 271–299.

LEWIS, CLAUDIA, 1946, *Children of the Cumberland*, New York: Columbia University Press.

LIDDLE, GORDON P., AND ROBERT E. ROCKWELL, 1966, "The Role of Parents and Family Life," in Staten W. Webster (ed.), *The Disadvantaged Learner: Knowing, Understanding, Educating*, San Francisco: Chandler Publishing Company.

LIPTON, EARLE L., ALFRED STEINSCHNEIDER, AND JULIUS B. RICHMOND, 1966, "Psychophysiologic Disorders in Children," in L. W. Hoffman and M. L. Hoffman (eds.), *Review of Child Development Research*, vol. 2, New York: Russell Sage Foundation.

LOCKE, ROBERT W., 1971, "Has the Education Industry Lost Its Nerve?" *Saturday Review*, vol. 54, no. 3, pp. 42–44, Jan. 16.

LOWRY, RITCHIE P., AND ROBERT P. RANKIN, 1969, *Sociology, The Science of Society*, New York: Charles Scribner's Sons.

LUCE, WILLIAM P., 1966, "Long Hair, the Long Green and the Youth Market," in Time-Life Special Report, *The Young Americans*, New York: Time, Inc.

LUNSTRUM, JOHN, 1966, "The Mystique of the Peace Corps: A Dilemma," *Phi Delta Kappan*, vol. 48, pp. 98–102.

LYNN, DAVID B., 1968, "Sex-Role and Parental Identification," in Ellis D. Evans (ed.), *Children: Readings in Behavior and Development*, New York: Holt, Rinehart and Winston, Inc.

LOEFFLER, DOROTHY, 1970, "Counseling and the Psychology of Communication," *Personnel and Guidance Journal*, vol. 48, pp. 629–636.

MCBRIDE, MARJORIE, 1963, "The School in the Life of Delinquent Girls," an address at the Portland Continuation Center, Oregon State System of Higher Education, March 6.

MCCANDLESS, BOYD R., 1967, *Children: Behavior and Development*, New York: Holt, Rinehart and Winston, Inc.

MACCOBY, MICHAEL, 1971, "The Three C's and Discipline for Freedom," *School Review*, vol. 79, pp. 227–242.

MCCLELLAND, DAVID C., 1971, "To Know Why Men Do What They Do," *Psychology Today*, vol. 4, no. 8, pp. 35–39+, January.

MCCREARY, EUGENE, 1967, "Pawns or Players," *Phi Delta Kappan*, vol. 49, pp. 138–142.

MCCREARY, EUGENE, 1966, "Some Positive Characteristics of Disadvantaged Learners and Their Implications for Education," in Staten W. Webster (ed.), *The Disadvantaged Learner*, San Francisco: Chandler Publishing Company.

MCCULLY, C. HAROLD, 1969, *Challenge for Change in Counselor Education*, compiled by Lyle L. Miller, Minneapolis: Burgess Publishing Company.

MCDAVID, RAVEN I., JR., 1970, "The Sociology of Education," in National Society for the Study of Education, 69th Yearbook, part II, *Linguistics In School Programs*, Chicago: University of Chicago Press.

MCDONALD, FREDERICK J., 1964, "The Influence of Learning Theories on Education (1900-1950)," in National Society for the Study of Education, 63d Yearbook, part I, *Theories of Learning and Instruction*, Chicago: University of Chicago Press.

MACGINITIE, WALTER H., AND SAMUEL BALL (eds.), 1968, *Readings in Psychological Foundations of Education*, New York: McGraw-Hill Book Company.

MACKINNON, DONALD W., 1962, "The Nature and Nurture of Creative Talent," *American Psychologist*, vol. 17, pp. 484-495.

MCMURRIN, STERLING M., 1969, "Introduction," in E. S. Mason (Chm.), *The Schools and the Challenge of Innovation*, New York: McGraw-Hill Book Company.

MCNEIL, JOHN D., 1964, "Programmed Instruction versus Usual Classroom Procedures in Teaching Boys to Read," *American Educational Research Journal*, vol. 1, pp. 113-119.

MCNEIL, KEITH A., AND BEEMAN N. PHILLIPS, 1969, "Scholastic Nature of Responses to the Environment in Selected Subcultures," *Journal of Educational Psychology*, vol. 60, pp. 79-85.

MCPHERSON, J. H., 1968, "The People, the Problems and the Problem-solving Methods," *The Journal of Creative Behavior*, vol. 2, pp. 103-110.

MAGER, ROBERT F., 1968, *Developing Attitude toward Learning*, Palo Alto, Calif.: Fearon Publishers.

MANNING, DUANE, 1971, *Toward a Humanistic Curriculum*, New York: Harper & Row, Publishers, Incorporated.

MANPOWER REPORT OF THE PRESIDENT, 1969, 1970, Washington, D.C.: U.S. Department of Labor, U.S. Government Printing Office.

MARX, MELVIN H., AND TOM N. TOMBAUGH, 1967, *Motivation*, San Francisco: Chandler Publishing Company.

MASLOW, ABRAHAM H., 1954, *Motivation and Personality*, New York: Harper and Row, Publishers, Incorporated.

MASLOW, ABRAHAM H., 1968a, "Music Education and Peak Experience," *Music Educators Journal*, vol. 54, no. 6, pp. 72-75, 163-171.

MASLOW, ABRAHAM H., 1968b, "Some Educational Implications of Humanistic Psychologies," *Harvard Educational Review*, vol. 38, pp. 685-696.

MASLOW, ABRAHAM H., 1969, "Toward a Humanistic Biology," *American Psychologist*, vol. 24, pp. 724-735.

MATHIS, B. CLAUDE, JOHN W. COTTON, AND LEE SECHREST, 1970, *Psychological Foundations of Education*, New York: Academic Press.

MEAD, MARGARET, 1970, "Youth Revolt: The Future Is Now," *Saturday Review*, vol. 53, no. 2, pp. 23–25+, Jan. 10.

MEDNICK, MARTHA T., AND FRANK M. ANDREWS, 1967, "Creative Thinking and Level of Intelligence," *Journal of Creative Behavior*, vol. 1, pp. 428–431.

MENNINGER, KARL A., 1953, Quotation in "Keeping Abreast in Education," *Phi Delta Kappan*, vol. 34, p. 156.

MENNINGER, KARL A., 1968, "The Crime of Punishment," *Saturday Review*, vol. 51, no. 36, pp. 21–25+, Sept. 7.

MENNINGER, KARL A., WITH M. MAYMAN AND P. PRUYSER, 1963, *The Vital Balance*, New York: Viking Press.

MERTON, ROBERT K., AND ROBERT A. NISBET, 1966, *Contemporary Social Problems*, New York: Harcourt, Brace & World, Inc.

MERWIN, JACK C., 1969, "Historical Review of Changing Concepts of Evaluation," in National Society for the Study of Education, 68th Yearbook, part II, *Educational Evaluation: New Roles, New Means*, Chicago: University of Chicago Press.

METCALF, LAWRENCE E., AND MAURICE P. HUNT, 1970, "Relevance and the Curriculum," *Phi Delta Kappan*, vol. 51, pp. 358–361.

MEYER, JAMES A., 1969, "Suburbia: A Wasteland of Disadvantaged Youth and Negligent Schools?" *Phi Delta Kappan*, vol. 50, pp. 575–578.

MILLER, GORDON W., 1970, "Factors in School Achievement and Social Class," *Journal of Educational Psychology*, vol. 61, pp. 260–269.

MONTAGU, ASHLEY, 1968, "Chromosomes and Crime," *Psychology Today*, vol. 2, no. 5, pp. 42–49, October.

MOORE, RAY, 1970, "Helping Adolescents Achieve Psychological Growth," *Adolescence*, vol. 5, no. 17, pp. 37–54.

MORGAN, C. D., AND H. A. MURRAY, 1935, "A Method for Investigating Fantasies: The Thematic Apperception Test," *Archives of Neurological Psychiatry*, vol. 34, pp. 289–306.

MOULY, GEORGE J., 1968, *Psychology for Effective Teaching*, New York: Holt, Rinehart and Winston, Inc.

MOUSTAKAS, CLARK, 1966, *The Authentic Teacher,* Cambridge, Mass.: Howard A. Doyle Publishing Company.

MOWRER, O. H., 1960, *Learning Theory and Behavior*, New York: John Wiley & Sons, Inc.

MULLIGAN, JAMES H., 1970, "Talent Lies Hidden in the Delta," *American Education*, vol. 6, no. 4, pp. 13–16, May.

MUNDAY, LEO A., 1970, "Factors Influencing the Predictability of College Grades," *American Educational Research Journal*, vol. 7, pp. 99–107.

MURRAY, H. A., 1938, *Explorations in Personality*, Fair Lawn, N.J.: Oxford University Press.

MUSGROVE, FRANK, 1969, "Why Youth Riot—The Adolescent Ghetto," in H. W. Bernard (ed.), *Readings in Adolescent Development*, Scranton,

Pa.: International Textbook Company. From *The Nation*, vol. 199, pp. 137–140, 1964.

MYRICK, ROBERT D., 1970, "The Counselor-Consultant and the Effeminate Boy," *Personnel and Guidance Journal*, vol. 48, pp. 355–361.

NASH, JOHN, 1970, *Developmental Psychology: A Psychobiological Approach*, Englewood Cliffs, N.J.: Prentice-Hall, Inc.

NATIONS, JIMMY E., 1967, "Caring for Individual Differences in Reading through Nongrading," address to Seattle, Wash., Teachers, May 3.

NEALE, DANIEL C., 1969, "Aversive Control of Behavior," *Phi Delta Kappan*, vol. 50, pp. 335–338, February.

NEILL, A. S., 1960, *Summerhill: A Radical Approach to Child Rearing*, New York: Hart Publishing Company.

NEWMAN, H. H., F. N. FREEMAN, AND K. H. HOLZINGER, 1937, *Twins: A Study of Heredity and Environment*, Chicago: The University of Chicago Press.

NORRIS, ELEANOR L., 1969, "The National Assessment," *American Education*, vol. 5, no. 8, pp. 20–23, October.

OHANIAN, VERA, 1971, "Educational Technology: A Critique," *Elementary School Journal*, vol. 71, pp. 182–197.

OLSEN, JAMES, 1965, "Challenge of the POOR to the Schools," *Phi Delta Kappan*, vol. 47, no. 2, pp. 79–84, October.

OSBORN, ALEX F., 1963, *Applied Imagination*, 3d ed., New York: Charles Scribner's Sons.

OSOFSKY, HOWARD J., BERNARD BRAEN, ROBERT DIFLORIO, JOHN H. HAGEN, AND PEGGY WOOD, 1968, "A Program for Pregnant Schoolgirls—A Progress Report," *Adolescence*, vol. 3, pp. 89–108.

OTTO, HERBERT A., 1969, "New Light on the Human Potential," *Saturday Review*, vol. 52, no. 51, pp. 14–17, Dec. 20.

OTTO, WAYNE, AND KARL KOENKE (eds.), 1969, *Remedial Teaching: Research and Comment*, Boston: Houghton Mifflin Company.

OWENS, W. A., 1966, "Age and Mental Abilities: A Second Adult Follow-up," *Journal of Educational Psychology*, vol. 57, pp. 311–325.

PARIS, NORMAN M., 1968, "T-Grouping: A Helping Movement," *Phi Delta Kappan*, vol. 49, pp. 460–462.

PARNES, SIDNEY J., 1971, "Creativity: Developing Human Potential," *Journal of Creative Behavior*, vol. 5, pp. 19–36.

PARSONS, TALCOTT, 1964, "Youth in the Context of American Society," in Henry Borow (ed.), *Man in a World at Work*, Boston: Houghton Mifflin Company.

PASSOW, A. HARRY, 1967a, "Early Childhood and Compensatory Education," in E. L. Morphet and C. O. Ryan (eds.), *Implications for Education of Prospective Changes in Society*, Denver: Designing Education for the Future.

PASSOW, A. HARRY, 1967*b*, "Instructional Content for Depressed Urban Centers: Problems and Approaches," in A. H. Passow, M. Goldberg and A. J. Tannenbaum (eds.), *Education of the Disadvantaged*, New York: Holt, Rinehart and Winston, Inc.

PATRICK, CATHERINE, 1955, *What Is Creative Thinking?* New York: Philosophical Library, Inc.

PATRICK, D., 1935, "Creative Thought in Poets," *Archives of Psychology*, no. 178, p. 30.

PAVLOV, IVAN P., 1927, *Conditioned Reflexes*, London: Oxford University Press (Translated by G. V. Anrep).

PEARSE, BENJAMIN H., 1969, "Dyslexia," *American Education*, vol. 5, no. 4, pp. 9-13, April.

PELTIER, GARY L., 1968, "Sex Differences in the School: Problem and Proposed Solution," *Phi Delta Kappan*, vol. 50, pp. 182-185.

PENFIELD, WILDER, 1967, "The Uncommitted Cortex, The Child's Changing Brain," in H. W. Bernard and W. C. Huckins (eds.), *Readings in Human Development*, Boston: Allyn and Bacon, Inc. From *The Atlantic*, vol. 214, no. 1, pp. 77-81, July 1964.

PENN, RICHARD, 1969, "Children Teach Each Other," *Christian Science Monitor*, April 29.

THE PEOPLE WHO SERVE EDUCATION, 1969, A report on the state of the Education Professions by the U.S. Commissioner of Education—1968, Washington, D.C.: U.S. Dept. of Health, Education, and Welfare.

PERSPECTIVES ON HUMAN DEPRIVATION, 1968, Washington, D.C.: U.S. Department of Health, Education, and Welfare.

PETREQUIN, GAYNOR, 1968, *Individualizing Learning through Modular-Flexible Programming*, New York: McGraw-Hill Book Company.

PFEIL, MARY PAT, 1969, "They Got the Feeling That Everybody's Somebody," *American Education*, vol. 5, no. 10, pp. 21-24.

PIAGET, JEAN, 1969, *The Theory of Stages in Cognitive Development*, Monterey, Calif.: CTB/McGraw-Hill. A booklet.

PIERSON, GEORGE A., 1965, *An Evaluation: Counselor Education in Regular Session Institutes*, Washington, D.C.: U.S. Department of Health, Education, and Welfare (OE-25042).

PILEGGI, NICHOLAS, 1969, "Revolutionaries Who Have to Be Home by 7:30," *Phi Delta Kappan*, vol. 50, pp. 561-569.

PINE, GERALD J., 1966, "The Affluent Delinquent," *Phi Delta Kappan*, vol. 48, pp. 138-143.

PINE, PATRICIA, 1969, "What's the IQ of the IQ Test?" *American Education*, vol. 5, no. 9, pp. 2-4.

PINES, MAYA, 1963, "How Three-year-olds Teach Themselves to Read—and Love It," *Harper's*, vol. 226, pp. 58-64, May.

PITTS, F. N., 1969, "The Biochemistry of Anxiety," *Scientific American*, vol. 220, pp. 69–75.

PLUNKETT, WILLIAM T., 1969, "Independent Study at Syosset High School," *Phi Delta Kappan*, vol. 50, pp. 350–352.

PORTER, BLAINE R., 1969, "American Teen-agers of the 1960's—Our Despair or Hope?" in H. W. Bernard (ed.), *Readings in Adolescent Development*, Scranton, Pa.: International Textbook Company. From *Journal of Marriage and the Family*, vol. 27, pp. 139–147, 1965.

PRESCOTT, DANIEL A., 1957, *The Child in the Educative Process*, New York: McGraw-Hill Book Company.

PROFF, FRED C., 1962, "Non-verbal Clues in Counseling," Lecture given at Portland Continuation Center, Oregon State System of Higher Education, July 26.

RATHS, JAMES, 1966, "Mutuality of Effective Functioning and School Experience," in W. B. Waetjen and R. R. Leeper (eds.), *Learning and Mental Health in the School*, Washington, D.C.: Association for Supervision and Curriculum Development, NEA.

READ, MERRILL S., 1969, "Malnutrition and Learning," *American Education*, vol. 5, no. 10, pp. 11–14, December.

RICHARDSON, ELLIOT L., 1971, "The Next Big Effort," *American Education*, vol. 7, no. 1, pp. 11–12, January–February.

RIESMAN, DAVID, 1969a, "The Search for Alternative Models in Education," *The American Scholar*, vol. 38, pp. 377–388.

RIESMAN, DAVID, 1969b, "The Young Are Captives of Each Other," *Psychology Today*, vol. 3, no. 5, pp. 28–31+.

RIESSMAN, FRANK, 1966a, "Styles of Learning," *NEA Journal*, vol. 55, no. 3, pp. 15–17, March.

RIESSMAN, FRANK, 1966b, "The Slow Gifted Child," in S. W. Webster (ed.), *The Disadvantaged Learner*, San Francisco: Chandler Publishing Company.

RIST, RAY C., 1970, "Student Social Class and Teacher Expectations: The Self-Fulfilling Prophecy in Ghetto Education," *Harvard Educational Review*, vol. 40, pp. 411–451.

RIVLIN, HARRY, 1965, "New Teachers for New Immigrants," *Teachers College Record*, vol. 66, pp. 707–718.

ROBBINS, MELVYN P., 1967, "Test of the Doman-Delacato Rationale with Retarded Readers," *Journal of the American Medical Association*, vol. 202, pp. 389–393.

ROBERTS, WALLACE, 1970, "No Place to Grow," *Saturday Review*, vol. 53, no. 12, pp. 62–67+, Mar. 21.

ROGERS, CARL R., no date, "The Process of the Basic Encounter Group," mimeographed, La Jolla, Calif.: Western Behavioral Sciences Institute.

ROGERS, CARL R., 1961, *On Becoming a Person*, Boston: Houghton Mifflin Company.

ROGERS, CARL R., 1968, *Freedom to Learn*, Columbus, Ohio: Charles E. Merrill Publishing Company.

ROGERS, CARL R., 1968, "Interpersonal Relationships: U.S.A. 2000," *Journal of Applied Behavioral Sciences*, vol. 4, pp. 265-280.

"CARL ROGERS: Joins Ranks of Radical Critics of the Public Schools," 1970, no author indicated, *Phi Delta Kappan*, vol. 51, no. 5, p. 294.

RORSCHACH, HERMANN, 1937, P*sychodiagnostik*, 3d ed., Bern, Switzerland: Hans Huber.

ROSENTHAL, M. J., M. K. FINKELSTEIN, E. NI, AND R. E. ROBERTSON, 1962, "Father-Child Relationships and Children's Problems," *American Archives of General Psychiatry*, vol. 7, pp. 360-373.

ROSENTHAL, ROBERT, AND LENORE JACOBSON, 1968, *Pygmalion in the the Classroom*, New York: Holt, Rinehart and Winston, Inc.

ROTHBART, MYRON, SUSAN DALFEN, AND ROBERT BARRETT, 1971, "Effects of Teacher's Expectancy on Student-Teacher Interaction," *Journal of Educational Psychology*, vol. 62, pp. 49-54.

ROTHNEY, JOHN W. M., PAUL DANIELSON, AND ROBERT A. HEIMANN, 1959, *Measurement for Guidance*, New York: Harper & Row, Publishers, Incorporated.

RUMMELL, FRANCES V., 1948, "What Are Good Teachers Like?" *School Life*, vol. 30, pp. 7-11, July.

RYAN, W. CARSON, 1938, *Mental Health through Education*, New York: The Commonwealth Fund.

SALTZMAN, HENRY, 1965, "The Poor and the Schools," in A. Pearl and F. Riesman, *New Careers for the Poor*, New York: The Free Press.

SARBIN, T. R., AND B. G. ROSENBERG, 1955, "Contributions to Role Taking Theory: IV. A Method for Obtaining a Quantitative Estimate of Self," *Journal of Social Psychology*, vol. 42, pp. 71-81.

SASSENRATH, JULIUS M., AND GEORGE D. YONGE, 1968, "Delayed Information Feedback, Feedback Cues, Retention Set, and Delayed Retention," *Journal of Educational Psychology*, vol. 59, pp. 69-73.

SAWREY, JAMES M., AND CHARLES W. TELFORD, 1968, *Educational Psychology*, 3d ed., Boston: Allyn and Bacon, Inc.

SCHILL, WILLIAM J., 1963, "Education and Occupational Success," *Personnel and Guidance Journal*, vol. 41, pp. 442-444.

SCHMUCK, R. A., AND E. VAN EGMOND, 1965, "Sex Differences in the Relationship of Interpersonal Perceptions to Academic Performance," *Psychology in the Schools*, vol. 2, pp. 32-40.

SCHRAG, PETER, 1969*a*, "The Forgotten American," *Harper's*, vol. 239, no. 1431, pp. 27-34, August.

SCHRAG, PETER, 1969*b*, "Gloom at the Top," *Saturday Review*, vol. 52, no. 33, pp. 50–51+, Aug. 16.

SCHREIBER, DANIEL, 1960, *The Higher Horizons Program: First Annual Progress Report*, New York: Board of Education of the City of New York (Pamphlet).

SCHREIBER, DANIEL, 1969, "Juvenile Delinquency and the School Dropout Problem," in H. W. Bernard (ed.), *Readings in Adolescent Development*, Scranton, Pa.: International Textbook Company. From *Federal Probation*, vol. 27, no. 2, pp. 15–19, 1963.

SCHREIBER, DANIEL, AND BERNARD A. KAPLAN (eds.), 1964, *Guidance and the School Dropout*, Washington, D.C.: National Education Association.

SEARS, PAULINE S., AND ERNEST R. HILGARD, 1964, "The Teacher's Role in the Motivation of the Learner," in National Society for the Study of Education, 63d Yearbook, part II, *Theories of Learning and Instruction*, Chicago: University of Chicago Press.

SECORD, PAUL F., AND CARL W. BACKMAN, 1964, *Social Psychology*, New York: McGraw-Hill Book Company.

SEGEL, DAVID, 1969, "Intellectual Abilities in the Adolescent Period," in H. W. Bernard (ed.), *Readings in Adolescent Development*, Scranton, Pa.: International Textbook Company. From Bulletin 1948, No. 6, Federal Security Agency, Office of Education, pp. 1–16.

SEXTON, PATRICIA C., 1961, *Education and Income*, New York: The Viking Press, Inc.

SHANNON, DAN C., 1957, "What Research Says about Acceleration," *Phi Delta Kappan*, vol. 39, pp. 7072.

SHAPLIN, JUDSON T., 1964, "Team Teaching," in R. Gross and J. Murphy (eds.), *The Revolution in the Schools*, New York: Harcourt, Brace & World, Inc.

SHELDON, W. H., AND S. S. STEVENS, 1942, *The Varieties of Temperament*, New York: Harper & Row, Publishers, Incorporated.

SHERIF, MUZAFER, AND CAROLYN W. SHERIF, 1964, *Reference Groups*, New York: Harper & Row, Publishers, Incorporated.

SHERMAN, MANDER, AND CORA B. KEY, 1932, "The Intelligence of Isolated Mountain Children," *Child Development*, vol. 3, pp. 279–290.

SHORE, MILTON F., AND JOSEPH L. MASSIMO, 1969, "The Alienated Adolescent: A Challenge to the Mental Health Professional," *Adolescence*, vol. 4, no. 13, pp. 19-34, Spring.

SHOSTROM, EVERETT L., 1969, "Group Therapy: Let the Buyer Beware," *Psychology Today*, vol. 2, no. 12, pp. 36–40, May.

SHRABLE, KENNETH, AND JULIUS M. SASSENRATH, 1970, "Effects of Achievement Motivation and Test Anxiety on Performance in Programmed Instruction," *American Educational Research Journal*, vol. 7, pp. 209–220.

SHUELL, THOMAS J., AND GEOFFREY KEPPEL, 1970, "Learning Ability and Retention," *Journal of Educational Psychology*, vol. 61, pp. 59–65.

SHULMAN, LEE S., AND EVAN R. KEISLAR (eds.), 1966, *Learning by Discovery: A Critical Appraisal*, Chicago: Rand McNally & Company.

SILBERMAN, MELVIN L., 1969, "Behavioral Expression of Teachers' Attitudes toward Elementary School Students," *Journal of Educational Psychology*, vol. 60, pp. 402–407.

SIMON, SIDNEY, 1966, "Wanted: New Education Professors for the Slums," *Teachers College Record*, vol. 67, pp. 271–275.

SIMON, SIDNEY B., 1970, "Grades Must Go," *School Review*, vol. 78, pp. 397–402.

SIMON, SIDNEY, HOWARD KIRSCHENBAUM, AND RODNEY NAPIER, 1970, "The Day the Consultant Looked at Our Grading System," *Phi Delta Kappan*, vol. 51, pp. 476–479, May.

SIMMS, MIMI, 1970, "Some Highlights from the Nutrition Conference," *Children*, vol. 17, no. 2, pp. 69–71.

SKINNER, B. F., 1967, "Why Teachers Fail," in H. W. Bernard and W. C. Huckins (eds.), *Readings in Educational Psychology*, Scranton, Pa.: International Textbook Company.

SKINNER, B. F., 1969, "The Machine That Is Man," *Psychology Today*, vol. 2, no. 11, pp. 20–25+, April.

SMITH, B. OTHANEL, 1967, "Conditions of Learning," in E. L. Morphet and C. O. Ryan (eds.), *Implications for Education of Prospective Changes in Society*, Denver, Colo.: Designing Education for the Future.

SMITH, KARL U., AND MARGARET F. SMITH, 1966, *Cybernetic Principles of Learning and Educational Design*, New York: Holt, Rinehart and Winston, Inc.

SMITH, MARSCHAL S., AND JOAN S. BISSELL, 1970, "Report Analysis: The Impact of Headstart," *Harvard Educational Review*, vol. 40, pp. 51–104.

SONTAG, L. W., 1963, "Somatopsychics of Personality and Bodily Function," *Vita Humana*, vol. 6, pp. 1–10.

SONTAG, L. W., C. T. BAKER, V. L. NELSON, 1958, *Mental Growth and Personality Development: A Longitudinal Study*, Monograph of the Society for Research in Child Development, vol. 23, no. 2, ser. no. 68.

SONTAG, LESTER AND JEROME KAGAN, 1968, "The Emergence of Intellectual-Achievement Motives," in Ellis D. Evans (ed.), *Children: Readings in Behavior and Development*, New York: Holt, Rinehart and Winston, Inc.

SROLE, LEO, T. S. LANGNER, S. T. MICHAEL, M. K. OPLER, AND T. A. C. RENNIE, 1962, *Mental Health in the Metropolis*, New York: McGraw-Hill Book Company.

"THE STAGES OF MAN," 1970, *Time*, vol. 96, no. 22, pp. 51–52, Nov. 30.

STATISTICAL ABSTRACTS OF THE UNITED STATES, 1967, Washington, D.C.: Bureau of the Census, U.S. Department of Commerce.

STERN, HELEN G., 1962, "Guidance for the Gifted Underachiever in High School," *NEA Journal*, vol. 51, no. 8, pp. 24–26.

STINCHCOMBE, ARTHUR L., 1969, "Environment: The Cumulation of Events," *Harvard Educational Review*, vol. 39, pp. 511–522.

STINNETT, T. M., 1970, "Reordering Goals and Roles: An Introduction," *Phi Delta Kappan*, vol. 52, pp. 1–3.

STOLUROW, LAWRENCE M., 1969, "Computer-assisted Instruction," in Edward S. Mason (Chm.), *The Schools and the Challenge of Innovation*, New York: McGraw-Hill Book Company.

STRAUSS, SAMUEL, 1969, "Looking Backward on Future Scientists," in H. W. Bernard (ed.) *Readings in Adolescent Development*, Scranton, Pa.: International Textbook Company. From *The Science Teacher*, vol. 24, pp. 385–387, 1957.

STROM, ROBERT D., 1969*a*, *Psychology for the Classroom*, Englewood Cliffs, N.J.: Prentice-Hall, Inc.

STROM, ROBERT D., 1969*b*, "Raising Aspirations of Youth: Implications for Community Organizations," in H. W. Bernard (ed.), *Readings in Adolescent Development*, Scranton, Pa.: International Textbook Company. From *Catholic Educational Review*, vol. 62, pp. 289–297, May 1964.

SUEHR, JOHN H., 1968, "A Response to Dr. Ebel on Marking," in Don E. Hamachek (ed.), *Human Dynamics in Psychology and Education*, Boston: Allyn and Bacon, Inc.

SUPPES, PATRICK, 1964, "Modern Learning Theory and the Elementary-school Curriculum," *American Educational Research Journal*, vol. 1, pp. 79–93.

TANNENBAUM, ABRAHAM J., 1967, "Social and Psychological Considerations in the Study of the Socially Disadvantaged," in National Society for the Study of Education, 66th Yearbook, part I, *The Educationally Retarded and Disadvantaged*, Chicago: University of Chicago Press.

TAYLOR, CALVIN W., 1961, "A Tentative Description of the Creative Individual," in *Human Variability and Learning*, Washington: National Education Association, Association for Supervision and Curriculum Development.

TAYLOR, CALVIN W., 1962, "Effects of Instructional Media on Creativity," *Educational Leadership*, vol. 19, pp. 453–458.

TAYLOR, CALVIN W., 1968, "Cultivating New Talents: A Way to Reach the Educationally Deprived," *Journal of Creative Behavior*, vol. 2, pp. 83–90.

TERMAN, LEWIS M., 1925, *Genetic Studies of Genius: I. Mental and Physical Traits of a Thousand Gifted Children*, Stanford, Calif.: Stanford University Press.

TERMAN, LEWIS M., AND MAUD A. MERRILL, 1960, *Stanford-Binet Intelligence Scale, Manual for Third Revision, Form L-M*, Boston: Houghton Mifflin Company.

THOMAS, EDWIN J., AND CLINTON F. FINK, 1968, "Effects of Group Size," in J. J. Muro and S. L. Freeman (eds.), *Readings in Group Counseling*, Scranton, Pa.: International Textbook Company. From *Psychological Bulletin*, vol. 60, pp. 371-384, 1963.

THOMAS, R. MURRAY, 1967, *Aiding the Maladjusted Pupil*, New York: David McKay Company, Inc.

THORNDIKE, E. L., 1932, *Fundamentals of Learning*, New York: Bureau of Publications, Teachers College, Columbia University.

THORNDIKE, E. L., et al., 1927, *The Measurement of Intelligence*, New York: Bureau of Publications, Teachers College, Columbia University.

THORNDIKE, R. L., 1948, "Growth of Intelligence during Adolescence," *Journal of Genetic Psychology*, vol. 72, pp. 11-15.

THORNDIKE, ROBERT L., 1969, "Book Review: Pygmalion in the Classroom," *Teachers College Record*, vol. 70, pp. 805-807.

TODD, RICHARD, 1970, "A Theory of the Lower Class—Edward Banfield: The Maverick of Urbanology," *The Atlantic*, vol. 226, no. 3, pp. 51-55, September.

TOMKINS, SYLVAN S., 1967, "Homo Patient: A Reexamination of the Concept of Drive," in James F. T. Bugenthal (ed.), *Challenges of Humanistic Psychology*, New York: McGraw-Hill Book Company.

TORRANCE, E. PAUL, 1962, *Guiding Creative Talent*, Englewood Cliffs, N.J.: Prentice-Hall, Inc.

TORRANCE, E. PAUL, 1966, "Problem-solving Attitudes and Self Concepts of Beginning Junior High School Students," *Guidance Journal*, vol. 4, pp. 74-86. Also in Bernard and Huckins, 1967, *Readings in Educational Psychology*, pp. 78-88.

TORRANCE, E. PAUL, 1968, "Examples and Rationales of Test Tasks for Assessing Creative Abilities," *Journal of Creative Behavior*, vol. 2, pp. 165-178.

TORRANCE, E. PAUL, 1969, "Foreword," in Robert C. Burkhart and High M. Neill, *Identity and Teacher Learning*, Scranton, Pa.: International Textbook Company.

TRAVERS, JOHN F., 1970, *Fundamentals of Educational Psychology*, Scranton, Pa.: International Textbook Company.

TRAVERS, ROBERT M. W., 1963, *Essentials of Learning*, New York: The Macmillan Company.

TROW, W. C., ALVIN F. ZANDER, WILLIAM C. MORSE, AND DAVID H. JENKINS, 1966, "Psychology of Group Behavior: The Class as a Group," in J. F. Rosenblith and W. Allinsmith (eds.), *The Causes of Behavior, II*, 2d ed., Boston: Allyn and Bacon, Inc. From *Journal of Educational Psychology*, vol. 41, pp. 322-338, 1950.

TUNLEY, ROUL, 1971, "Smooth Path at Rough Rock," *American Education*, vol. 7, no. 2, pp. 15-20, March.

200 MILLION AMERICANS, 1967, Washington, D.C.: U.S. Department of Commerce, Bureau of the Census.

TYLER, LEONA E., 1963, *Tests and Measurements*, Englewood Cliffs, N.J.: Prentice-Hall, Inc.

TYLER, RALPH W., 1967, "Purposes, Scope and Organization of Education," in E. L. Morphet and C. O. Ryan (eds.), *Implications for Education of Prospective Changes in Society*, Denver: Designing Education for the Future.

TYLER, RALPH W., 1969, "Introduction," in National Society for the Study of Education, 68th Yearbook, part II, *Educational Evaluation: New Roles, New Means*, Chicago: University of Chicago Press.

VELDMAN, DONALD J., AND ROBERT F. PECK, 1969, "Influences on Pupil Evaluations of Student Teachers," *Journal of Educational Psychology*, vol. 60, pp. 103-108.

VENN, GRANT, 1969, "Eye on Tomorrow's Jobs," *American Education*, vol. 5, no. 3, pp. 12-15, March.

VOELKER, PAUL H., AND FRANCES A. MULLEN, 1963, "Organization, Administration, and Supervision of Special Education," *Review of Educational Research*, vol. 33, pp. 5-19.

WADE, SERENA, 1969, "Differences between Intelligence and Creativity: Some Speculation on the Role of Environment," *The Journal of Creative Behavior*, vol. 2, pp. 97-101.

WALBERG, HERBERT J., 1969, "Social Environment as a Mediator of Classroom Learning," *Journal of Educational Psychology*, vol. 60, pp. 443-448.

WALBERG, HERBERT J., AND GARY J. ANDERSON, 1968, "Classroom Climate and Individual Learning," *Journal of Educational Psychology*, vol. 59, pp. 414-419.

WALLAS, GRAHAM, 1926, *The Art of Thought*, New York: Harcourt, Brace and World, Inc.

WANN, KENNETH D., M. S. DORN, AND E. A. LIDDLE, 1962, *Fostering Intellectual Development in Young Children*, New York: Bureau of Publications, Teachers College, Columbia University.

WASSERMAN, SIDNEY, 1967, "The Abused Parent of the Abused Child," *Children*, vol. 14, pp. 175-179.

WATZLAWICK, PAUL, JANET H. BEAVIN, AND DON D. JACKSON, 1967, *Pragmatics of Human Communication,* New York: W. W. Norton & Company.

WEBSTER, STATEN W. (ed.), 1966, *The Disadvantaged Learner: Knowing, Understanding, Educating*, San Francisco: Chandler Publishing Company.

WECHSLER, DAVID, 1951, *Wechsler Adult Intelligence Scale*, New York: Psychological Corporation.

WEINER, BERNARD, AND PENELOPE A. POTEPAN, 1970, "Personality Characteristics and Affective Reactions toward Exams of Superior and Failing College Students," *Journal of Educational Psychology*, vol. 61, pp. 133–151.

WELLMAN, BETH L., 1940, "Iowa Studies on the Effects of School," in National Society for the Study of Education, 39th Yearbook, Part II, *Intelligence: Its Nature and Nurture*," Chicago: University of Chicago Press.

WESMAN, ALEXANDER G., 1968, "Intelligent Testing," *American Psychologist*, vol. 23, pp. 267–274.

WESTLEY, WILLIAM A., AND NATHAN B. EPSTEIN, 1969, *The Silent Majority: Families of Emotionally Healthy Children*, San Francisco: Jossey-Bass, Inc.

WHITE, WILLIAM F., 1969, *Psychosocial Principles Applied to Classroom Teaching*, New York: McGraw-Hill Book Company.

WHITLA, DEAN K., 1969, "Research in College Admissions," in National Society for the Study of Education, 68th Yearbook, Part II, *Educational Evaluation: New Roles, New Means*, Chicago: University of Chicago Press.

WINICK, CHARLES, ASYA L. KADIS, AND EILEEN CLARK, 1969, "The Teachers' Educational Workshop," *Teacher College Record*, vol. 70, pp. 297–311.

WICKMAN, E. K., 1928, *Children's Behavior and Teachers' Attitudes*, Cambridge, Mass.: Published for the Commonwealth Fund by Harvard University Press.

WILLIAMS, ROGER J., 1971, "The Biology of Behavior," *Saturday Review*, vol. 54, no. 5, pp. 17–19, Jan. 30.

WILSON, JOHN A. R., MILDRED C. ROBECK, AND WILLIAM B. MICHAEL, 1969, *Psychological Foundations of Learning and Teaching*, New York: McGraw-Hill Book Company.

WINDER, ALVIN E., AND NICHOLAI SAVENKO, 1970, "Group Counseling with Neighborhood Youth Corps Trainees," *Personnel and Guidance Journal*, vol. 48, pp. 561–567.

WOODRING, PAUL, 1970, "Retrospect and Prospect," *Saturday Review*, vol. 53, no. 38, p. 66, Sept. 19.

WRIGHT, STEPHEN J., 1970, "Black Studies and Sound Scholarship," *Phi Delta Kappan*, vol. 51, pp. 365–368.

WYZANSKI, CHARLES E., JR., 1969, "A Federal Judge Digs the Young," in H. W. Bernard (ed.), *Readings in Adolescent Development*, Scranton, Pa.: International Textbook Company. From *Saturday Review*, vol. 51, no. 29, pp. 14-16+, 1968.

YAMAMOTO, AAORU, 1964, "Creative Thinking: Some Thoughts on Research," *Exceptional Children*, vol. 30, pp. 403-410.

ZIGLER, EDWARD, 1966, "Mental Retardation: Current Issues and Approaches," in L. W. Hoffman and M.L . Hoffman (eds.), *Review of Child Development Research*, vol. 2, New York: Russell Sage Foundation.

ZIGLER, EDWARD F., 1970, "A National Priority: Raising the Quality of Children's Lives," *Children*, vol. 17, no. 5, pp. 166-170.

ZILLER, R. C., AND R. D. BEHRINGE, 1960, "Assimilation of the Knowledgeable Newcomer under Conditions of Success and Failure," *Journal of Abnormal and Social Psychology*, vol. 60, pp. 288-291.

ZILLER, R. C., AND OTHERS, 1962, "Group Creativity under Conditions of Success or Failure and Variations in Group Stability," *Journal of Applied Psychology*, vol. 46, pp. 43-49.

Name Index

Subject Index

493